by HIROMU ARAKAWA

FULLMETAL ALCHEMIST

FULLMETAL EDITION

05

05

FULLMETAL EDITION

FULLMETAL ALCHEMIST

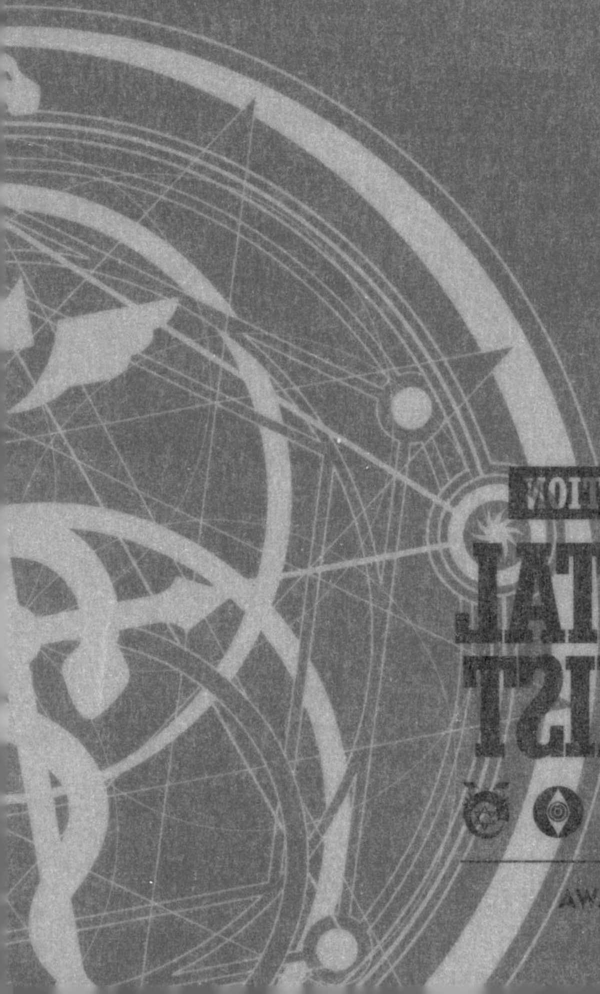

by HIROMU ARAKAWA

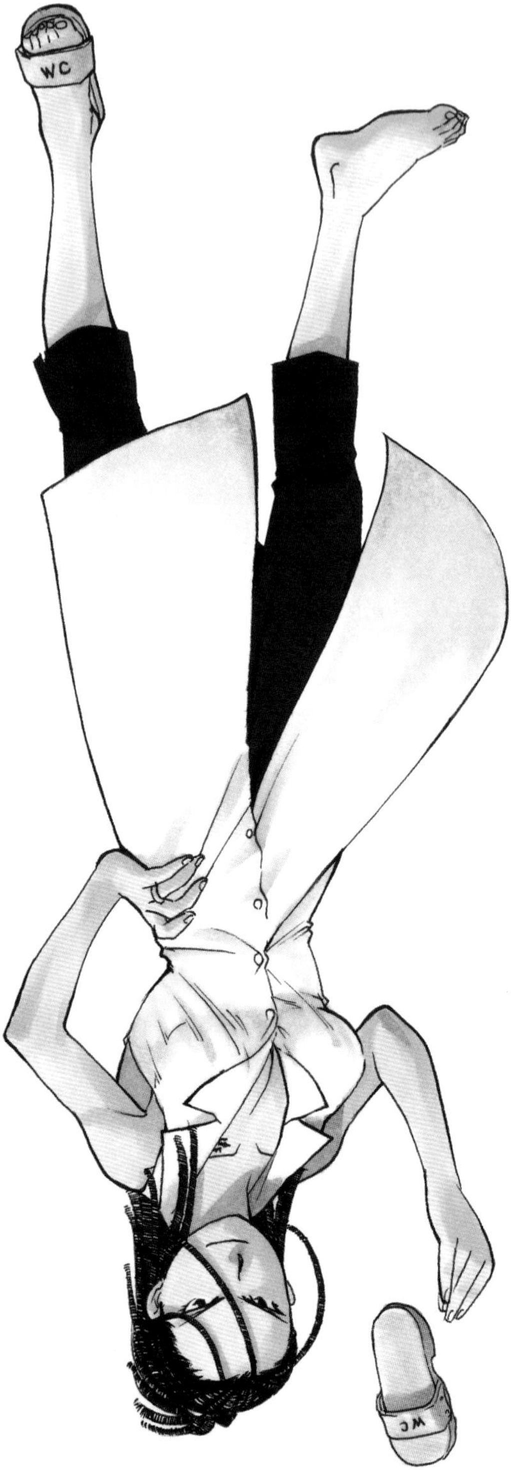
WC
WC

FULLMETAL EDITION

FULLMETAL ALCHEMIST

05 CONTENTS

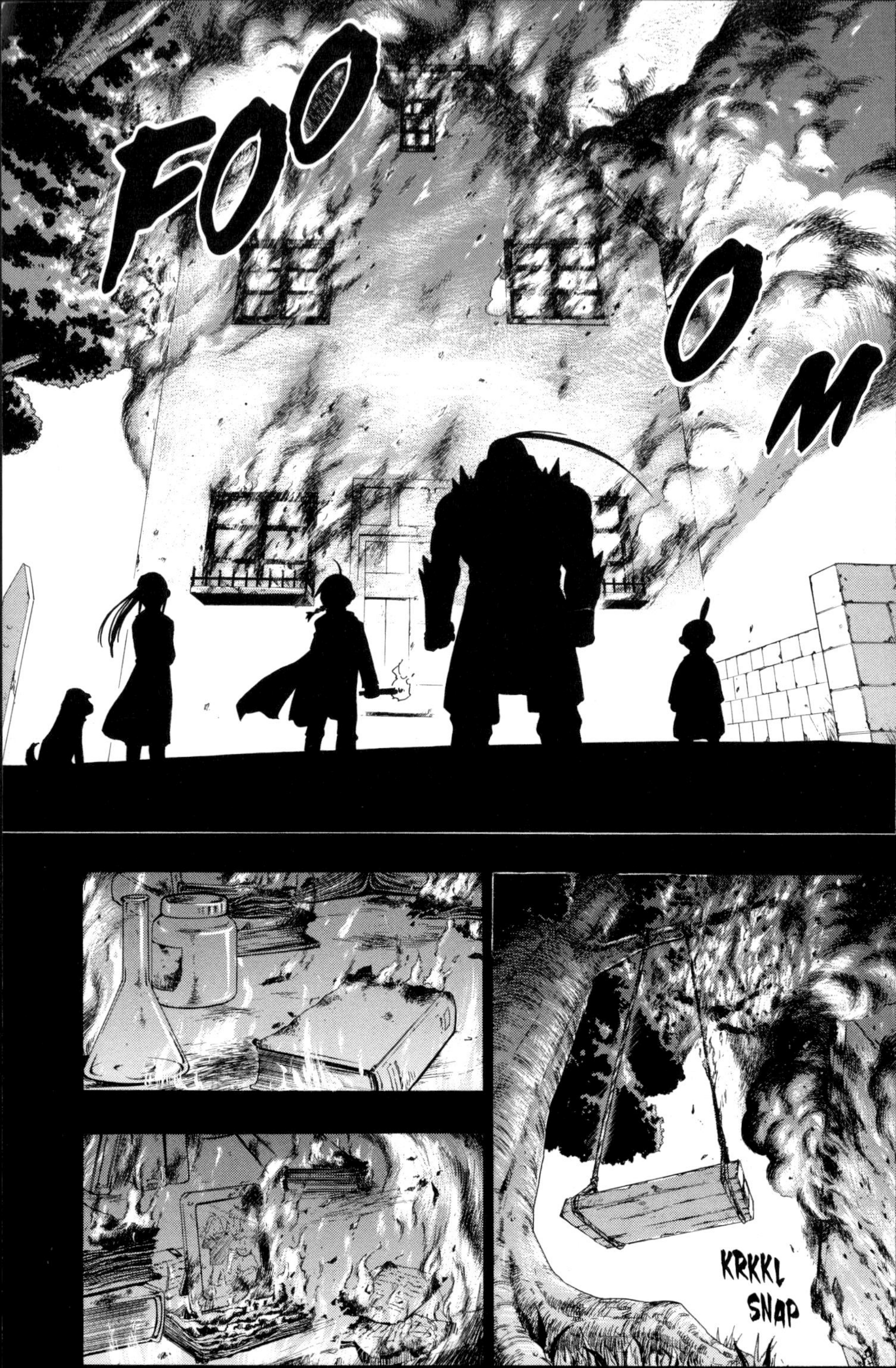
FOOOM
KRKKL
SNAP

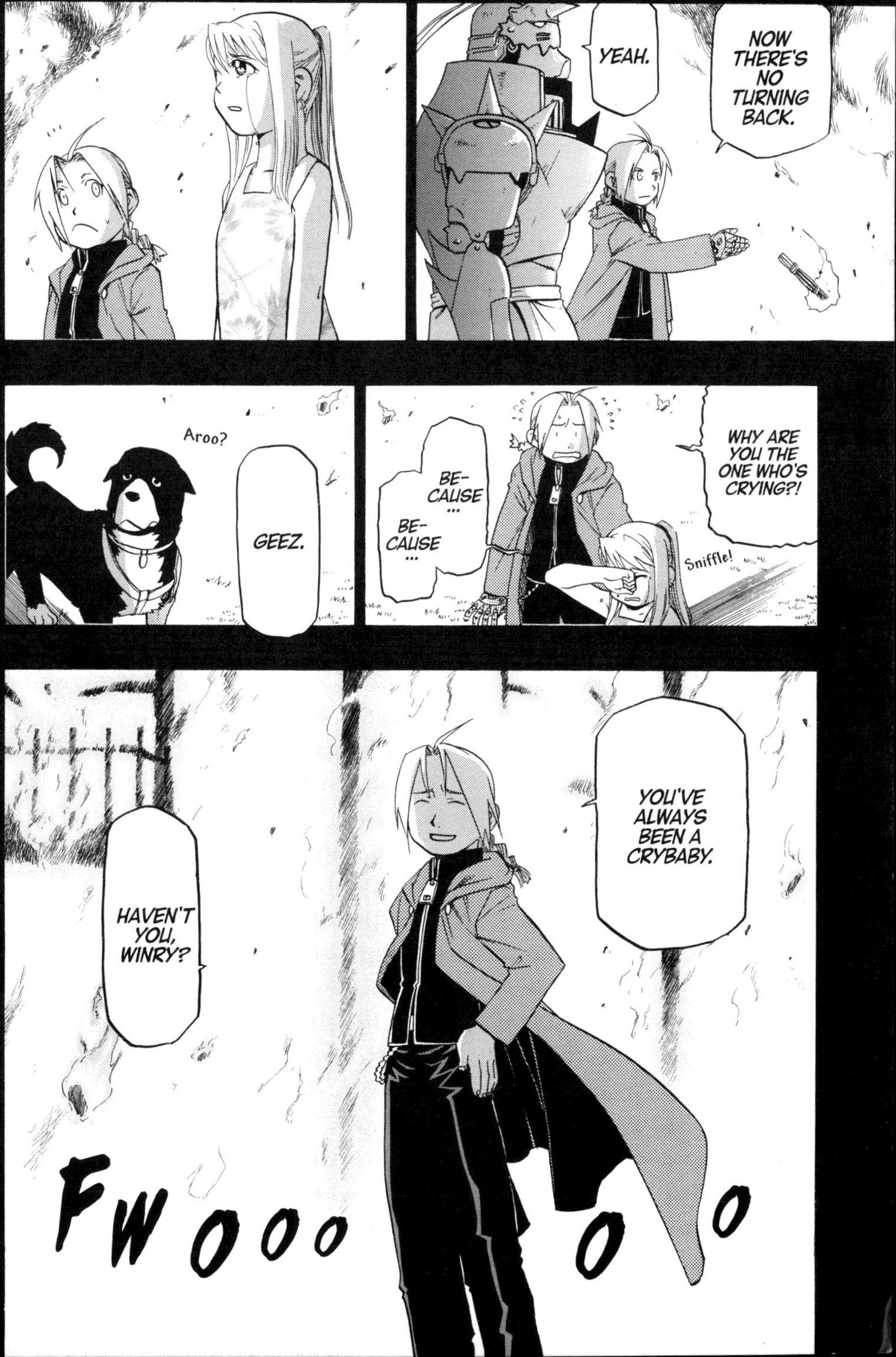
NOW THERE'S NO TURNING BACK.
YEAH.
WHY ARE YOU THE ONE WHO'S CRYING?!
BE-CAUSE ...
BE-CAUSE ...
Sniffle!
GEEZ.
Aroo?
YOU'VE ALWAYS BEEN A CRYBABY.
HAVEN'T YOU, WINRY?
FWOOOOOO

CHAPTER 25 MASTER AND APPRENTICE

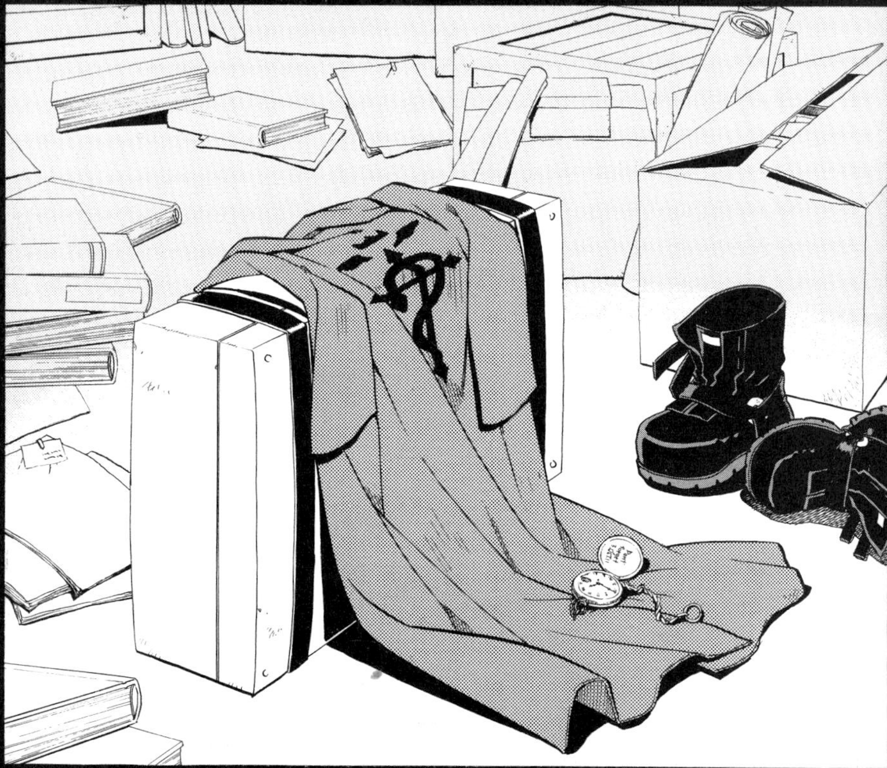

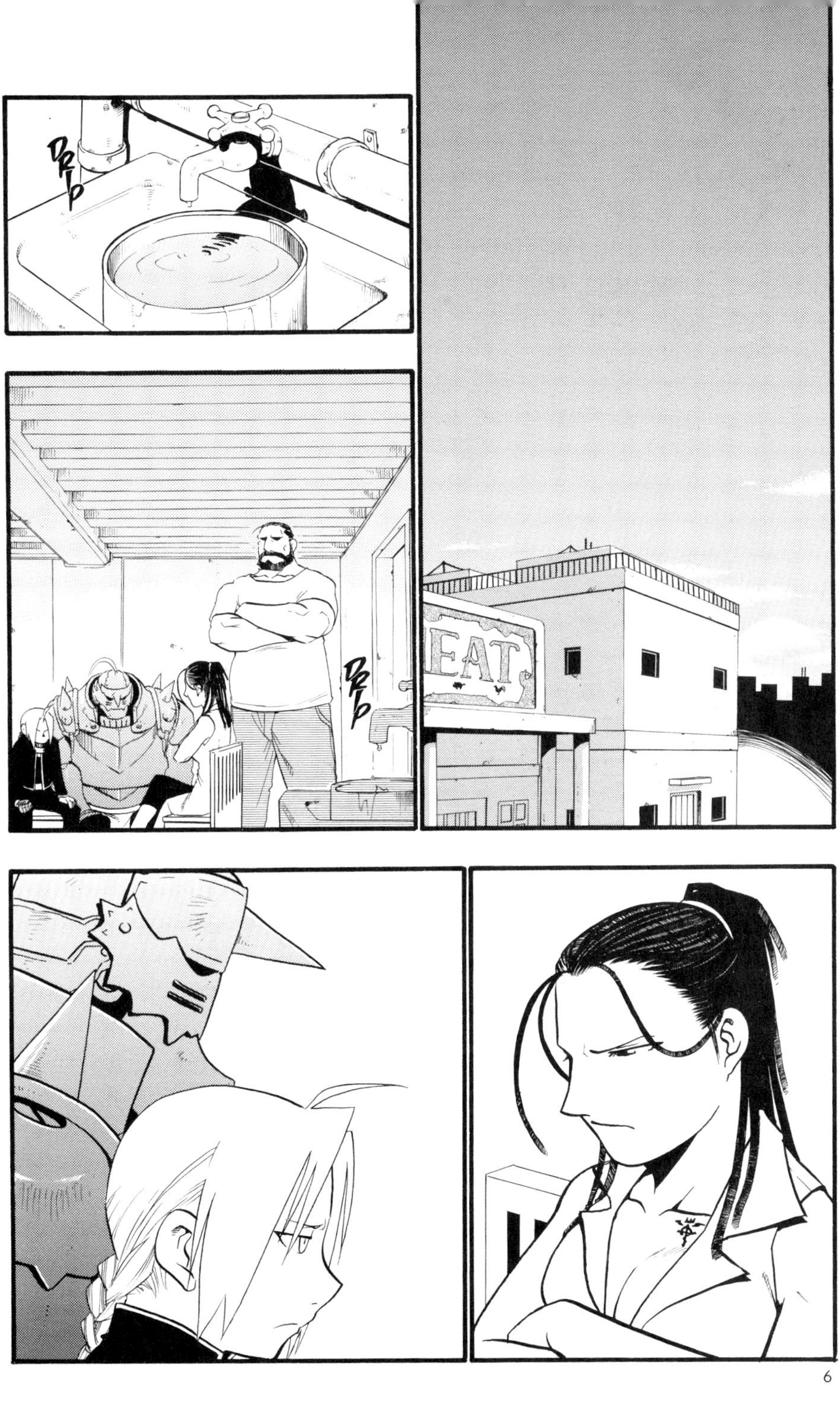
EAT
DRIP
DRIP

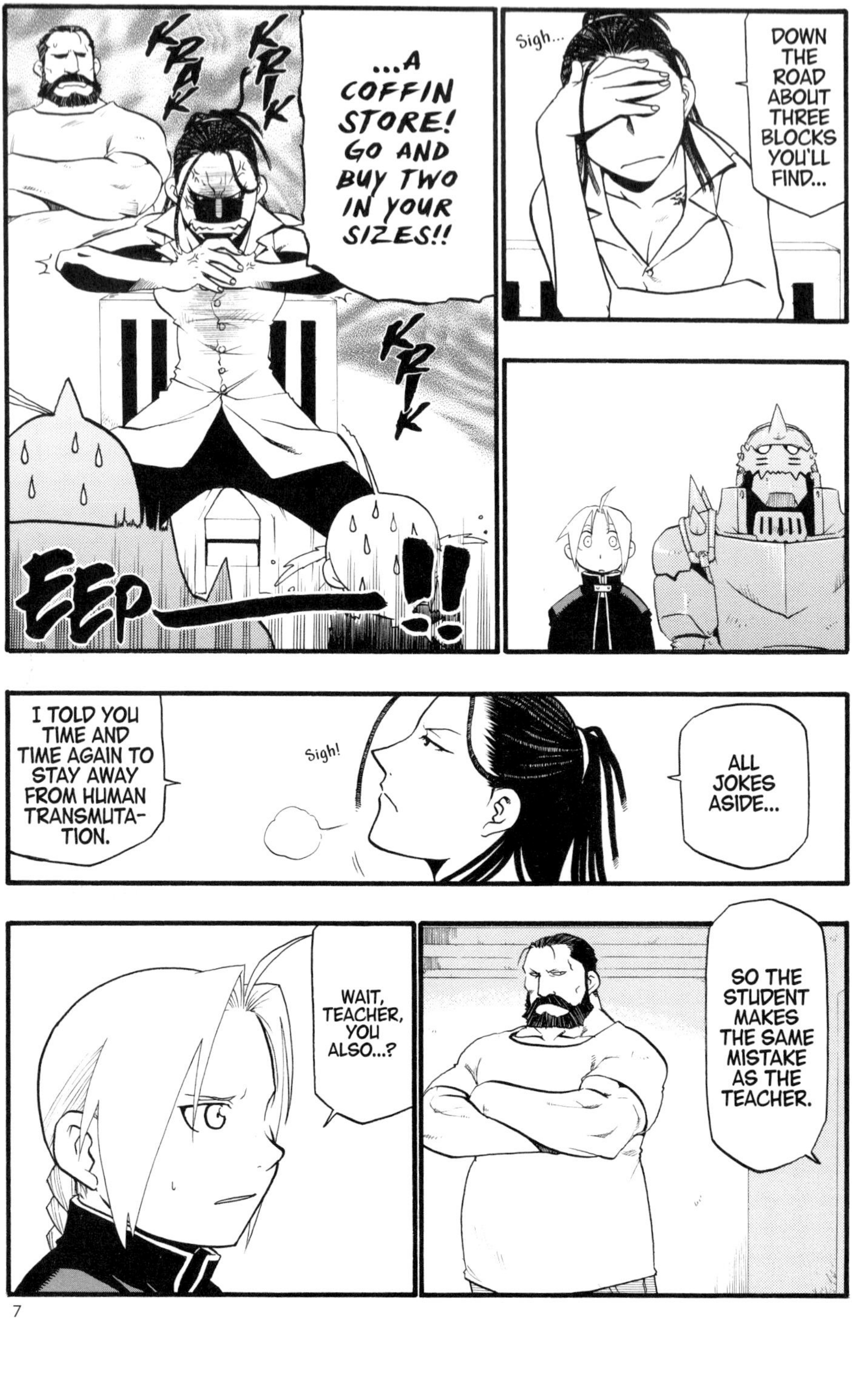
Sigh...
DOWN THE ROAD ABOUT THREE BLOCKS YOU'LL FIND...
...A COFFIN STORE! GO AND BUY TWO IN YOUR SIZES!!
KRIK
KRAK
KRIK
EEP—!!
ALL JOKES ASIDE...
Sigh!
I TOLD YOU TIME AND TIME AGAIN TO STAY AWAY FROM HUMAN TRANSMUTA-TION.
SO THE STUDENT MAKES THE SAME MISTAKE AS THE TEACHER.
WAIT, TEACHER, YOU ALSO...?

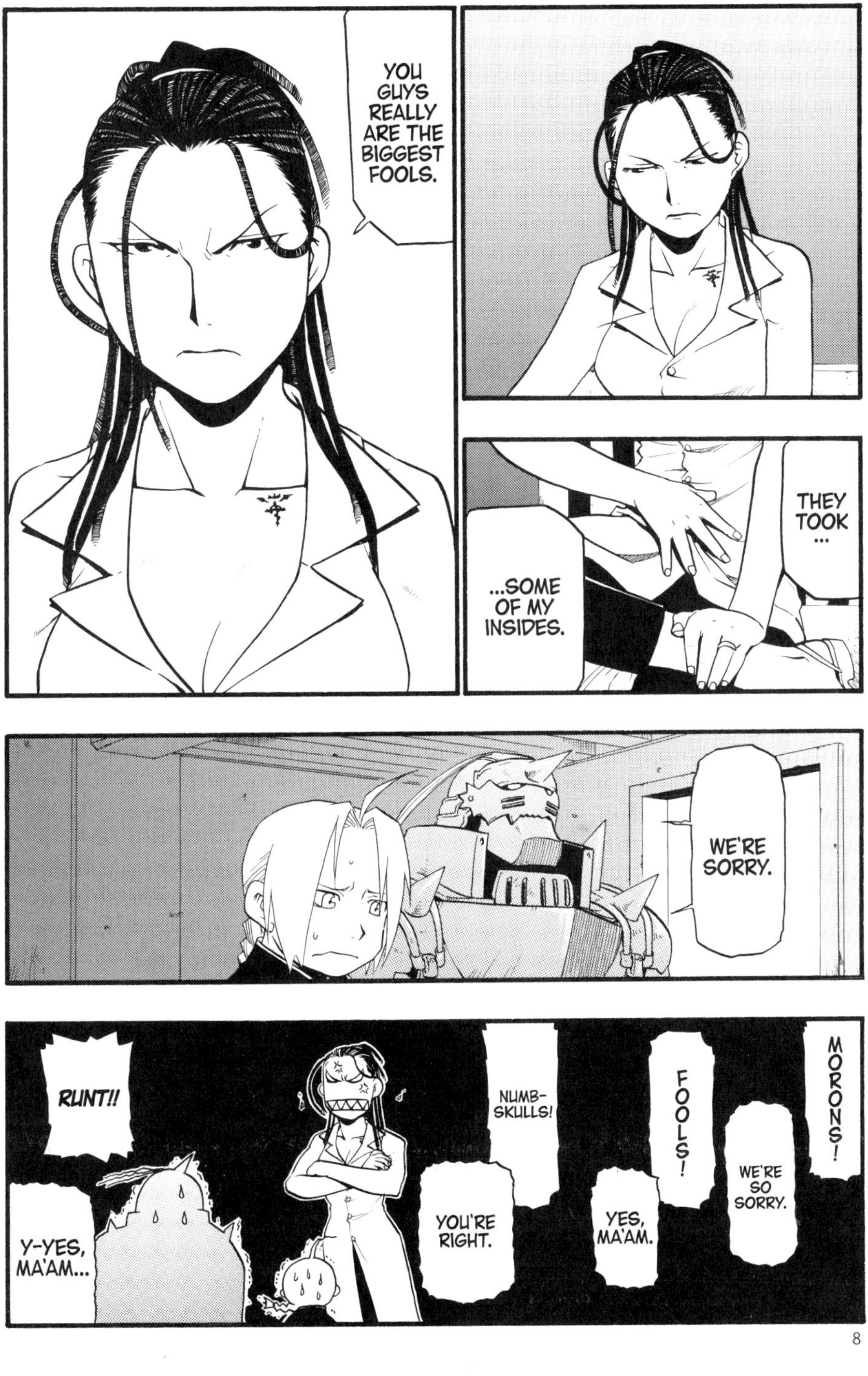
THEY TOOK...
...SOME OF MY INSIDES.
YOU GUYS REALLY ARE THE BIGGEST FOOLS.
WE'RE SORRY.
MORONS!
WE'RE SO SORRY.
FOOLS!
YES, MA'AM.
NUMB-SKULLS!
YOU'RE RIGHT.
RUNT!!
Y-YES, MA'AM...

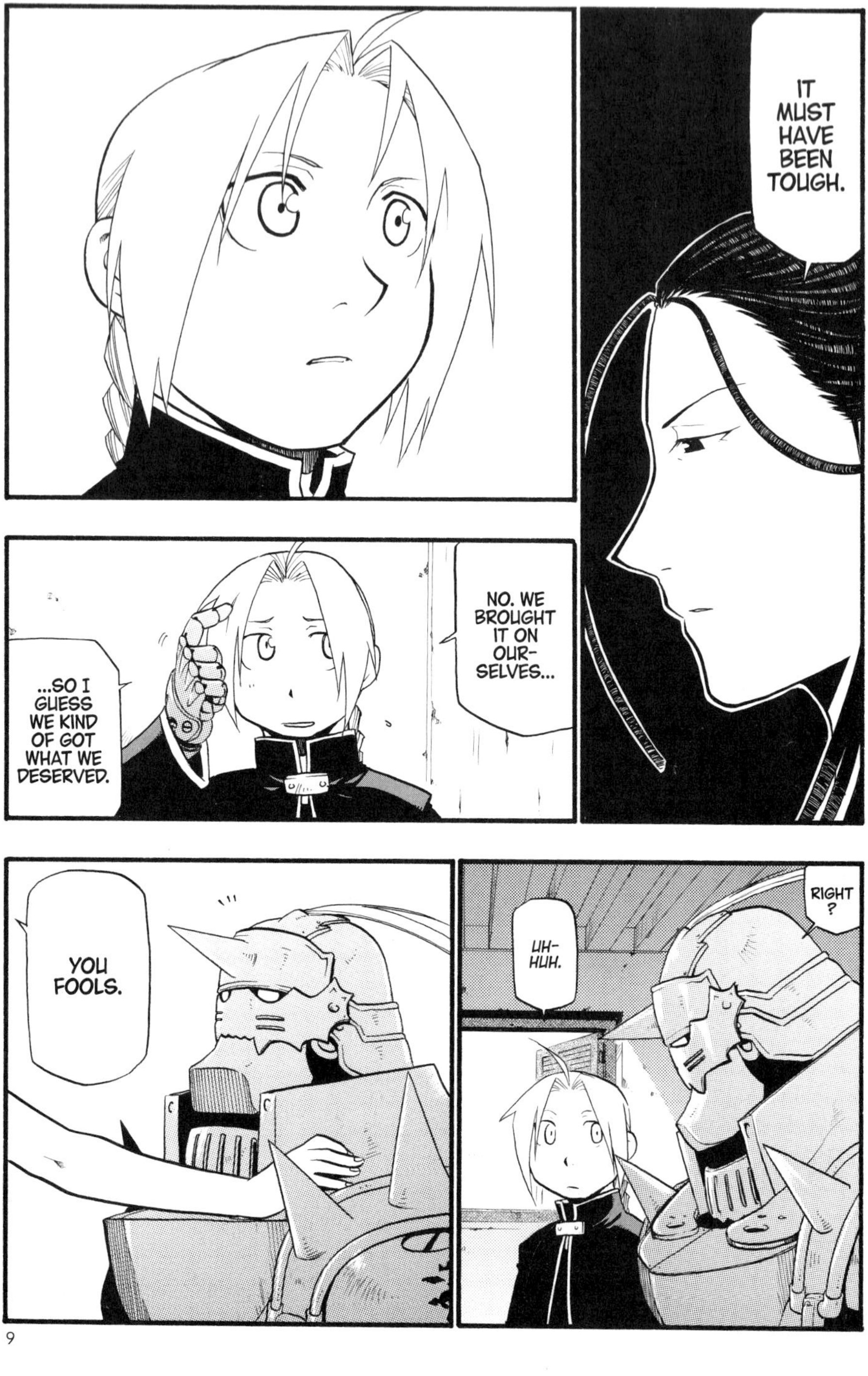
IT MUST HAVE BEEN TOUGH.
NO. WE BROUGHT IT ON OUR-SELVES...
...SO I GUESS WE KIND OF GOT WHAT WE DESERVED.
RIGHT?
UH-HUH.
YOU FOOLS.

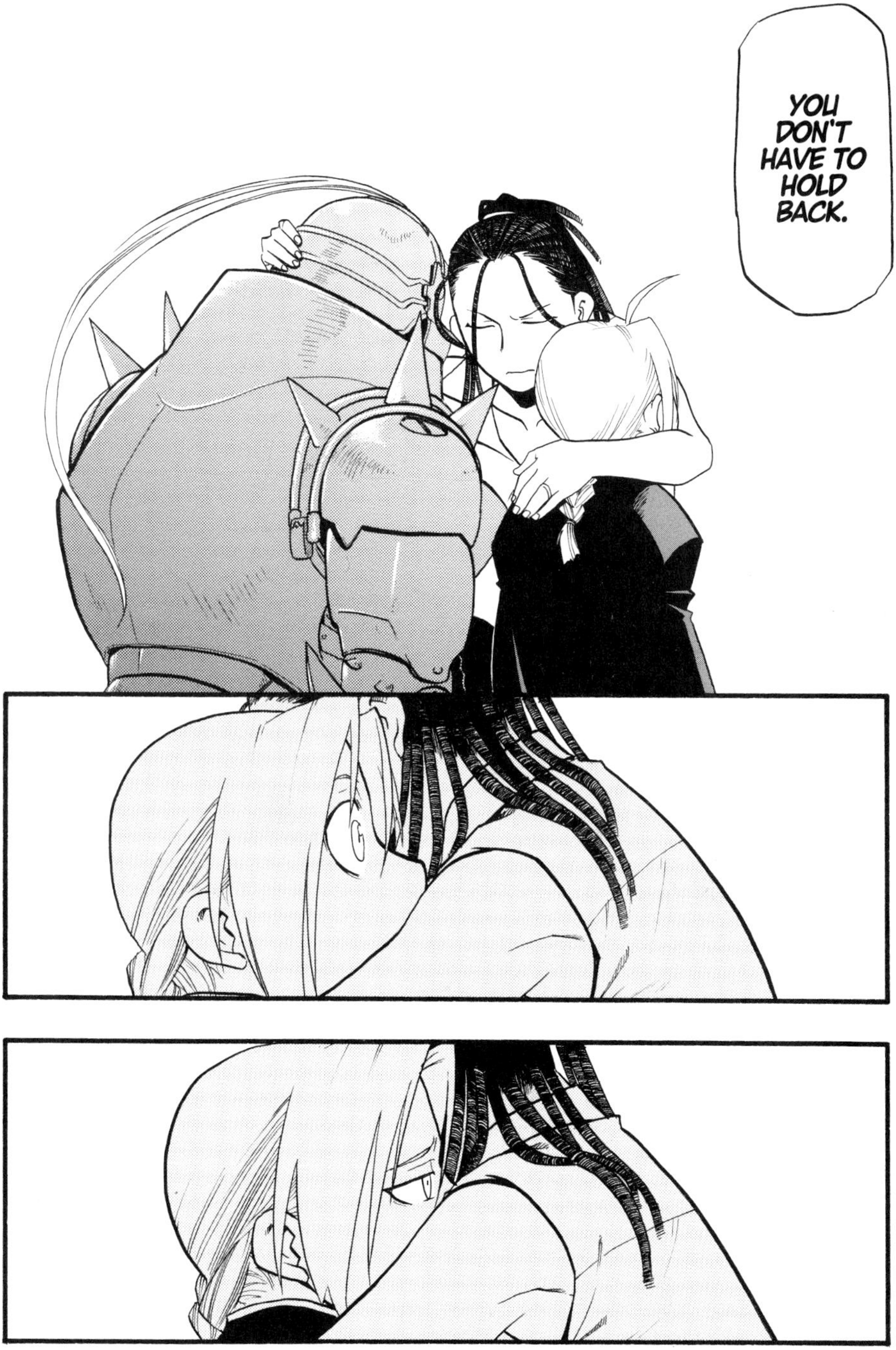
YOU DON'T HAVE TO HOLD BACK.

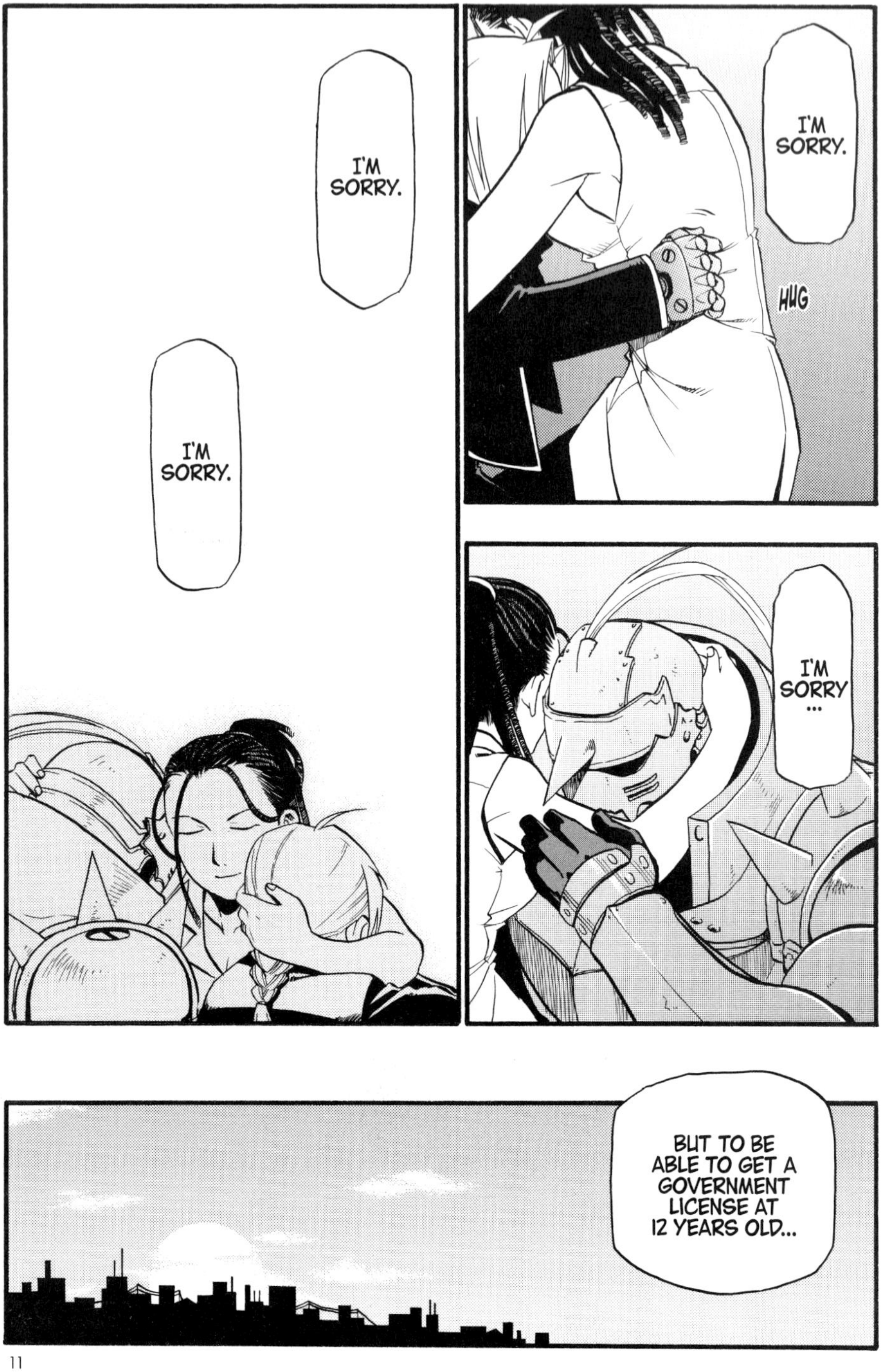
I'M SORRY.
HUG
I'M SORRY ...
I'M SORRY.
I'M SORRY.
BUT TO BE ABLE TO GET A GOVERNMENT LICENSE AT 12 YEARS OLD...

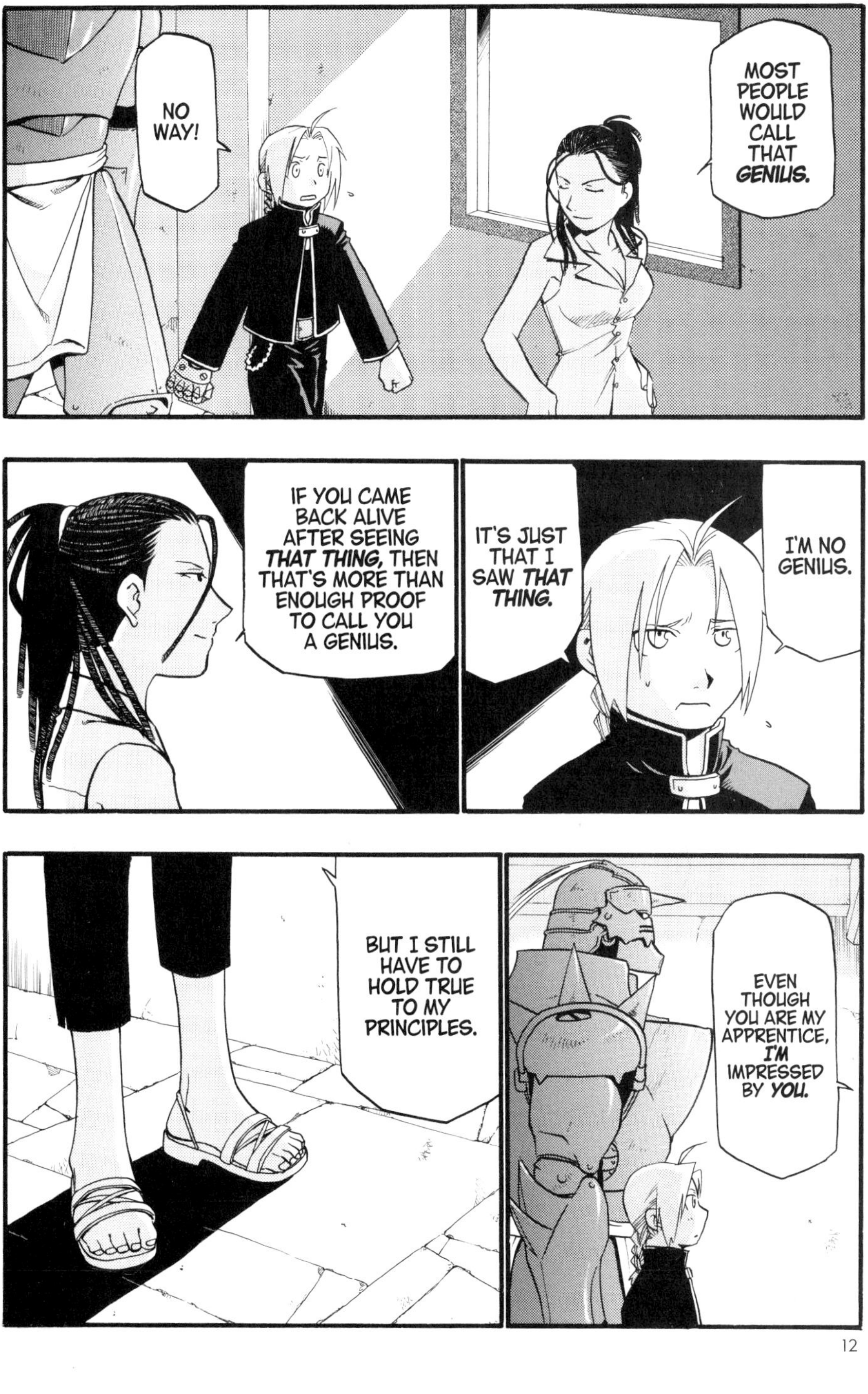
MOST PEOPLE WOULD CALL THAT GENIUS.
NO WAY!
I'M NO GENIUS.
IT'S JUST THAT I SAW THAT THING.
IF YOU CAME BACK ALIVE AFTER SEEING THAT THING, THEN THAT'S MORE THAN ENOUGH PROOF TO CALL YOU A GENIUS.
EVEN THOUGH YOU ARE MY APPRENTICE, I'M IMPRESSED BY YOU.
BUT I STILL HAVE TO HOLD TRUE TO MY PRINCIPLES.

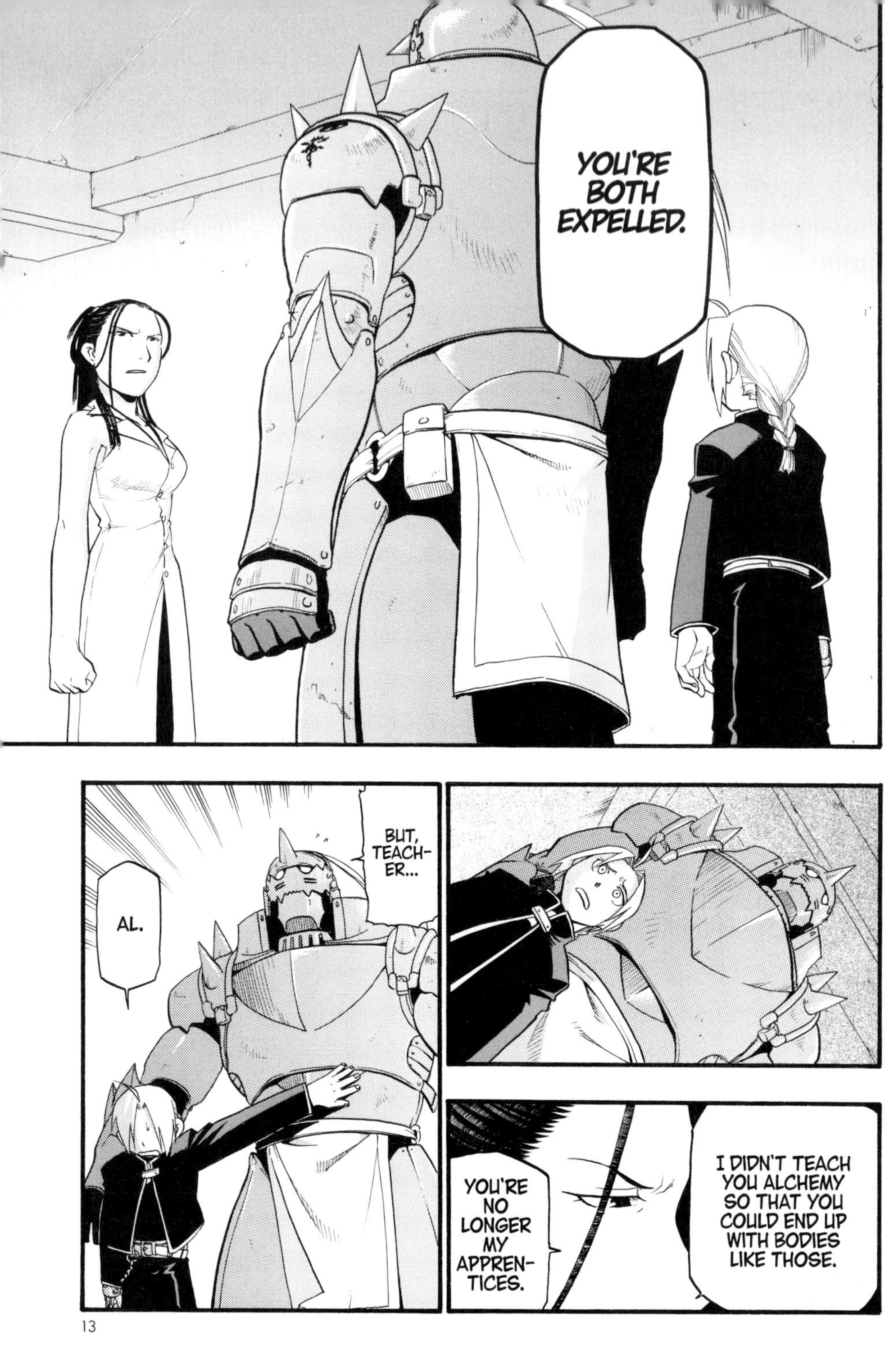
YOU'RE BOTH EXPELLED.
I DIDN'T TEACH YOU ALCHEMY SO THAT YOU COULD END UP WITH BODIES LIKE THOSE.
YOU'RE NO LONGER MY APPREN-TICES.
BUT, TEACH-ER...
AL.

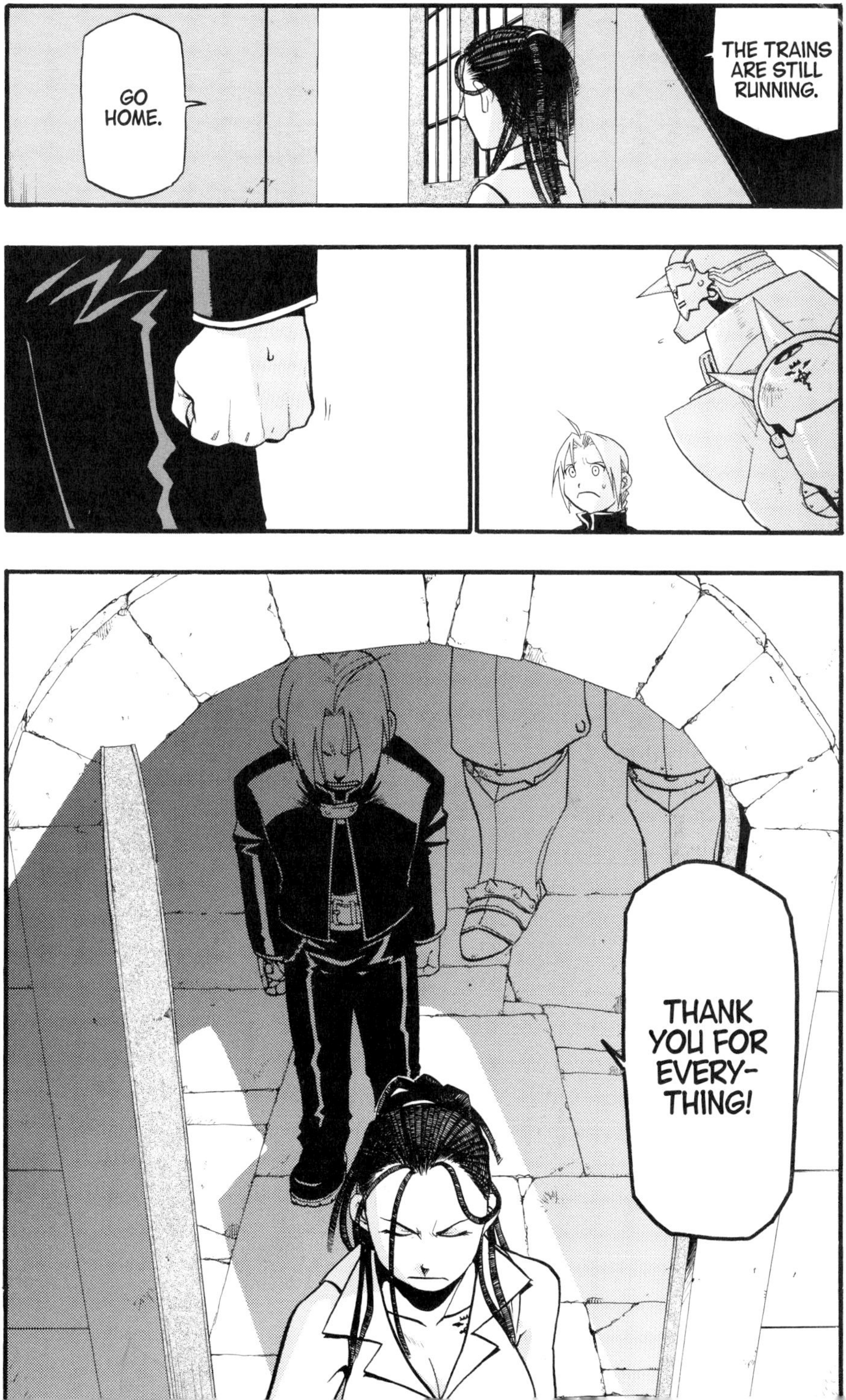
THE TRAINS ARE STILL RUNNING.
GO HOME.
THANK YOU FOR EVERY-THING!

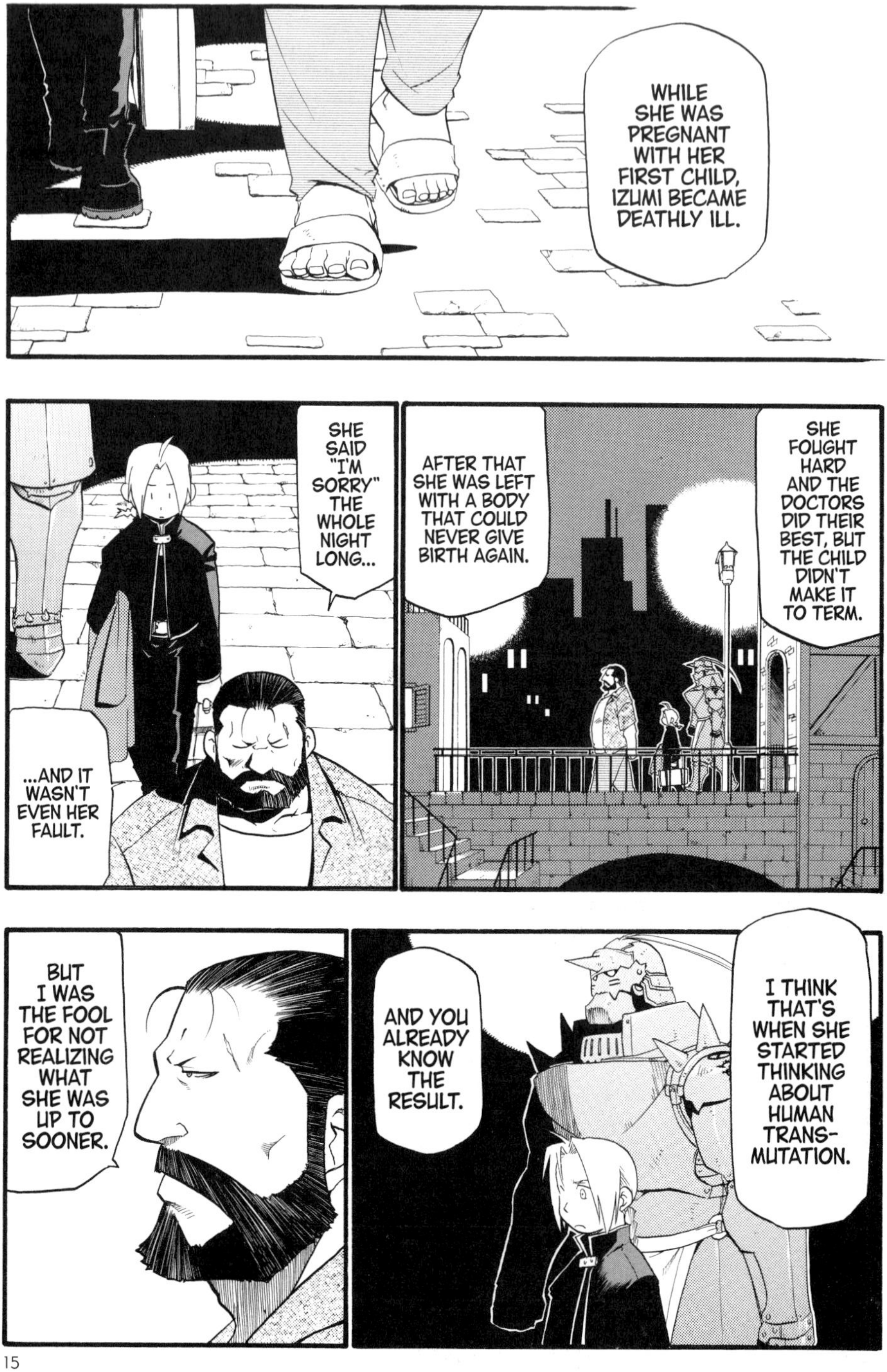
WHILE SHE WAS PREGNANT WITH HER FIRST CHILD, IZUMI BECAME DEATHLY ILL.
SHE FOUGHT HARD AND THE DOCTORS DID THEIR BEST, BUT THE CHILD DIDN'T MAKE IT TO TERM.
AFTER THAT SHE WAS LEFT WITH A BODY THAT COULD NEVER GIVE BIRTH AGAIN.
SHE SAID "I'M SORRY" THE WHOLE NIGHT LONG...
...AND IT WASN'T EVEN HER FAULT.
I THINK THAT'S WHEN SHE STARTED THINKING ABOUT HUMAN TRANS-MUTATION.
AND YOU ALREADY KNOW THE RESULT.
BUT I WAS THE FOOL FOR NOT REALIZING WHAT SHE WAS UP TO SOONER.

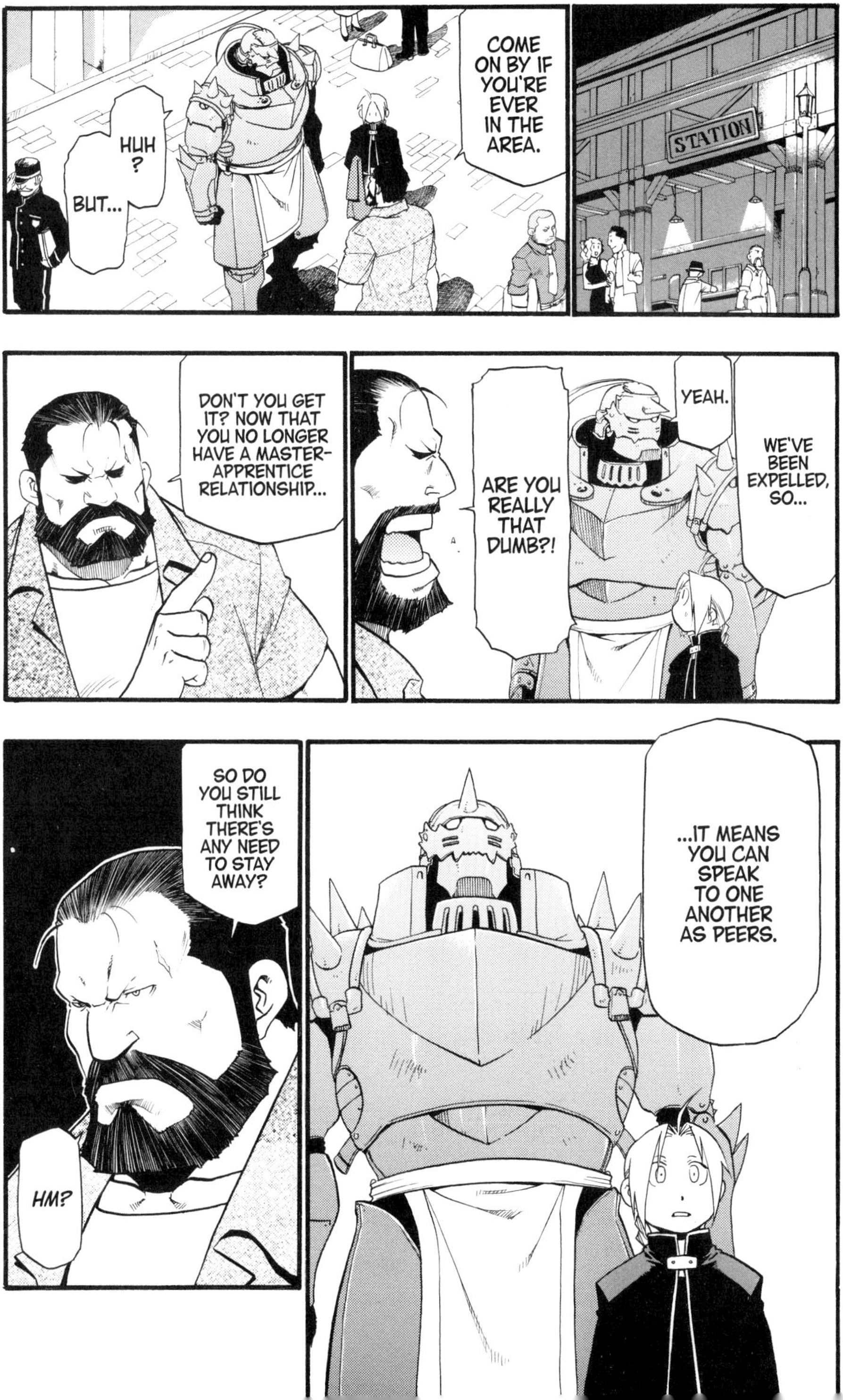
STATION
COME ON BY IF YOU'RE EVER IN THE AREA.
HUH?
BUT...
YEAH.
WE'VE BEEN EXPELLED, SO...
ARE YOU REALLY THAT DUMB?!
DON'T YOU GET IT? NOW THAT YOU NO LONGER HAVE A MASTER-APPRENTICE RELATIONSHIP...
...IT MEANS YOU CAN SPEAK TO ONE ANOTHER AS PEERS.
SO DO YOU STILL THINK THERE'S ANY NEED TO STAY AWAY?
HM?

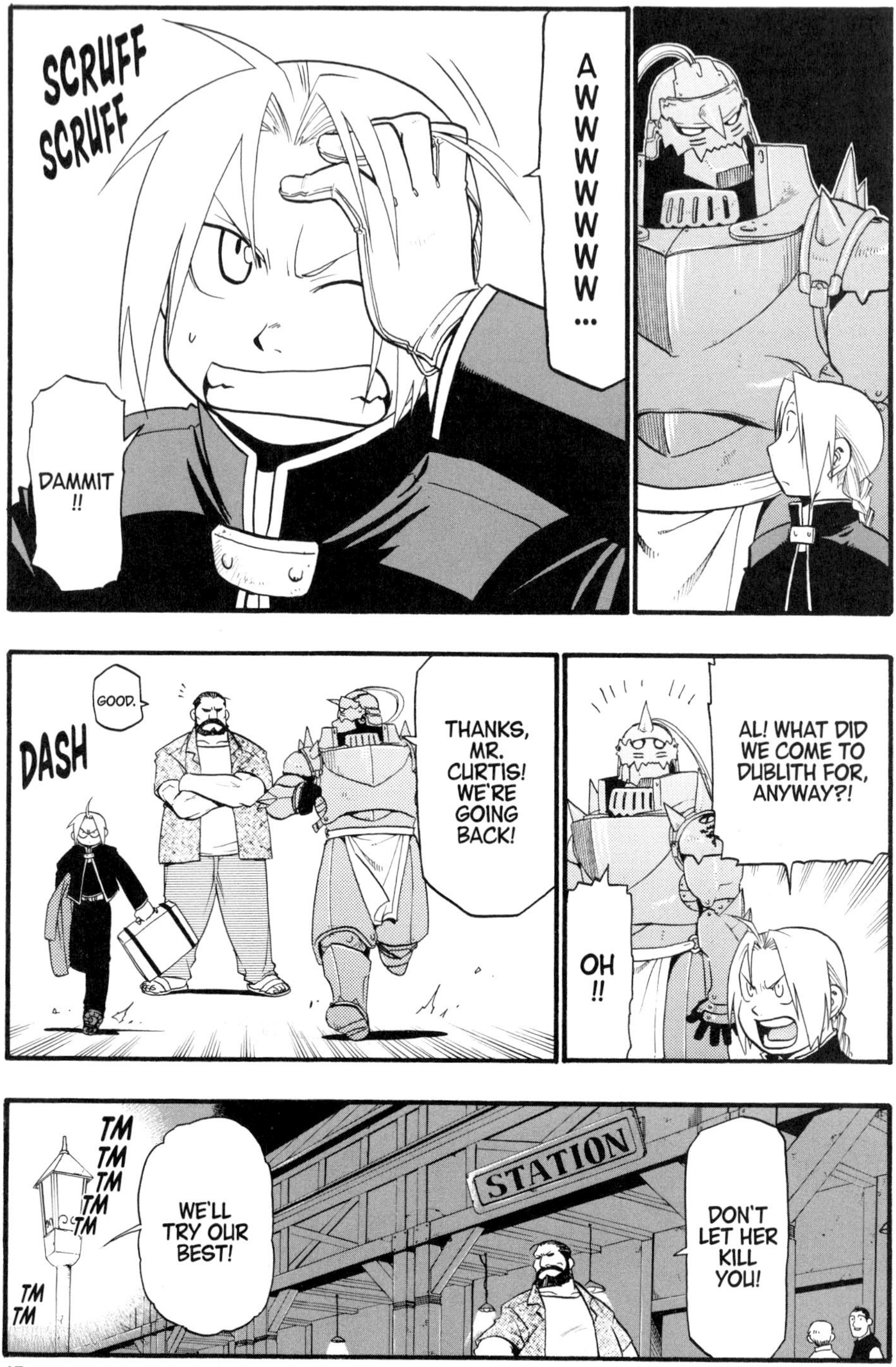
AWWWWWWWWW...
SCRUFF SCRUFF
DAMMIT!!
AL! WHAT DID WE COME TO DUBLITH FOR, ANYWAY?!
OH!!
THANKS, MR. CURTIS! WE'RE GOING BACK!
GOOD.
DASH
DON'T LET HER KILL YOU!
STATION
WE'LL TRY OUR BEST!
TM TM TM TM TM
TM TM

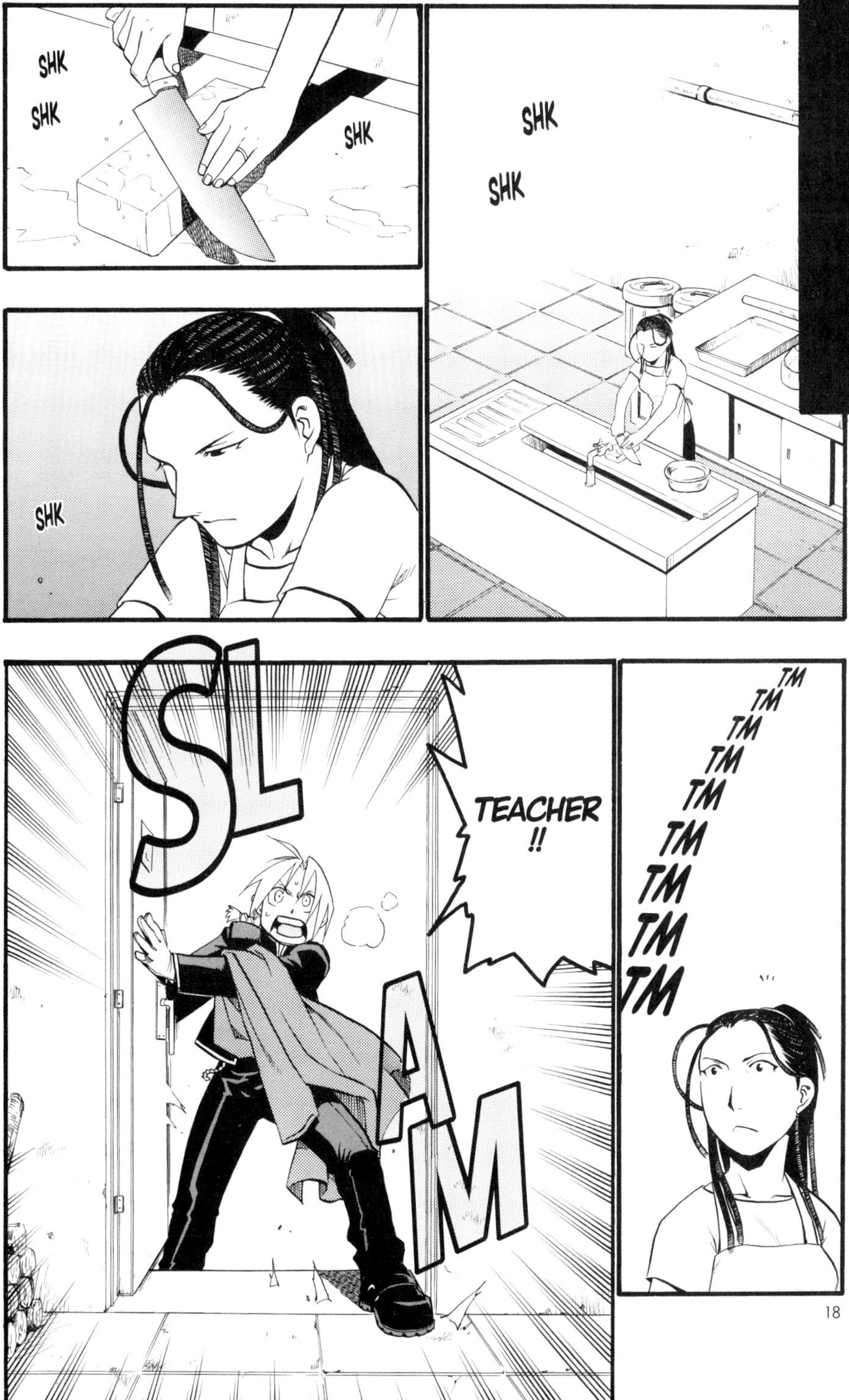
SHK
SHK
SHK
SHK
SHK
SHK
TM
TM
TM
TM
TM
TM
TM
TM
TM
SLAM
TEACHER !!

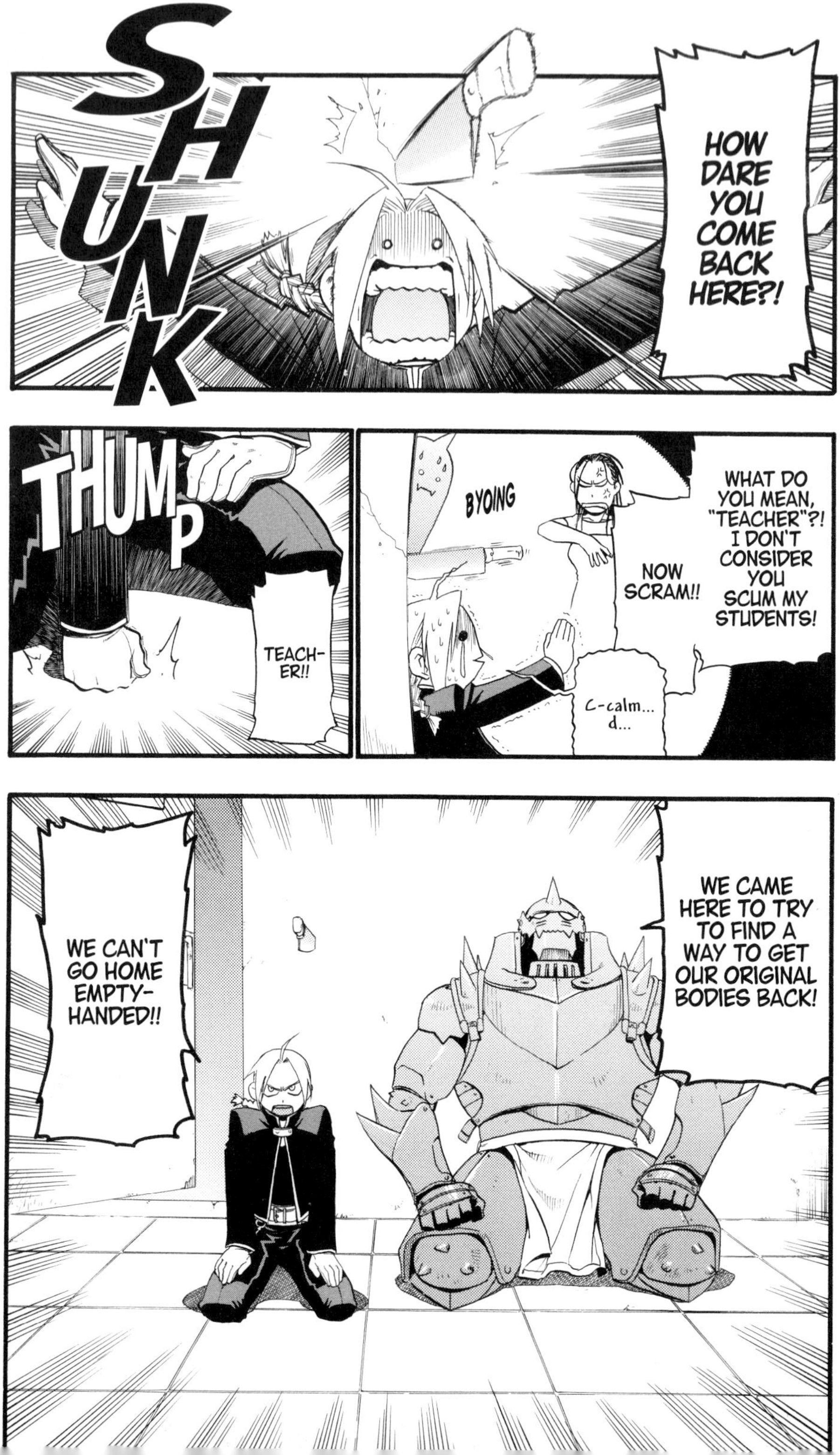
HOW DARE YOU COME BACK HERE?!
SHUNK
WHAT DO YOU MEAN, "TEACHER"?! I DON'T CONSIDER YOU SCUM MY STUDENTS!
NOW SCRAM!!
BYOING
C-calm... d...
THUMP
TEACHER!!
WE CAME HERE TO TRY TO FIND A WAY TO GET OUR ORIGINAL BODIES BACK!
WE CAN'T GO HOME EMPTY-HANDED!!

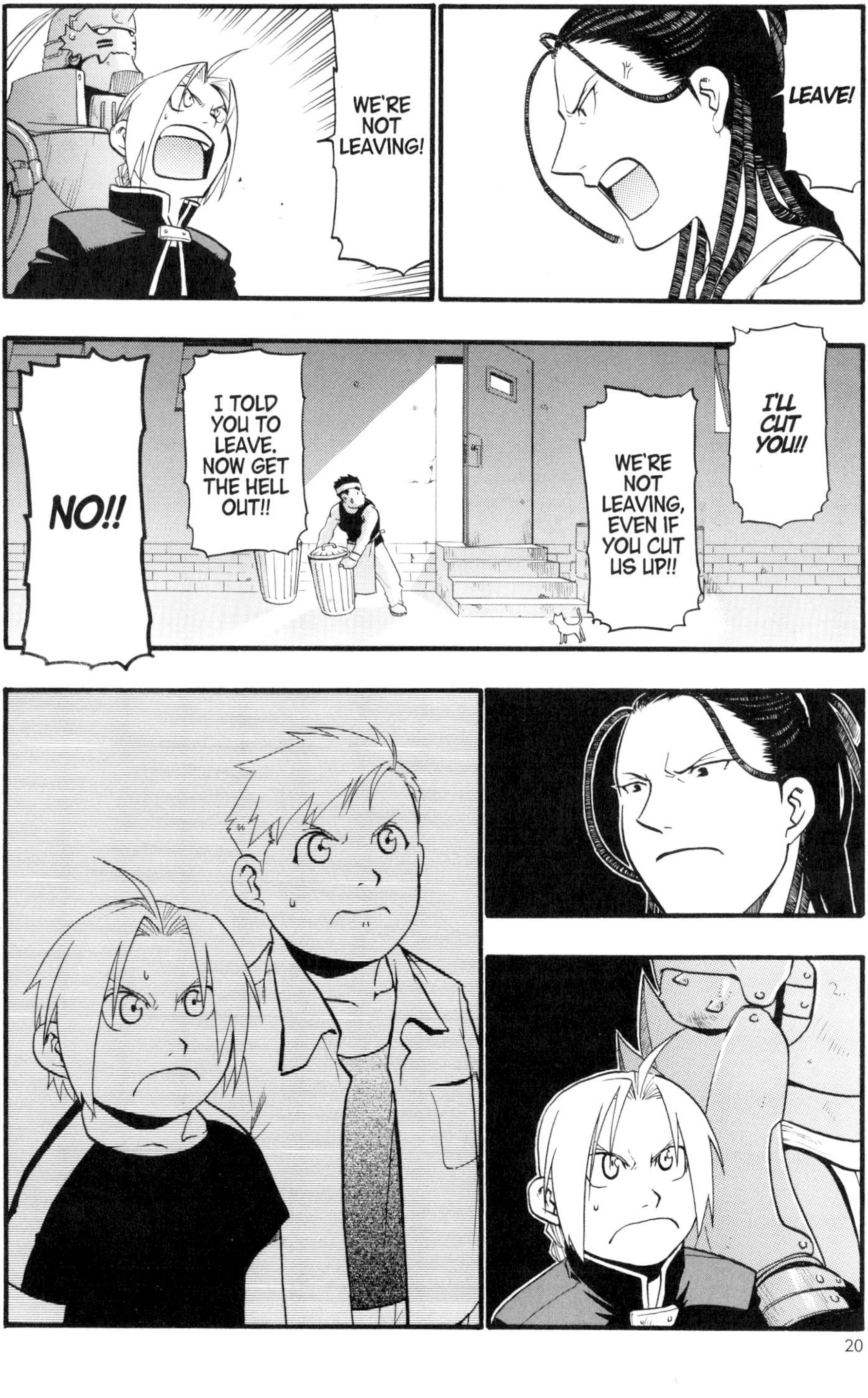
LEAVE!
WE'RE NOT LEAVING!
I'LL CUT YOU!!
WE'RE NOT LEAVING, EVEN IF YOU CUT US UP!!
I TOLD YOU TO LEAVE. NOW GET THE HELL OUT!!
NO!!

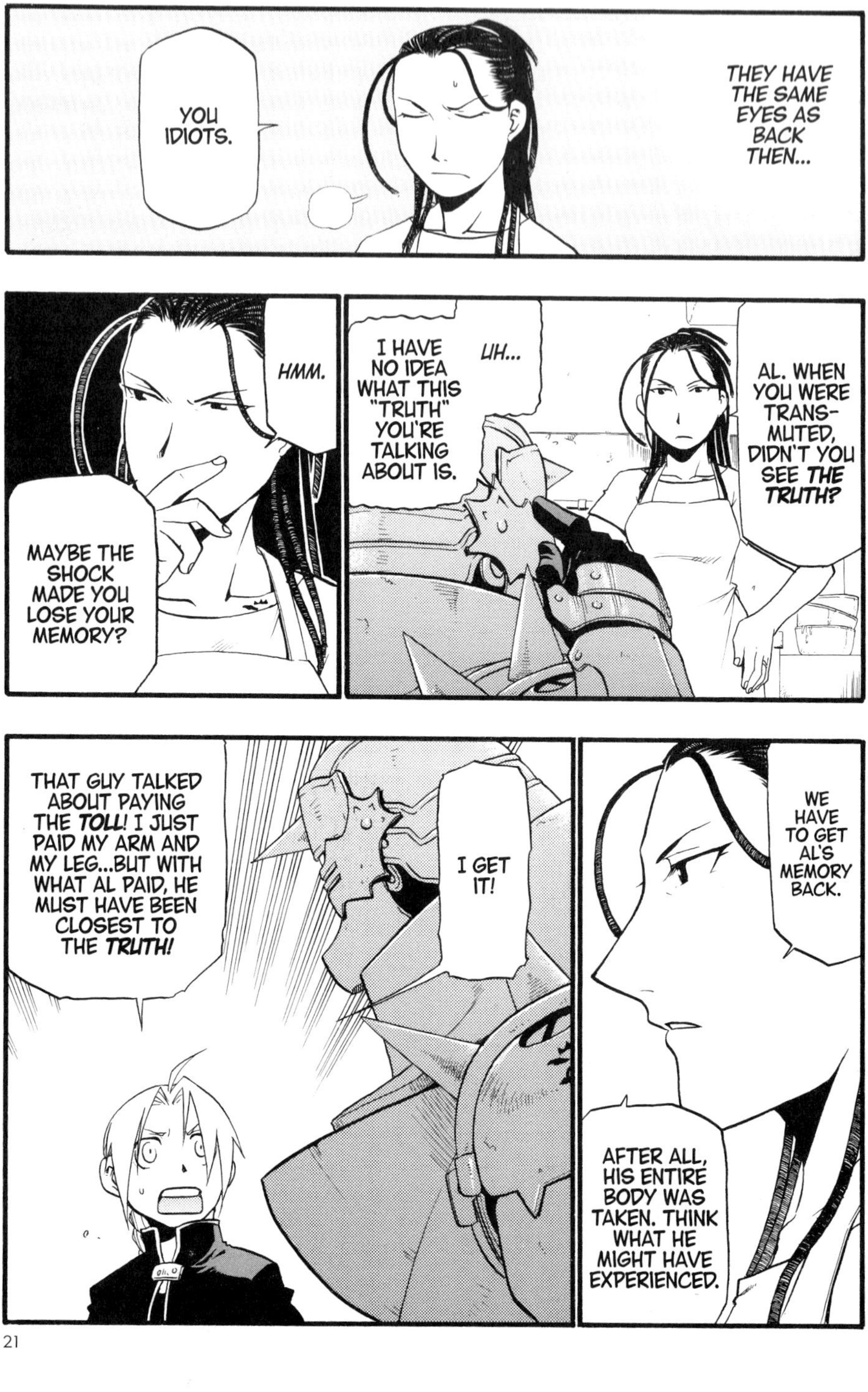
THEY HAVE THE SAME EYES AS BACK THEN...
YOU IDIOTS.
AL. WHEN YOU WERE TRANS-MUTED, DIDN'T YOU SEE *THE TRUTH?*
UH...
I HAVE NO IDEA WHAT THIS "TRUTH" YOU'RE TALKING ABOUT IS.
HMM.
MAYBE THE SHOCK MADE YOU LOSE YOUR MEMORY?
WE HAVE TO GET AL'S MEMORY BACK.
AFTER ALL, HIS ENTIRE BODY WAS TAKEN. THINK WHAT HE MIGHT HAVE EXPERIENCED.
I GET IT!
THAT GUY TALKED ABOUT PAYING THE *TOLL!* I JUST PAID MY ARM AND MY LEG...BUT WITH WHAT AL PAID, HE MUST HAVE BEEN CLOSEST TO THE *TRUTH!*

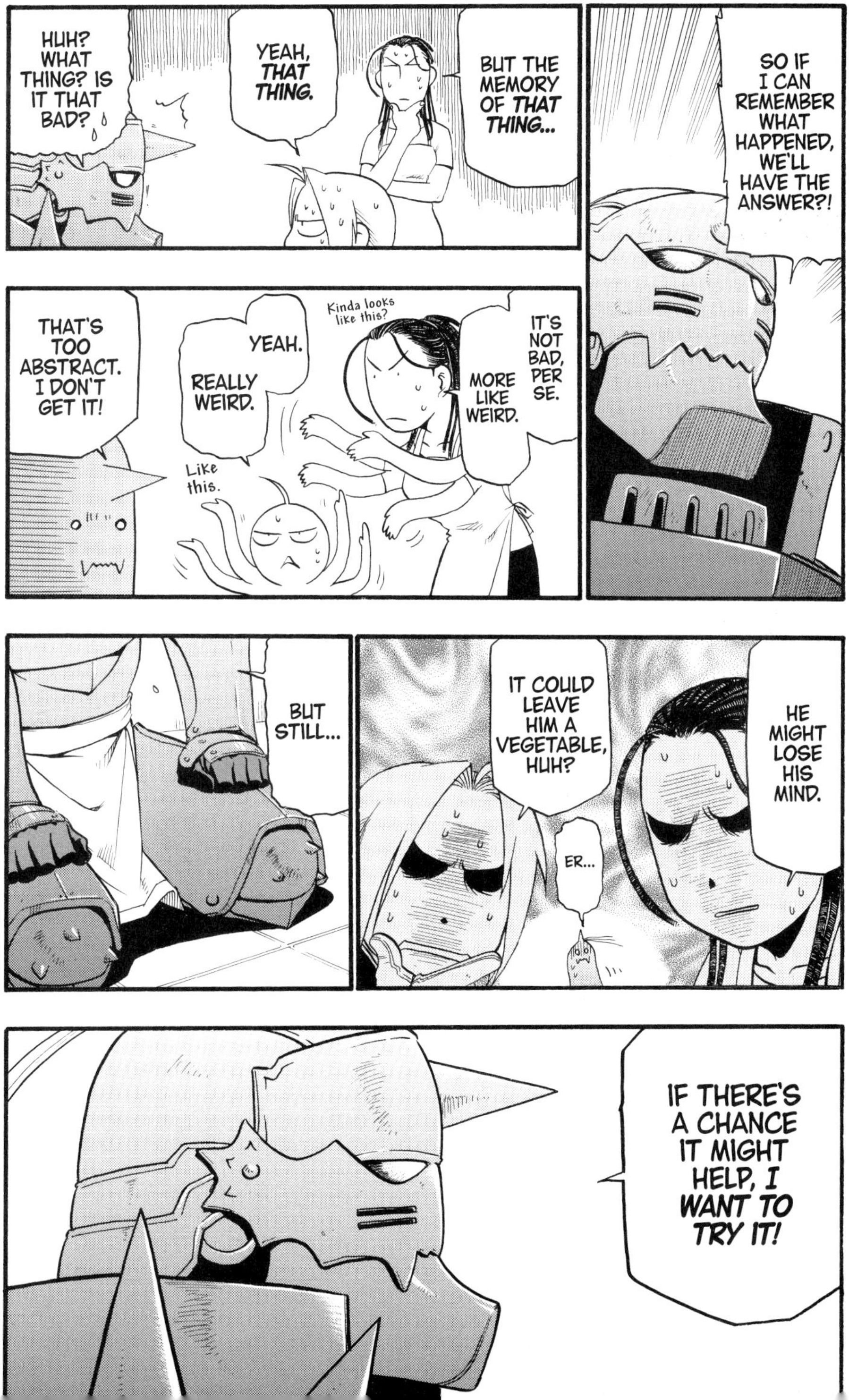
SO IF I CAN REMEMBER WHAT HAPPENED, WE'LL HAVE THE ANSWER?!
BUT THE MEMORY OF THAT THING...
YEAH, THAT THING.
HUH? WHAT THING? IS IT THAT BAD?
IT'S NOT BAD, PER SE.
MORE LIKE WEIRD.
Kinda looks like this?
YEAH.
REALLY WEIRD.
Like this.
THAT'S TOO ABSTRACT. I DON'T GET IT!
HE MIGHT LOSE HIS MIND.
IT COULD LEAVE HIM A VEGETABLE, HUH?
ER...
BUT STILL...
IF THERE'S A CHANCE IT MIGHT HELP, I WANT TO TRY IT!

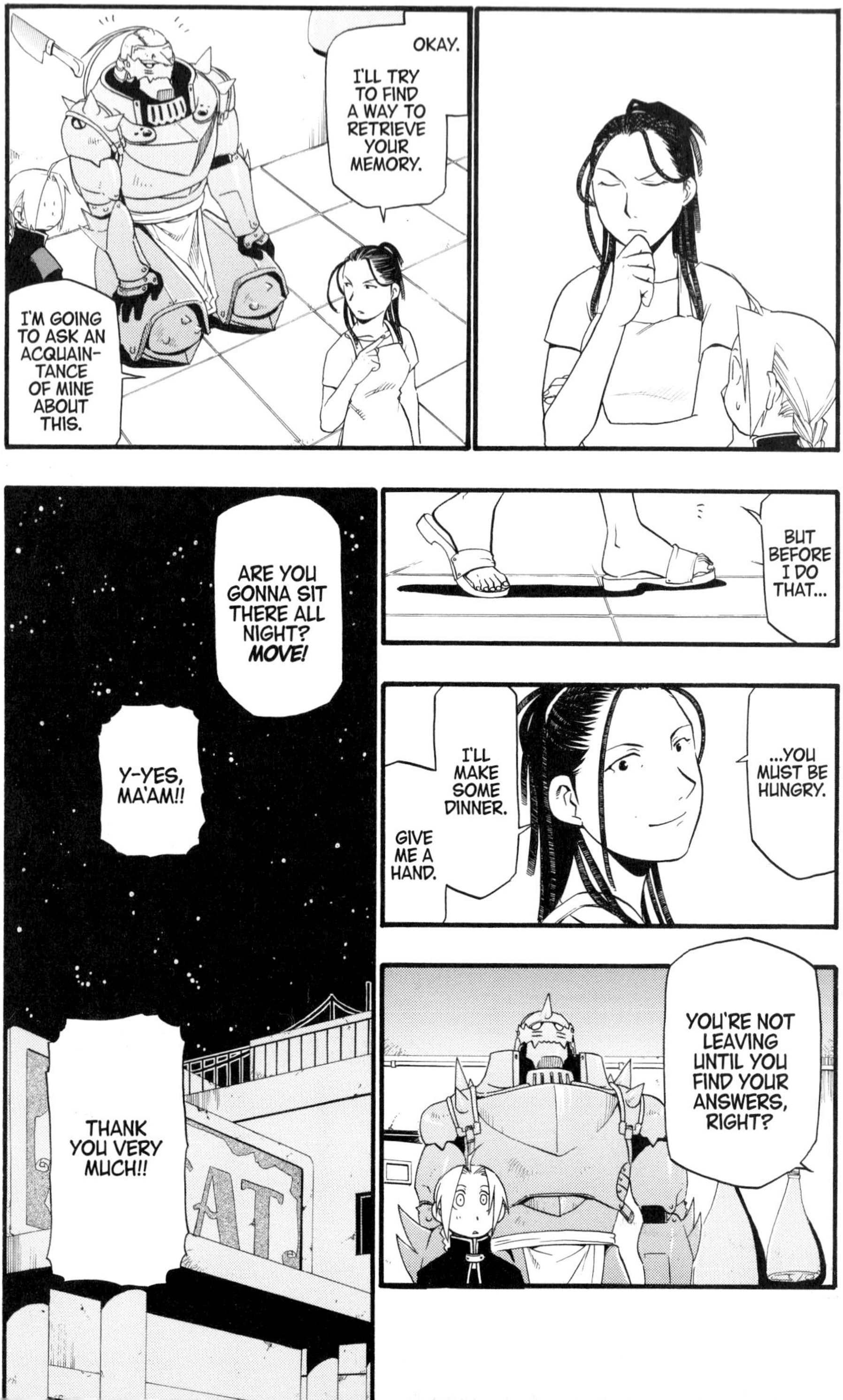
OKAY.
I'LL TRY TO FIND A WAY TO RETRIEVE YOUR MEMORY.
I'M GOING TO ASK AN ACQUAIN-TANCE OF MINE ABOUT THIS.
BUT BEFORE I DO THAT...
...YOU MUST BE HUNGRY.
I'LL MAKE SOME DINNER.
GIVE ME A HAND.
YOU'RE NOT LEAVING UNTIL YOU FIND YOUR ANSWERS, RIGHT?
ARE YOU GONNA SIT THERE ALL NIGHT? *MOVE!*
Y-YES, MA'AM!!
THANK YOU VERY MUCH!!

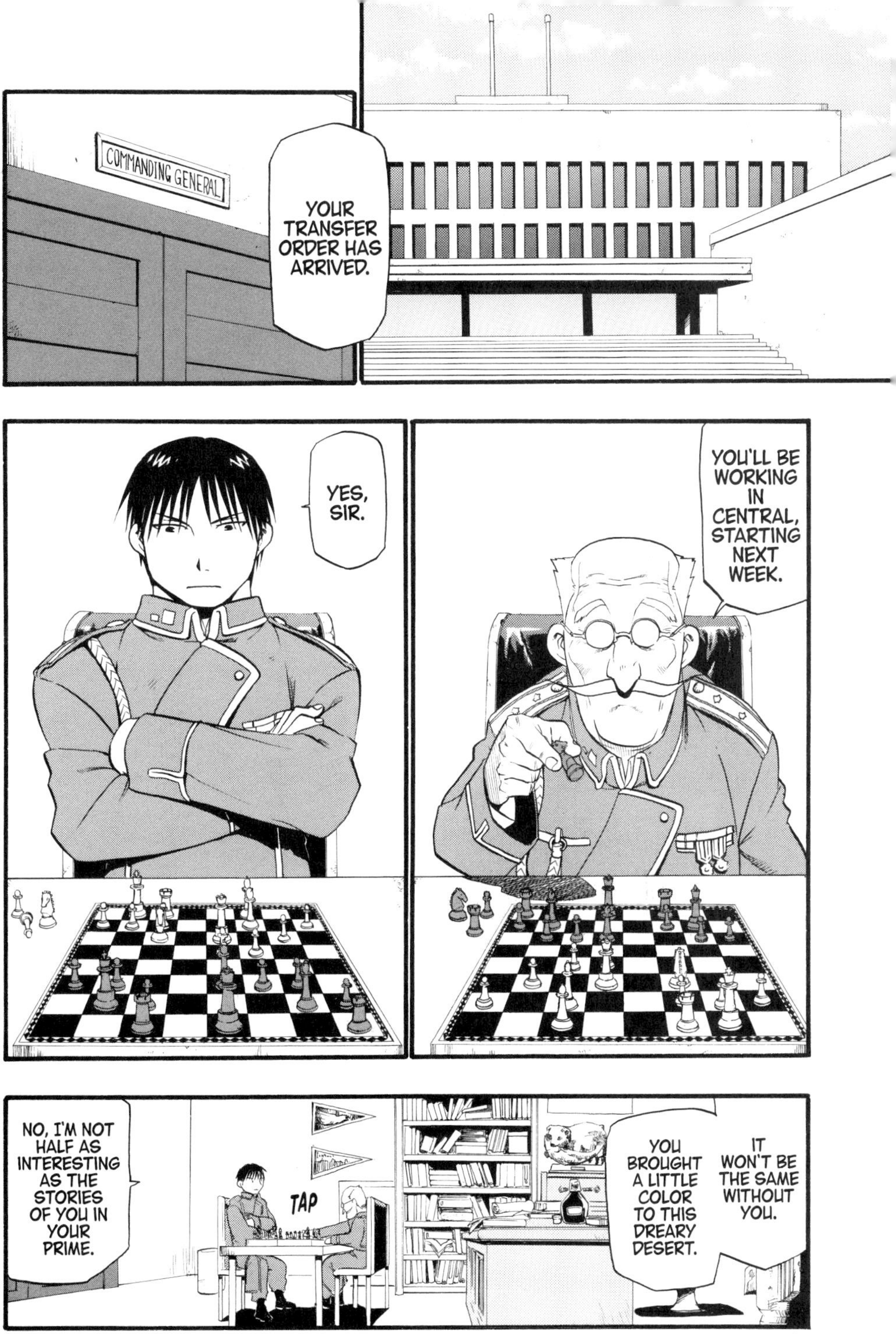
YOUR TRANSFER ORDER HAS ARRIVED.
COMMANDING GENERAL
YOU'LL BE WORKING IN CENTRAL, STARTING NEXT WEEK.
YES, SIR.
IT WON'T BE THE SAME WITHOUT YOU.
YOU BROUGHT A LITTLE COLOR TO THIS DREARY DESERT.
TAP
NO, I'M NOT HALF AS INTERESTING AS THE STORIES OF YOU IN YOUR PRIME.

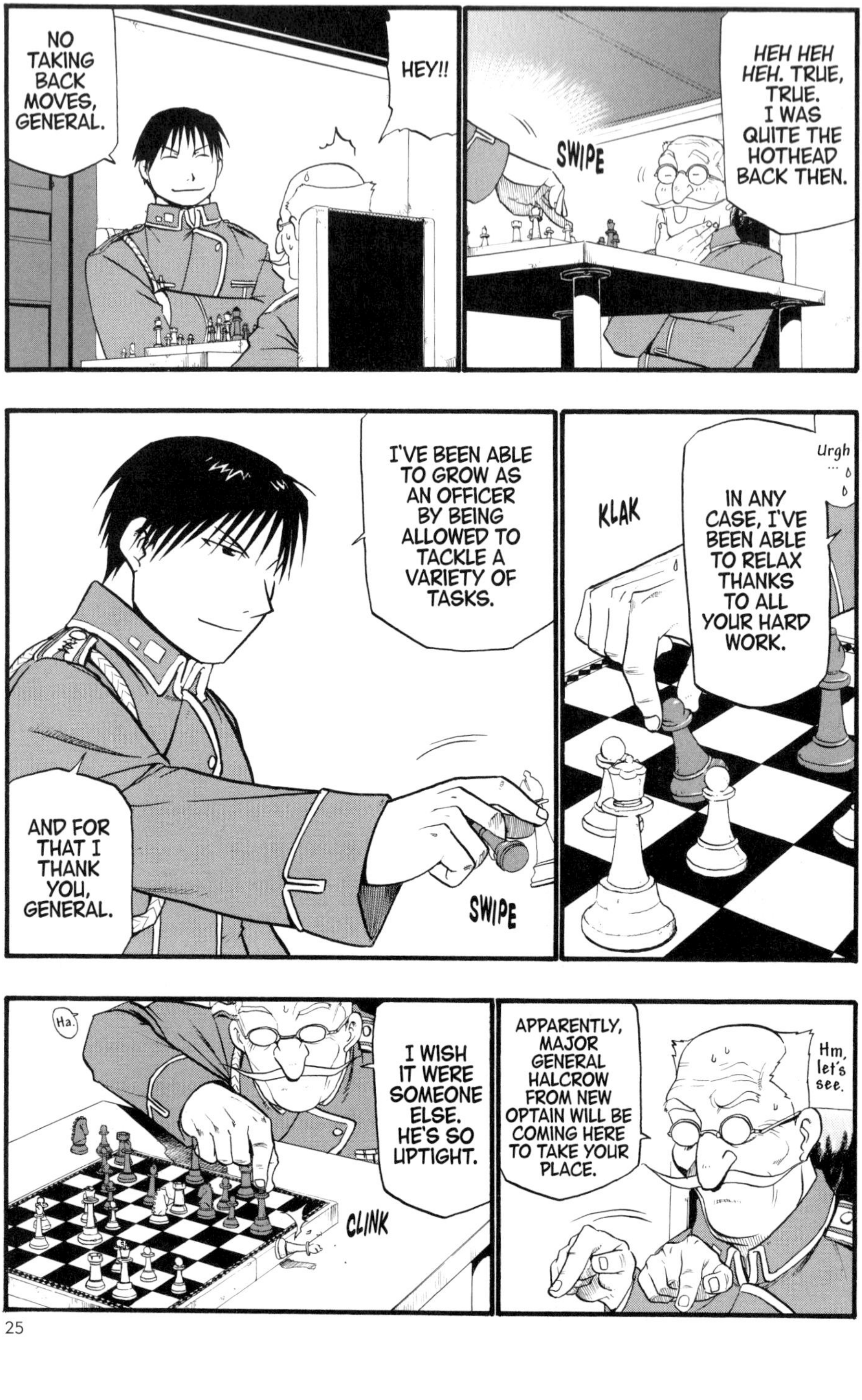
HEH HEH HEH. TRUE, TRUE. I WAS QUITE THE HOTHEAD BACK THEN.
SWIPE
HEY!!
NO TAKING BACK MOVES, GENERAL.
Urgh...
IN ANY CASE, I'VE BEEN ABLE TO RELAX THANKS TO ALL YOUR HARD WORK.
KLAK
I'VE BEEN ABLE TO GROW AS AN OFFICER BY BEING ALLOWED TO TACKLE A VARIETY OF TASKS.
AND FOR THAT I THANK YOU, GENERAL.
SWIPE
Hm, let's see.
APPARENTLY, MAJOR GENERAL HALCROW FROM NEW OPTAIN WILL BE COMING HERE TO TAKE YOUR PLACE.
I WISH IT WERE SOMEONE ELSE. HE'S SO UPTIGHT.
Ha.
CLINK

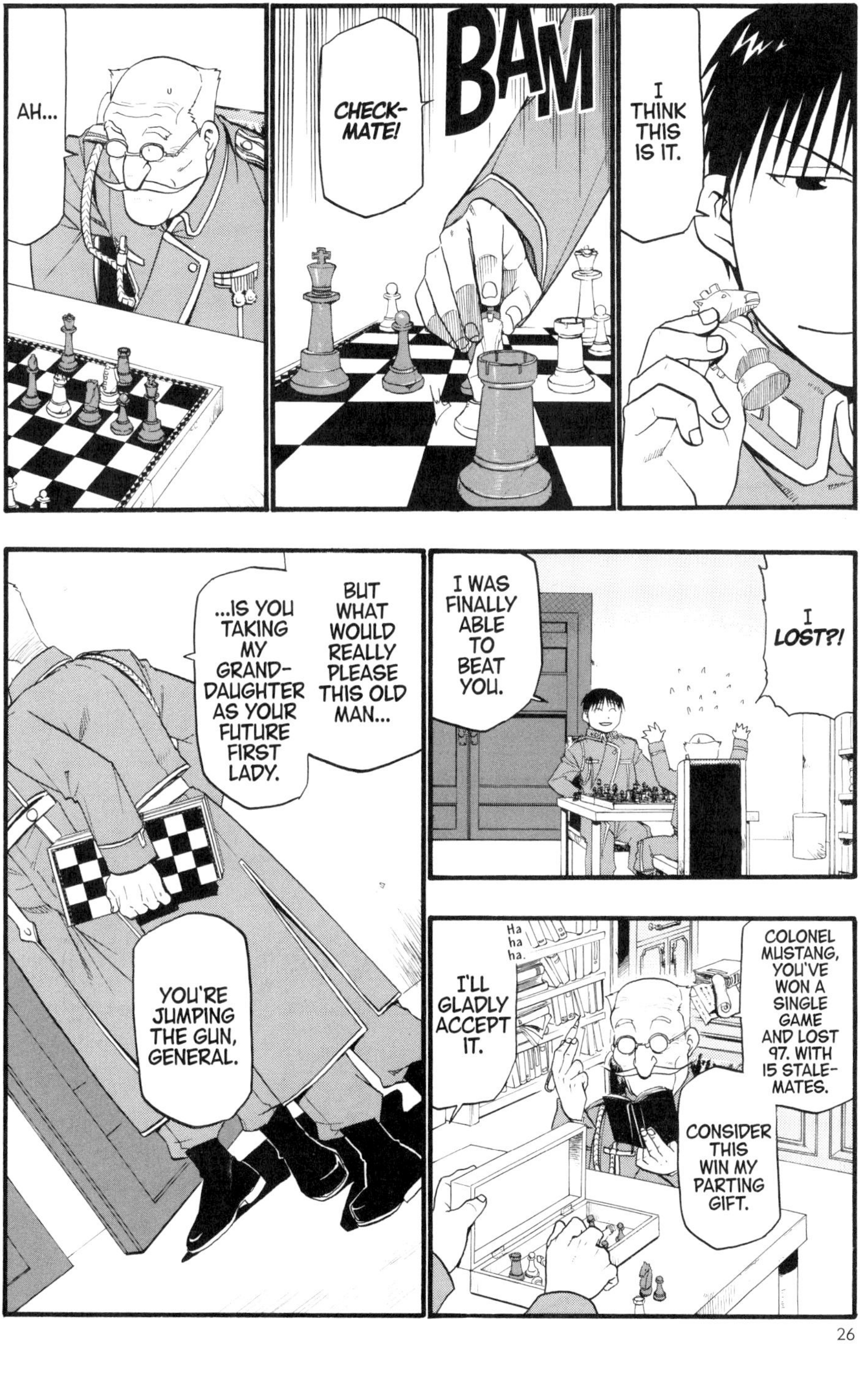
I THINK THIS IS IT.
BAM
CHECK-MATE!
AH...
I LOST?!
I WAS FINALLY ABLE TO BEAT YOU.
COLONEL MUSTANG, YOU'VE WON A SINGLE GAME AND LOST 97. WITH 15 STALE-MATES.
CONSIDER THIS WIN MY PARTING GIFT.
Ha ha ha.
I'LL GLADLY ACCEPT IT.
BUT WHAT WOULD REALLY PLEASE THIS OLD MAN...
...IS YOU TAKING MY GRAND-DAUGHTER AS YOUR FUTURE FIRST LADY.
YOU'RE JUMPING THE GUN, GENERAL.

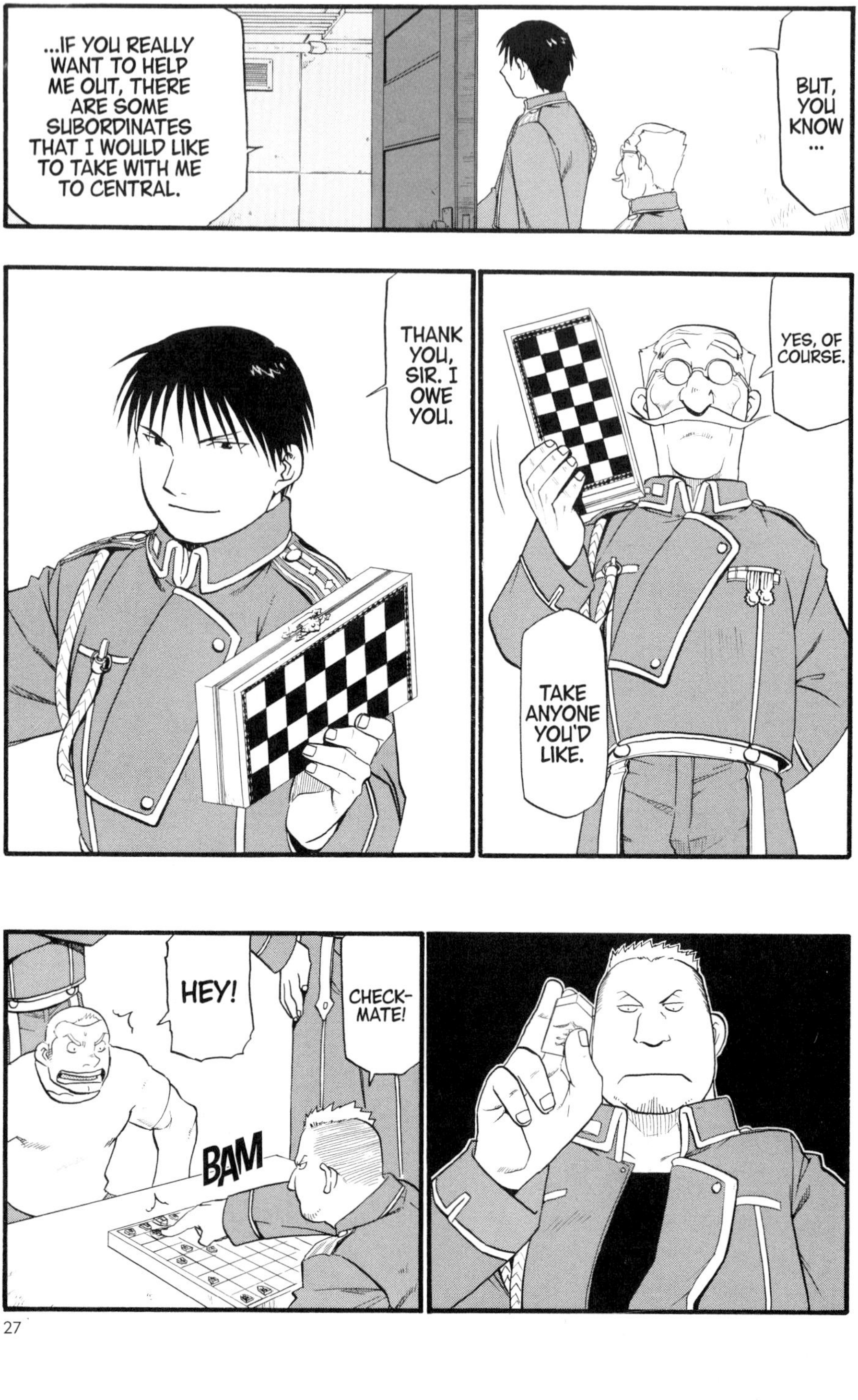
BUT, YOU KNOW ...
...IF YOU REALLY WANT TO HELP ME OUT, THERE ARE SOME SUBORDINATES THAT I WOULD LIKE TO TAKE WITH ME TO CENTRAL.
YES, OF COURSE.
TAKE ANYONE YOU'D LIKE.
THANK YOU, SIR. I OWE YOU.
CHECK-MATE!
HEY!
BAM

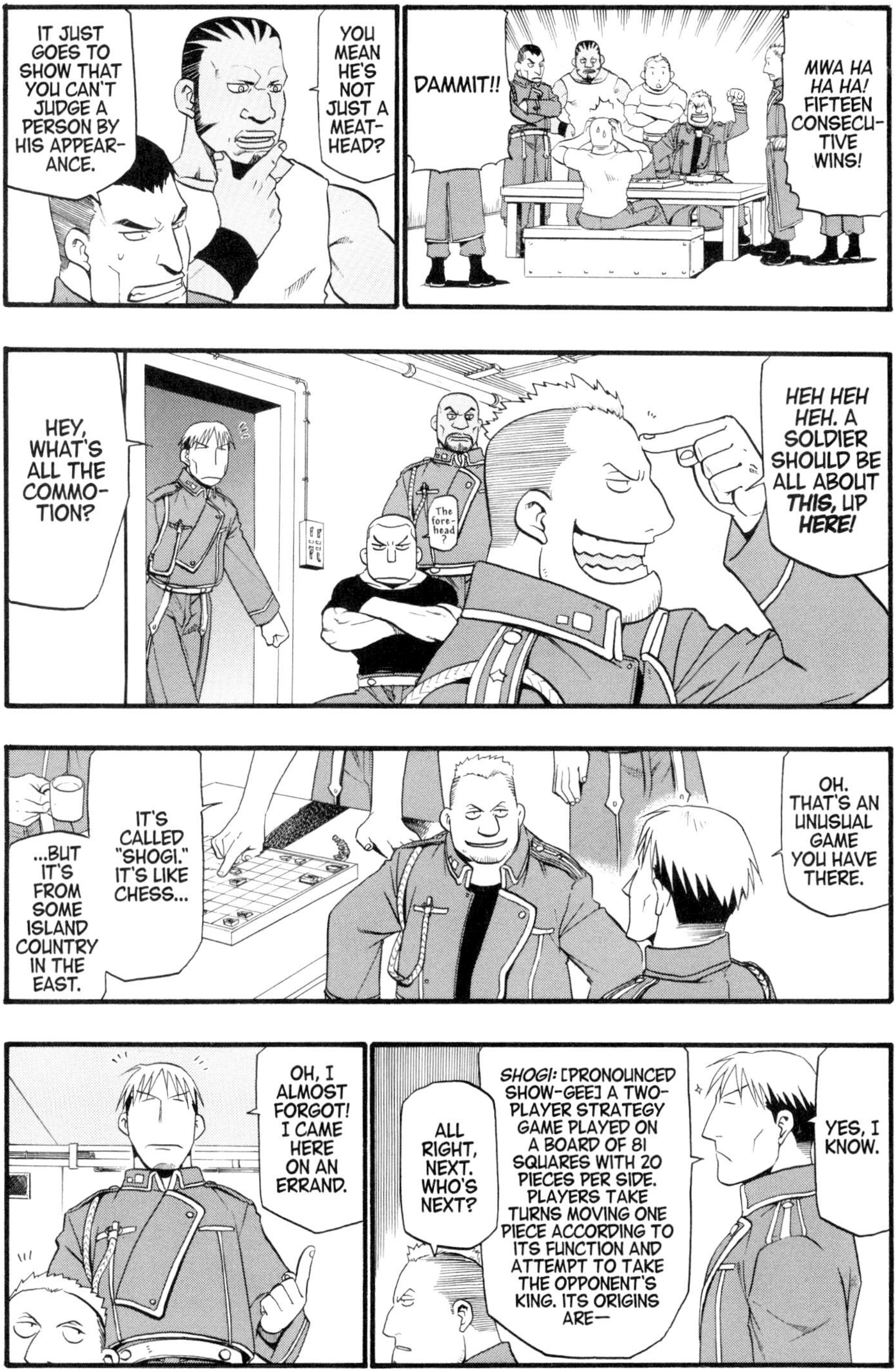
MWA HA HA HA! FIFTEEN CONSECUTIVE WINS!
DAMMIT!!
YOU MEAN HE'S NOT JUST A MEATHEAD?
IT JUST GOES TO SHOW THAT YOU CAN'T JUDGE A PERSON BY HIS APPEARANCE.
HEH HEH HEH. A SOLDIER SHOULD BE ALL ABOUT THIS, UP HERE!
The forehead?
HEY, WHAT'S ALL THE COMMOTION?
OH. THAT'S AN UNUSUAL GAME YOU HAVE THERE.
IT'S CALLED "SHOGI." IT'S LIKE CHESS...
...BUT IT'S FROM SOME ISLAND COUNTRY IN THE EAST.
YES, I KNOW.
SHOGI: [PRONOUNCED SHOW-GEE] A TWO-PLAYER STRATEGY GAME PLAYED ON A BOARD OF 81 SQUARES WITH 20 PIECES PER SIDE. PLAYERS TAKE TURNS MOVING ONE PIECE ACCORDING TO ITS FUNCTION AND ATTEMPT TO TAKE THE OPPONENT'S KING. ITS ORIGINS ARE—
ALL RIGHT, NEXT. WHO'S NEXT?
OH, I ALMOST FORGOT! I CAME HERE ON AN ERRAND.

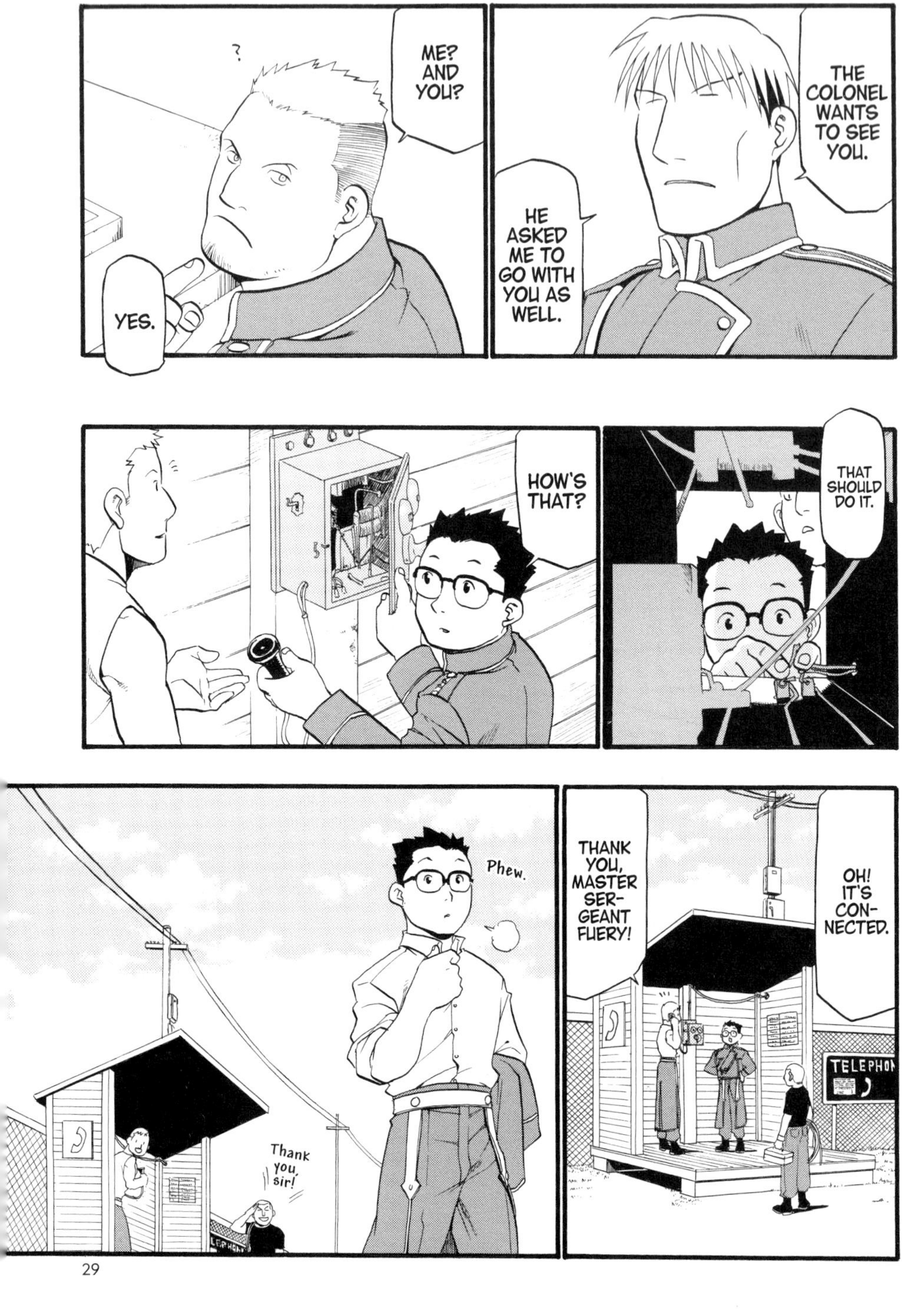
THE COLONEL WANTS TO SEE YOU.
HE ASKED ME TO GO WITH YOU AS WELL.
ME? AND YOU?
YES.
THAT SHOULD DO IT.
HOW'S THAT?
OH! IT'S CONNECTED.
THANK YOU, MASTER SERGEANT FUERY!
Phew.
Thank you, sir!

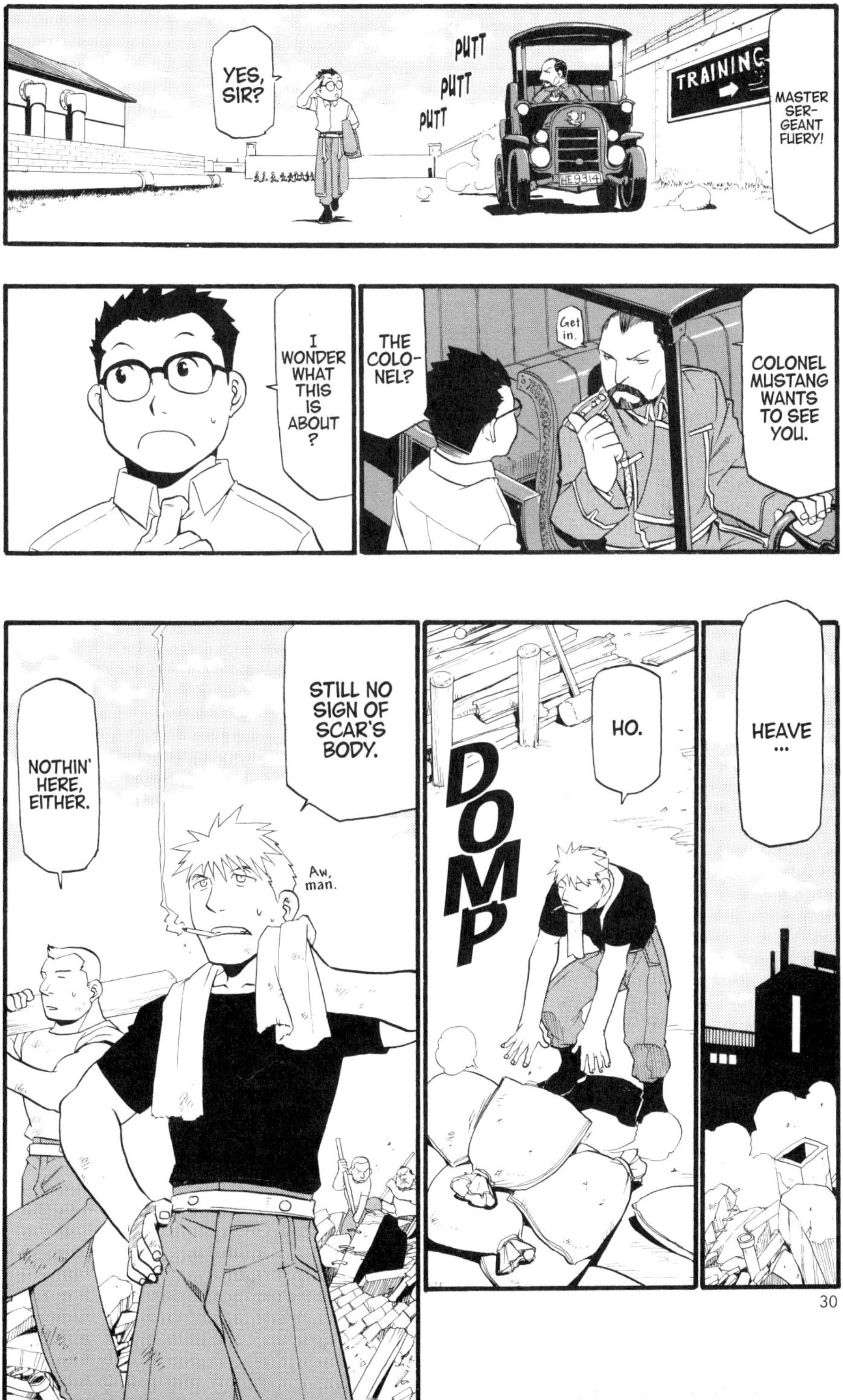
TRAINING
MASTER SER-GEANT FUERY!
PUTT
PUTT
PUTT
YES, SIR?
COLONEL MUSTANG WANTS TO SEE YOU.
Get in.
THE COLO-NEL?
I WONDER WHAT THIS IS ABOUT?
HEAVE...
HO.
DOMP
STILL NO SIGN OF SCAR'S BODY.
Aw, man.
NOTHIN' HERE, EITHER.

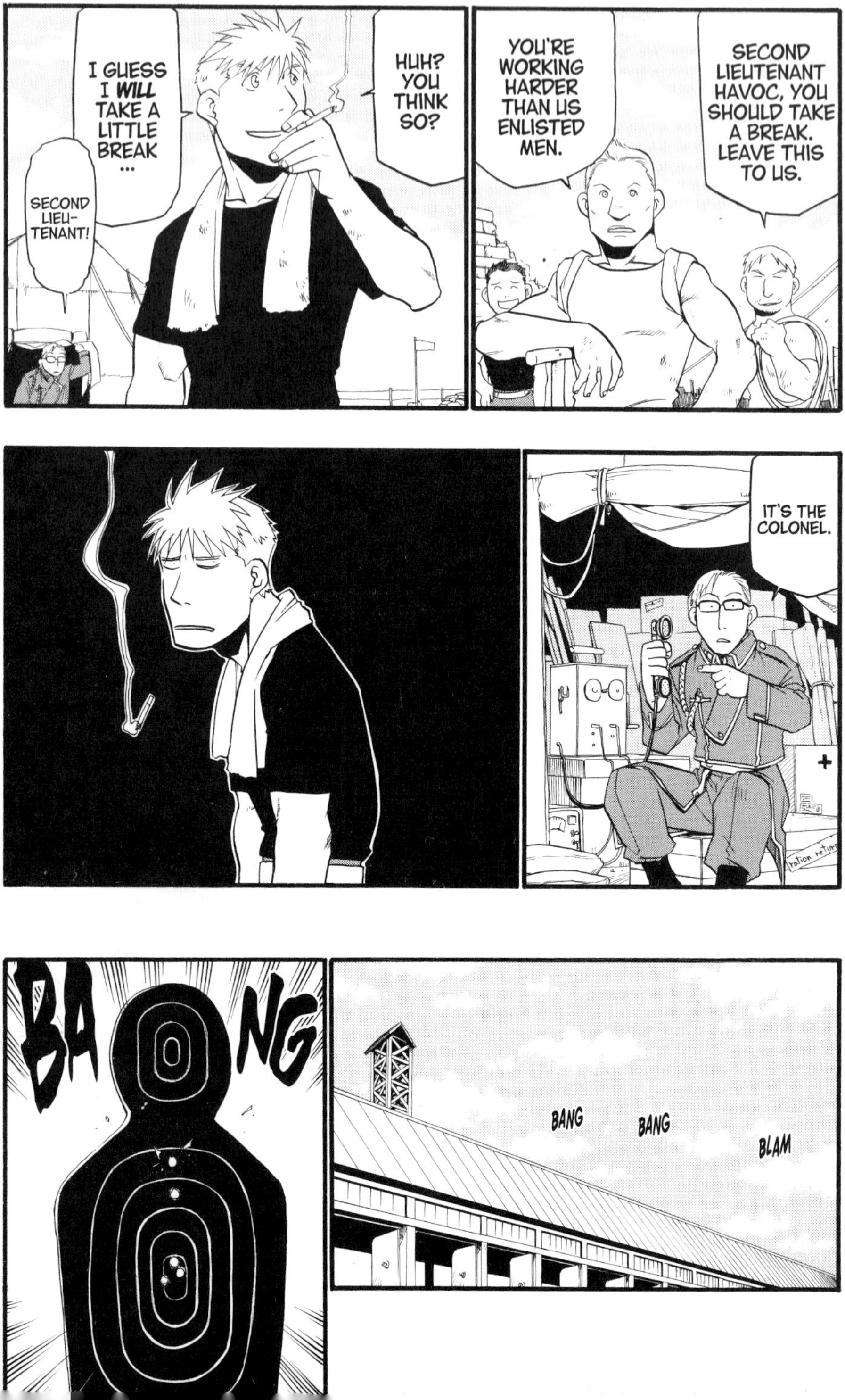
SECOND LIEUTENANT HAVOC, YOU SHOULD TAKE A BREAK. LEAVE THIS TO US.
YOU'RE WORKING HARDER THAN US ENLISTED MEN.
HUH? YOU THINK SO?
I GUESS I *WILL* TAKE A LITTLE BREAK ...
SECOND LIEU-TENANT!
IT'S THE COLONEL.
BANG
BANG
BLAM
BANG

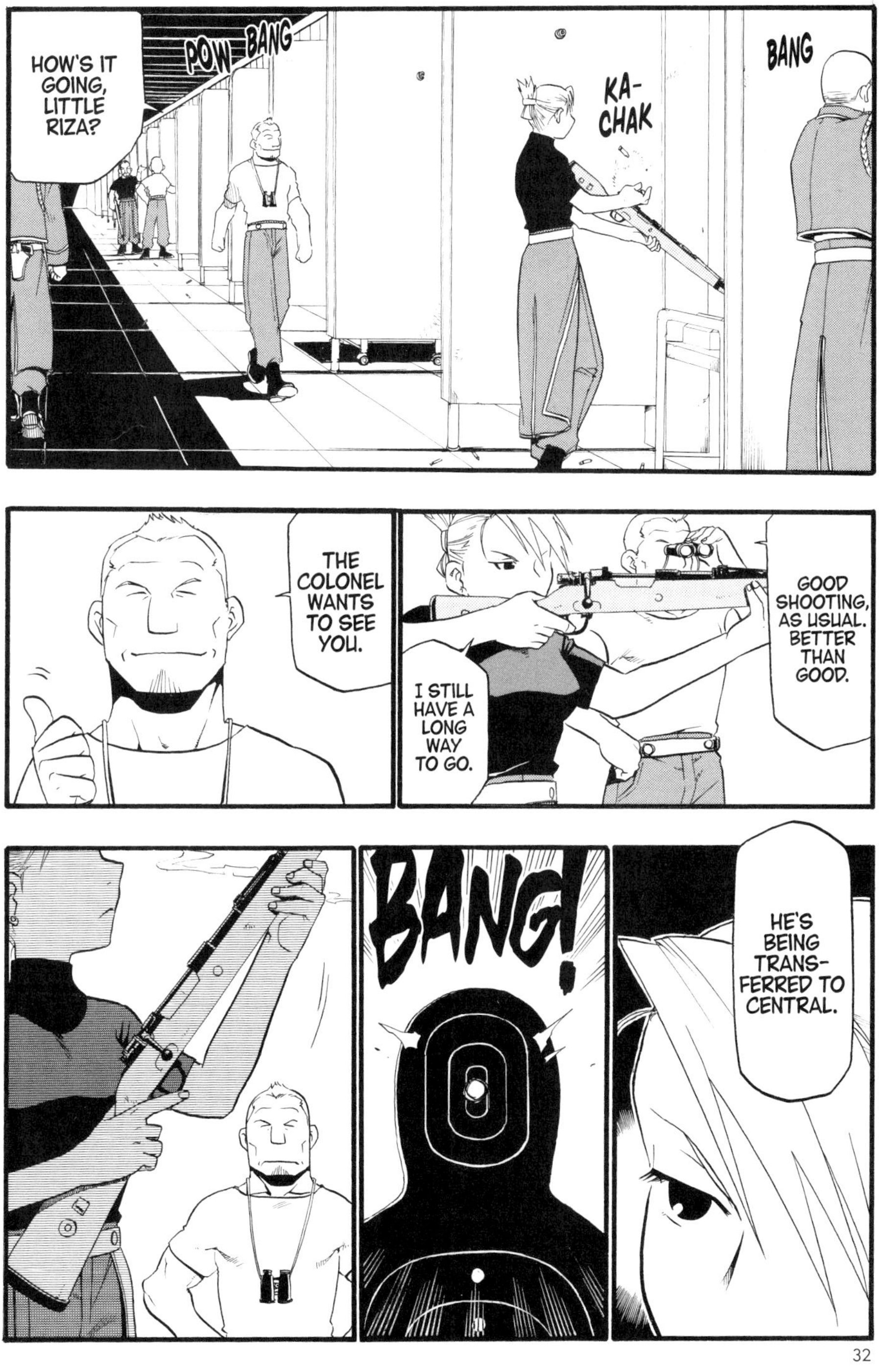
BANG
KA-CHAK
POW
BANG
HOW'S IT GOING, LITTLE RIZA?
GOOD SHOOTING, AS USUAL. BETTER THAN GOOD.
I STILL HAVE A LONG WAY TO GO.
THE COLONEL WANTS TO SEE YOU.
HE'S BEING TRANSFERRED TO CENTRAL.
BANG!

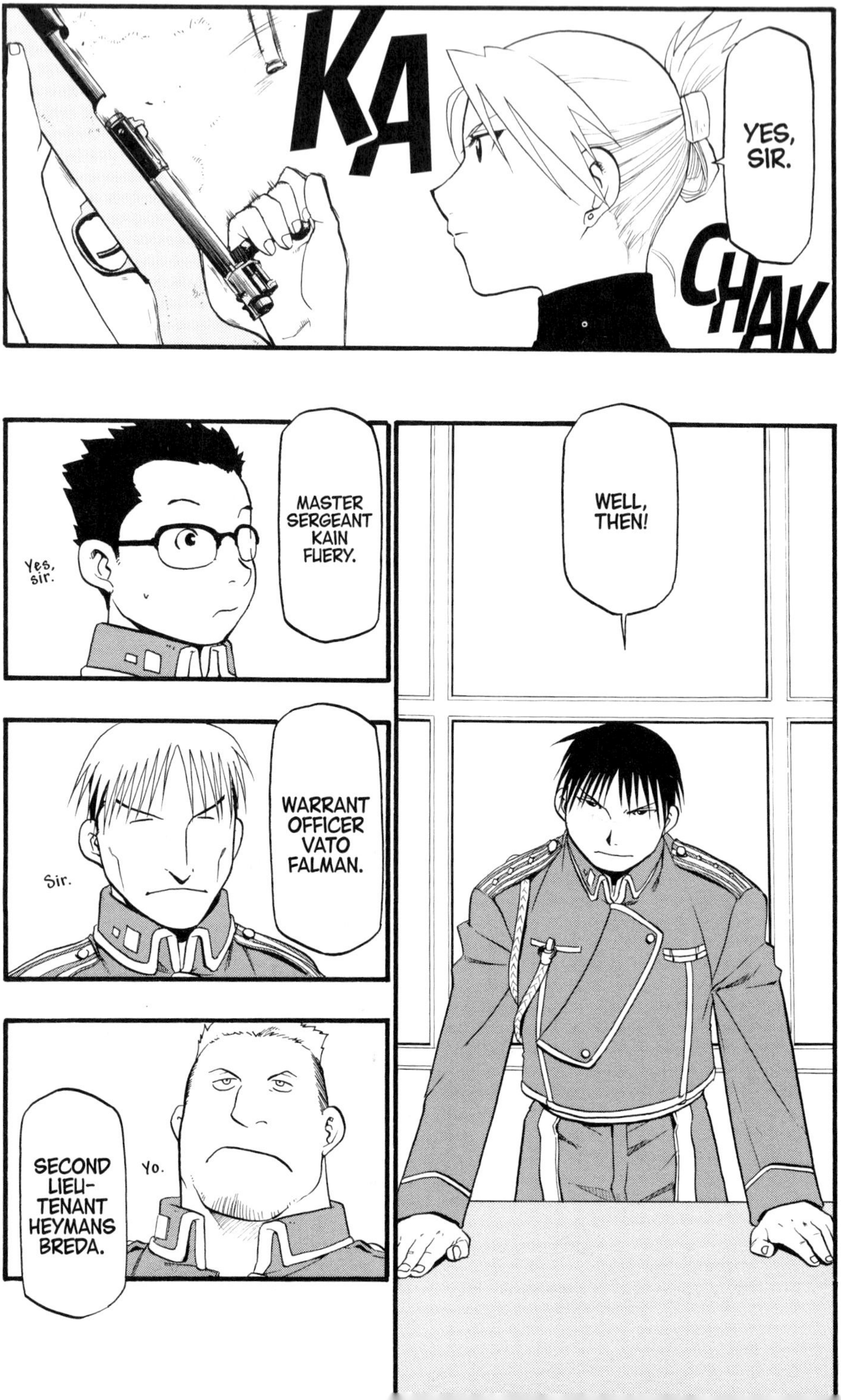
YES, SIR.
KA
CHAK
WELL, THEN!
MASTER SERGEANT KAIN FUERY.
Yes, sir.
WARRANT OFFICER VATO FALMAN.
Sir.
SECOND LIEU-TENANT HEYMANS BREDA.
Yo.

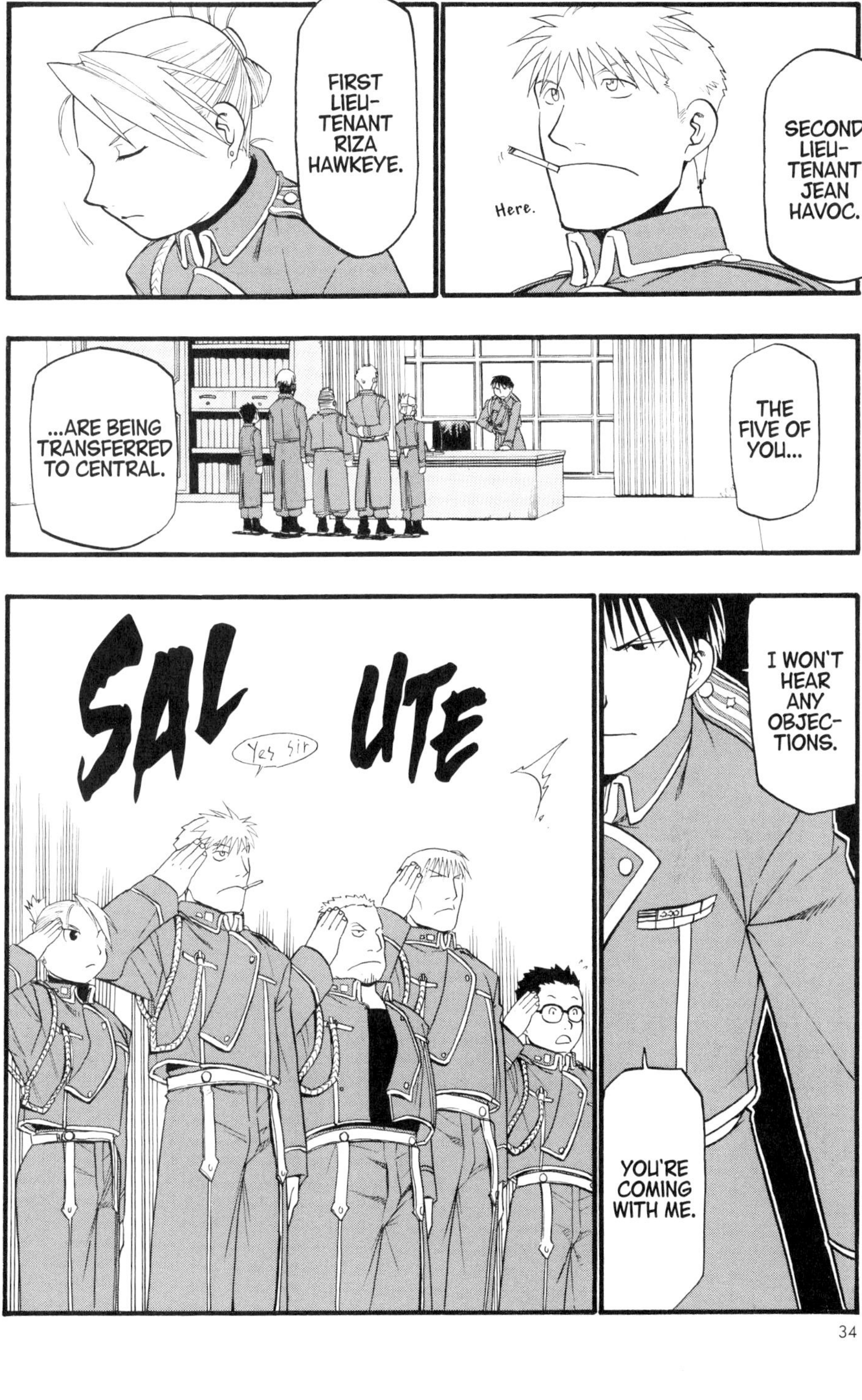
SECOND LIEU-TENANT JEAN HAVOC.
Here.
FIRST LIEU-TENANT RIZA HAWKEYE.
THE FIVE OF YOU...
...ARE BEING TRANSFERRED TO CENTRAL.
I WON'T HEAR ANY OBJECTIONS.
YOU'RE COMING WITH ME.
SALUTE
Yes sir

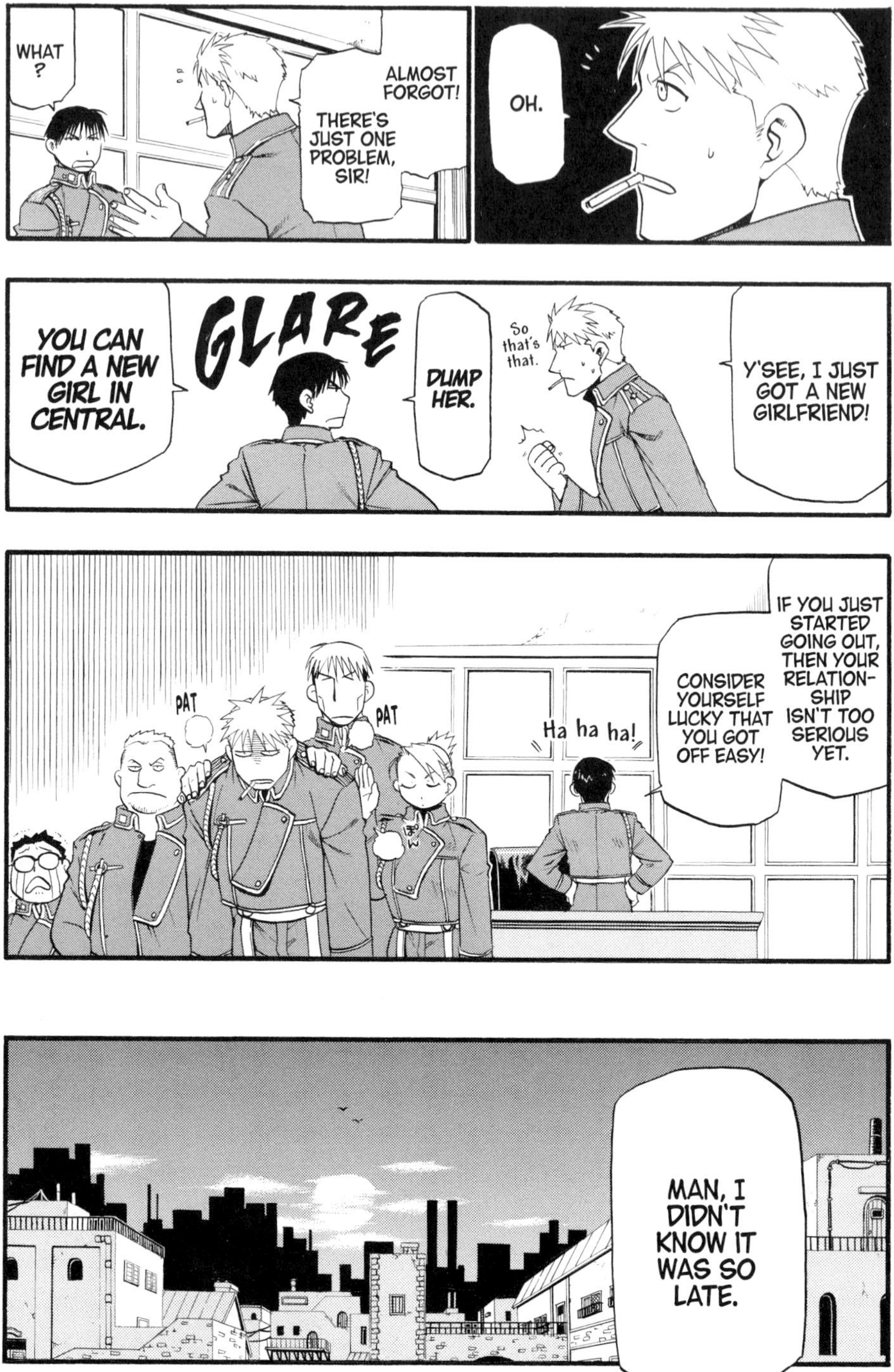
OH.
ALMOST FORGOT!
THERE'S JUST ONE PROBLEM, SIR!
WHAT ?
Y'SEE, I JUST GOT A NEW GIRLFRIEND!
So that's that.
DUMP HER.
GLARE
YOU CAN FIND A NEW GIRL IN CENTRAL.
IF YOU JUST STARTED GOING OUT, THEN YOUR RELATION-SHIP ISN'T TOO SERIOUS YET.
CONSIDER YOURSELF LUCKY THAT YOU GOT OFF EASY!
Ha ha ha!
PAT
PAT
MAN, I DIDN'T KNOW IT WAS SO LATE.

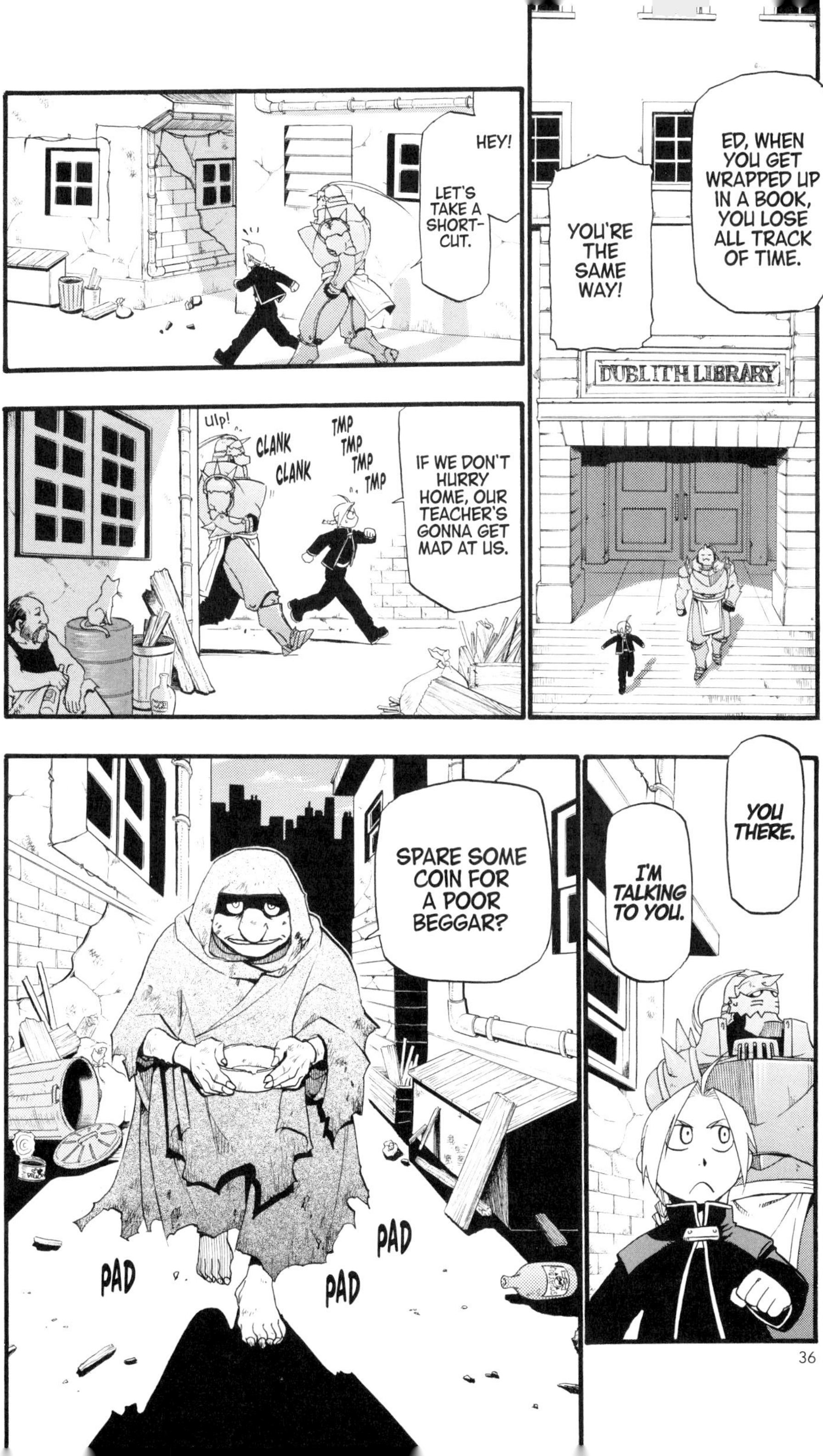
ED, WHEN YOU GET WRAPPED UP IN A BOOK, YOU LOSE ALL TRACK OF TIME.
YOU'RE THE SAME WAY!
DUBLITH LIBRARY
HEY!
LET'S TAKE A SHORT-CUT.
IF WE DON'T HURRY HOME, OUR TEACHER'S GONNA GET MAD AT US.
TMP TMP TMP TMP
CLANK CLANK
Ulp!
YOU THERE.
I'M TALKING TO YOU.
SPARE SOME COIN FOR A POOR BEGGAR?
PAD
PAD
PAD

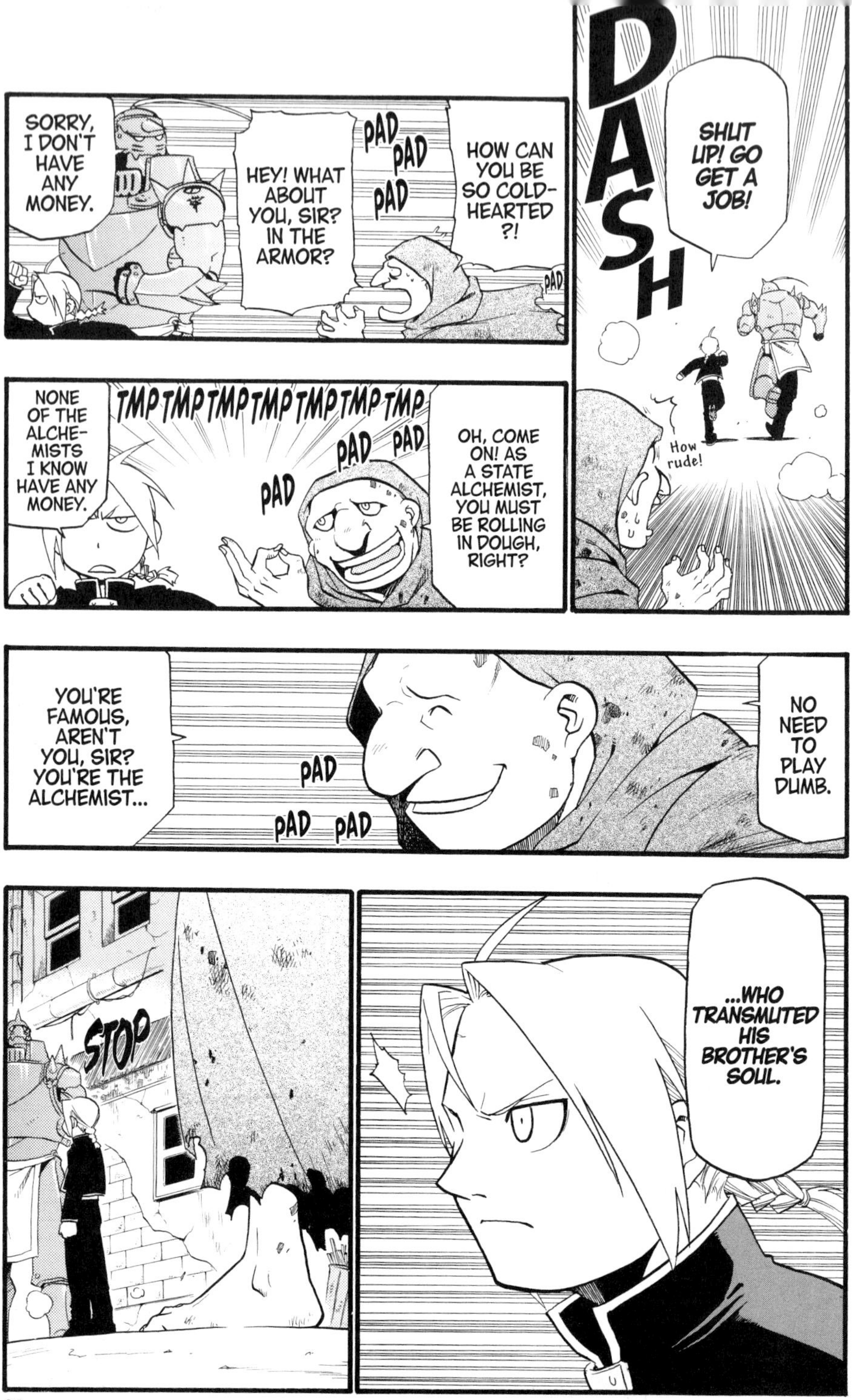
DASH
SHUT UP! GO GET A JOB!
How rude!
HOW CAN YOU BE SO COLD-HEARTED?!
PAD
PAD PAD PAD
HEY! WHAT ABOUT YOU, SIR? IN THE ARMOR?
SORRY, I DON'T HAVE ANY MONEY.
OH, COME ON! AS A STATE ALCHEMIST, YOU MUST BE ROLLING IN DOUGH, RIGHT?
PAD PAD PAD
TMP TMP TMP TMP TMP TMP TMP
NONE OF THE ALCHEMISTS I KNOW HAVE ANY MONEY.
NO NEED TO PLAY DUMB.
PAD PAD PAD
YOU'RE FAMOUS, AREN'T YOU, SIR? YOU'RE THE ALCHEMIST...
...WHO TRANSMUTED HIS BROTHER'S SOUL.
STOP

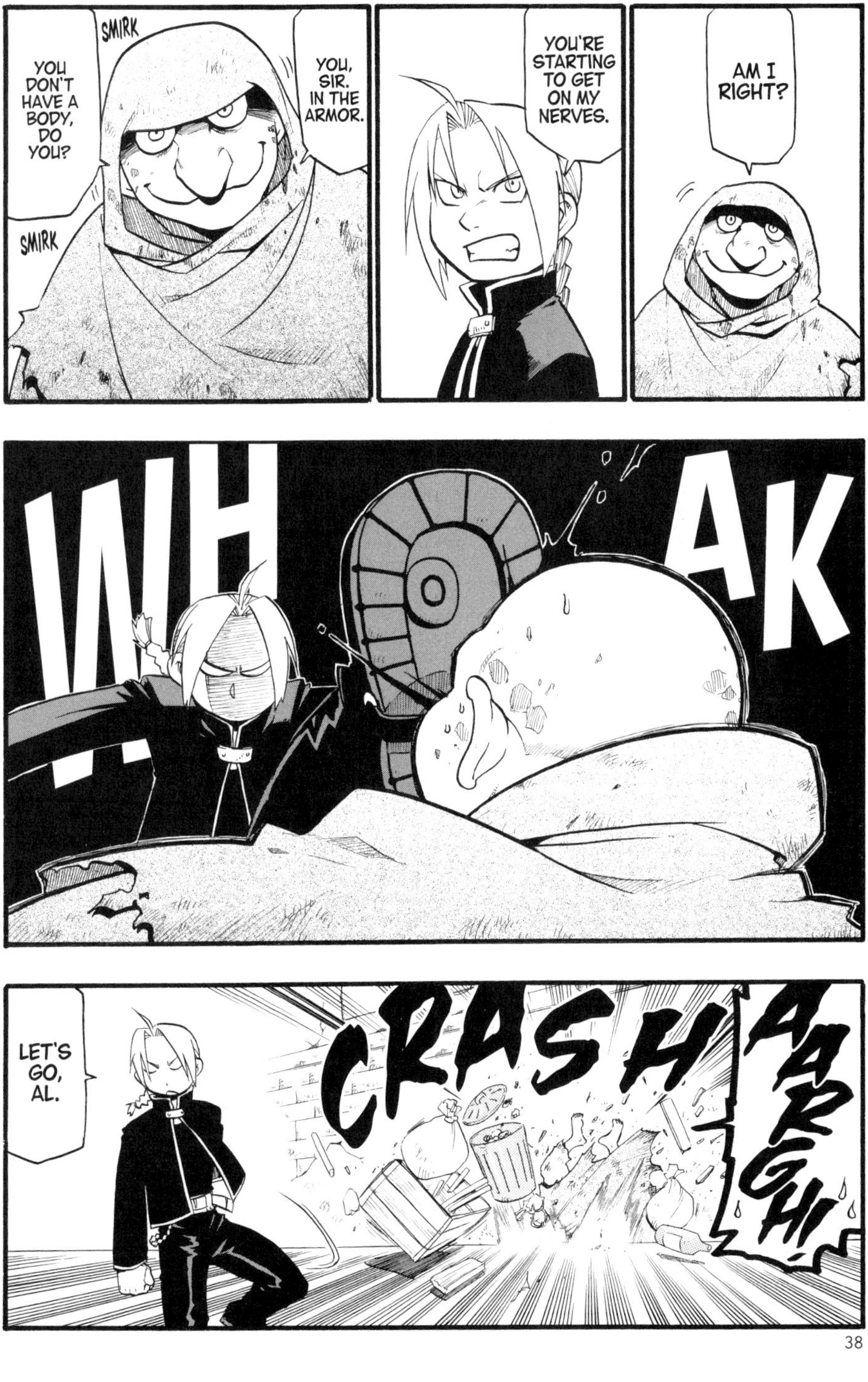
YOU, SIR. IN THE ARMOR.
YOU DON'T HAVE A BODY, DO YOU?
SMIRK
SMIRK
YOU'RE STARTING TO GET ON MY NERVES.
AM I RIGHT?
WHAK
LET'S GO, AL.
CRASH
AARGH!

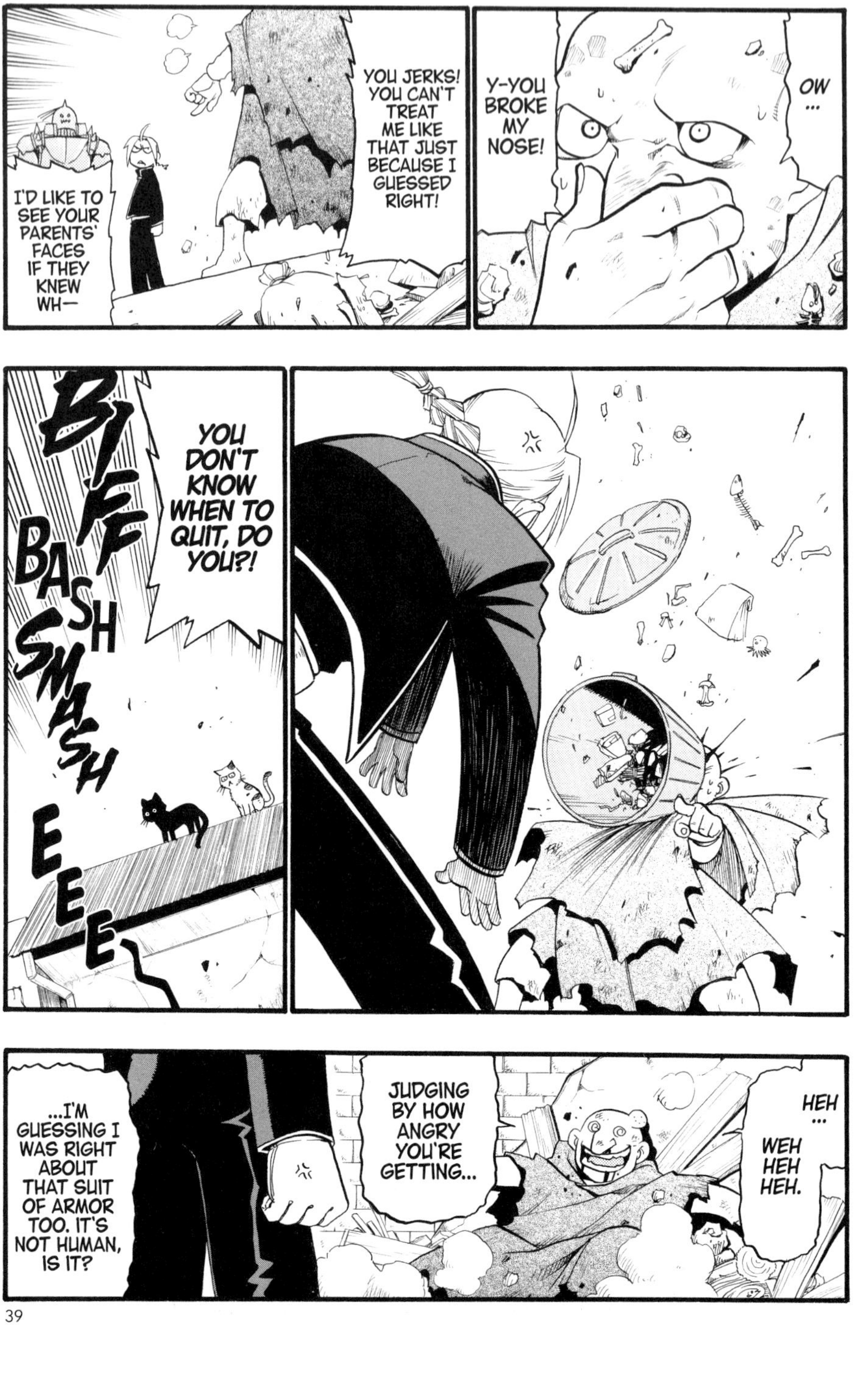
OW ...
Y-YOU BROKE MY NOSE!
YOU JERKS! YOU CAN'T TREAT ME LIKE THAT JUST BECAUSE I GUESSED RIGHT!
I'D LIKE TO SEE YOUR PARENTS' FACES IF THEY KNEW WH—
YOU DON'T KNOW WHEN TO QUIT, DO YOU?!
BIFF
BASH
SMASH
EEEE
HEH ...
WEH HEH HEH.
JUDGING BY HOW ANGRY YOU'RE GETTING...
...I'M GUESSING I WAS RIGHT ABOUT THAT SUIT OF ARMOR TOO. IT'S NOT HUMAN, IS IT?

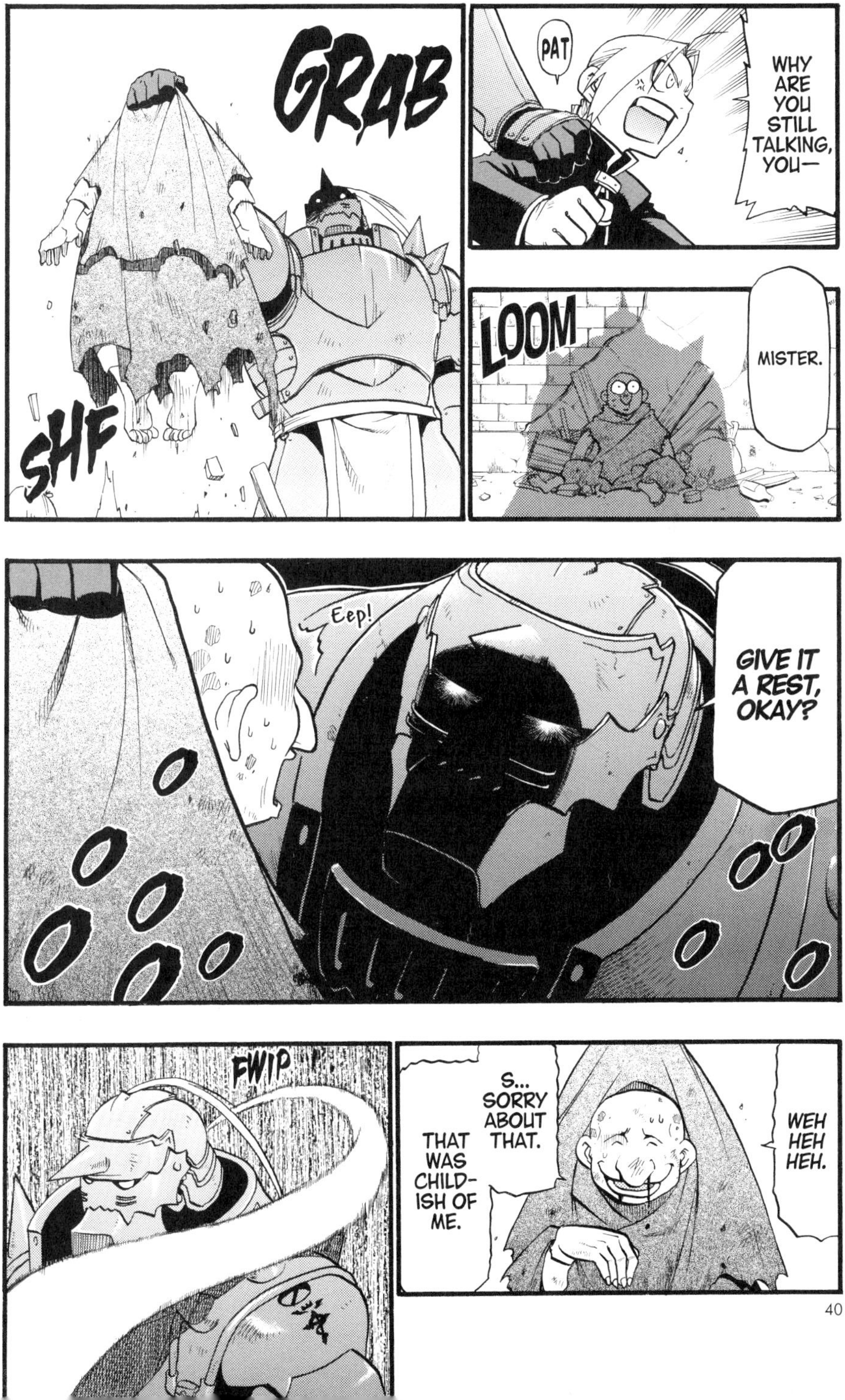

PAT
WHY ARE YOU STILL TALKING, YOU—
MISTER.
LOOM
GRAB
SHF
GIVE IT A REST, OKAY?
Eep!
WEH HEH HEH.
S... SORRY ABOUT THAT.
THAT WAS CHILD-ISH OF ME.
FWIP

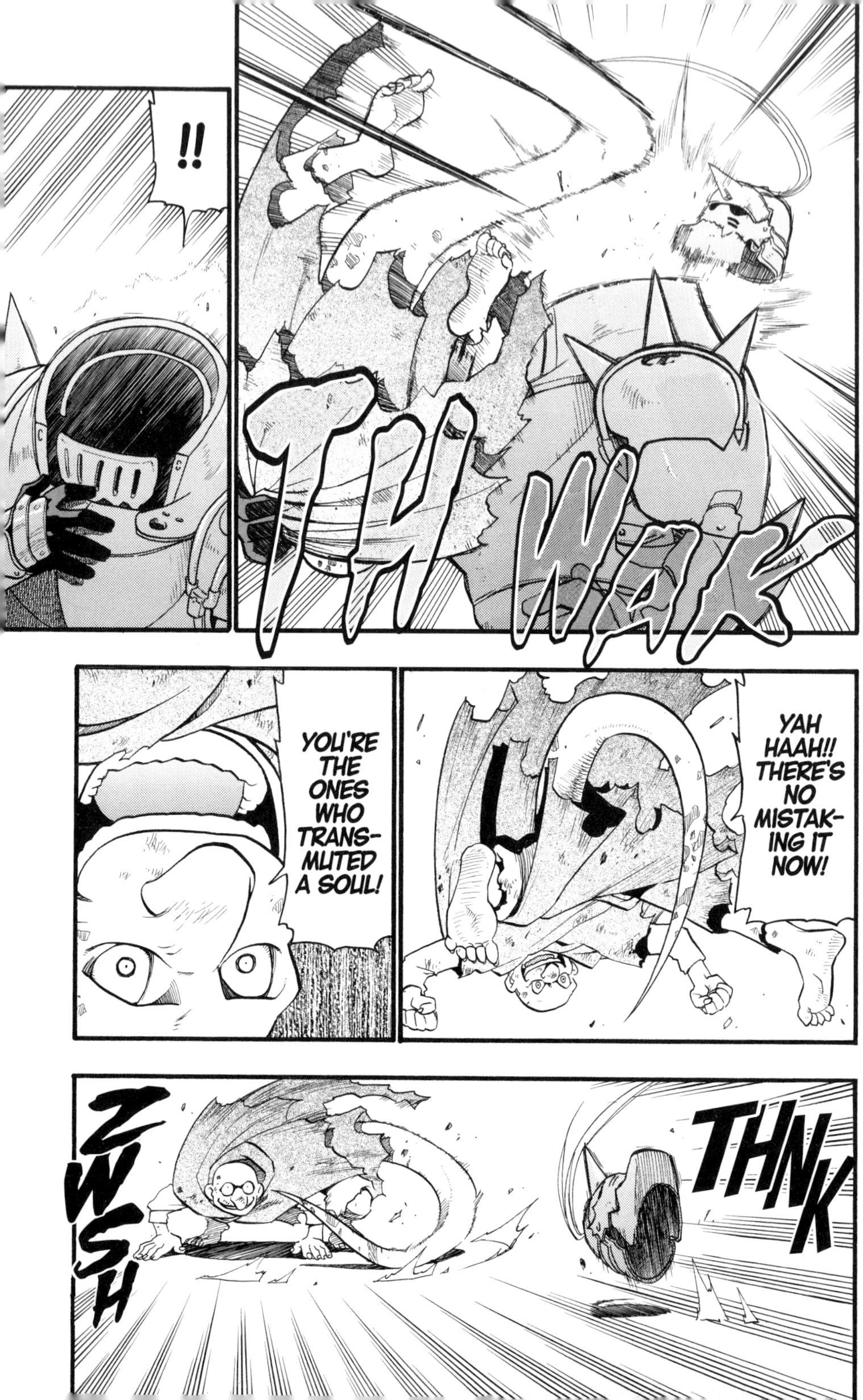
THWAK
!!
YAH HAAH!! THERE'S NO MISTAK-ING IT NOW!
YOU'RE THE ONES WHO TRANS-MUTED A SOUL!
THNK
ZWSH

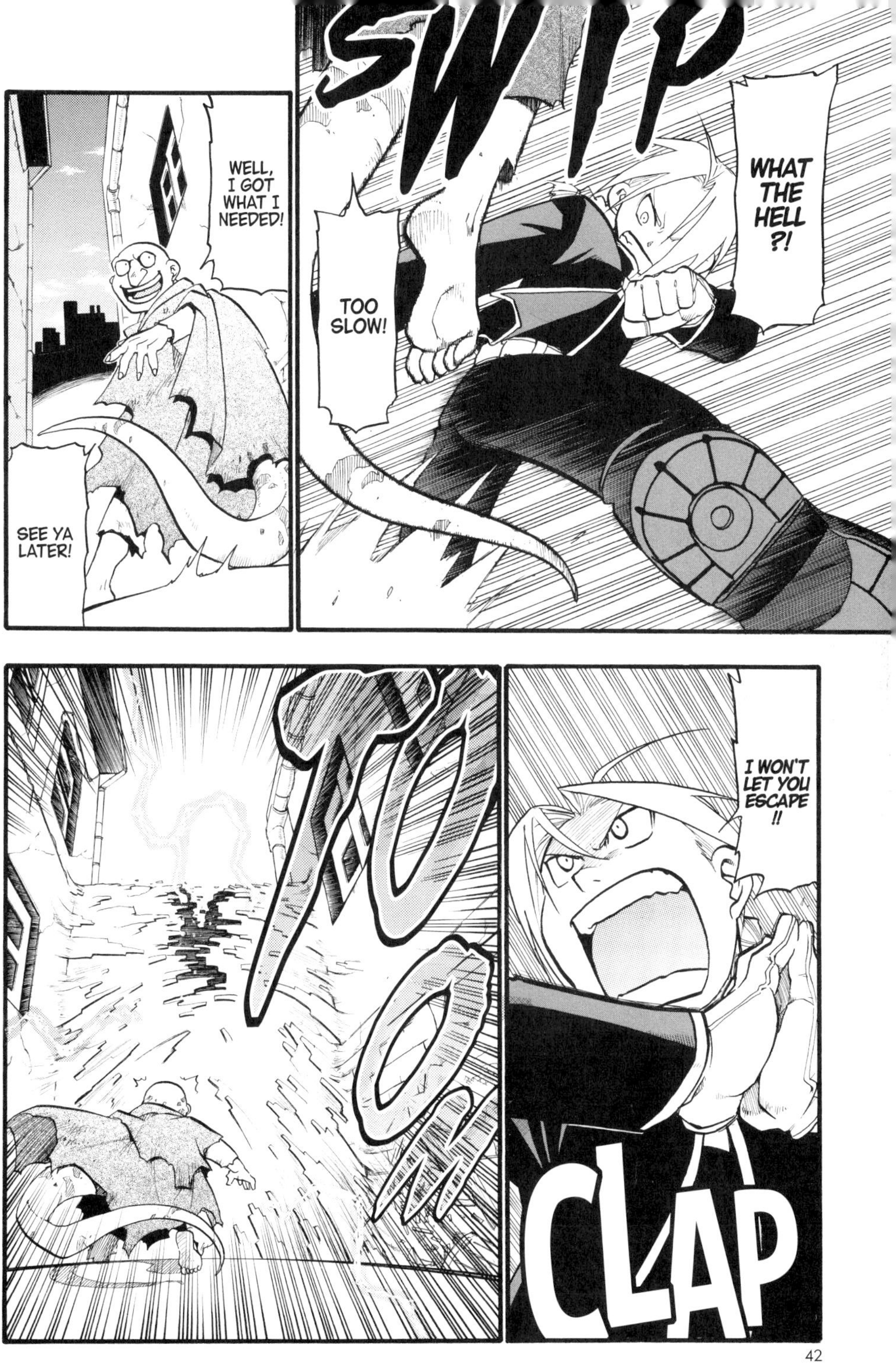
SWIP
WHAT THE HELL?!
TOO SLOW!
WELL, I GOT WHAT I NEEDED!
SEE YA LATER!
I WON'T LET YOU ESCAPE!!
CLAP

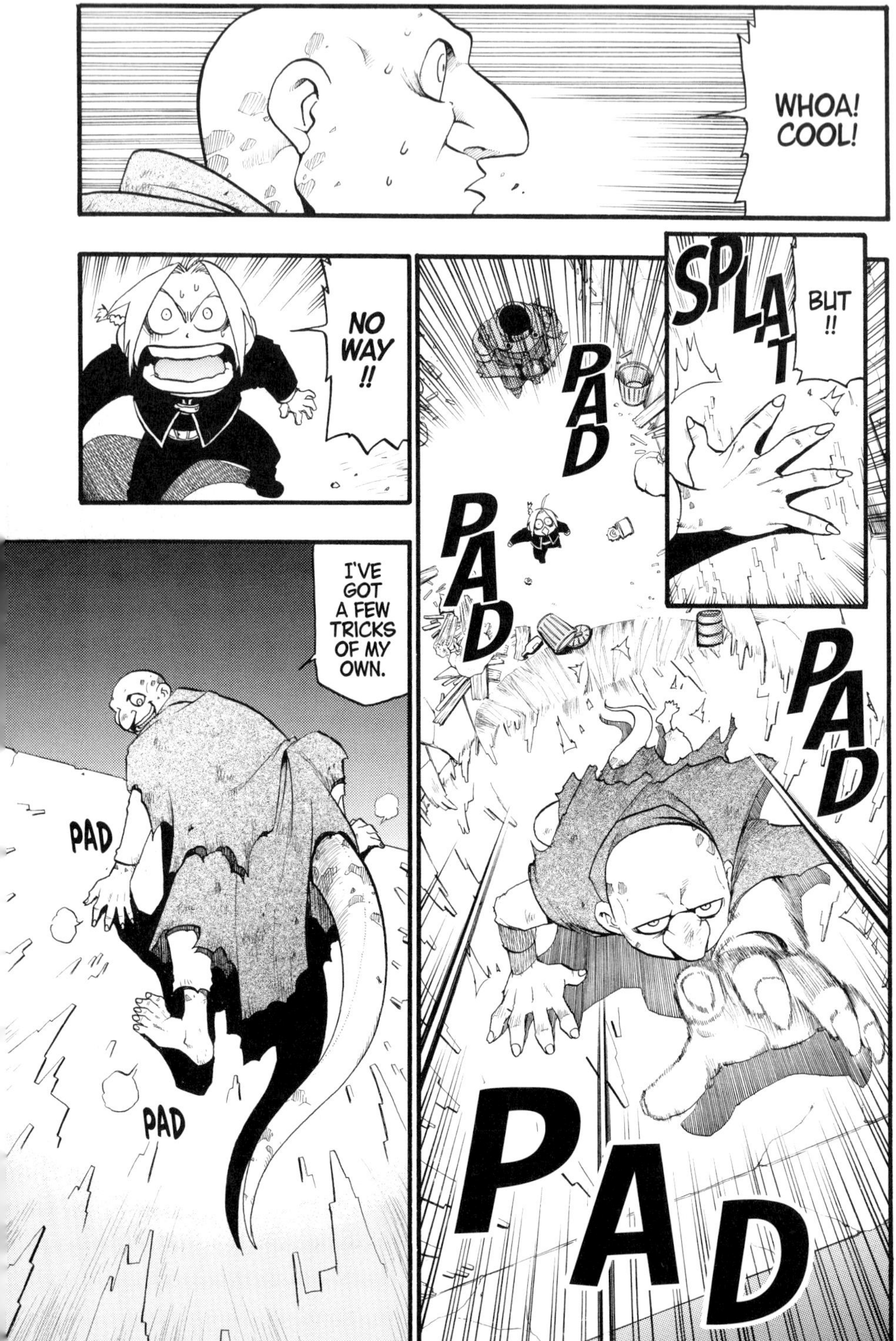
WHOA! COOL!
SPLAT
BUT !!
PAD PAD
PAD PAD
PAD PAD
PAD
NO WAY !!
I'VE GOT A FEW TRICKS OF MY OWN.
PAD
PAD

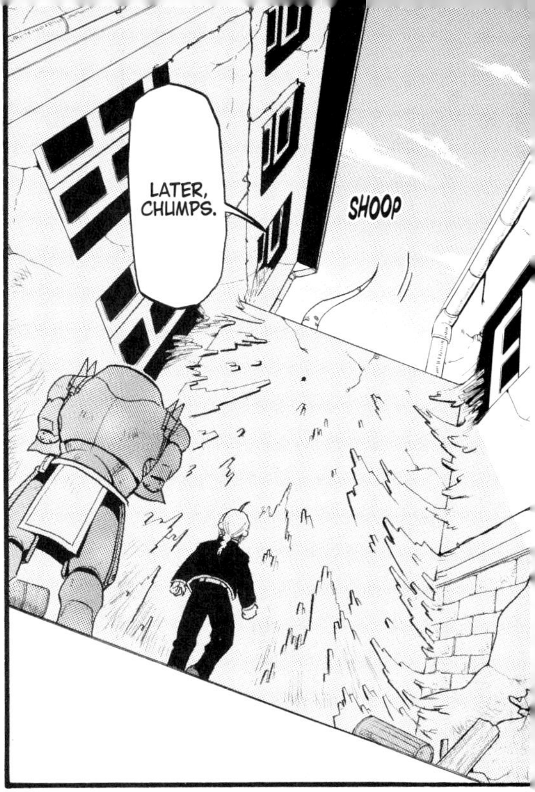
LATER, CHUMPS.
SHOOP

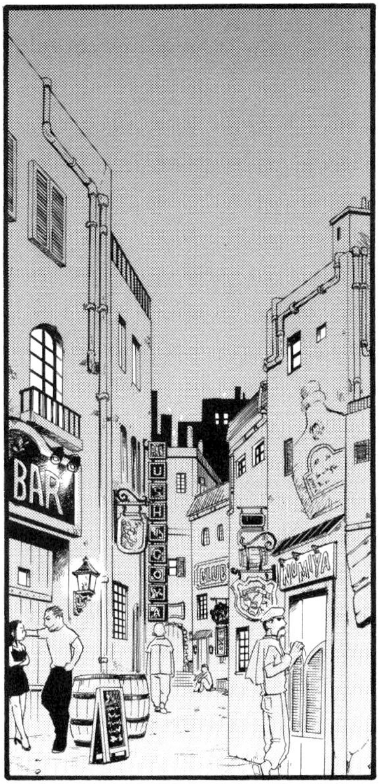
BAR
CLUB
NOMIYA

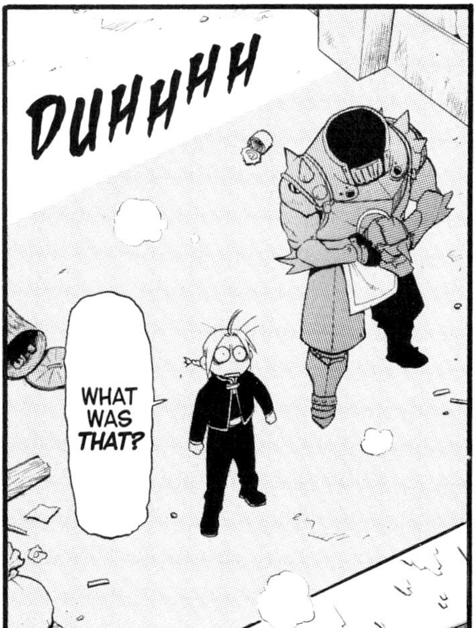
DUHHHH
WHAT WAS *THAT?*

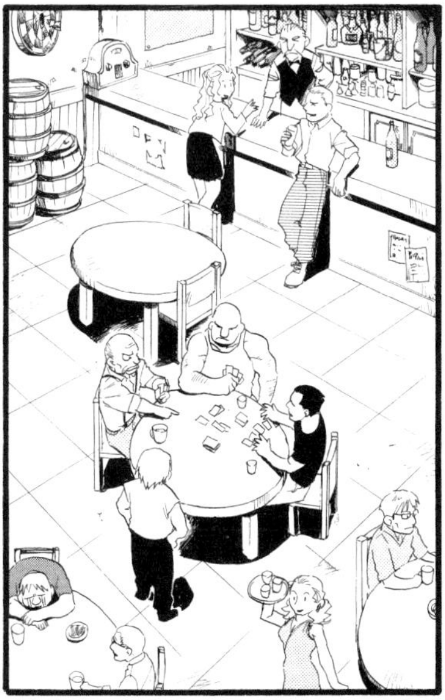

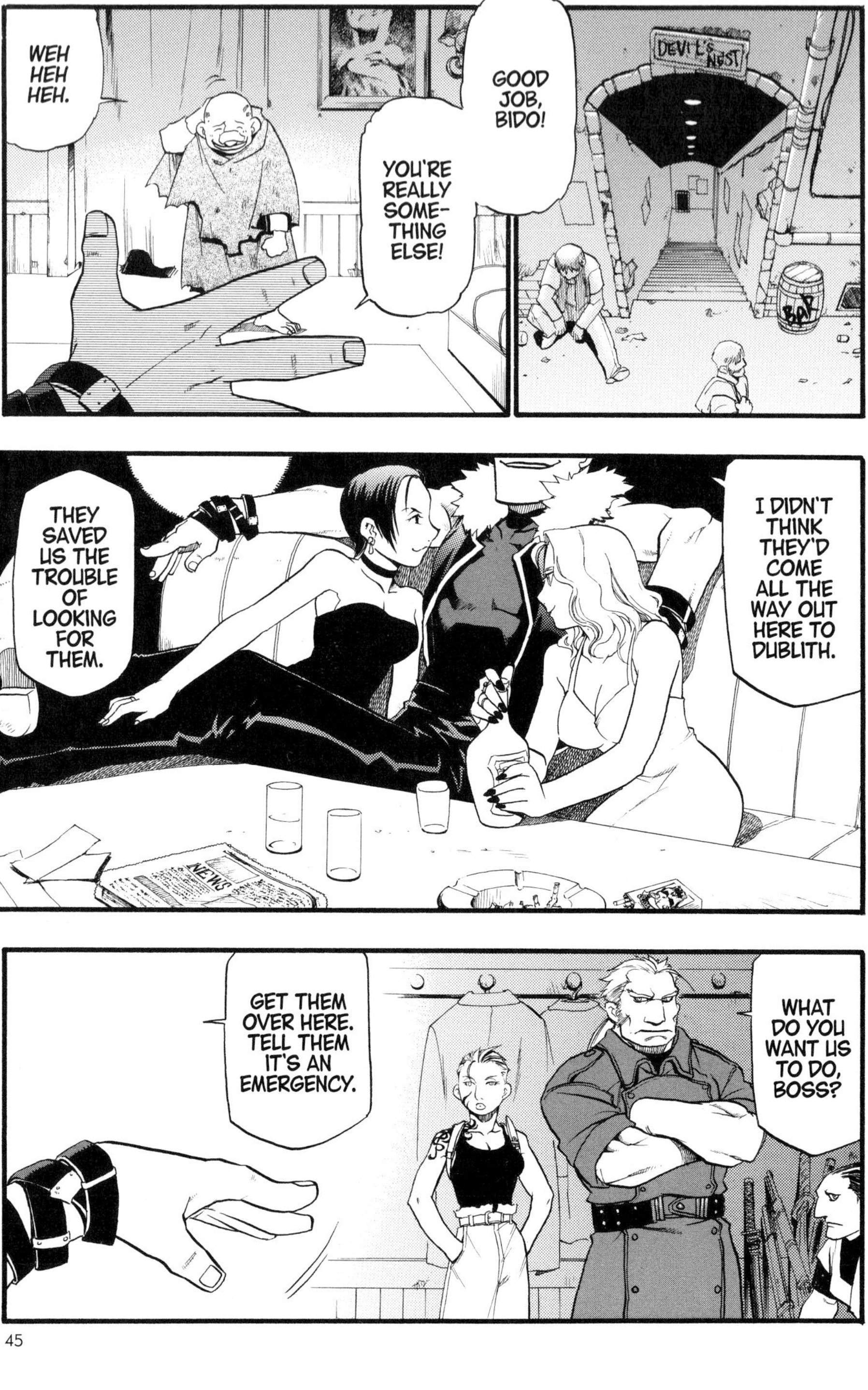
DEVIL'S NEST
GOOD JOB, BIDO!
YOU'RE REALLY SOMETHING ELSE!
WEH HEH HEH.
I DIDN'T THINK THEY'D COME ALL THE WAY OUT HERE TO DUBLITH.
THEY SAVED US THE TROUBLE OF LOOKING FOR THEM.
NEWS
WHAT DO YOU WANT US TO DO, BOSS?
GET THEM OVER HERE. TELL THEM IT'S AN EMERGENCY.

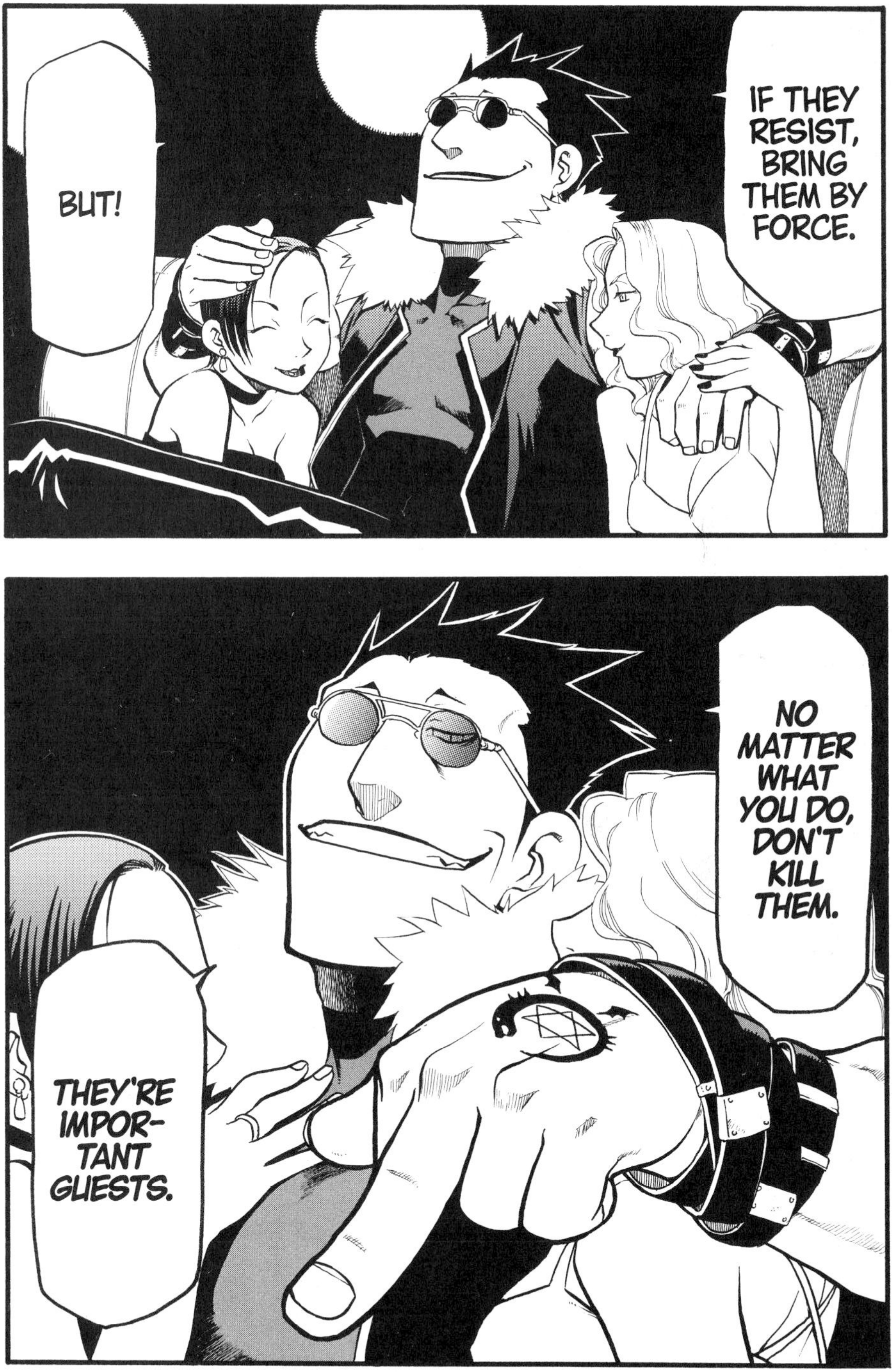
IF THEY RESIST, BRING THEM BY FORCE.
BUT!
NO MATTER WHAT YOU DO, DON'T KILL THEM.
THEY'RE IMPOR-TANT GUESTS.

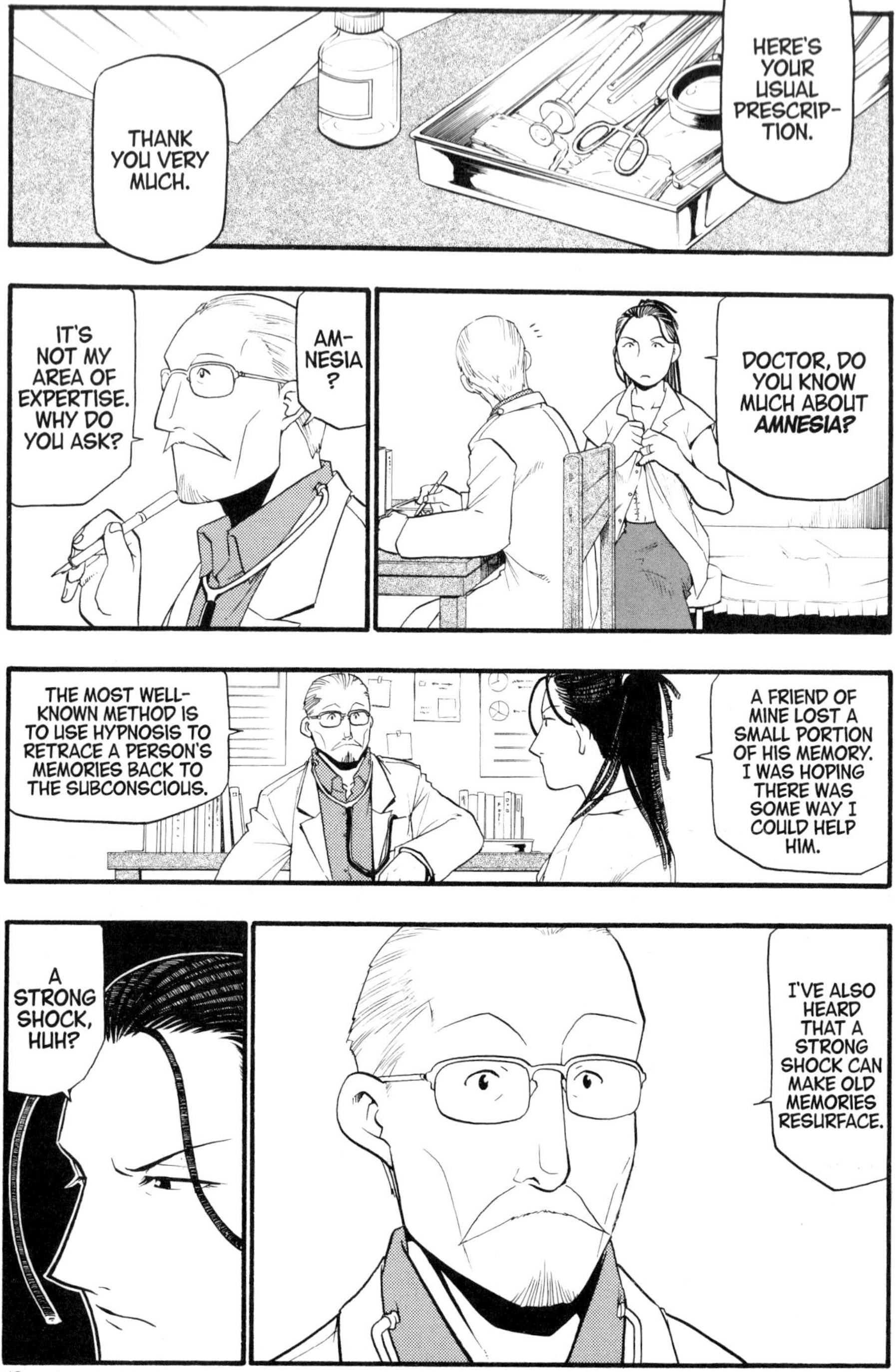
HERE'S YOUR USUAL PRESCRIPTION.
THANK YOU VERY MUCH.
DOCTOR, DO YOU KNOW MUCH ABOUT AMNESIA?
AMNESIA?
IT'S NOT MY AREA OF EXPERTISE. WHY DO YOU ASK?
A FRIEND OF MINE LOST A SMALL PORTION OF HIS MEMORY. I WAS HOPING THERE WAS SOME WAY I COULD HELP HIM.
THE MOST WELL-KNOWN METHOD IS TO USE HYPNOSIS TO RETRACE A PERSON'S MEMORIES BACK TO THE SUBCONSCIOUS.
I'VE ALSO HEARD THAT A STRONG SHOCK CAN MAKE OLD MEMORIES RESURFACE.
A STRONG SHOCK, HUH?

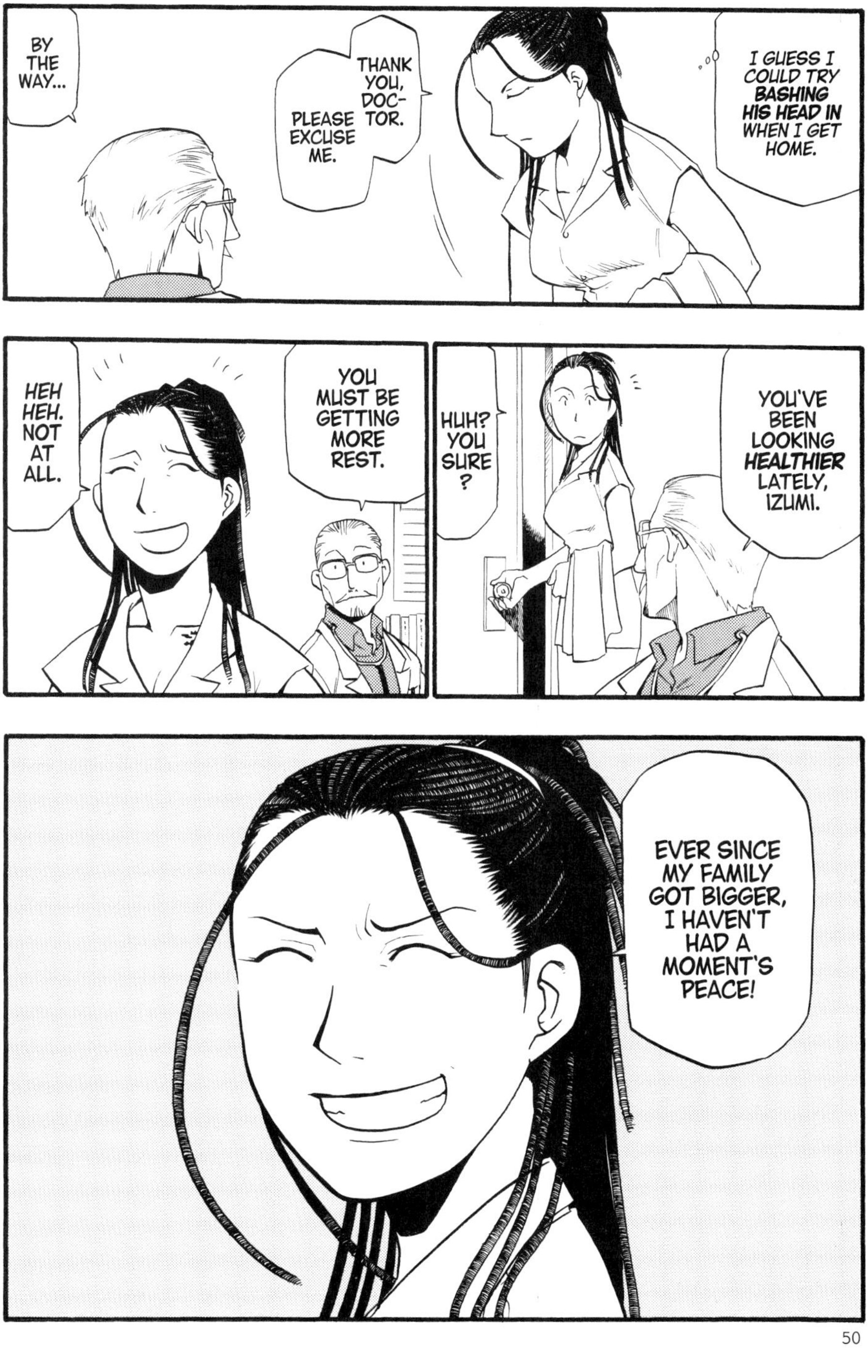
I GUESS I COULD TRY **BASHING HIS HEAD IN** WHEN I GET HOME.
THANK YOU, DOCTOR. PLEASE EXCUSE ME.
BY THE WAY...
YOU'VE BEEN LOOKING **HEALTHIER** LATELY, IZUMI.
HUH? YOU SURE?
YOU MUST BE GETTING MORE REST.
HEH HEH. NOT AT ALL.
EVER SINCE MY FAMILY GOT BIGGER, I HAVEN'T HAD A MOMENT'S PEACE!

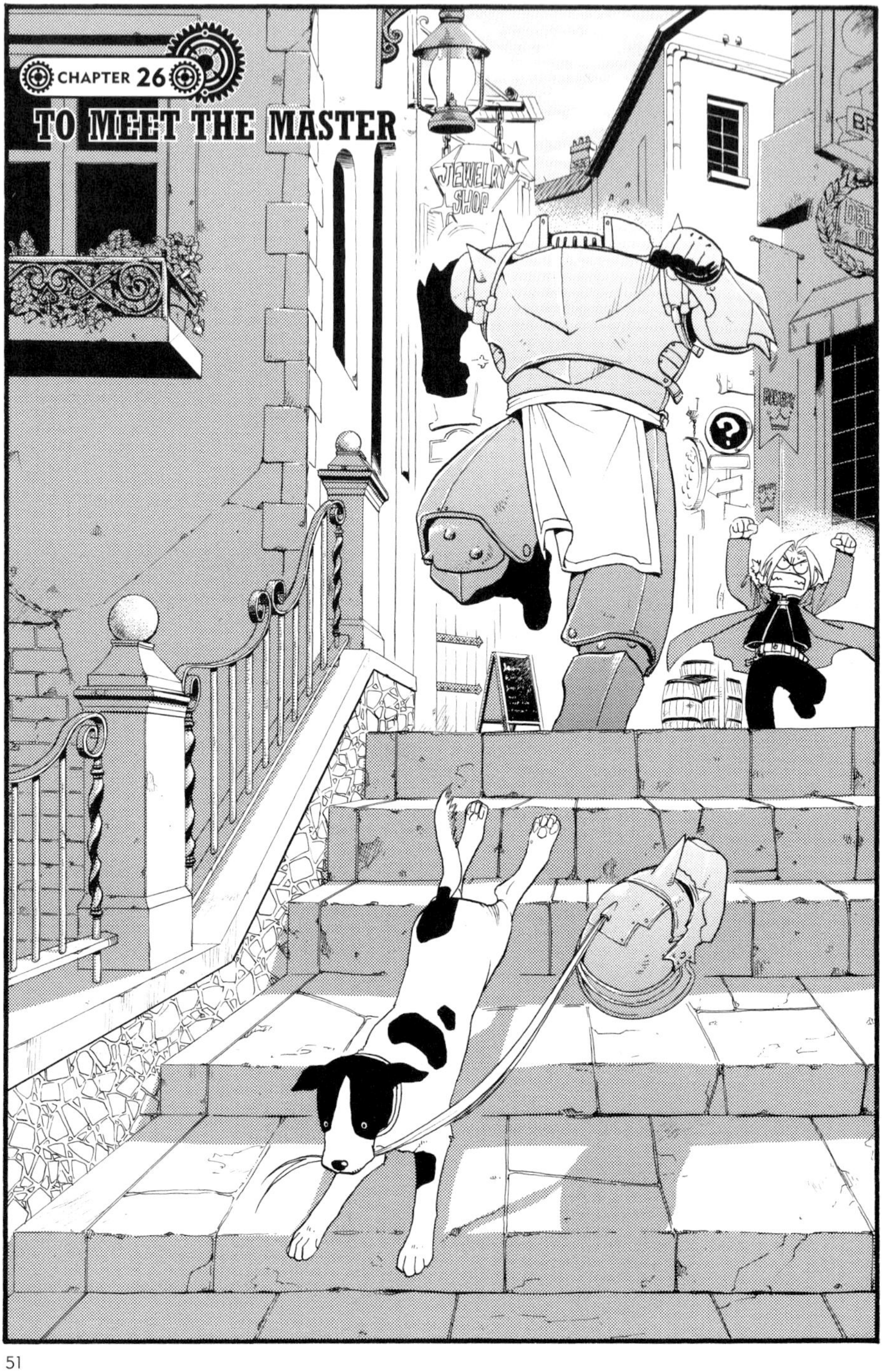
CHAPTER 26
TO MEET THE MASTER
JEWELRY SHOP

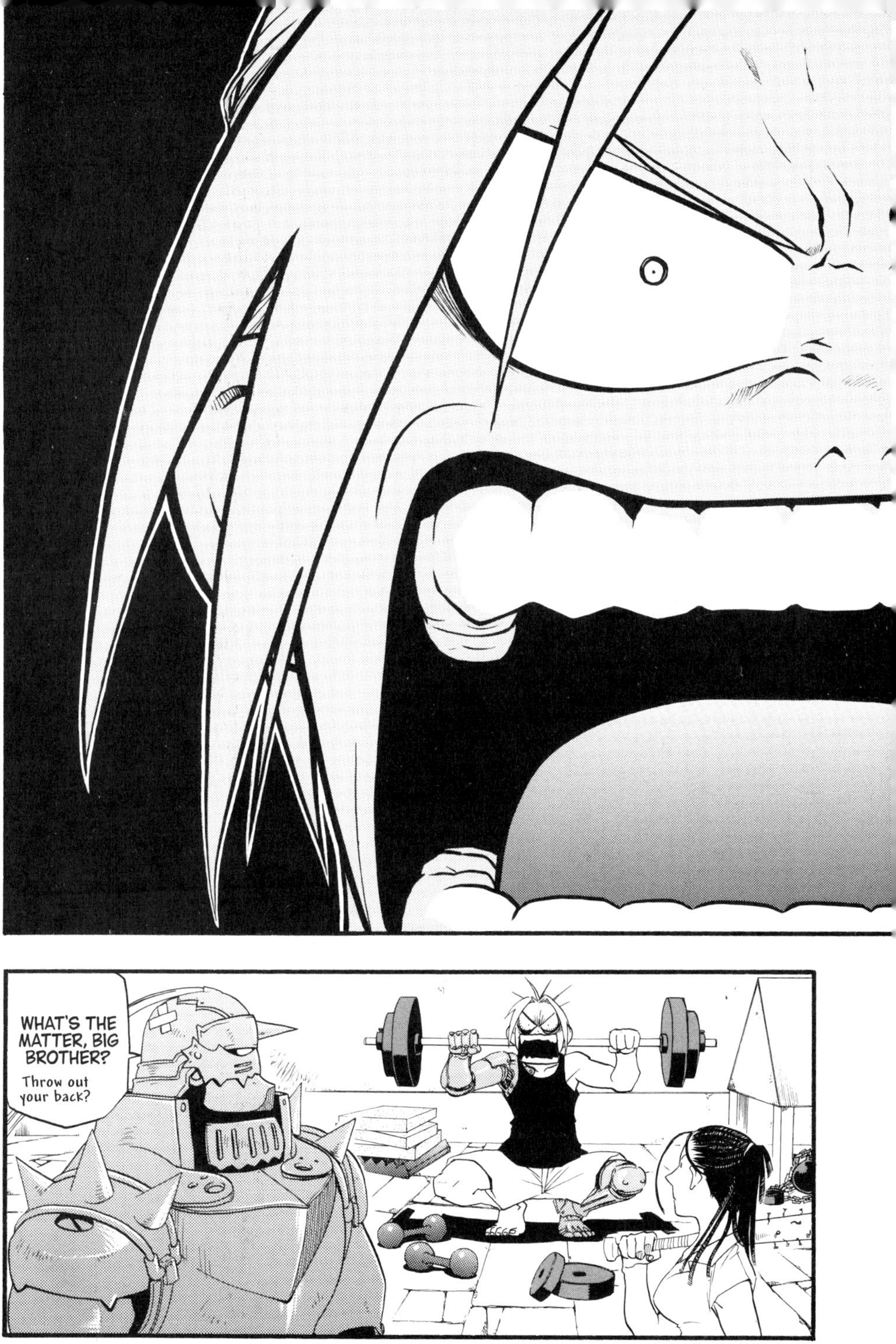
WHAT'S THE MATTER, BIG BROTHER?
Throw out your back?

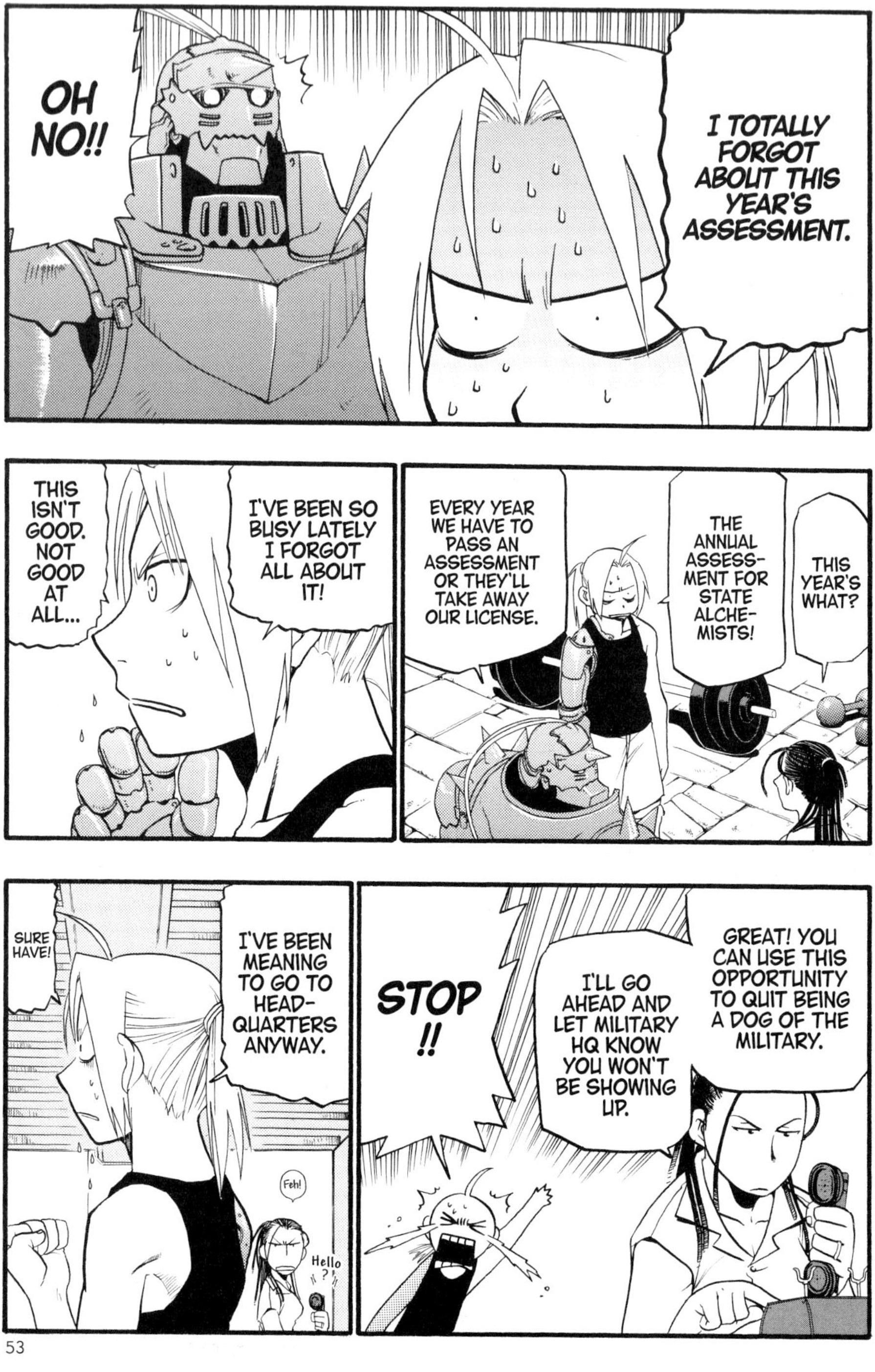
I TOTALLY FORGOT ABOUT THIS YEAR'S ASSESSMENT.
OH NO!!
THIS YEAR'S WHAT?
THE ANNUAL ASSESSMENT FOR STATE ALCHEMISTS!
EVERY YEAR WE HAVE TO PASS AN ASSESSMENT OR THEY'LL TAKE AWAY OUR LICENSE.
I'VE BEEN SO BUSY LATELY I FORGOT ALL ABOUT IT!
THIS ISN'T GOOD. NOT GOOD AT ALL...
GREAT! YOU CAN USE THIS OPPORTUNITY TO QUIT BEING A DOG OF THE MILITARY.
I'LL GO AHEAD AND LET MILITARY HQ KNOW YOU WON'T BE SHOWING UP.
STOP!!
I'VE BEEN MEANING TO GO TO HEAD-QUARTERS ANYWAY.
SURE HAVE!
Feh!
Hello ?!

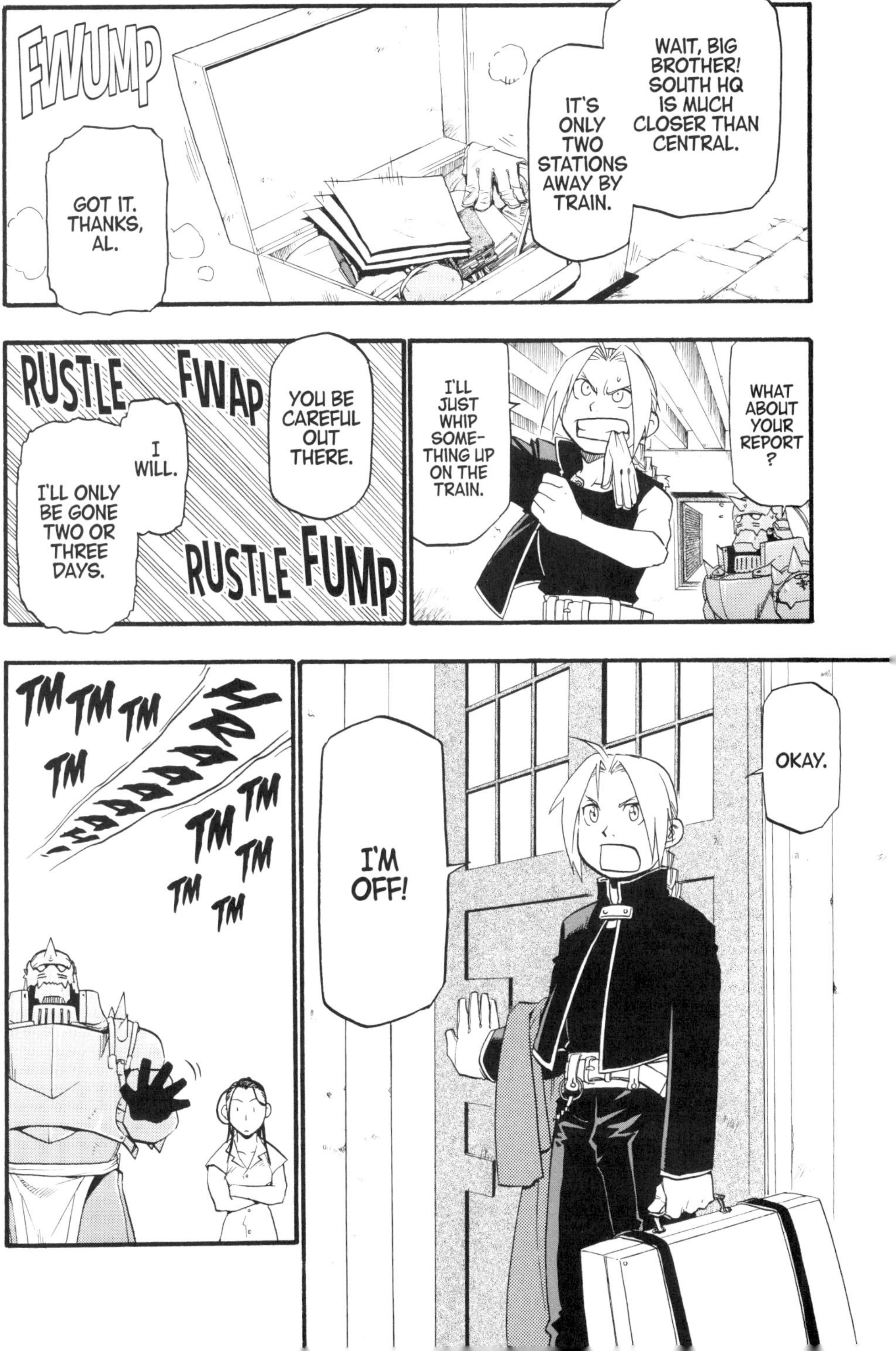

WAIT, BIG BROTHER! SOUTH HQ IS MUCH CLOSER THAN CENTRAL.
IT'S ONLY TWO STATIONS AWAY BY TRAIN.
FWUMP
GOT IT. THANKS, AL.
WHAT ABOUT YOUR REPORT?
I'LL JUST WHIP SOME-THING UP ON THE TRAIN.
FWAP
YOU BE CAREFUL OUT THERE.
RUSTLE
I WILL.
I'LL ONLY BE GONE TWO OR THREE DAYS.
RUSTLE FUMP
OKAY.
I'M OFF!
HRAAAAAAH!
TM TM TM TM TM TM TM TM TM TM

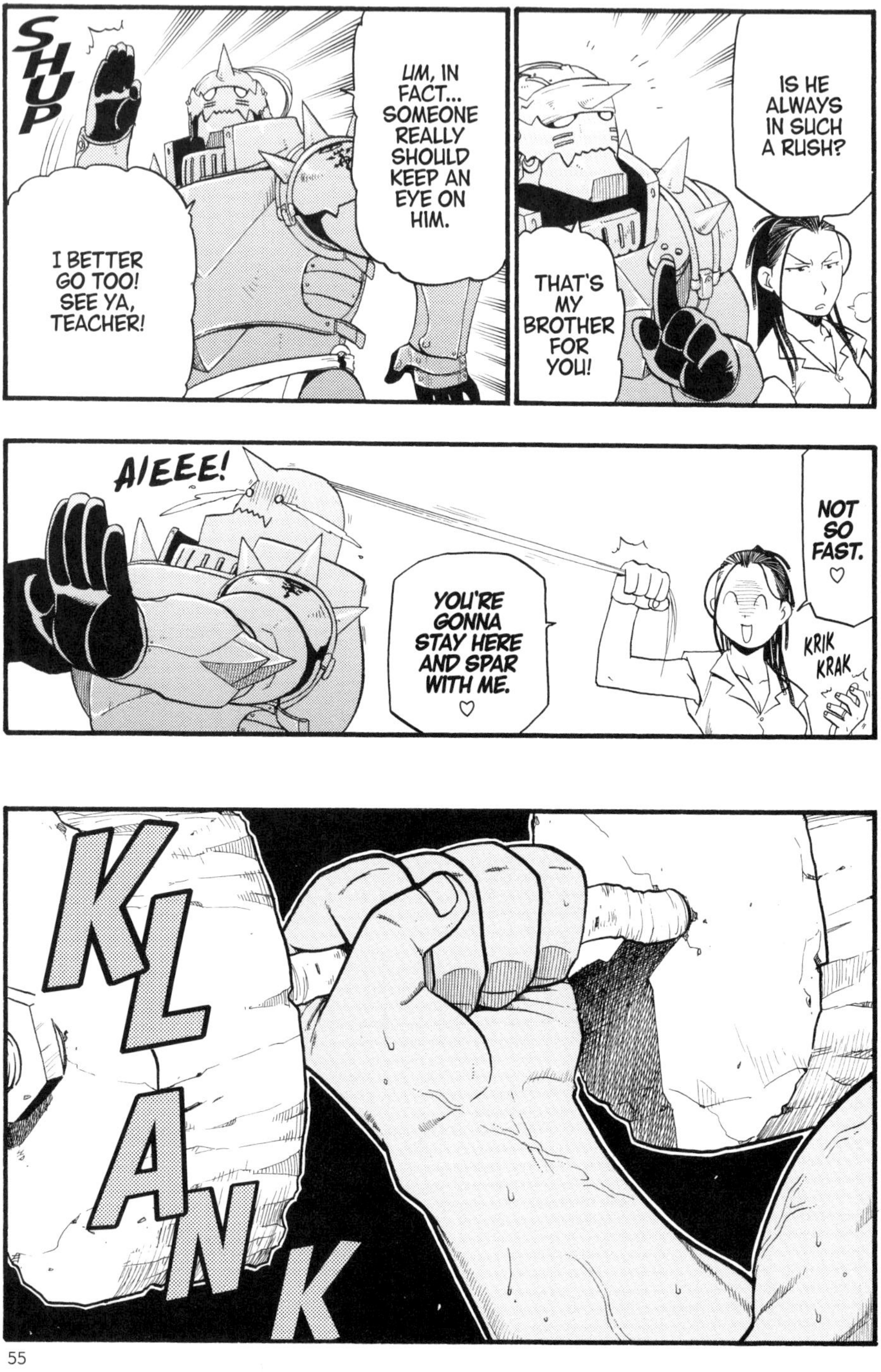
IS HE ALWAYS IN SUCH A RUSH?
THAT'S MY BROTHER FOR YOU!
UM, IN FACT... SOMEONE REALLY SHOULD KEEP AN EYE ON HIM.
SHUP
I BETTER GO TOO! SEE YA, TEACHER!
NOT SO FAST. ♡
KRIK KRAK
YOU'RE GONNA STAY HERE AND SPAR WITH ME. ♡
AIEEE!
KLANK

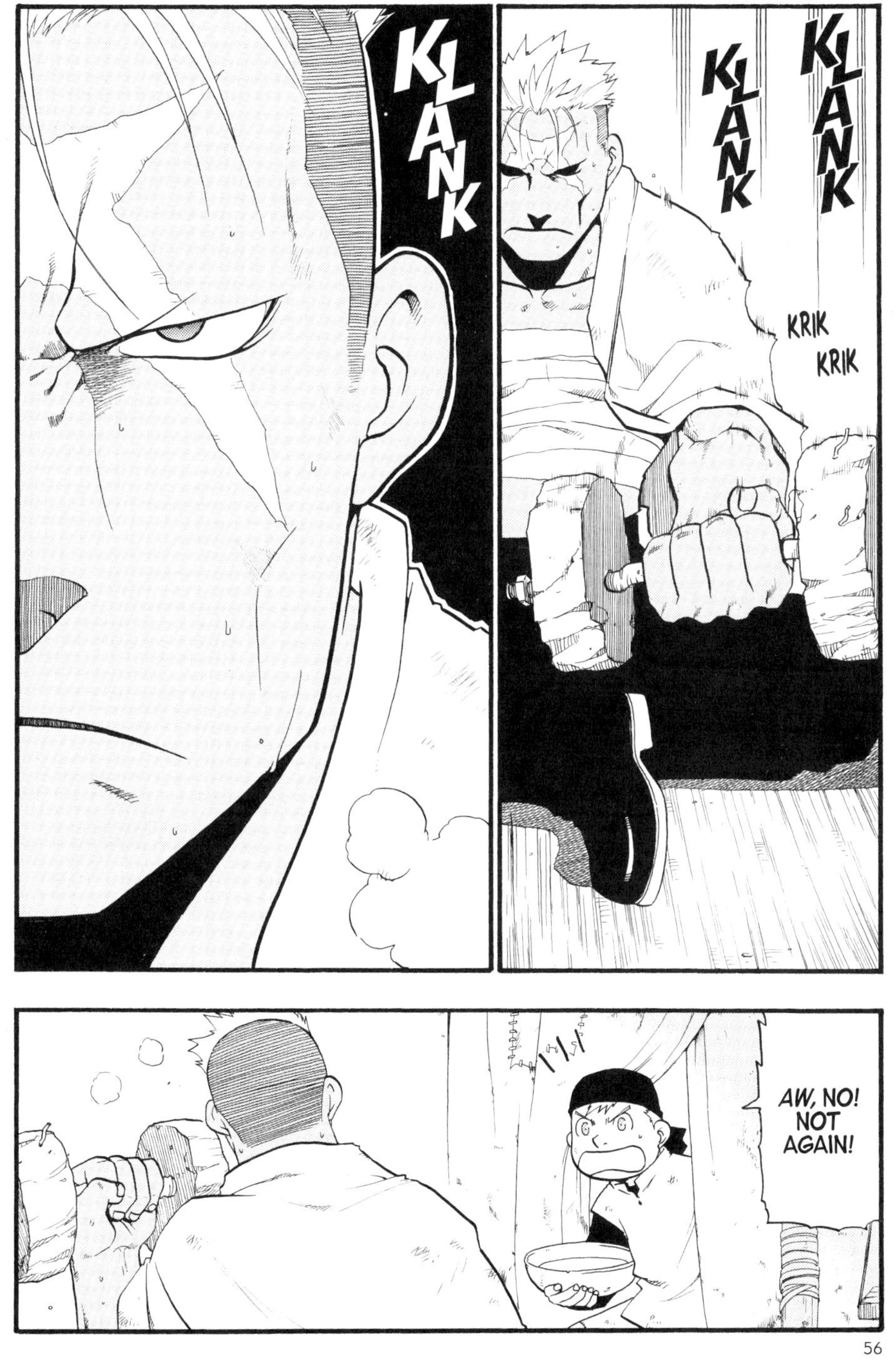
KLANK
KLANK
KRIK
KRIK
KLANK
AW, NO! NOT AGAIN!

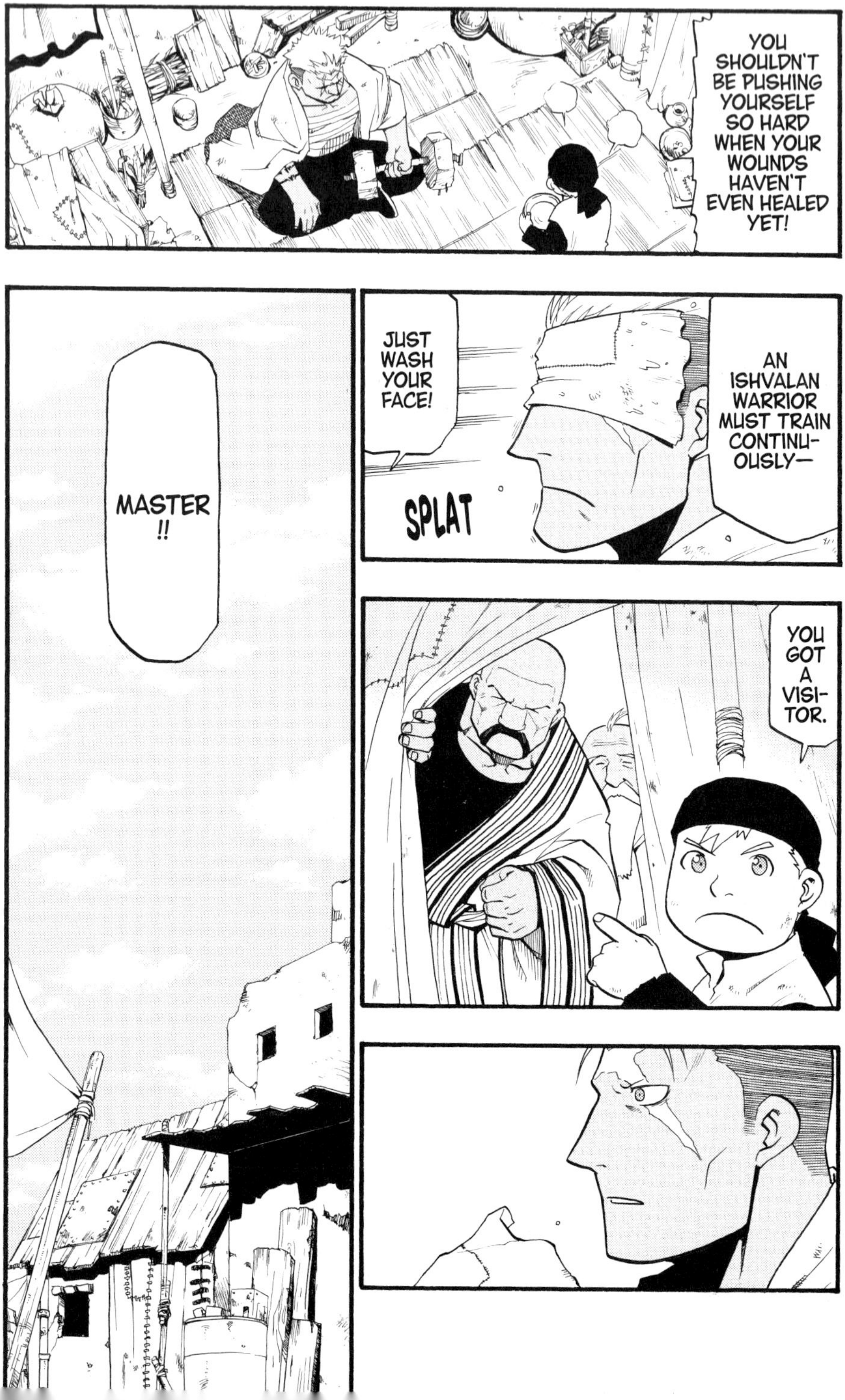
YOU SHOULDN'T BE PUSHING YOURSELF SO HARD WHEN YOUR WOUNDS HAVEN'T EVEN HEALED YET!
AN ISHVALAN WARRIOR MUST TRAIN CONTINU-OUSLY—
JUST WASH YOUR FACE!
SPLAT
YOU GOT A VISI-TOR.
MASTER!!

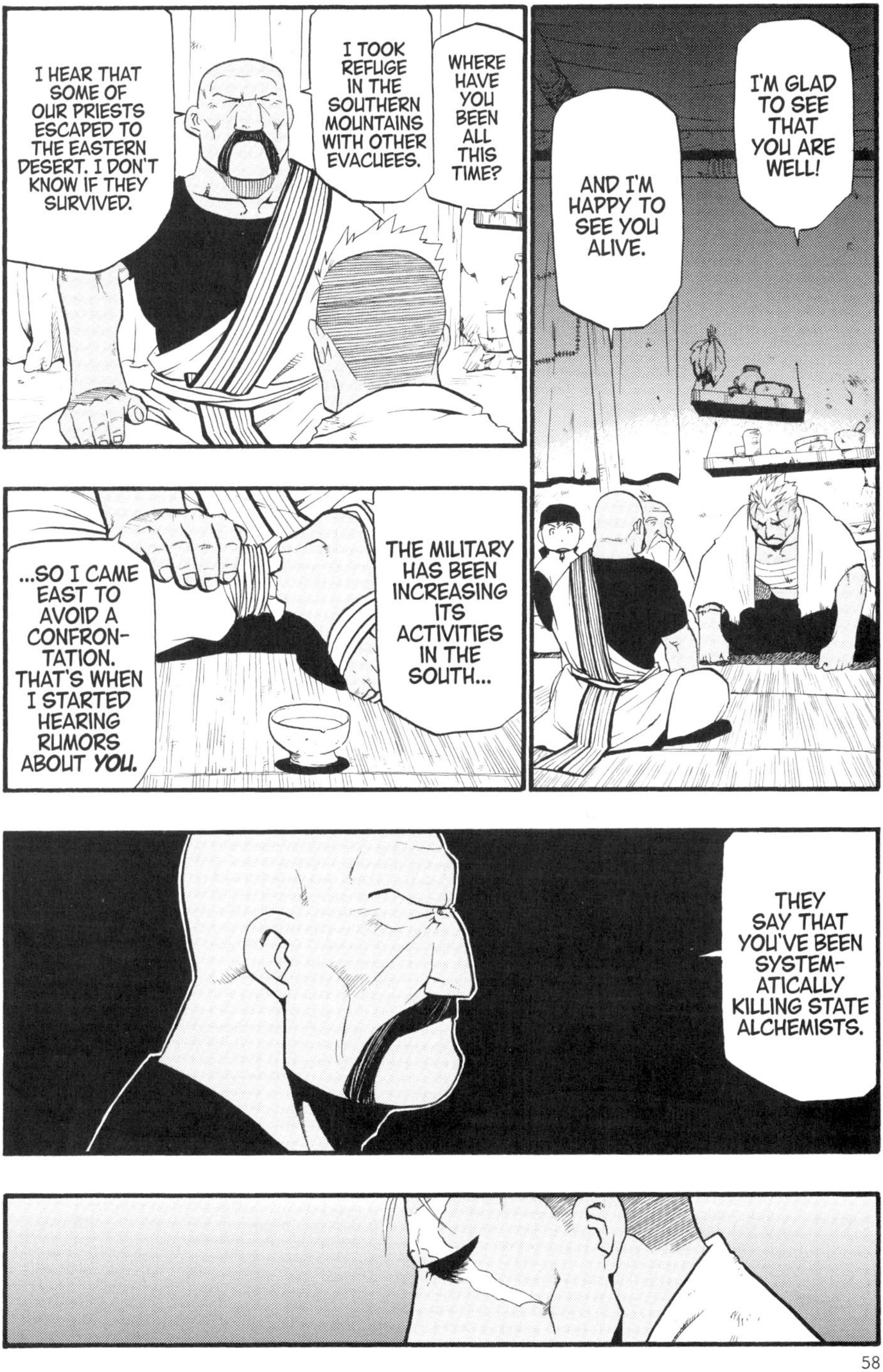
I'M GLAD TO SEE THAT YOU ARE WELL!
AND I'M HAPPY TO SEE YOU ALIVE.
WHERE HAVE YOU BEEN ALL THIS TIME?
I TOOK REFUGE IN THE SOUTHERN MOUNTAINS WITH OTHER EVACUEES.
I HEAR THAT SOME OF OUR PRIESTS ESCAPED TO THE EASTERN DESERT. I DON'T KNOW IF THEY SURVIVED.
THE MILITARY HAS BEEN INCREASING ITS ACTIVITIES IN THE SOUTH...
...SO I CAME EAST TO AVOID A CONFRON-TATION. THAT'S WHEN I STARTED HEARING RUMORS ABOUT *YOU.*
THEY SAY THAT YOU'VE BEEN SYSTEM-ATICALLY KILLING STATE ALCHEMISTS.

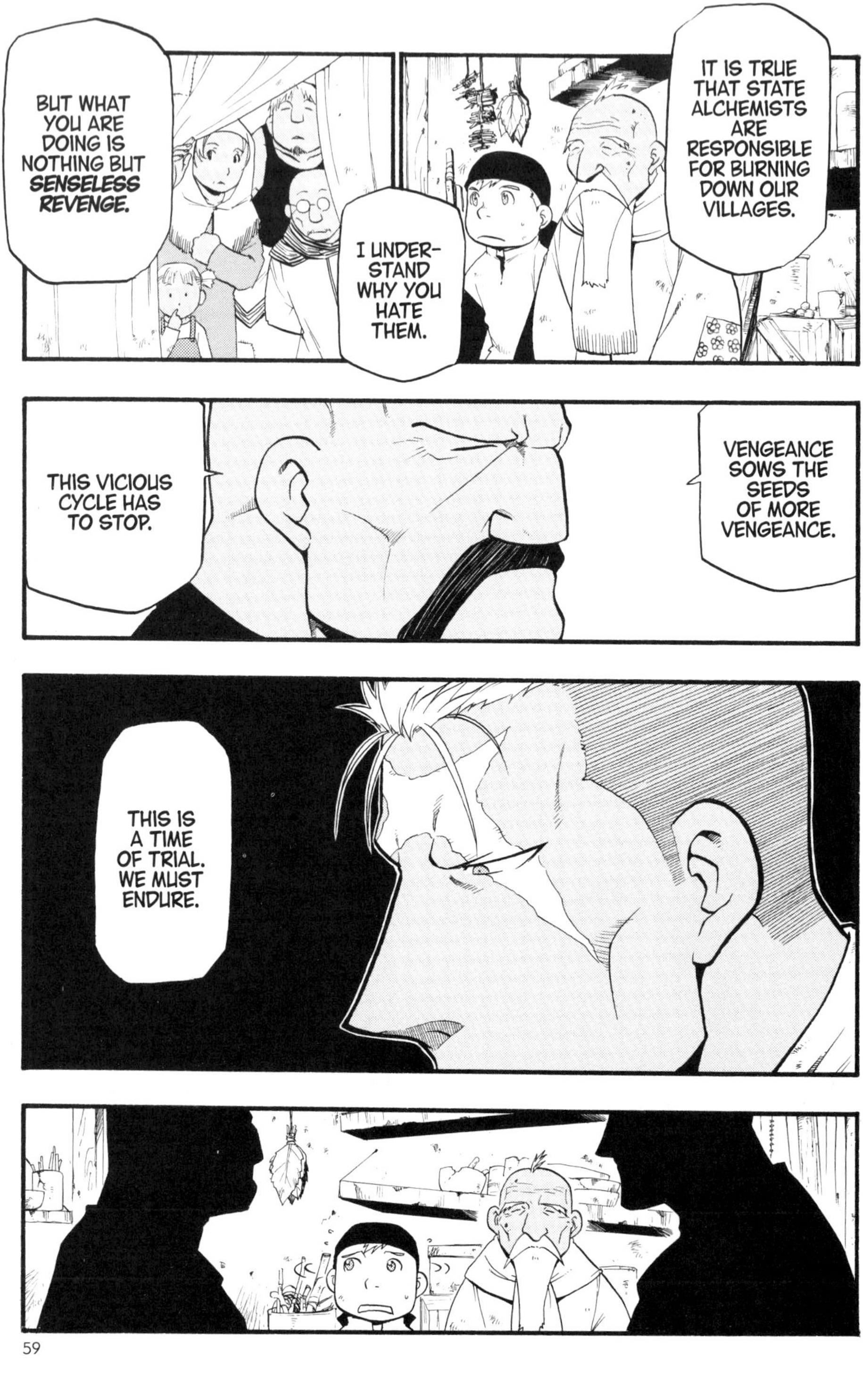
IT IS TRUE THAT STATE ALCHEMISTS ARE RESPONSIBLE FOR BURNING DOWN OUR VILLAGES.
I UNDER-STAND WHY YOU HATE THEM.
BUT WHAT YOU ARE DOING IS NOTHING BUT SENSELESS REVENGE.
VENGEANCE SOWS THE SEEDS OF MORE VENGEANCE.
THIS VICIOUS CYCLE HAS TO STOP.
THIS IS A TIME OF TRIAL. WE MUST ENDURE.

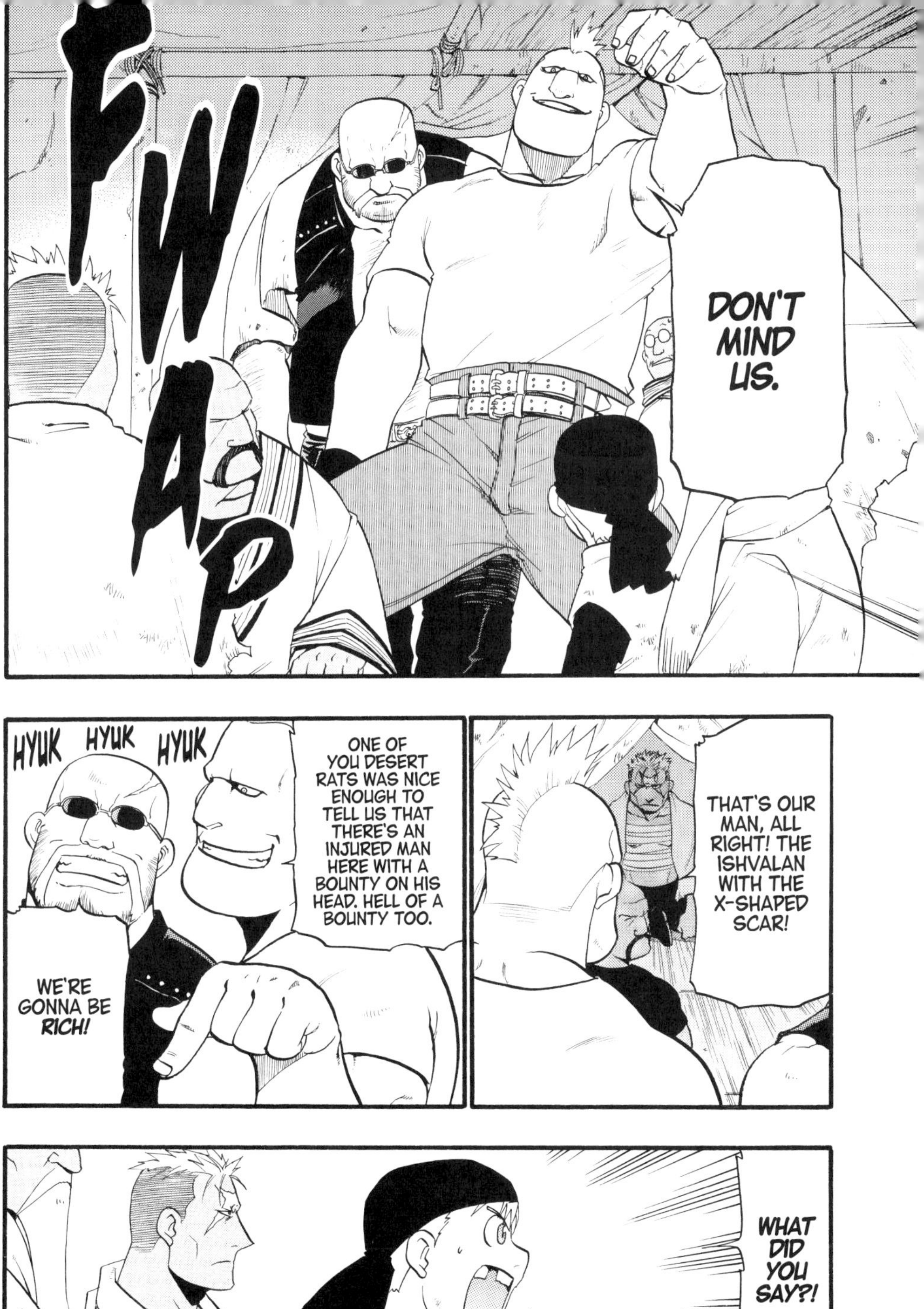

DON'T MIND US.
FWAP
THAT'S OUR MAN, ALL RIGHT! THE ISHVALAN WITH THE X-SHAPED SCAR!
ONE OF YOU DESERT RATS WAS NICE ENOUGH TO TELL US THAT THERE'S AN INJURED MAN HERE WITH A BOUNTY ON HIS HEAD. HELL OF A BOUNTY TOO.
HYUK HYUK HYUK
WE'RE GONNA BE RICH!
WHAT DID YOU SAY?!

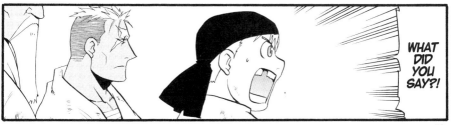

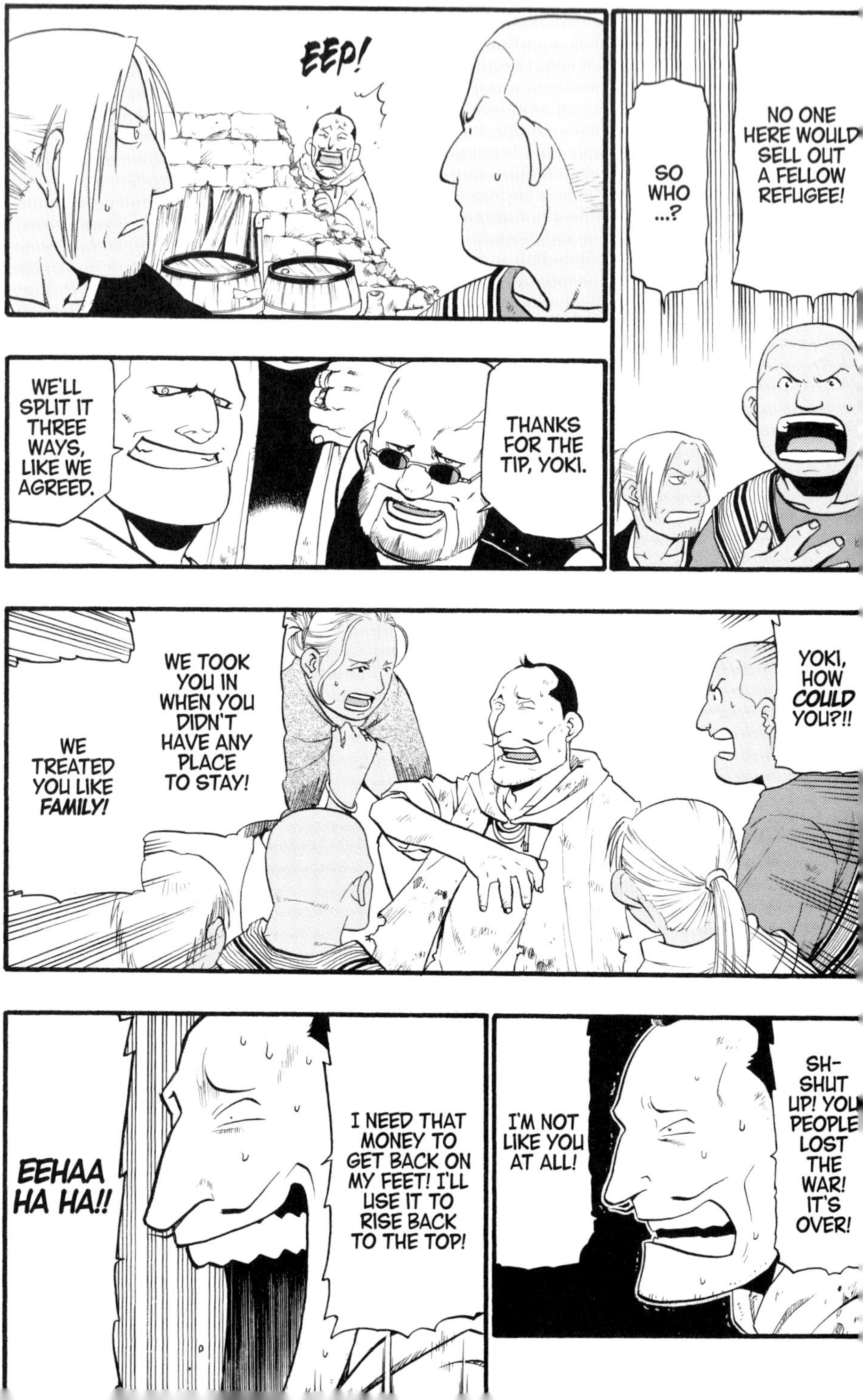
NO ONE HERE WOULD SELL OUT A FELLOW REFUGEE!
SO WHO ...?
EEP!
THANKS FOR THE TIP, YOKI.
WE'LL SPLIT IT THREE WAYS, LIKE WE AGREED.
YOKI, HOW COULD YOU?!!
WE TOOK YOU IN WHEN YOU DIDN'T HAVE ANY PLACE TO STAY!
WE TREATED YOU LIKE FAMILY!
SH-SHUT UP! YOU PEOPLE LOST THE WAR! IT'S OVER!
I'M NOT LIKE YOU AT ALL!
I NEED THAT MONEY TO GET BACK ON MY FEET! I'LL USE IT TO RISE BACK TO THE TOP!
EEHAA HA HA!!

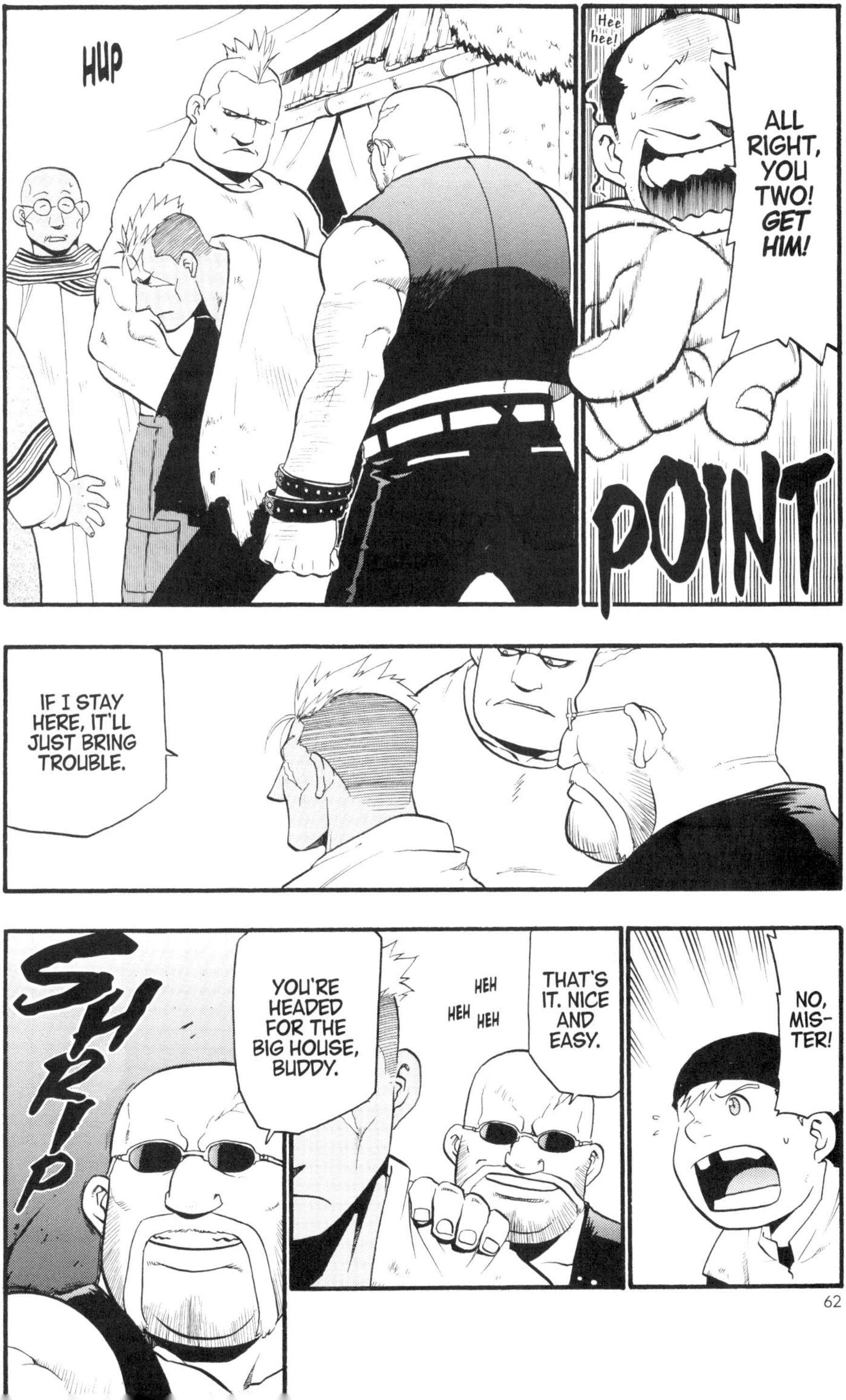
Hee hee!
ALL RIGHT, YOU TWO! GET HIM!
POINT
HUP
IF I STAY HERE, IT'LL JUST BRING TROUBLE.
NO, MISTER!
THAT'S IT. NICE AND EASY.
HEH HEH HEH
YOU'RE HEADED FOR THE BIG HOUSE, BUDDY.
SHRIP

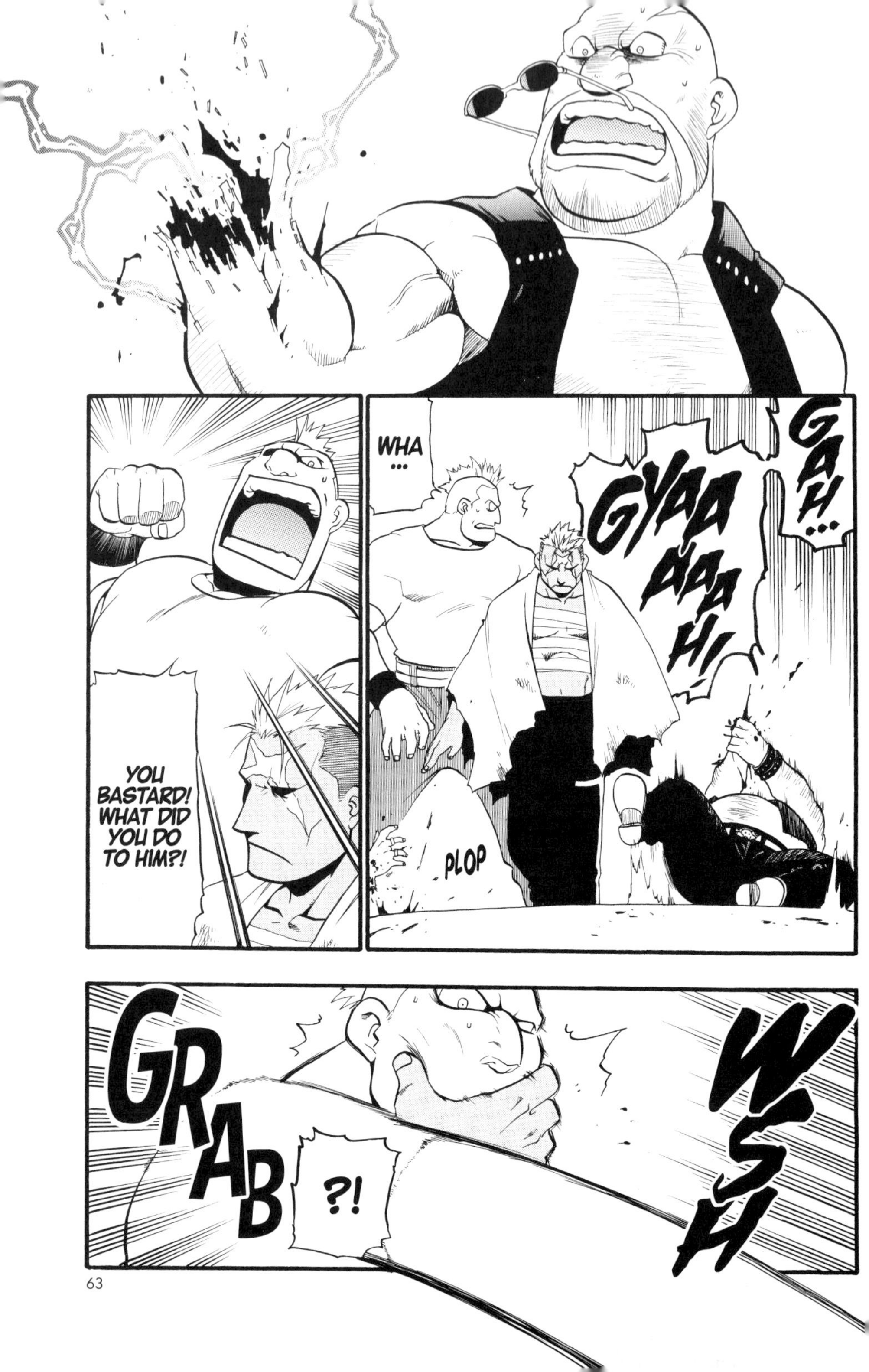
GAH...
GYAAAAAH!
WHA...
PLOP
YOU BASTARD! WHAT DID YOU DO TO HIM?!
WSH
?!
GRAB

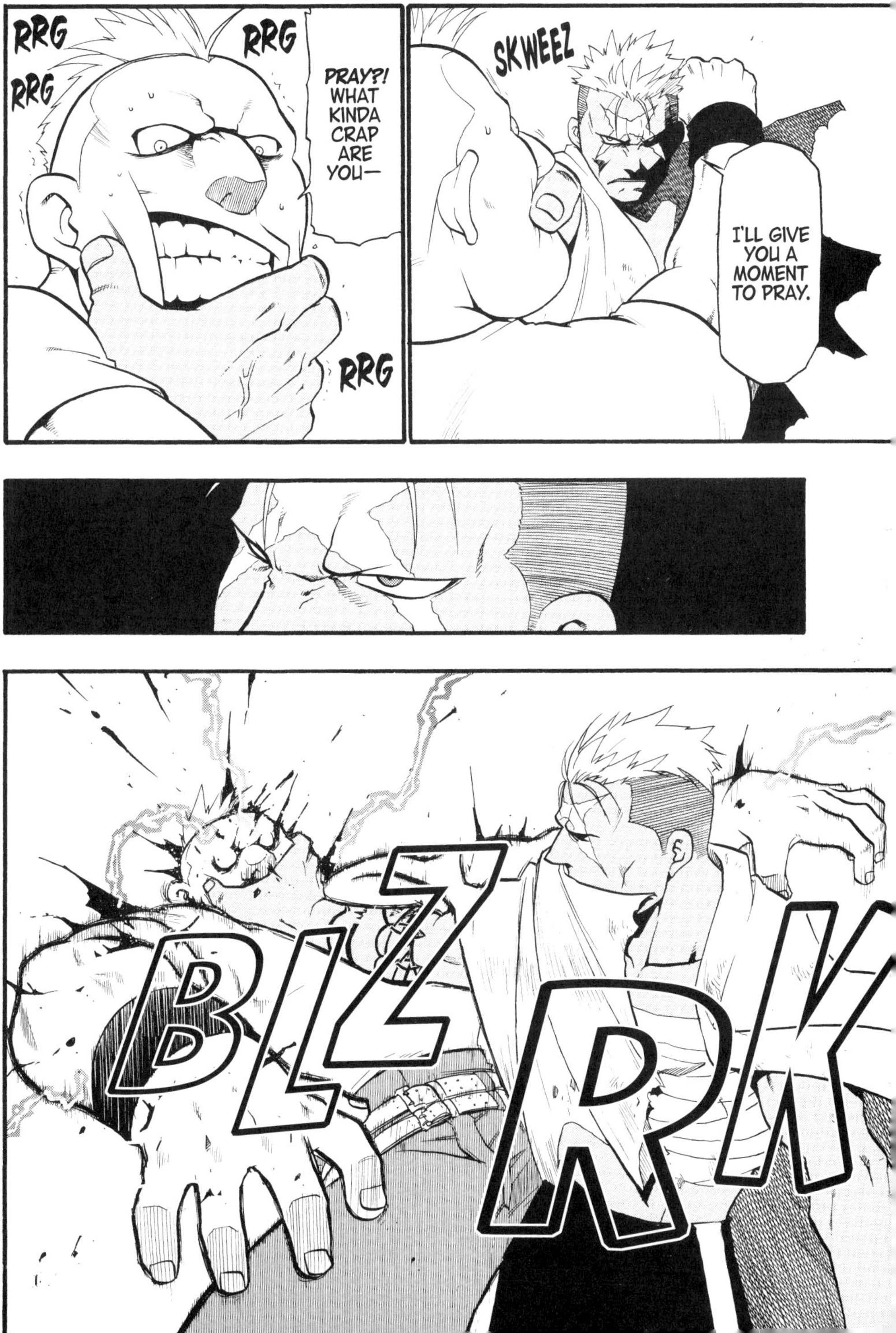
SKWEEZ
I'LL GIVE YOU A MOMENT TO PRAY.
RRG
RRG
RRG
PRAY?! WHAT KINDA CRAP ARE YOU—
RRG
BLZRK

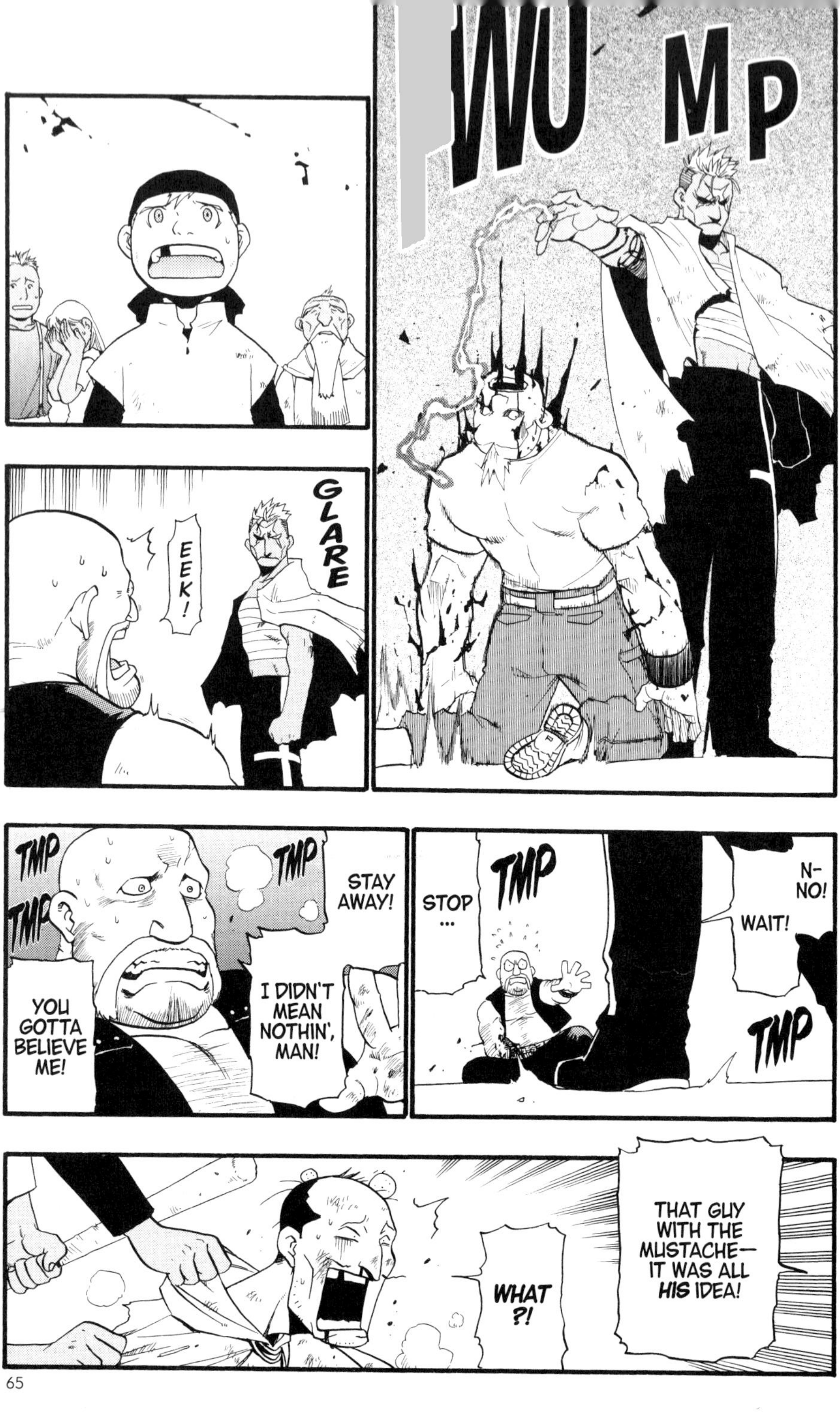
WUMP
GLARE
EEK!
N-NO!
WAIT!
TMP
STOP ...
TMP
STAY AWAY!
TMP
TMP
TMP
I DIDN'T MEAN NOTHIN', MAN!
YOU GOTTA BELIEVE ME!
THAT GUY WITH THE MUSTACHE— IT WAS ALL **HIS** IDEA!
WHAT?!

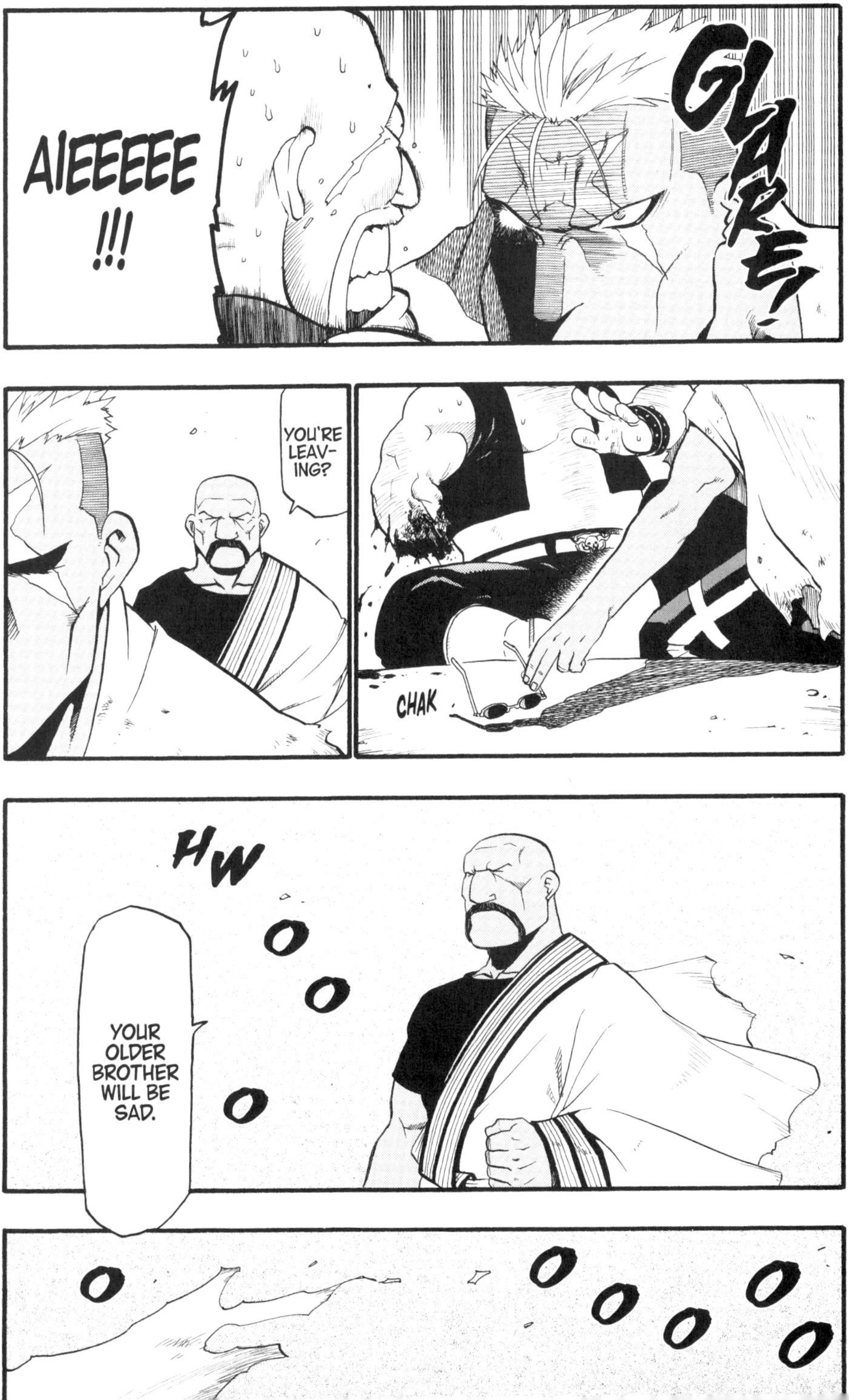
GLARE!
AIEEEEE!!!
CHAK
YOU'RE LEAV-ING?
HWOOO
YOUR OLDER BROTHER WILL BE SAD.
OOOOOO

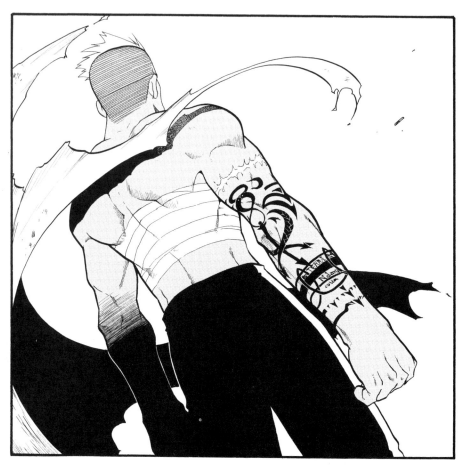

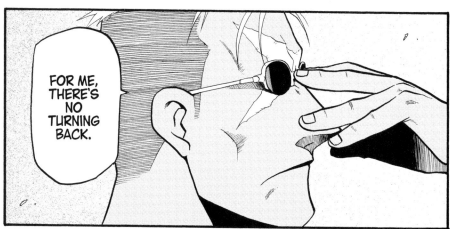

FOR ME, THERE'S NO TURNING BACK.

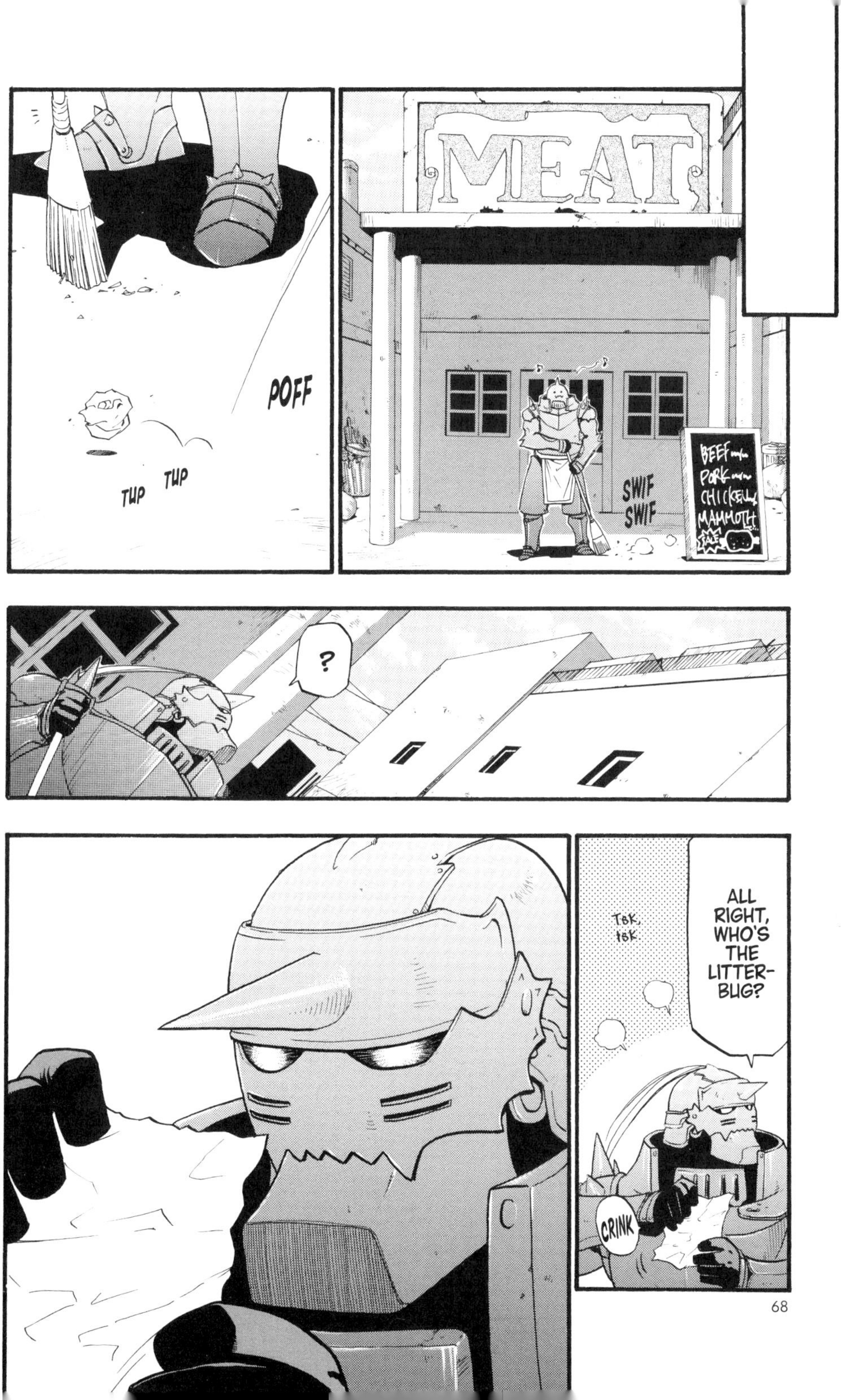
MEAT
BEEF
PORK
MAMMOTH
SALE
SWIF SWIF
POFF
TUP TUP
?
ALL RIGHT, WHO'S THE LITTER-BUG?
TBK, TBK
CRINK

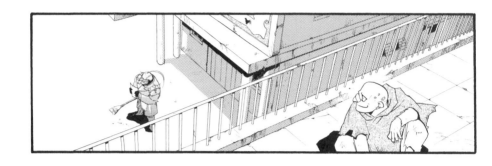

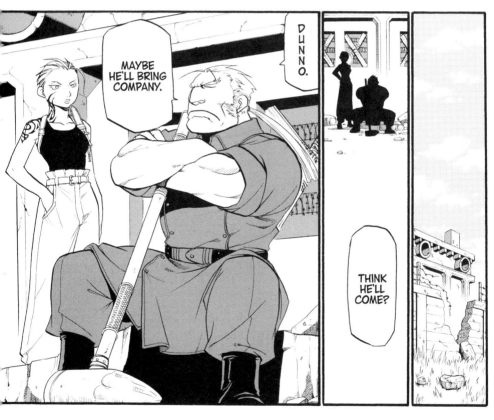

THINK HE'LL COME?
DUNNO.
MAYBE HE'LL BRING COMPANY.
SNIFF
HE'S HERE.

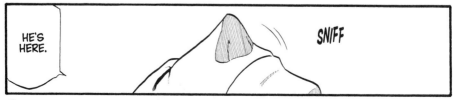

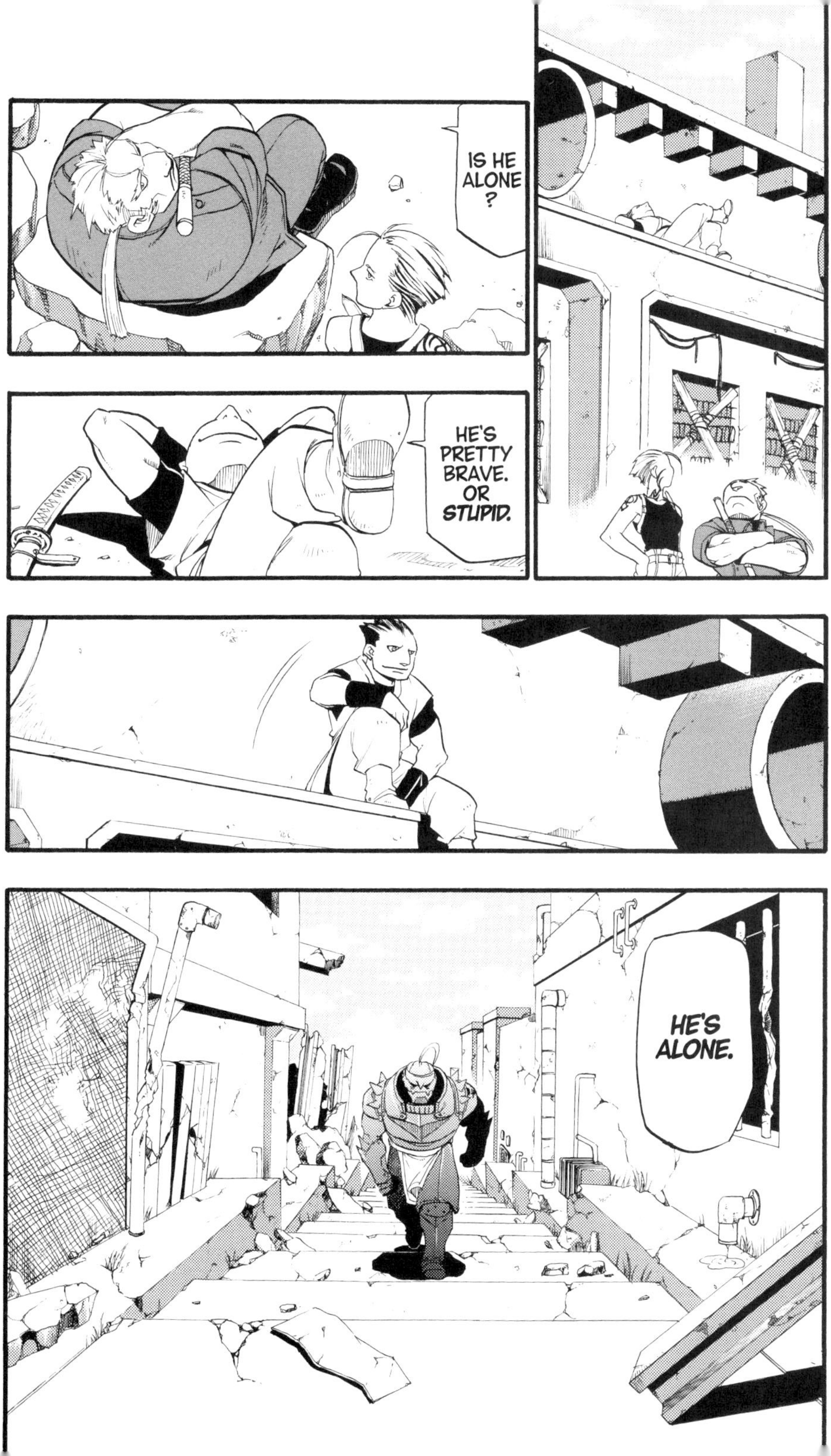
IS HE ALONE?
HE'S PRETTY BRAVE. OR STUPID.
HE'S ALONE.

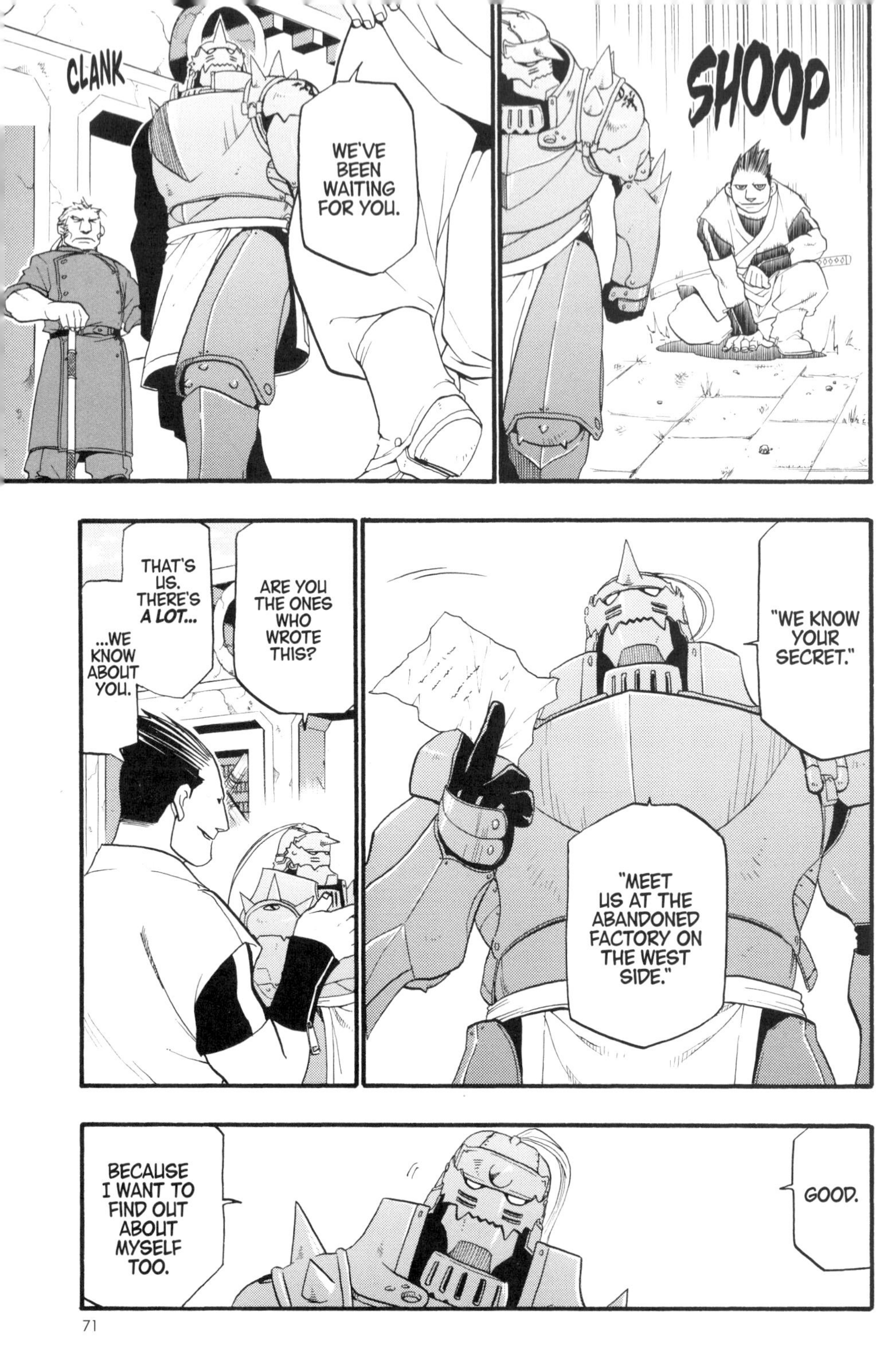
SHOOP
CLANK
WE'VE BEEN WAITING FOR YOU.
"WE KNOW YOUR SECRET."
"MEET US AT THE ABANDONED FACTORY ON THE WEST SIDE."
ARE YOU THE ONES WHO WROTE THIS?
THAT'S US. THERE'S A LOT...
...WE KNOW ABOUT YOU.
GOOD.
BECAUSE I WANT TO FIND OUT ABOUT MYSELF TOO.

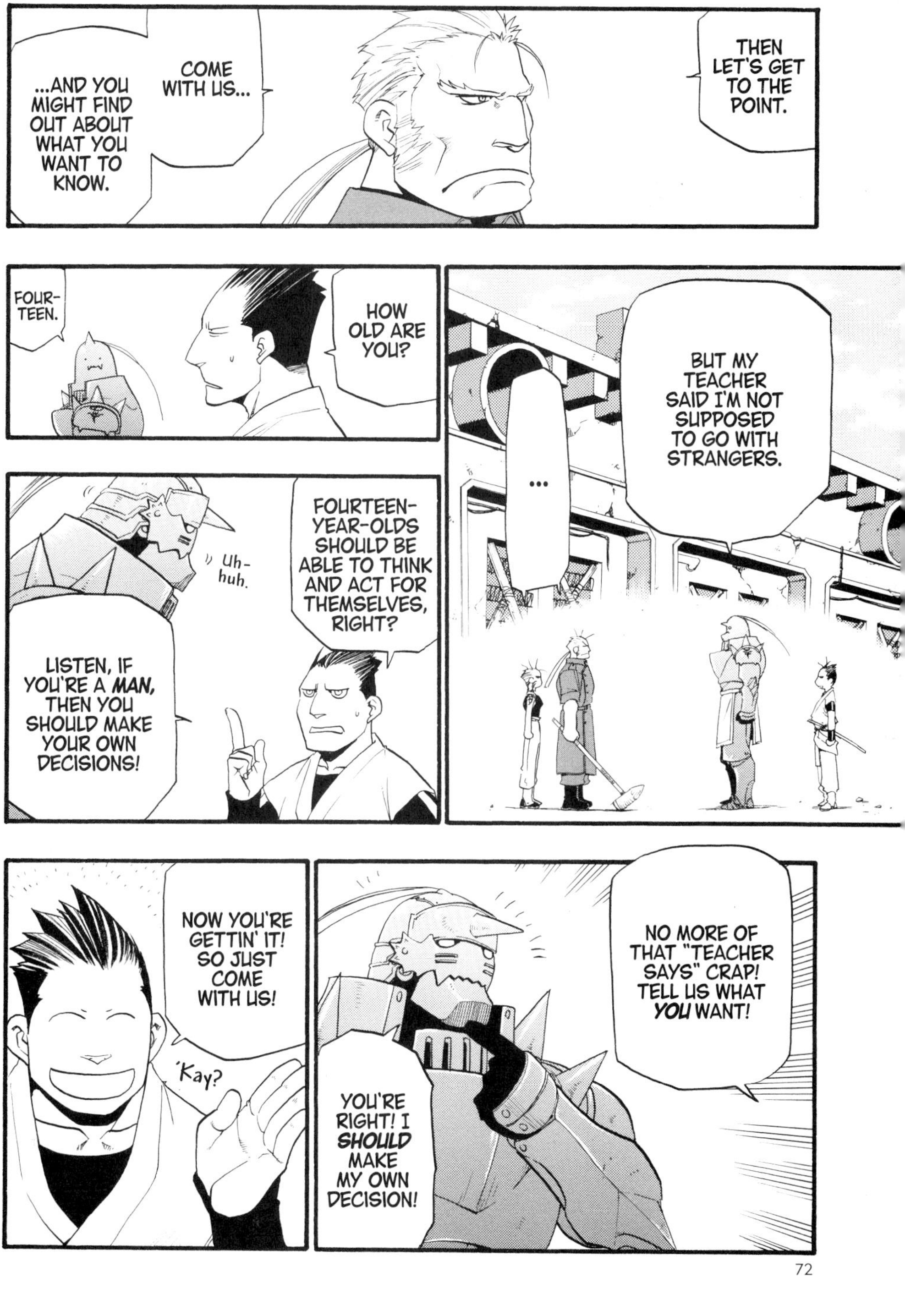
THEN LET'S GET TO THE POINT.
COME WITH US...
...AND YOU MIGHT FIND OUT ABOUT WHAT YOU WANT TO KNOW.
BUT MY TEACHER SAID I'M NOT SUPPOSED TO GO WITH STRANGERS.
...
HOW OLD ARE YOU?
FOURTEEN.
FOURTEEN-YEAR-OLDS SHOULD BE ABLE TO THINK AND ACT FOR THEMSELVES, RIGHT?
Uh-huh.
LISTEN, IF YOU'RE A ***MAN***, THEN YOU SHOULD MAKE YOUR OWN DECISIONS!
NO MORE OF THAT "TEACHER SAYS" CRAP! TELL US WHAT ***YOU*** WANT!
YOU'RE RIGHT! I **SHOULD** MAKE MY OWN DECISION!
NOW YOU'RE GETTIN' IT! SO JUST COME WITH US!
'Kay?

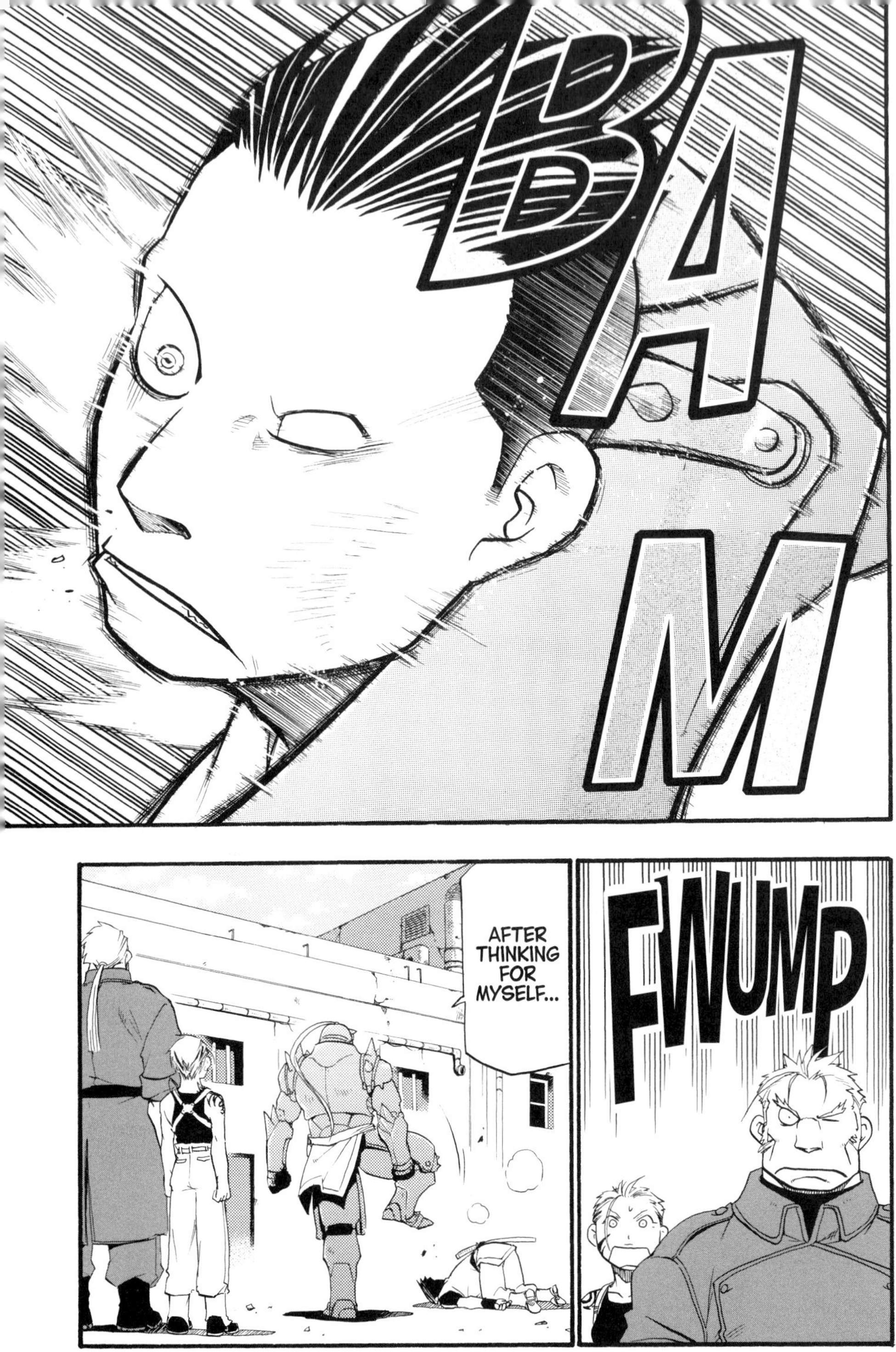
BAM
FWUMP
AFTER THINKING FOR MYSELF...

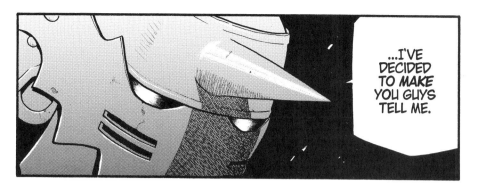

...I'VE DECIDED TO MAKE YOU GUYS TELL ME.

SO IT COMES DOWN TO FORCE, DOES IT?

THUNK

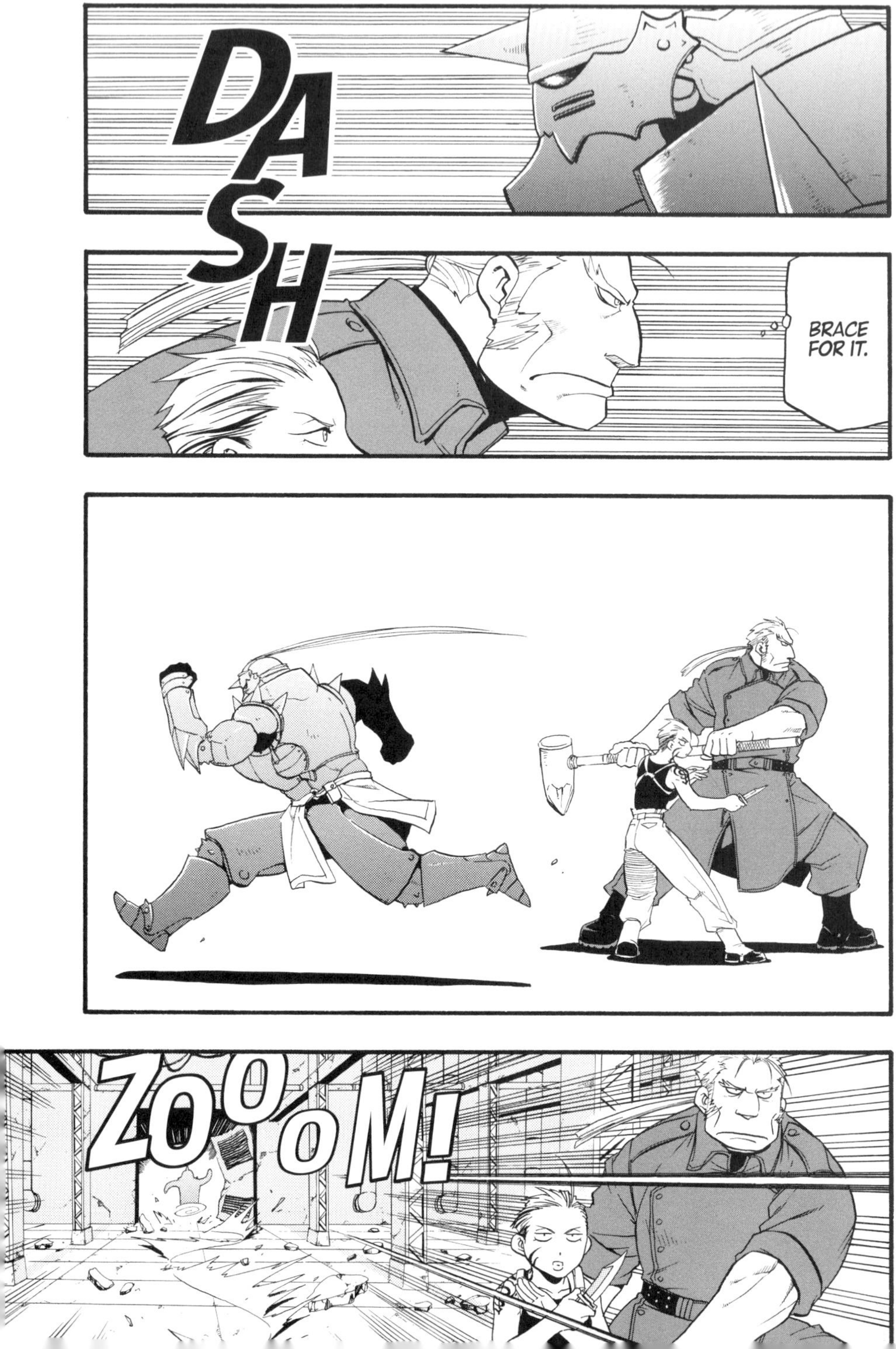
DASH
BRACE FOR IT.
ZOOOM!

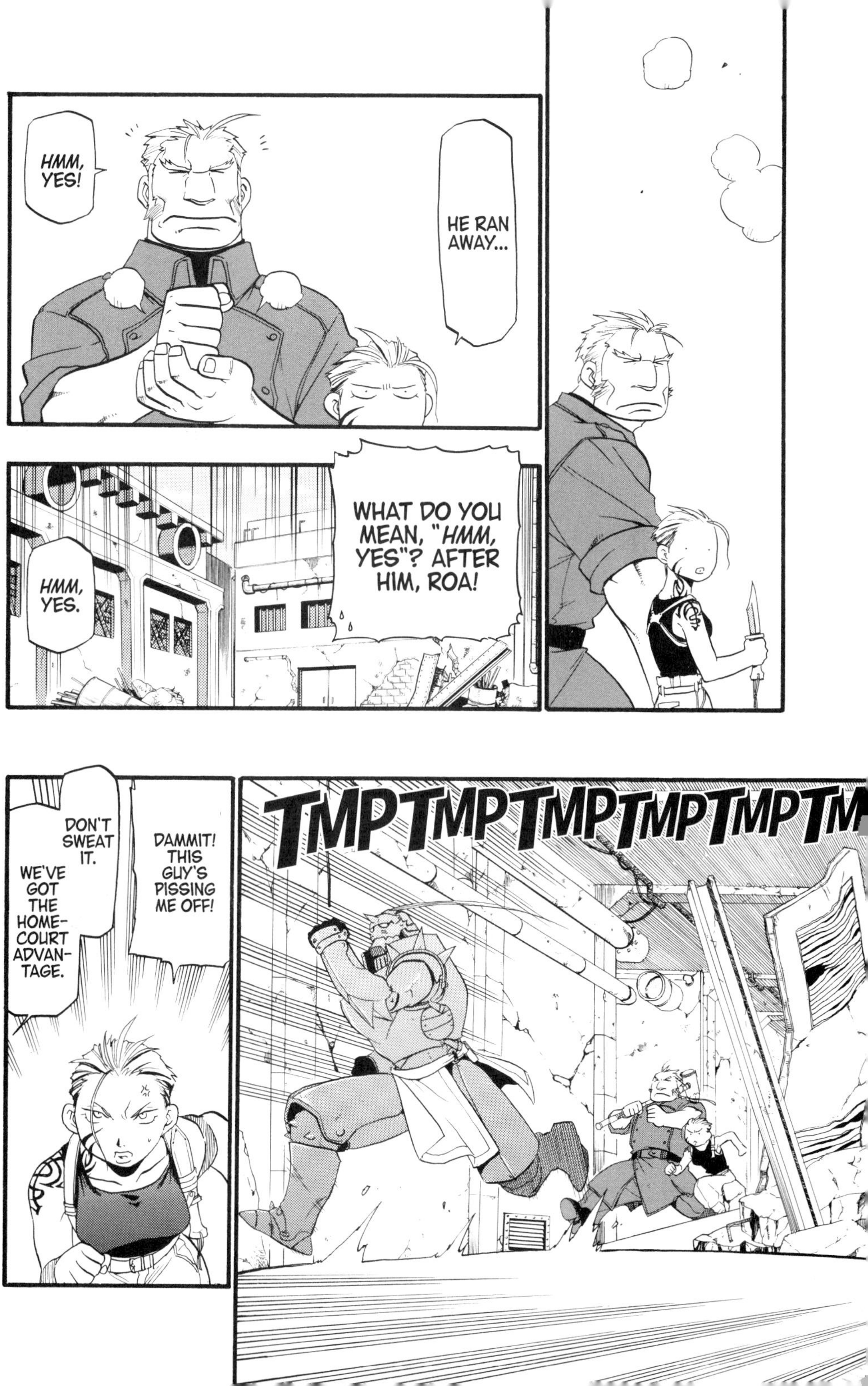
HE RAN AWAY...
HMM, YES!
WHAT DO YOU MEAN, "HMM, YES"? AFTER HIM, ROA!
HMM, YES.
TMPTMPTMPTMPTMPTM
DAMMIT! THIS GUY'S PISSING ME OFF!
DON'T SWEAT IT. WE'VE GOT THE HOME-COURT ADVANTAGE.

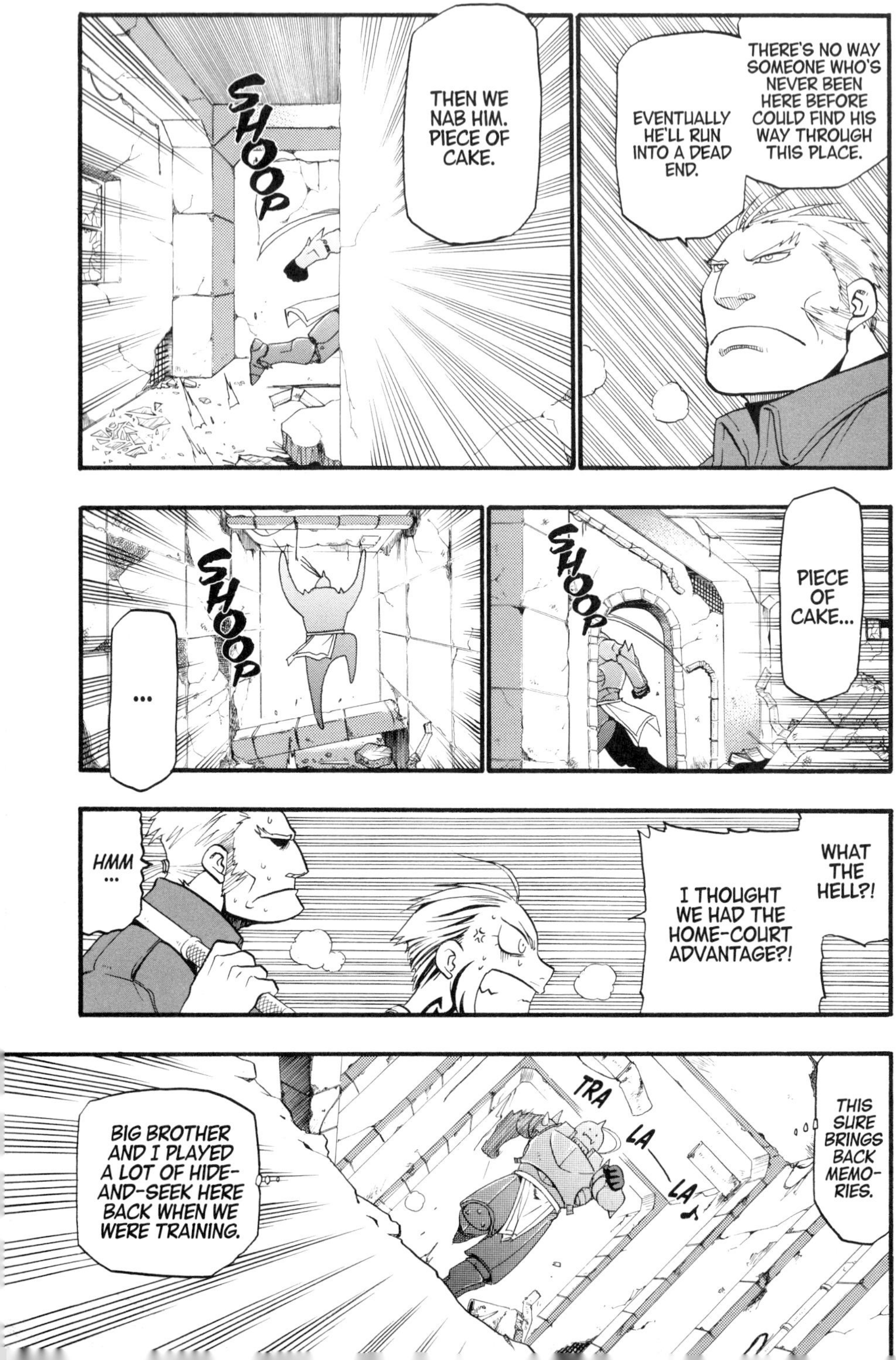
THERE'S NO WAY SOMEONE WHO'S NEVER BEEN HERE BEFORE COULD FIND HIS WAY THROUGH THIS PLACE.
EVENTUALLY HE'LL RUN INTO A DEAD END.
THEN WE NAB HIM. PIECE OF CAKE.
SHOOP
PIECE OF CAKE...
SHOOP
SHOOP
...
WHAT THE HELL?!
I THOUGHT WE HAD THE HOME-COURT ADVANTAGE?!
HMM...
THIS SURE BRINGS BACK MEMORIES.
TRA LA LA
BIG BROTHER AND I PLAYED A LOT OF HIDE-AND-SEEK HERE BACK WHEN WE WERE TRAINING.

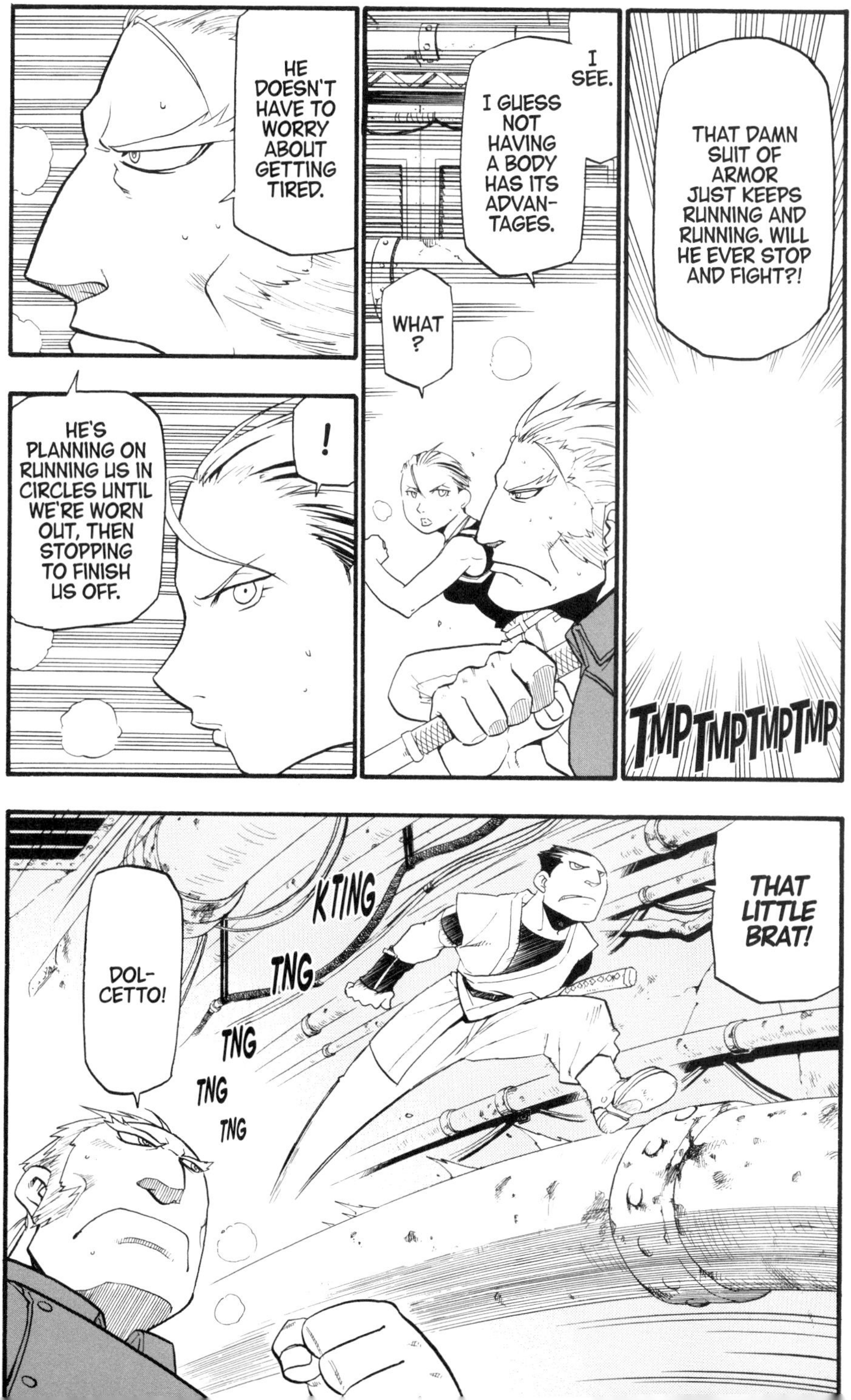
THAT DAMN SUIT OF ARMOR JUST KEEPS RUNNING AND RUNNING. WILL HE EVER STOP AND FIGHT?!
TMPTMPTMPTMP
I SEE.
I GUESS NOT HAVING A BODY HAS ITS ADVANTAGES.
WHAT?
HE DOESN'T HAVE TO WORRY ABOUT GETTING TIRED.
!
HE'S PLANNING ON RUNNING US IN CIRCLES UNTIL WE'RE WORN OUT, THEN STOPPING TO FINISH US OFF.
THAT LITTLE BRAT!
KTING
TNG
TNG
TNG
TNG
DOL-CETTO!

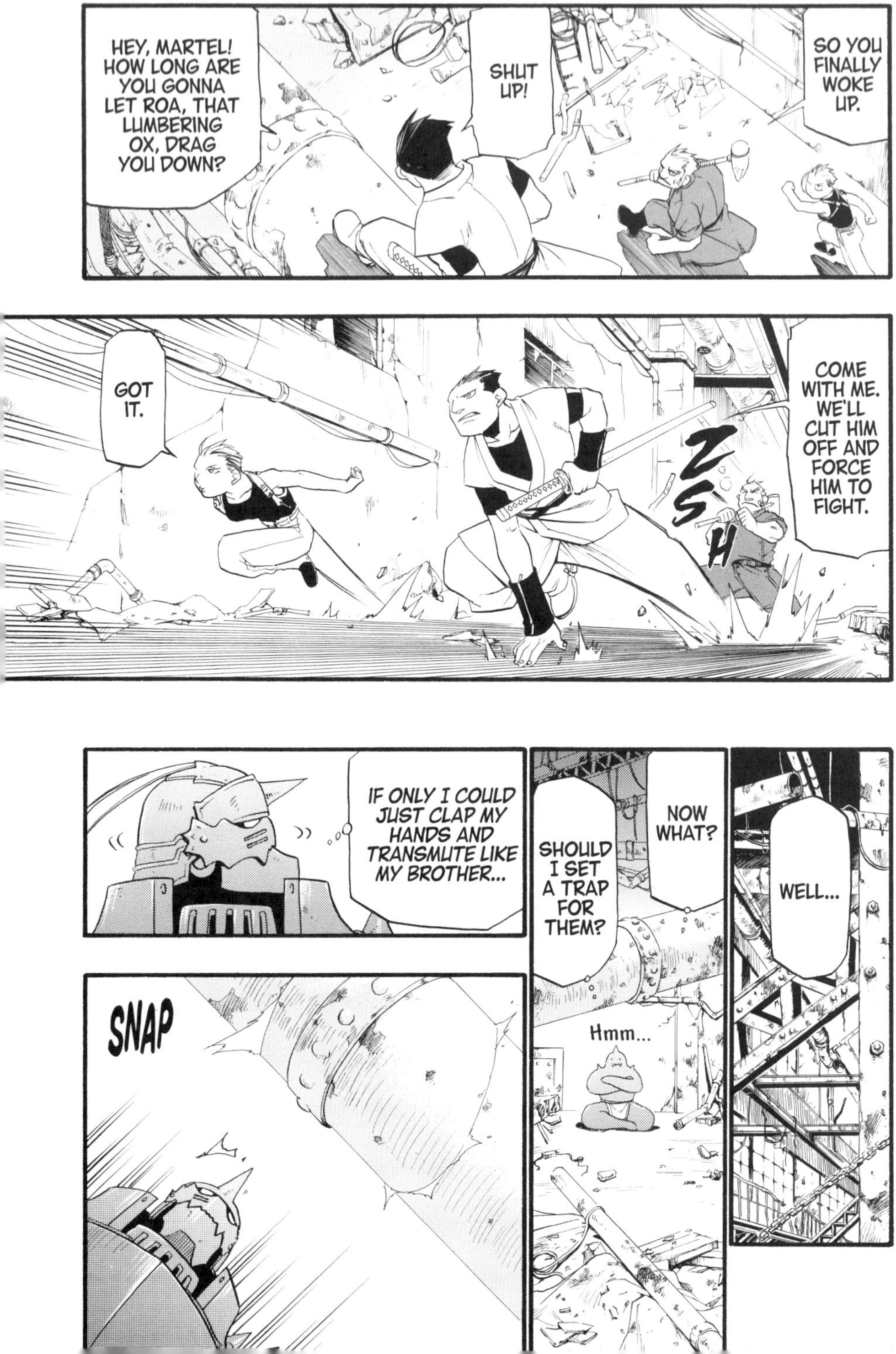
SO YOU FINALLY WOKE UP.
SHUT UP!
HEY, MARTEL! HOW LONG ARE YOU GONNA LET ROA, THAT LUMBERING OX, DRAG YOU DOWN?
COME WITH ME. WE'LL CUT HIM OFF AND FORCE HIM TO FIGHT.
ZSH
GOT IT.
WELL...
NOW WHAT?
SHOULD I SET A TRAP FOR THEM?
Hmm...
IF ONLY I COULD JUST CLAP MY HANDS AND TRANSMUTE LIKE MY BROTHER...
SNAP

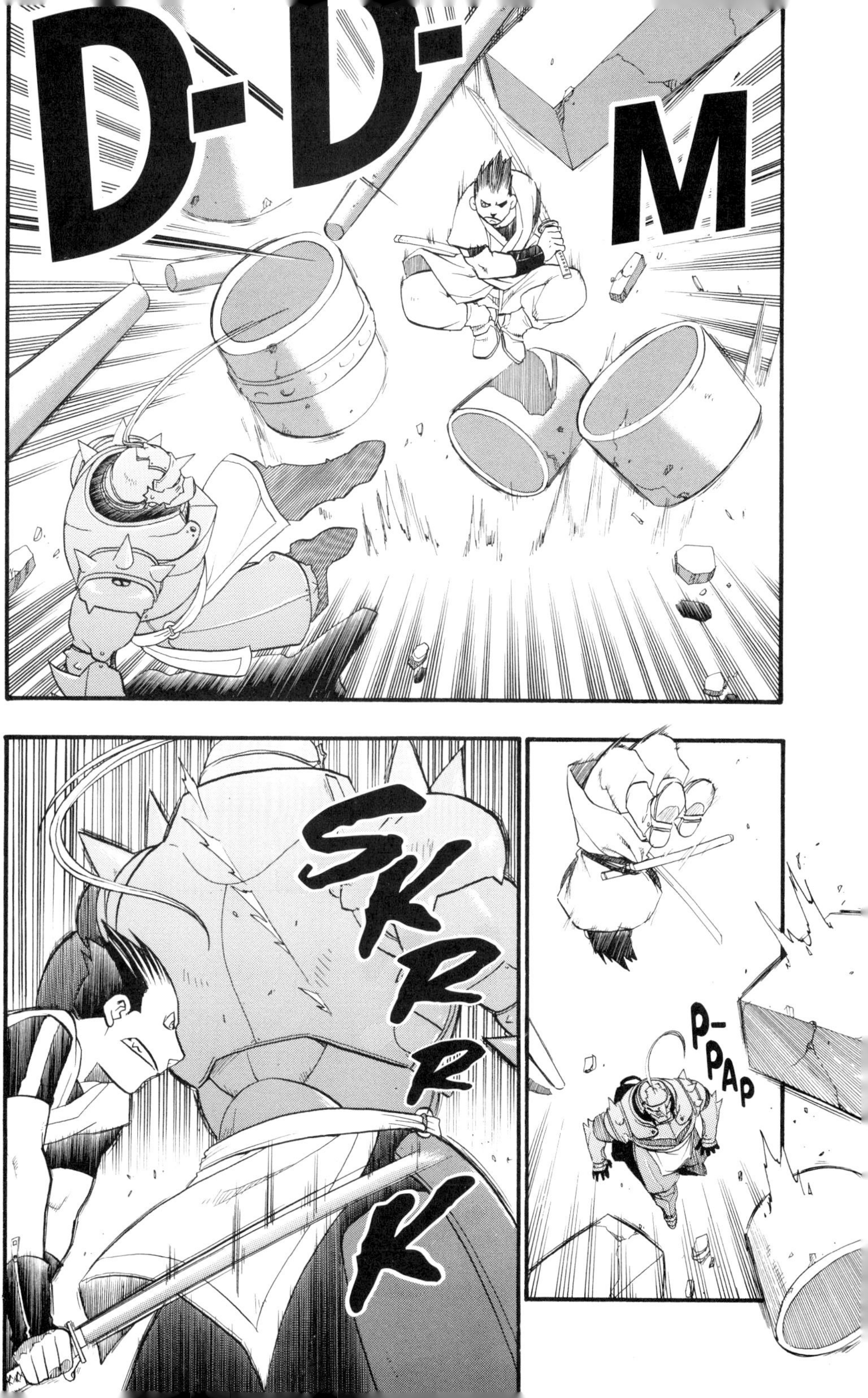
D-D-M
P-PPAP
SKRRK

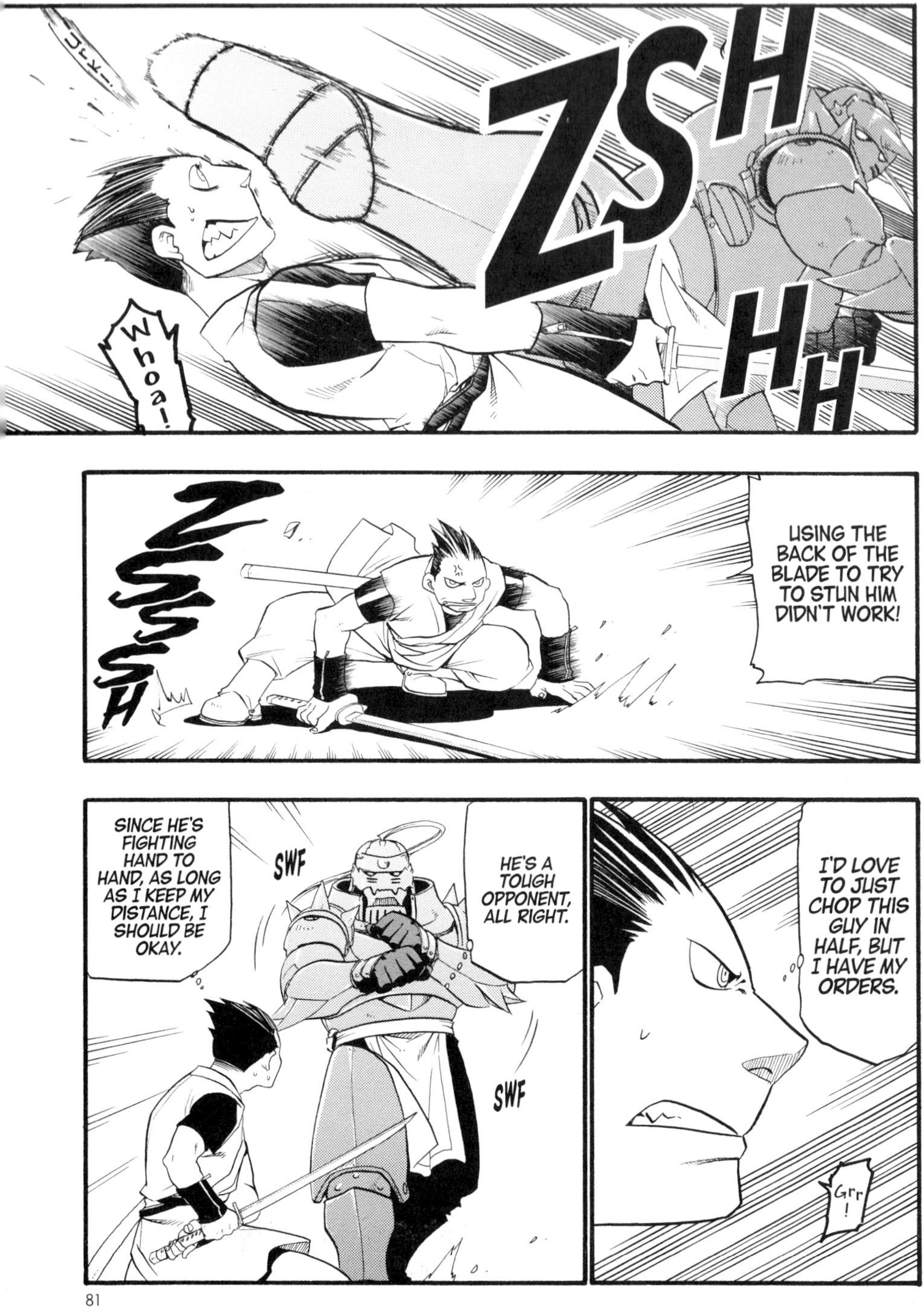
ZSH
HHH
Whoa!
USING THE BACK OF THE BLADE TO TRY TO STUN HIM DIDN'T WORK!
ZSSSH
I'D LOVE TO JUST CHOP THIS GUY IN HALF, BUT I HAVE MY ORDERS.
Grr!
HE'S A TOUGH OPPONENT, ALL RIGHT.
SWF
SINCE HE'S FIGHTING HAND TO HAND, AS LONG AS I KEEP MY DISTANCE, I SHOULD BE OKAY.
SWF

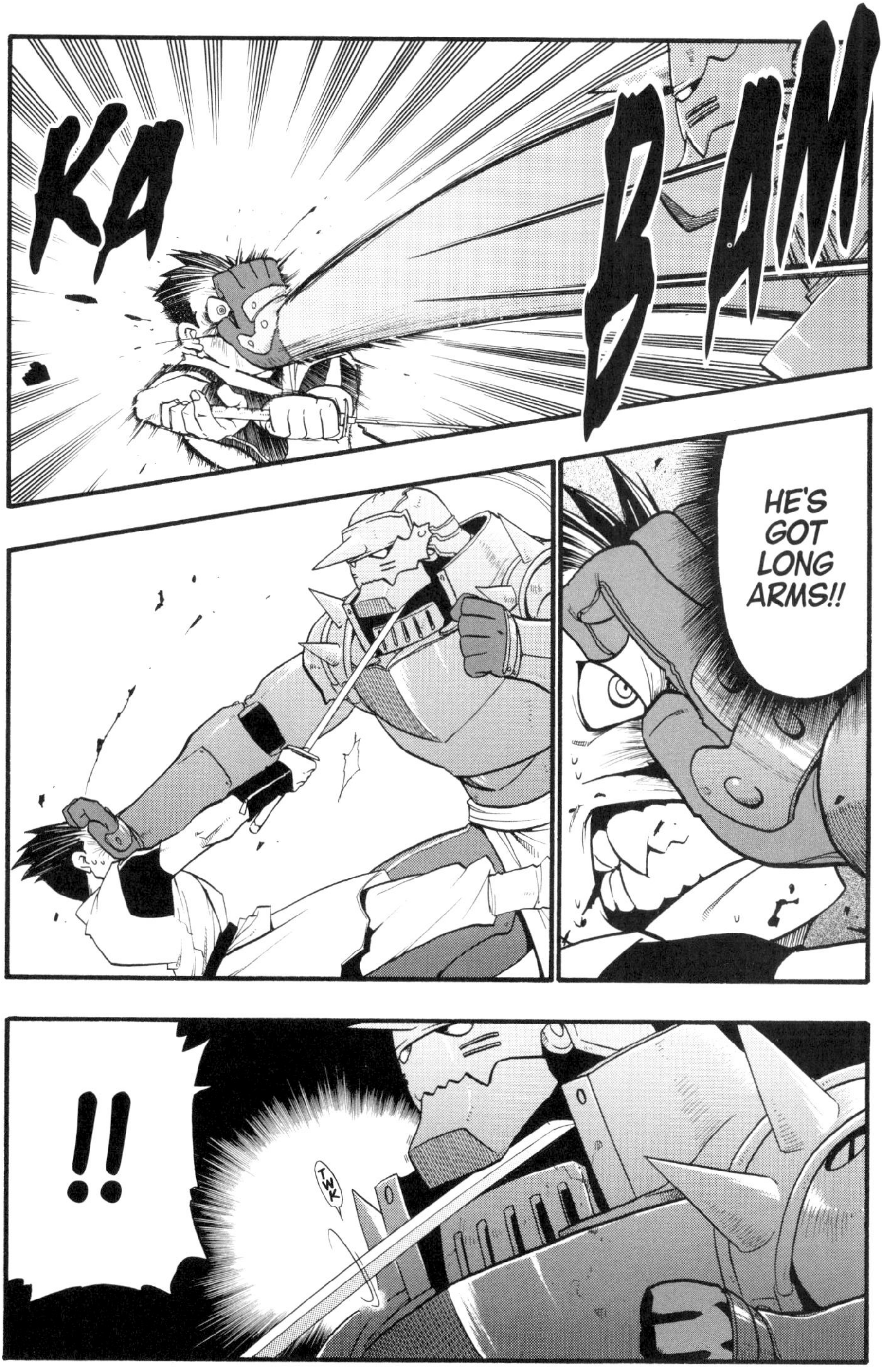
KA
BAM
HE'S GOT LONG ARMS!!
TWK
!!

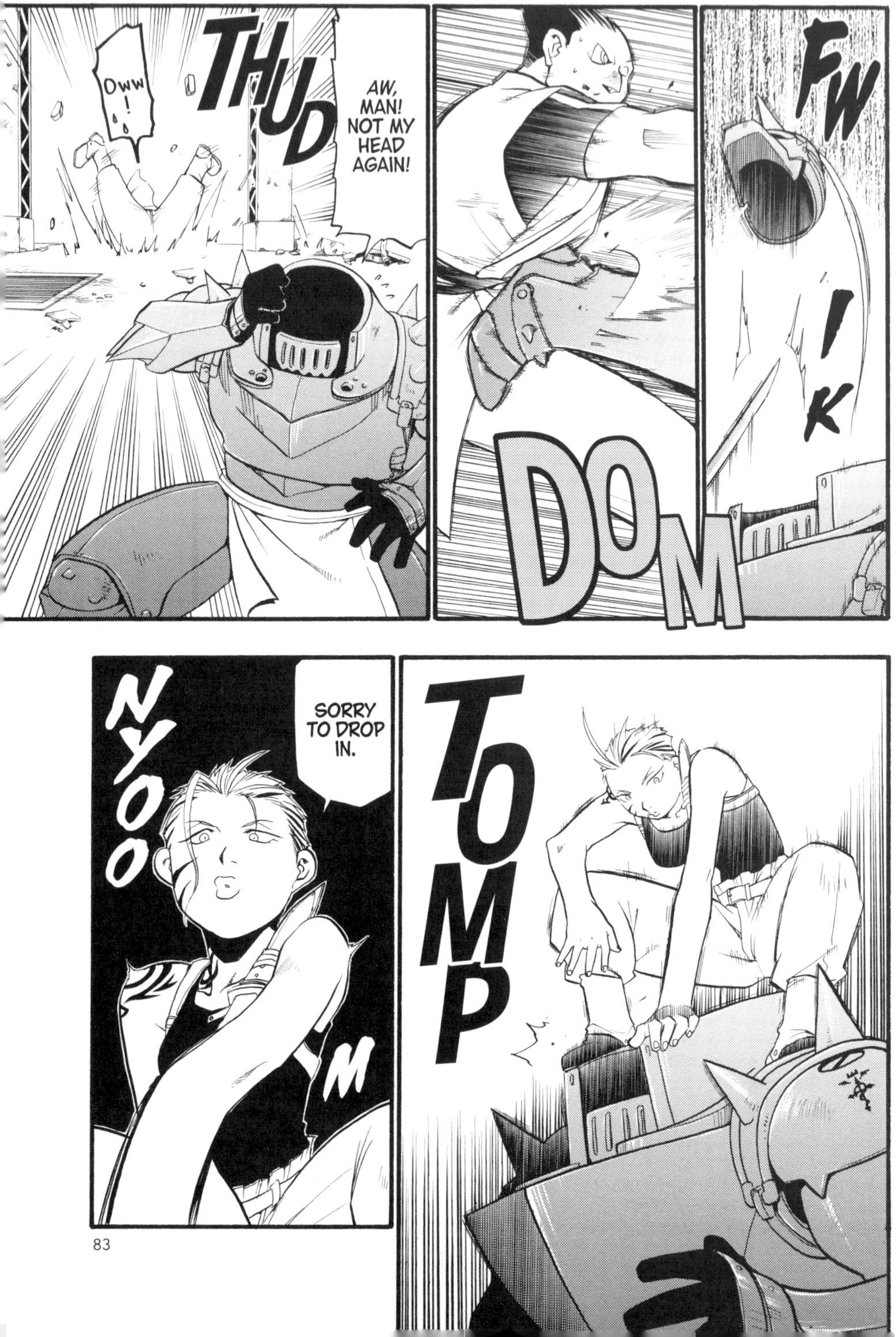
FWIK
DOM
AW, MAN! NOT MY HEAD AGAIN!
THUD
Oww!
TOMP
SORRY TO DROP IN.
NYOO
M

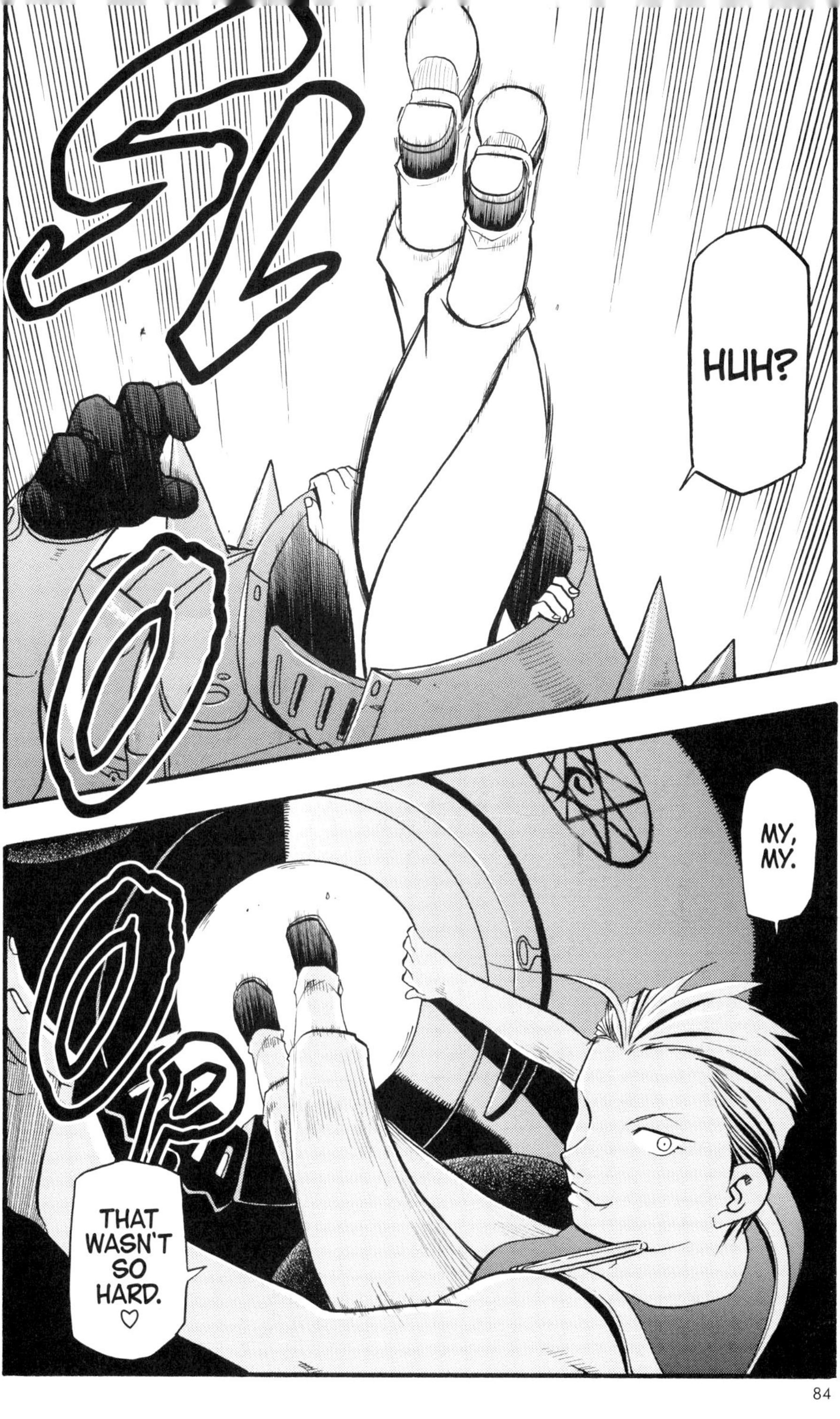

SHA
HUH?
MY, MY.
THAT WASN'T SO HARD. ♡

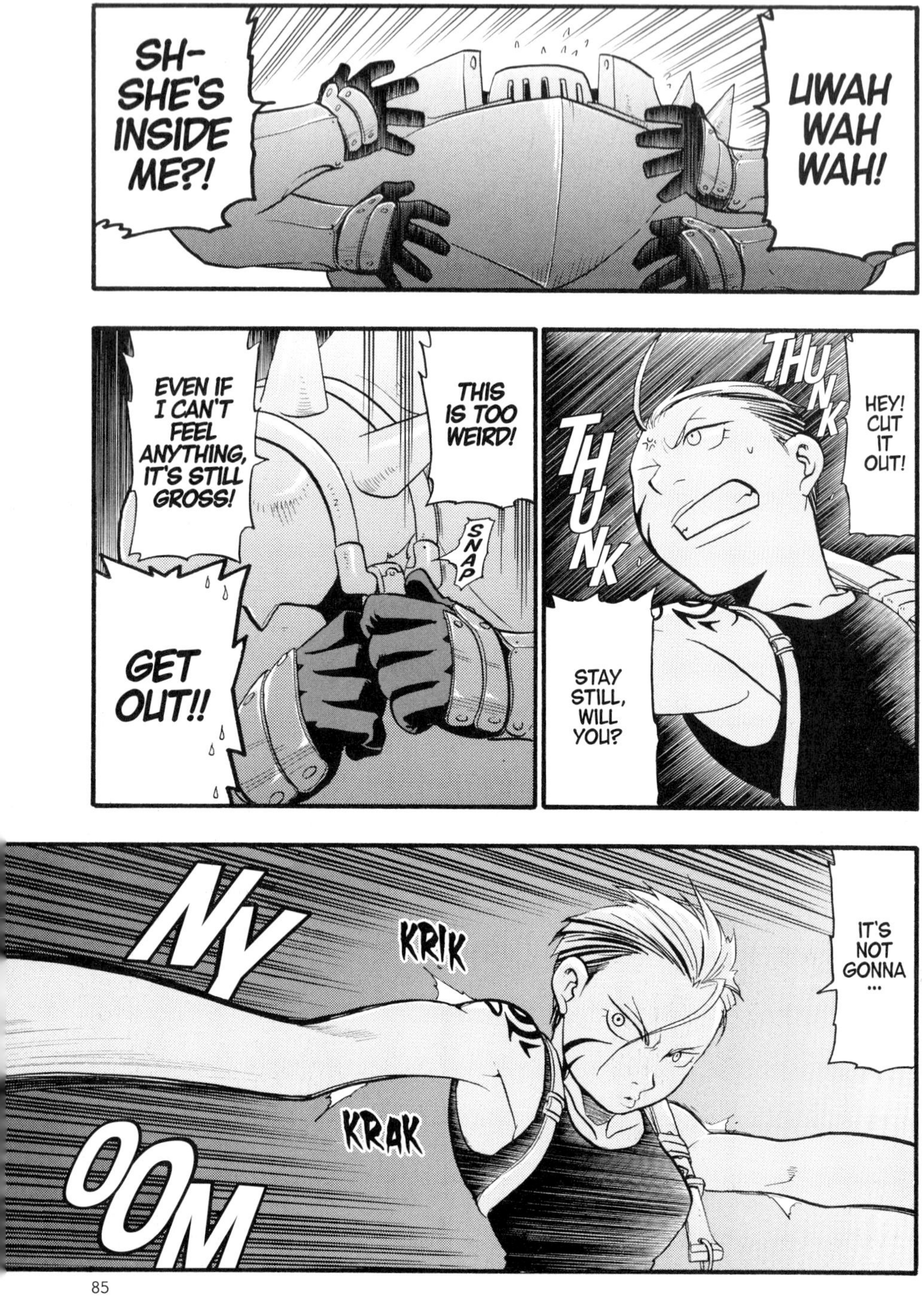
UWAH WAH WAH!
SH- SHE'S INSIDE ME?!
THUNK
HEY! CUT IT OUT!
THUNK
STAY STILL, WILL YOU?
THIS IS TOO WEIRD!
EVEN IF I CAN'T FEEL ANYTHING, IT'S STILL GROSS!
SNAP
GET OUT!!
IT'S NOT GONNA...
KRIK
NY
KRAK
OOM

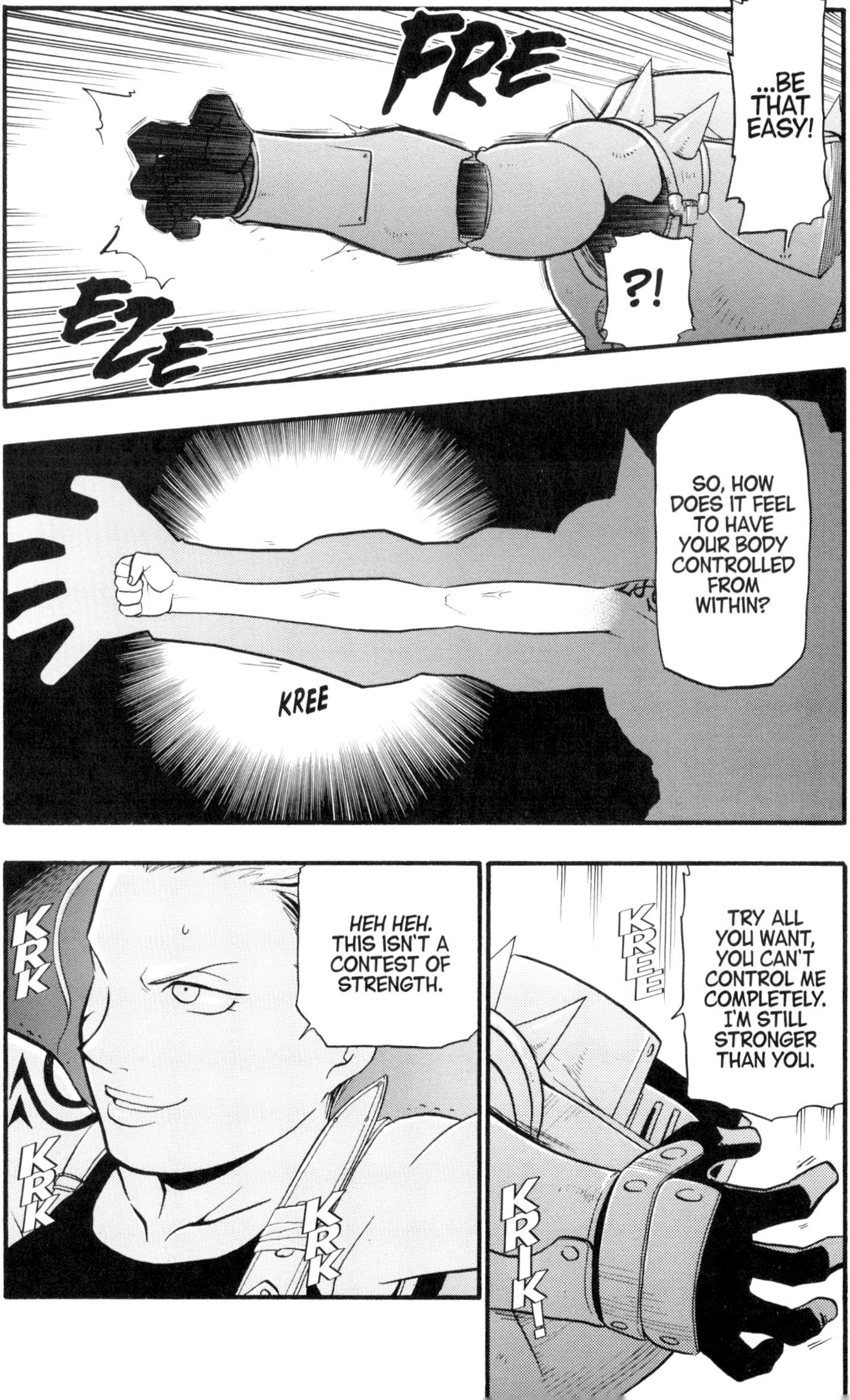
...BE THAT EASY!
?!
FREEZE
SO, HOW DOES IT FEEL TO HAVE YOUR BODY CONTROLLED FROM WITHIN?
KREE
KREE
TRY ALL YOU WANT, YOU CAN'T CONTROL ME COMPLETELY. I'M STILL STRONGER THAN YOU.
KRIK!
HEH HEH. THIS ISN'T A CONTEST OF STRENGTH.
KRK
KRK
KRK

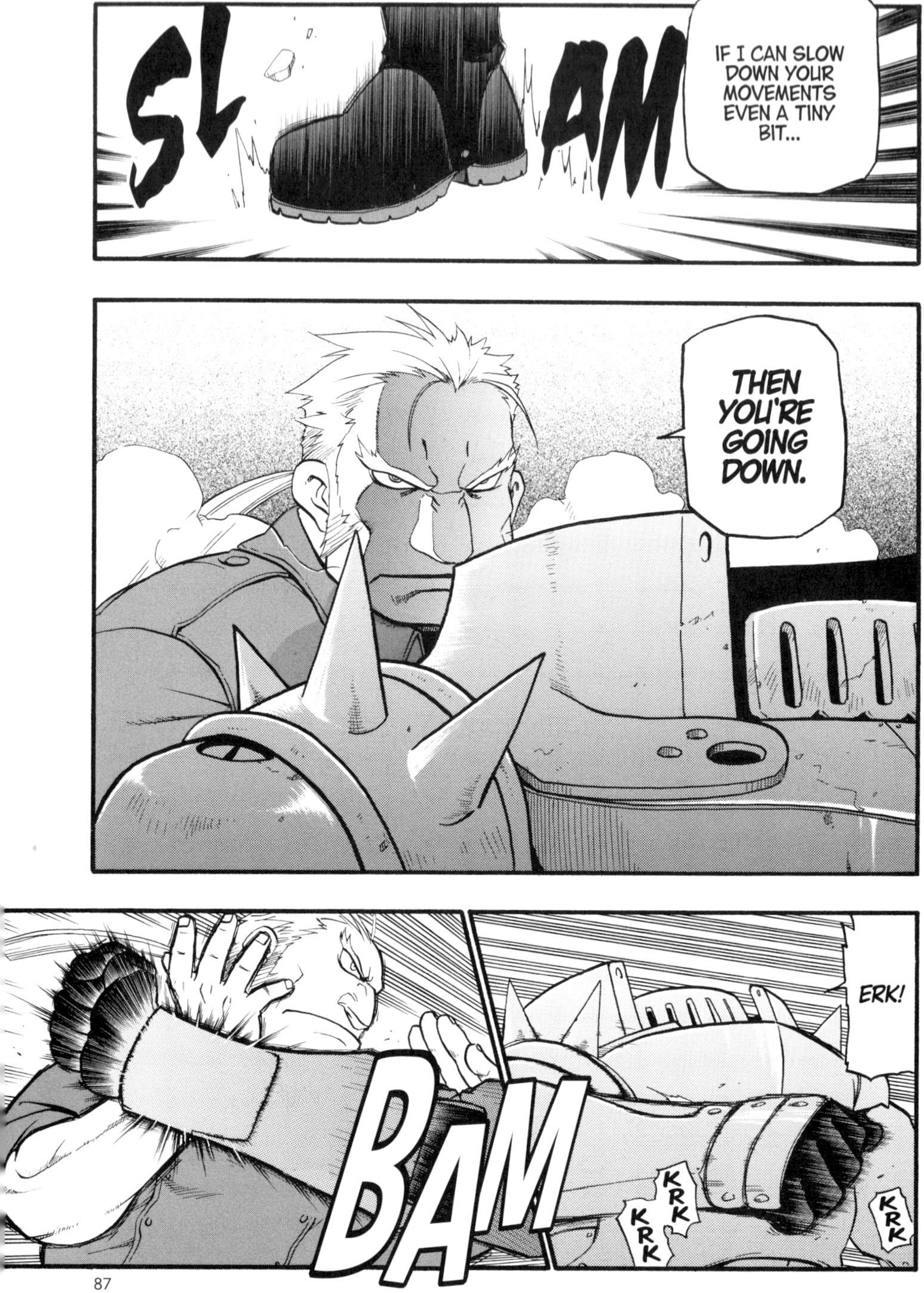
SL AM
IF I CAN SLOW DOWN YOUR MOVEMENTS EVEN A TINY BIT...
THEN YOU'RE GOING DOWN.
ERK!
KRK KRK
KRK
BAM

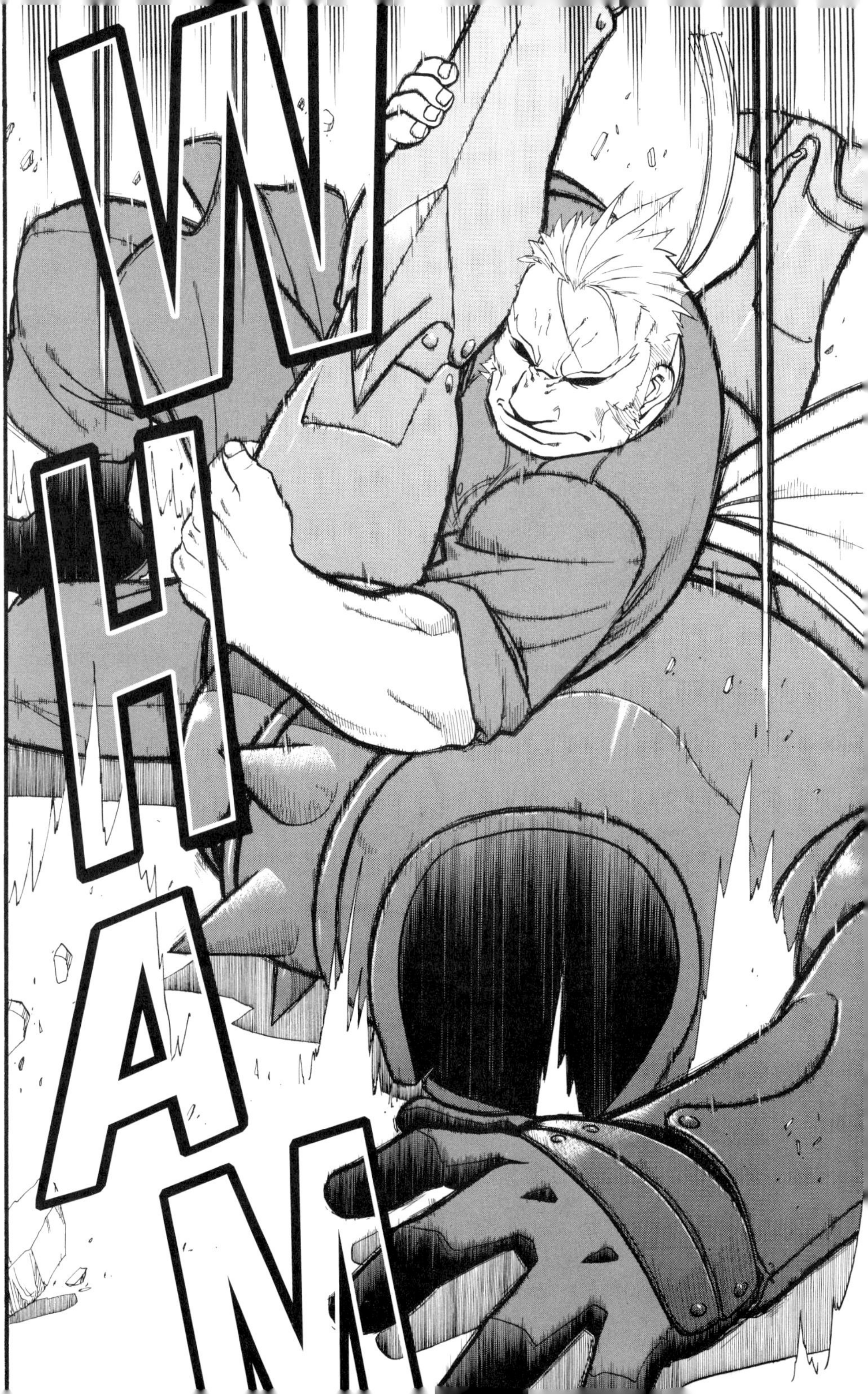
WHAM

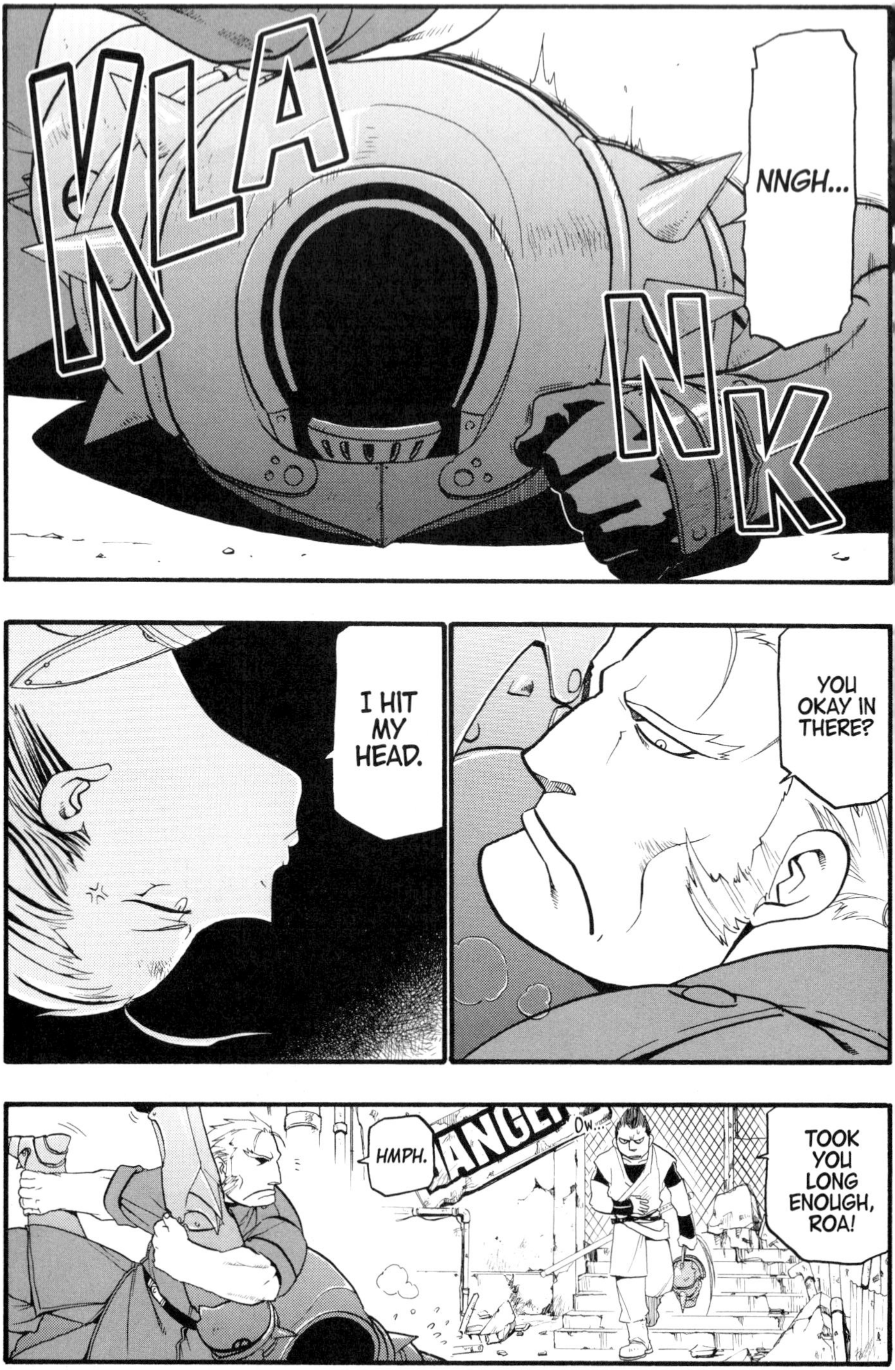
NNGH...
KLANK
YOU OKAY IN THERE?
I HIT MY HEAD.
TOOK YOU LONG ENOUGH, ROA!
OW...
HMPH.

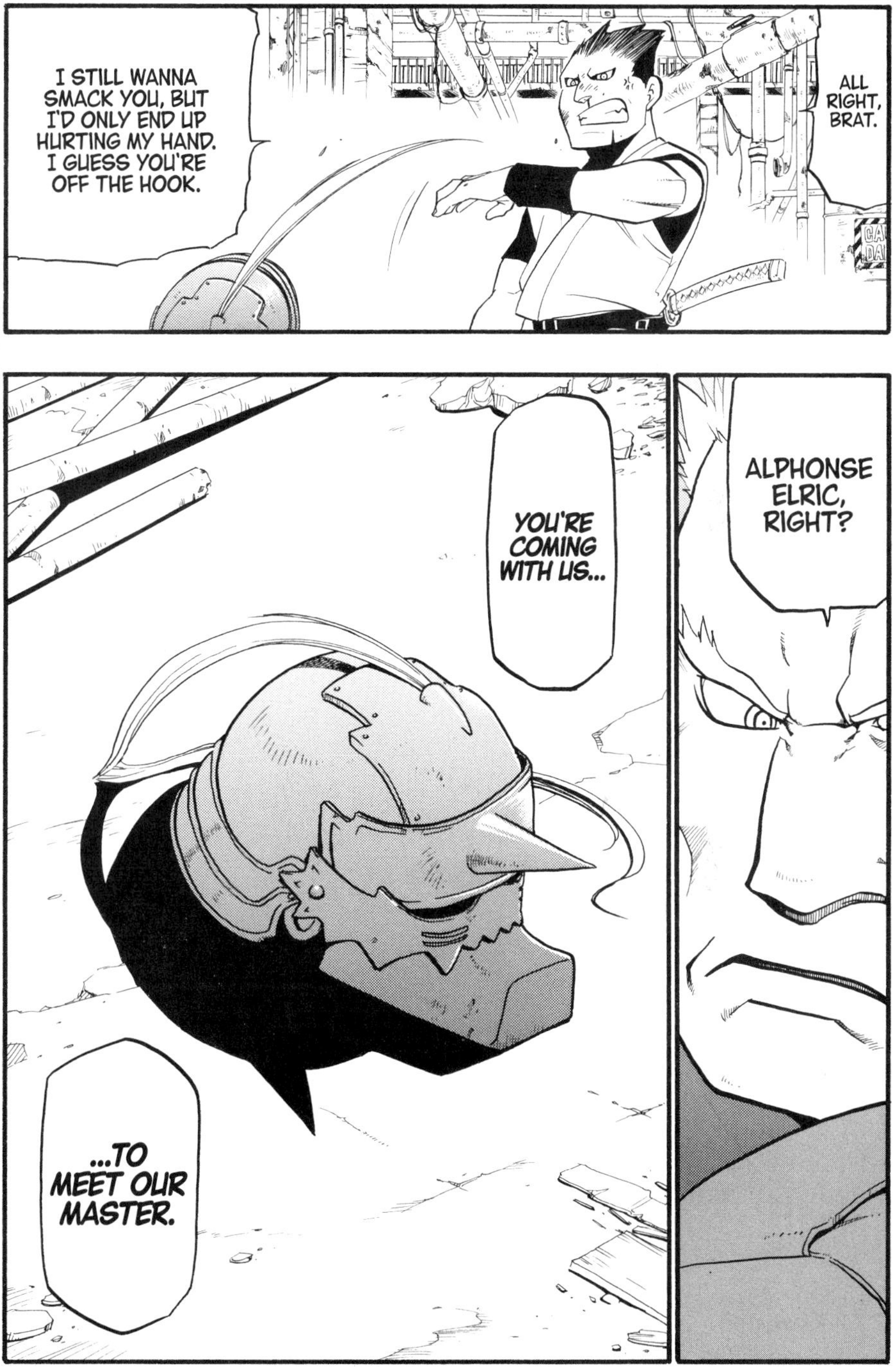
ALL RIGHT, BRAT.
I STILL WANNA SMACK YOU, BUT I'D ONLY END UP HURTING MY HAND. I GUESS YOU'RE OFF THE HOOK.
ALPHONSE ELRIC, RIGHT?
YOU'RE COMING WITH US...
...TO MEET OUR MASTER.

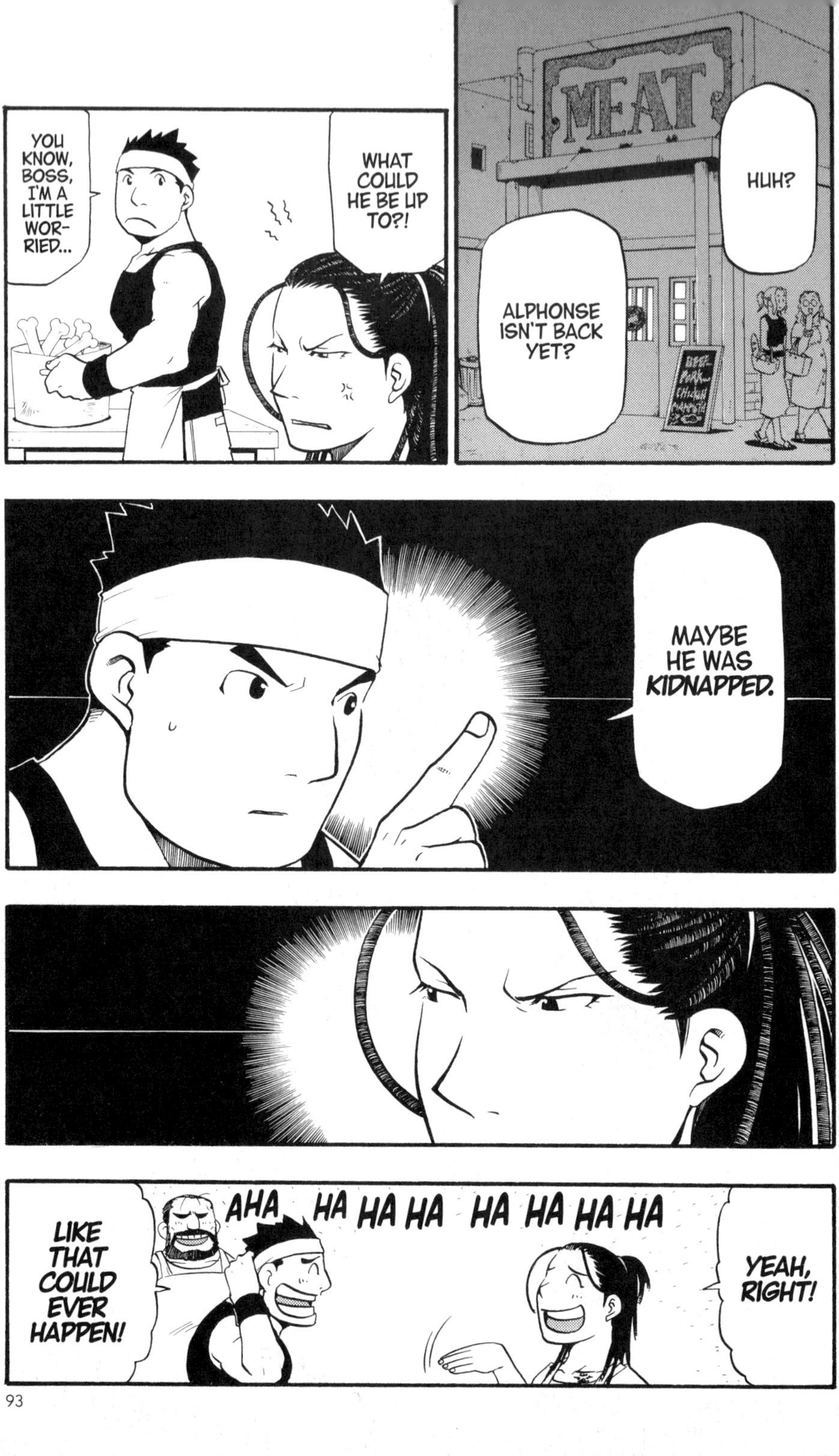
MEAT
HUH?
ALPHONSE ISN'T BACK YET?
WHAT COULD HE BE UP TO?!
YOU KNOW, BOSS, I'M A LITTLE WOR-RIED...
MAYBE HE WAS KIDNAPPED.
YEAH, RIGHT!
AHA HA HA HA HA HA HA HA
LIKE THAT COULD EVER HAPPEN!

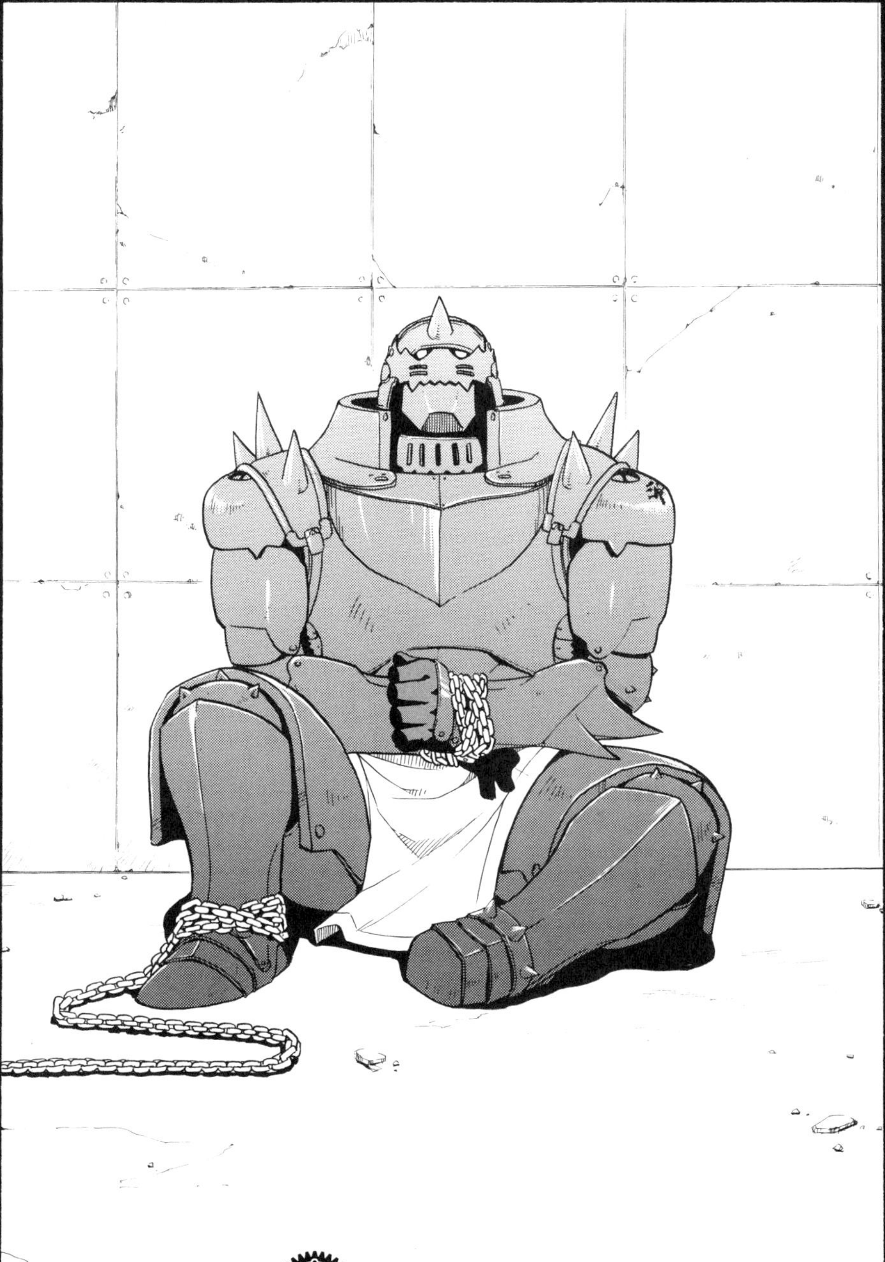

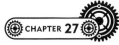

CHAPTER 27 THE BEASTS OF DUBLITH

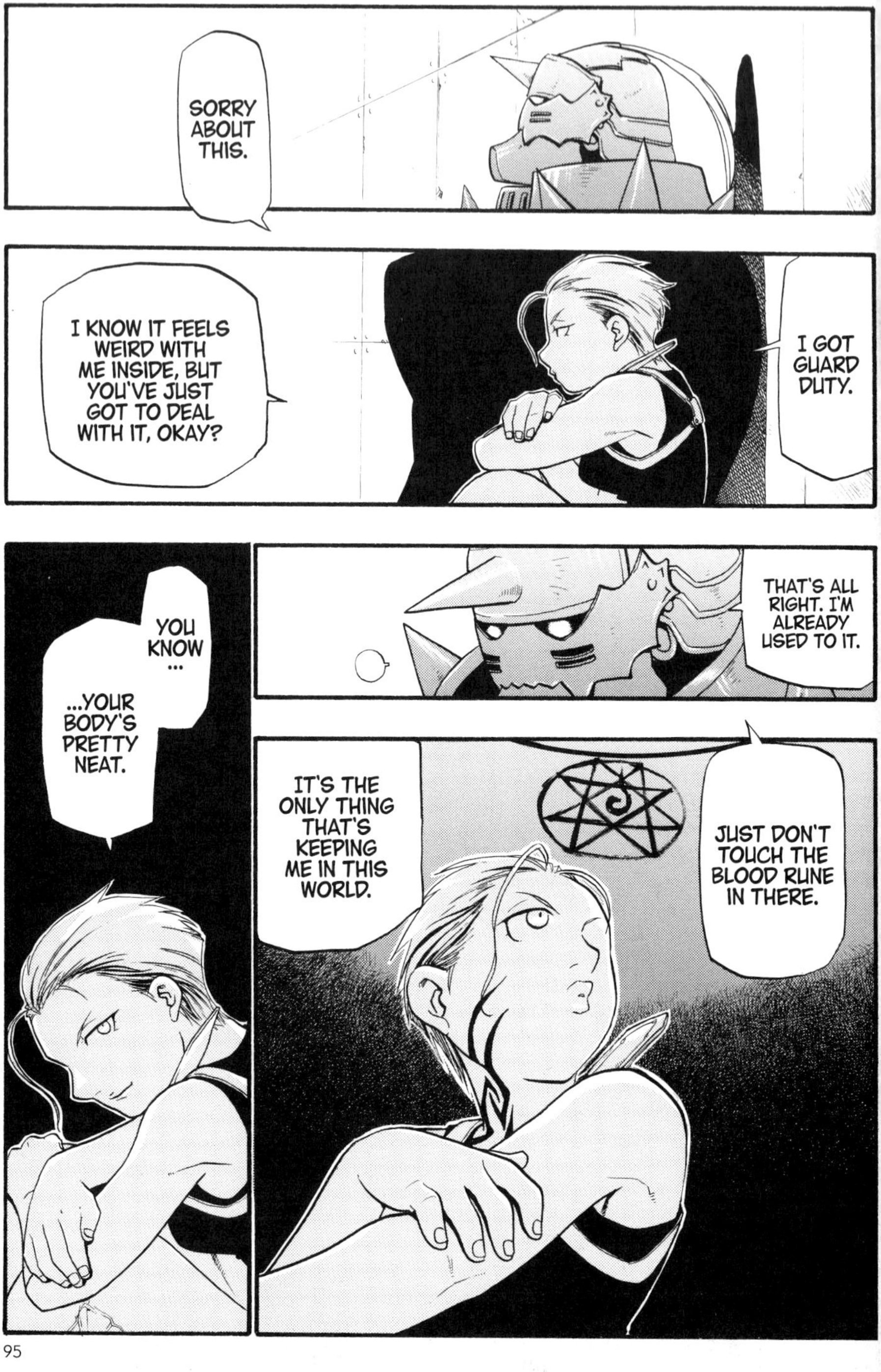
SORRY ABOUT THIS.
I GOT GUARD DUTY.
I KNOW IT FEELS WEIRD WITH ME INSIDE, BUT YOU'VE JUST GOT TO DEAL WITH IT, OKAY?
THAT'S ALL RIGHT. I'M ALREADY USED TO IT.
JUST DON'T TOUCH THE BLOOD RUNE IN THERE.
IT'S THE ONLY THING THAT'S KEEPING ME IN THIS WORLD.
YOU KNOW...
...YOUR BODY'S PRETTY NEAT.

YOU'RE PRETTY UNUSUAL YOURSELF, AREN'T YOU, MISS?
DO YOU KNOW WHAT A CHIMERA IS?
MY BODY...
...IS PART SNAKE.
TWIST
B-BUT THAT'S IMPOSSIBLE!
I THOUGHT YOU COULDN'T MAKE HUMAN-ANIMAL CHIMERAS! NO ONE'S EVER SUCCEEDED!
HOW RUDE! IF I'M NOT A SUCCESS, THEN WHAT AM I?
I USED TO BE A SOLDIER.
I WAS CRITICALLY WOUNDED IN THE SOUTH BORDER WAR.
THE MILITARY DRAGGED MY HALF-DEAD BODY TO THEIR LABORATORIES AND USED ME IN THEIR EXPERIMENTS.
THAT'S...
...HOW I GOT LIKE THIS.

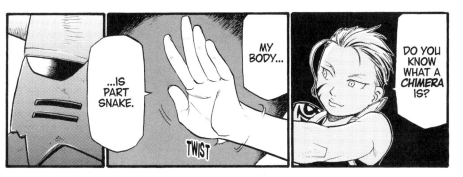

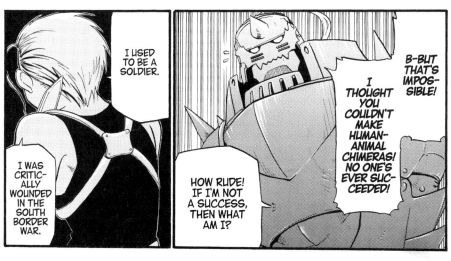

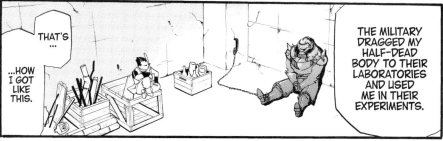

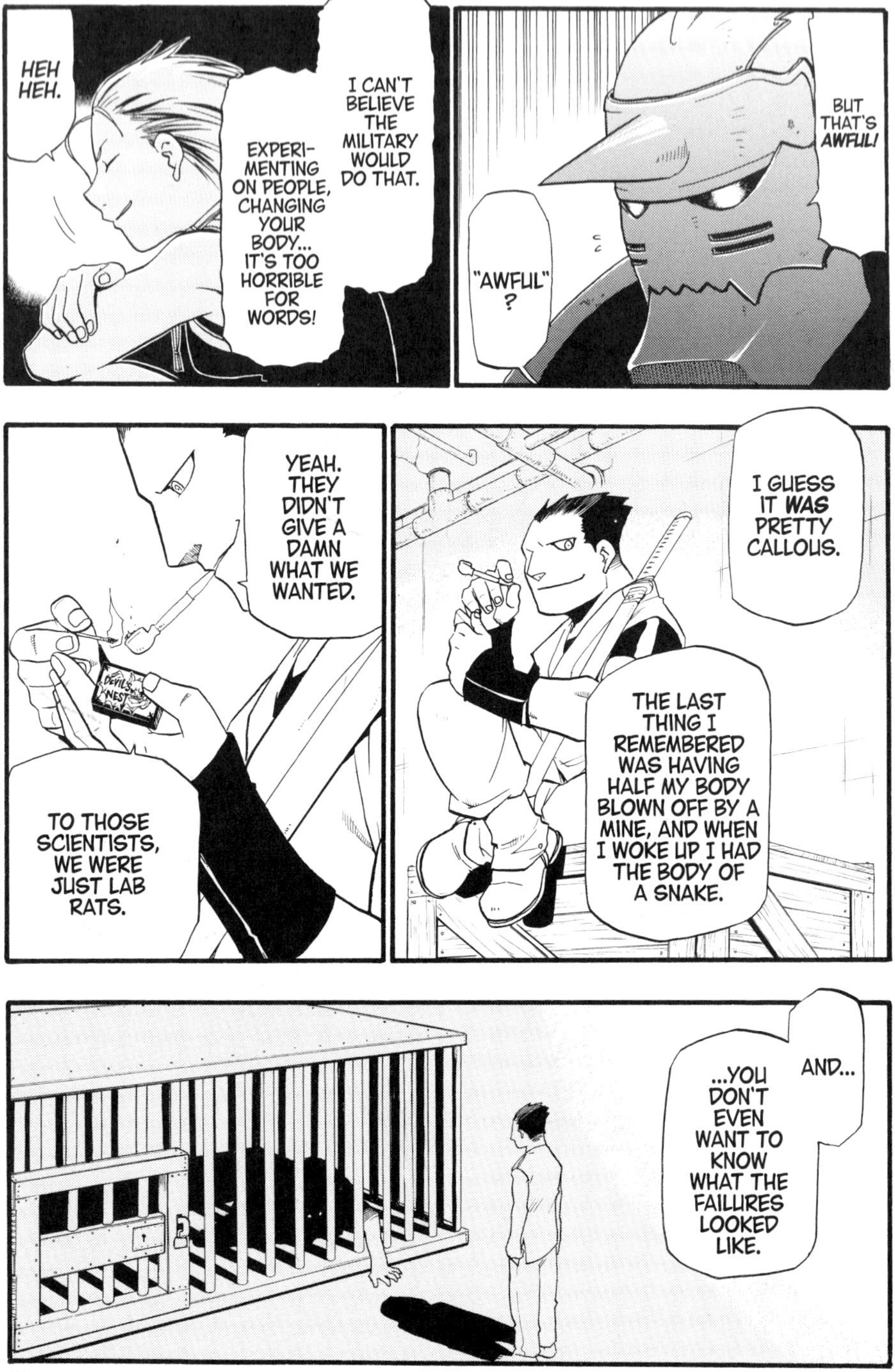
BUT THAT'S **AWFUL!**
"AWFUL"?
I CAN'T BELIEVE THE MILITARY WOULD DO THAT.
EXPERIMENTING ON PEOPLE, CHANGING YOUR BODY... IT'S TOO HORRIBLE FOR WORDS!
HEH HEH.
I GUESS IT **WAS** PRETTY CALLOUS.
THE LAST THING I REMEMBERED WAS HAVING HALF MY BODY BLOWN OFF BY A MINE, AND WHEN I WOKE UP I HAD THE BODY OF A SNAKE.
YEAH. THEY DIDN'T GIVE A DAMN WHAT WE WANTED.
DEVIL'S NEST
TO THOSE SCIENTISTS, WE WERE JUST LAB RATS.
AND...
...YOU DON'T EVEN WANT TO KNOW WHAT THE FAILURES LOOKED LIKE.

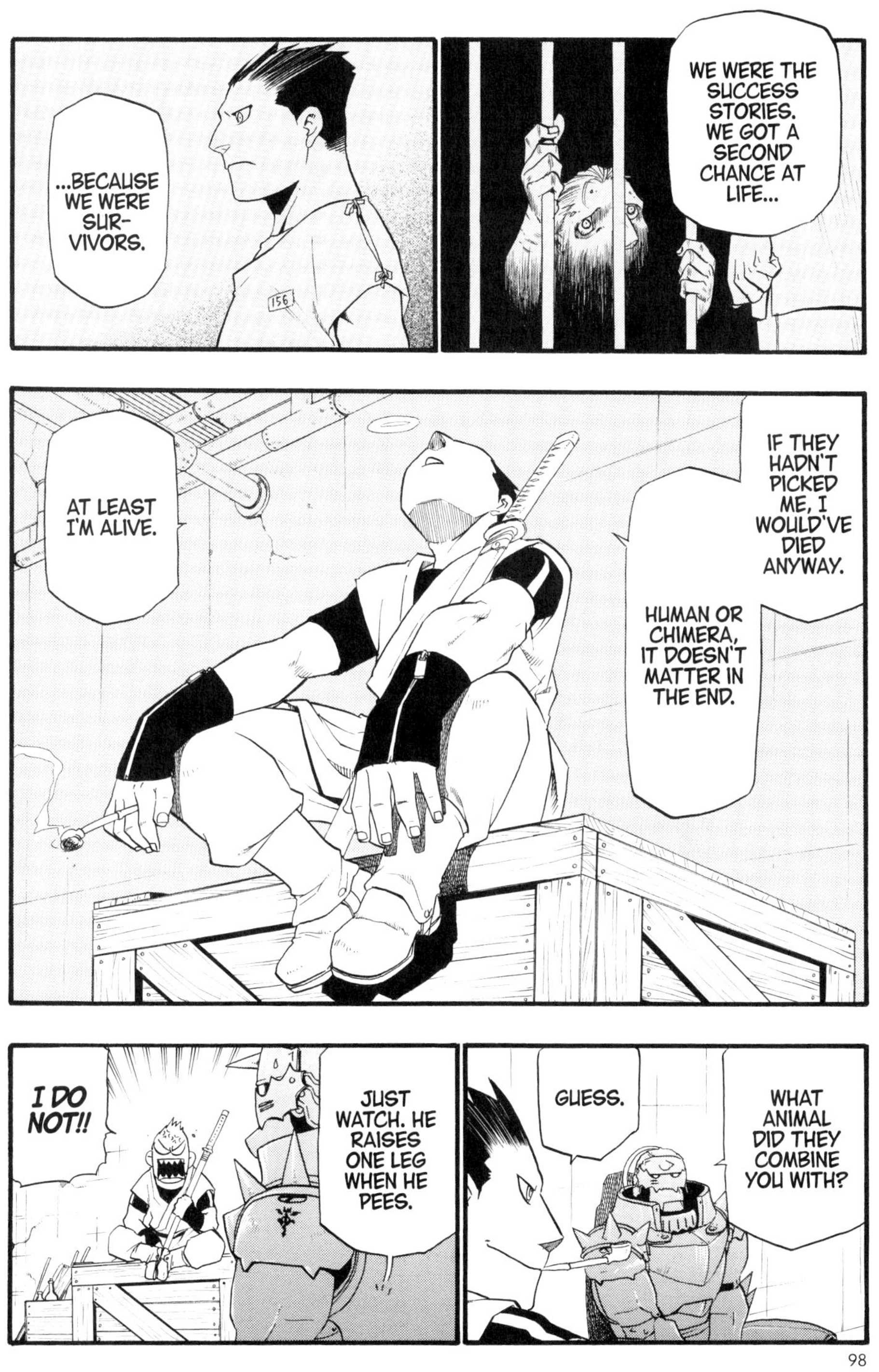
WE WERE THE SUCCESS STORIES. WE GOT A SECOND CHANCE AT LIFE...
...BECAUSE WE WERE SUR-VIVORS.
IF THEY HADN'T PICKED ME, I WOULD'VE DIED ANYWAY.
HUMAN OR CHIMERA, IT DOESN'T MATTER IN THE END.
AT LEAST I'M ALIVE.
WHAT ANIMAL DID THEY COMBINE YOU WITH?
GUESS.
JUST WATCH. HE RAISES ONE LEG WHEN HE PEES.
I DO NOT!!

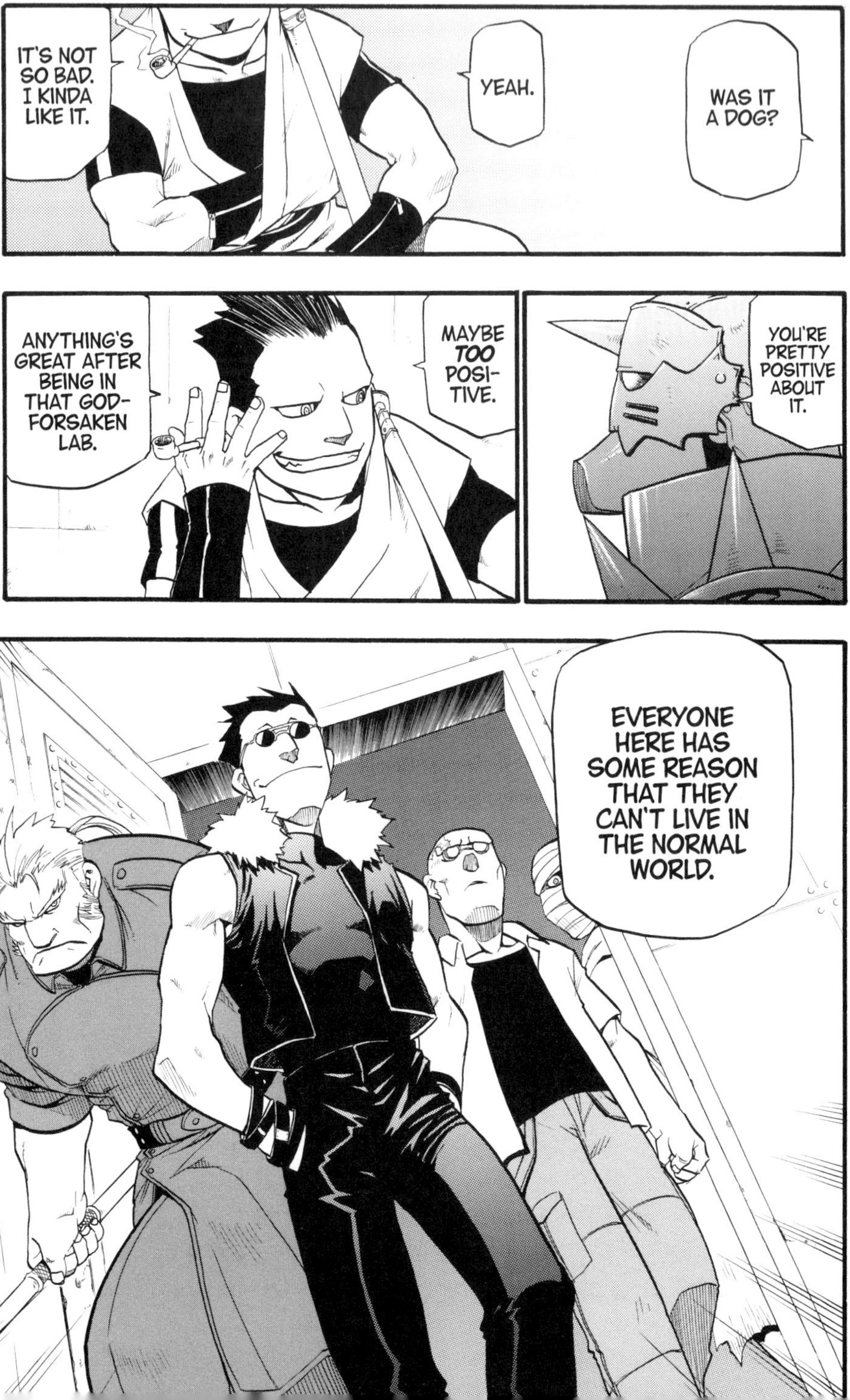
WAS IT A DOG?
YEAH.
IT'S NOT SO BAD. I KINDA LIKE IT.
YOU'RE PRETTY POSITIVE ABOUT IT.
MAYBE *TOO* POSI-TIVE.
ANYTHING'S GREAT AFTER BEING IN THAT GOD-FORSAKEN LAB.
EVERYONE HERE HAS SOME REASON THAT THEY CAN'T LIVE IN THE NORMAL WORLD.

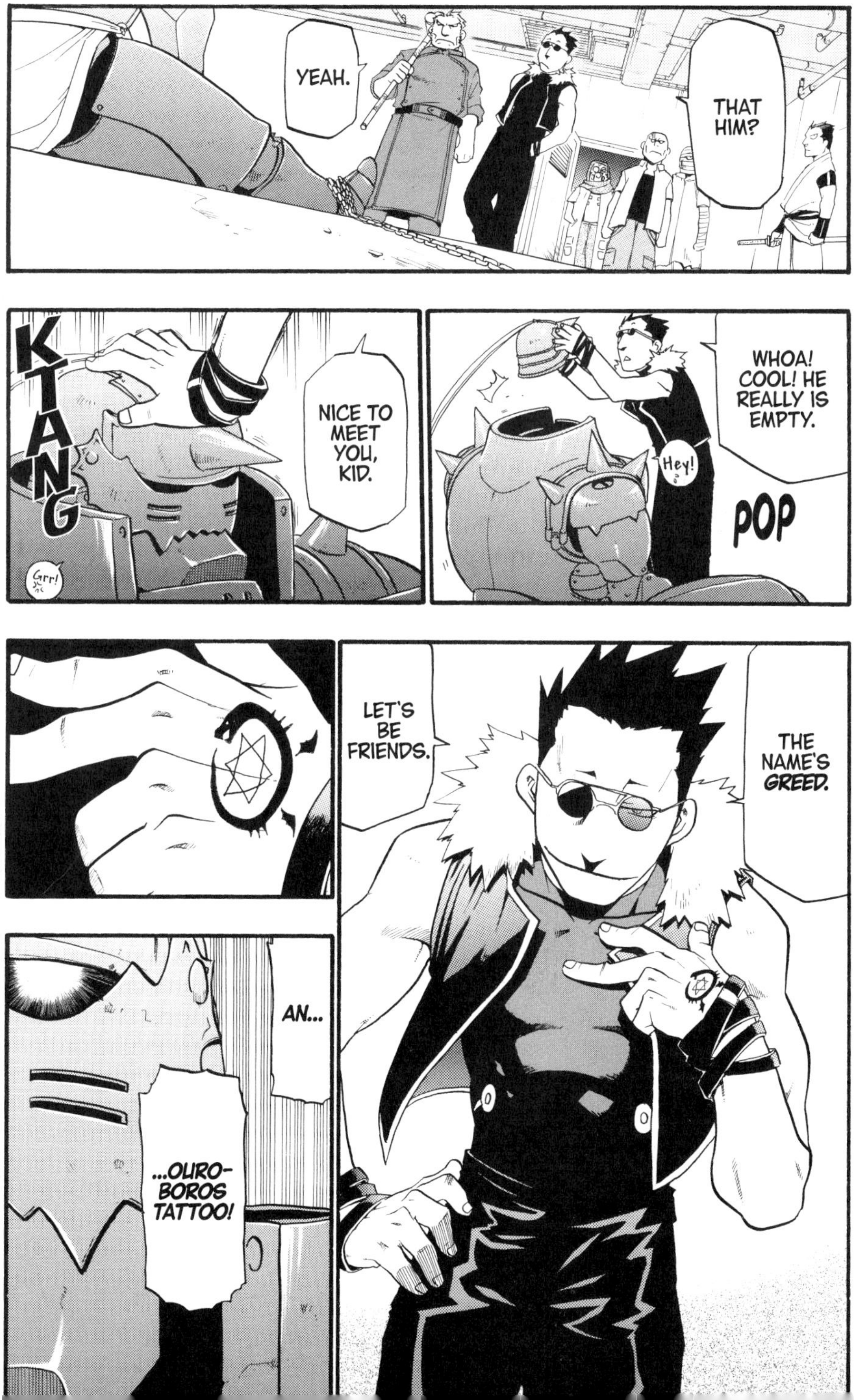
THAT HIM?
YEAH.
WHOA! COOL! HE REALLY IS EMPTY.
Hey!
POP
NICE TO MEET YOU, KID.
KTANG
Grr!
THE NAME'S GREED.
LET'S BE FRIENDS.
AN...
...OURO-BOROS TATTOO!

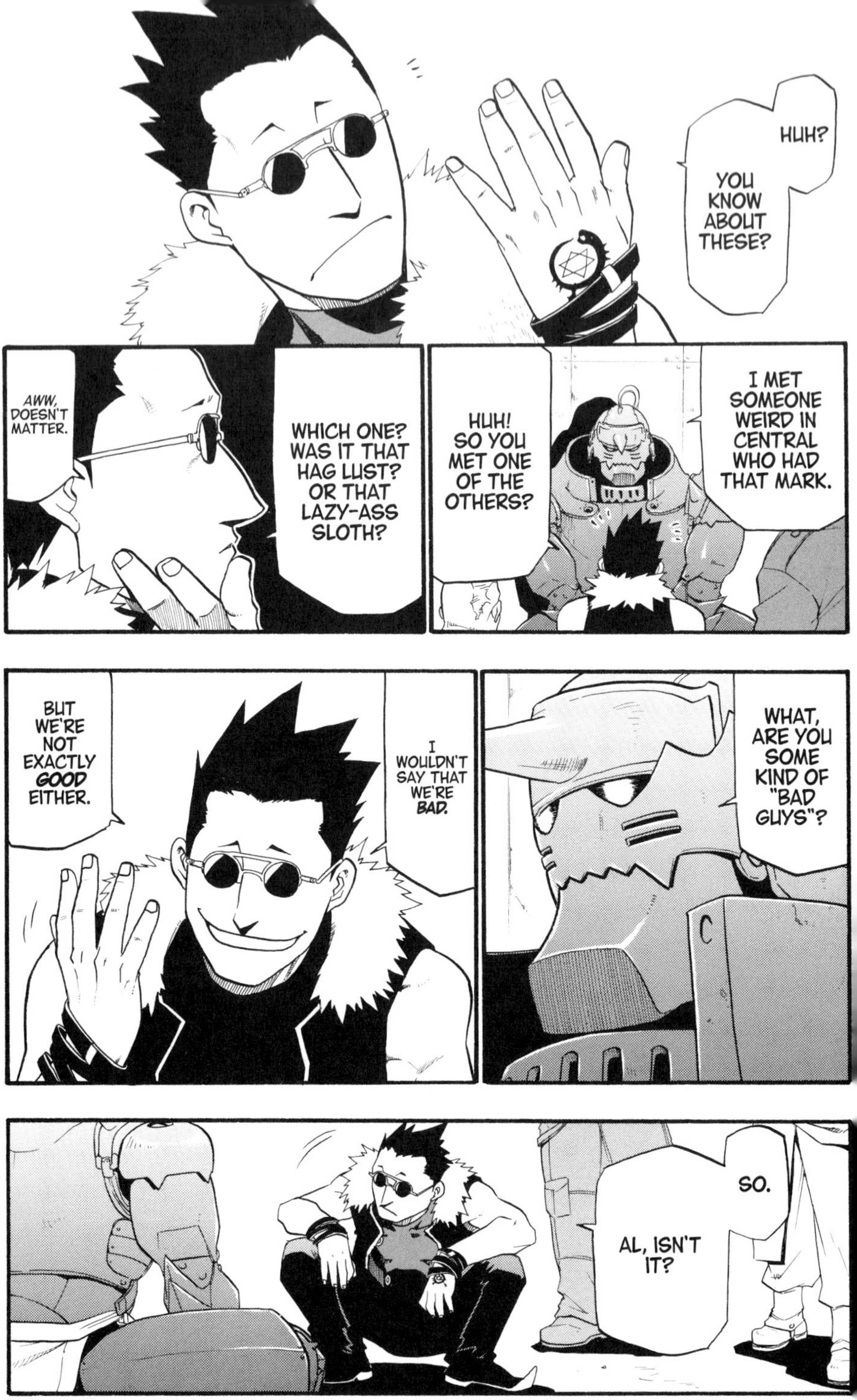
HUH?
YOU KNOW ABOUT THESE?
I MET SOMEONE WEIRD IN CENTRAL WHO HAD THAT MARK.
HUH! SO YOU MET ONE OF THE OTHERS?
WHICH ONE? WAS IT THAT HAG LUST? OR THAT LAZY-ASS SLOTH?
AWW, DOESN'T MATTER.
WHAT, ARE YOU SOME KIND OF "BAD GUYS"?
I WOULDN'T SAY THAT WE'RE BAD.
BUT WE'RE NOT EXACTLY GOOD EITHER.
SO.
AL, ISN'T IT?

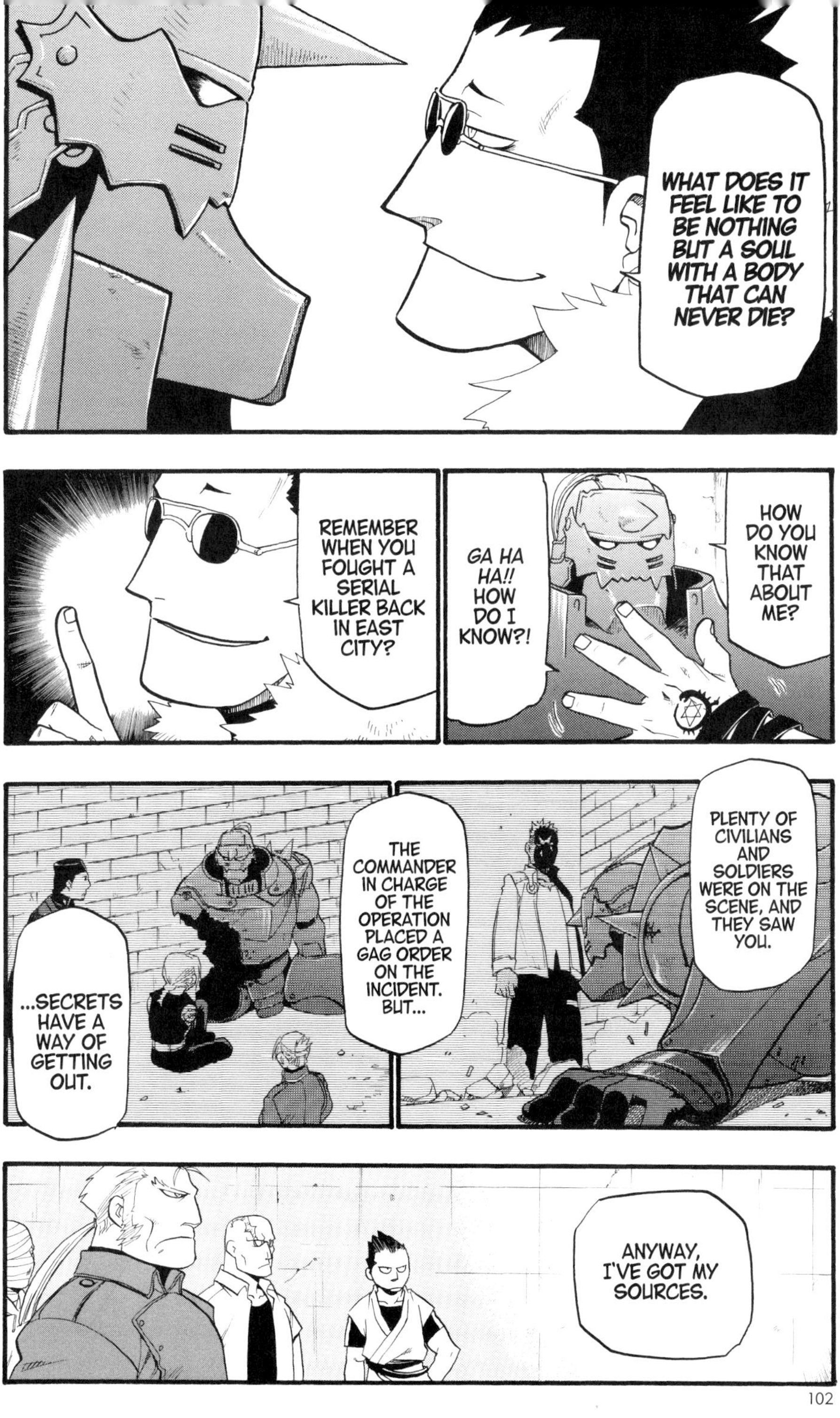
WHAT DOES IT FEEL LIKE TO BE NOTHING BUT A SOUL WITH A BODY THAT CAN NEVER DIE?
HOW DO YOU KNOW THAT ABOUT ME?
GA HA HA!! HOW DO I KNOW?!
REMEMBER WHEN YOU FOUGHT A SERIAL KILLER BACK IN EAST CITY?
PLENTY OF CIVILIANS AND SOLDIERS WERE ON THE SCENE, AND THEY SAW YOU.
THE COMMANDER IN CHARGE OF THE OPERATION PLACED A GAG ORDER ON THE INCIDENT. BUT...
...SECRETS HAVE A WAY OF GETTING OUT.
ANYWAY, I'VE GOT MY SOURCES.

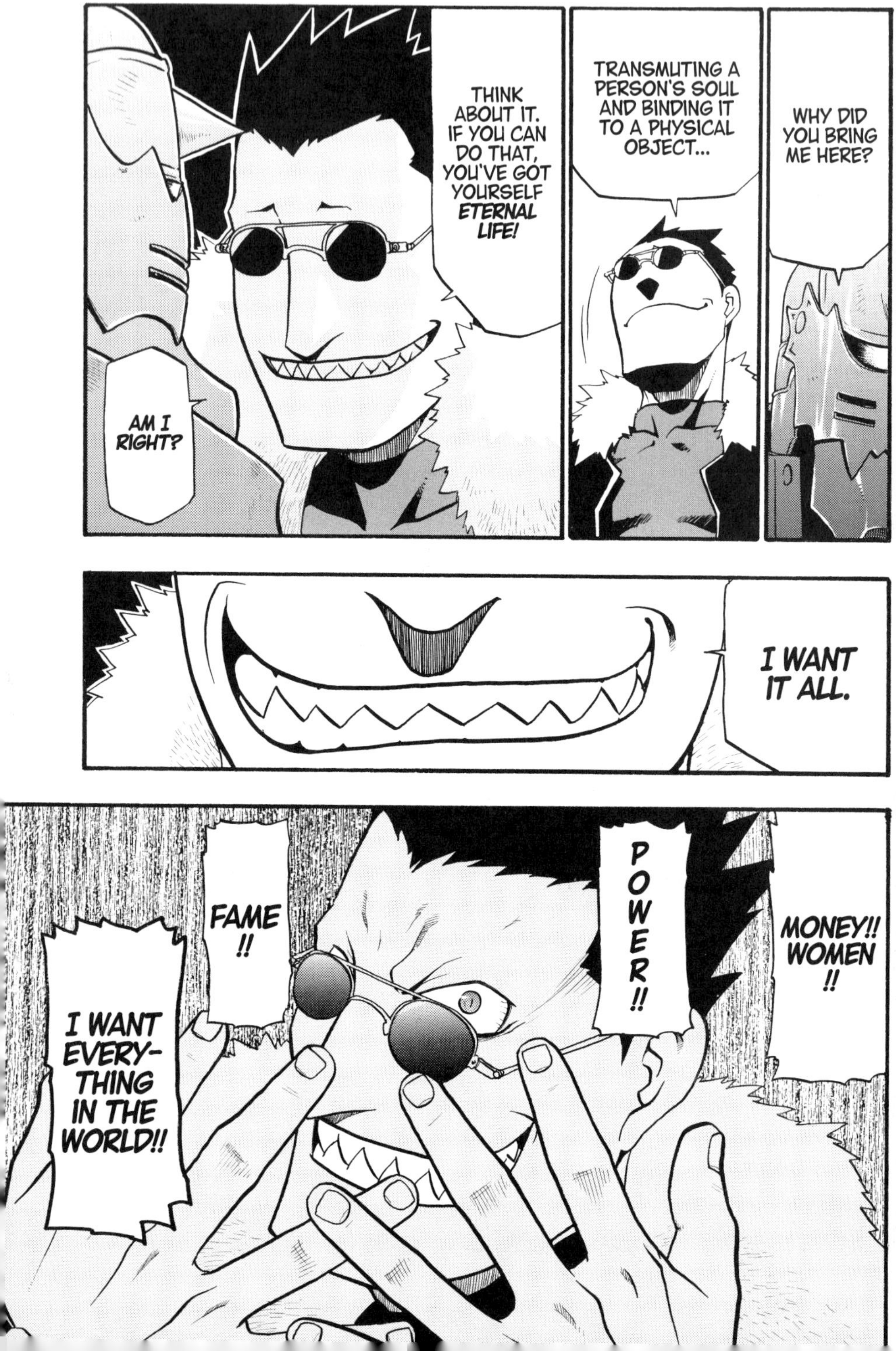
WHY DID YOU BRING ME HERE?
TRANSMUTING A PERSON'S SOUL AND BINDING IT TO A PHYSICAL OBJECT...
THINK ABOUT IT. IF YOU CAN DO THAT, YOU'VE GOT YOURSELF ETERNAL LIFE!
AM I RIGHT?
I WANT IT ALL.
MONEY!! WOMEN !!
POWER!!
FAME !!
I WANT EVERY-THING IN THE WORLD!!

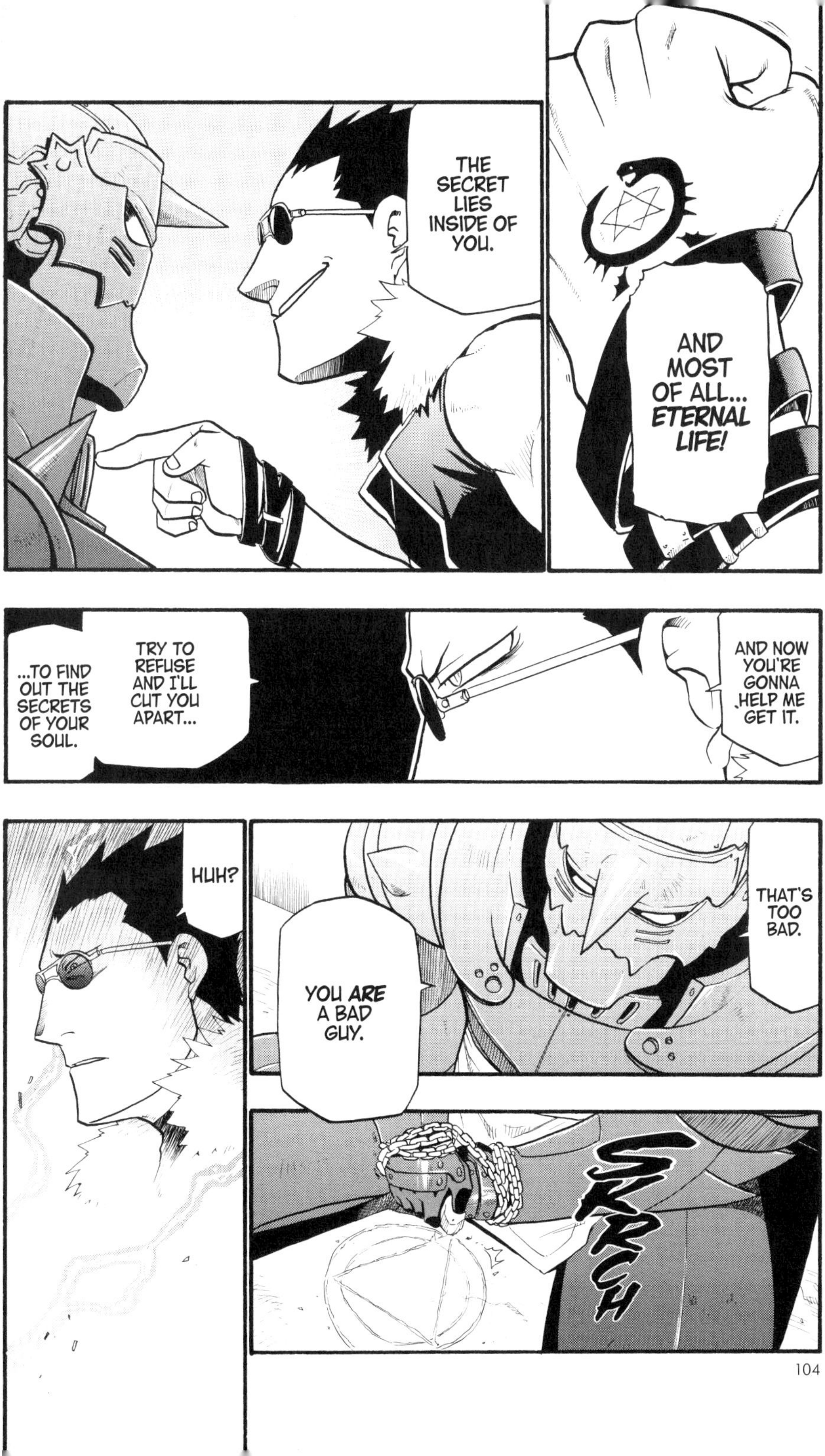
AND MOST OF ALL... ETERNAL LIFE!
THE SECRET LIES INSIDE OF YOU.
AND NOW YOU'RE GONNA HELP ME GET IT.
TRY TO REFUSE AND I'LL CUT YOU APART...
...TO FIND OUT THE SECRETS OF YOUR SOUL.
THAT'S TOO BAD.
YOU ARE A BAD GUY.
SKRCH
HUH?

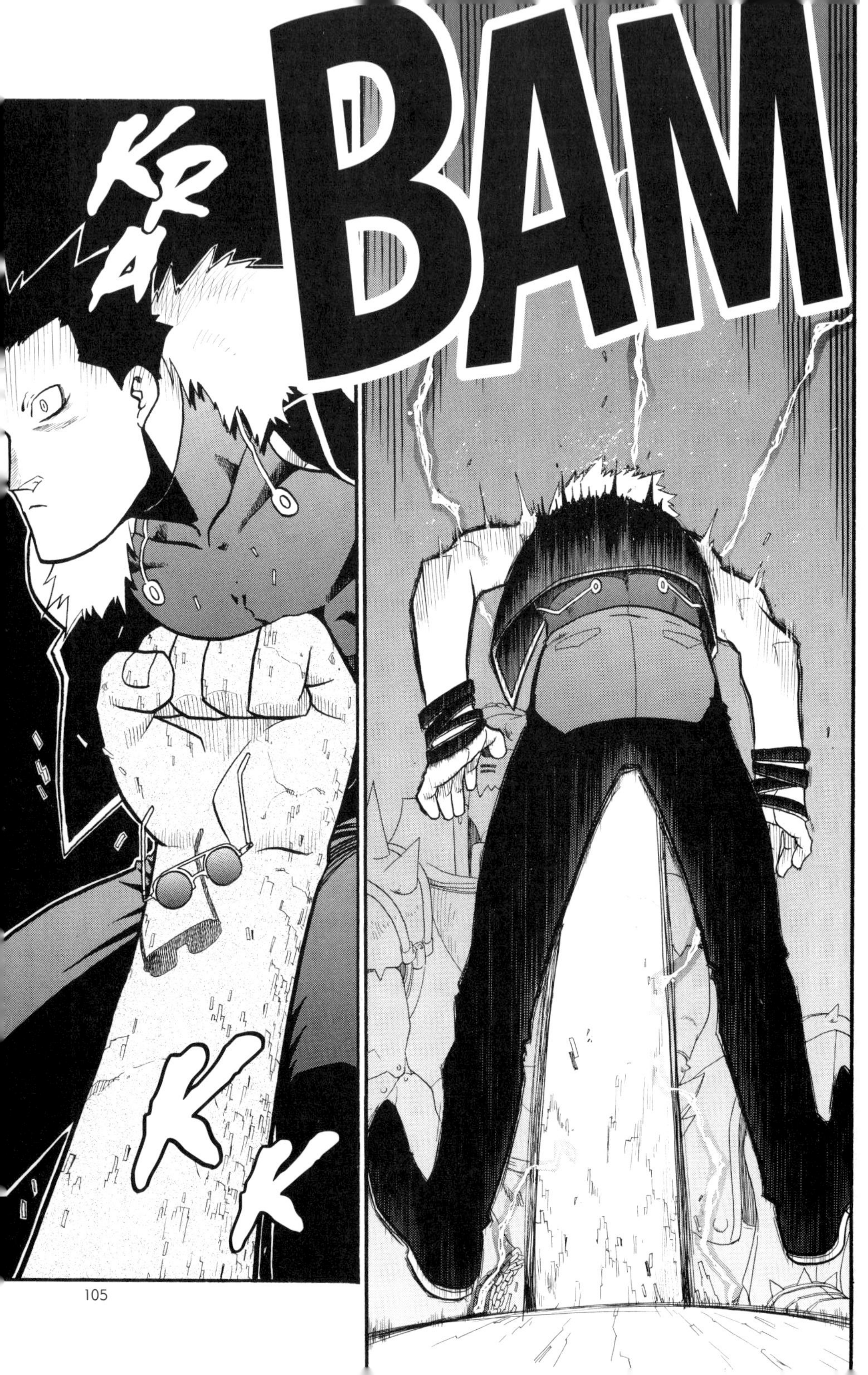
KRA BAM
KKK

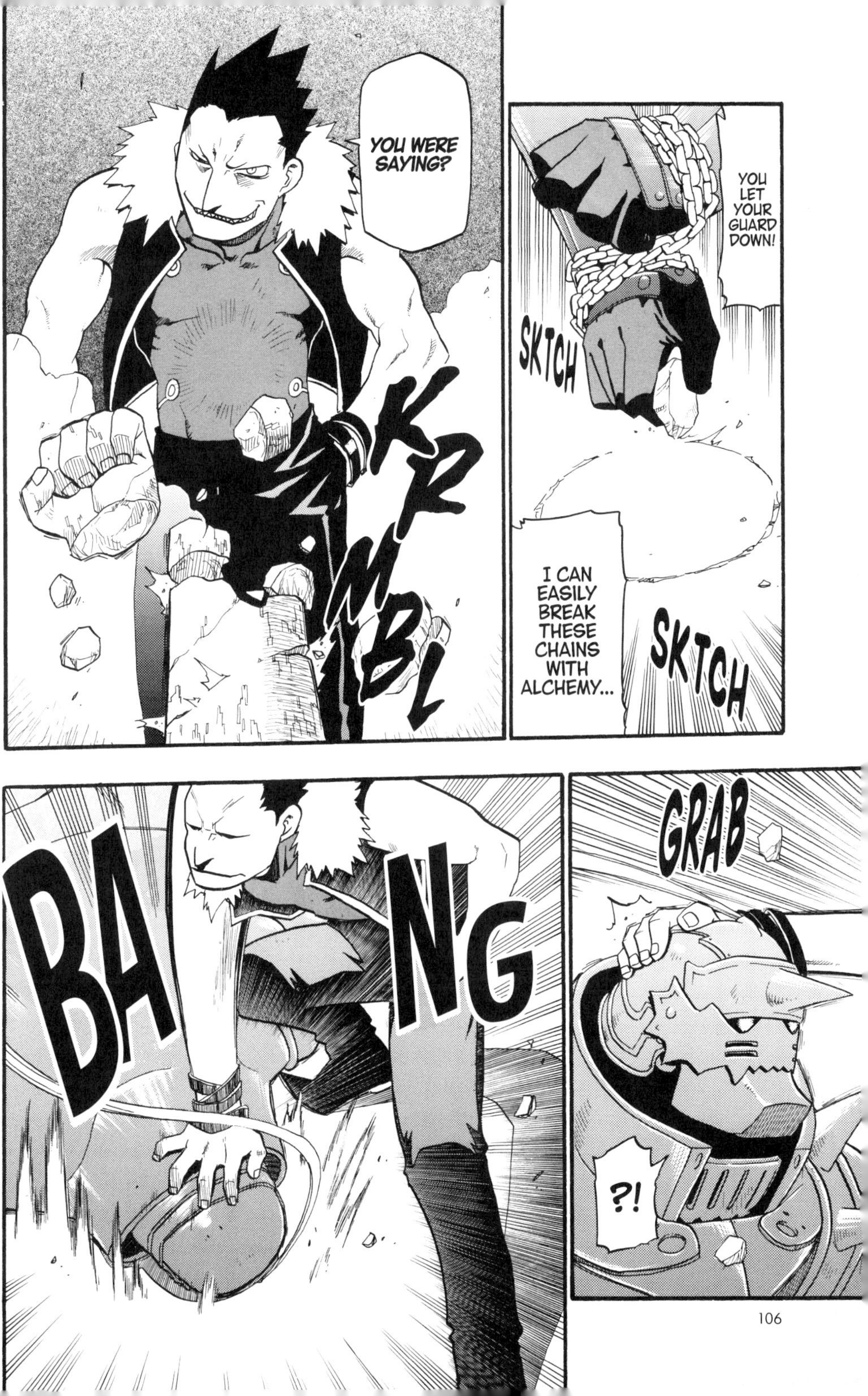
YOU LET YOUR GUARD DOWN!
SKTCH
I CAN EASILY BREAK THESE CHAINS WITH ALCHEMY...
SKTCH
YOU WERE SAYING?
KRMBL
GRAB
?!
BANG

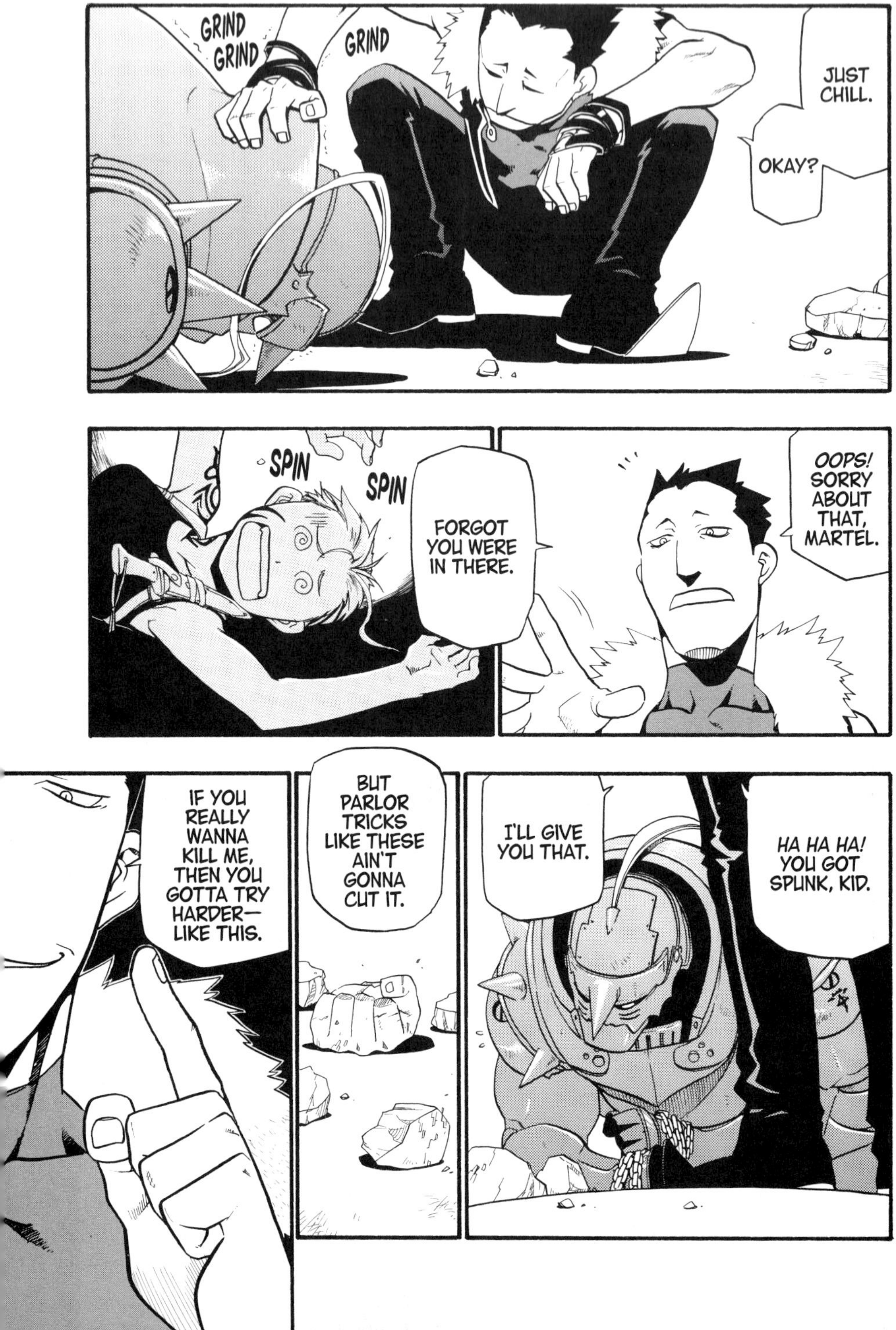
JUST CHILL.
OKAY?
GRIND
GRIND GRIND
OOPS! SORRY ABOUT THAT, MARTEL.
FORGOT YOU WERE IN THERE.
SPIN
SPIN
HA HA HA! YOU GOT SPUNK, KID.
I'LL GIVE YOU THAT.
BUT PARLOR TRICKS LIKE THESE AIN'T GONNA CUT IT.
IF YOU REALLY WANNA KILL ME, THEN YOU GOTTA TRY HARDER—LIKE THIS.

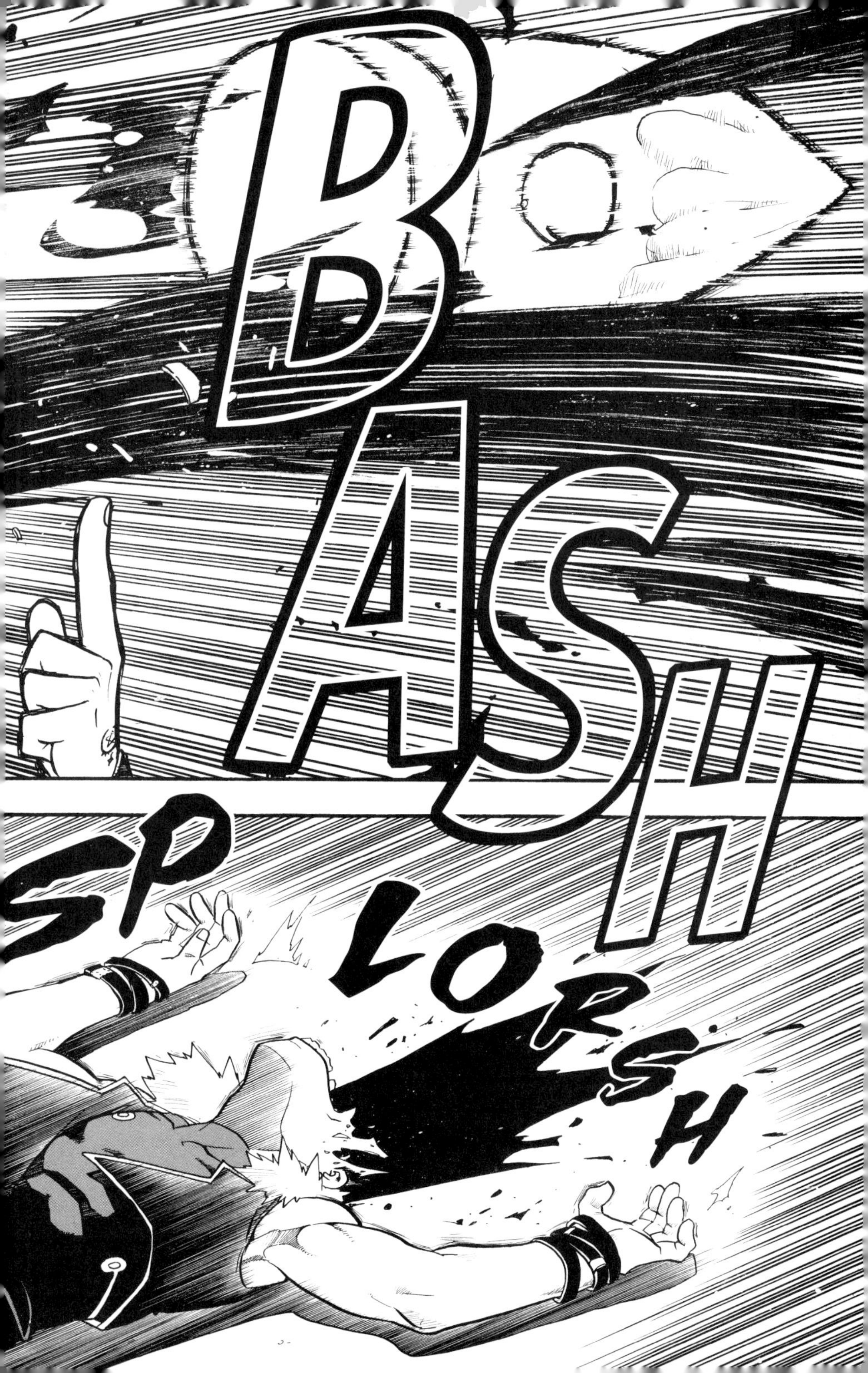
BASH
SPLORSH

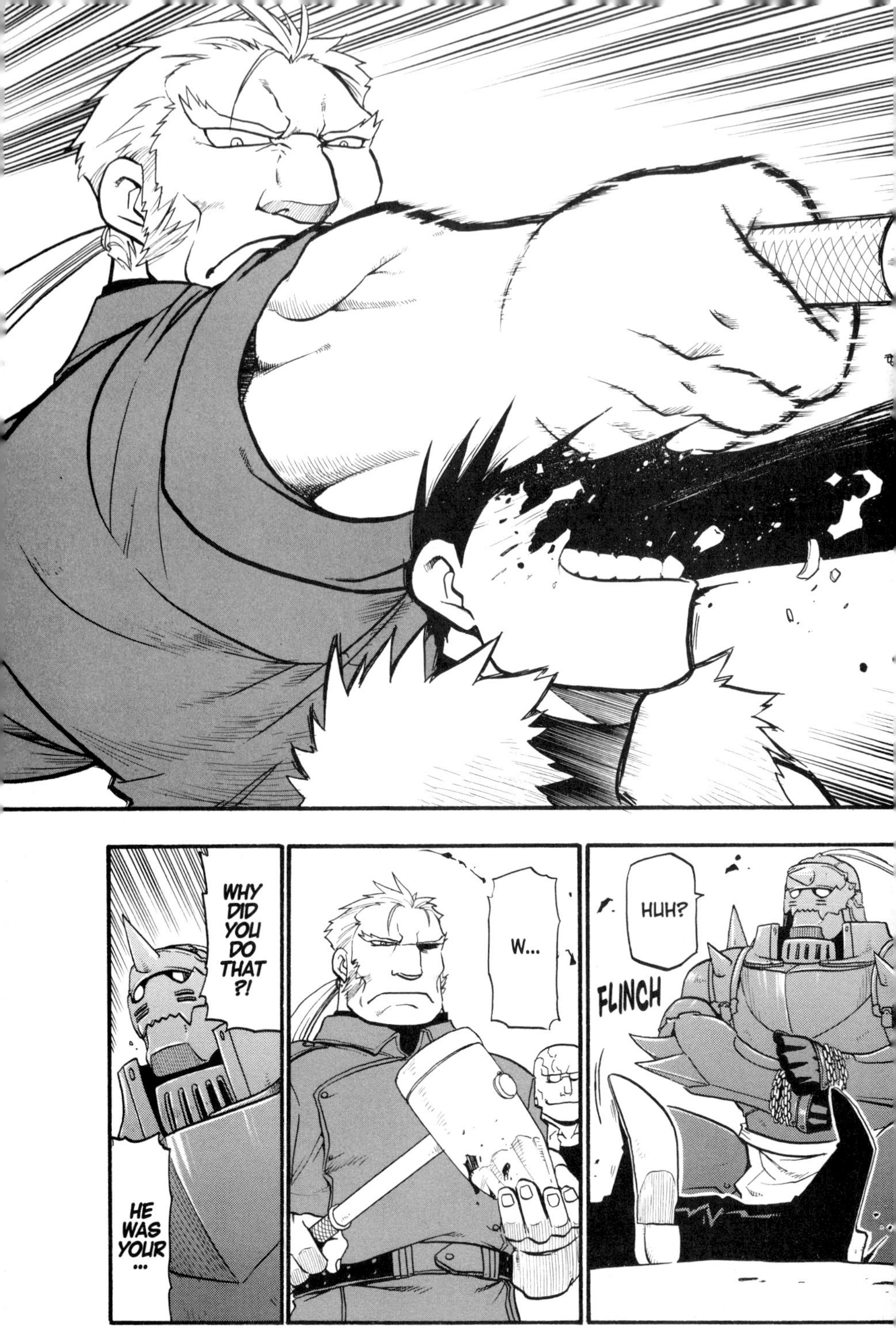
HUH?
FLINCH
W...
WHY DID YOU DO THAT?!
HE WAS YOUR ...

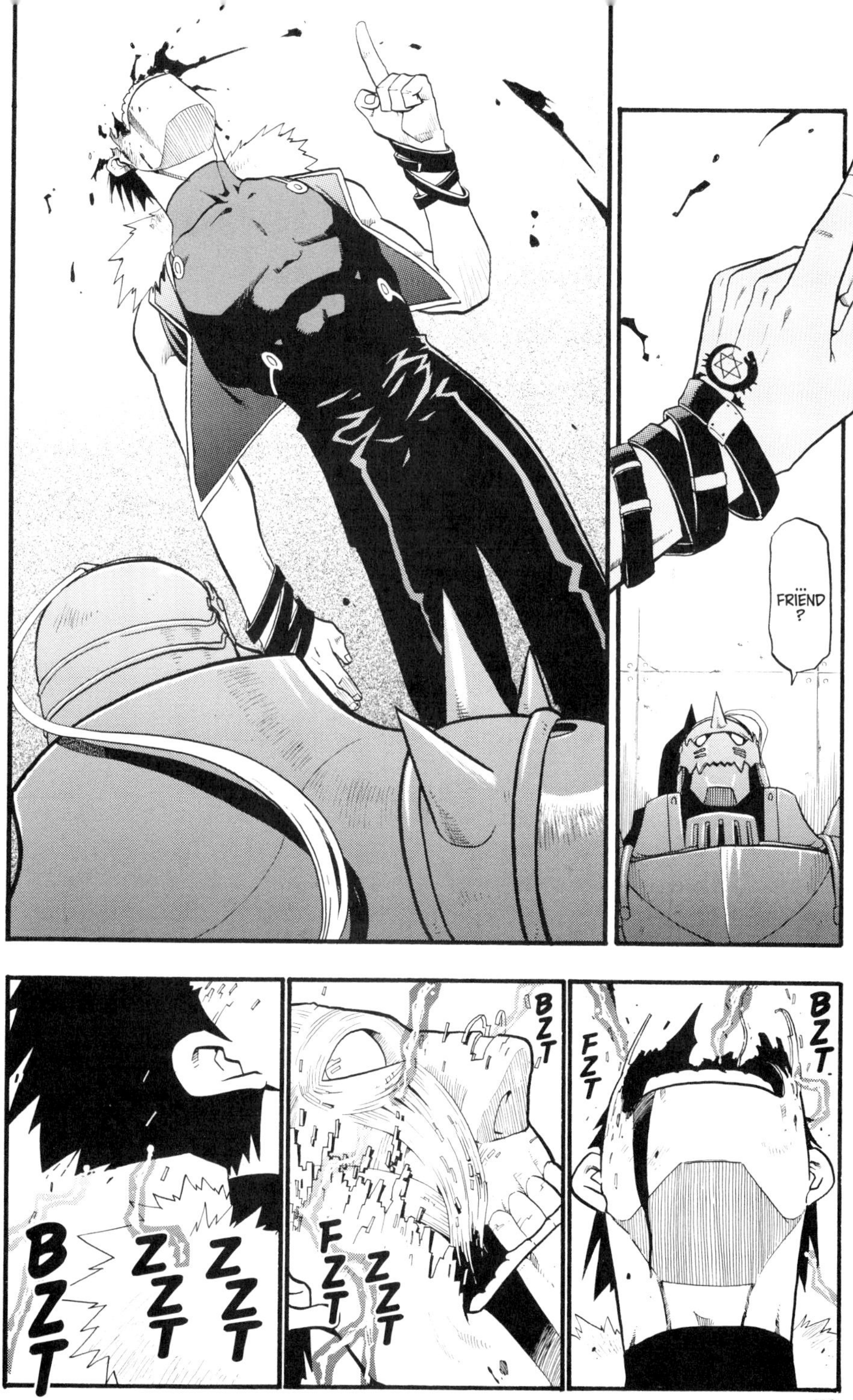
...FRIEND?
BZT
FZT
FZT
ZZT
BZT
ZZT
ZZT

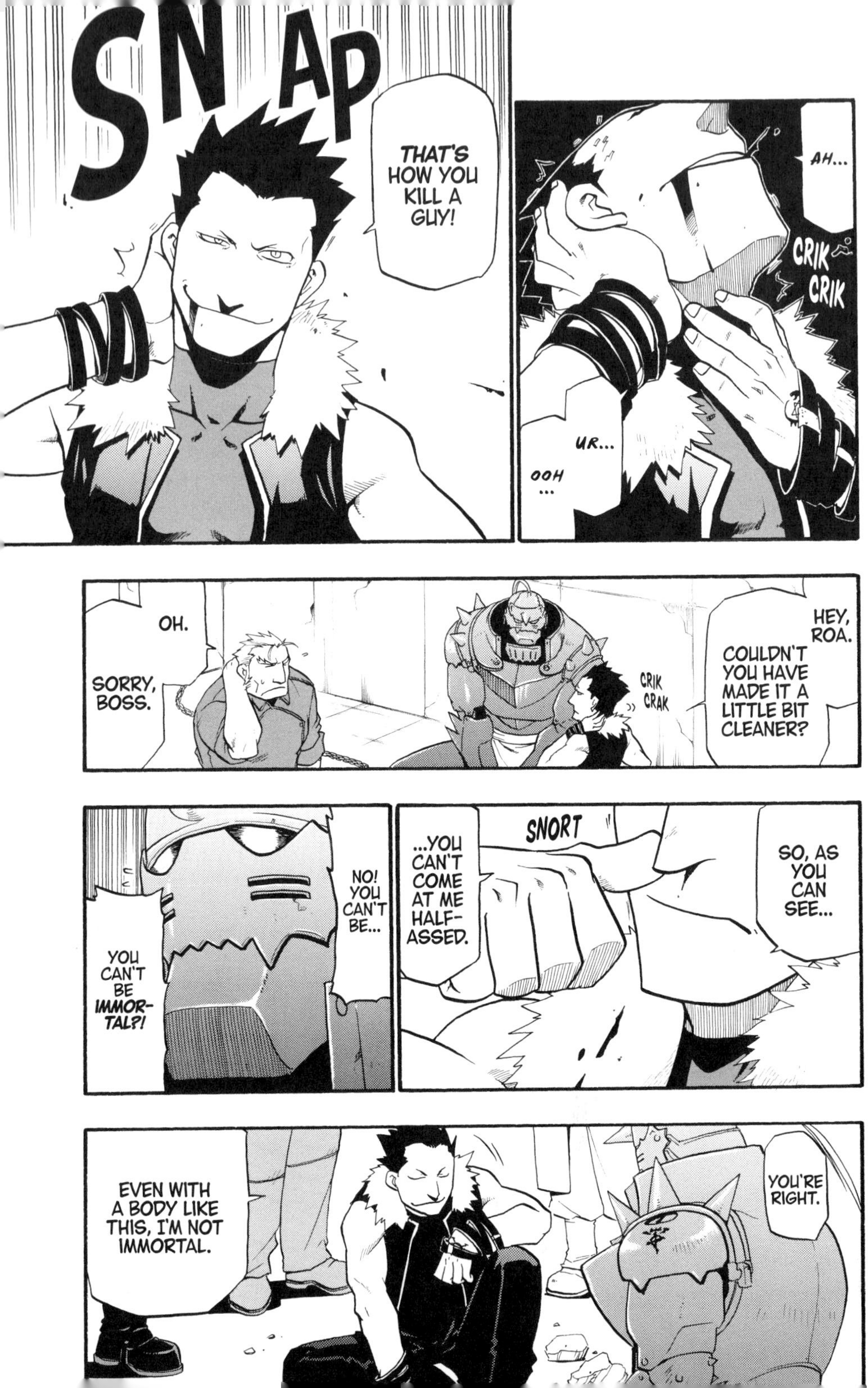
AH...
CRIK CRIK
UR...
OOH ...
SNAP
THAT'S HOW YOU KILL A GUY!
HEY, ROA. COULDN'T YOU HAVE MADE IT A LITTLE BIT CLEANER?
CRIK CRAK
OH.
SORRY, BOSS.
SO, AS YOU CAN SEE...
SNORT
...YOU CAN'T COME AT ME HALF-ASSED.
NO! YOU CAN'T BE...
YOU CAN'T BE IMMORTAL?!
YOU'RE RIGHT.
EVEN WITH A BODY LIKE THIS, I'M NOT IMMORTAL.

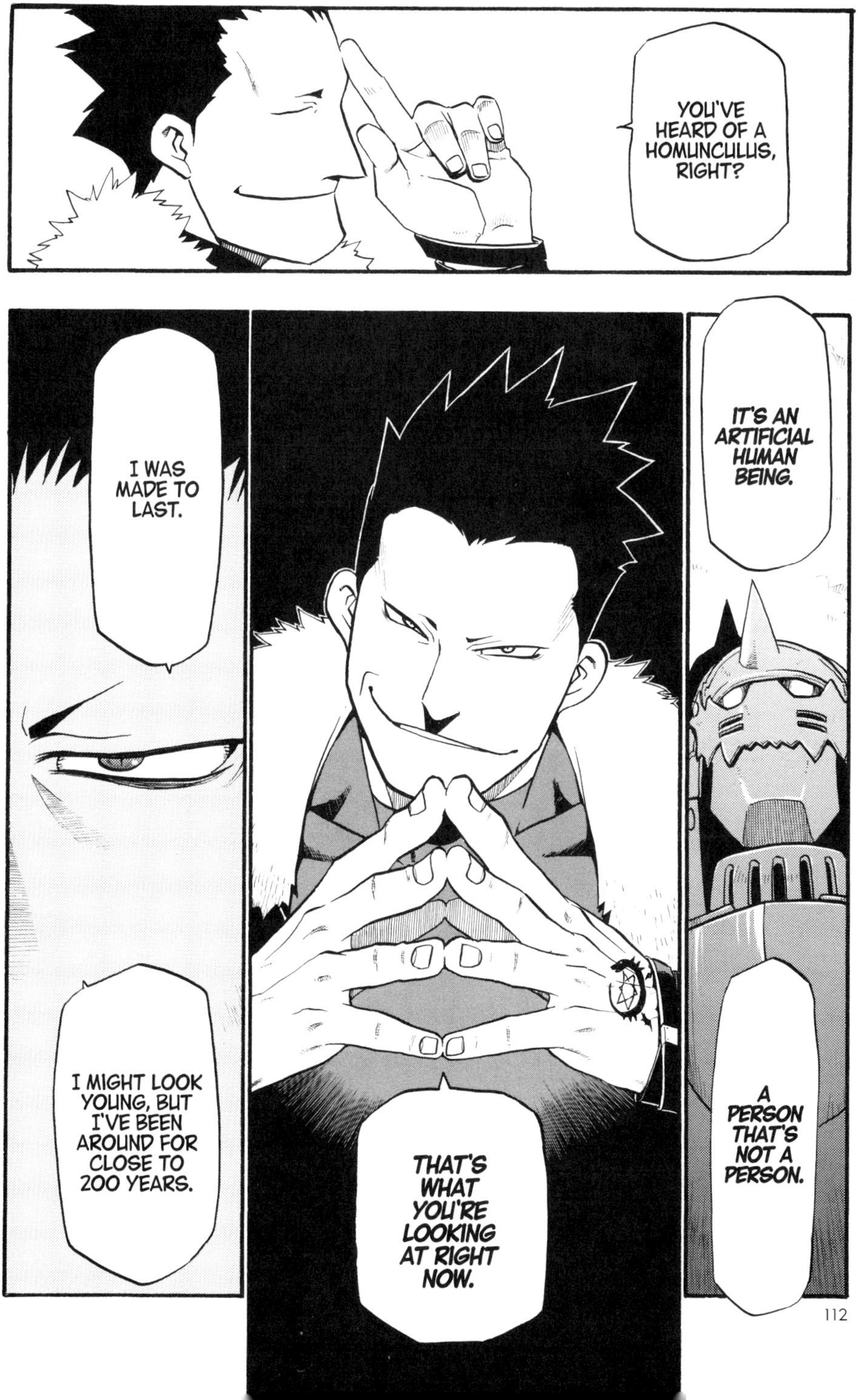
YOU'VE HEARD OF A HOMUNCULUS, RIGHT?
IT'S AN ARTIFICIAL HUMAN BEING.
A PERSON THAT'S NOT A PERSON.
THAT'S WHAT YOU'RE LOOKING AT RIGHT NOW.
I WAS MADE TO LAST.
I MIGHT LOOK YOUNG, BUT I'VE BEEN AROUND FOR CLOSE TO 200 YEARS.

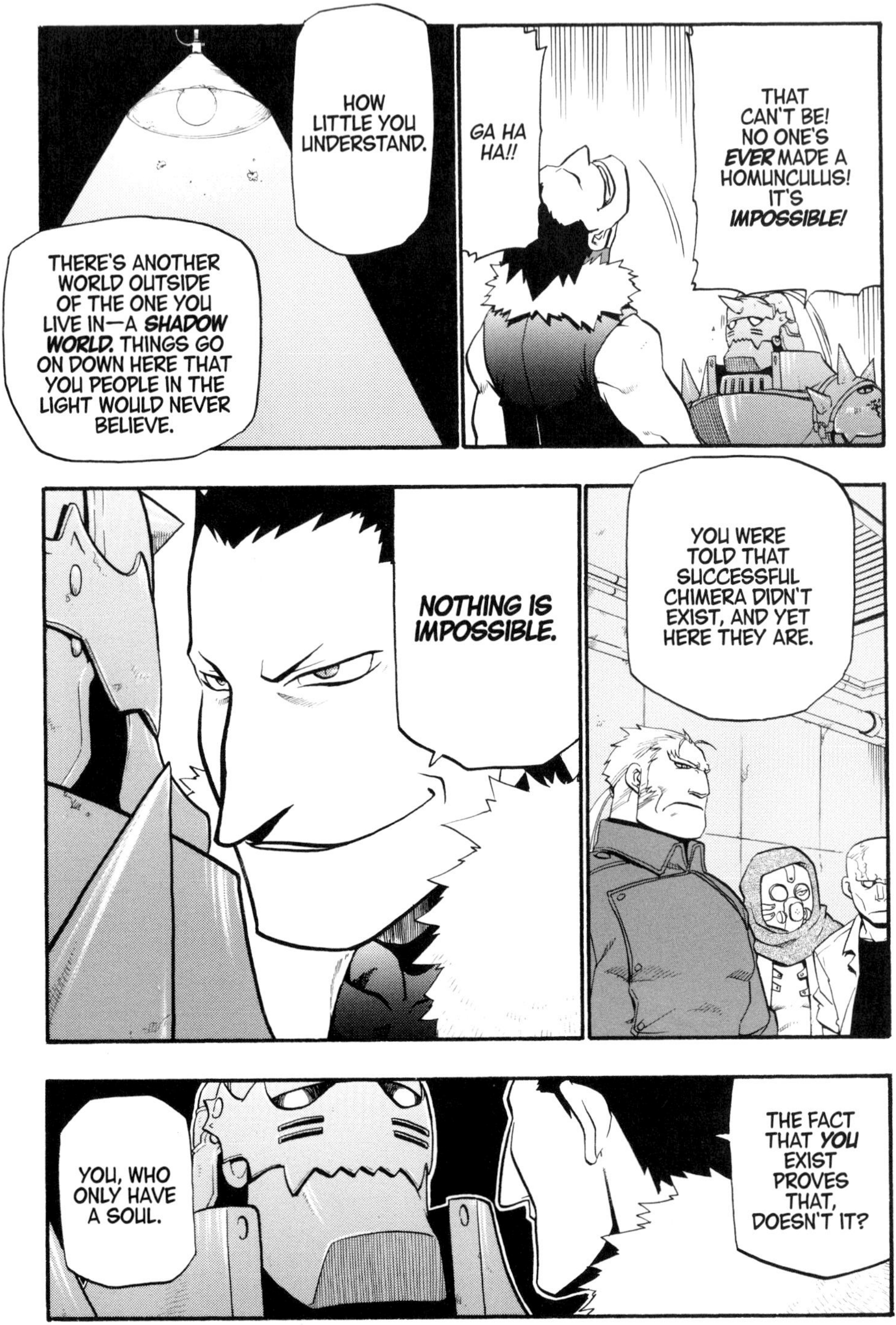
THAT CAN'T BE! NO ONE'S **EVER** MADE A HOMUNCULUS! IT'S **IMPOSSIBLE!**
GA HA HA!!
HOW LITTLE YOU UNDERSTAND.
THERE'S ANOTHER WORLD OUTSIDE OF THE ONE YOU LIVE IN—A **SHADOW WORLD.** THINGS GO ON DOWN HERE THAT YOU PEOPLE IN THE LIGHT WOULD NEVER BELIEVE.
YOU WERE TOLD THAT SUCCESSFUL CHIMERA DIDN'T EXIST, AND YET HERE THEY ARE.
NOTHING IS IMPOSSIBLE.
THE FACT THAT **YOU** EXIST PROVES THAT, DOESN'T IT?
YOU, WHO ONLY HAVE A SOUL.

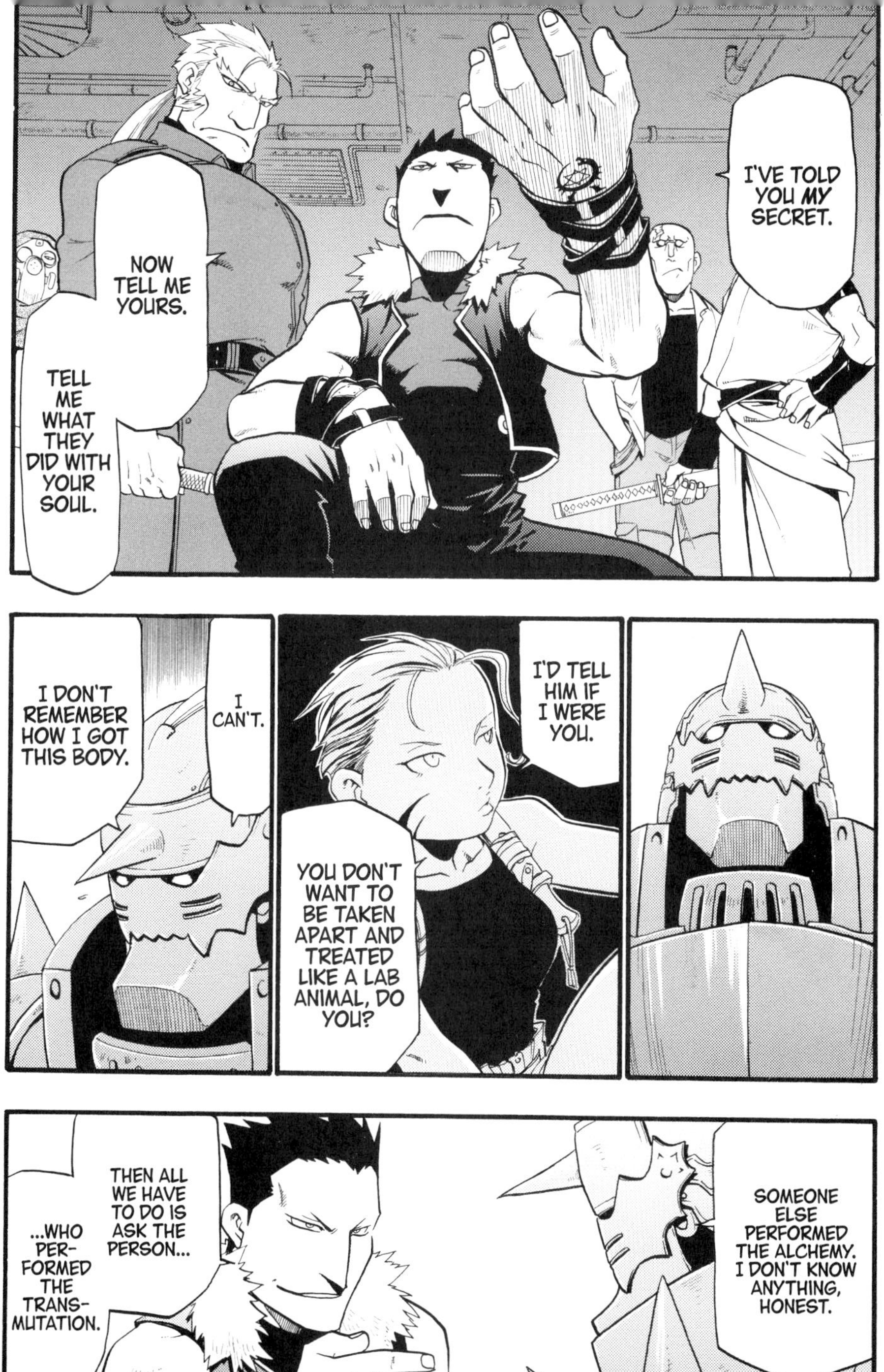
I'VE TOLD YOU MY SECRET.
NOW TELL ME YOURS.
TELL ME WHAT THEY DID WITH YOUR SOUL.
I'D TELL HIM IF I WERE YOU.
YOU DON'T WANT TO BE TAKEN APART AND TREATED LIKE A LAB ANIMAL, DO YOU?
I CAN'T.
I DON'T REMEMBER HOW I GOT THIS BODY.
SOMEONE ELSE PERFORMED THE ALCHEMY. I DON'T KNOW ANYTHING, HONEST.
THEN ALL WE HAVE TO DO IS ASK THE PERSON...
...WHO PER-FORMED THE TRANS-MUTATION.

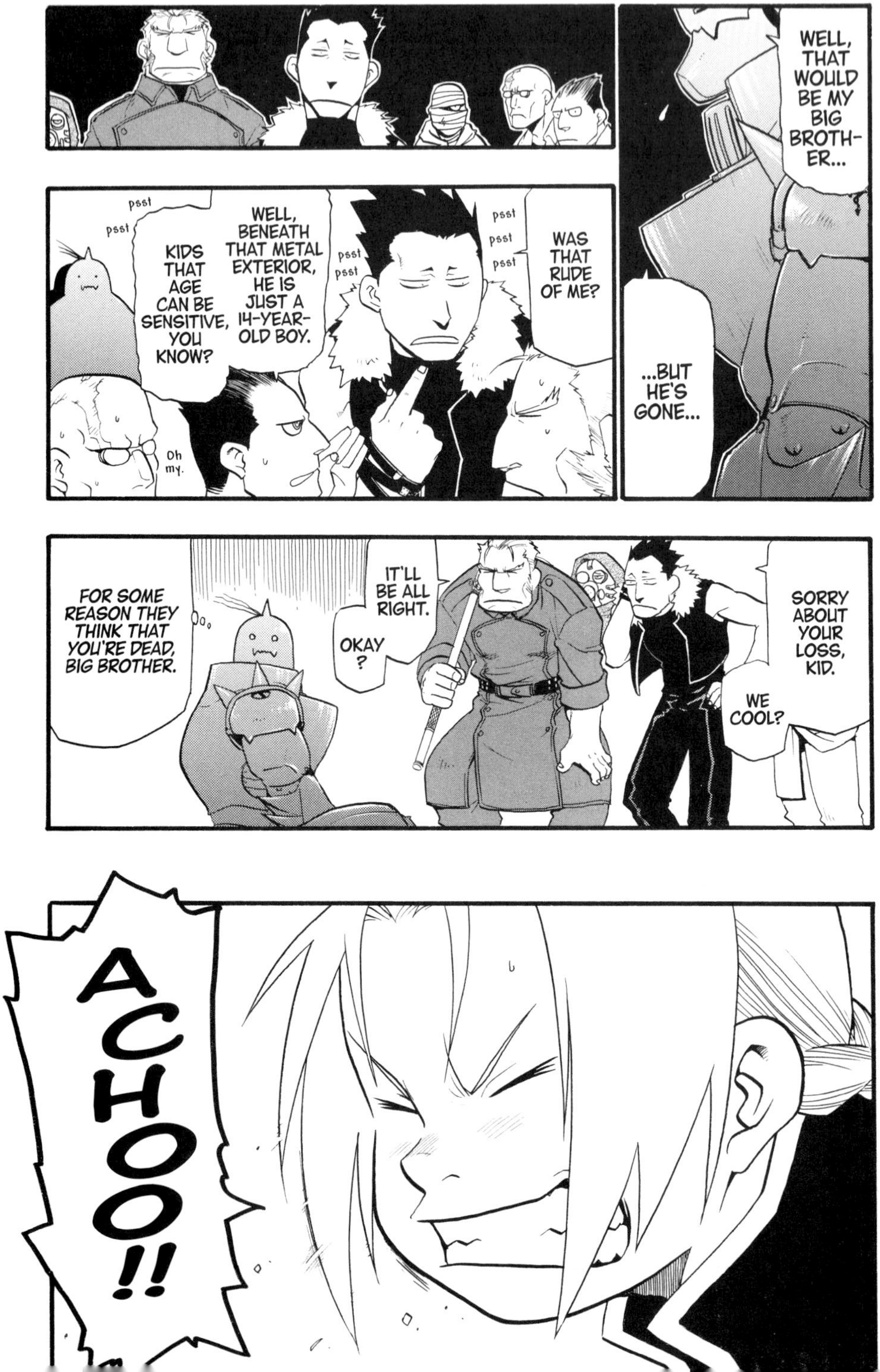
WELL, THAT WOULD BE MY BIG BROTHER...
...BUT HE'S GONE...
psst psst psst
WAS THAT RUDE OF ME?
psst psst
WELL, BENEATH THAT METAL EXTERIOR, HE IS JUST A 14-YEAR-OLD BOY.
KIDS THAT AGE CAN BE SENSITIVE, YOU KNOW?
psst psst
Oh my.
SORRY ABOUT YOUR LOSS, KID.
WE COOL?
IT'LL BE ALL RIGHT.
OKAY?
FOR SOME REASON THEY THINK THAT YOU'RE DEAD, BIG BROTHER.
ACHOO!!

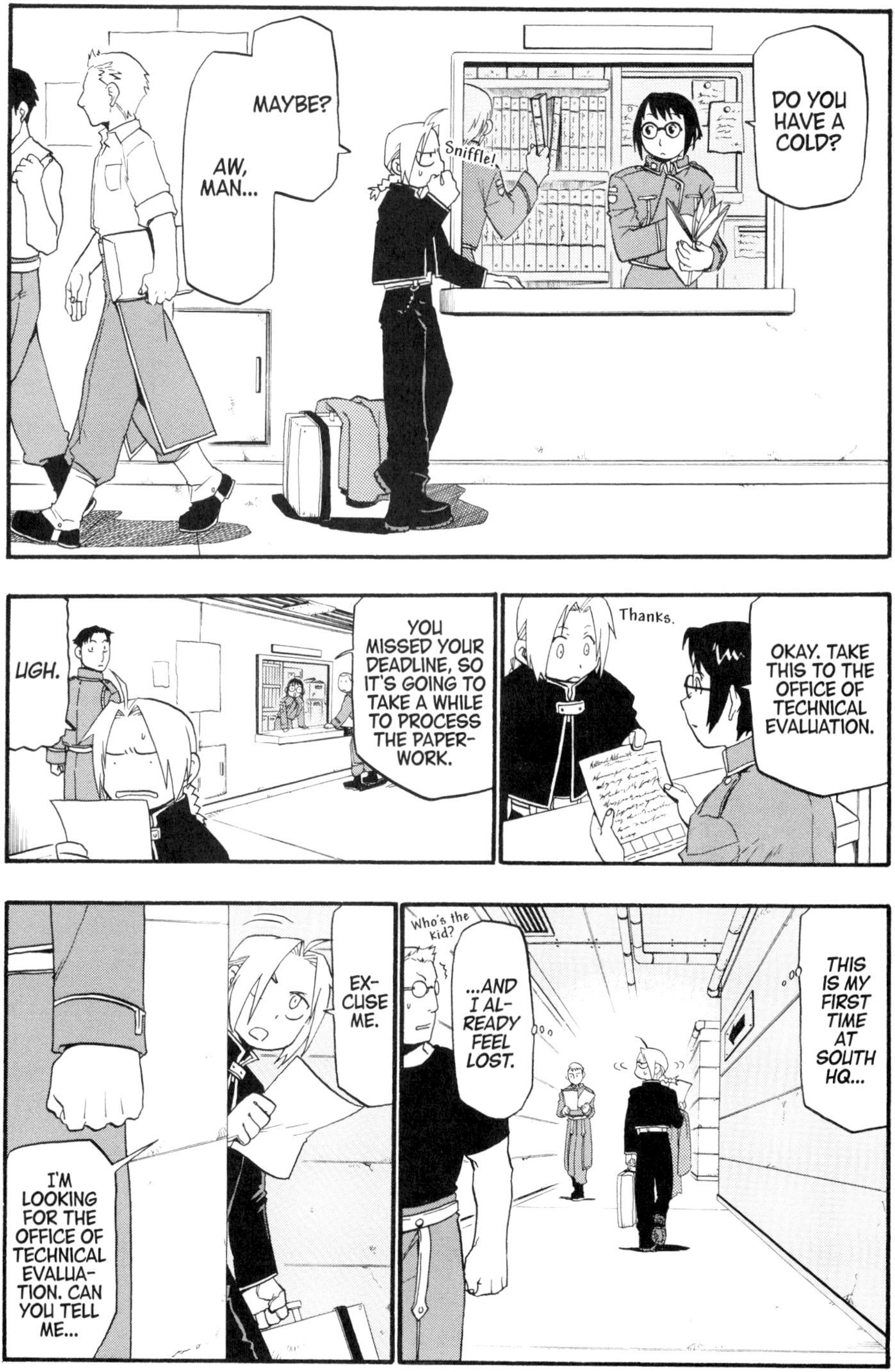
DO YOU HAVE A COLD?
Sniffle!
MAYBE?
AW, MAN...
OKAY. TAKE THIS TO THE OFFICE OF TECHNICAL EVALUATION.
Thanks.
YOU MISSED YOUR DEADLINE, SO IT'S GOING TO TAKE A WHILE TO PROCESS THE PAPERWORK.
UGH.
THIS IS MY FIRST TIME AT SOUTH HQ...
...AND I ALREADY FEEL LOST.
Who's the kid?
EXCUSE ME.
I'M LOOKING FOR THE OFFICE OF TECHNICAL EVALUATION. CAN YOU TELL ME...

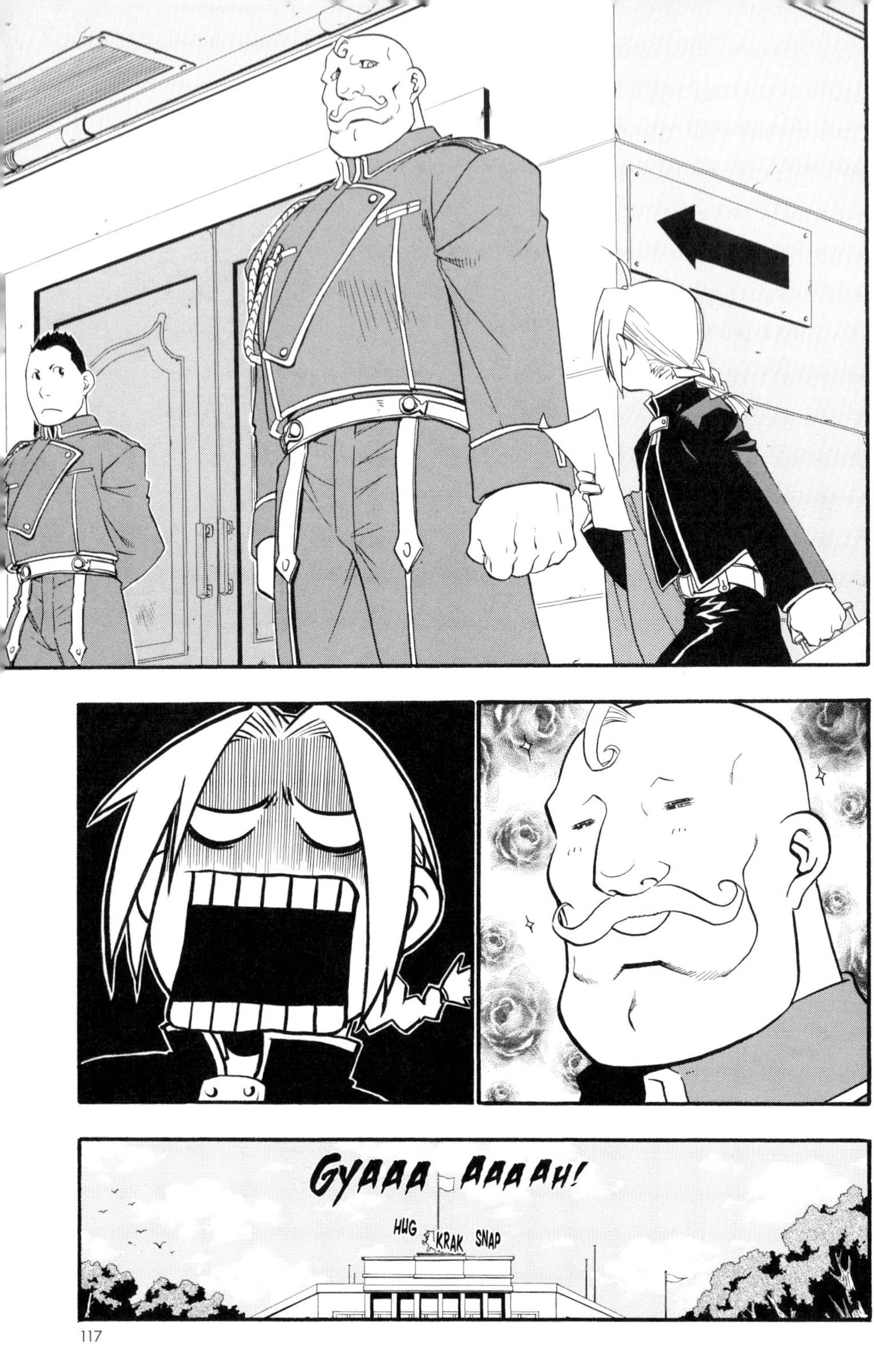
GYAAA AAAAH!
HUG
KRAK
SNAP

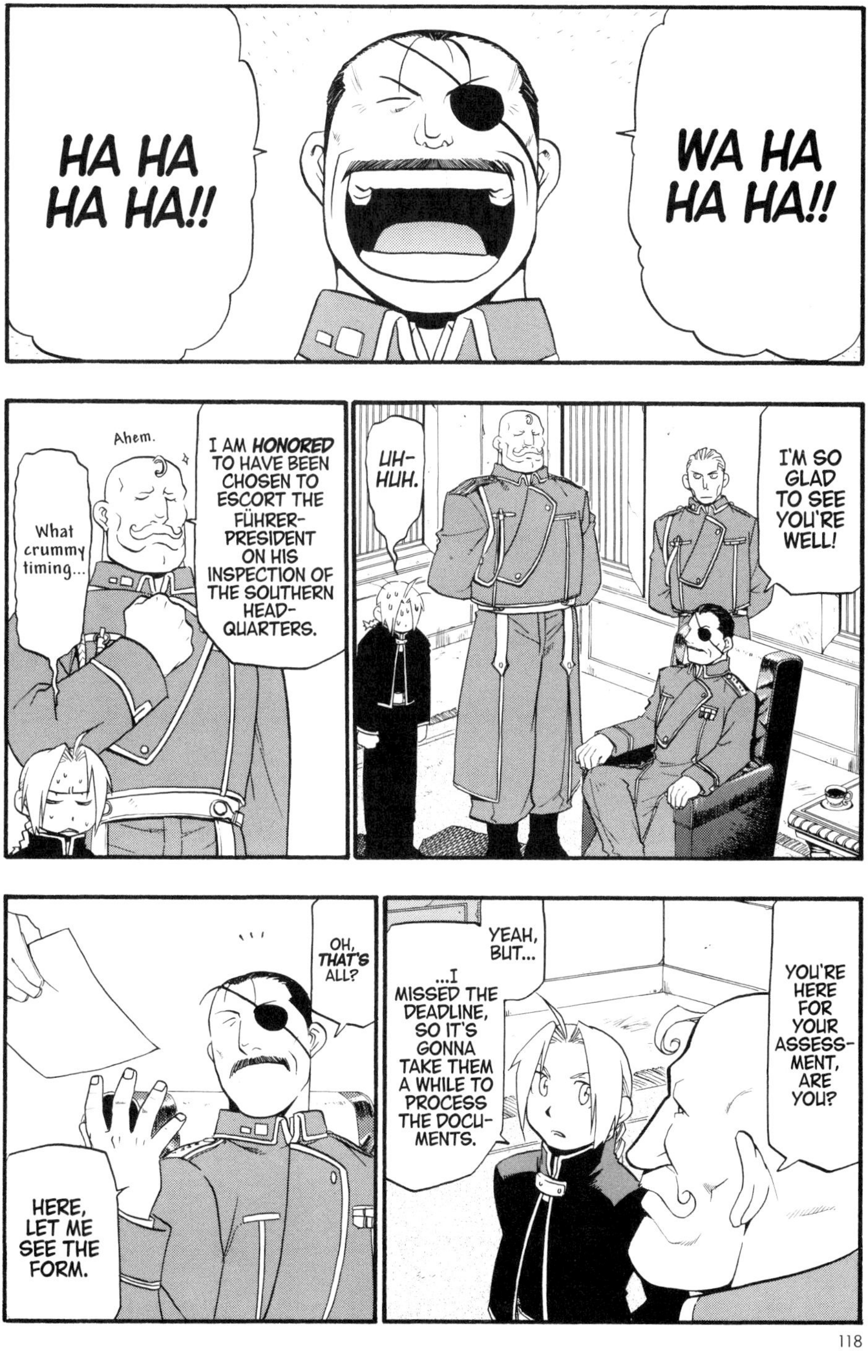
WA HA HA HA!!
HA HA HA HA!!
I'M SO GLAD TO SEE YOU'RE WELL!
UH-HUH.
I AM **HONORED** TO HAVE BEEN CHOSEN TO ESCORT THE FÜHRER-PRESIDENT ON HIS INSPECTION OF THE SOUTHERN HEAD-QUARTERS.
Ahem.
What crummy timing...
YOU'RE HERE FOR YOUR ASSESS-MENT, ARE YOU?
YEAH, BUT...
...I MISSED THE DEADLINE, SO IT'S GONNA TAKE THEM A WHILE TO PROCESS THE DOCU-MENTS.
OH, **THAT'S** ALL?
HERE, LET ME SEE THE FORM.

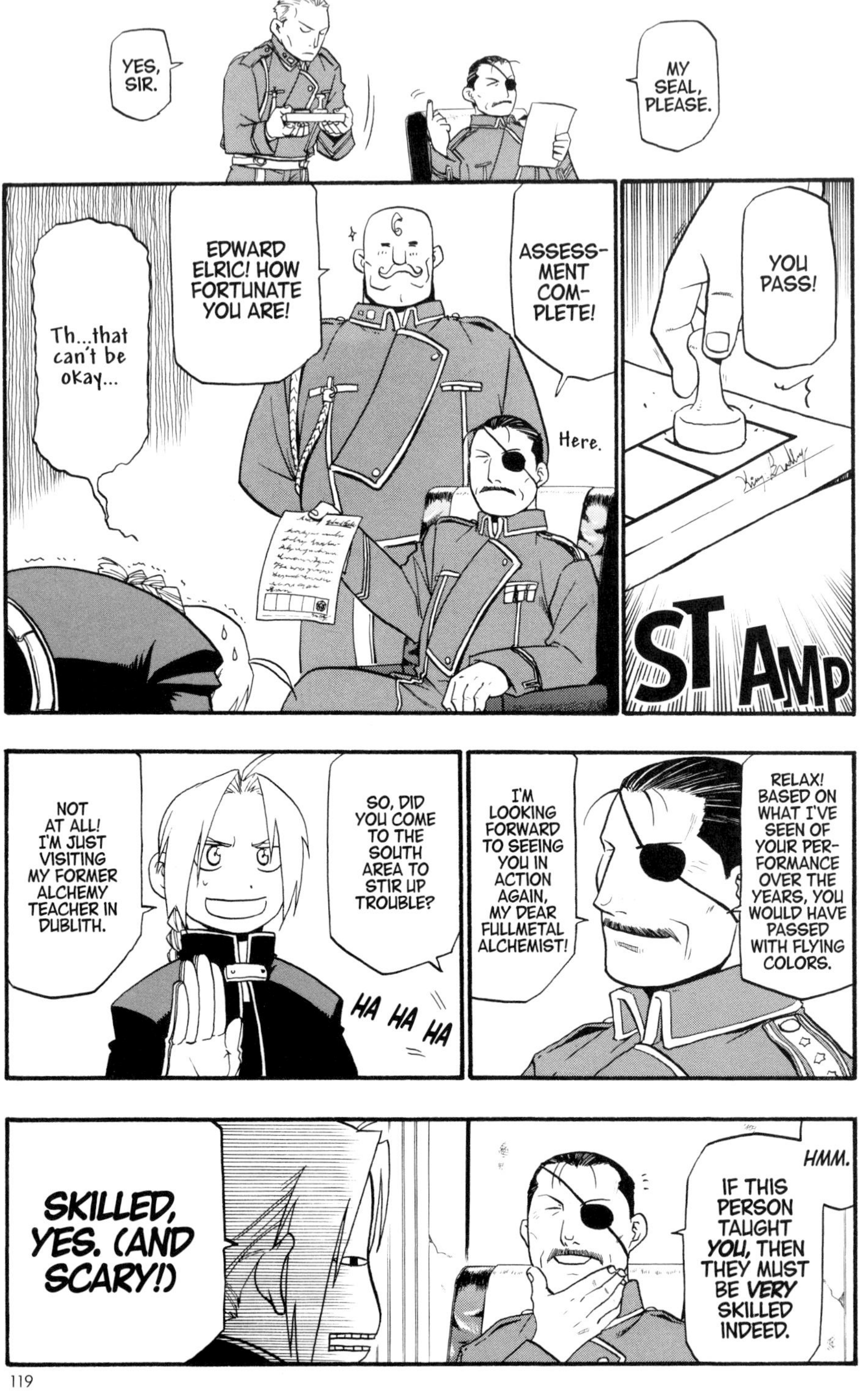
MY SEAL, PLEASE.
YES, SIR.
YOU PASS!
STAMP
ASSESSMENT COMPLETE!
Here.
EDWARD ELRIC! HOW FORTUNATE YOU ARE!
Th...that can't be okay...
RELAX! BASED ON WHAT I'VE SEEN OF YOUR PERFORMANCE OVER THE YEARS, YOU WOULD HAVE PASSED WITH FLYING COLORS.
I'M LOOKING FORWARD TO SEEING YOU IN ACTION AGAIN, MY DEAR FULLMETAL ALCHEMIST!
SO, DID YOU COME TO THE SOUTH AREA TO STIR UP TROUBLE?
HA HA HA
NOT AT ALL! I'M JUST VISITING MY FORMER ALCHEMY TEACHER IN DUBLITH.
HMM.
IF THIS PERSON TAUGHT *YOU*, THEN THEY MUST BE *VERY* SKILLED INDEED.
SKILLED, YES. (AND SCARY!)

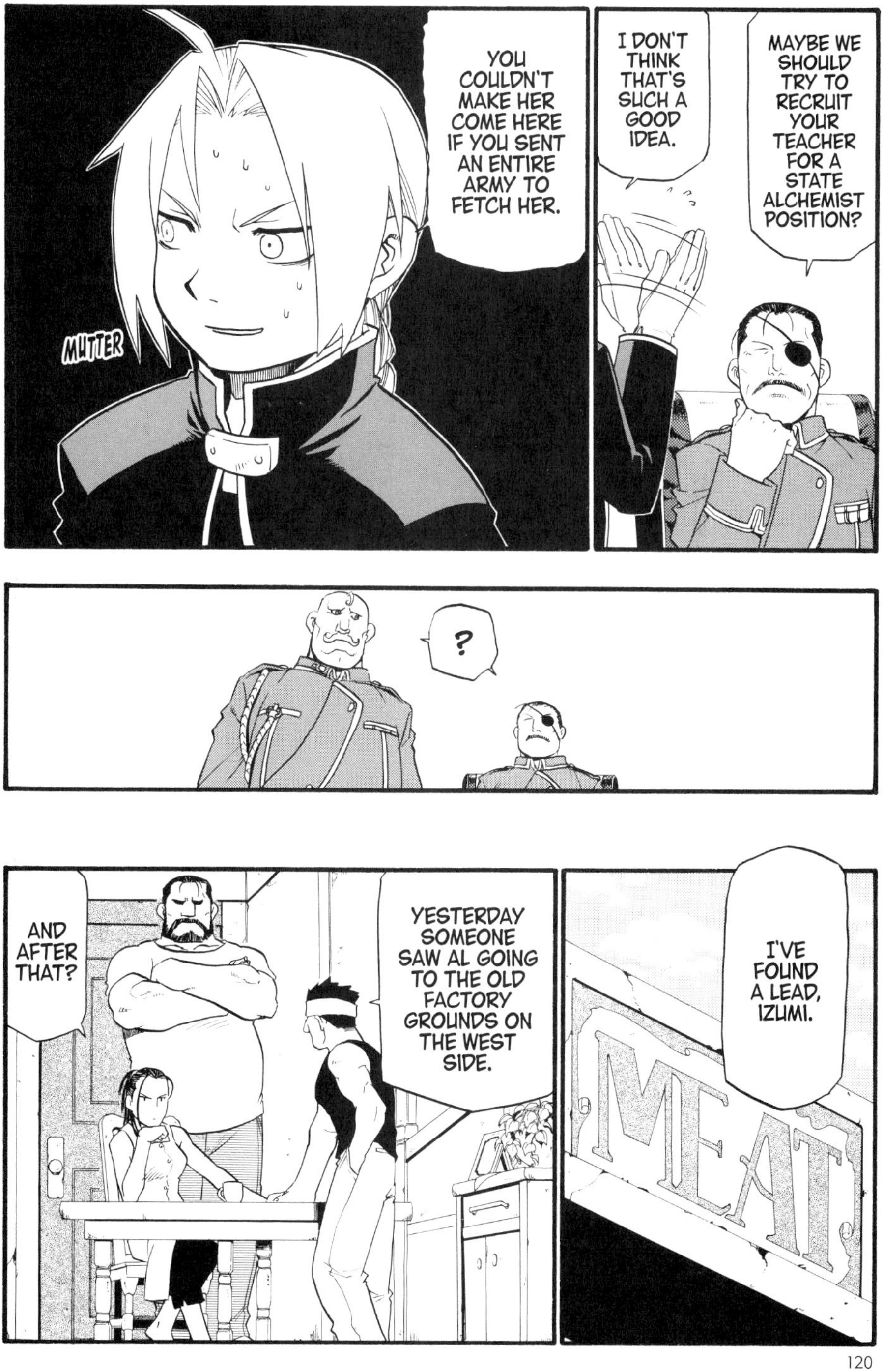
MAYBE WE SHOULD TRY TO RECRUIT YOUR TEACHER FOR A STATE ALCHEMIST POSITION?
I DON'T THINK THAT'S SUCH A GOOD IDEA.
YOU COULDN'T MAKE HER COME HERE IF YOU SENT AN ENTIRE ARMY TO FETCH HER.
MUTTER
?
I'VE FOUND A LEAD, IZUMI.
MEAT
YESTERDAY SOMEONE SAW AL GOING TO THE OLD FACTORY GROUNDS ON THE WEST SIDE.
AND AFTER THAT?

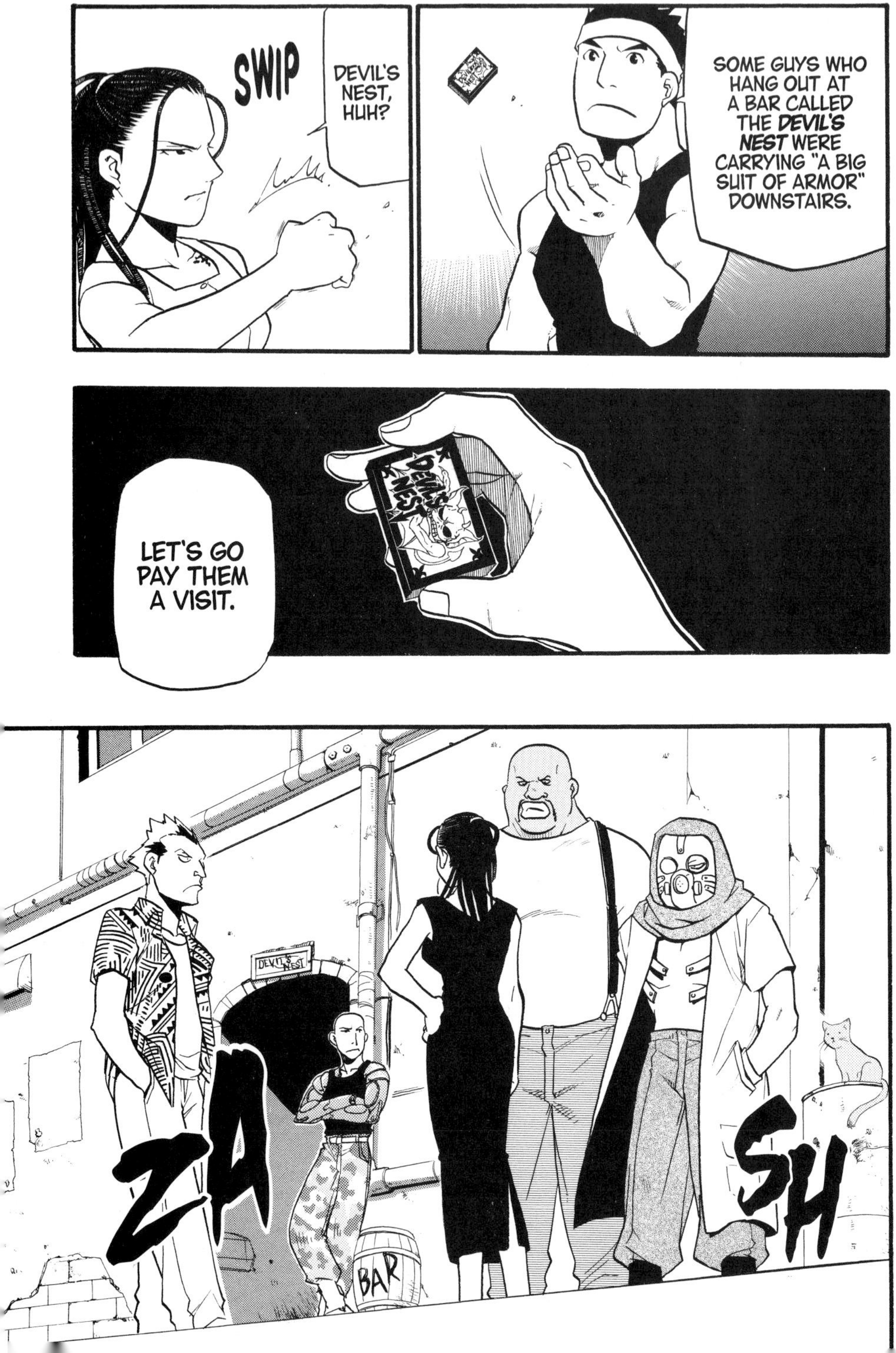
SOME GUYS WHO HANG OUT AT A BAR CALLED THE **DEVIL'S NEST** WERE CARRYING "A BIG SUIT OF ARMOR" DOWNSTAIRS.
SWIP
DEVIL'S NEST, HUH?
DEVIL'S NEST
LET'S GO PAY THEM A VISIT.
DEVIL'S NEST
ZA
SH
BAR

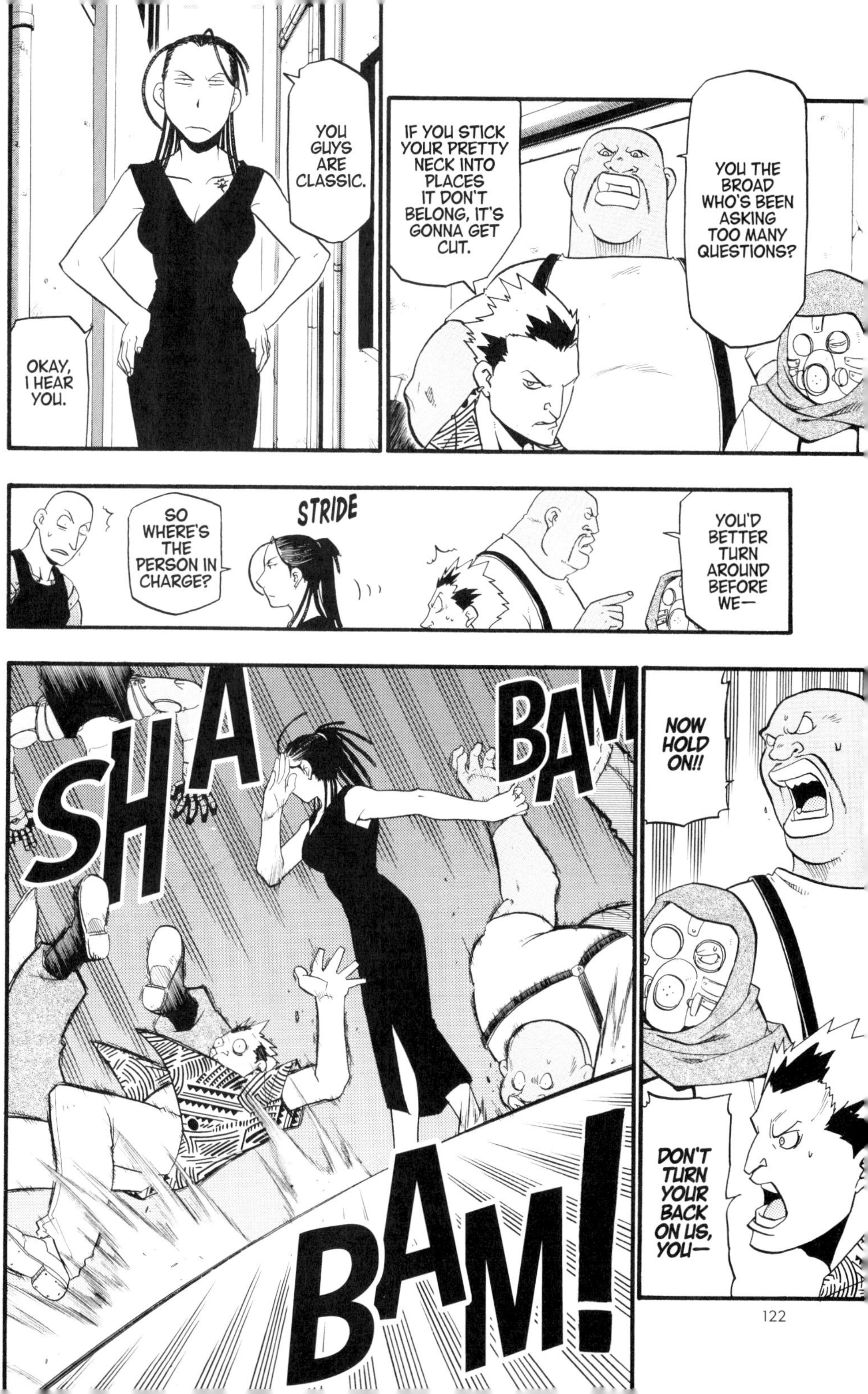
YOU THE BROAD WHO'S BEEN ASKING TOO MANY QUESTIONS?
IF YOU STICK YOUR PRETTY NECK INTO PLACES IT DON'T BELONG, IT'S GONNA GET CUT.
YOU GUYS ARE CLASSIC.
OKAY, I HEAR YOU.
YOU'D BETTER TURN AROUND BEFORE WE—
STRIDE
SO WHERE'S THE PERSON IN CHARGE?
NOW HOLD ON!!
DON'T TURN YOUR BACK ON US, YOU—
SHA
BAM
BAM!

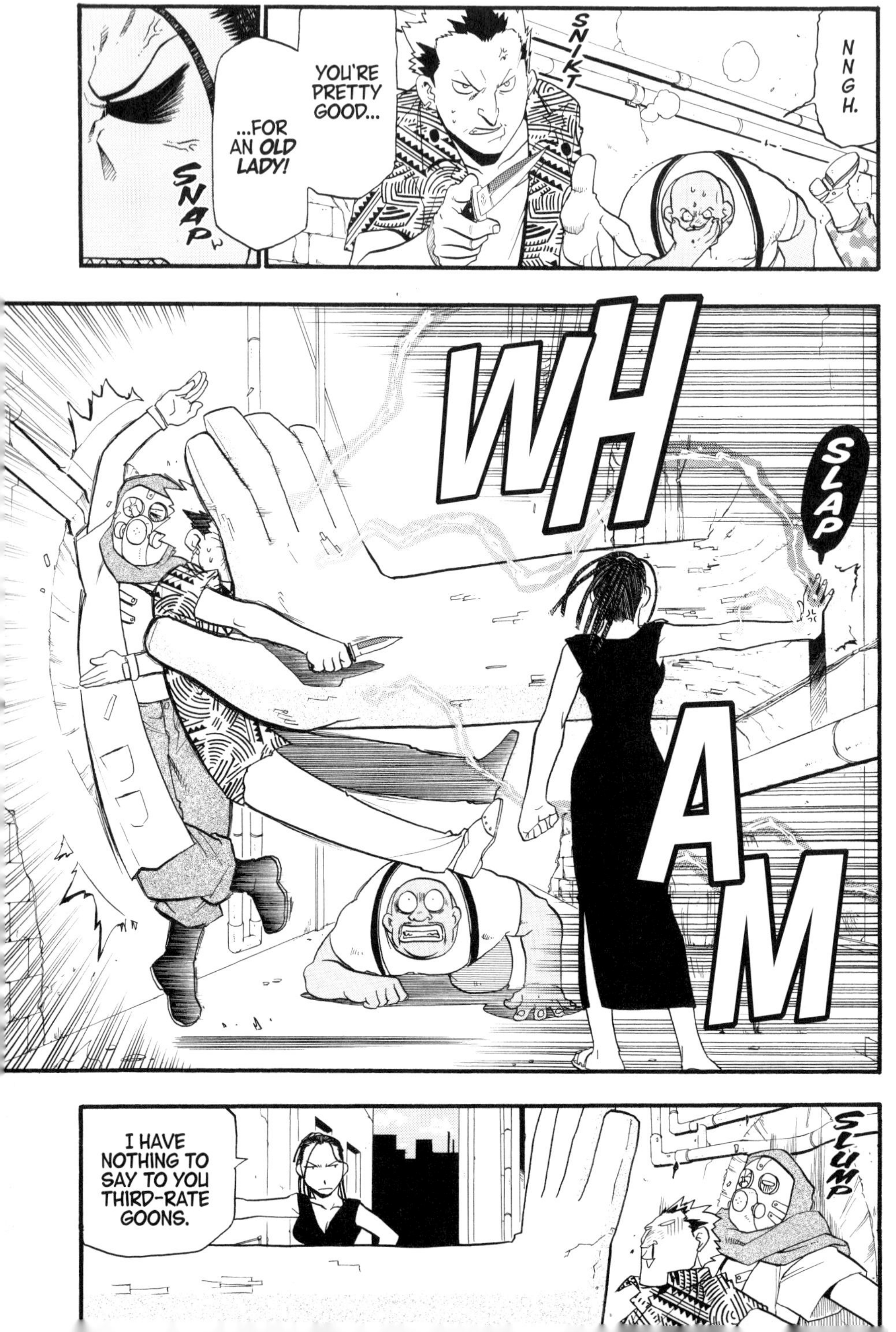
NNGH.
SNIKT
YOU'RE PRETTY GOOD...
...FOR AN OLD LADY!
SNAP
SLAP
WHAM
SLUMP
I HAVE NOTHING TO SAY TO YOU THIRD-RATE GOONS.

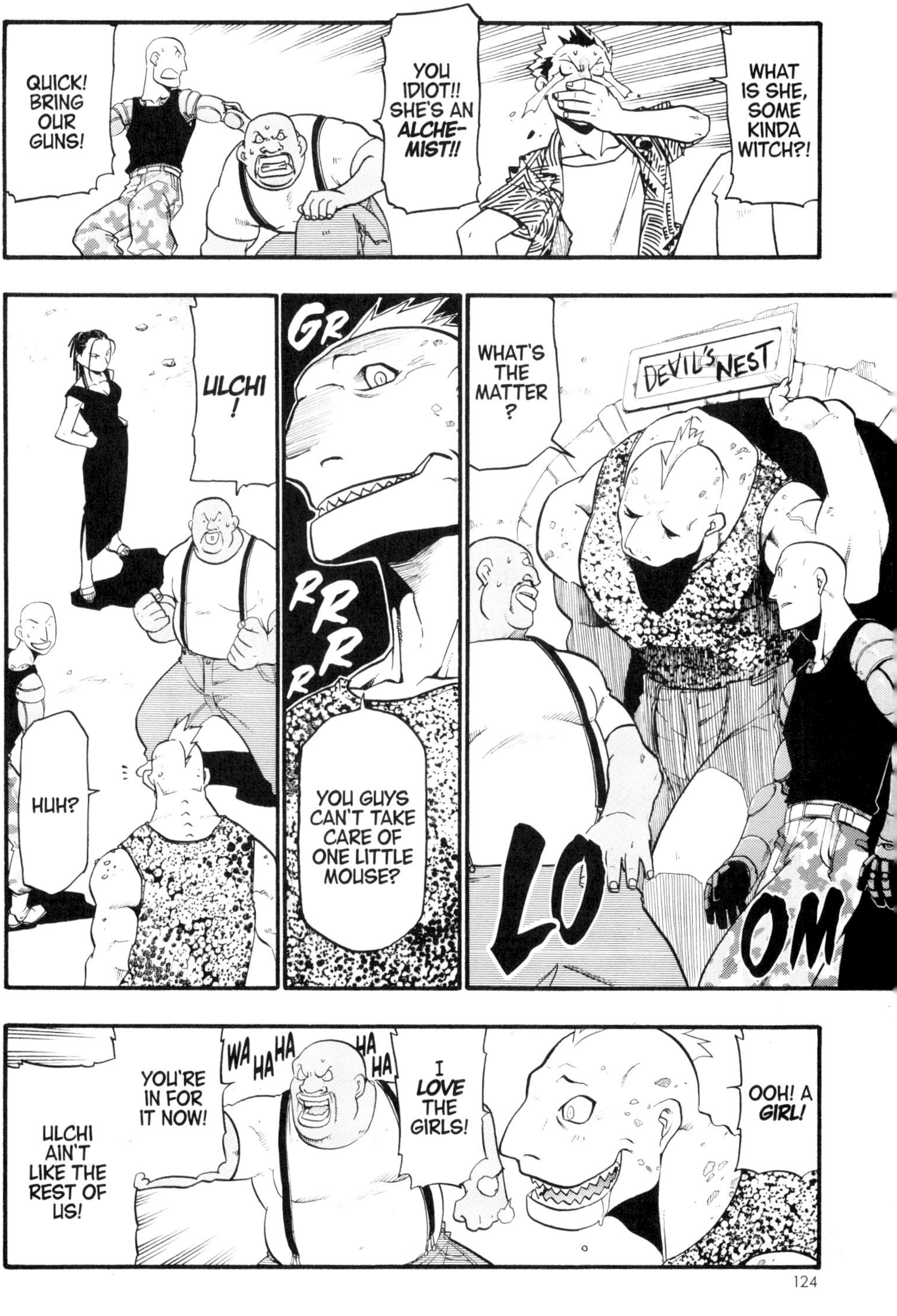
WHAT IS SHE, SOME KINDA WITCH?!
YOU IDIOT!! SHE'S AN ALCHEMIST!!
QUICK! BRING OUR GUNS!
WHAT'S THE MATTER?
DEVIL'S NEST
LOOM
GRRRRRR
YOU GUYS CAN'T TAKE CARE OF ONE LITTLE MOUSE?
ULCHI!
HUH?
OOH! A GIRL!
I LOVE THE GIRLS!
WAHAHAHAHA
YOU'RE IN FOR IT NOW!
ULCHI AIN'T LIKE THE REST OF US!

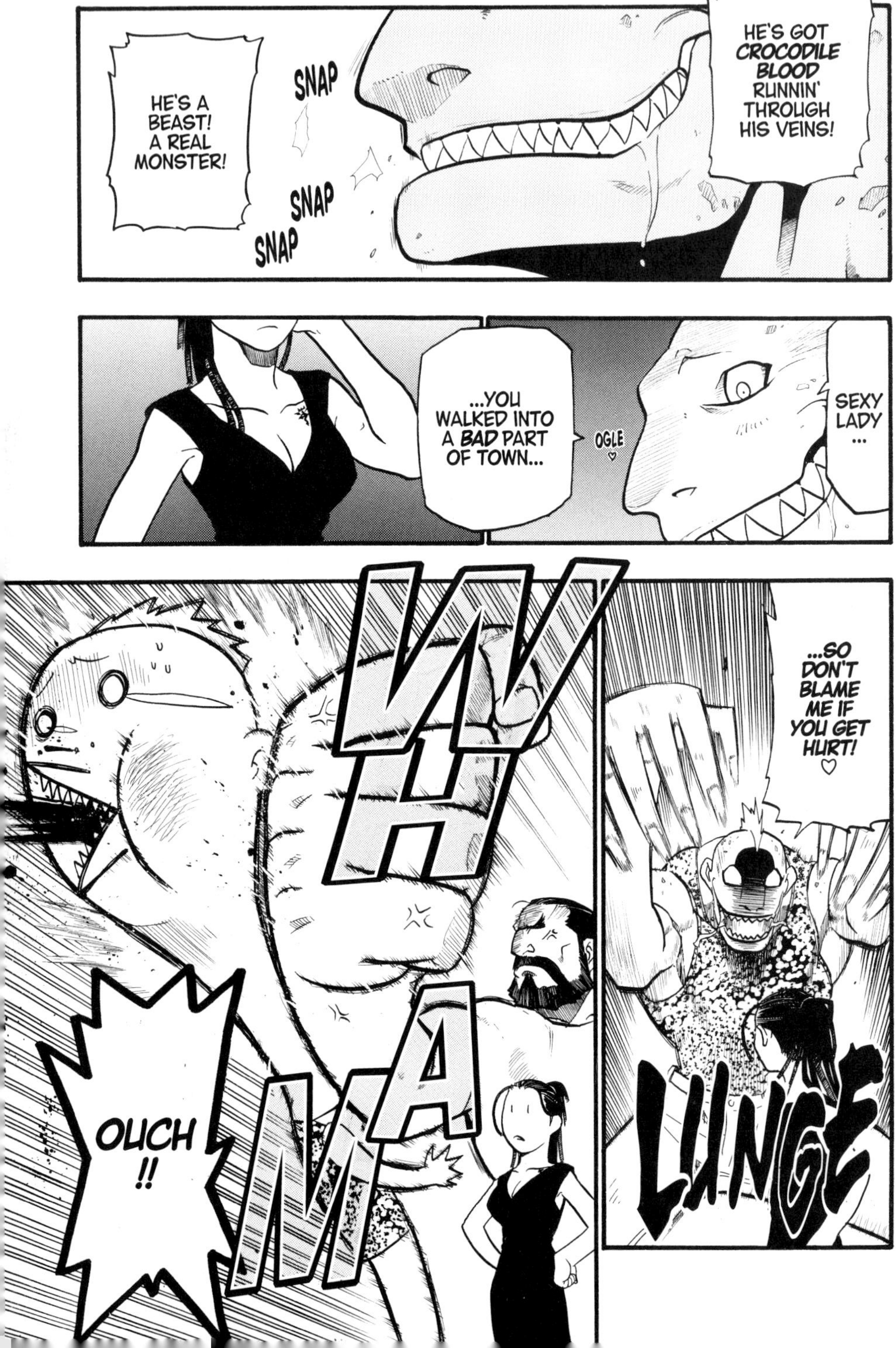
HE'S GOT CROCODILE BLOOD RUNNIN' THROUGH HIS VEINS!
SNAP
HE'S A BEAST! A REAL MONSTER!
SNAP
SNAP
SEXY LADY...
OGLE ♡
...YOU WALKED INTO A BAD PART OF TOWN...
...SO DON'T BLAME ME IF YOU GET HURT! ♡
LUNGE
WHAM
OUCH!!

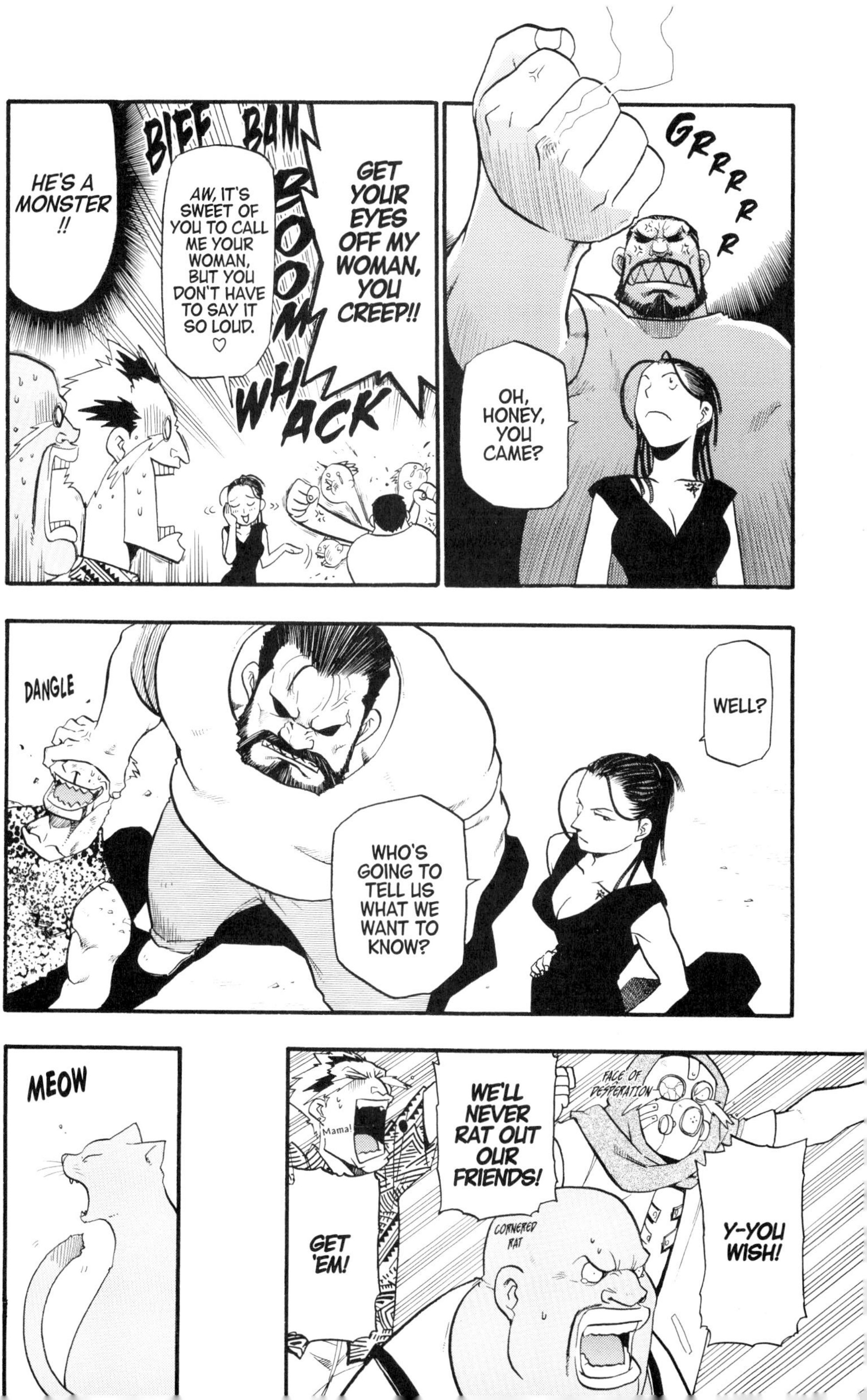
GRRRRR
OH, HONEY, YOU CAME?
GET YOUR EYES OFF MY WOMAN, YOU CREEP!!
BOOM
WHACK
BIFF BAM
AW, IT'S SWEET OF YOU TO CALL ME YOUR WOMAN, BUT YOU DON'T HAVE TO SAY IT SO LOUD. ♡
HE'S A MONSTER!!
WELL?
WHO'S GOING TO TELL US WHAT WE WANT TO KNOW?
DANGLE
FACE OF DESPERATION
Y-YOU WISH!
WE'LL NEVER RAT OUT OUR FRIENDS!
CORNERED RAT
Mama!
GET 'EM!
MEOW

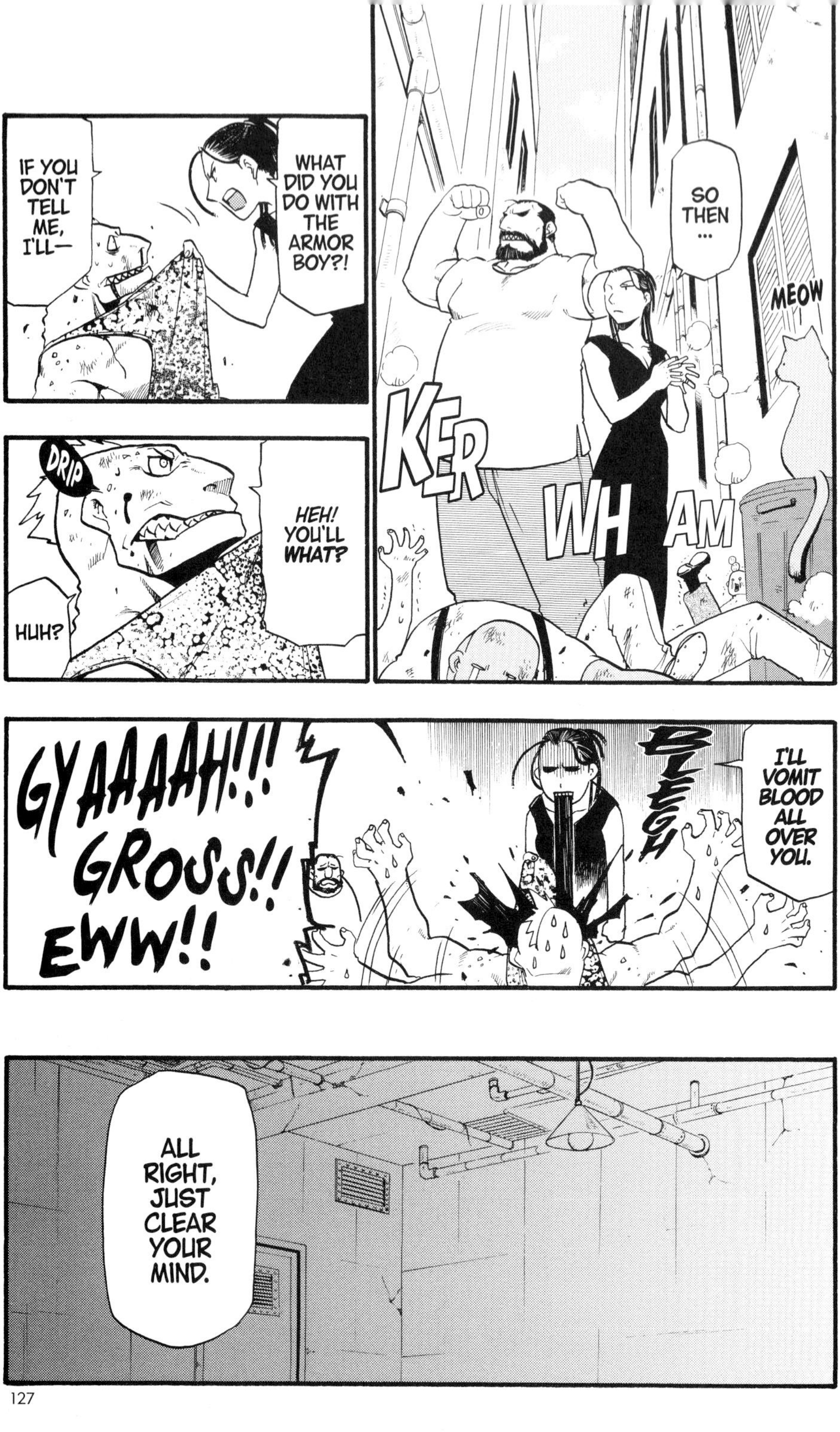
SO THEN...
MEOW
KER WHAM
WHAT DID YOU DO WITH THE ARMOR BOY?!
IF YOU DON'T TELL ME, I'LL—
DRIP
HEH! YOU'LL WHAT?
HUH?
I'LL VOMIT BLOOD ALL OVER YOU.
BLEGH
GYAAAAH!!! GROSS!! EWW!!
ALL RIGHT, JUST CLEAR YOUR MIND.

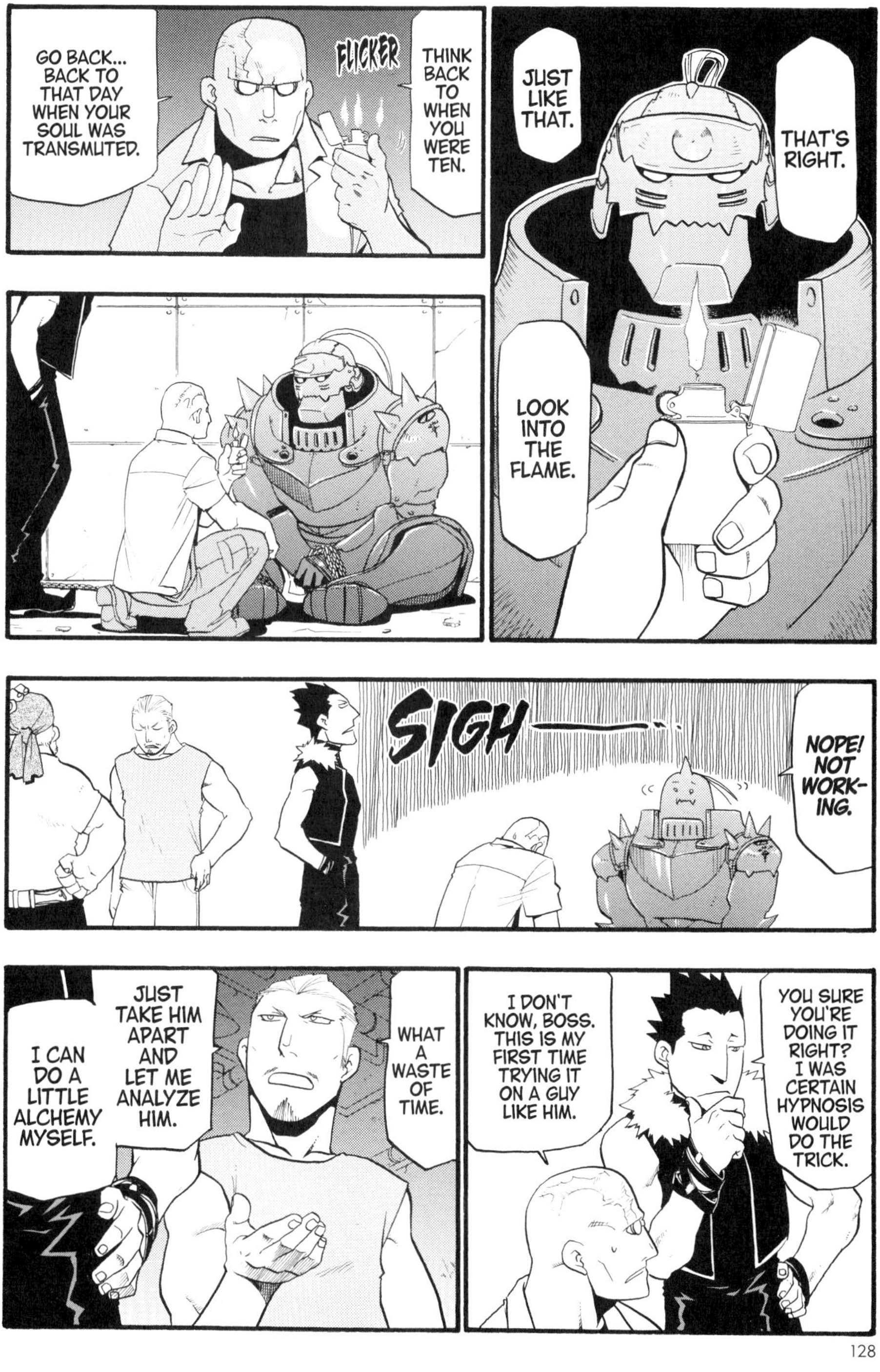
THAT'S RIGHT.
JUST LIKE THAT.
LOOK INTO THE FLAME.
THINK BACK TO WHEN YOU WERE TEN.
FLICKER
GO BACK... BACK TO THAT DAY WHEN YOUR SOUL WAS TRANSMUTED.
NOPE! NOT WORKING.
SIGH——
YOU SURE YOU'RE DOING IT RIGHT? I WAS CERTAIN HYPNOSIS WOULD DO THE TRICK.
I DON'T KNOW, BOSS. THIS IS MY FIRST TIME TRYING IT ON A GUY LIKE HIM.
WHAT A WASTE OF TIME.
JUST TAKE HIM APART AND LET ME ANALYZE HIM.
I CAN DO A LITTLE ALCHEMY MYSELF.

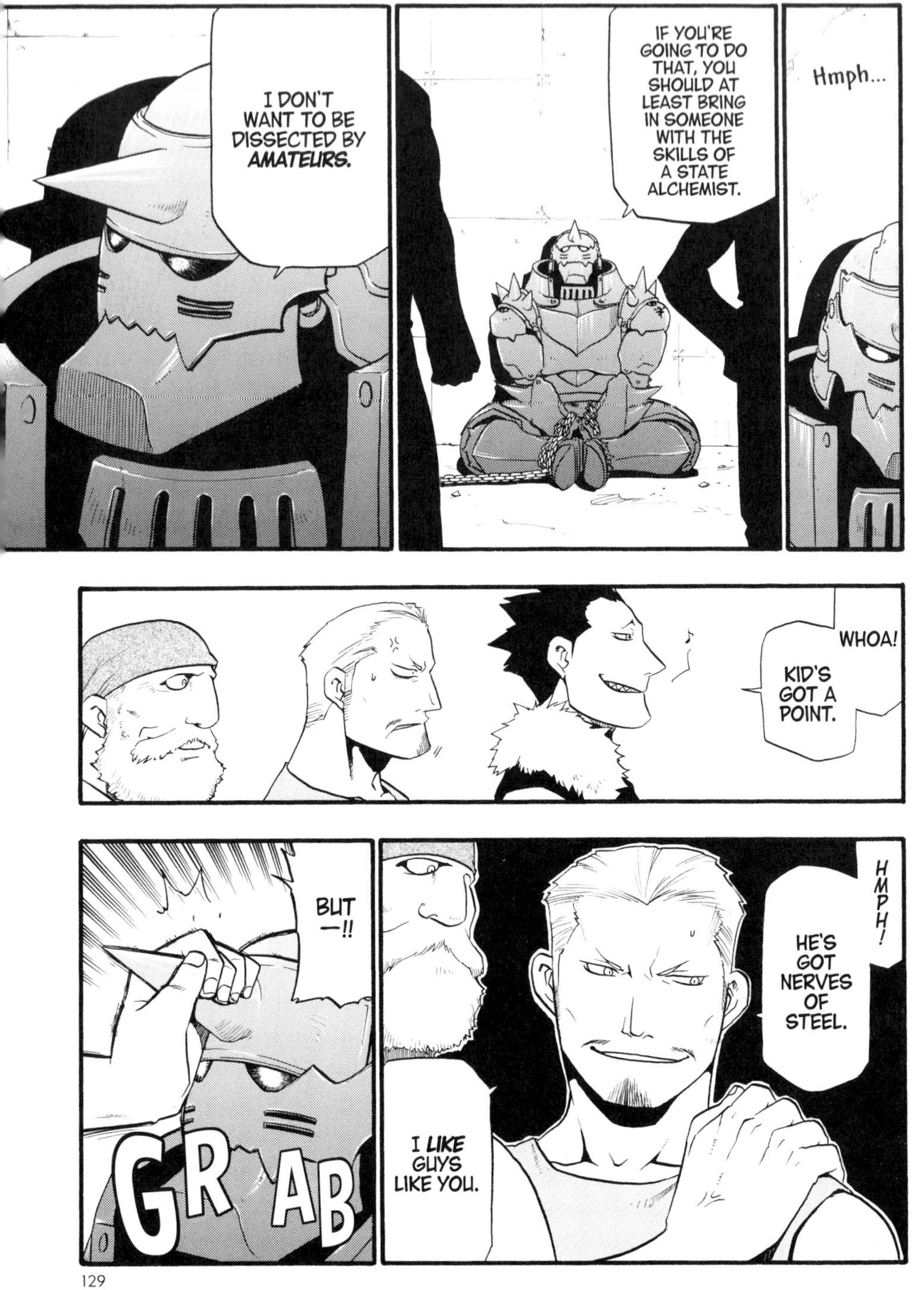
Hmph...
IF YOU'RE GOING TO DO THAT, YOU SHOULD AT LEAST BRING IN SOMEONE WITH THE SKILLS OF A STATE ALCHEMIST.
I DON'T WANT TO BE DISSECTED BY AMATEURS.
WHOA!
KID'S GOT A POINT.
HMPH!
HE'S GOT NERVES OF STEEL.
I LIKE GUYS LIKE YOU.
BUT—!!
GRAB

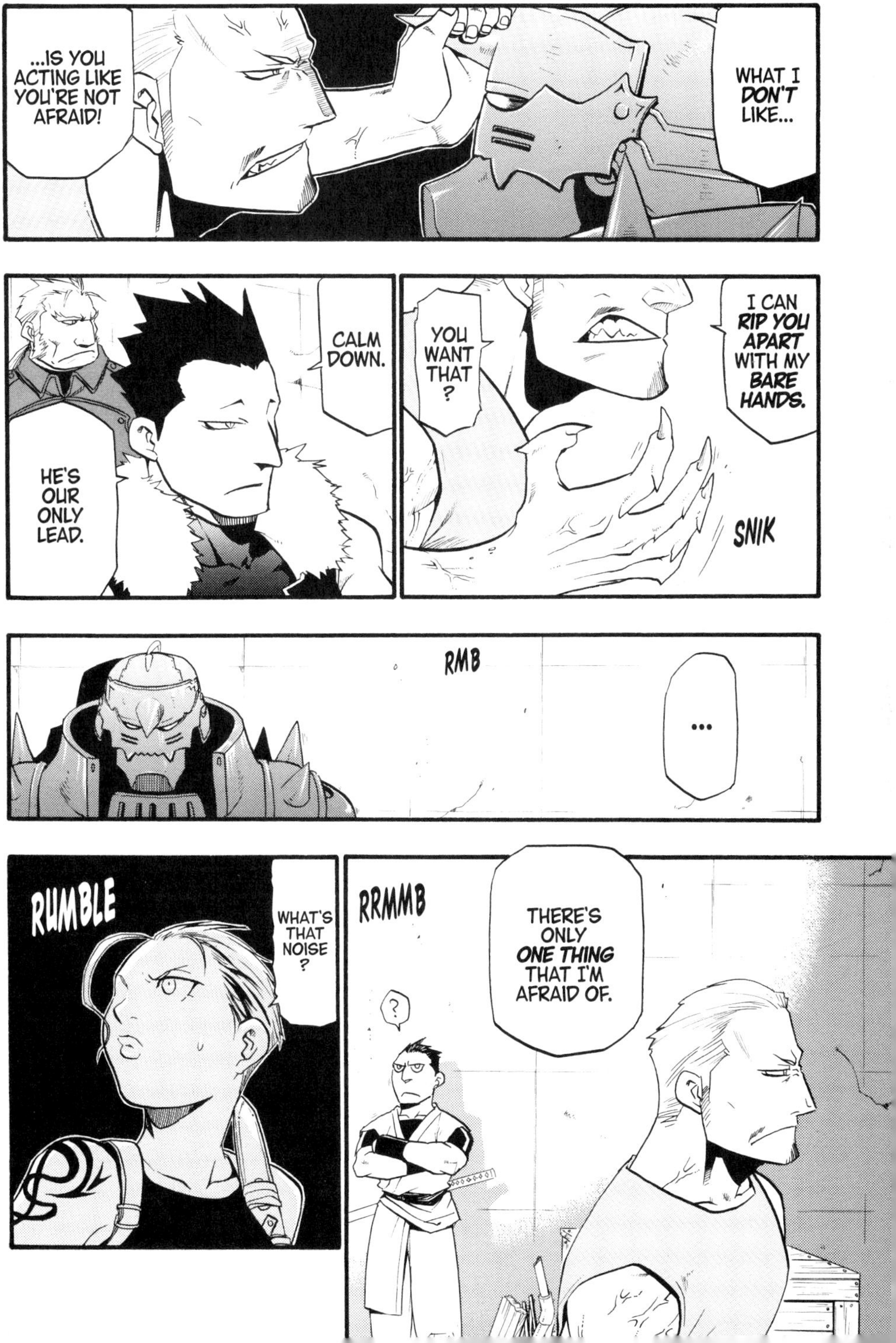
WHAT I DON'T LIKE...
...IS YOU ACTING LIKE YOU'RE NOT AFRAID!
I CAN RIP YOU APART WITH MY BARE HANDS.
YOU WANT THAT?
SNIK
CALM DOWN.
HE'S OUR ONLY LEAD.
...
RMB
THERE'S ONLY ONE THING THAT I'M AFRAID OF.
RRMMB
?
WHAT'S THAT NOISE?
RUMBLE

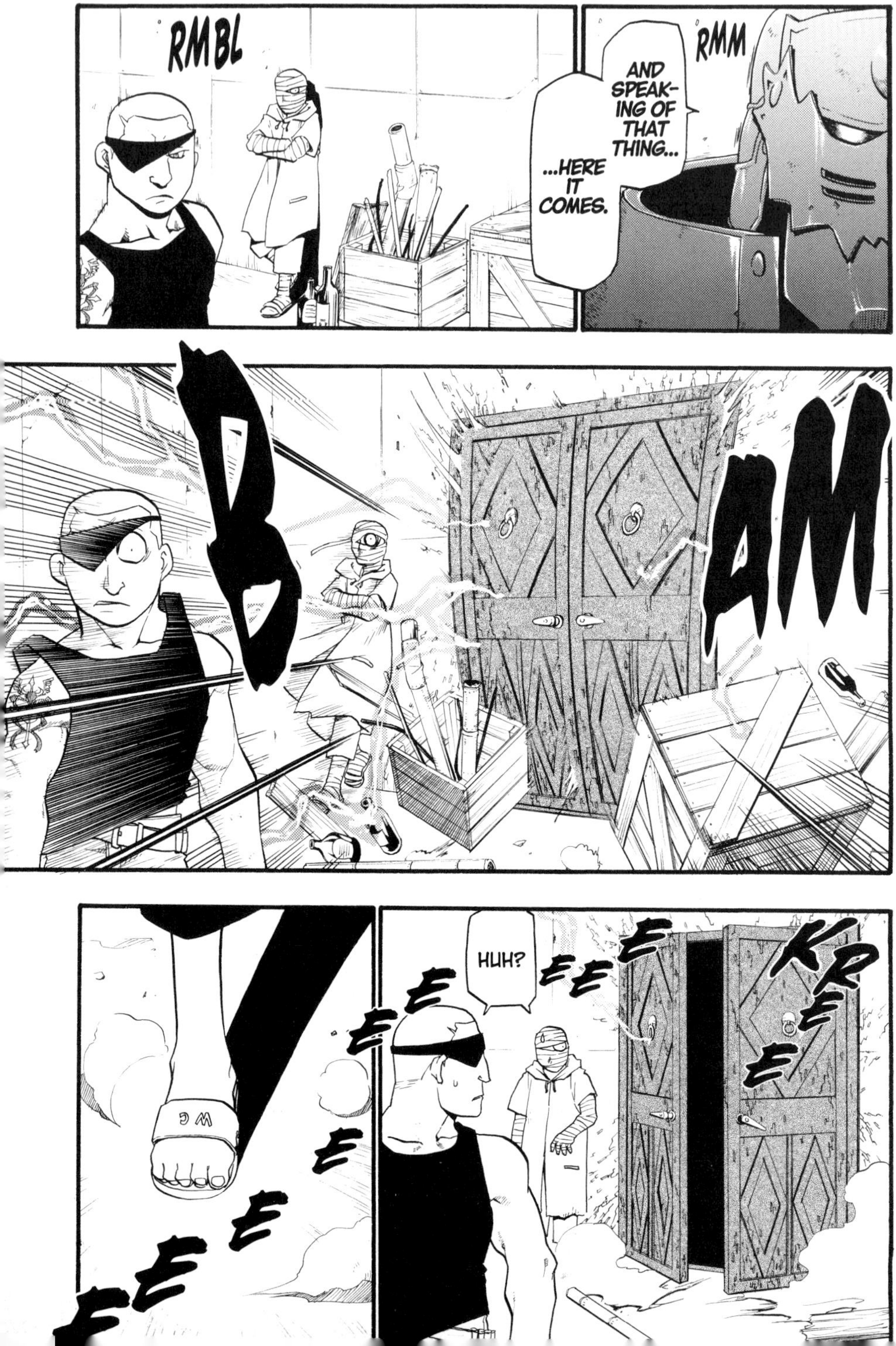
RMM
AND SPEAK-ING OF THAT THING...
...HERE IT COMES.
RMBL
BAM
KREEE
EEEE
HUH?
EE
EEEEE

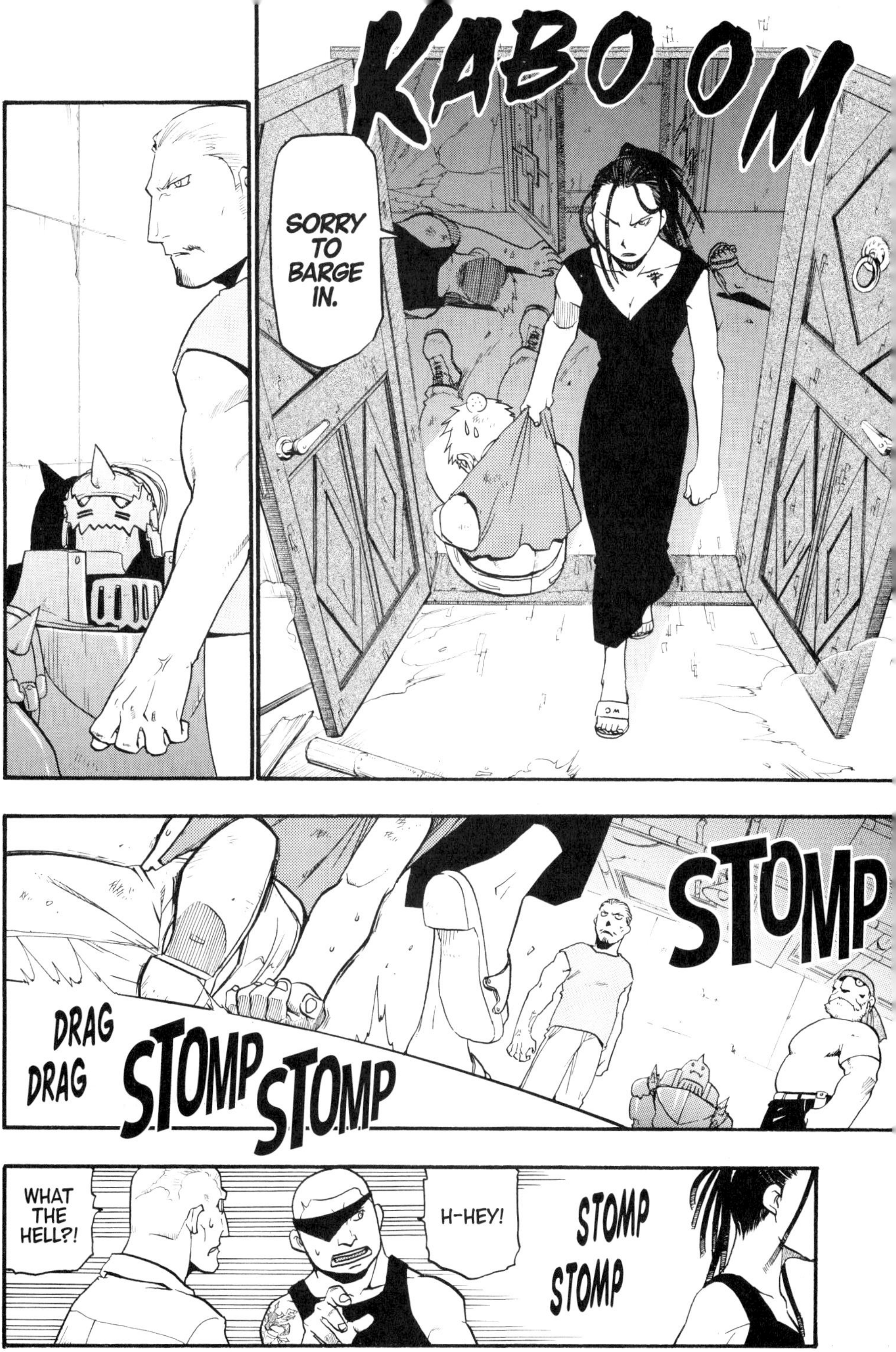
KABOOM
SORRY TO BARGE IN.
STOMP
DRAG DRAG
STOMP STOMP
STOMP STOMP
H-HEY!
WHAT THE HELL?!

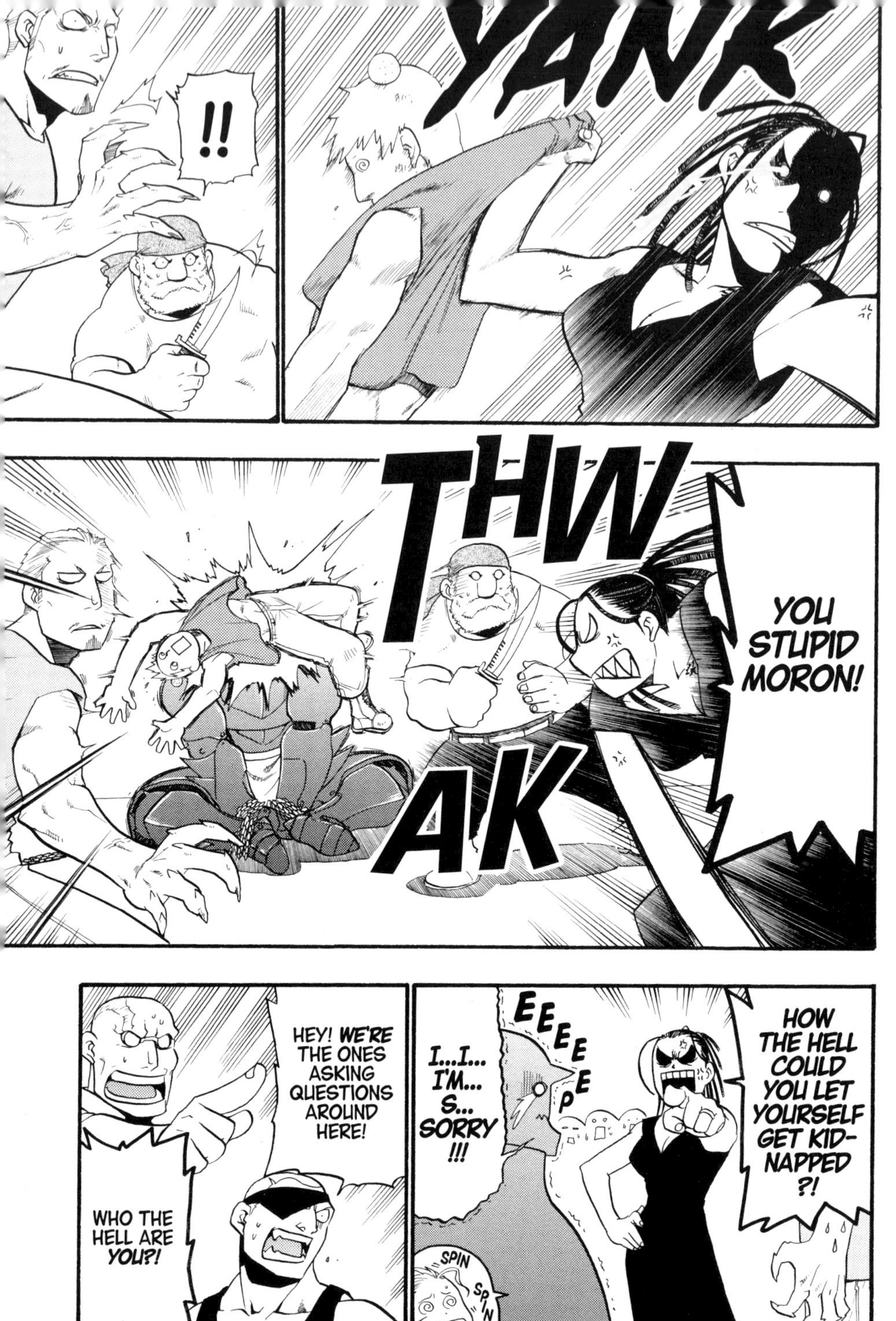
YANK
!!
THWAK
YOU STUPID MORON!
HOW THE HELL COULD YOU LET YOURSELF GET KID-NAPPED?!
EEEEEEP
I...I... I'M... S... SORRY!!!
SPIN SPIN
HEY! WE'RE THE ONES ASKING QUESTIONS AROUND HERE!
WHO THE HELL ARE YOU?!

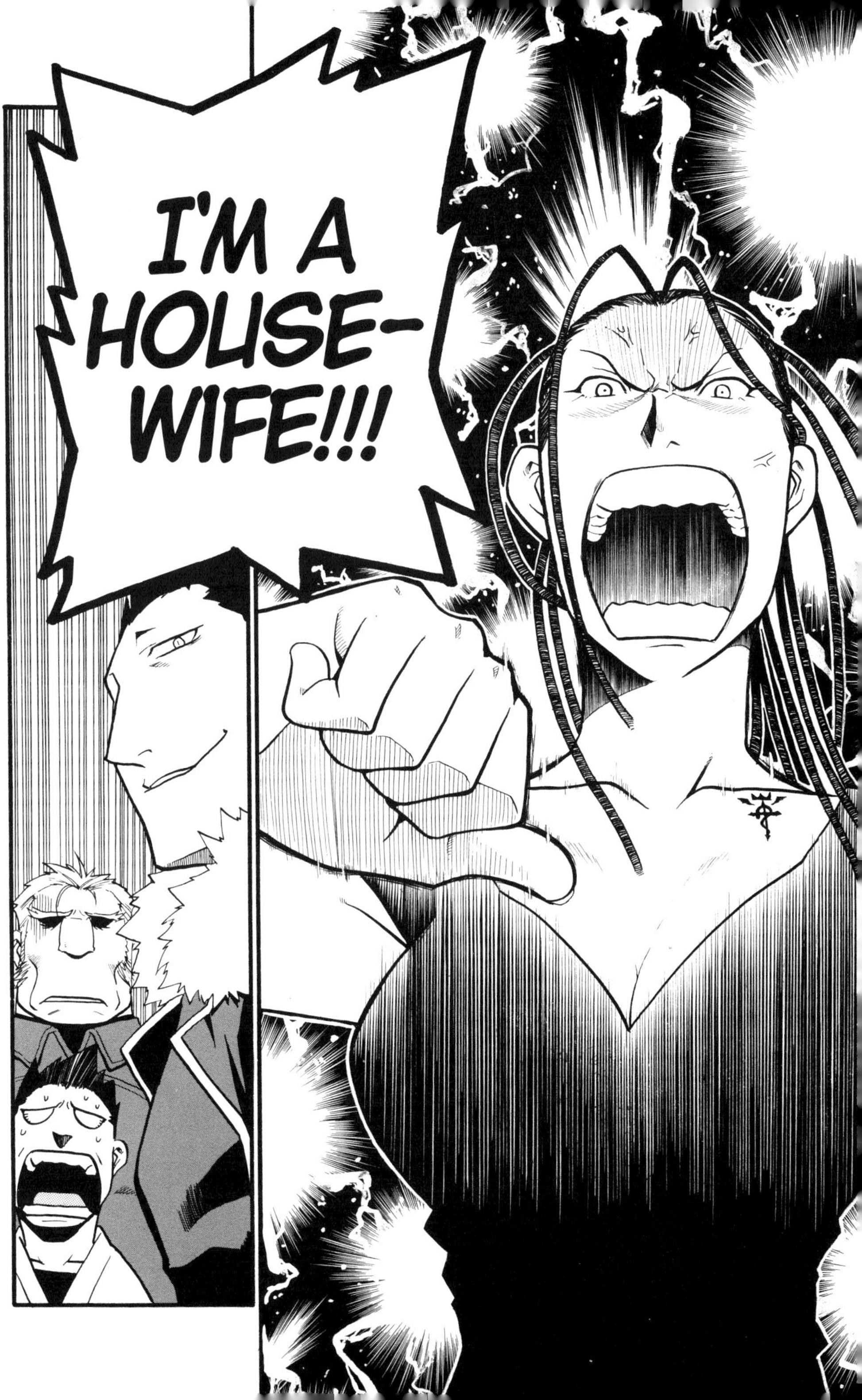
I'M A HOUSE-WIFE!!!

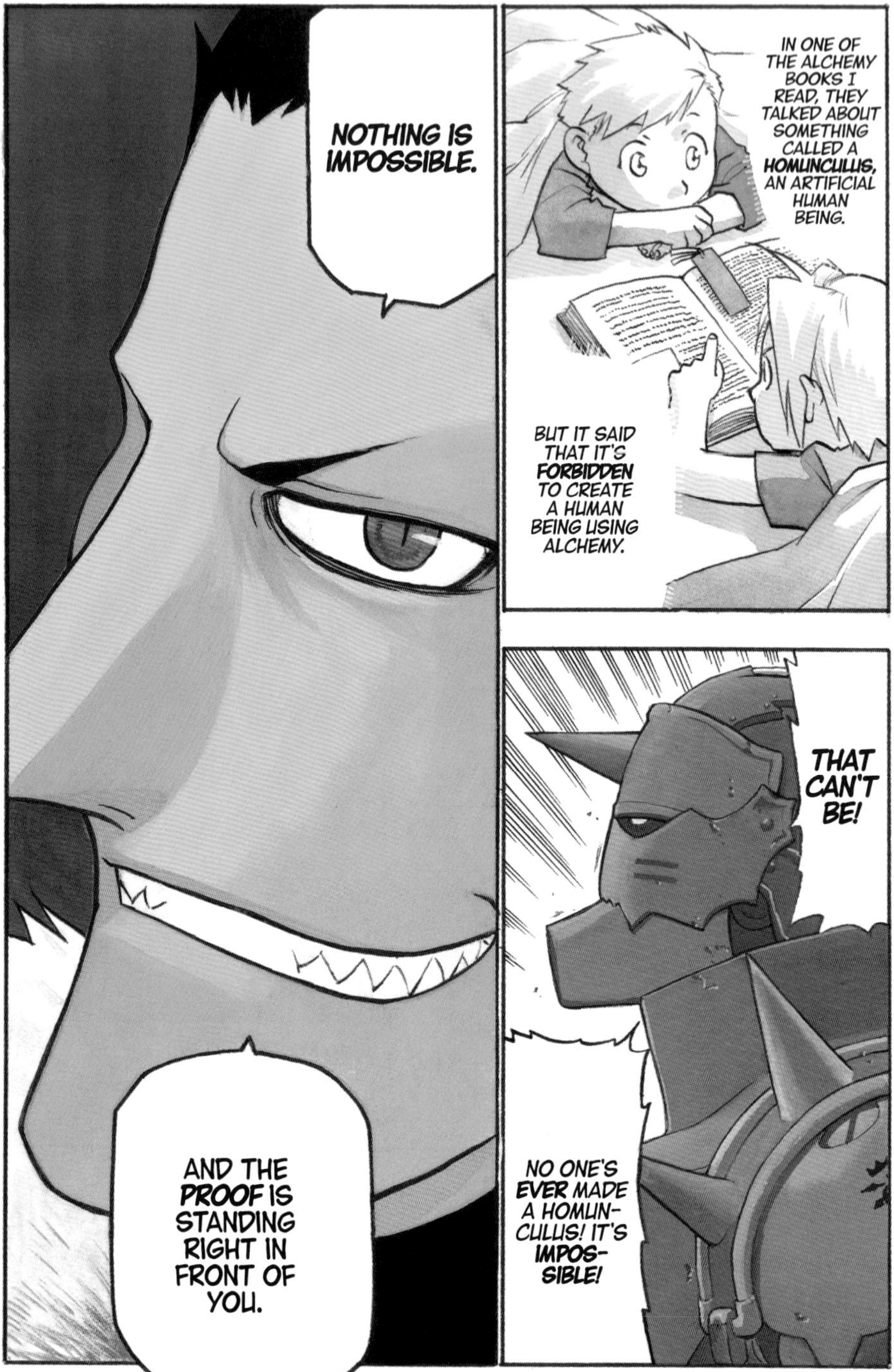
IN ONE OF THE ALCHEMY BOOKS I READ, THEY TALKED ABOUT SOMETHING CALLED A **HOMUNCULUS,** AN ARTIFICIAL HUMAN BEING.
BUT IT SAID THAT IT'S **FORBIDDEN** TO CREATE A HUMAN BEING USING ALCHEMY.
THAT CAN'T BE!
NO ONE'S **EVER** MADE A HOMUNCULUS! IT'S **IMPOSSIBLE!**
NOTHING IS IMPOSSIBLE.
AND THE **PROOF** IS STANDING RIGHT IN FRONT OF YOU.

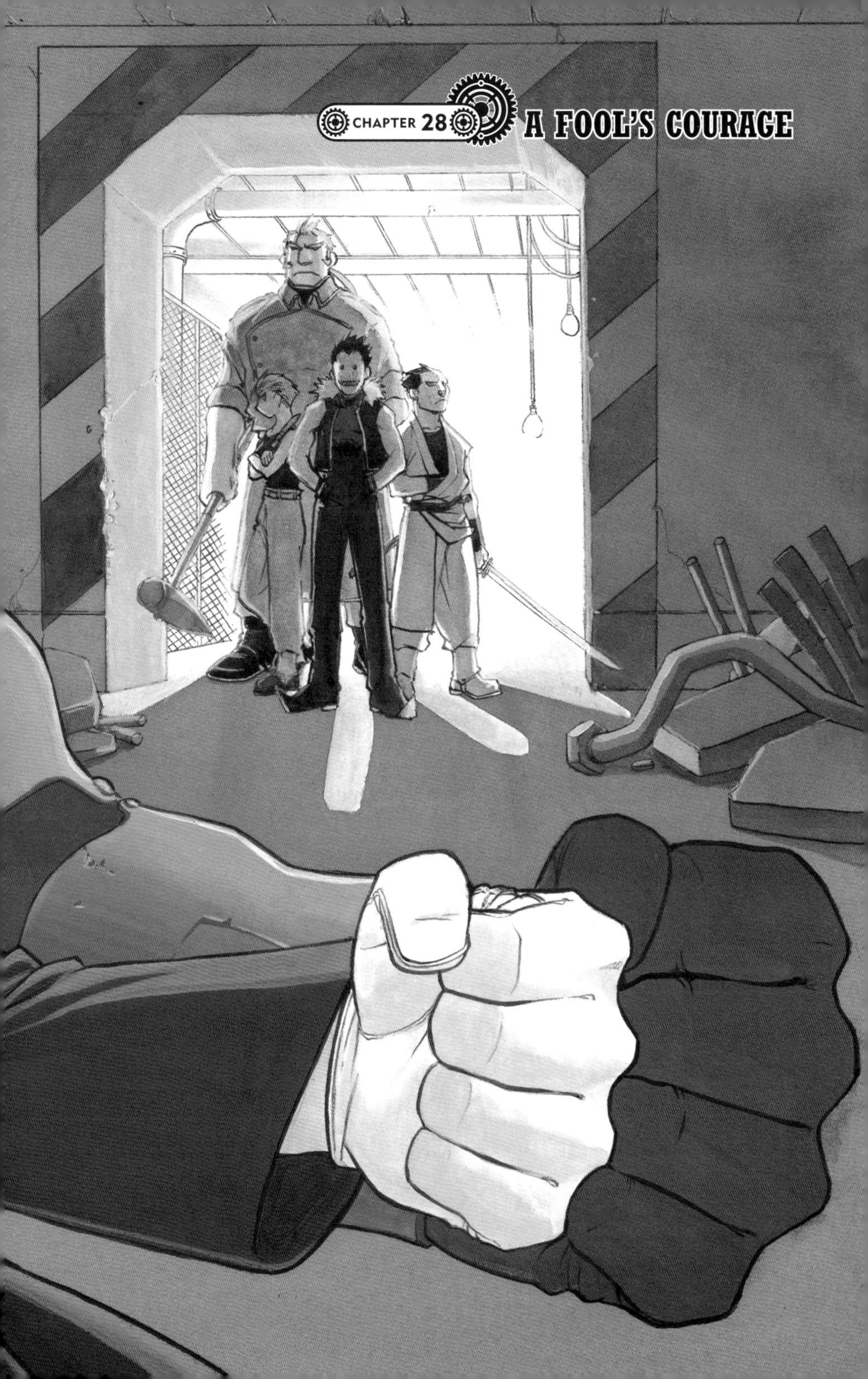
CHAPTER 28
A FOOL'S COURAGE

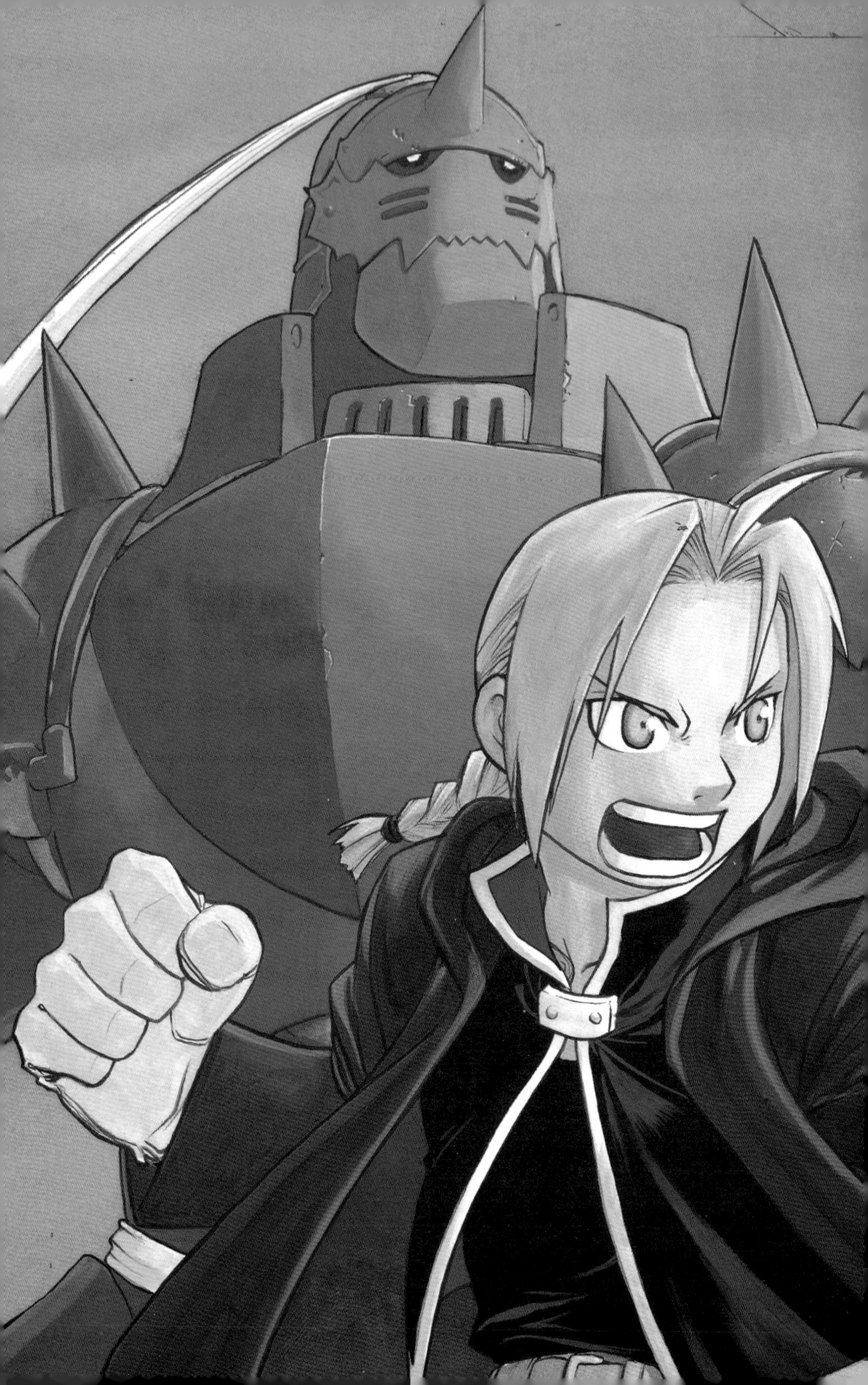

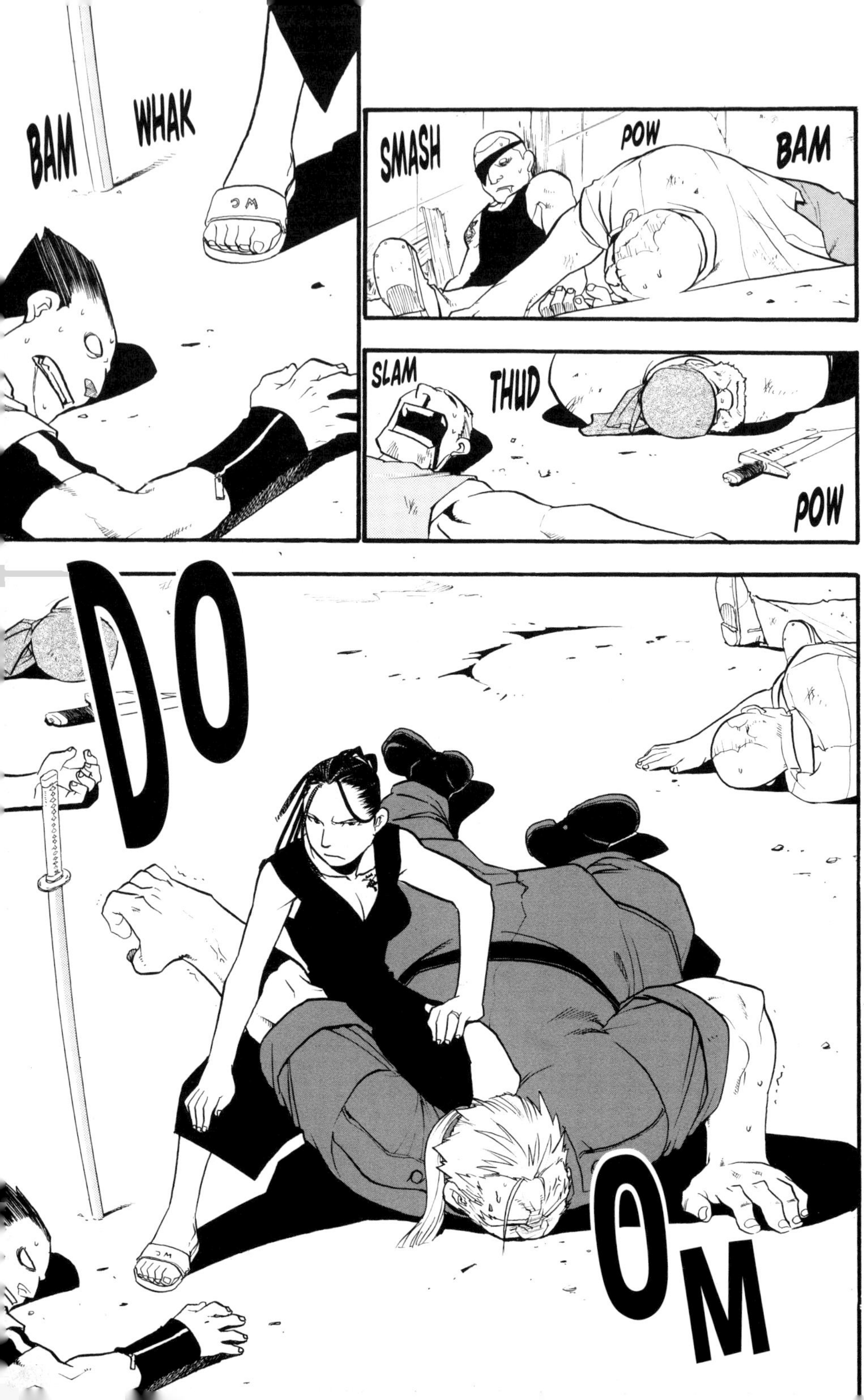
BAM
POW
SMASH
THUD
SLAM
POW
WHAK
BAM
DO
OM

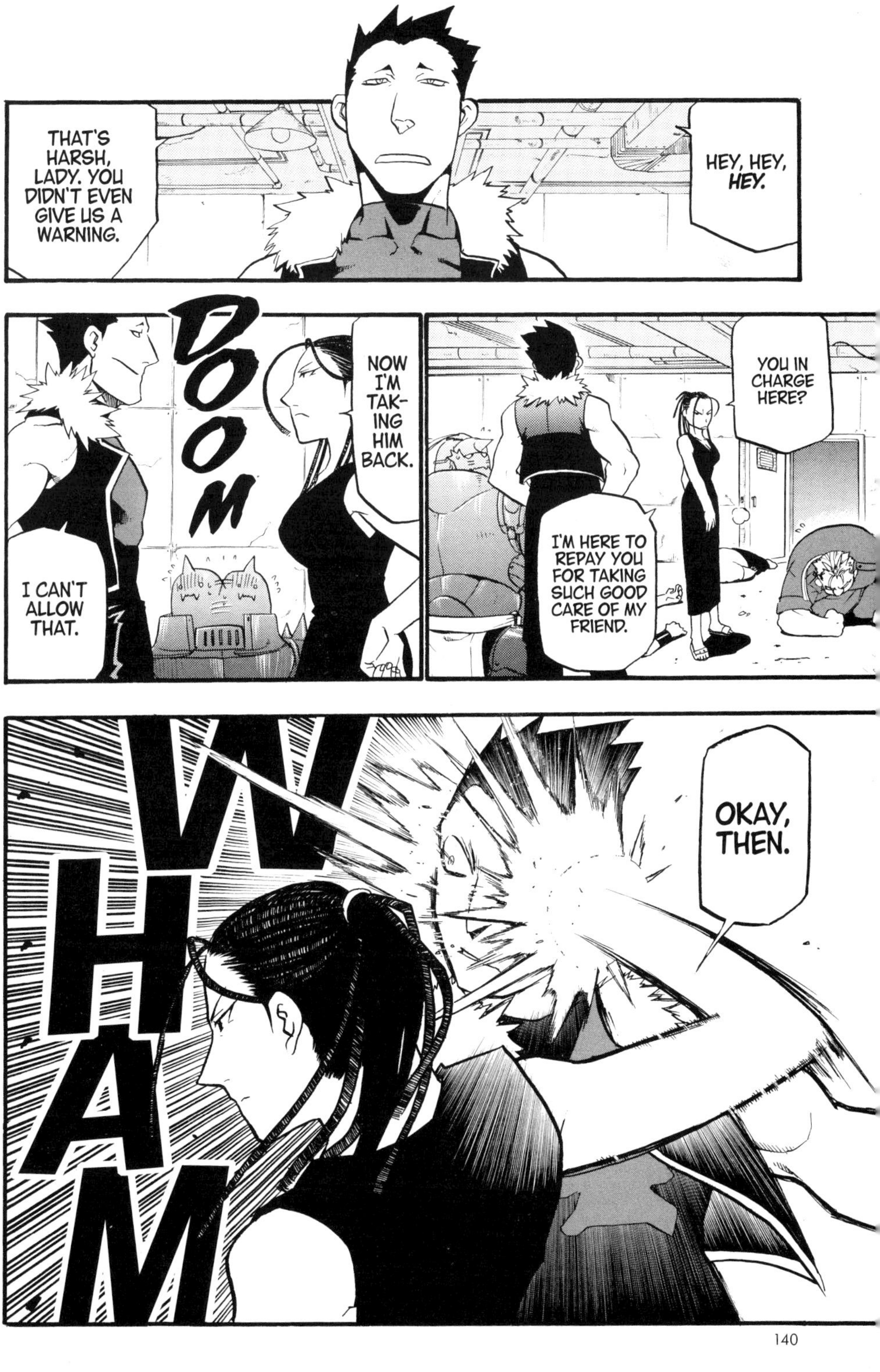
HEY, HEY, HEY.
THAT'S HARSH, LADY. YOU DIDN'T EVEN GIVE US A WARNING.
YOU IN CHARGE HERE?
I'M HERE TO REPAY YOU FOR TAKING SUCH GOOD CARE OF MY FRIEND.
NOW I'M TAKING HIM BACK.
DOOM
I CAN'T ALLOW THAT.
OKAY, THEN.
WHAM

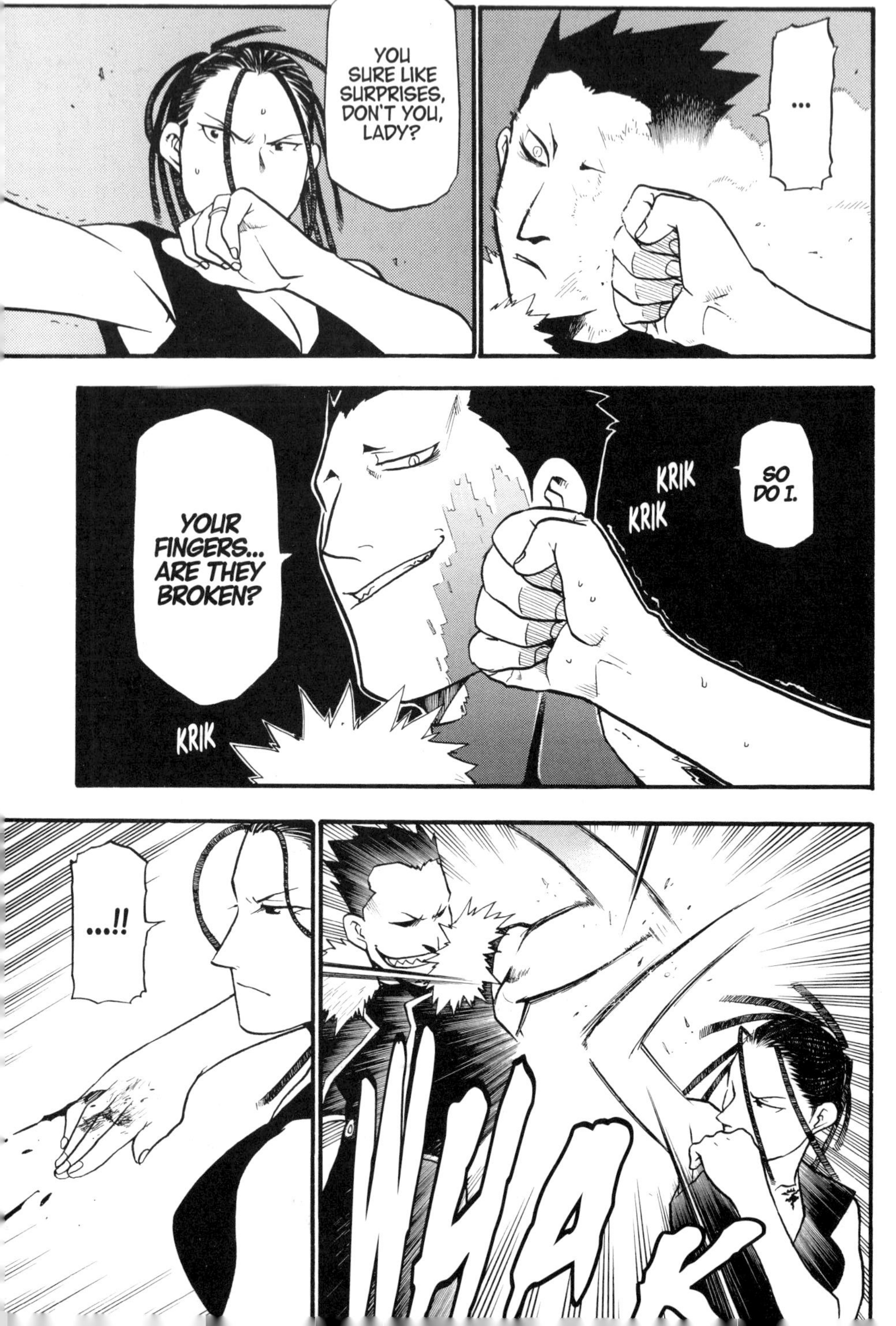

...
YOU SURE LIKE SURPRISES, DON'T YOU, LADY?
SO DO I.
KRIK
KRIK
YOUR FINGERS... ARE THEY BROKEN?
KRIK
WHAK
...!!

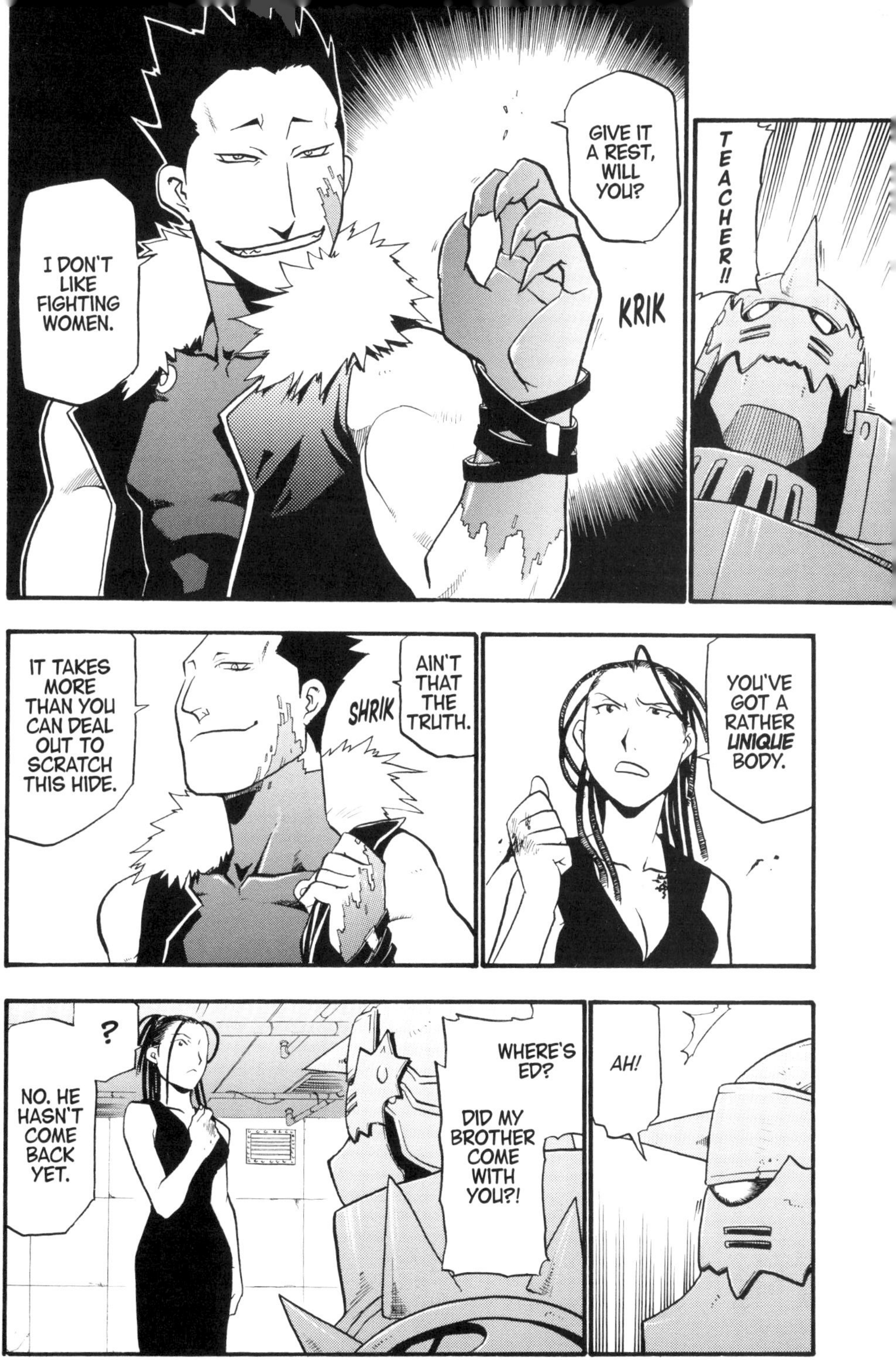
TEACHER!!
GIVE IT A REST, WILL YOU?
KRIK
I DON'T LIKE FIGHTING WOMEN.
YOU'VE GOT A RATHER UNIQUE BODY.
AIN'T THAT THE TRUTH.
SHRIK
IT TAKES MORE THAN YOU CAN DEAL OUT TO SCRATCH THIS HIDE.
AH!
WHERE'S ED?
DID MY BROTHER COME WITH YOU?!
?
NO. HE HASN'T COME BACK YET.

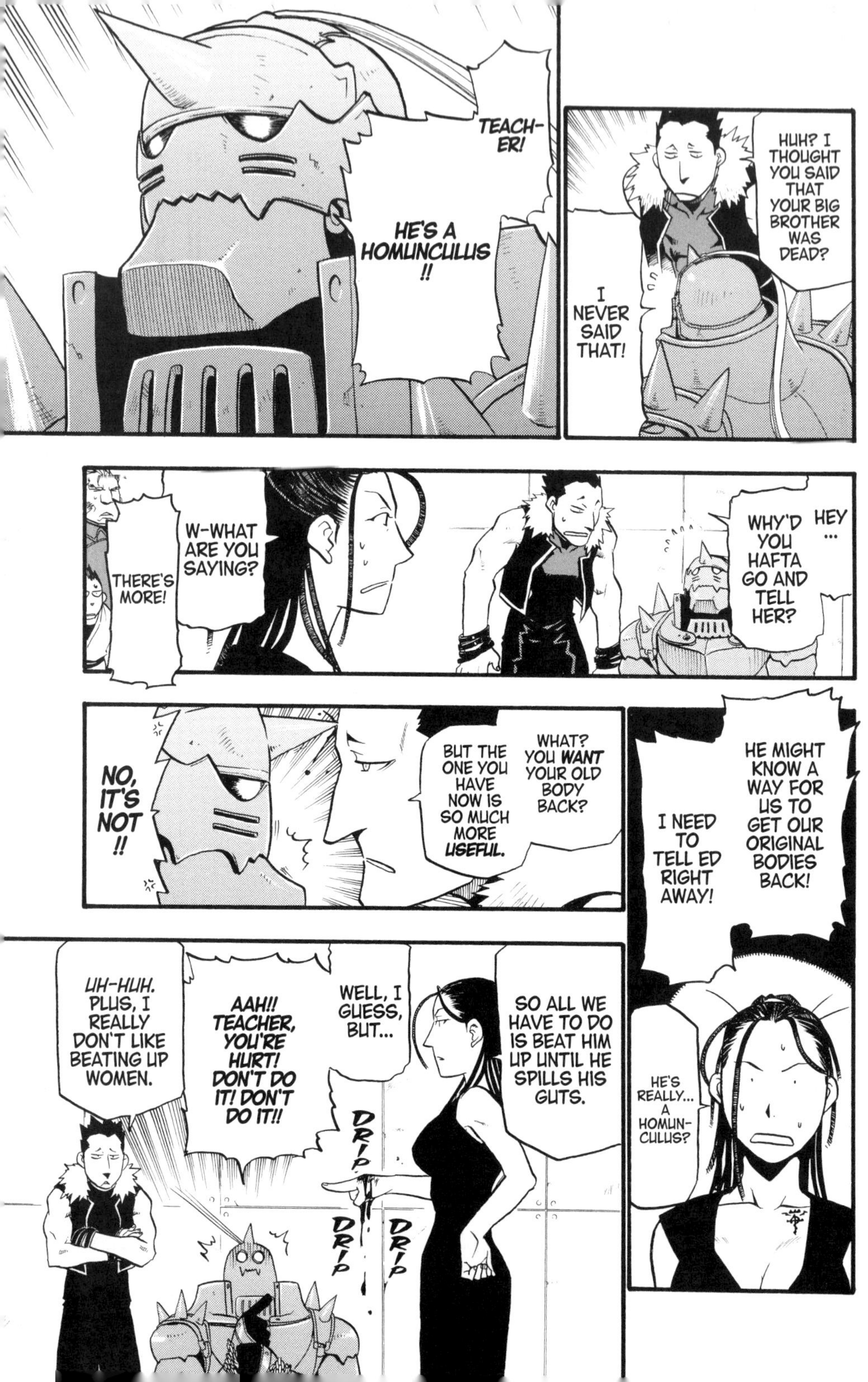
HUH? I THOUGHT YOU SAID THAT YOUR BIG BROTHER WAS DEAD?
I NEVER SAID THAT!
TEACHER-ER!
HE'S A HOMUNCULUS!!
HEY...
WHY'D YOU HAFTA GO AND TELL HER?
W-WHAT ARE YOU SAYING?
THERE'S MORE!
HE MIGHT KNOW A WAY FOR US TO GET OUR ORIGINAL BODIES BACK!
I NEED TO TELL ED RIGHT AWAY!
HE'S REALLY... A HOMUNCULUS?
WHAT? YOU WANT YOUR OLD BODY BACK?
BUT THE ONE YOU HAVE NOW IS SO MUCH MORE USEFUL.
NO, IT'S NOT!!
SO ALL WE HAVE TO DO IS BEAT HIM UP UNTIL HE SPILLS HIS GUTS.
WELL, I GUESS, BUT...
DRIP
DRIP
DRIP
AAH!! TEACHER, YOU'RE HURT! DON'T DO IT! DON'T DO IT!!
UH-HUH. PLUS, I REALLY DON'T LIKE BEATING UP WOMEN.

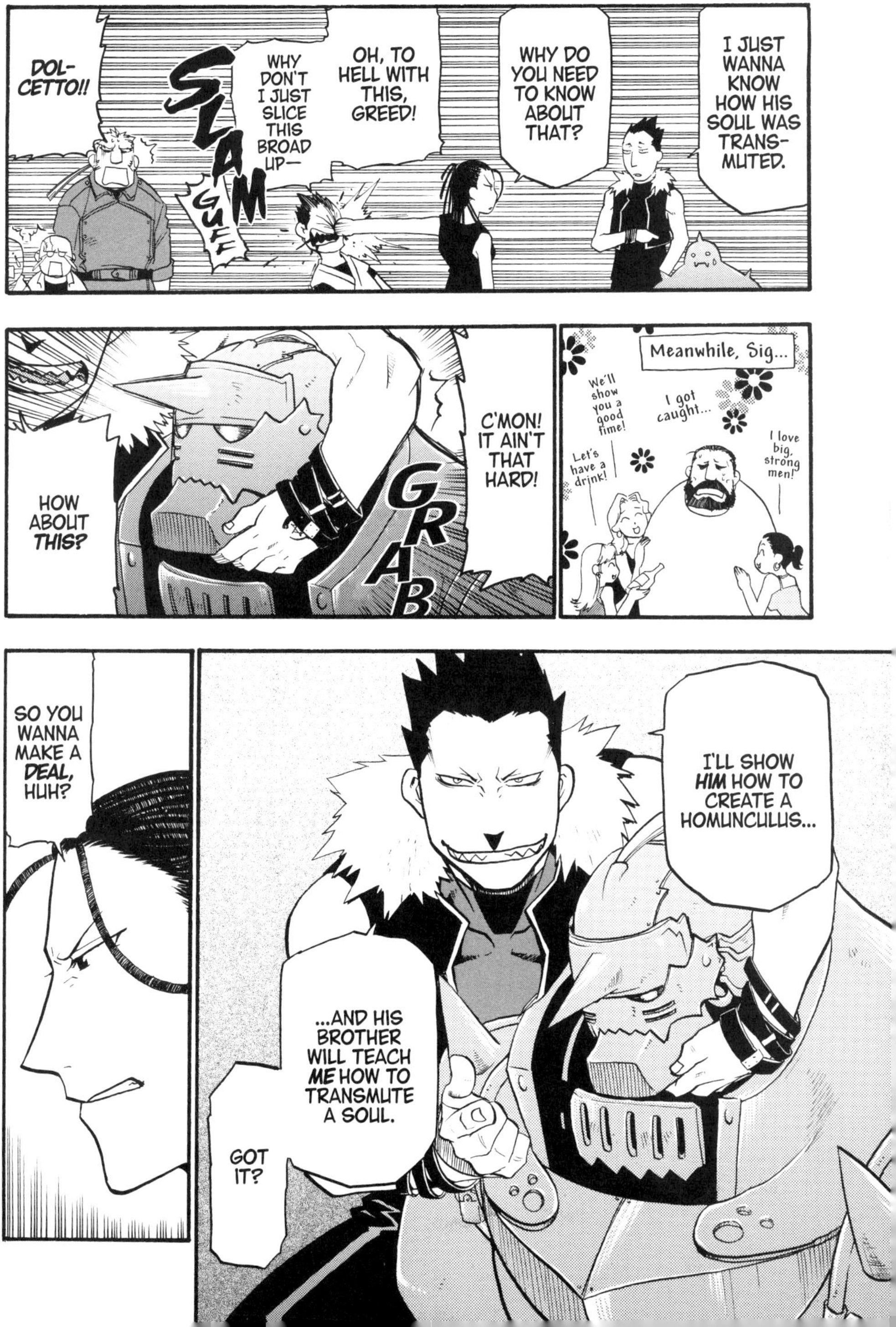
I JUST WANNA KNOW HOW HIS SOUL WAS TRANS-MUTED.
WHY DO YOU NEED TO KNOW ABOUT THAT?
OH, TO HELL WITH THIS, GREED!
WHY DON'T I JUST SLICE THIS BROAD UP—
SLAM
GUFF
DOL-CETTO!!
Meanwhile, Sig...
I got caught...
We'll show you a good time!
I love big, strong men!
Let's have a drink!
C'MON! IT AIN'T THAT HARD!
GRAB
HOW ABOUT THIS?
I'LL SHOW HIM HOW TO CREATE A HOMUNCULUS...
...AND HIS BROTHER WILL TEACH ME HOW TO TRANSMUTE A SOUL.
GOT IT?
SO YOU WANNA MAKE A DEAL, HUH?

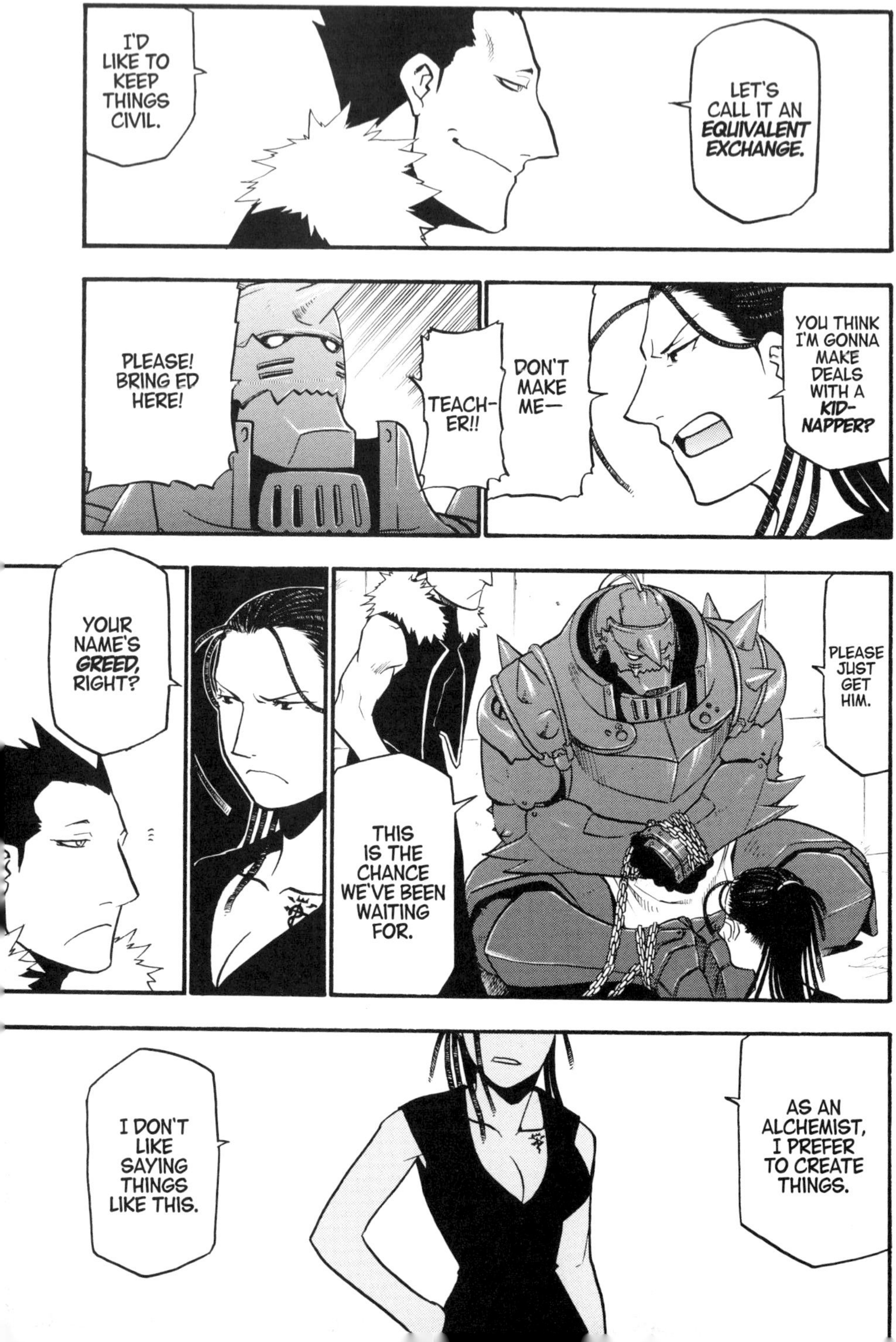
LET'S CALL IT AN **EQUIVALENT EXCHANGE.**
I'D LIKE TO KEEP THINGS CIVIL.
YOU THINK I'M GONNA MAKE DEALS WITH A ***KID-NAPPER?***
DON'T MAKE ME—
TEACHER!!
PLEASE! BRING ED HERE!
PLEASE JUST GET HIM.
THIS IS THE CHANCE WE'VE BEEN WAITING FOR.
YOUR NAME'S ***GREED,*** RIGHT?
AS AN ALCHEMIST, I PREFER TO CREATE THINGS.
I DON'T LIKE SAYING THINGS LIKE THIS.

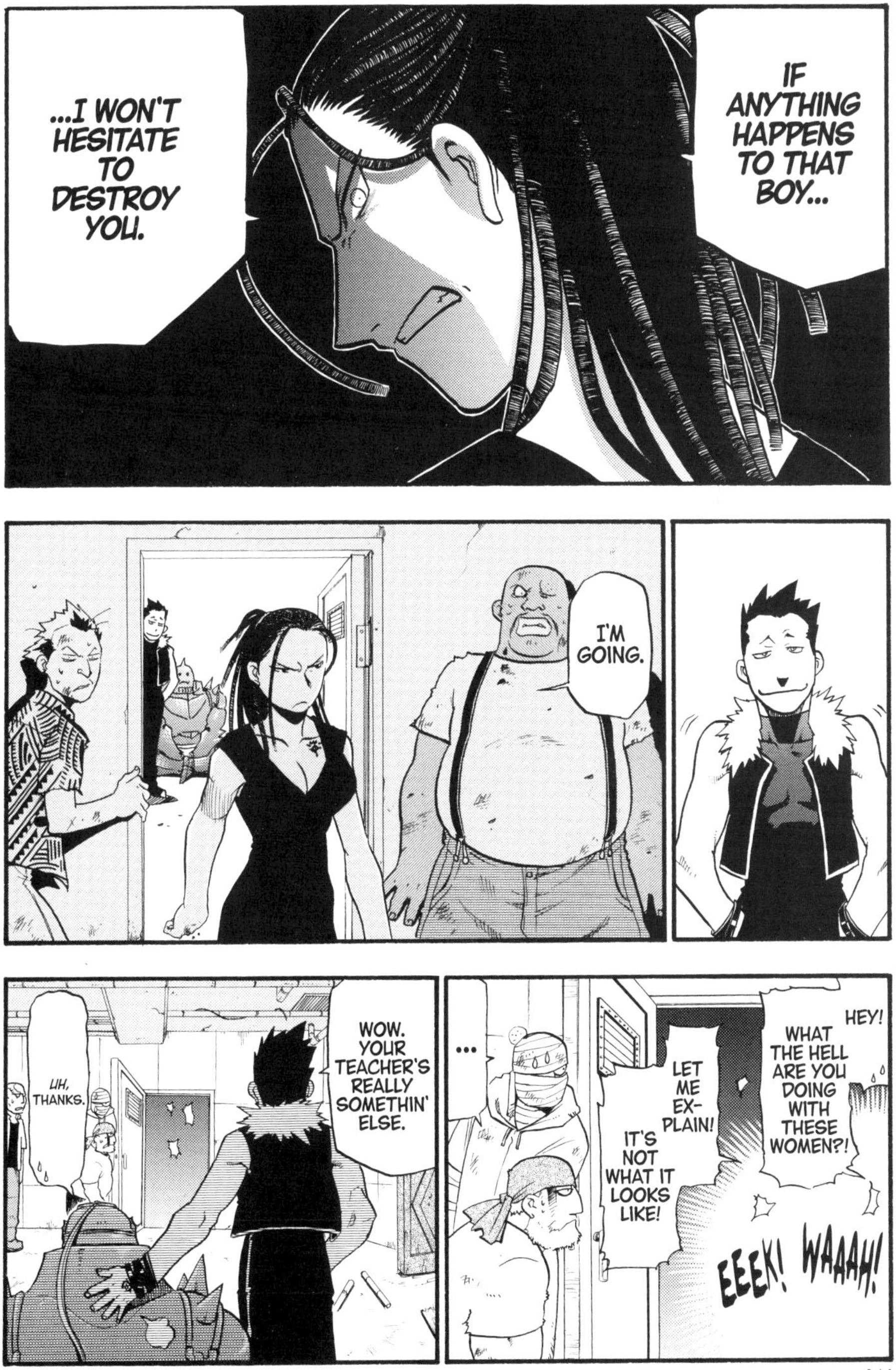
IF ANYTHING HAPPENS TO THAT BOY...
...I WON'T HESITATE TO DESTROY YOU.
I'M GOING.
HEY! WHAT THE HELL ARE YOU DOING WITH THESE WOMEN?!
LET ME EX-PLAIN!
IT'S NOT WHAT IT LOOKS LIKE!
EEEK! WAAAH!
...
WOW. YOUR TEACHER'S REALLY SOMETHIN' ELSE.
UH, THANKS.

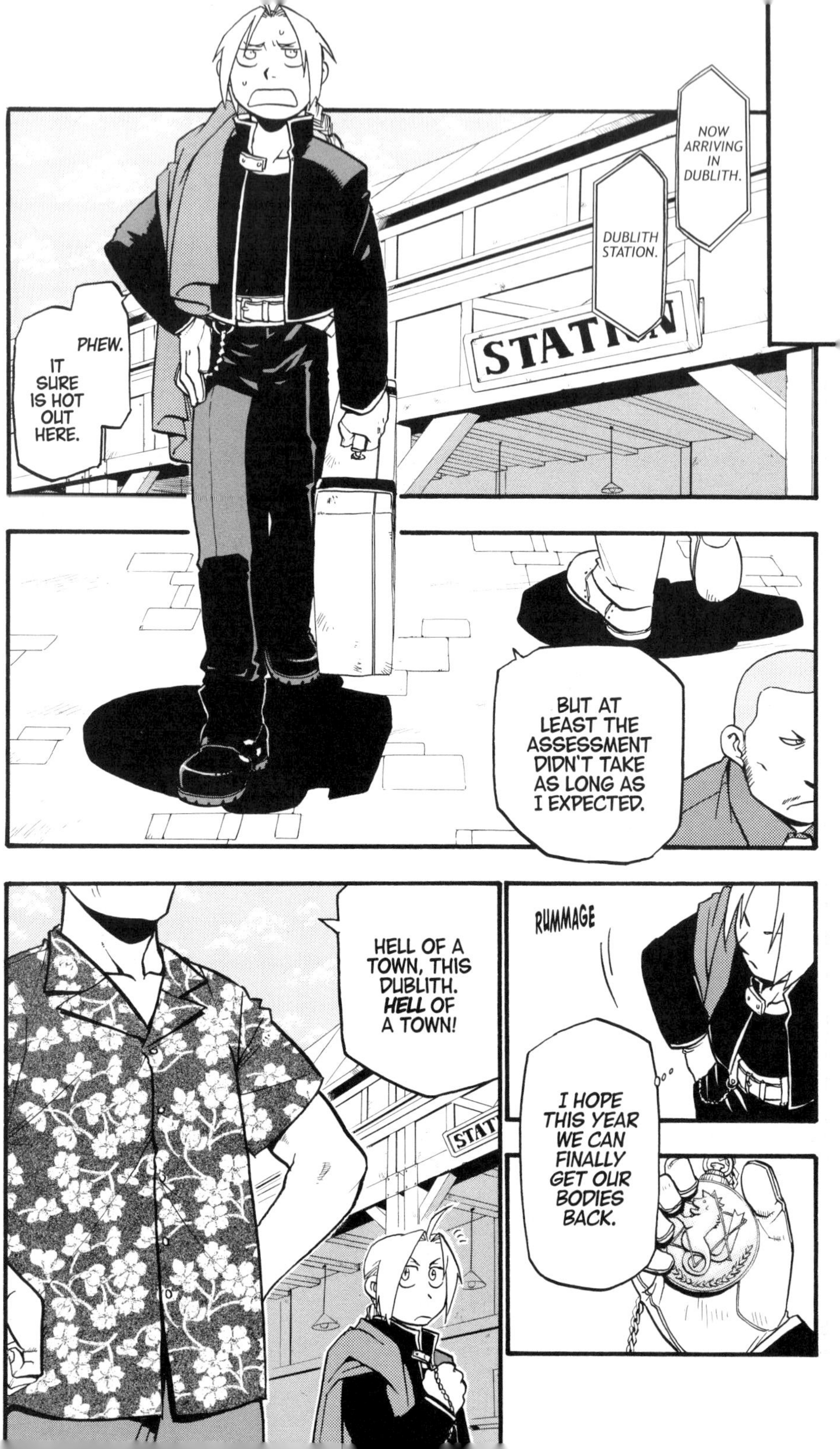
NOW ARRIVING IN DUBLITH.
DUBLITH STATION.
PHEW. IT SURE IS HOT OUT HERE.
BUT AT LEAST THE ASSESSMENT DIDN'T TAKE AS LONG AS I EXPECTED.
RUMMAGE
I HOPE THIS YEAR WE CAN FINALLY GET OUR BODIES BACK.
HELL OF A TOWN, THIS DUBLITH. HELL OF A TOWN!

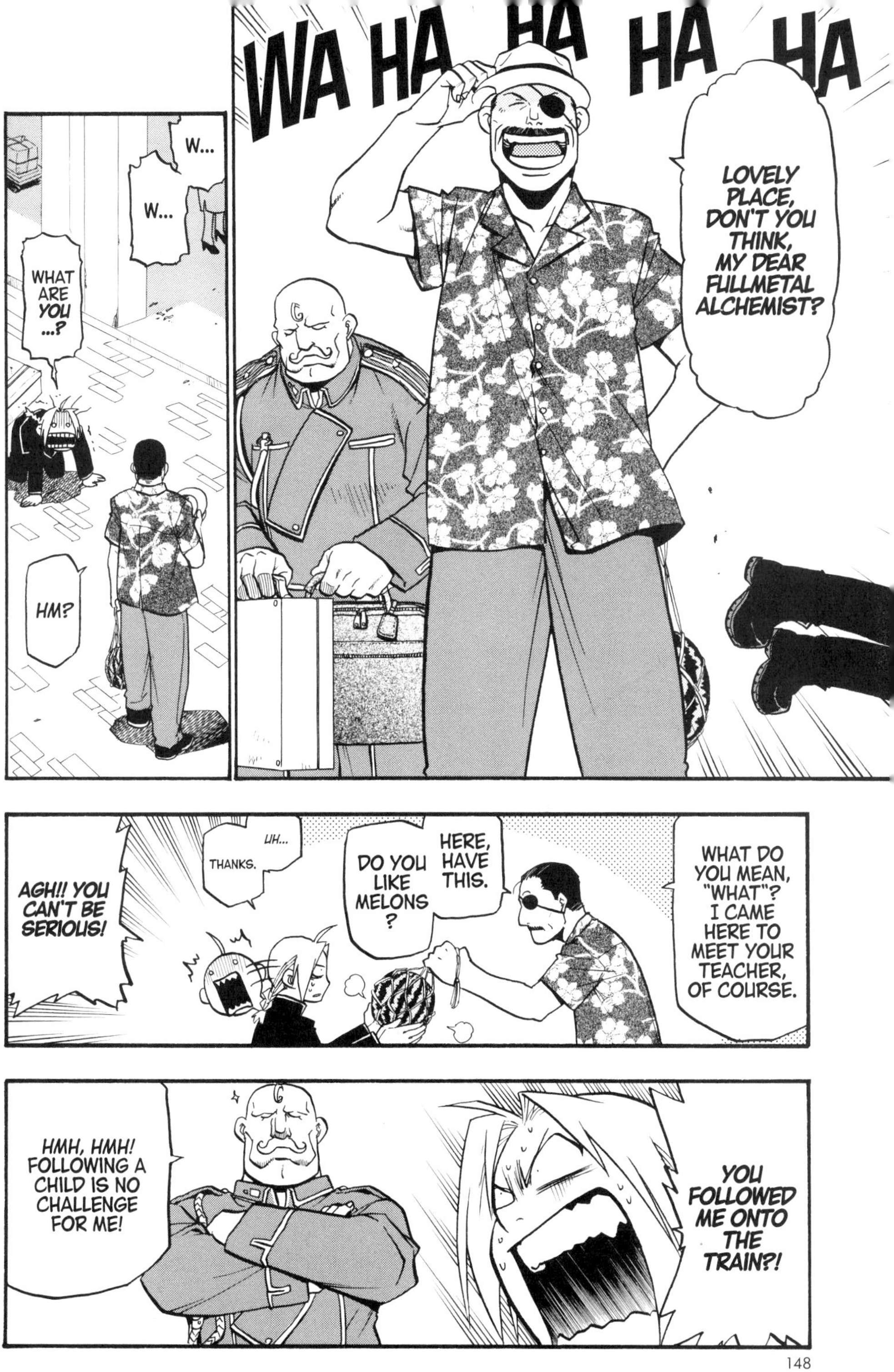
WA HA HA HA HA
LOVELY PLACE, DON'T YOU THINK, MY DEAR FULLMETAL ALCHEMIST?
W...
W...
WHAT ARE YOU ...?
HM?
WHAT DO YOU MEAN, "WHAT"? I CAME HERE TO MEET YOUR TEACHER, OF COURSE.
HERE, HAVE THIS.
DO YOU LIKE MELONS?
UH... THANKS.
AGH!! YOU CAN'T BE SERIOUS!
YOU FOLLOWED ME ONTO THE TRAIN?!
HMH, HMH! FOLLOWING A CHILD IS NO CHALLENGE FOR ME!

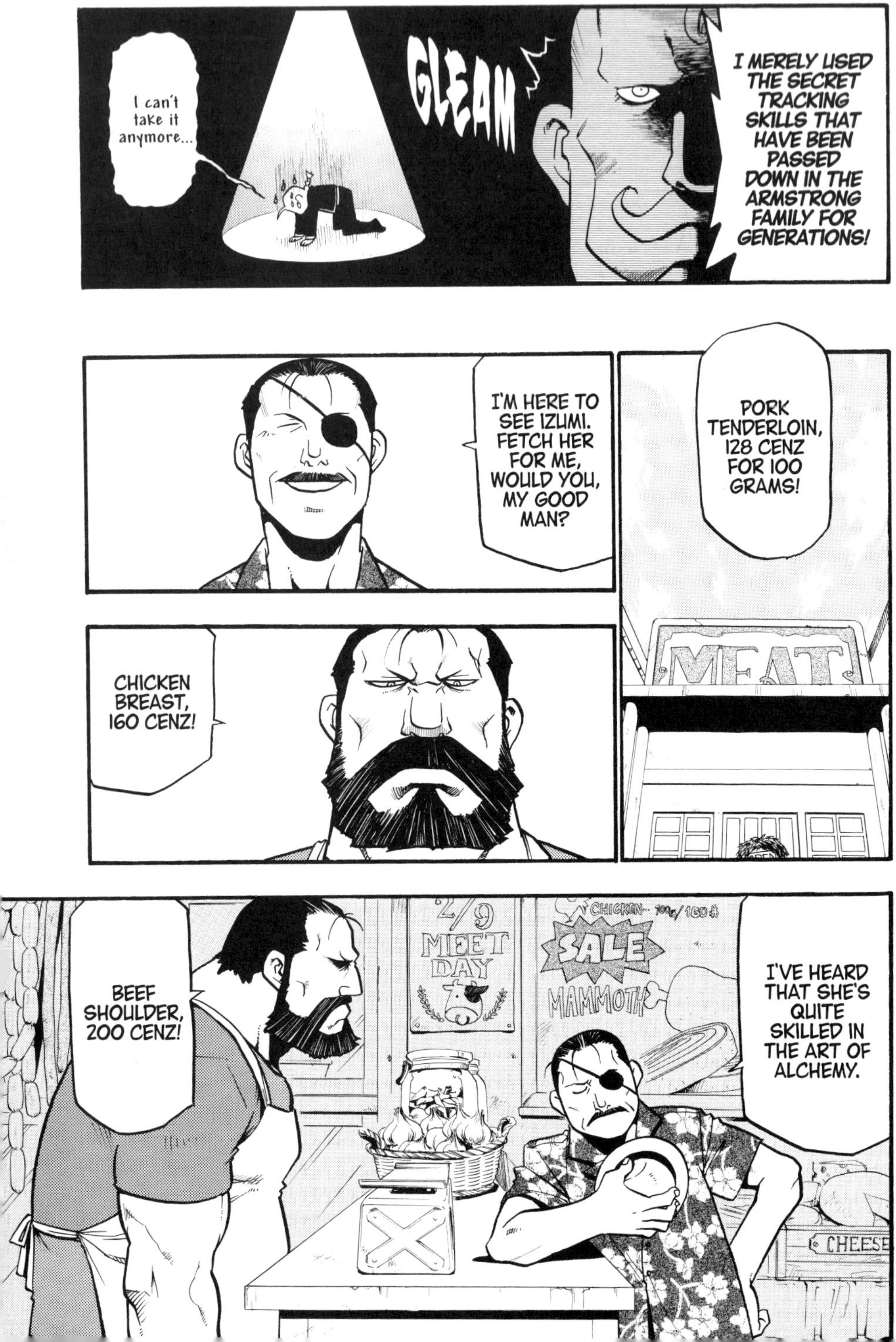

I MERELY USED THE SECRET TRACKING SKILLS THAT HAVE BEEN PASSED DOWN IN THE ARMSTRONG FAMILY FOR GENERATIONS!
GLEAM
I can't take it anymore...
PORK TENDERLOIN, 128 CENZ FOR 100 GRAMS!
MEAT
I'M HERE TO SEE IZUMI. FETCH HER FOR ME, WOULD YOU, MY GOOD MAN?
CHICKEN BREAST, 160 CENZ!
I'VE HEARD THAT SHE'S QUITE SKILLED IN THE ART OF ALCHEMY.
CHICKEN
SALE
MAMMOTH
2/9 MEET DAY
CHEESE
BEEF SHOULDER, 200 CENZ!

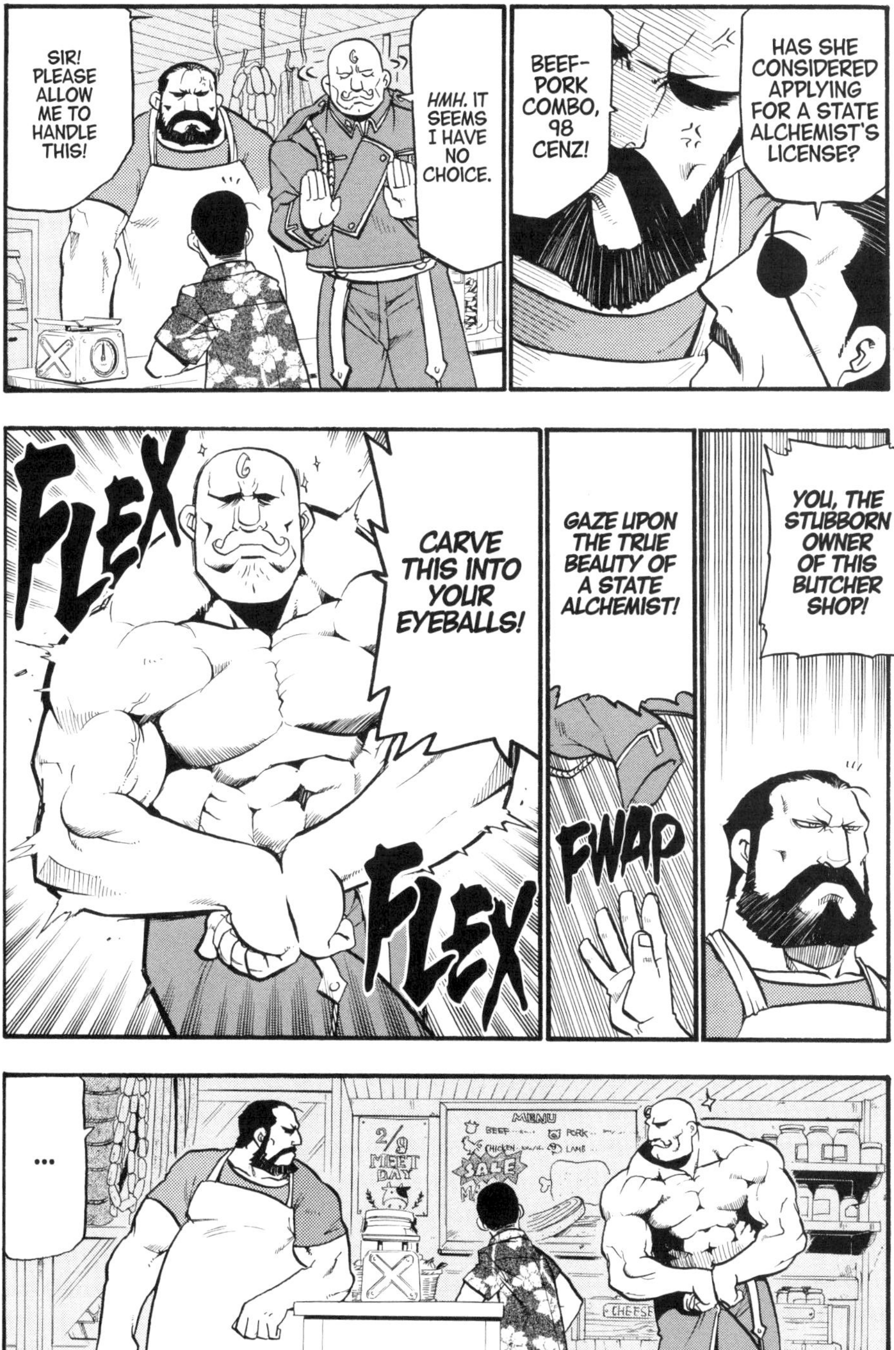
HAS SHE CONSIDERED APPLYING FOR A STATE ALCHEMIST'S LICENSE?
BEEF-PORK COMBO, 98 CENZ!
HMH. IT SEEMS I HAVE NO CHOICE.
SIR! PLEASE ALLOW ME TO HANDLE THIS!
YOU, THE STUBBORN OWNER OF THIS BUTCHER SHOP!
GAZE UPON THE TRUE BEAUTY OF A STATE ALCHEMIST!
FWAP
CARVE THIS INTO YOUR EYEBALLS!
FLEX
FLEX
MENU
BEEF
PORK
CHICKEN
LAMB
SALE
2/9 MEET DAY
CHEESE
...

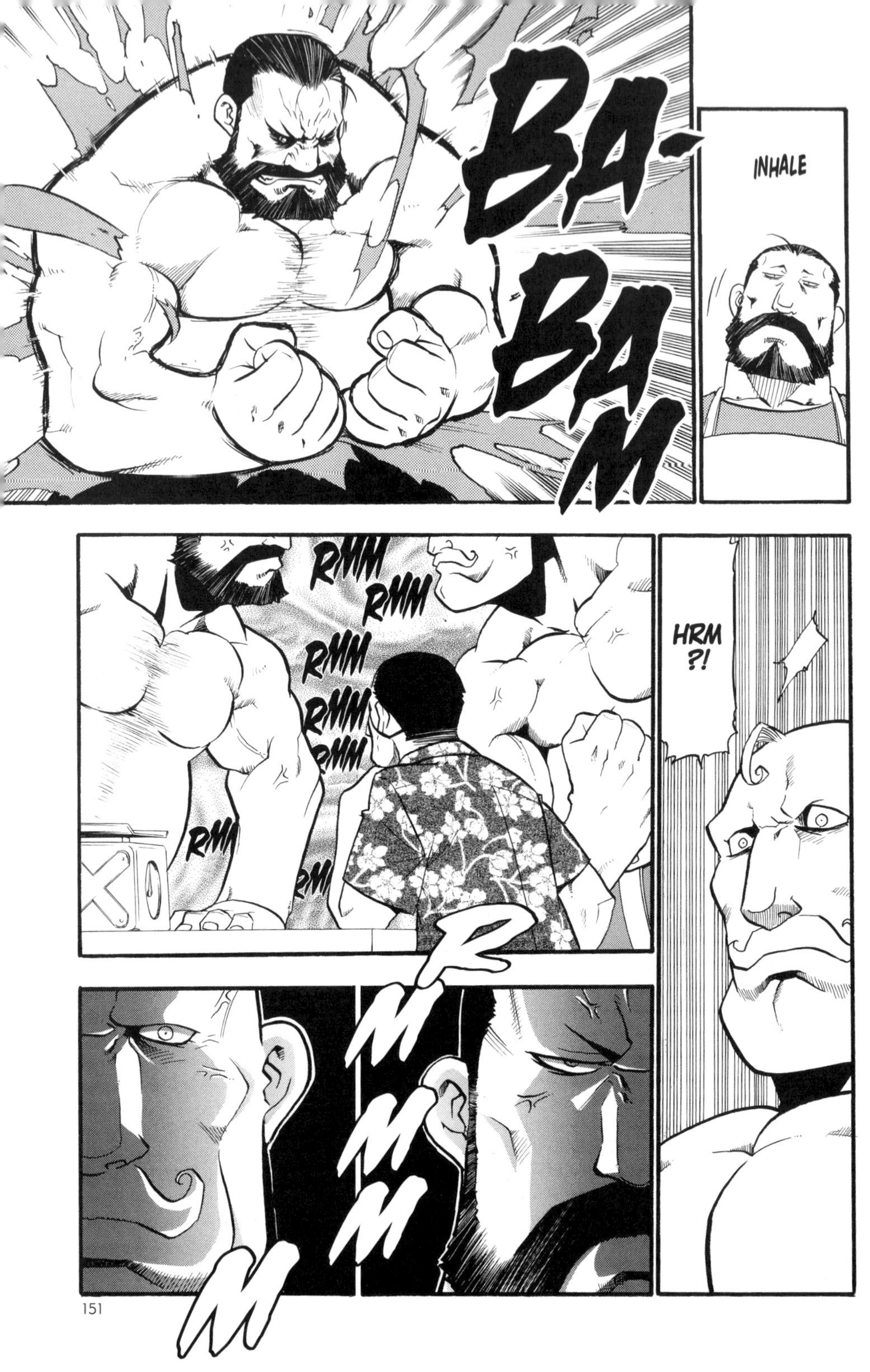
INHALE
BA-BA-BAM
HRM ?!
RMM
RMM
RMM
RMM
RMMMM

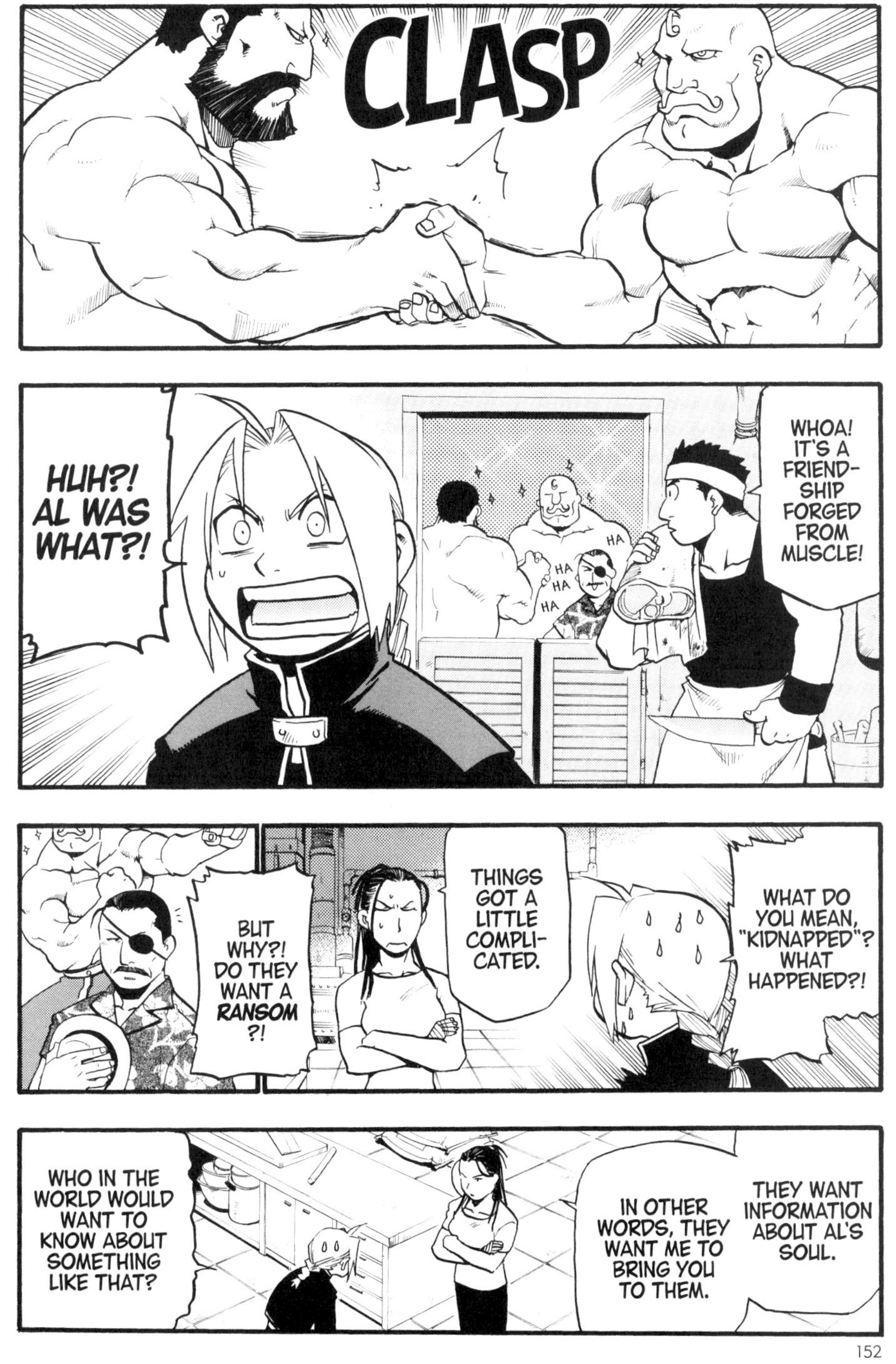
CLASP
WHOA! IT'S A FRIEND-SHIP FORGED FROM MUSCLE!
HA HA HA HA
HUH?! AL WAS WHAT?!
WHAT DO YOU MEAN, "KIDNAPPED"? WHAT HAPPENED?!
THINGS GOT A LITTLE COMPLI-CATED.
BUT WHY?! DO THEY WANT A RANSOM?!
THEY WANT INFORMATION ABOUT AL'S SOUL.
IN OTHER WORDS, THEY WANT ME TO BRING YOU TO THEM.
WHO IN THE WORLD WOULD WANT TO KNOW ABOUT SOMETHING LIKE THAT?

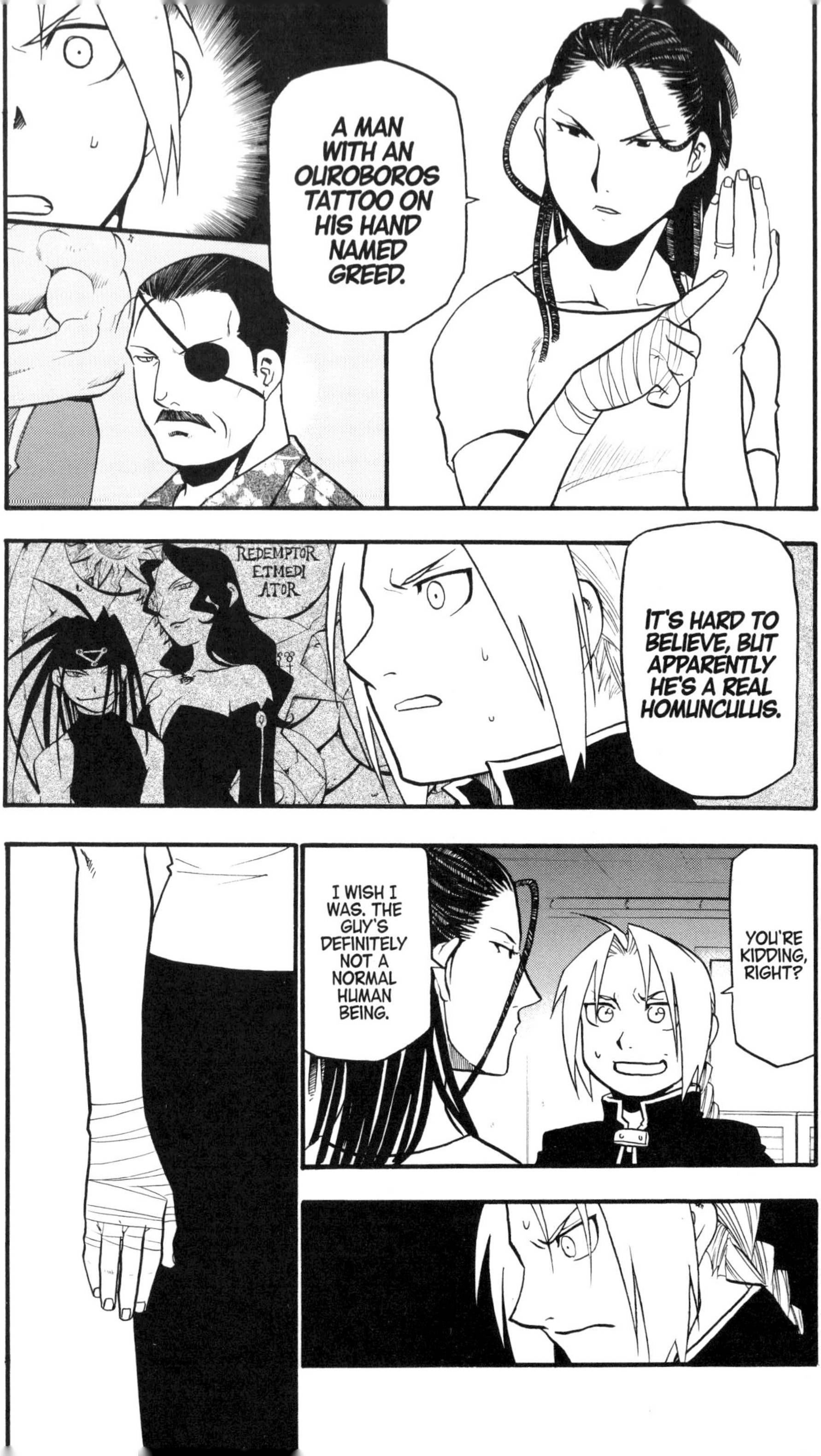
A MAN WITH AN OUROBOROS TATTOO ON HIS HAND NAMED GREED.
IT'S HARD TO BELIEVE, BUT APPARENTLY HE'S A REAL HOMUNCULUS.
REDEMPTOR ETMEDI ATOR
YOU'RE KIDDING, RIGHT?
I WISH I WAS. THE GUY'S DEFINITELY NOT A NORMAL HUMAN BEING.

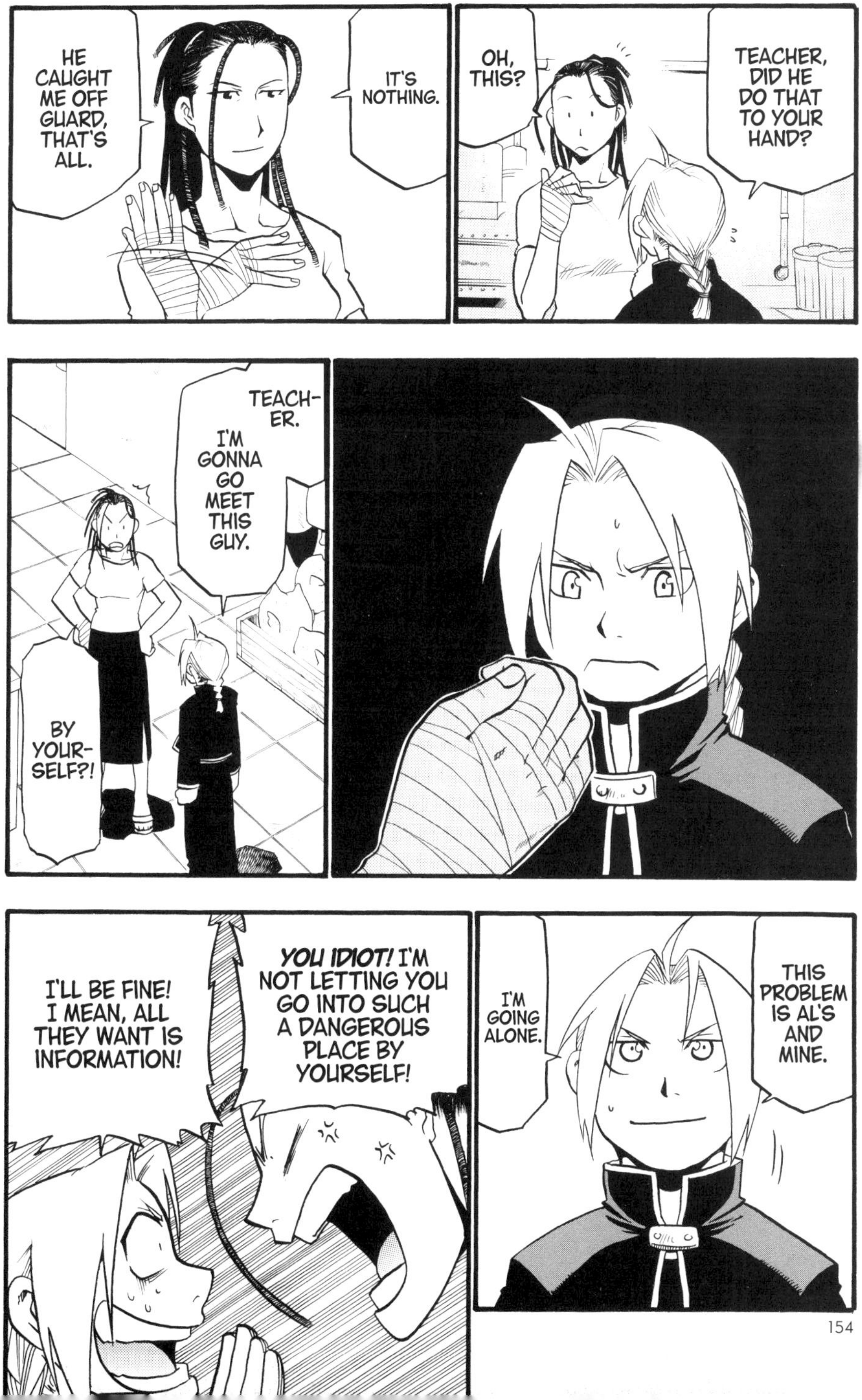

TEACHER, DID HE DO THAT TO YOUR HAND?
OH, THIS?
IT'S NOTHING.
HE CAUGHT ME OFF GUARD, THAT'S ALL.
TEACHER. I'M GONNA GO MEET THIS GUY.
BY YOURSELF?!
THIS PROBLEM IS AL'S AND MINE.
I'M GOING ALONE.
YOU IDIOT! I'M NOT LETTING YOU GO INTO SUCH A DANGEROUS PLACE BY YOURSELF!
I'LL BE FINE! I MEAN, ALL THEY WANT IS INFORMATION!

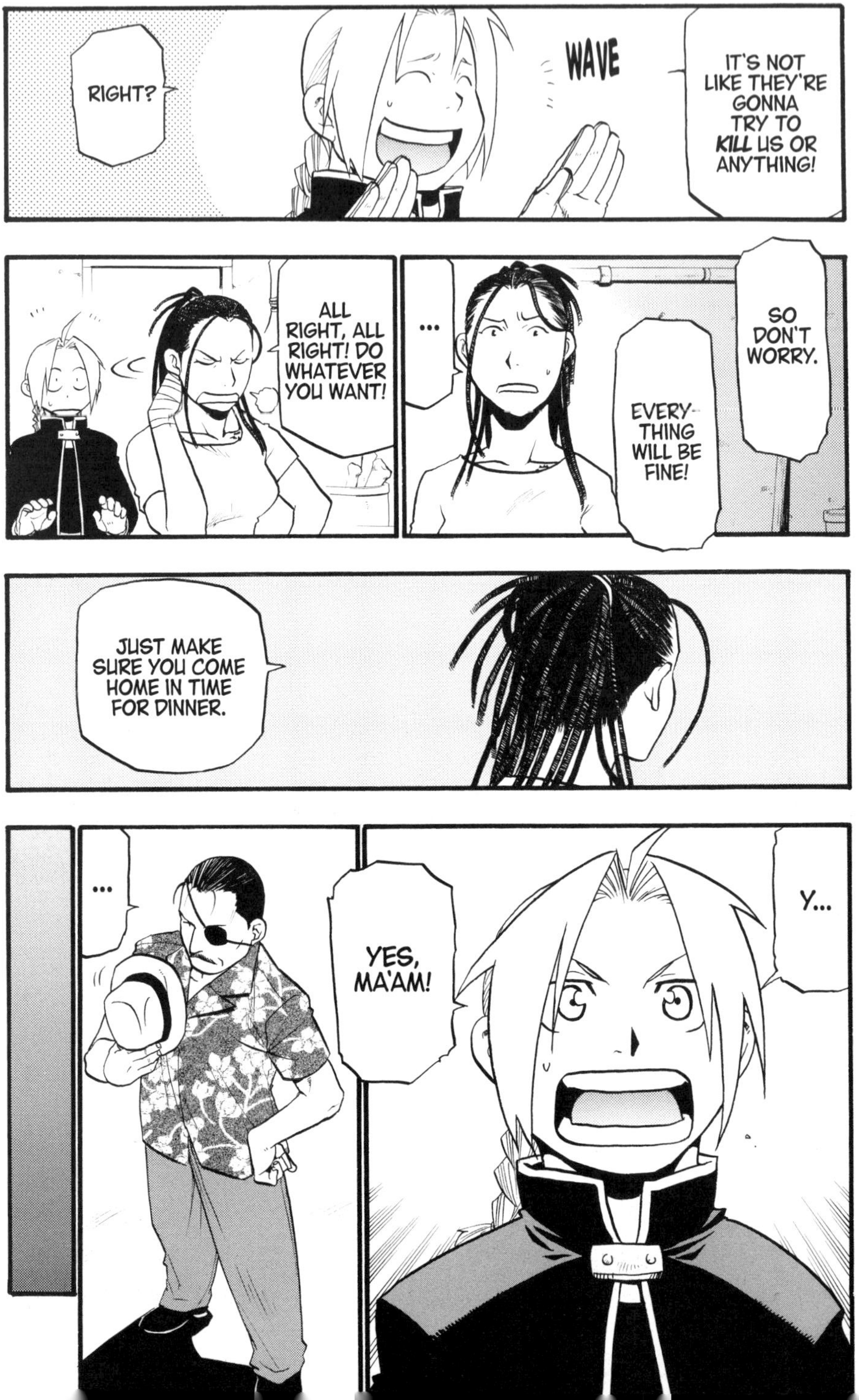
IT'S NOT LIKE THEY'RE GONNA TRY TO KILL US OR ANYTHING!
WAVE
RIGHT?
SO DON'T WORRY.
EVERYTHING WILL BE FINE!
...
ALL RIGHT, ALL RIGHT! DO WHATEVER YOU WANT!
JUST MAKE SURE YOU COME HOME IN TIME FOR DINNER.
Y...
YES, MA'AM!
...

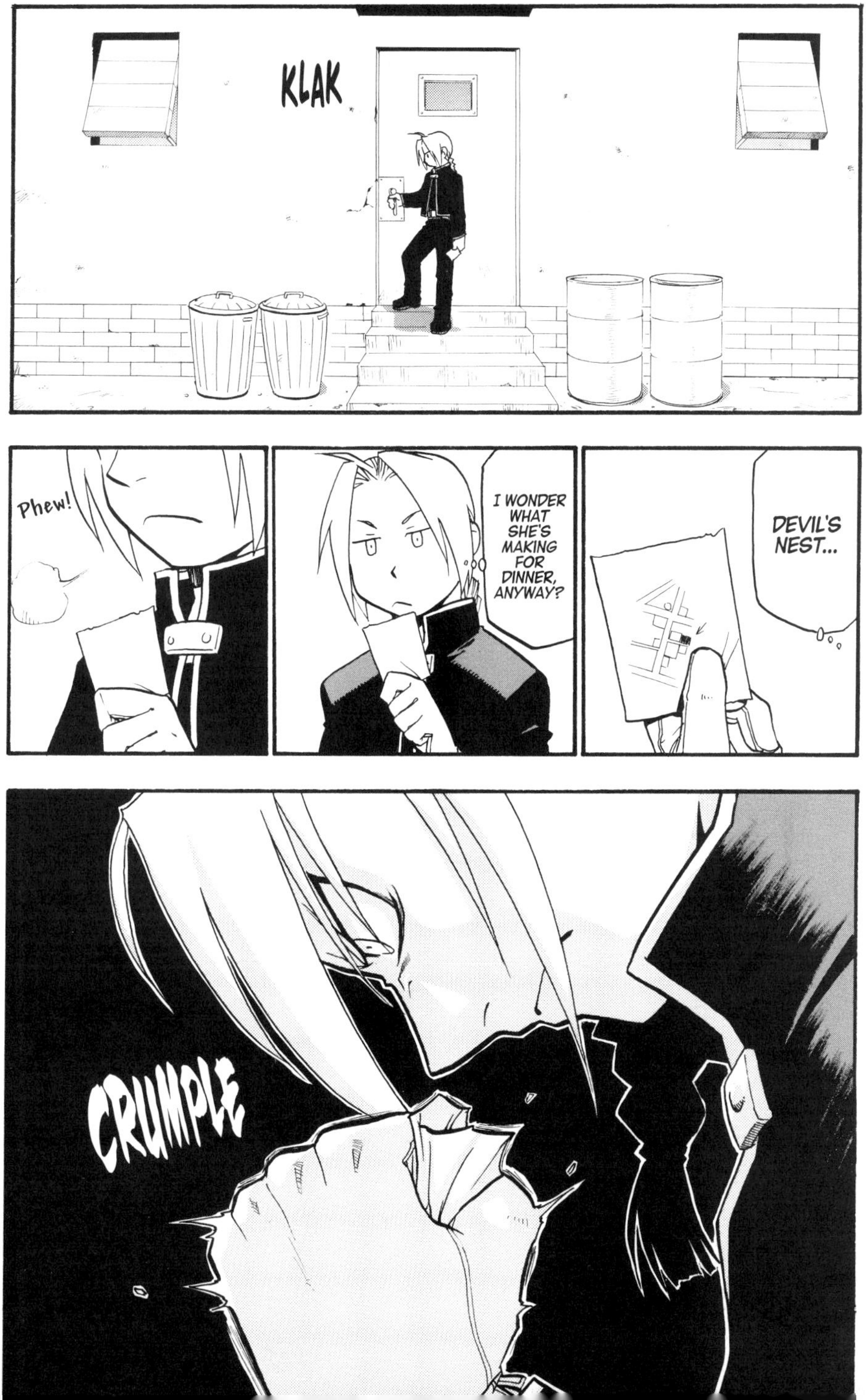
KLAK
DEVIL'S NEST...
I WONDER WHAT SHE'S MAKING FOR DINNER, ANYWAY?
Phew!
CRUMPLE

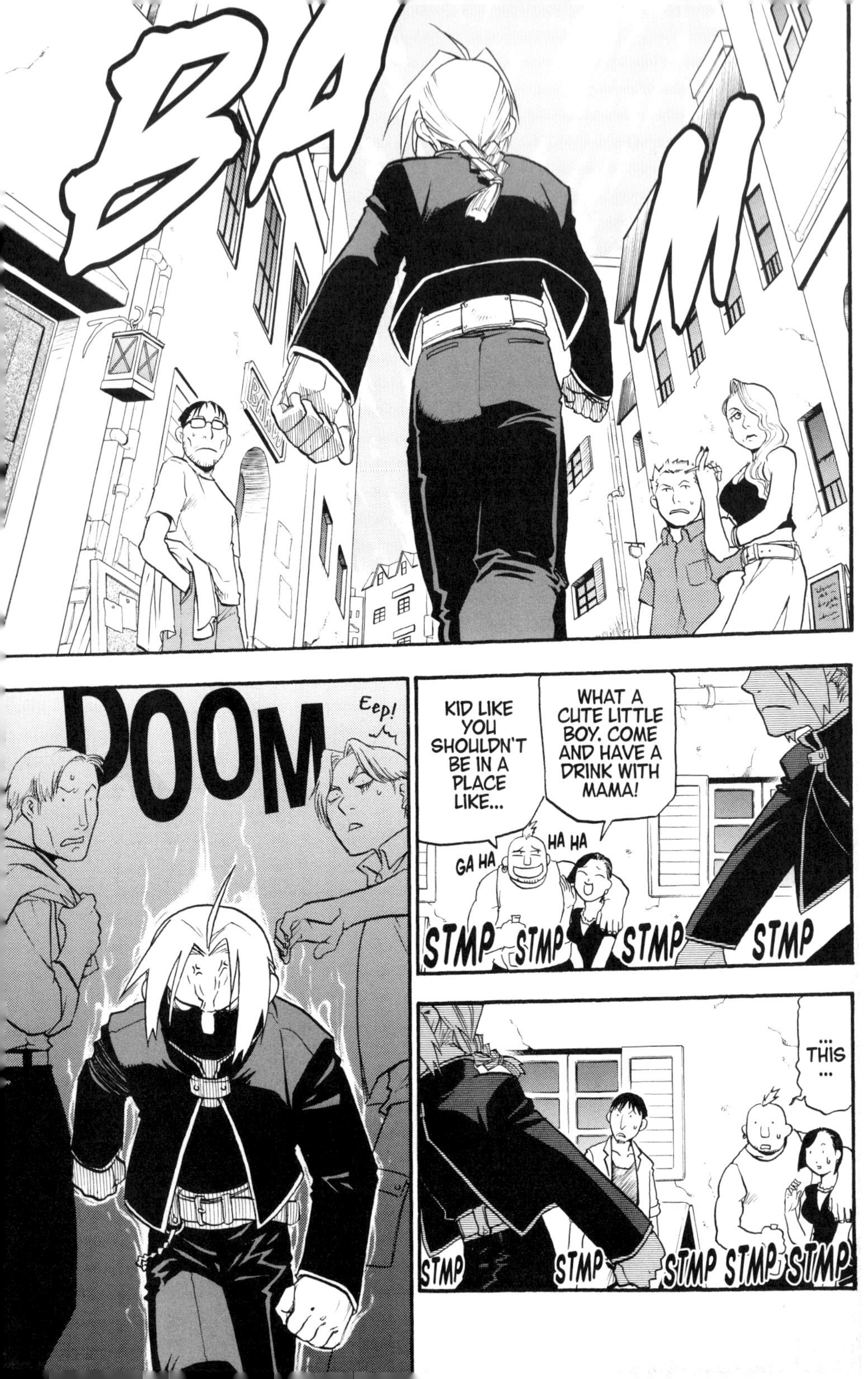
BAM
WHAT A CUTE LITTLE BOY. COME AND HAVE A DRINK WITH MAMA!
KID LIKE YOU SHOULDN'T BE IN A PLACE LIKE...
HA HA
GA HA
STMP
STMP
STMP
STMP
... THIS ...
STMP
STMP
STMP
STMP
STMP
Eep!
DOOM

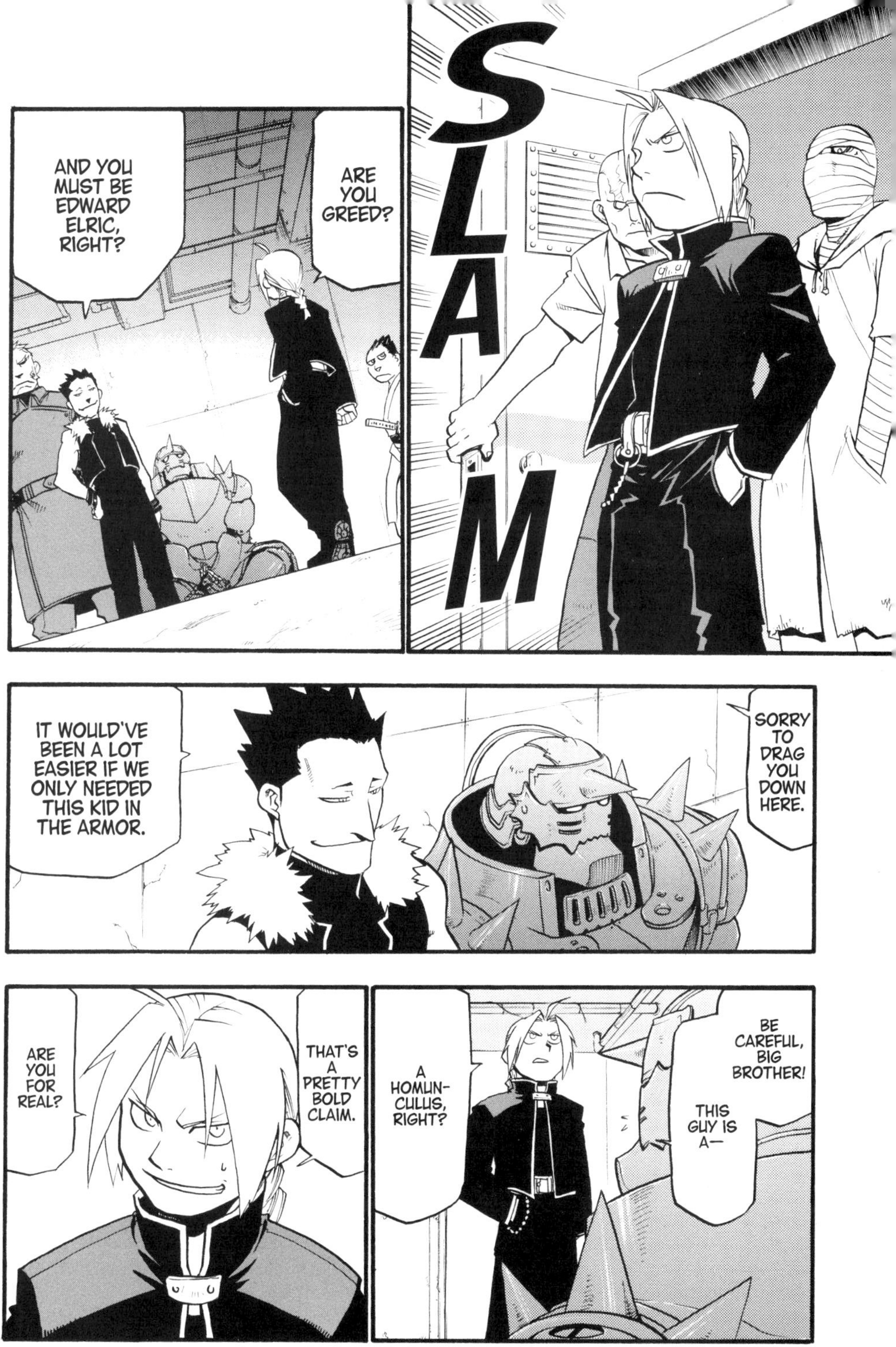
SLAM
ARE YOU GREED?
AND YOU MUST BE EDWARD ELRIC, RIGHT?
SORRY TO DRAG YOU DOWN HERE.
IT WOULD'VE BEEN A LOT EASIER IF WE ONLY NEEDED THIS KID IN THE ARMOR.
BE CAREFUL, BIG BROTHER!
THIS GUY IS A—
A HOMUN-CULUS, RIGHT?
THAT'S A PRETTY BOLD CLAIM.
ARE YOU FOR REAL?

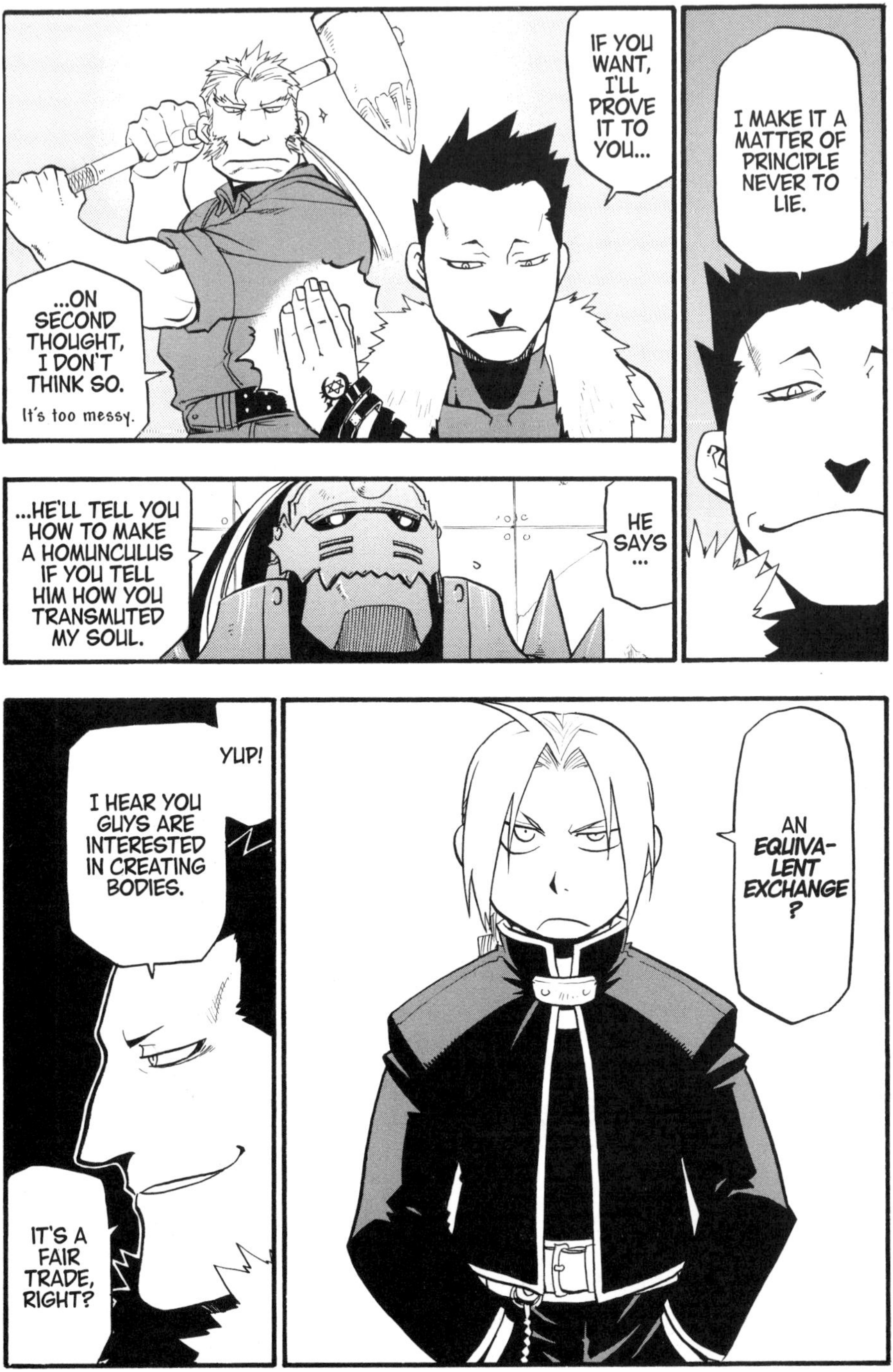

I MAKE IT A MATTER OF PRINCIPLE NEVER TO LIE.
IF YOU WANT, I'LL PROVE IT TO YOU...
...ON SECOND THOUGHT, I DON'T THINK SO.
It's too messy.
HE SAYS...
...HE'LL TELL YOU HOW TO MAKE A HOMUNCULUS IF YOU TELL HIM HOW YOU TRANSMUTED MY SOUL.
AN EQUIVALENT EXCHANGE?
YUP!
I HEAR YOU GUYS ARE INTERESTED IN CREATING BODIES.
IT'S A FAIR TRADE, RIGHT?

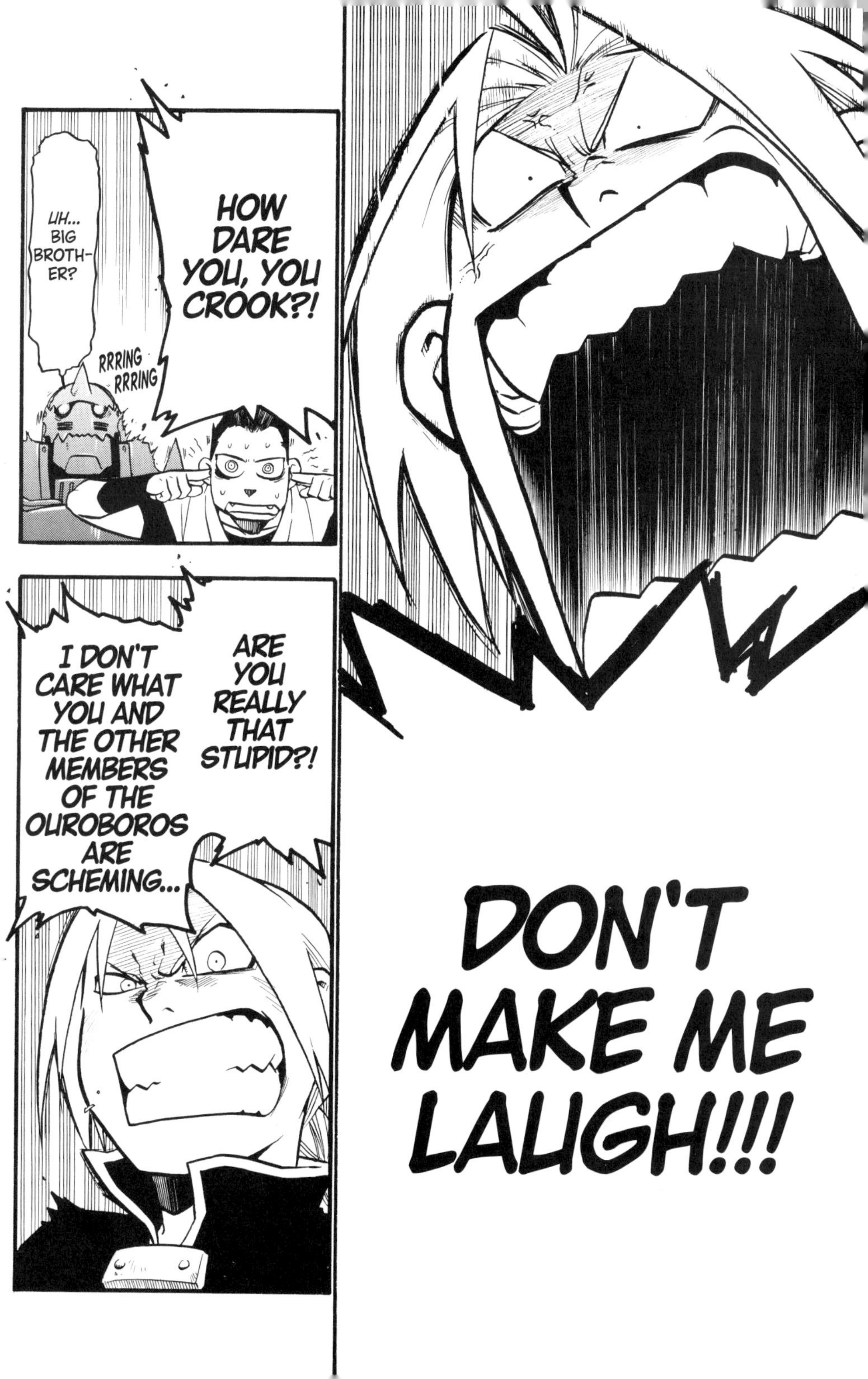
UH... BIG BROTH-ER?
HOW DARE YOU, YOU CROOK?!
RRRING RRRING
I DON'T CARE WHAT YOU AND THE OTHER MEMBERS OF THE OUROBOROS ARE SCHEMING...
ARE YOU REALLY THAT STUPID?!
DON'T MAKE ME LAUGH!!!

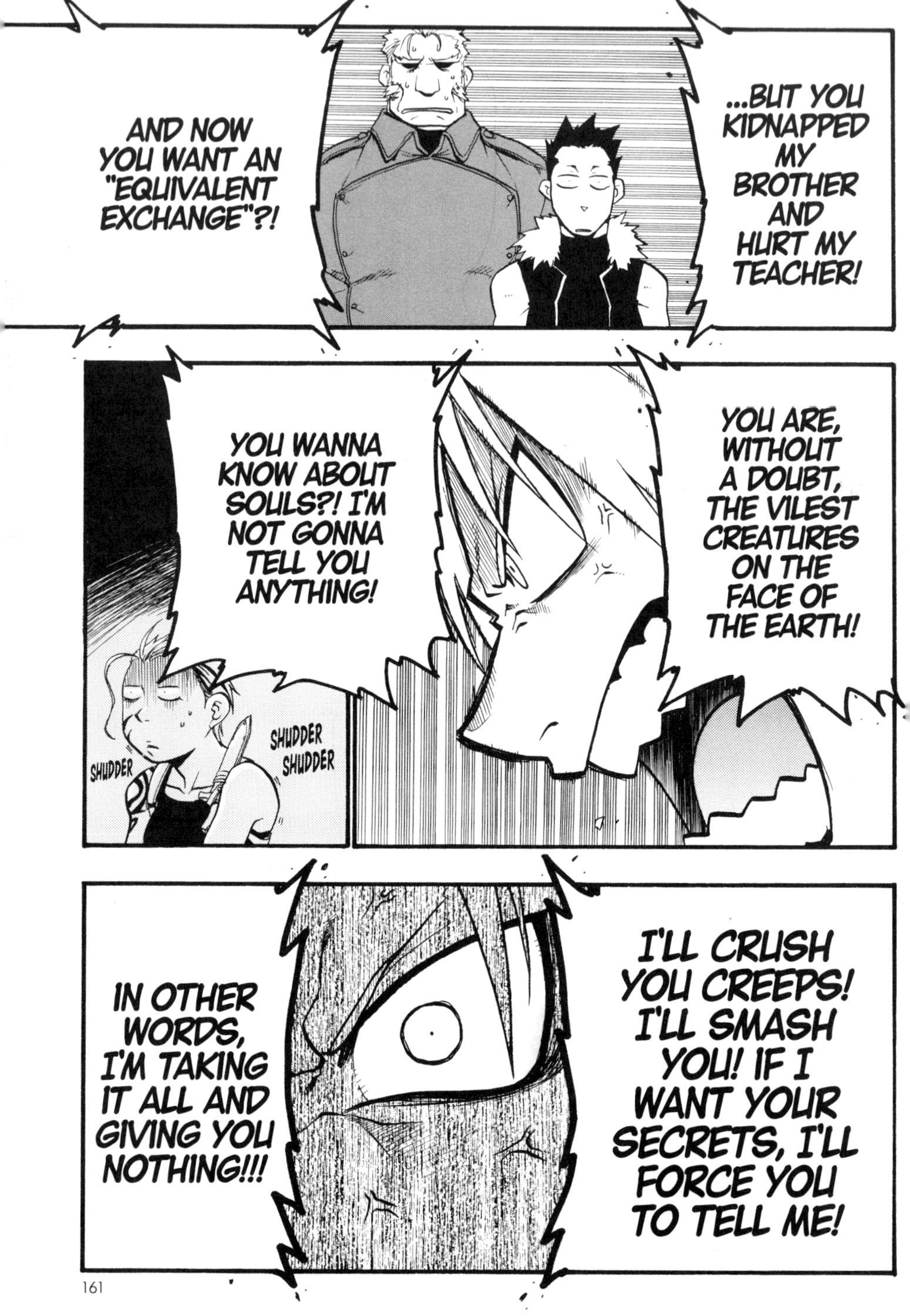
...BUT YOU KIDNAPPED MY BROTHER AND HURT MY TEACHER!
AND NOW YOU WANT AN "EQUIVALENT EXCHANGE"?!
YOU ARE, WITHOUT A DOUBT, THE VILEST CREATURES ON THE FACE OF THE EARTH!
YOU WANNA KNOW ABOUT SOULS?! I'M NOT GONNA TELL YOU ANYTHING!
SHUDDER SHUDDER
SHUDDER
I'LL CRUSH YOU CREEPS! I'LL SMASH YOU! IF I WANT YOUR SECRETS, I'LL FORCE YOU TO TELL ME!
IN OTHER WORDS, I'M TAKING IT ALL AND GIVING YOU NOTHING!!!

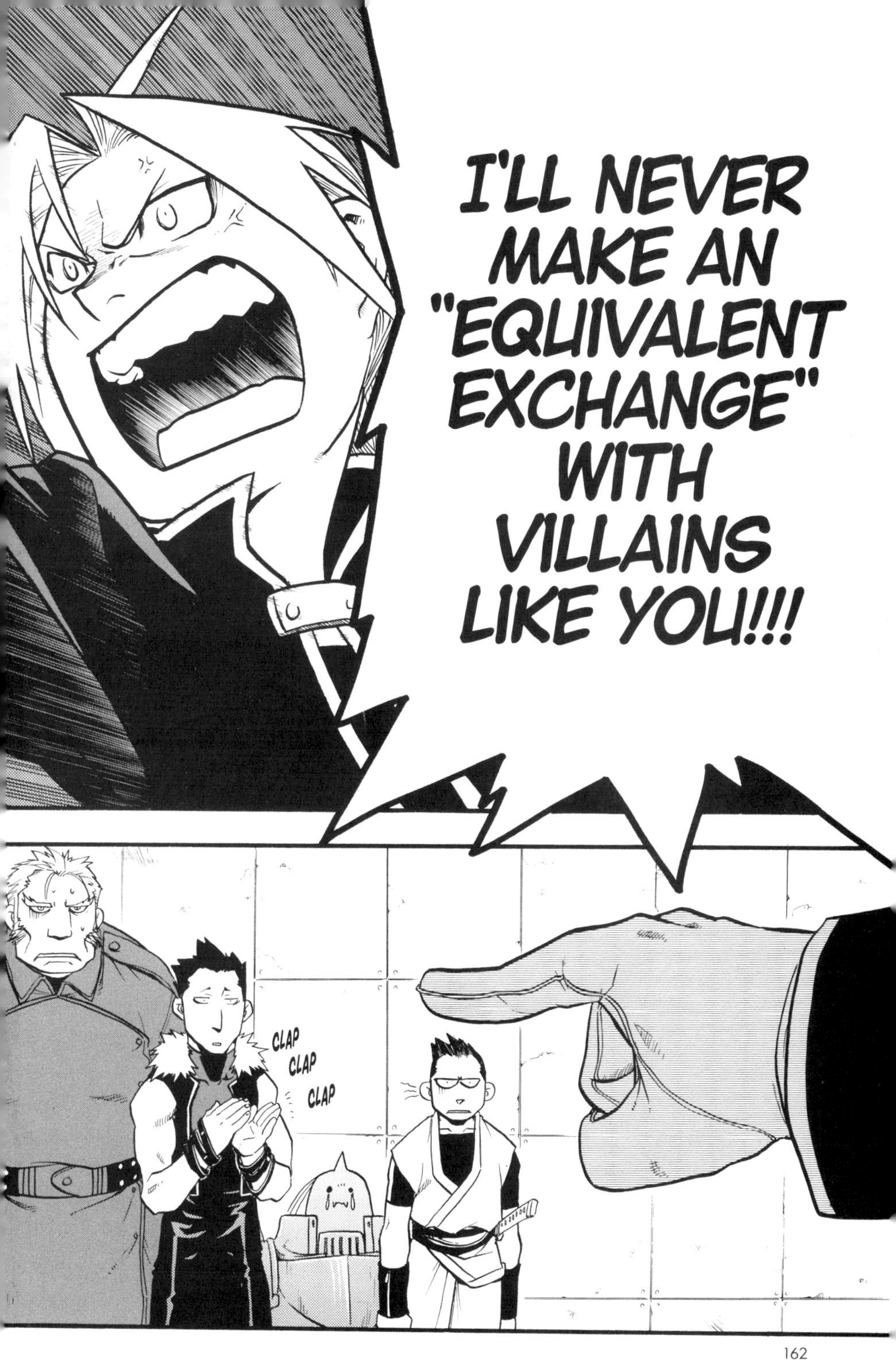
I'LL NEVER MAKE AN "EQUIVALENT EXCHANGE" WITH VILLAINS LIKE YOU!!!
CLAP
CLAP
CLAP

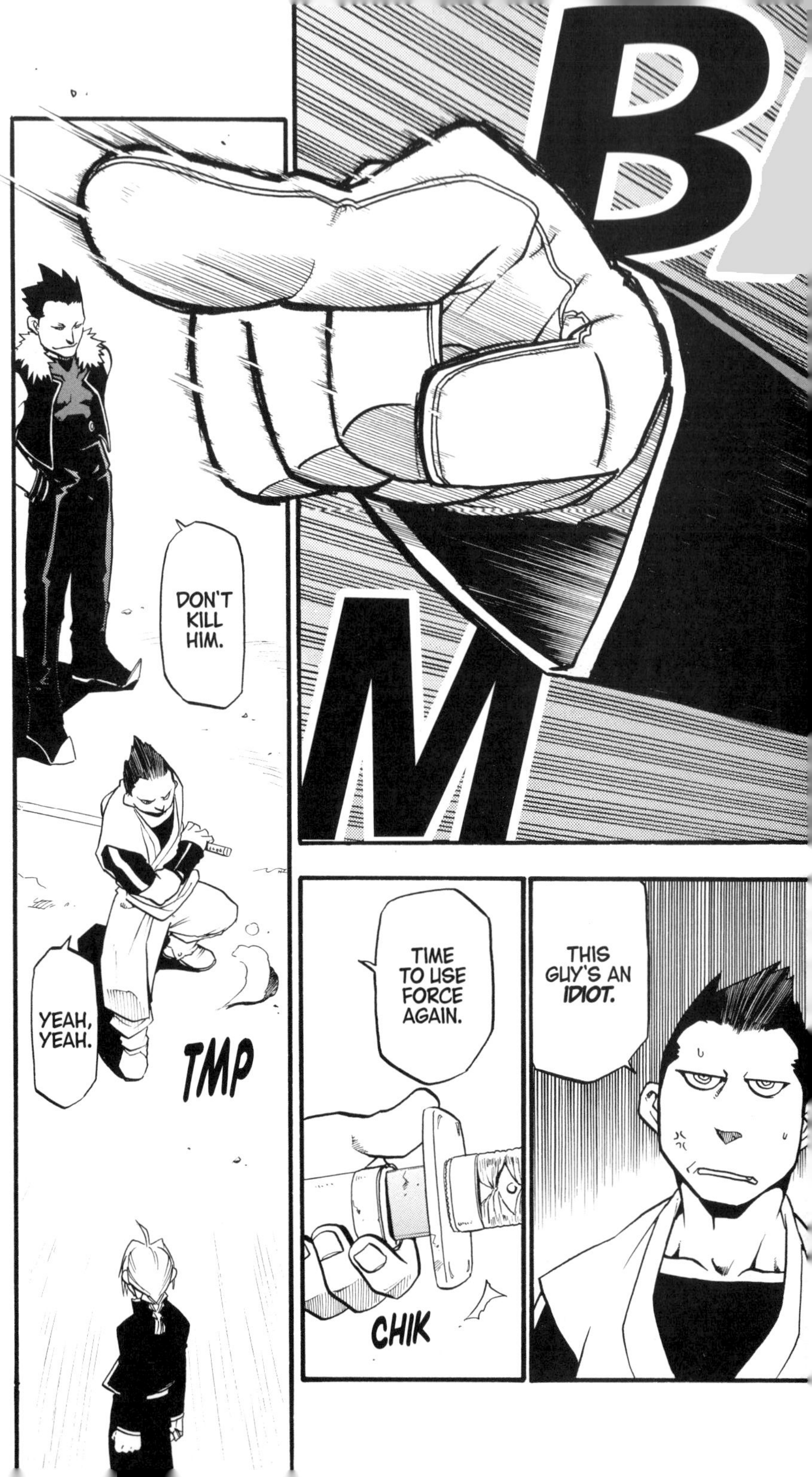
B
M
THIS GUY'S AN IDIOT.
TIME TO USE FORCE AGAIN.
CHIK
DON'T KILL HIM.
YEAH, YEAH.
TMP

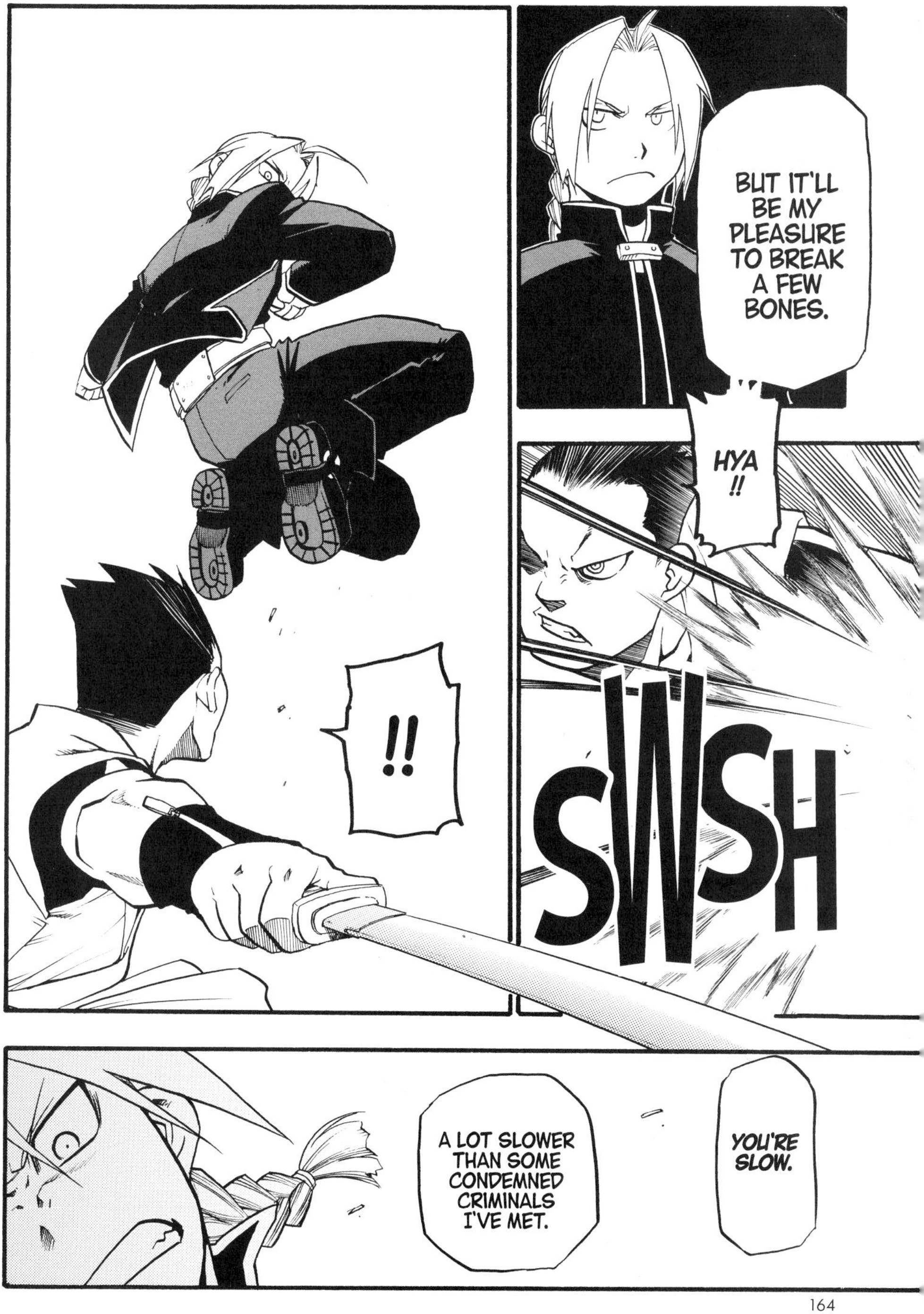
BUT IT'LL BE MY PLEASURE TO BREAK A FEW BONES.
HYA !!
SWSH
!!
YOU'RE SLOW.
A LOT SLOWER THAN SOME CONDEMNED CRIMINALS I'VE MET.

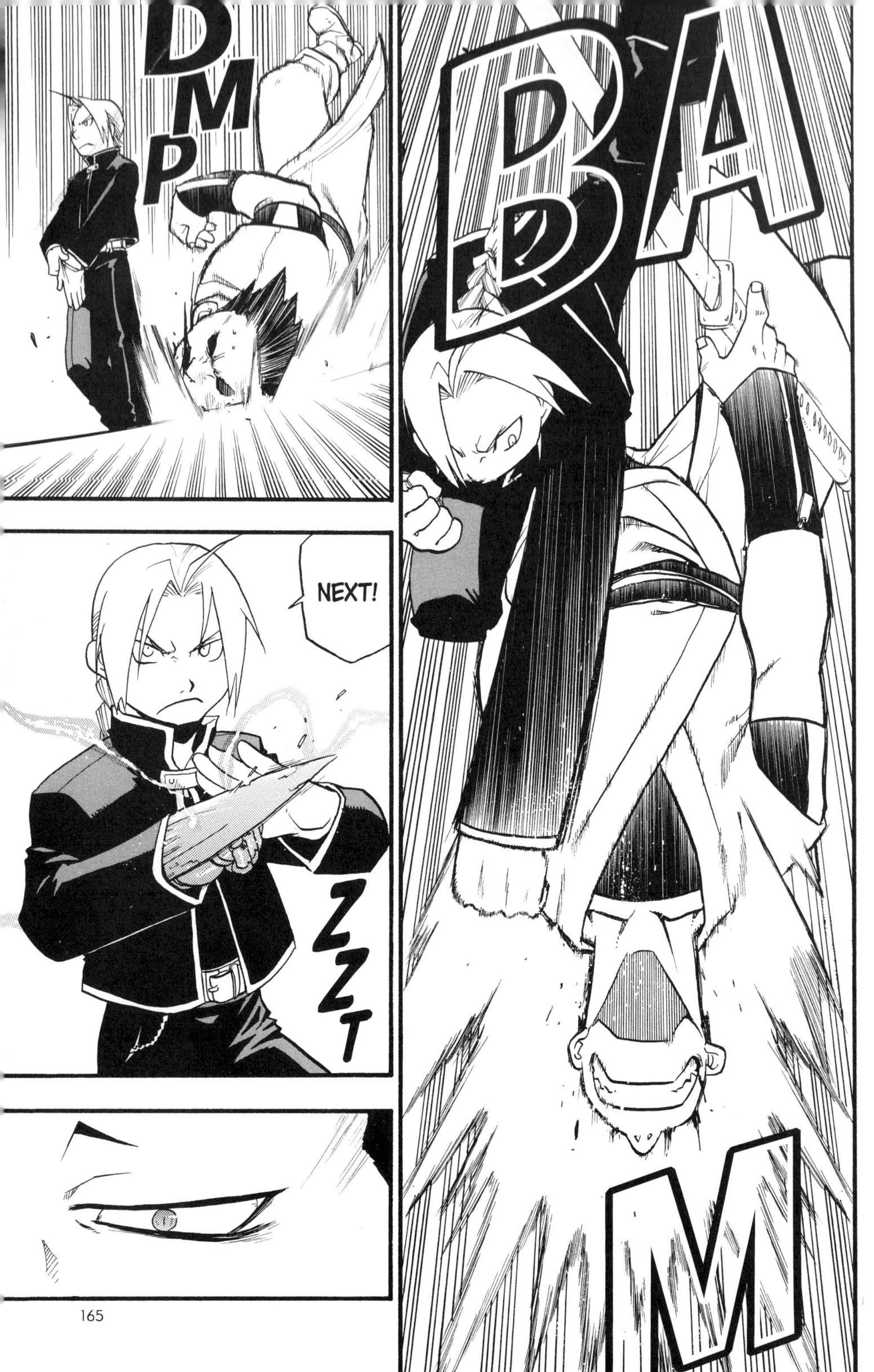
BAM
DMP
NEXT!
ZZT

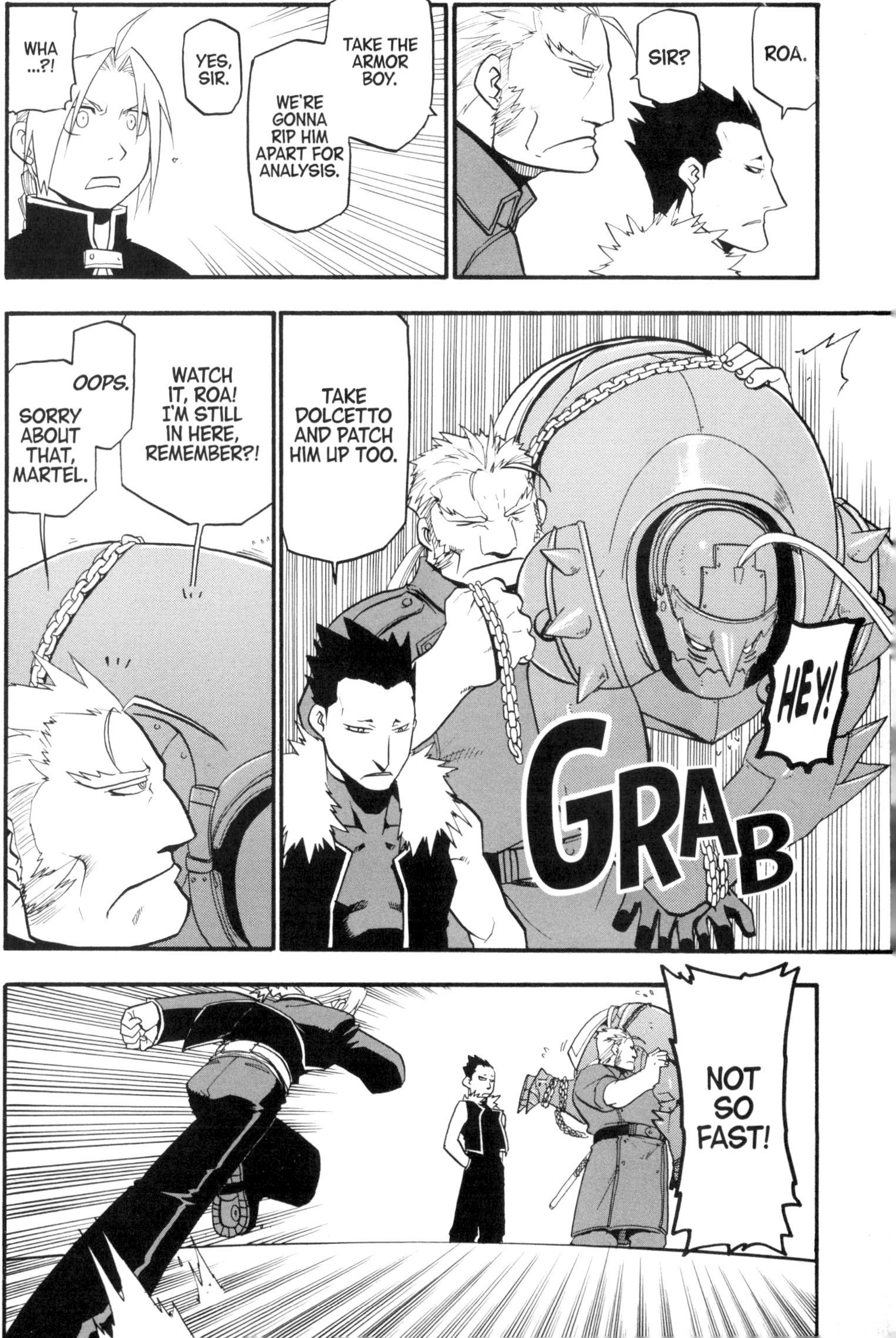
ROA.
SIR?
TAKE THE ARMOR BOY.
WE'RE GONNA RIP HIM APART FOR ANALYSIS.
YES, SIR.
WHA ...?!
TAKE DOLCETTO AND PATCH HIM UP TOO.
HEY!
GRAB
WATCH IT, ROA! I'M STILL IN HERE, REMEMBER?!
OOPS.
SORRY ABOUT THAT, MARTEL.
NOT SO FAST!

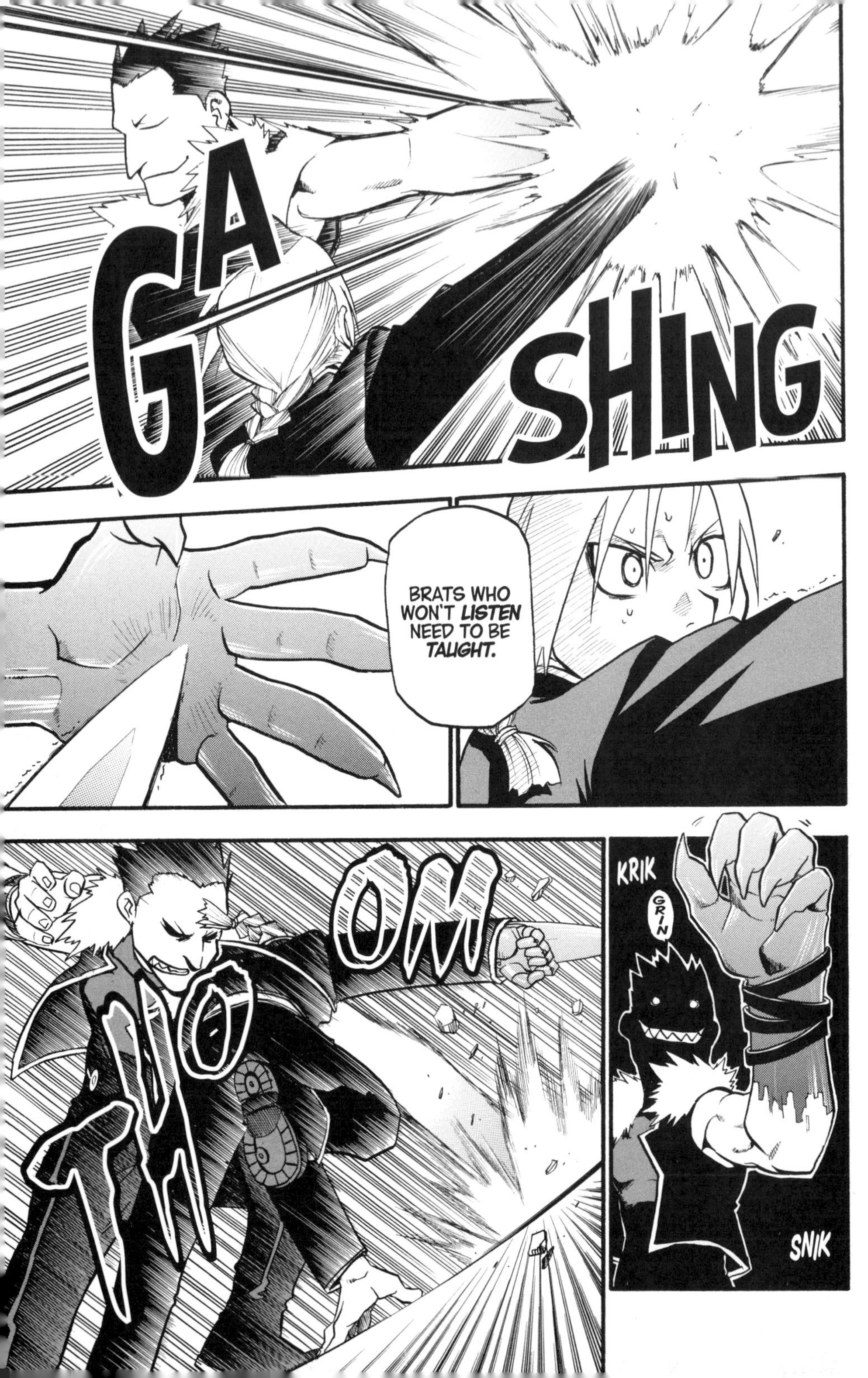
GASHING
BRATS WHO WON'T *LISTEN* NEED TO BE *TAUGHT.*
KRIK
GRIN
SNIK
WHOOM

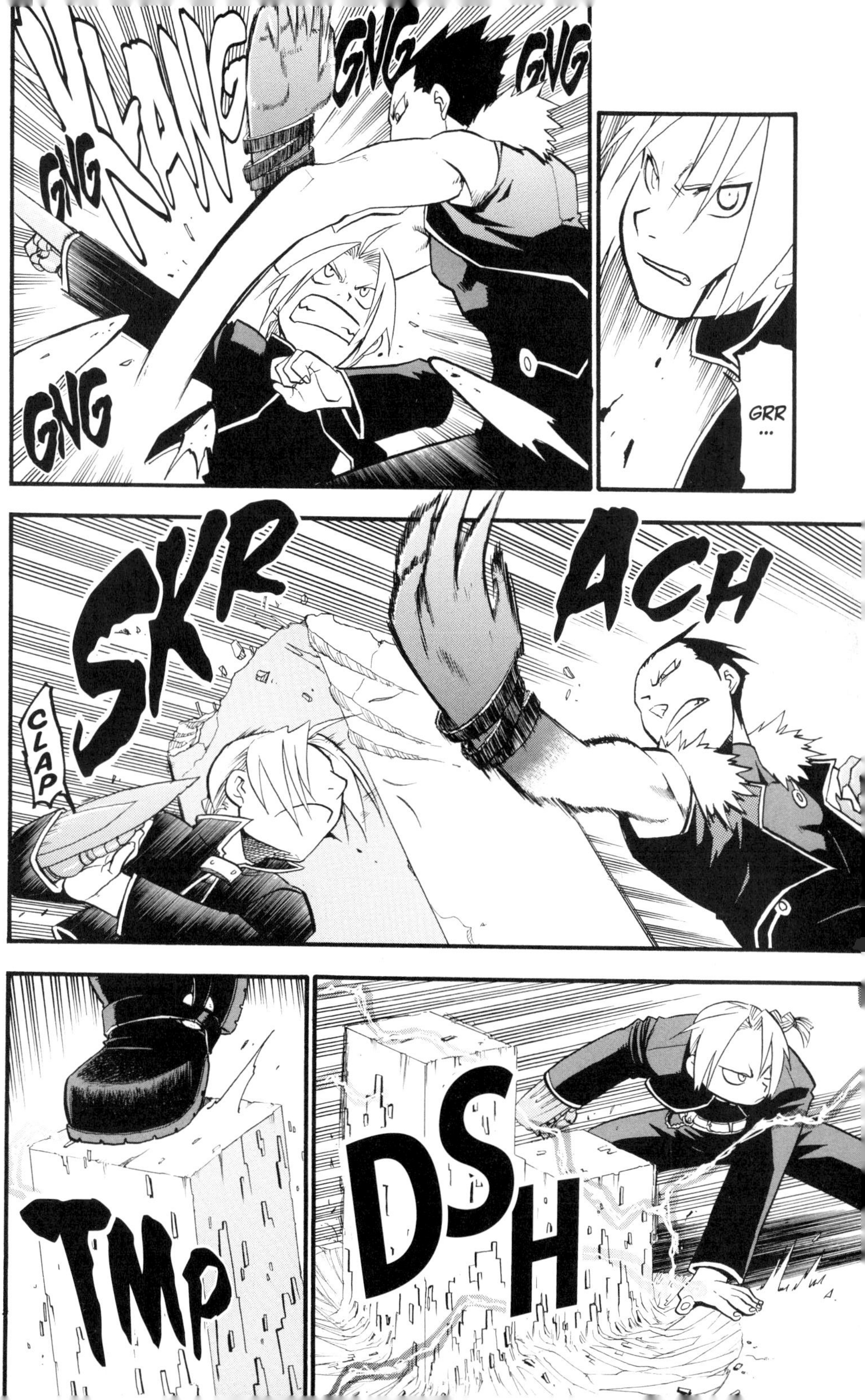
GRR ...
GNG
GNG
GNG
GNG
SKR ACH
CLAP
DSH
TMP

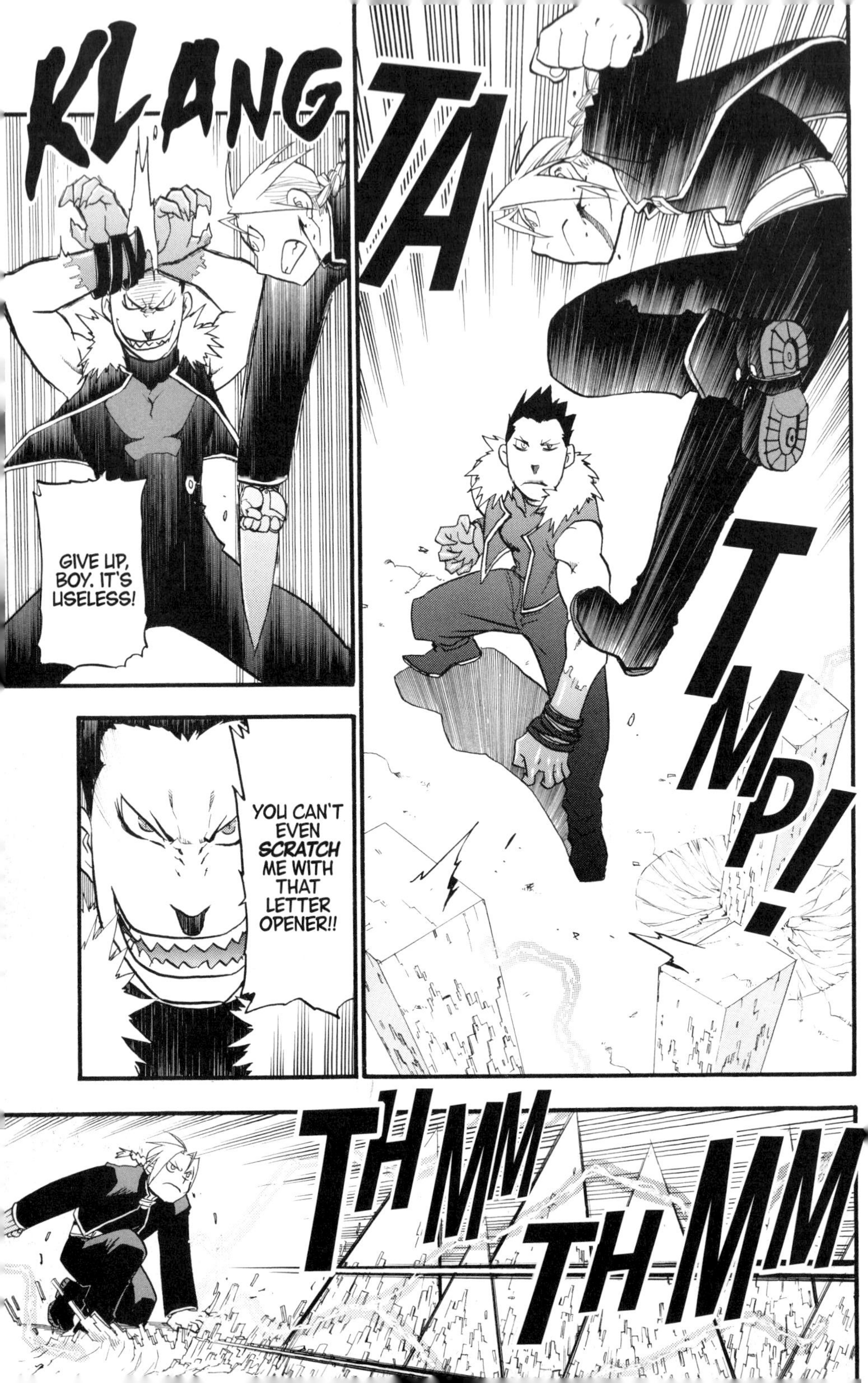
TA
TMP!
KLANG
GIVE UP, BOY. IT'S USELESS!
YOU CAN'T EVEN **SCRATCH** ME WITH THAT LETTER OPENER!!
THMM
THMM

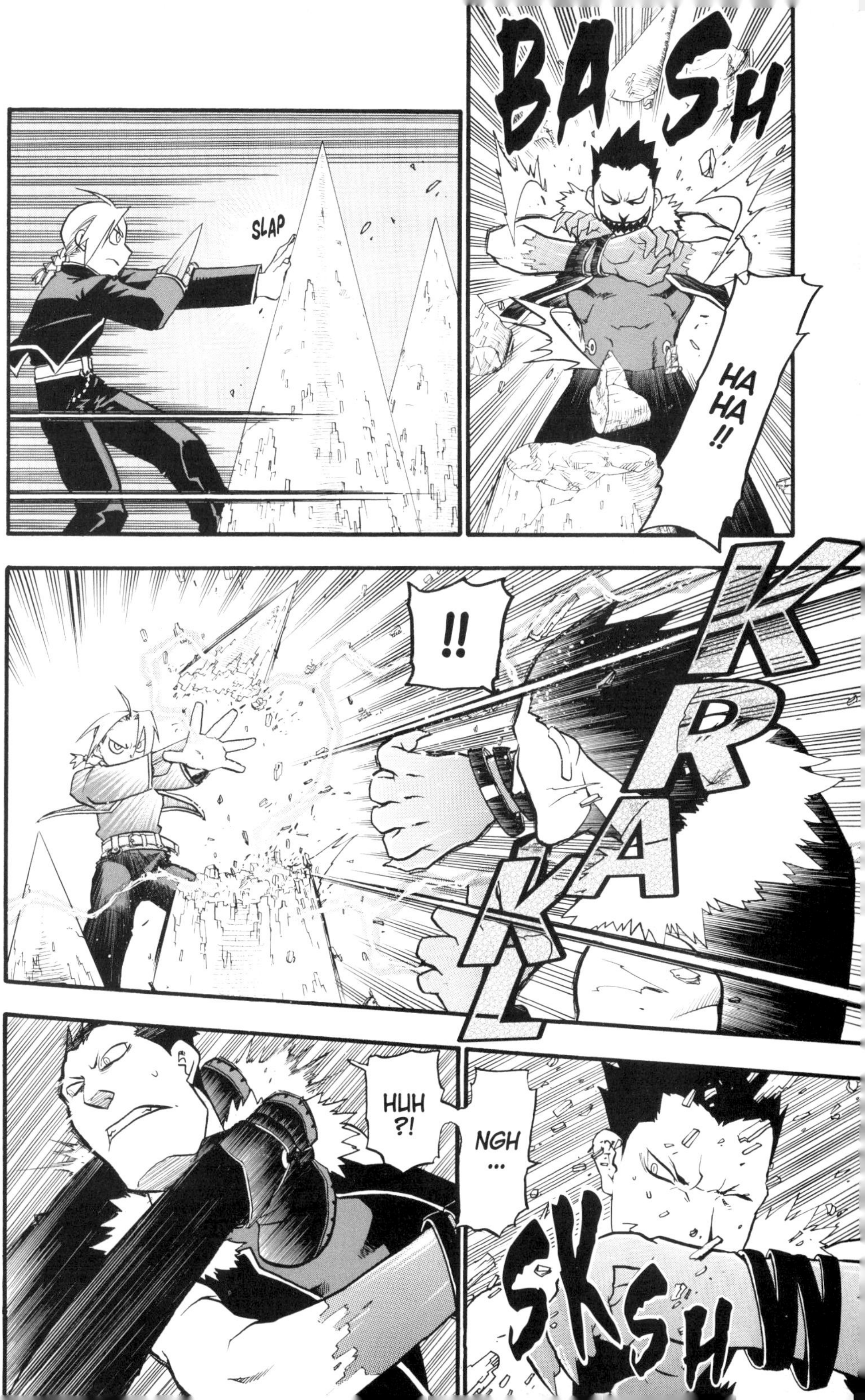
BASH
HAHA !!
SLAP
KRAKL
!!
NGH ...
SKSH
HUH ?!

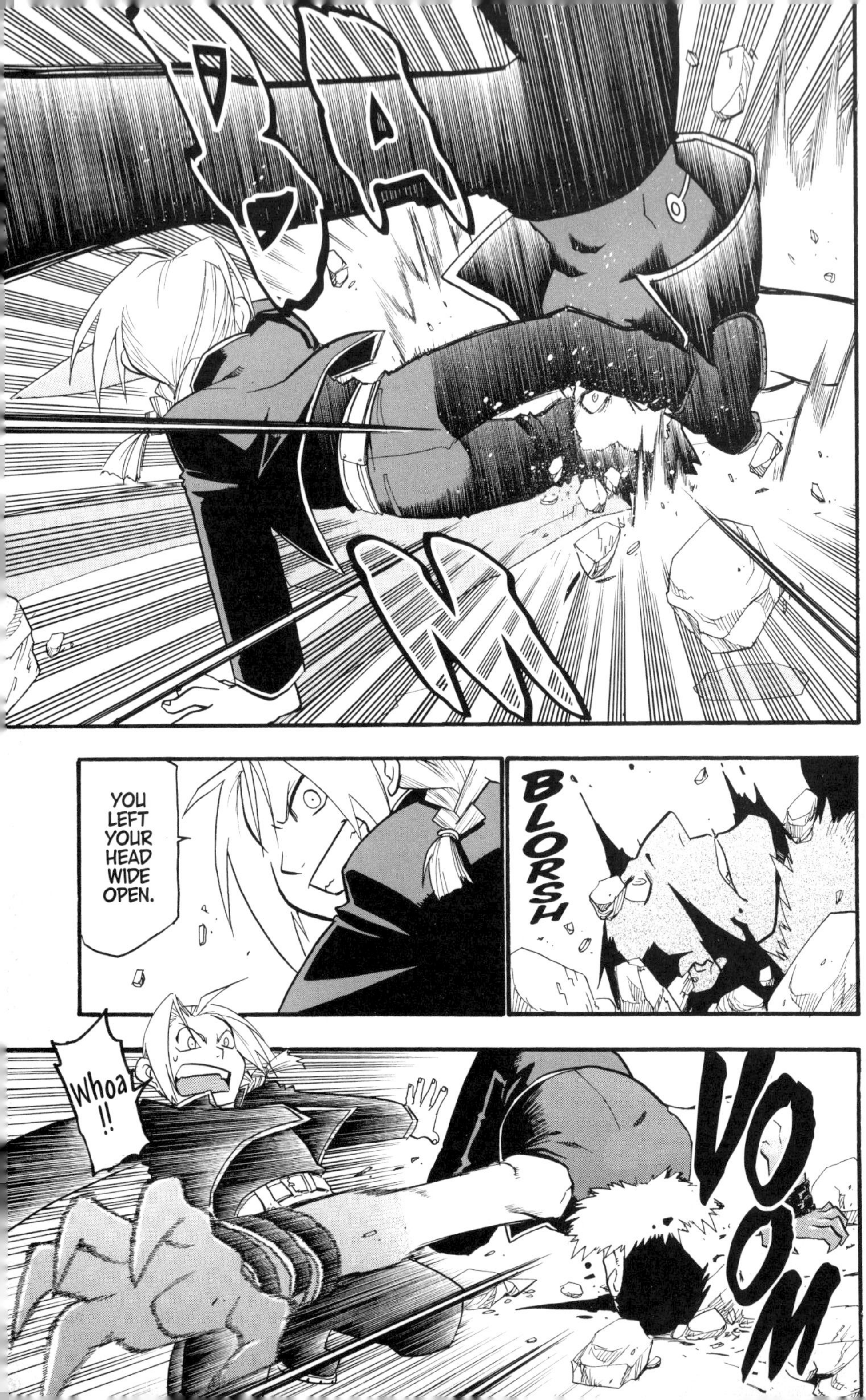
BAM
BLORSH
YOU LEFT YOUR HEAD WIDE OPEN.
VOOM
Whoa!!

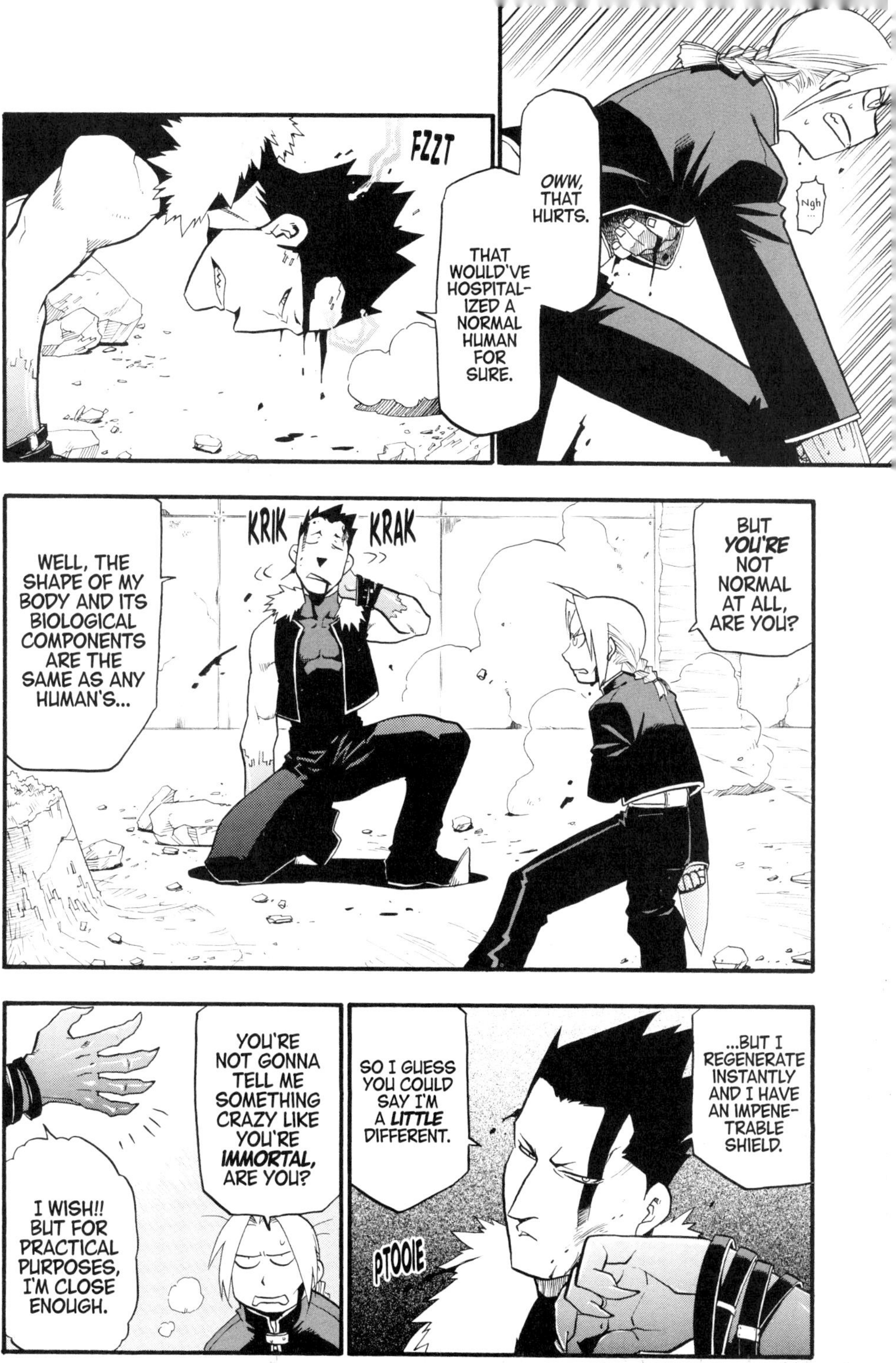

Ngh...
OWW, THAT HURTS.
THAT WOULD'VE HOSPITAL-IZED A NORMAL HUMAN FOR SURE.
FZZT
BUT YOU'RE NOT NORMAL AT ALL, ARE YOU?
KRIK KRAK
WELL, THE SHAPE OF MY BODY AND ITS BIOLOGICAL COMPONENTS ARE THE SAME AS ANY HUMAN'S...
...BUT I REGENERATE INSTANTLY AND I HAVE AN IMPENE-TRABLE SHIELD.
SO I GUESS YOU COULD SAY I'M A LITTLE DIFFERENT.
PTOOIE
YOU'RE NOT GONNA TELL ME SOMETHING CRAZY LIKE YOU'RE IMMORTAL, ARE YOU?
I WISH!! BUT FOR PRACTICAL PURPOSES, I'M CLOSE ENOUGH.

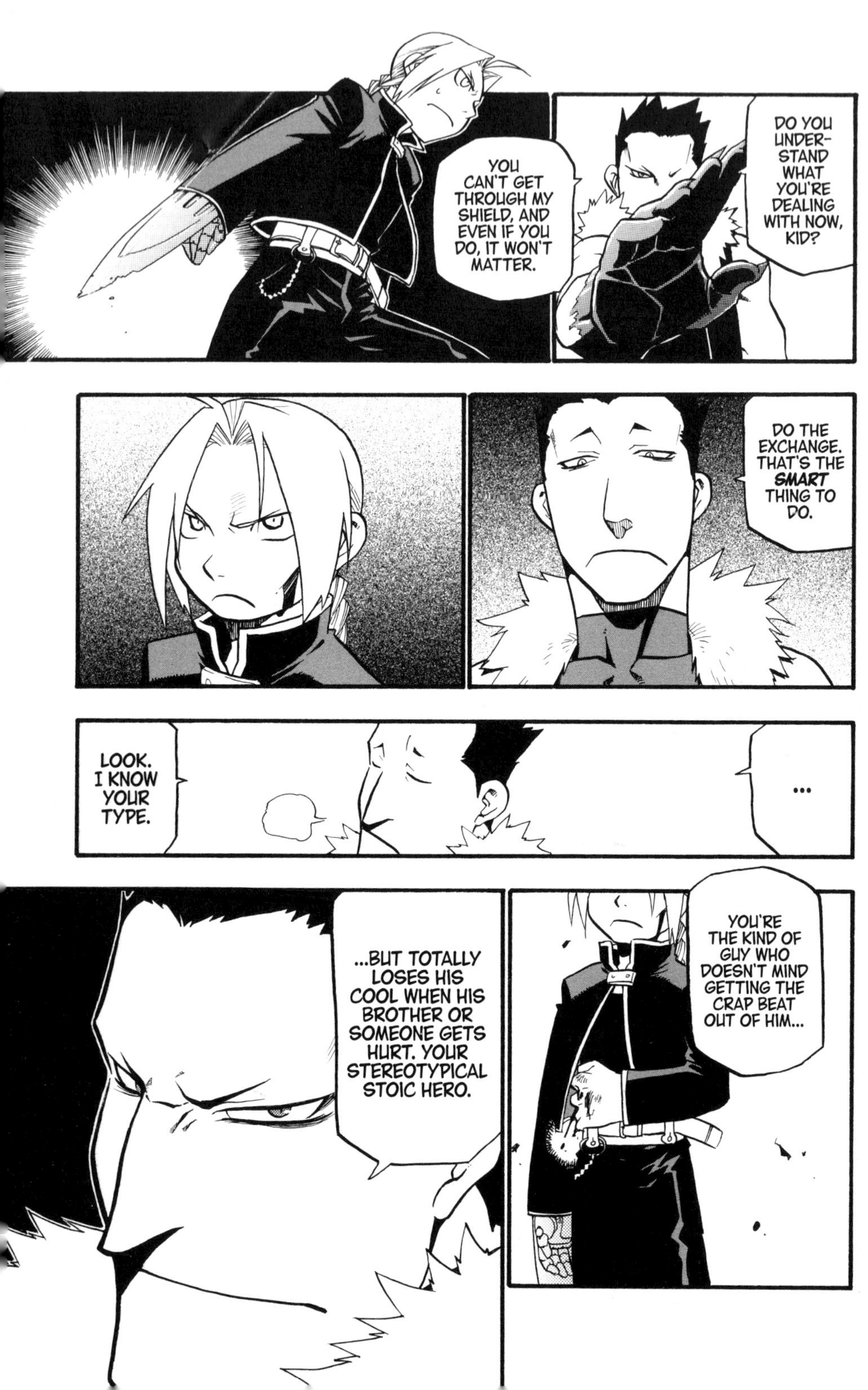
DO YOU UNDER-STAND WHAT YOU'RE DEALING WITH NOW, KID?
YOU CAN'T GET THROUGH MY SHIELD, AND EVEN IF YOU DO, IT WON'T MATTER.
DO THE EXCHANGE. THAT'S THE **SMART** THING TO DO.
...
LOOK. I KNOW YOUR TYPE.
YOU'RE THE KIND OF GUY WHO DOESN'T MIND GETTING THE CRAP BEAT OUT OF HIM...
...BUT TOTALLY LOSES HIS COOL WHEN HIS BROTHER OR SOMEONE GETS HURT. YOUR STEREOTYPICAL STOIC HERO.

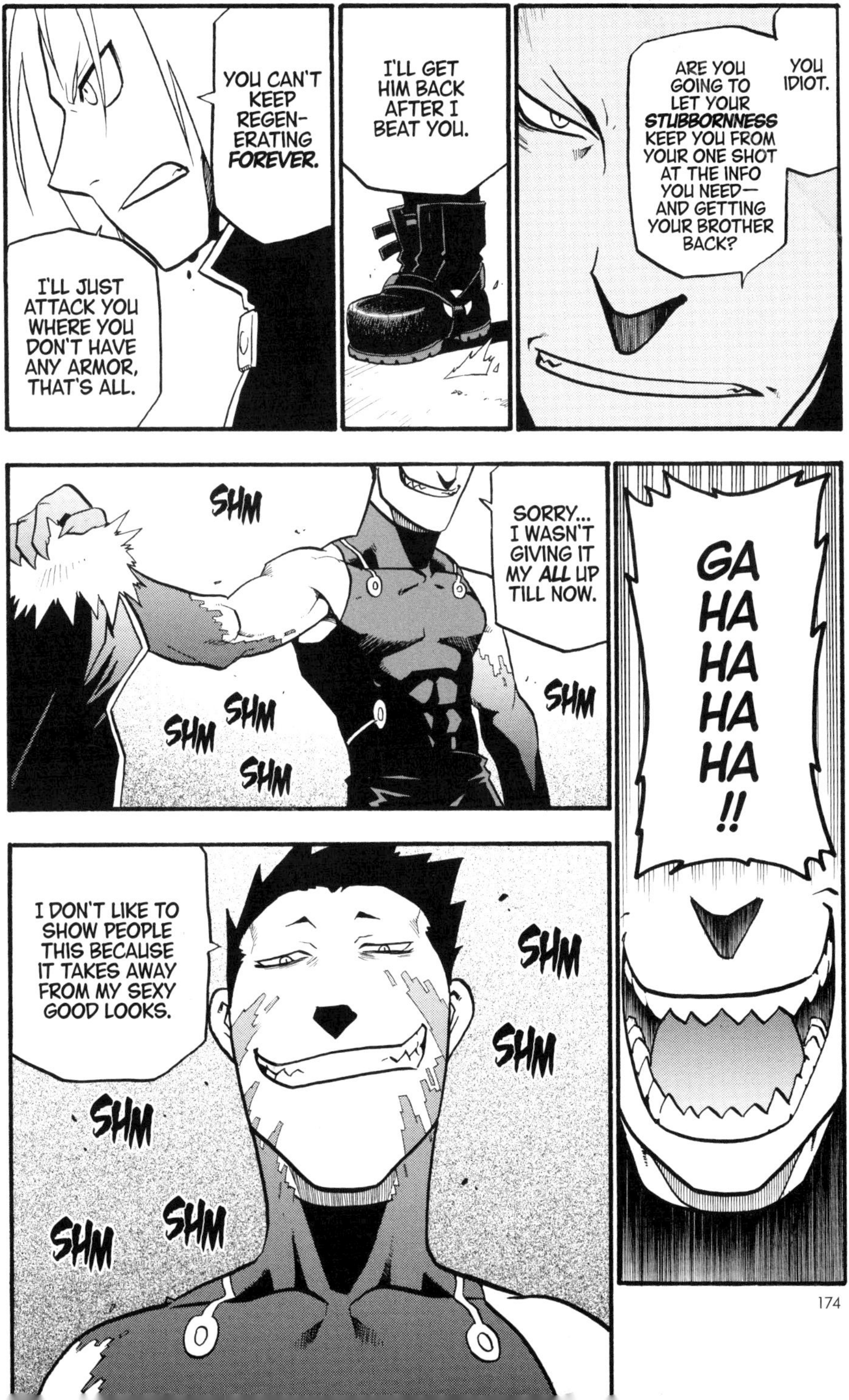

YOU IDIOT.
ARE YOU GOING TO LET YOUR **STUBBORNNESS** KEEP YOU FROM YOUR ONE SHOT AT THE INFO YOU NEED— AND GETTING YOUR BROTHER BACK?
I'LL GET HIM BACK AFTER I BEAT YOU.
YOU CAN'T KEEP REGEN-ERATING **FOREVER.**
I'LL JUST ATTACK YOU WHERE YOU DON'T HAVE ANY ARMOR, THAT'S ALL.
GA HA HA HA HA HA !!
SORRY... I WASN'T GIVING IT MY **ALL** UP TILL NOW.
SHM
SHM
SHM
SHM
SHM
I DON'T LIKE TO SHOW PEOPLE THIS BECAUSE IT TAKES AWAY FROM MY SEXY GOOD LOOKS.
SHM
SHM
SHM
SHM
SHM

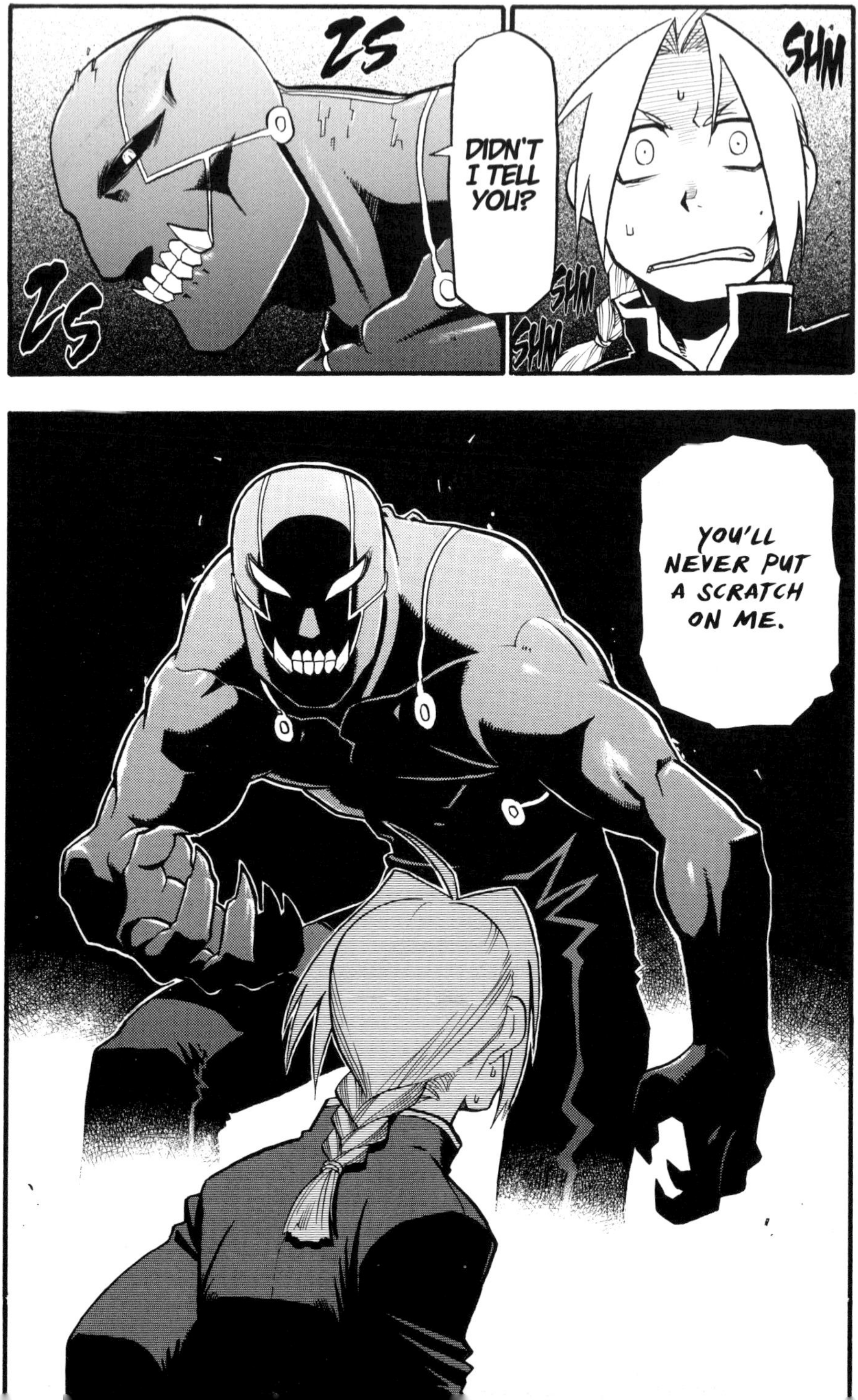
SHM
SHM
SHM
ZS
DIDN'T I TELL YOU?
ZS
YOU'LL NEVER PUT A SCRATCH ON ME.

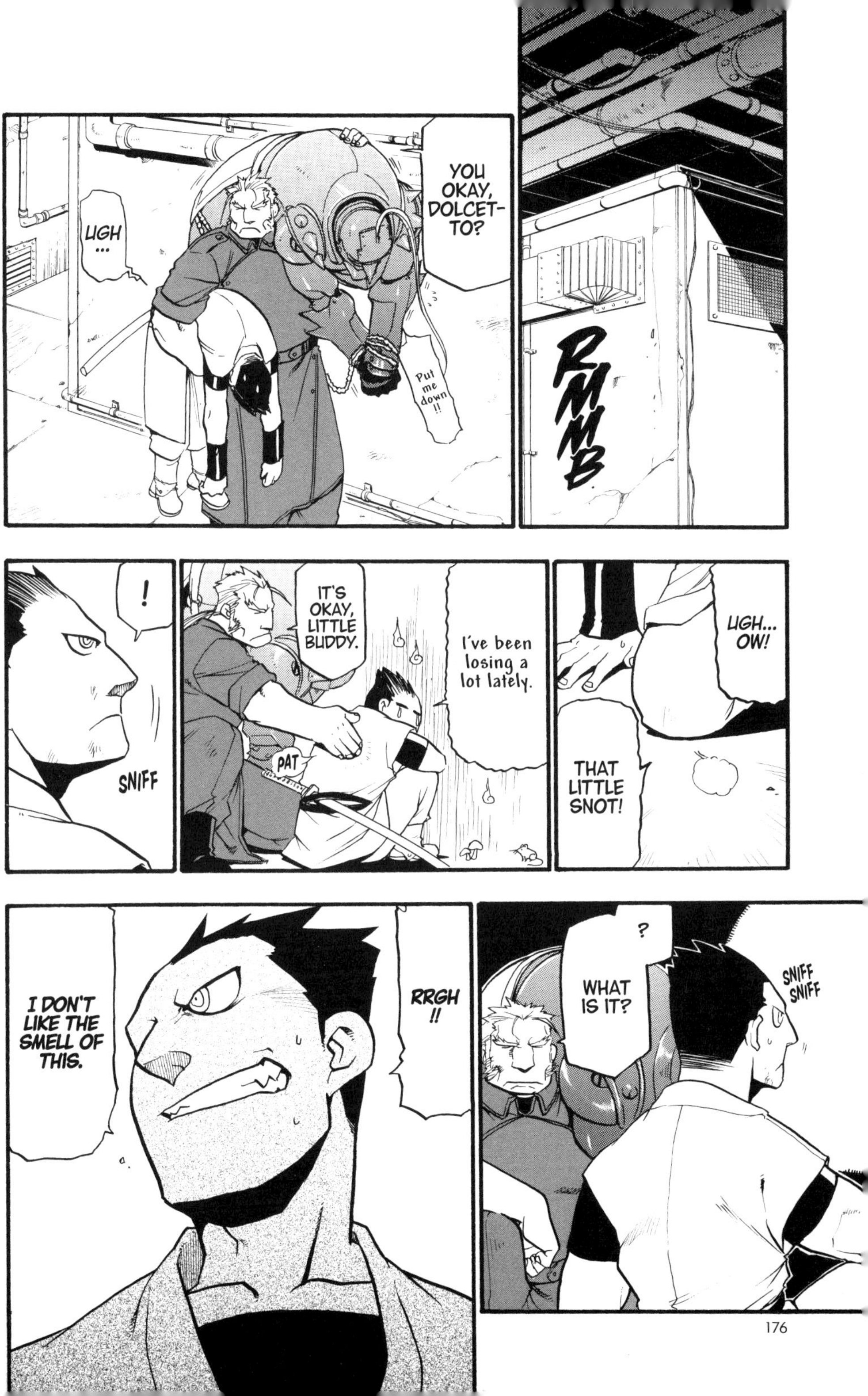
RMMMB
YOU OKAY, DOLCETTO?
UGH...
Put me down!!
UGH... OW!
THAT LITTLE SNOT!
I've been losing a lot lately.
IT'S OKAY, LITTLE BUDDY.
PAT
!
SNIFF
?
WHAT IS IT?
SNIFF SNIFF
RRGH!!
I DON'T LIKE THE SMELL OF THIS.

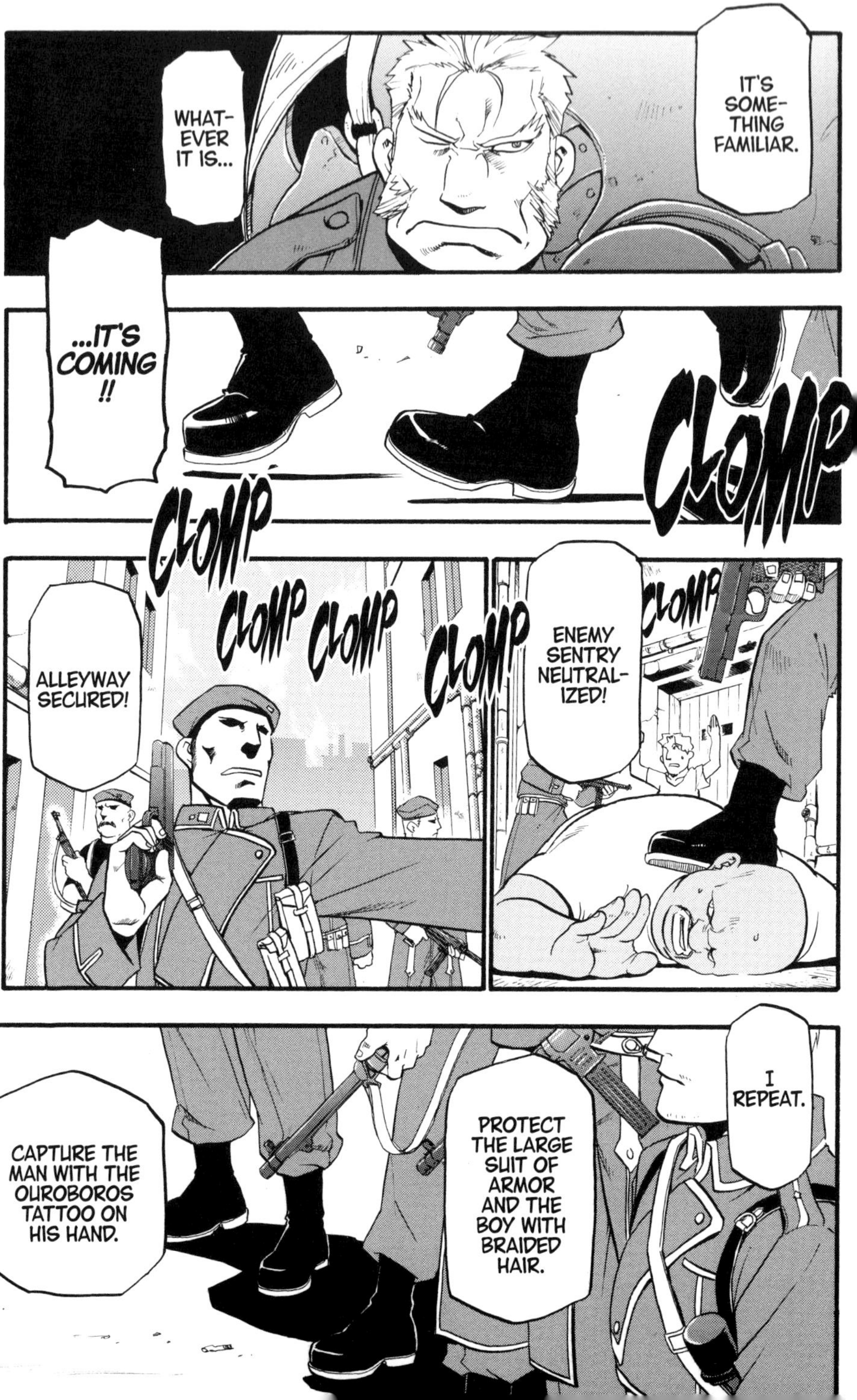
IT'S SOMETHING FAMILIAR.
WHATEVER IT IS...
CLOMP
...IT'S COMING!!
CLOMP
CLOMP
ENEMY SENTRY NEUTRALIZED!
CLOMP
CLOMP
CLOMP
ALLEYWAY SECURED!
I REPEAT.
PROTECT THE LARGE SUIT OF ARMOR AND THE BOY WITH BRAIDED HAIR.
CAPTURE THE MAN WITH THE OUROBOROS TATTOO ON HIS HAND.

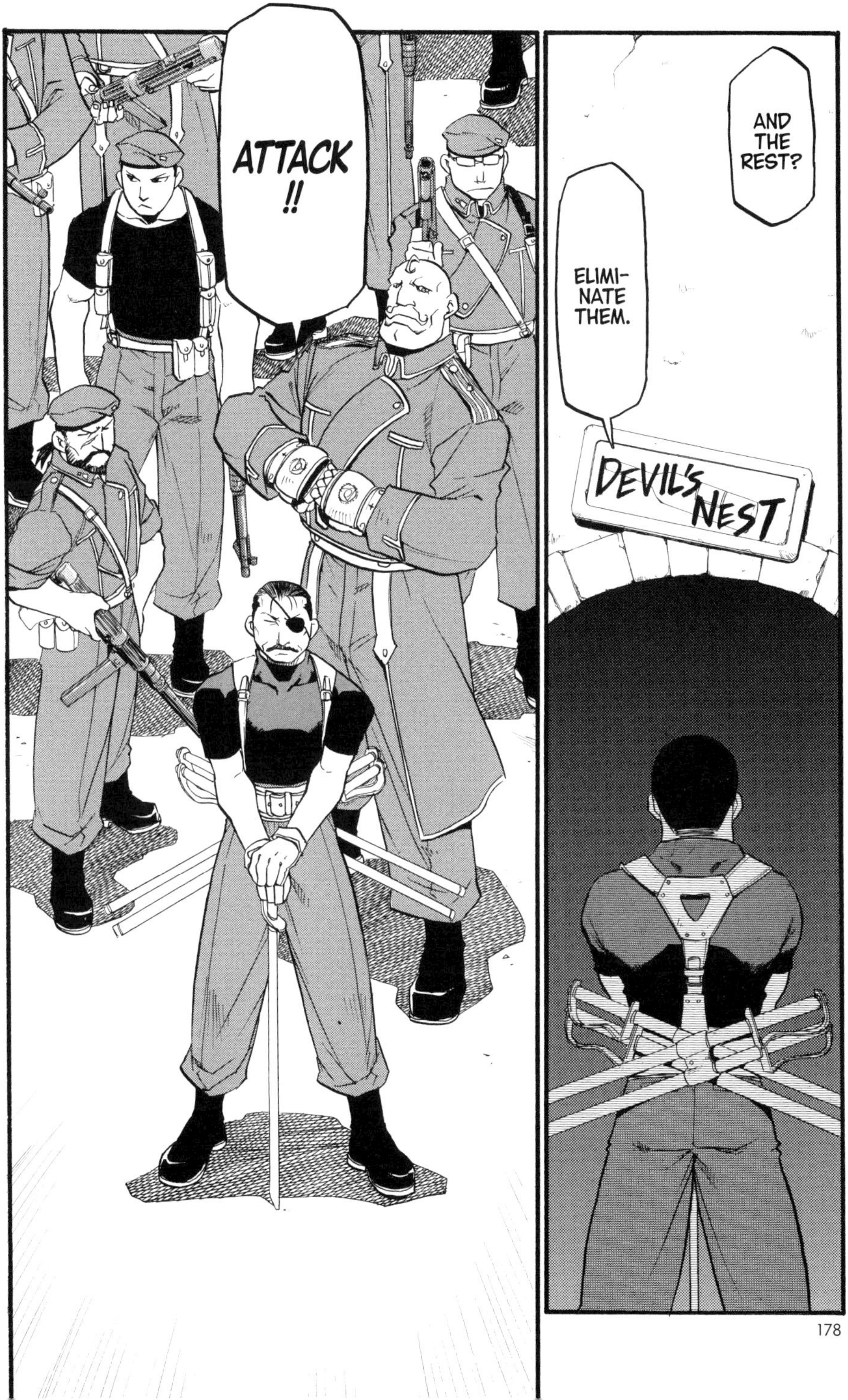
AND THE REST?
ELIMINATE THEM.
DEVIL'S NEST
ATTACK!!

CHAPTER 29 THE EYE OF THE KING

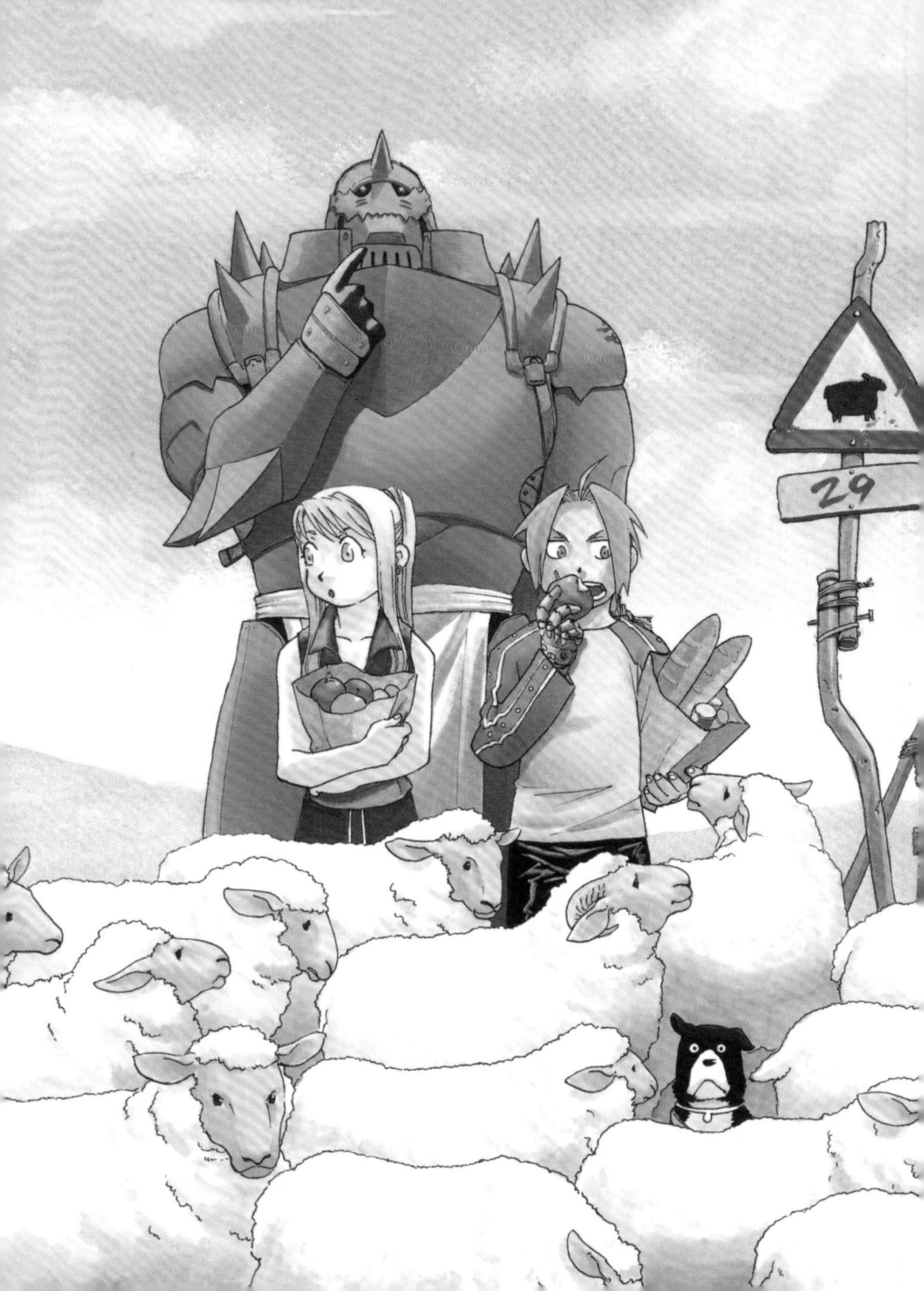
29

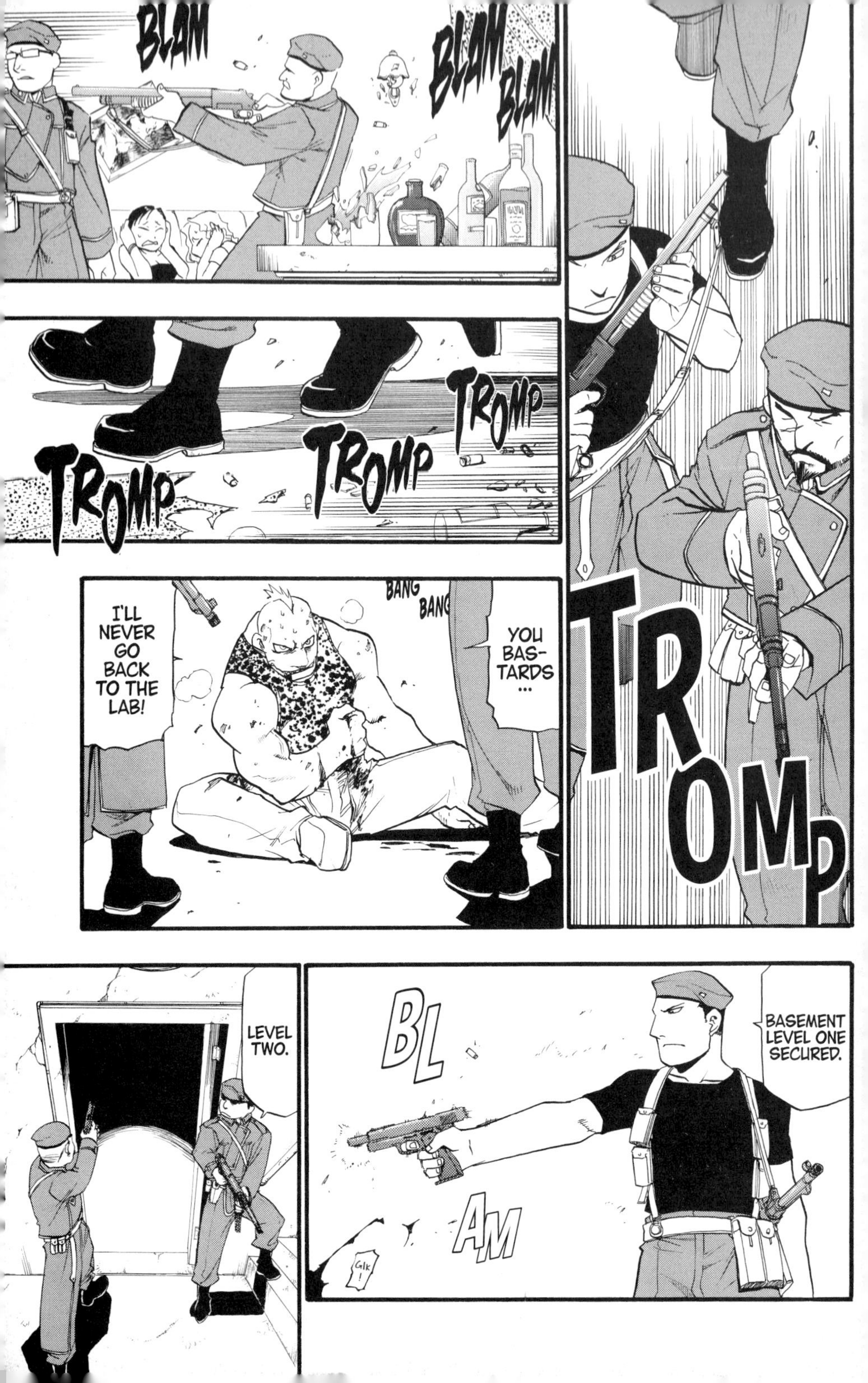
TROMP
BLAM
BLAM
BLAM
TROMP
TROMP
TROMP
BANG
BANG
YOU BASTARDS...
I'LL NEVER GO BACK TO THE LAB!
BASEMENT LEVEL ONE SECURED.
BLAM
Glk!
LEVEL TWO.

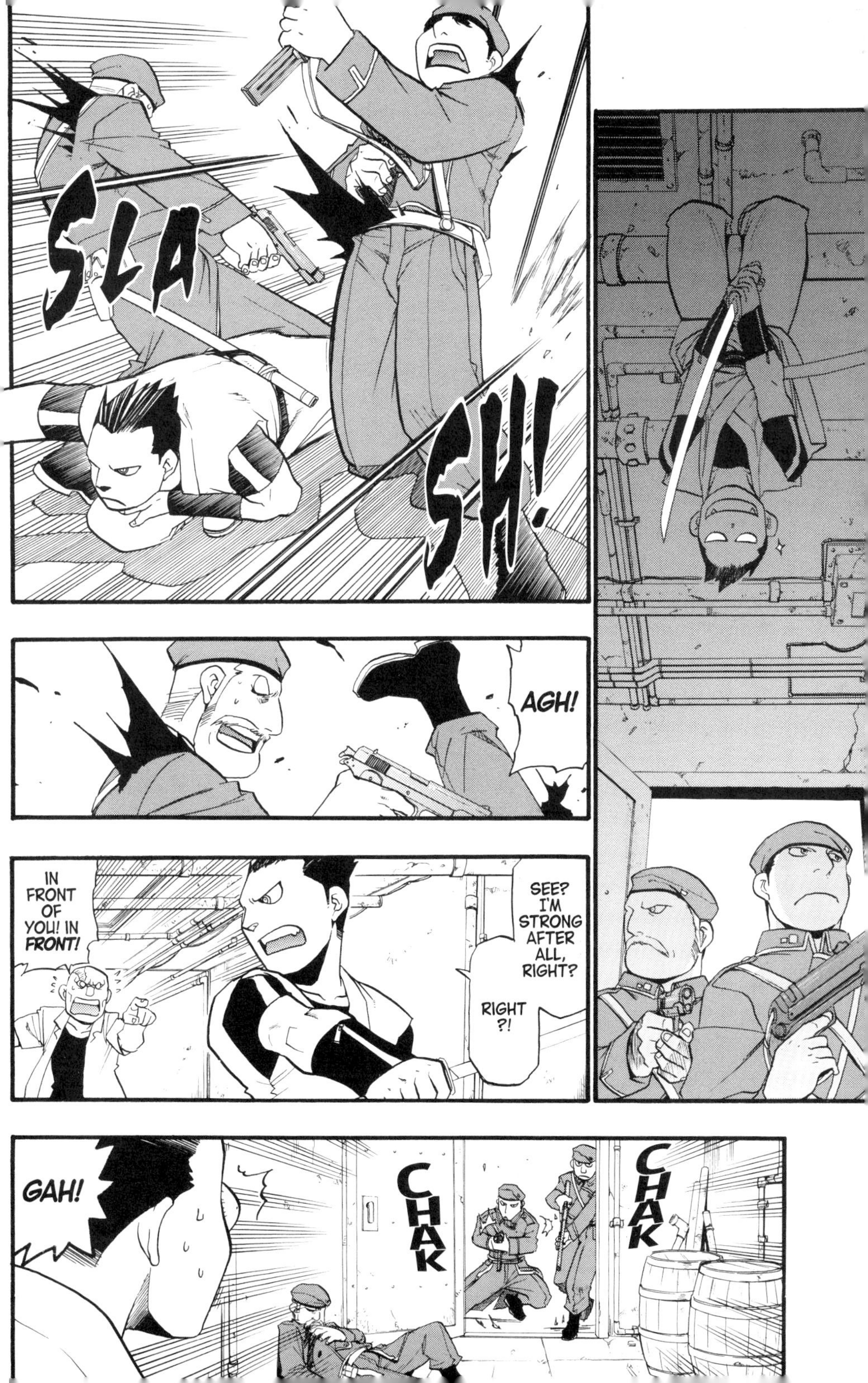
SLASH!
AGH!
SEE? I'M STRONG AFTER ALL, RIGHT?
RIGHT?!
IN FRONT OF YOU! IN FRONT!
CHAK
CHAK
GAH!

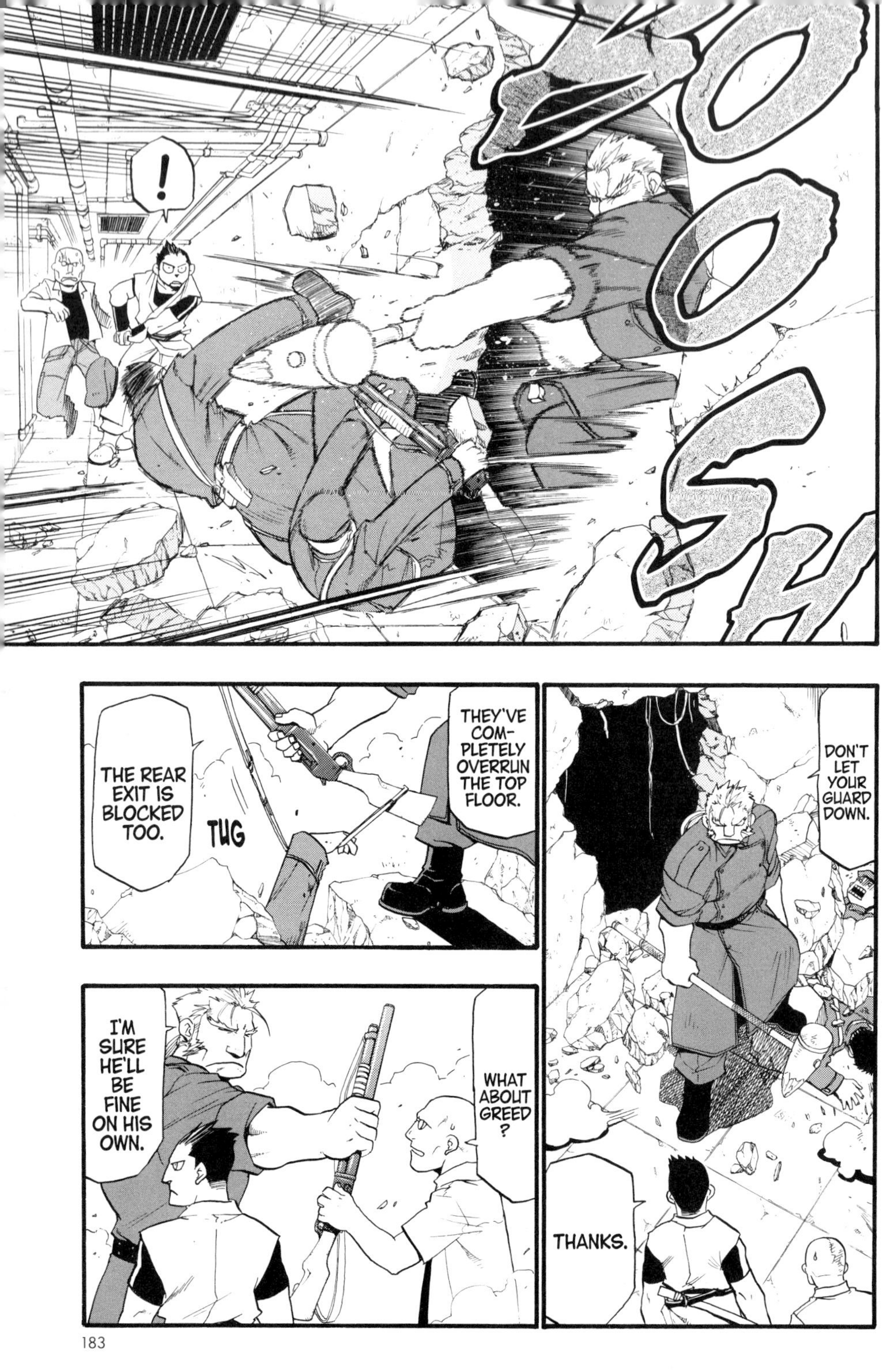
!
BOOSH
DON'T LET YOUR GUARD DOWN.
THANKS.
THEY'VE COMPLETELY OVERRUN THE TOP FLOOR.
TUG
THE REAR EXIT IS BLOCKED TOO.
WHAT ABOUT GREED?
I'M SURE HE'LL BE FINE ON HIS OWN.

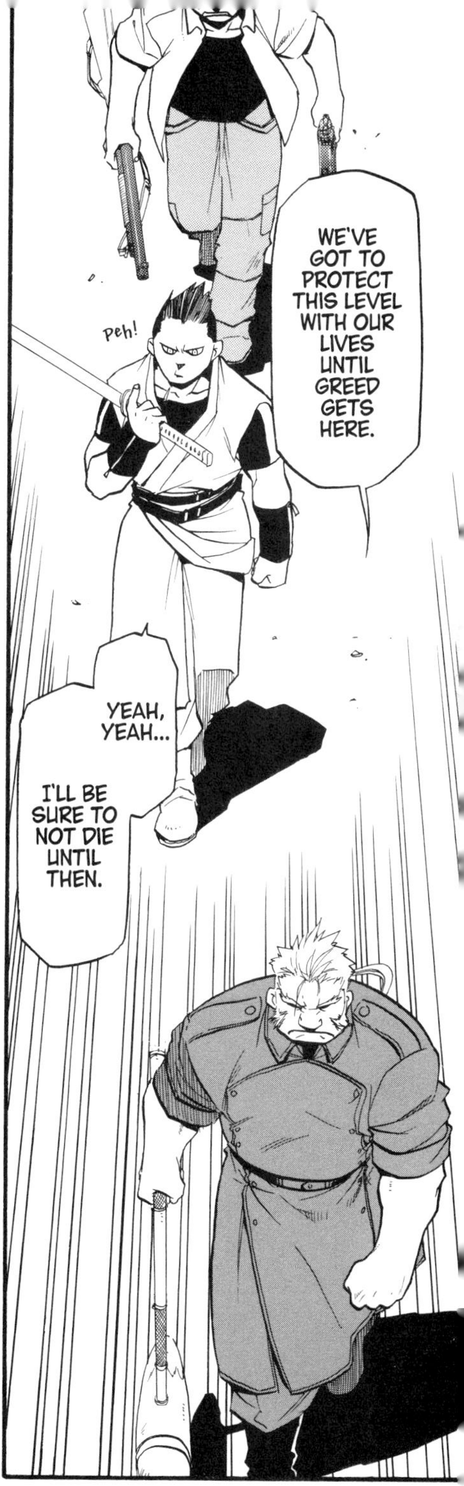
WE'VE GOT TO PROTECT THIS LEVEL WITH OUR LIVES UNTIL GREED GETS HERE.
Peh!
YEAH, YEAH...
I'LL BE SURE TO NOT DIE UNTIL THEN.

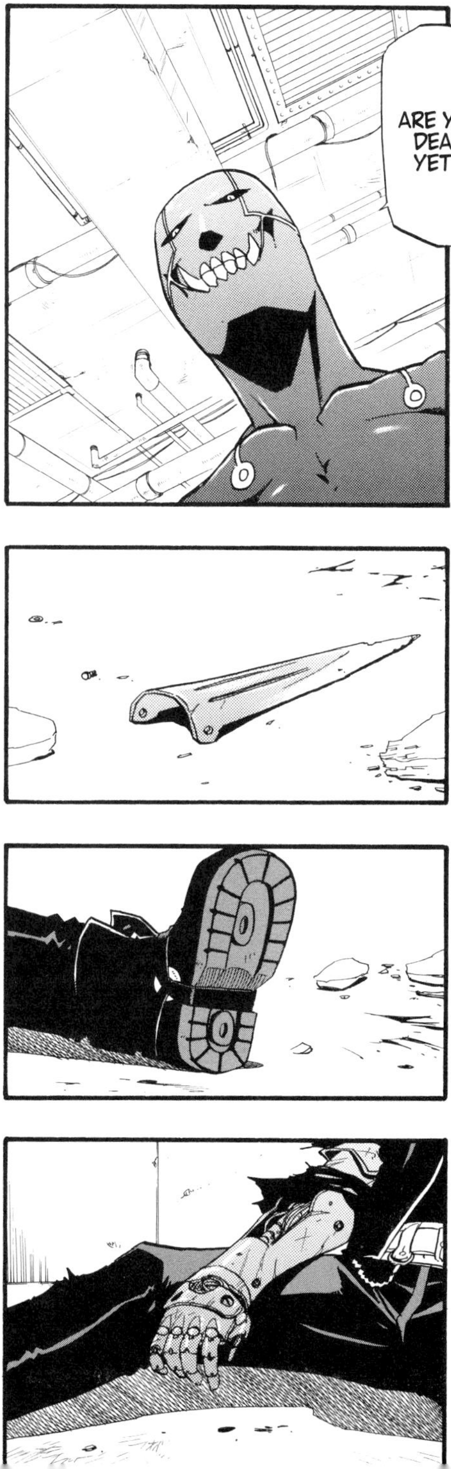
ARE YOU DEAD YET?

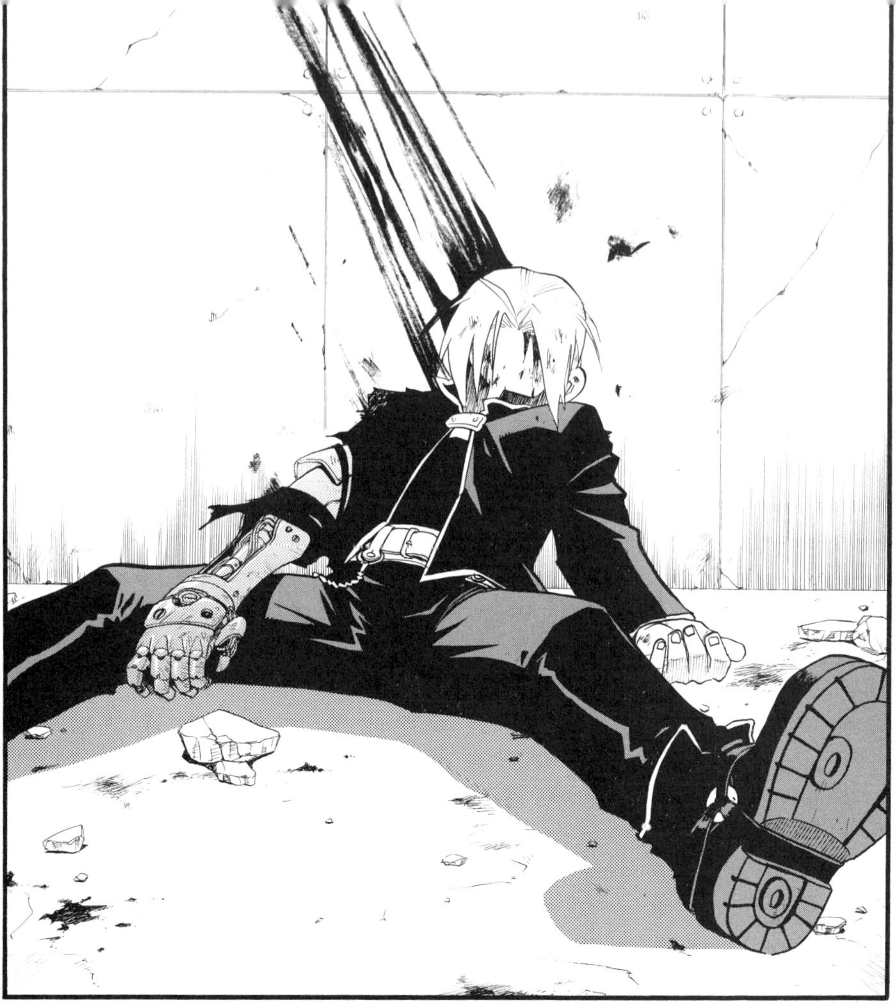

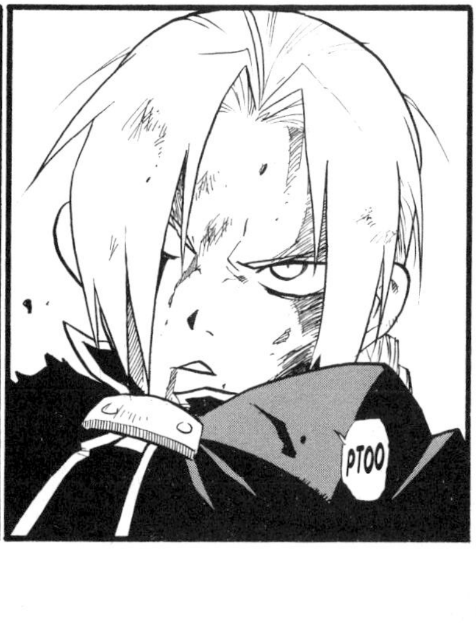
PTOO

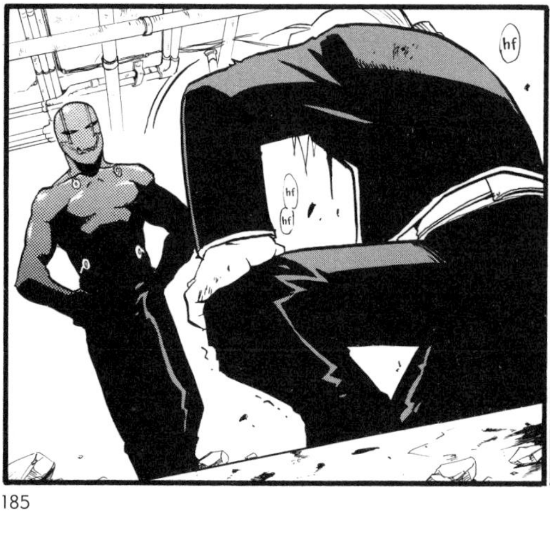
hf
hf
hf

THAT'S THE SPIRIT! KIDS **SHOULD** BE FULL OF ENERGY.

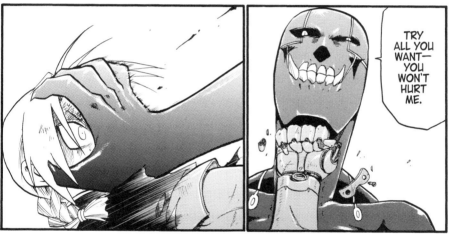

TRY ALL YOU WANT— YOU WON'T HURT ME.

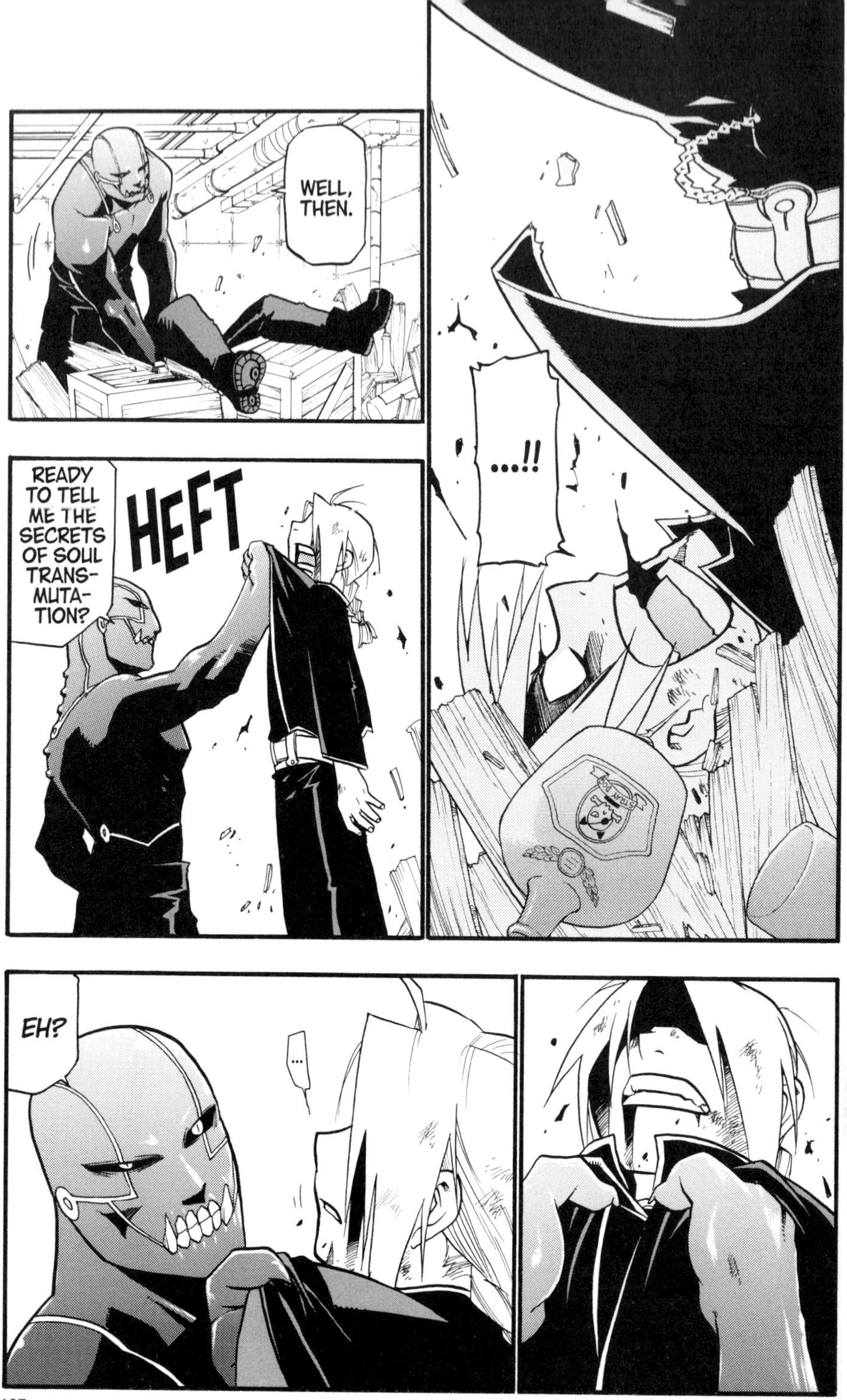
...!!
WELL, THEN.
HEFT
READY TO TELL ME THE SECRETS OF SOUL TRANSMUTATION?
...
EH?

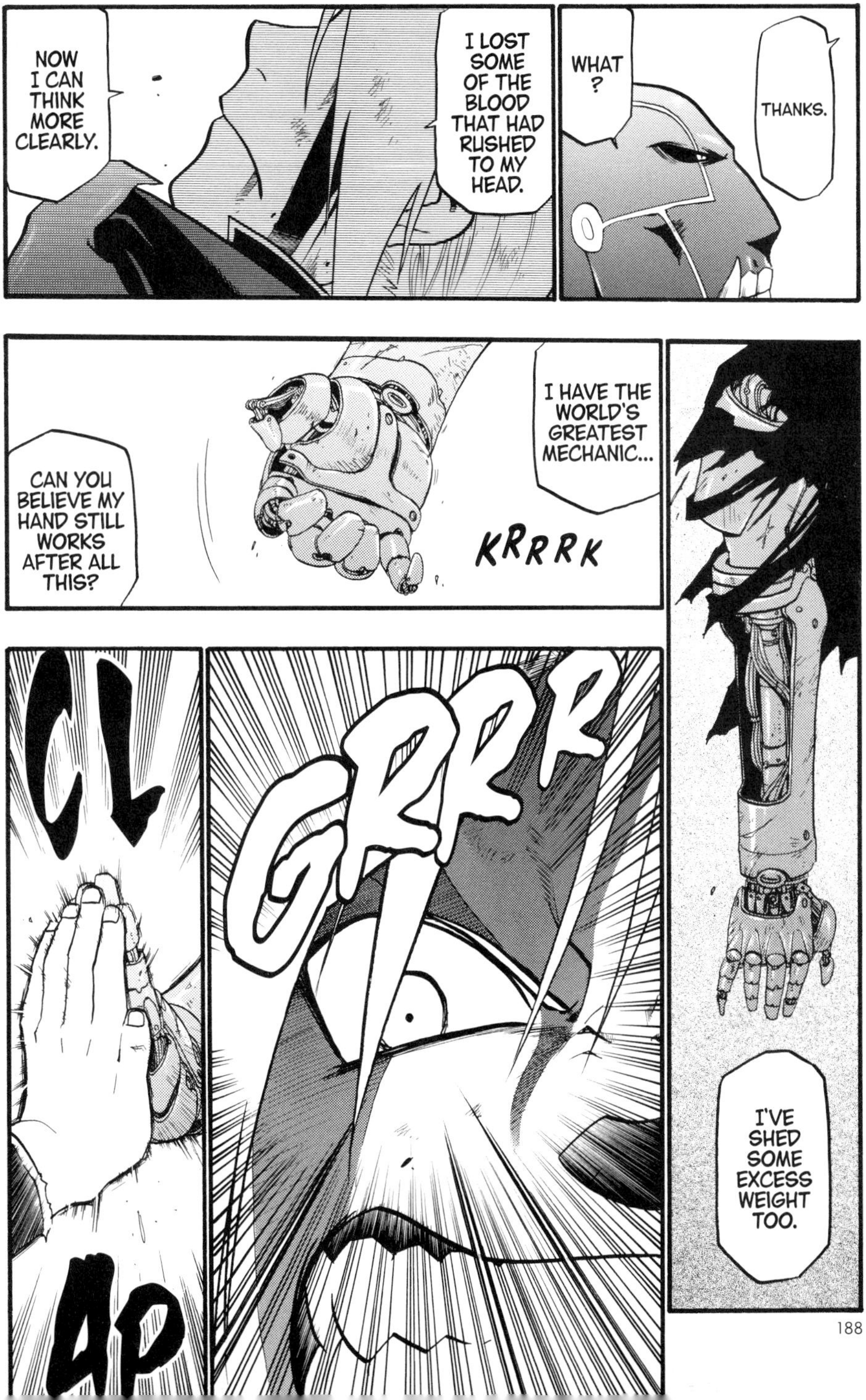
THANKS.
WHAT ?
I LOST SOME OF THE BLOOD THAT HAD RUSHED TO MY HEAD.
NOW I CAN THINK MORE CLEARLY.
I'VE SHED SOME EXCESS WEIGHT TOO.
I HAVE THE WORLD'S GREATEST MECHANIC...
KRRRK
CAN YOU BELIEVE MY HAND STILL WORKS AFTER ALL THIS?
GRRR
CL
AP

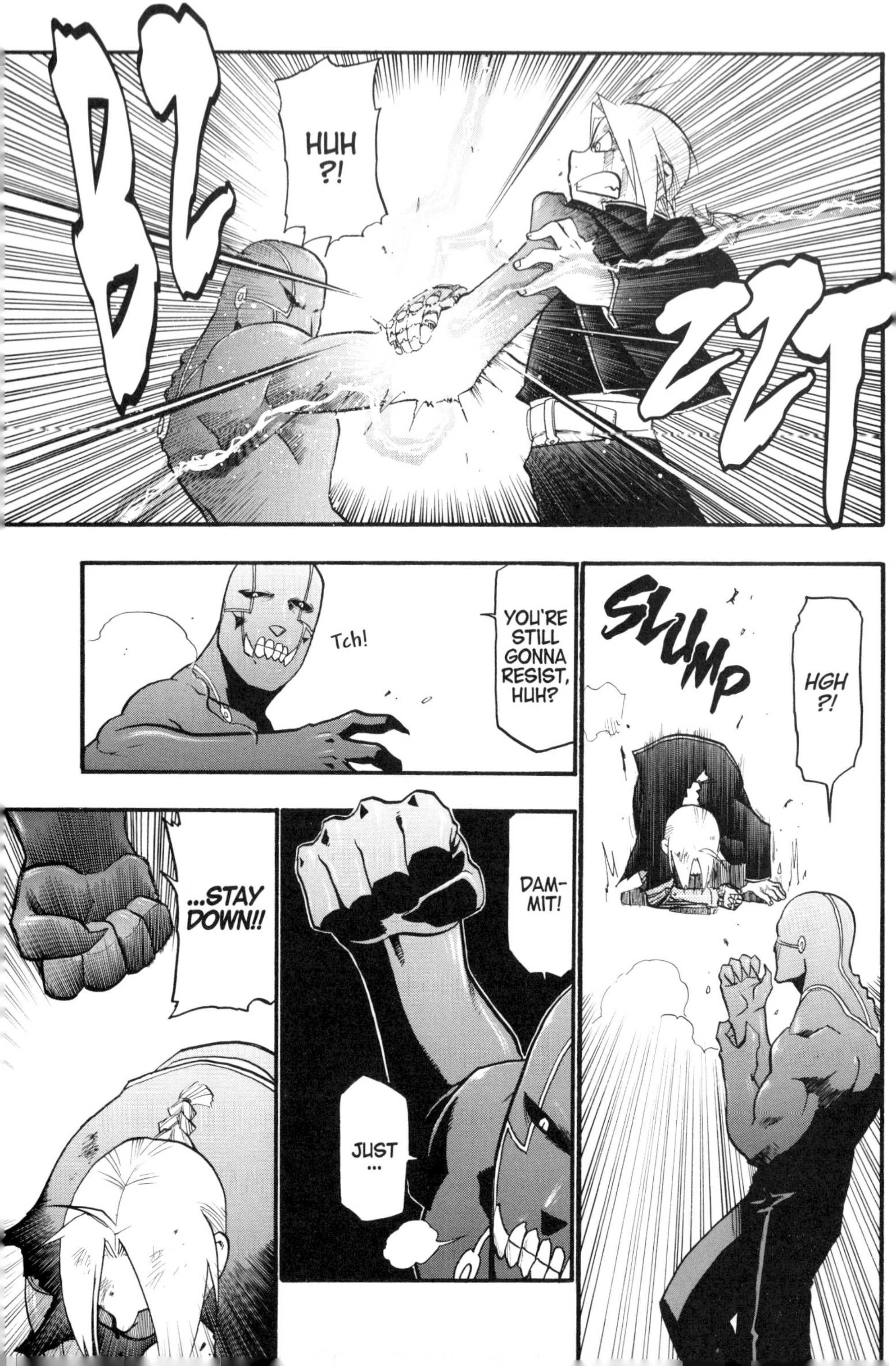
BZ ZZT
HUH ?!
HGH ?!
SLUMP
YOU'RE STILL GONNA RESIST, HUH?
Tch!
DAM-MIT!
JUST ...
...STAY DOWN!!

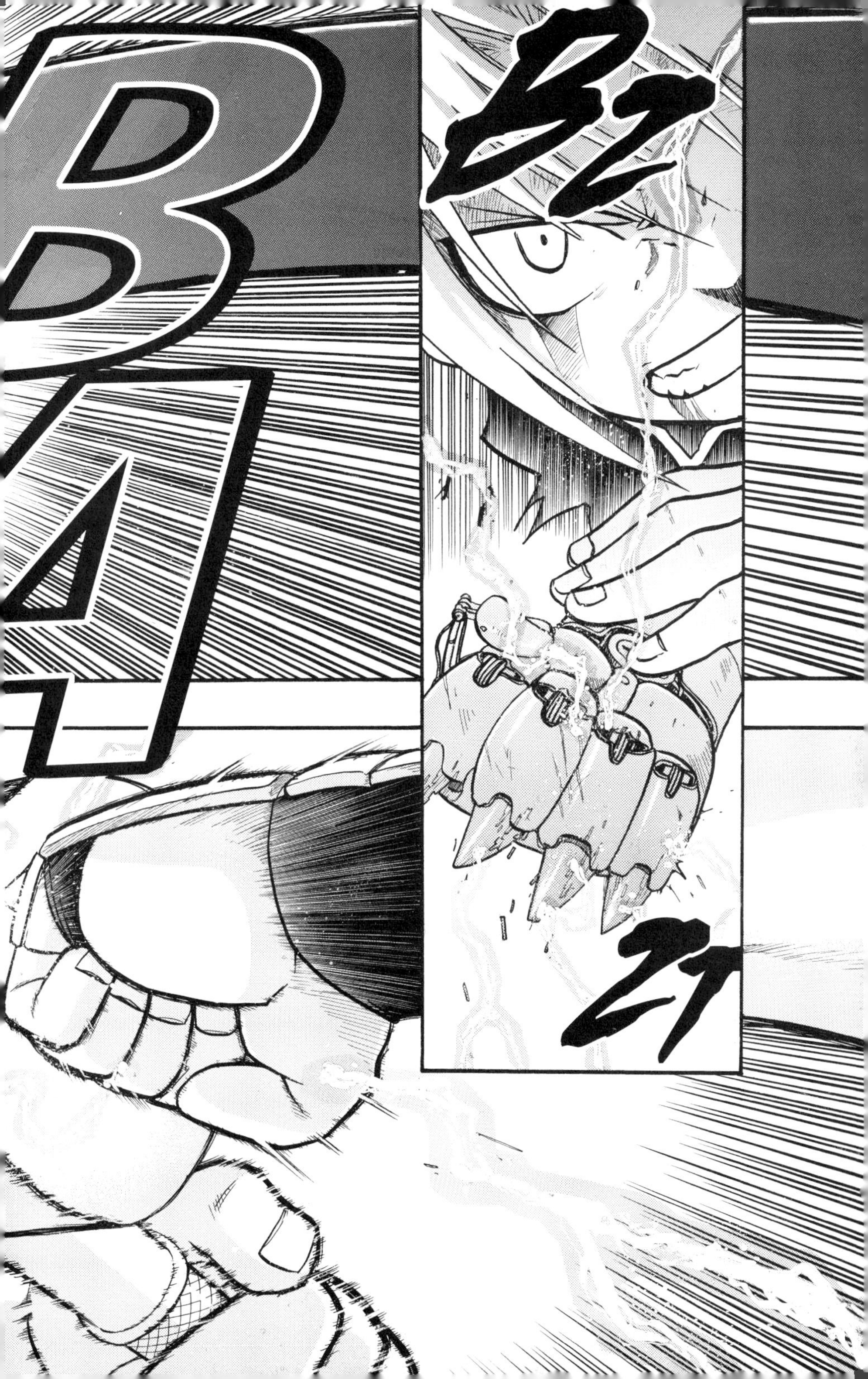
BA

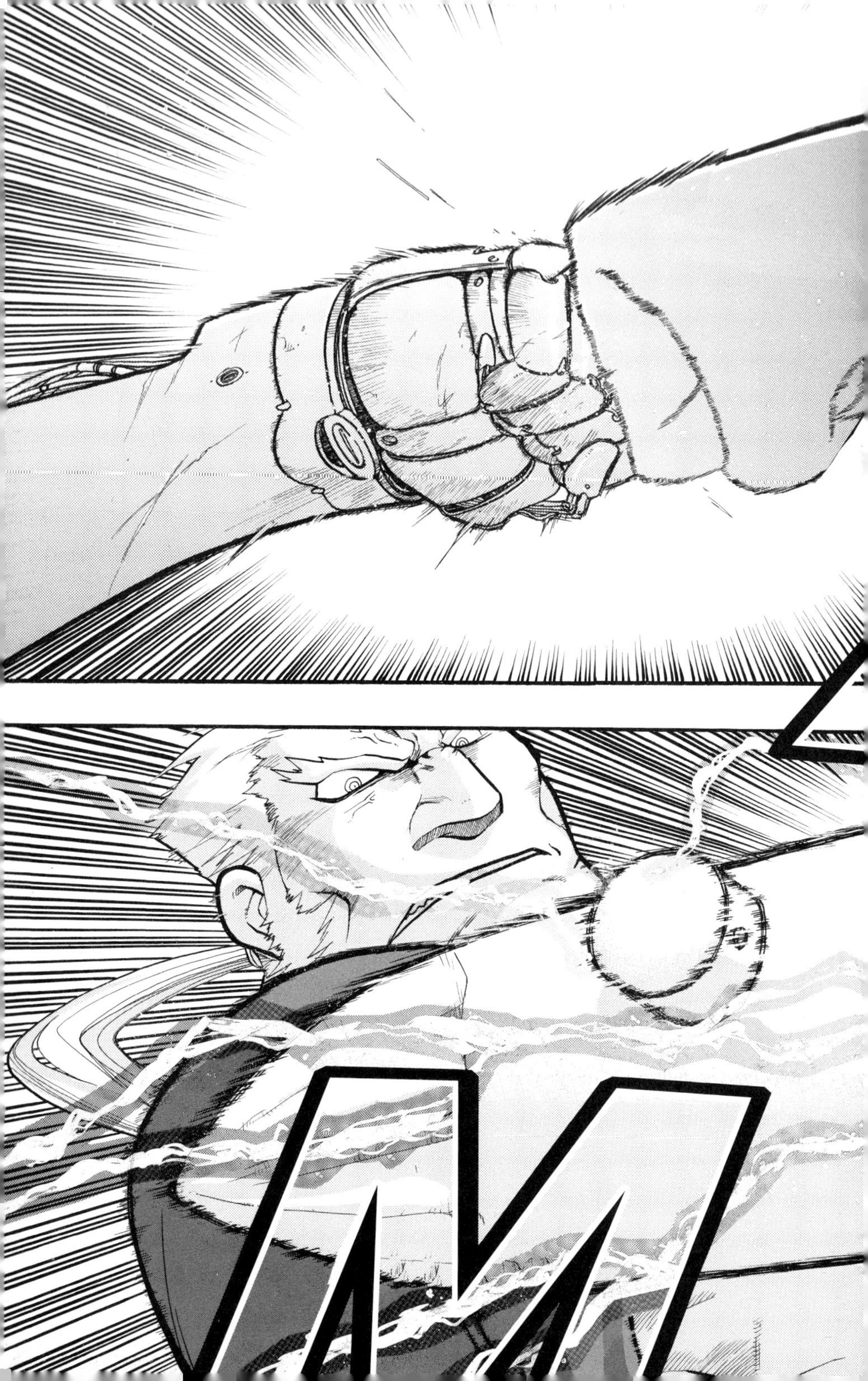
M

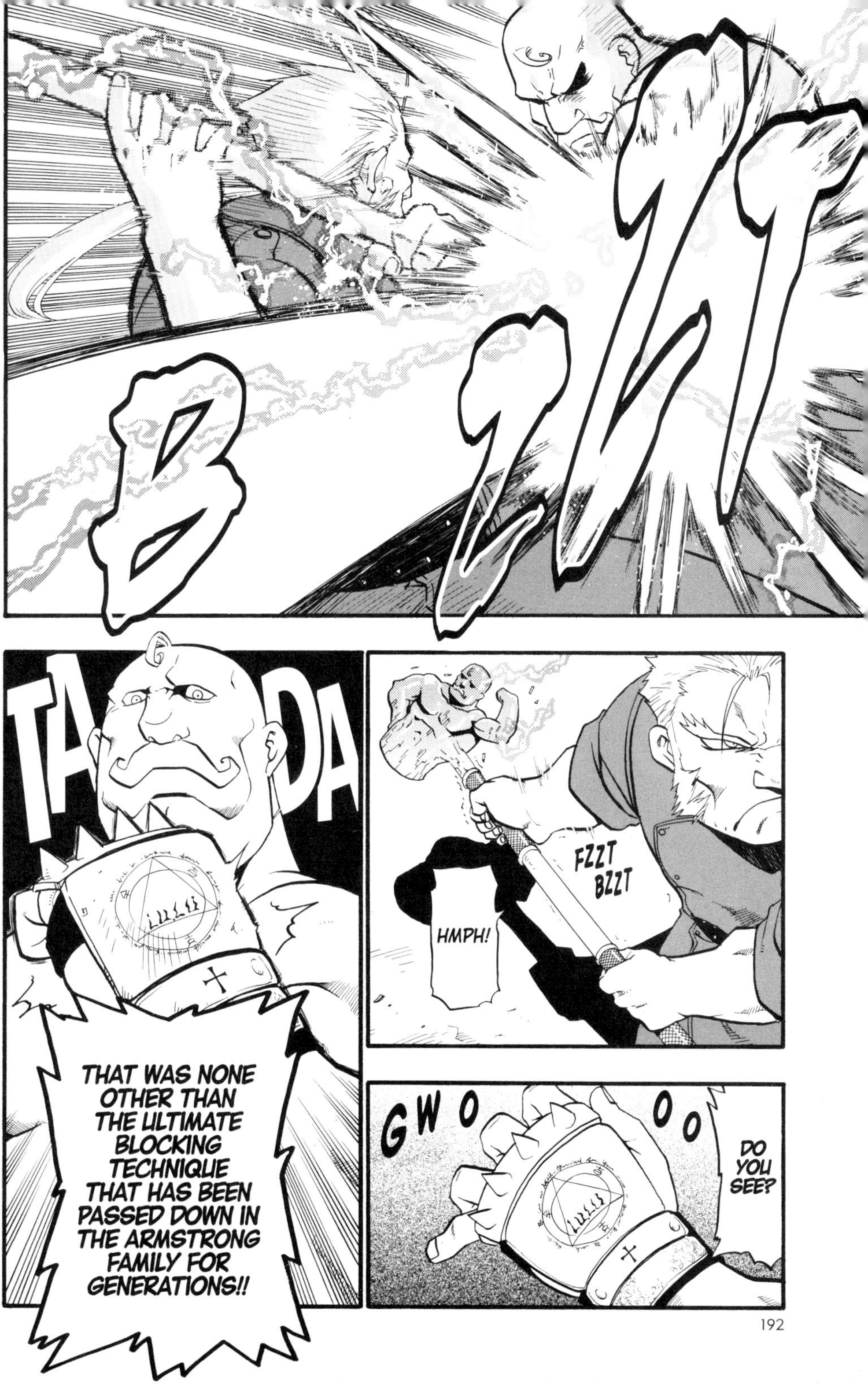
BZZT
FZZT
BZZT
HMPH!
GWOOO
DO YOU SEE?
TA DA
THAT WAS NONE OTHER THAN THE ULTIMATE BLOCKING TECHNIQUE THAT HAS BEEN PASSED DOWN IN THE ARMSTRONG FAMILY FOR GENERATIONS!!

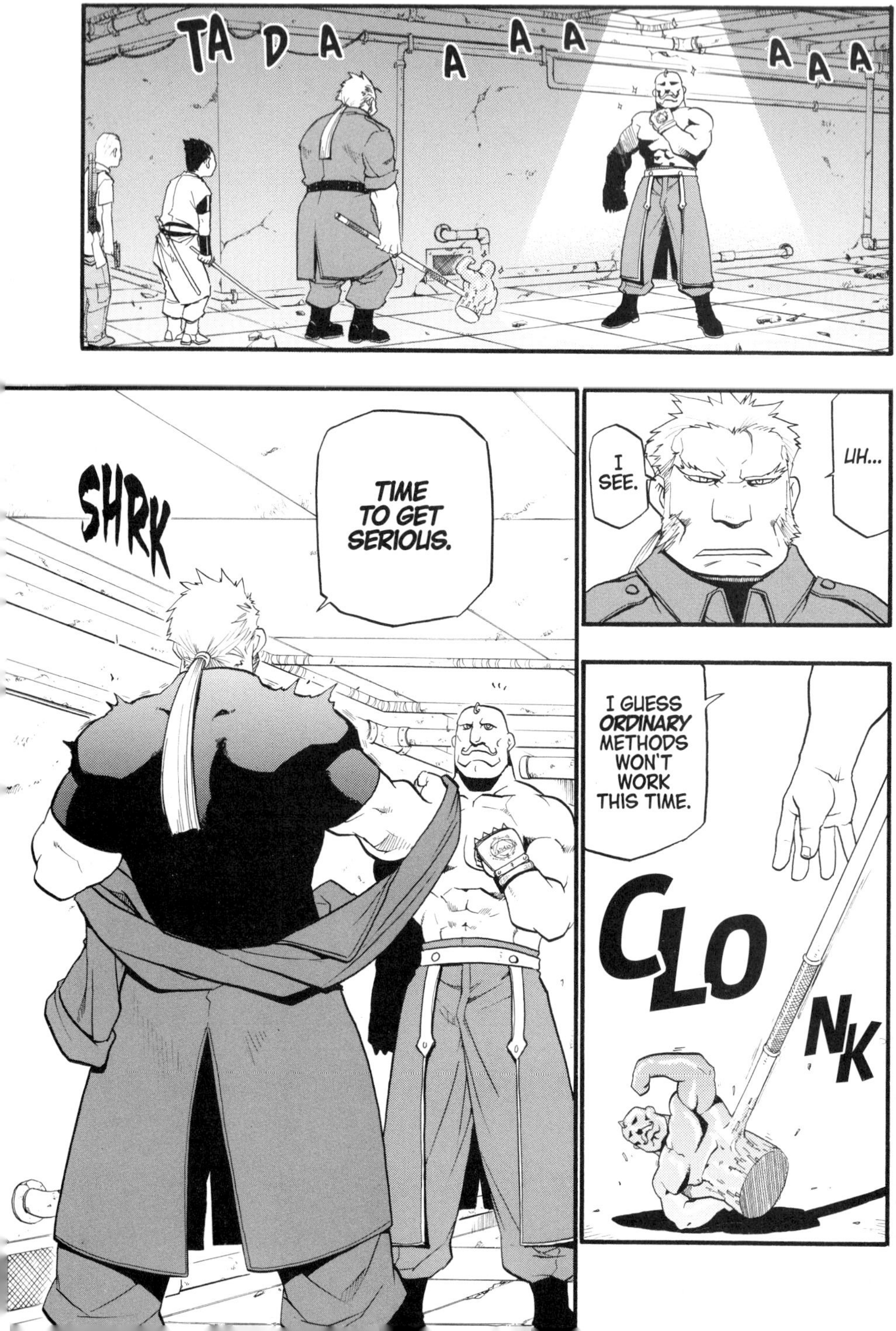
TA DA A A A A AAA
UH...
I SEE.
I GUESS ORDINARY METHODS WON'T WORK THIS TIME.
CLONK
SHRK
TIME TO GET SERIOUS.

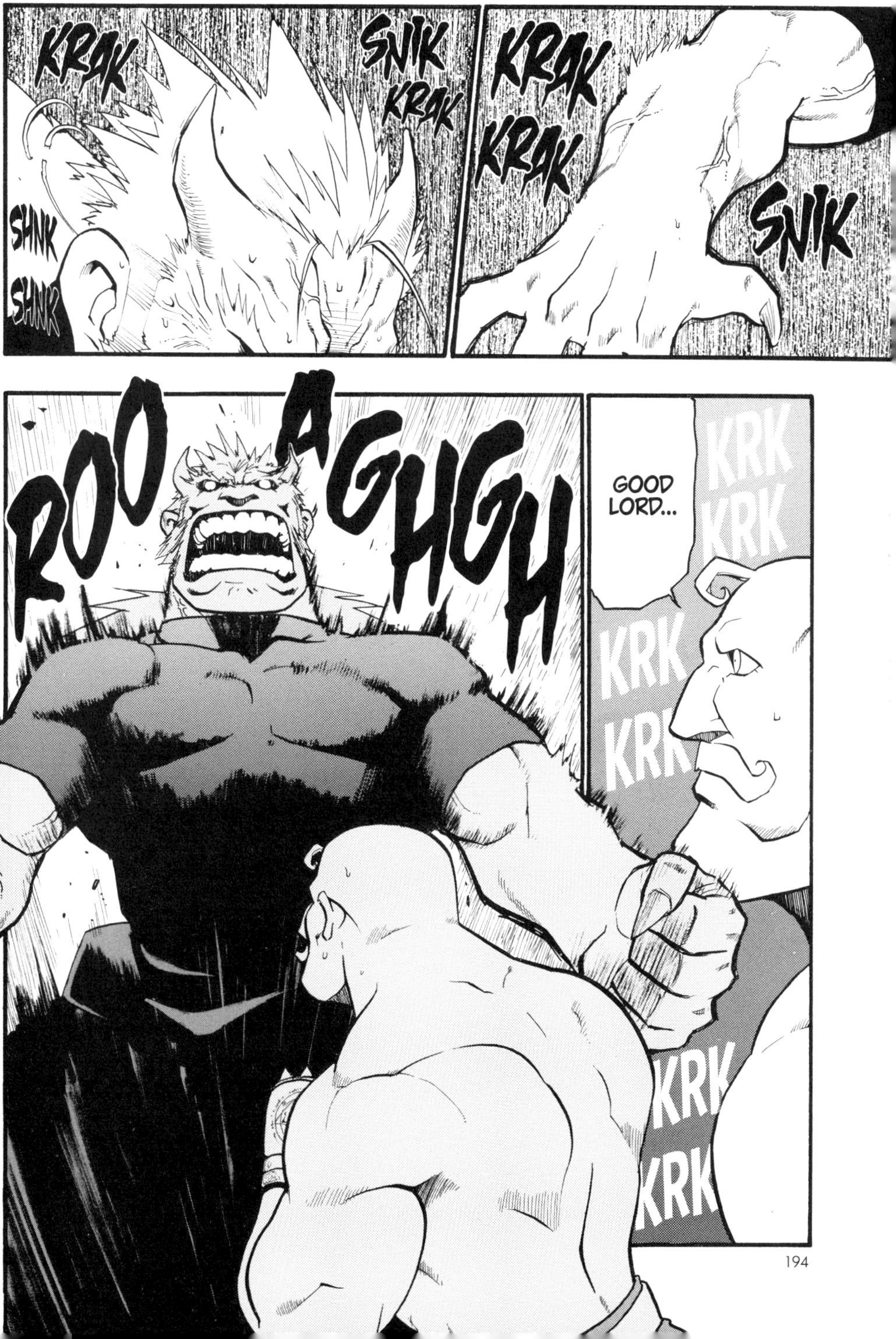
KRAK
KRAK
SNIK
KRAK
SNIK
KRAK
SHNK
SHNK
GOOD LORD...
KRK
KRK
KRK
KRK
KRK
KRK
ROOAGHGH

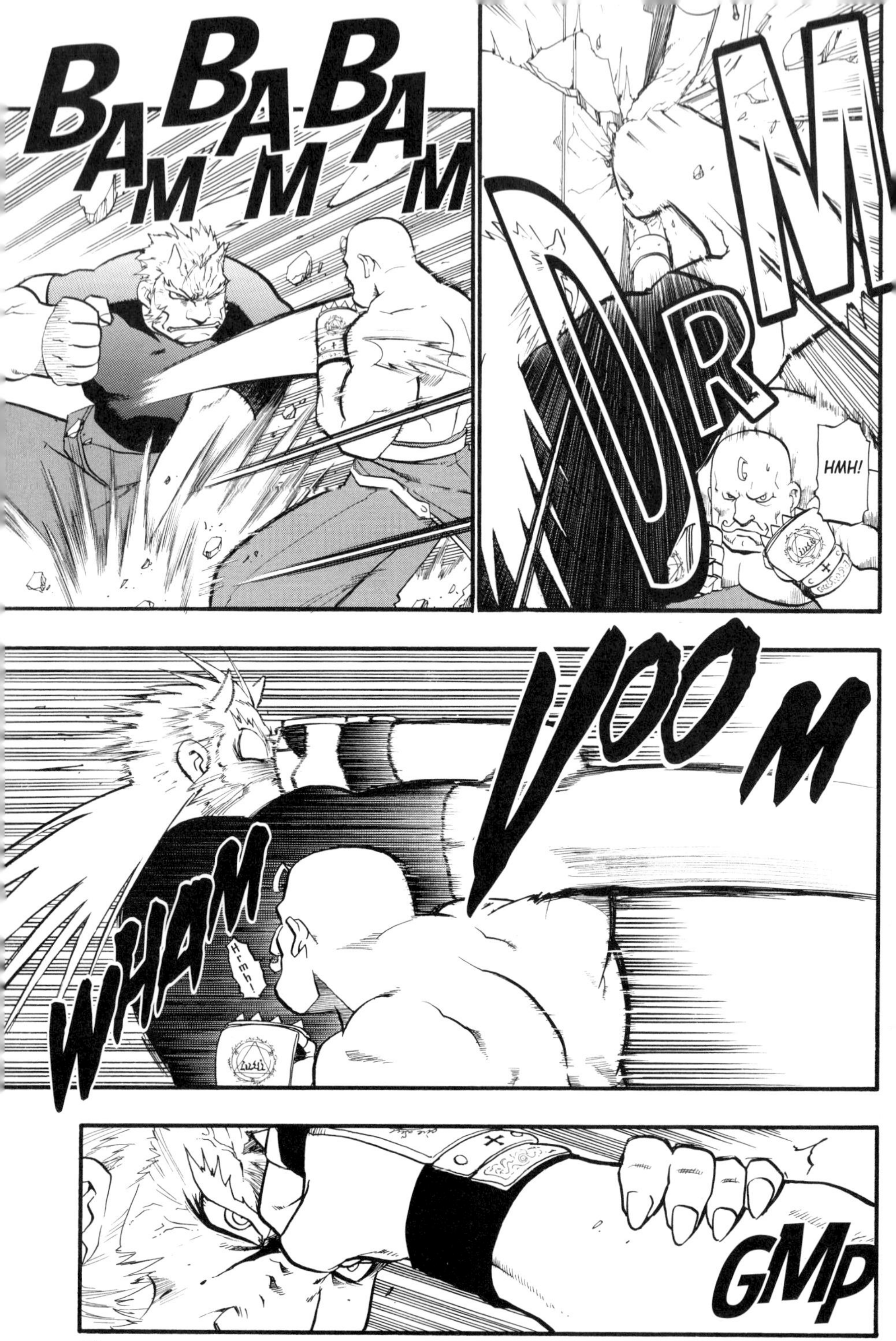
DRMM
HMH!
BAMBAMBAM
VOOM
WHAM
Hrmh!
GMP

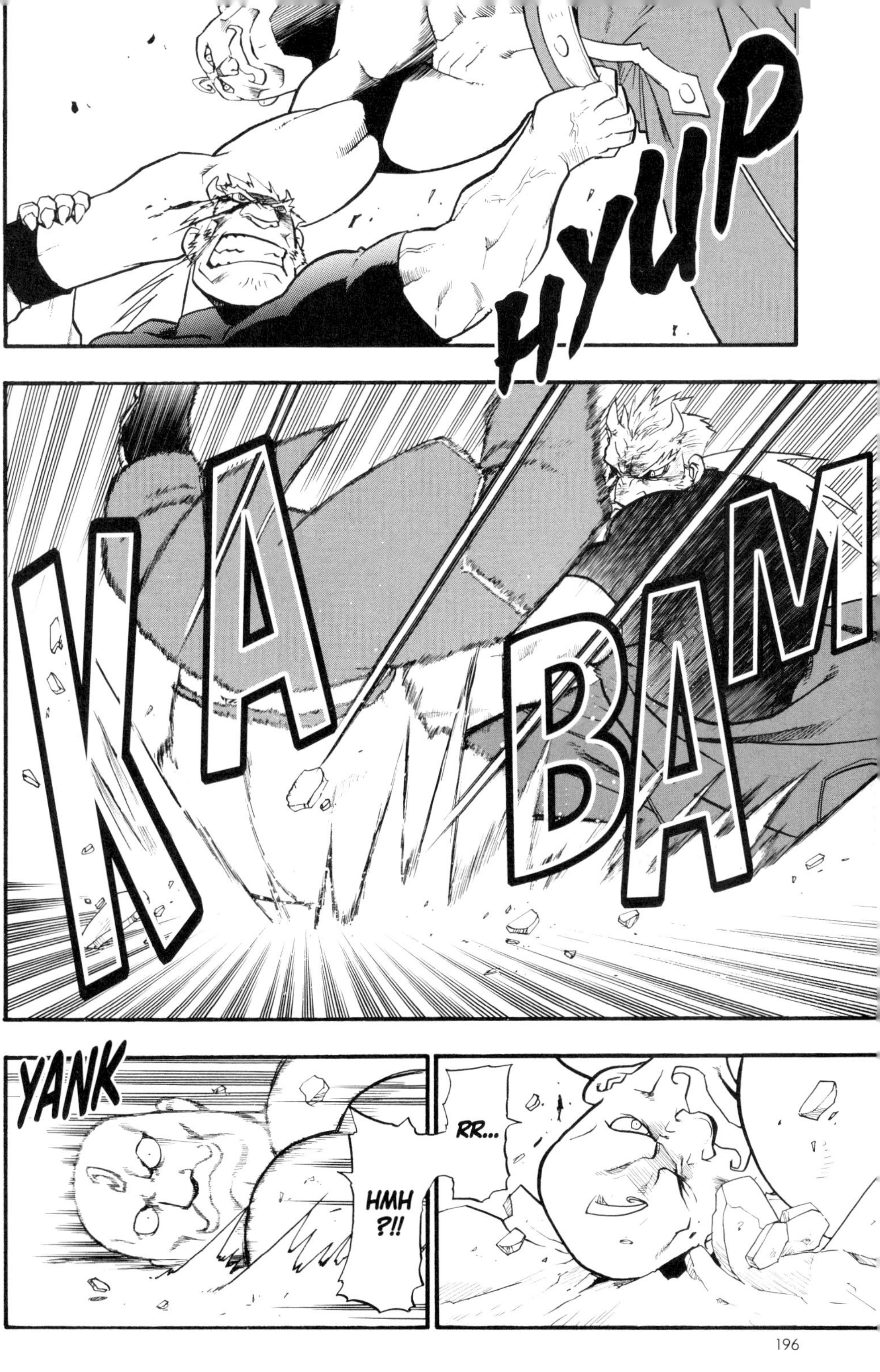
HYUP
KA BAM
RR...
HMH ?!!
YANK

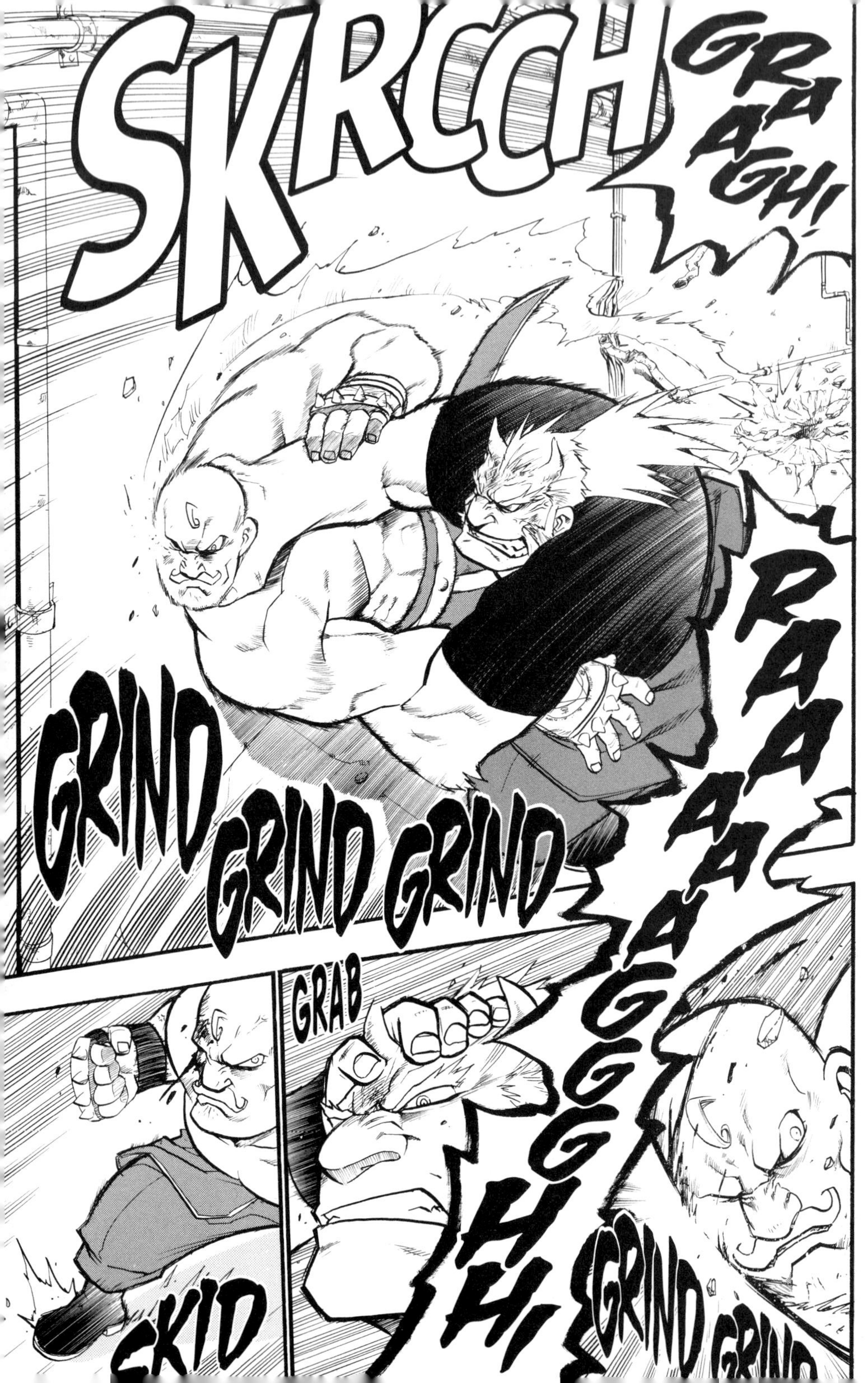
SKRCCH
GRAAAGH!
GRIND GRIND GRIND
RAAAAAGGGGHHH!
GRIND GRIND
GRAB
SKID

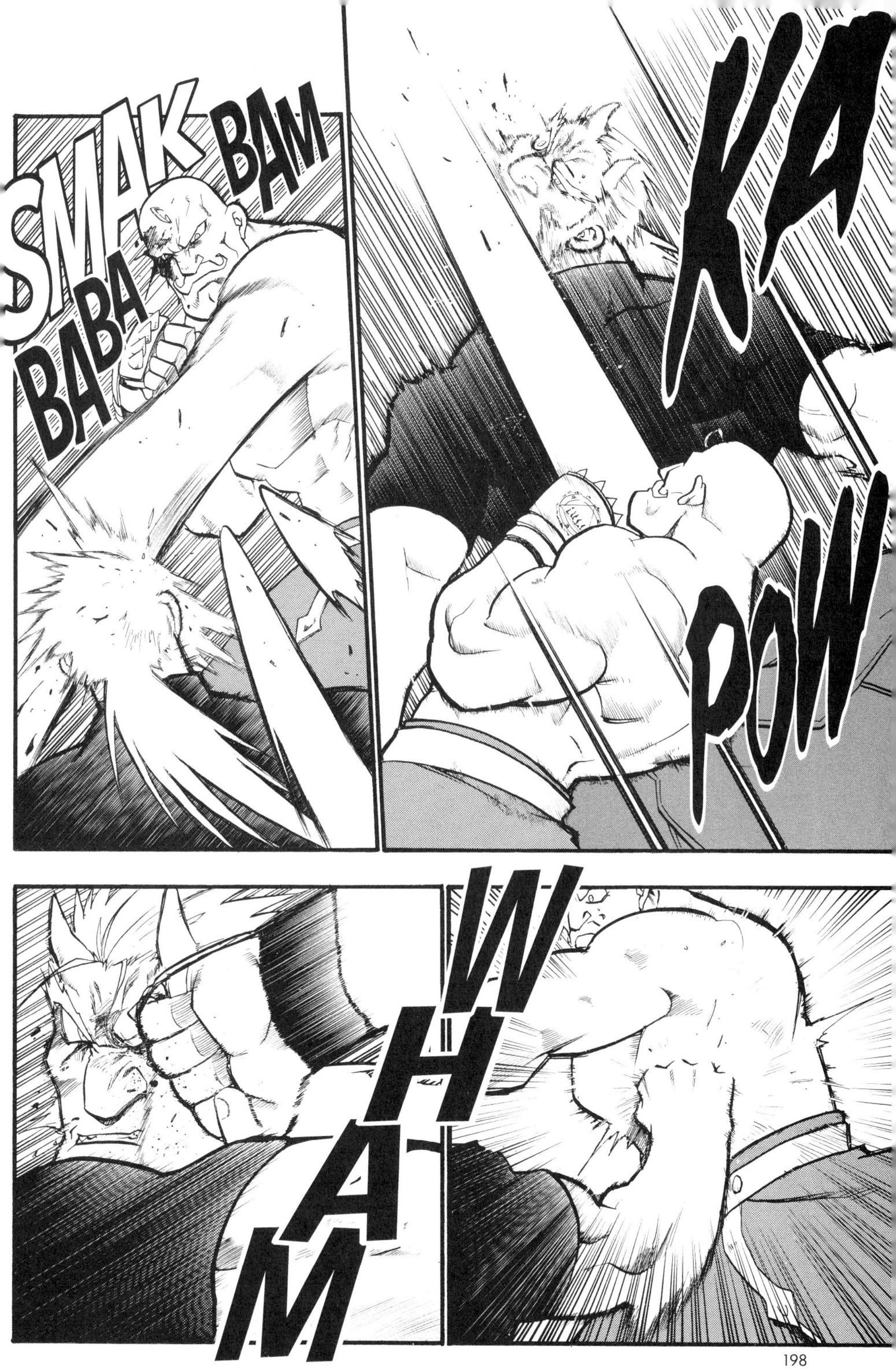
KA
POW
SMAK
BAM
BABA
WHAM

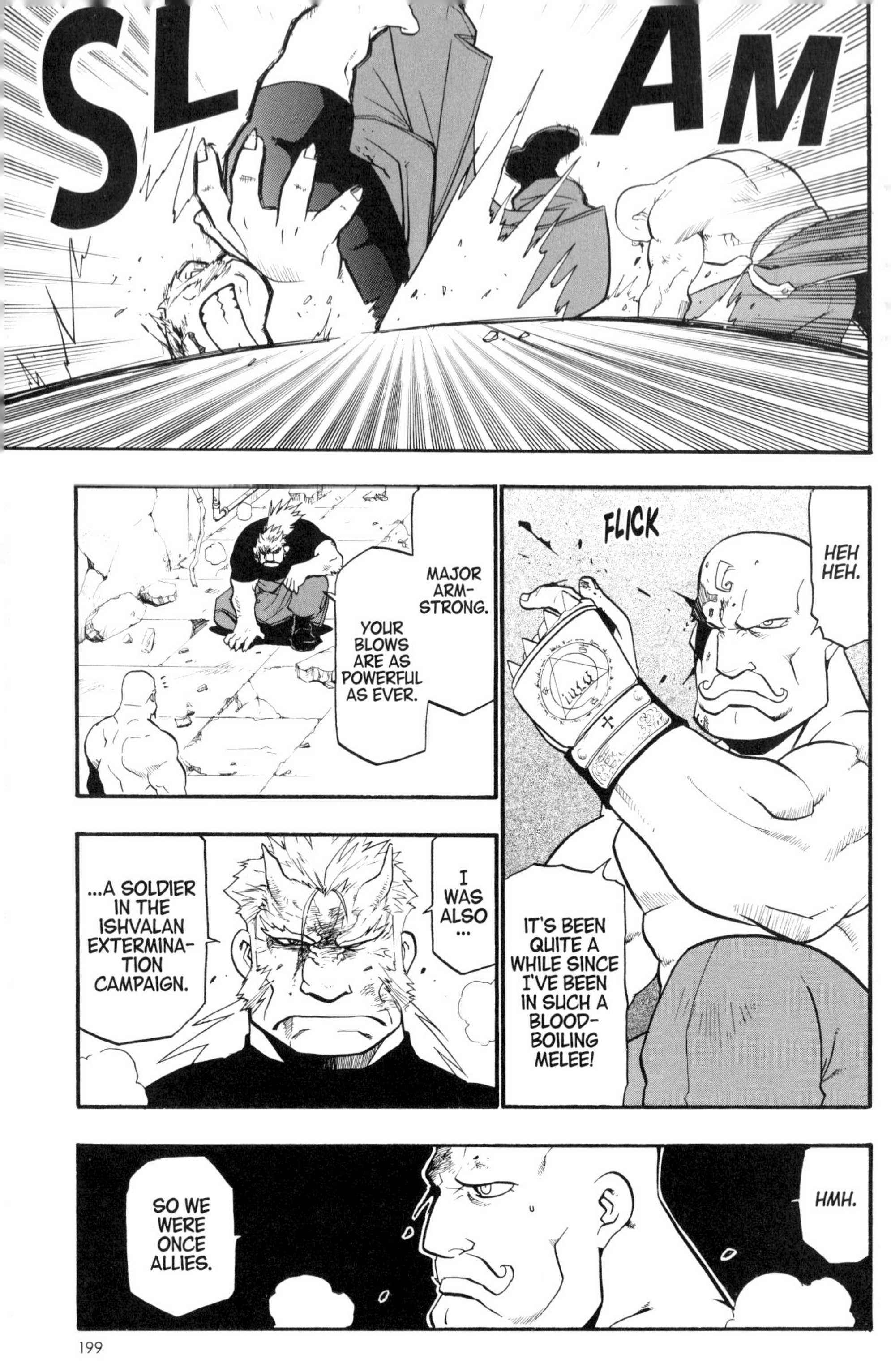
SLAM
FLICK
HEH HEH.
IT'S BEEN QUITE A WHILE SINCE I'VE BEEN IN SUCH A BLOOD-BOILING MELEE!
MAJOR ARM-STRONG.
YOUR BLOWS ARE AS POWERFUL AS EVER.
I WAS ALSO ...
...A SOLDIER IN THE ISHVALAN EXTERMINA-TION CAMPAIGN.
HMH.
SO WE WERE ONCE ALLIES.

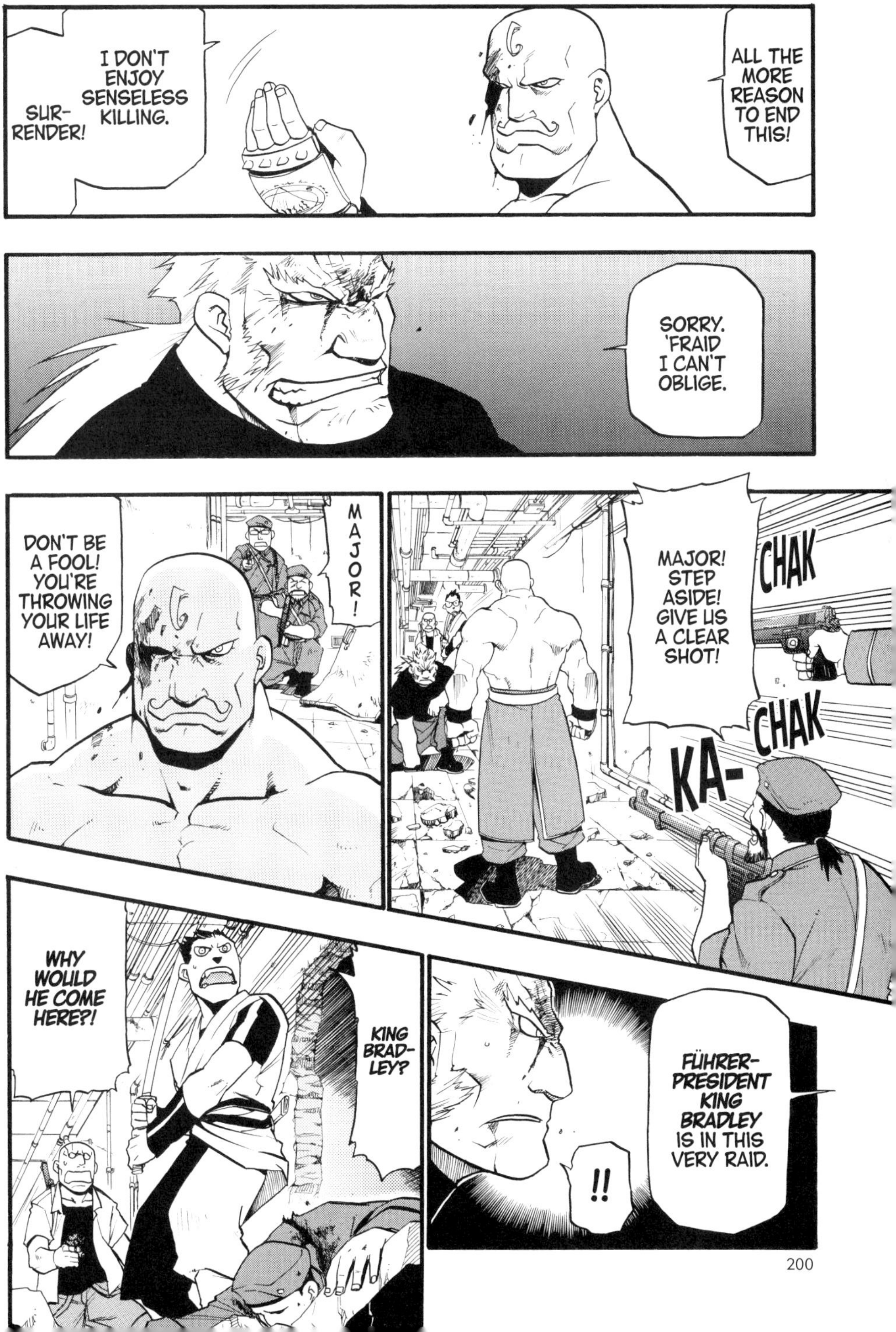
ALL THE MORE REASON TO END THIS!
SUR-RENDER! I DON'T ENJOY SENSELESS KILLING.
SORRY. 'FRAID I CAN'T OBLIGE.
MAJOR! STEP ASIDE! GIVE US A CLEAR SHOT!
CHAK
KA-CHAK
MAJOR!
DON'T BE A FOOL! YOU'RE THROWING YOUR LIFE AWAY!
FÜHRER-PRESIDENT KING BRADLEY IS IN THIS VERY RAID.
!!
KING BRADLEY?
WHY WOULD HE COME HERE?!

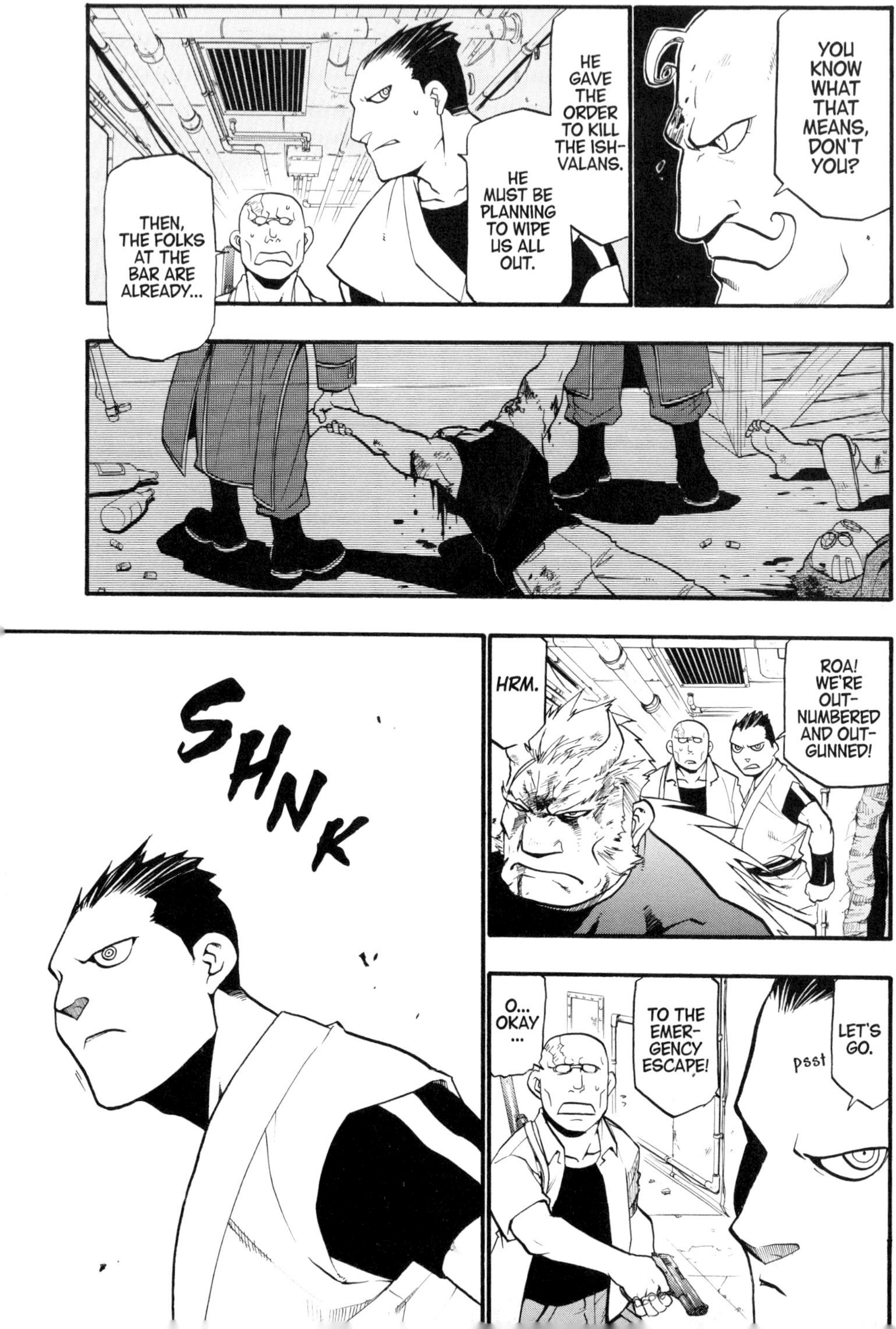
YOU KNOW WHAT THAT MEANS, DON'T YOU?
HE GAVE THE ORDER TO KILL THE ISH-VALANS.
HE MUST BE PLANNING TO WIPE US ALL OUT.
THEN, THE FOLKS AT THE BAR ARE ALREADY...
ROA! WE'RE OUT-NUMBERED AND OUT-GUNNED!
HRM.
LET'S GO.
psst
TO THE EMER-GENCY ESCAPE!
O... OKAY ...
SHNK

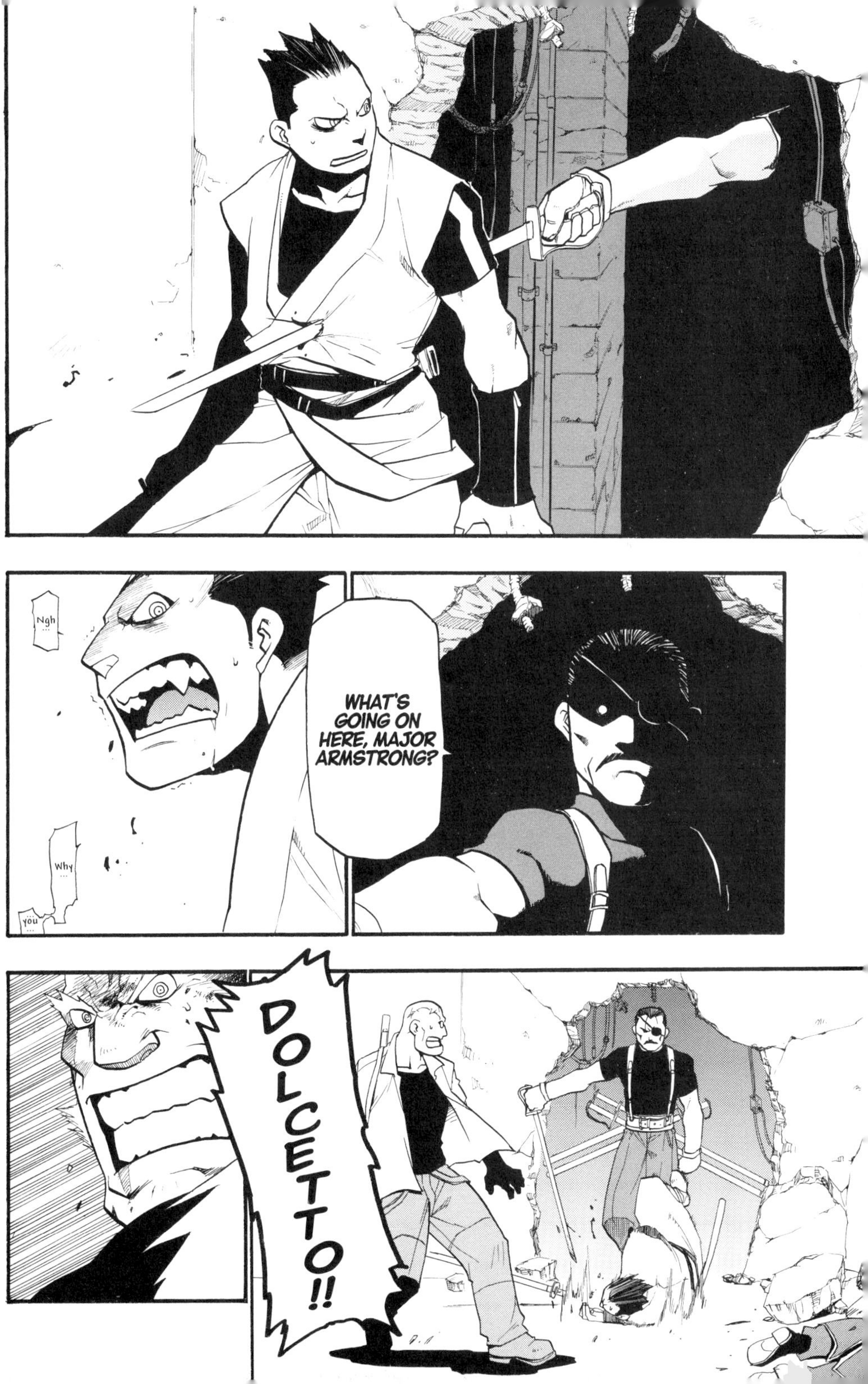
WHAT'S GOING ON HERE, MAJOR ARMSTRONG?
Ngh...
Why...
...you...
DOLCETTO!!

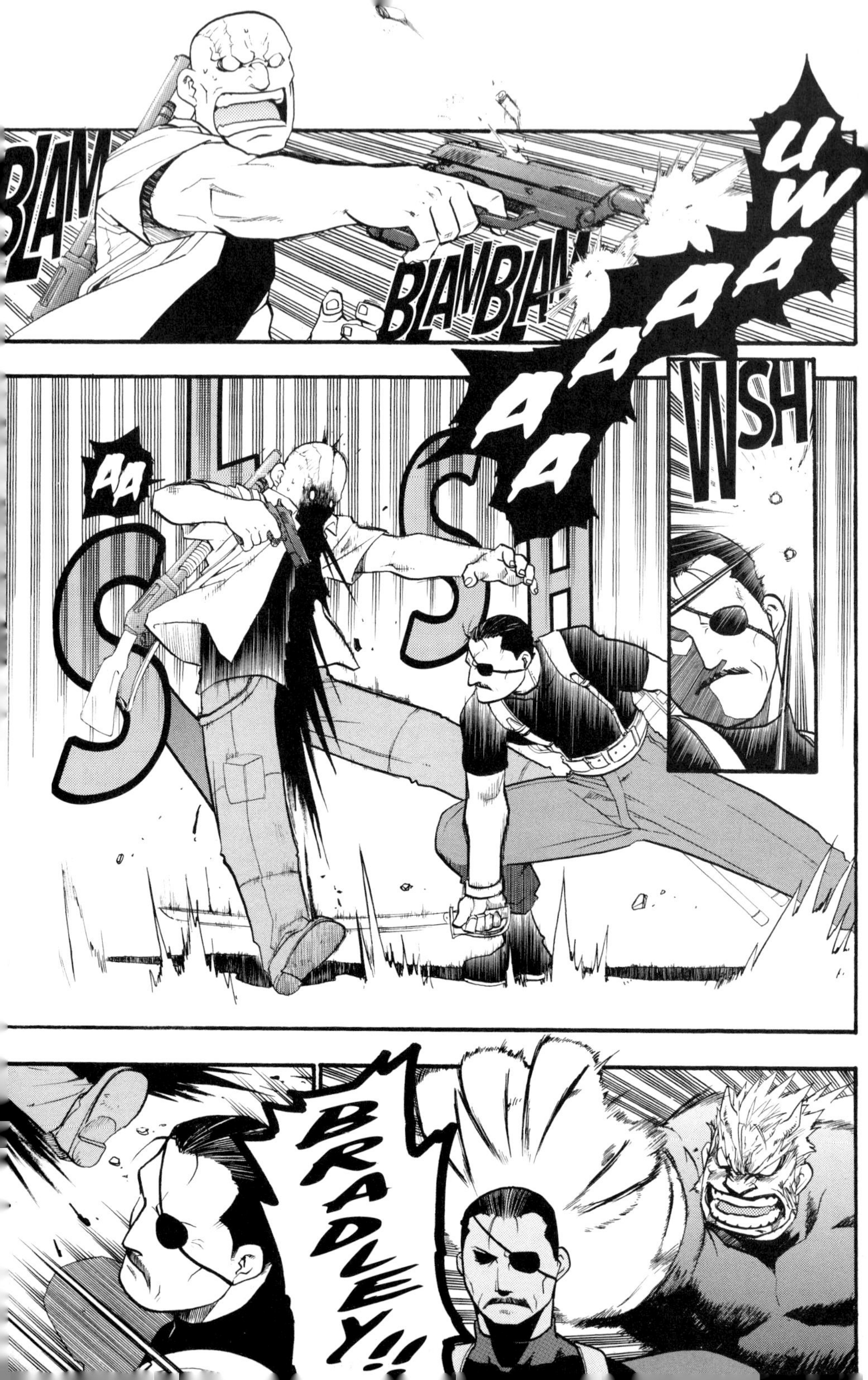
UWAAAAAA
BLAM
BLAMBLAM
WSH
AA
SLSH
BRADLEY!!

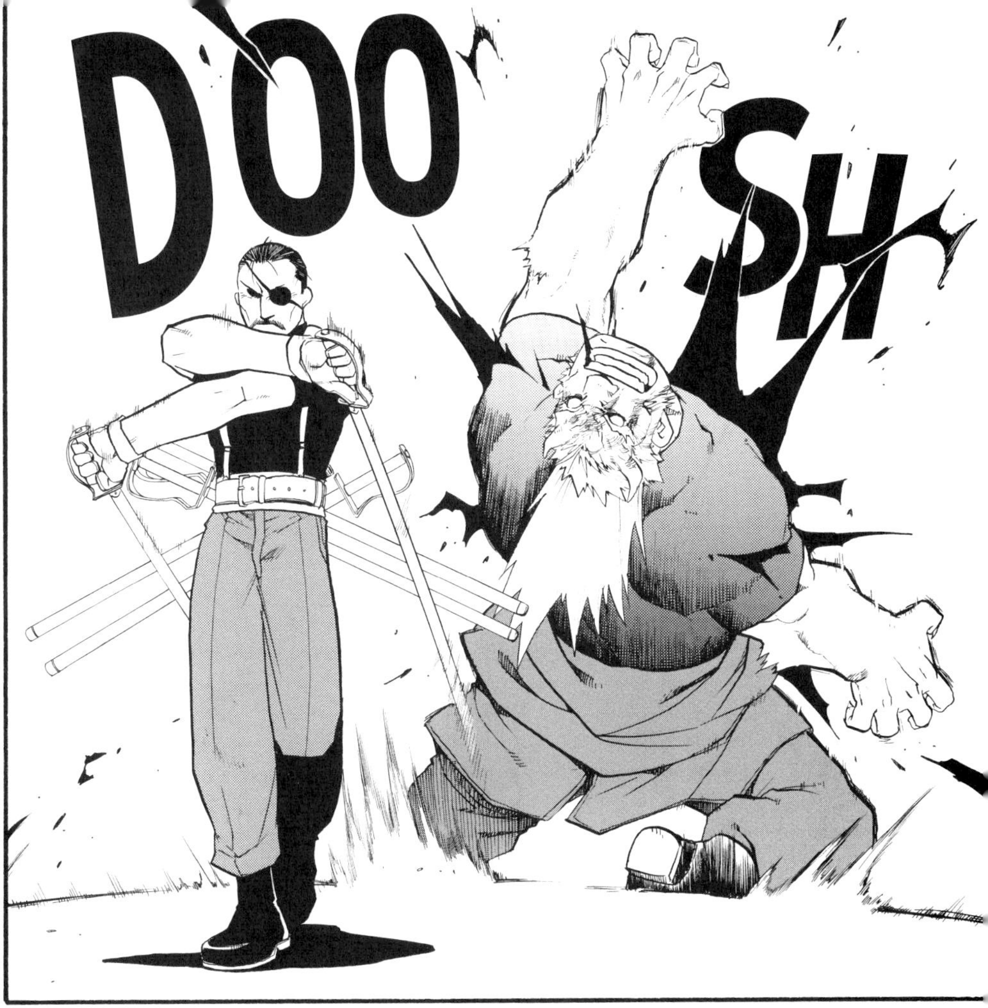
DOOSH

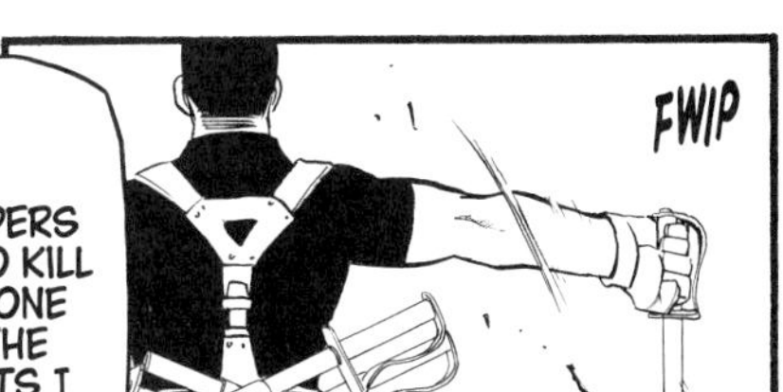
FWIP

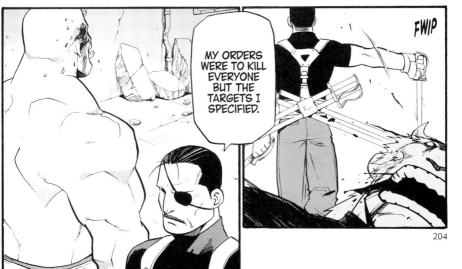

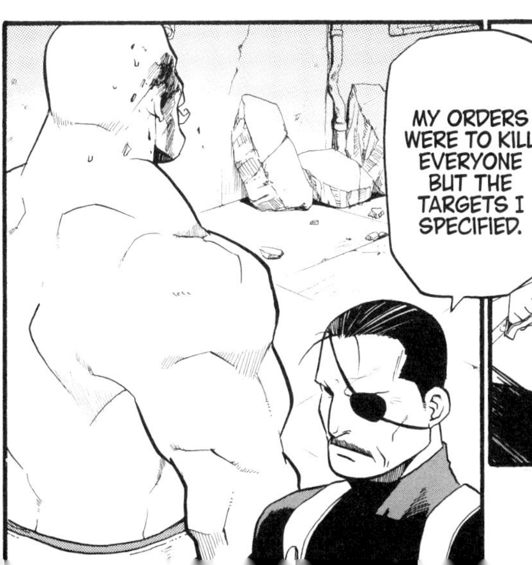
MY ORDERS WERE TO KILL EVERYONE BUT THE TARGETS I SPECIFIED.

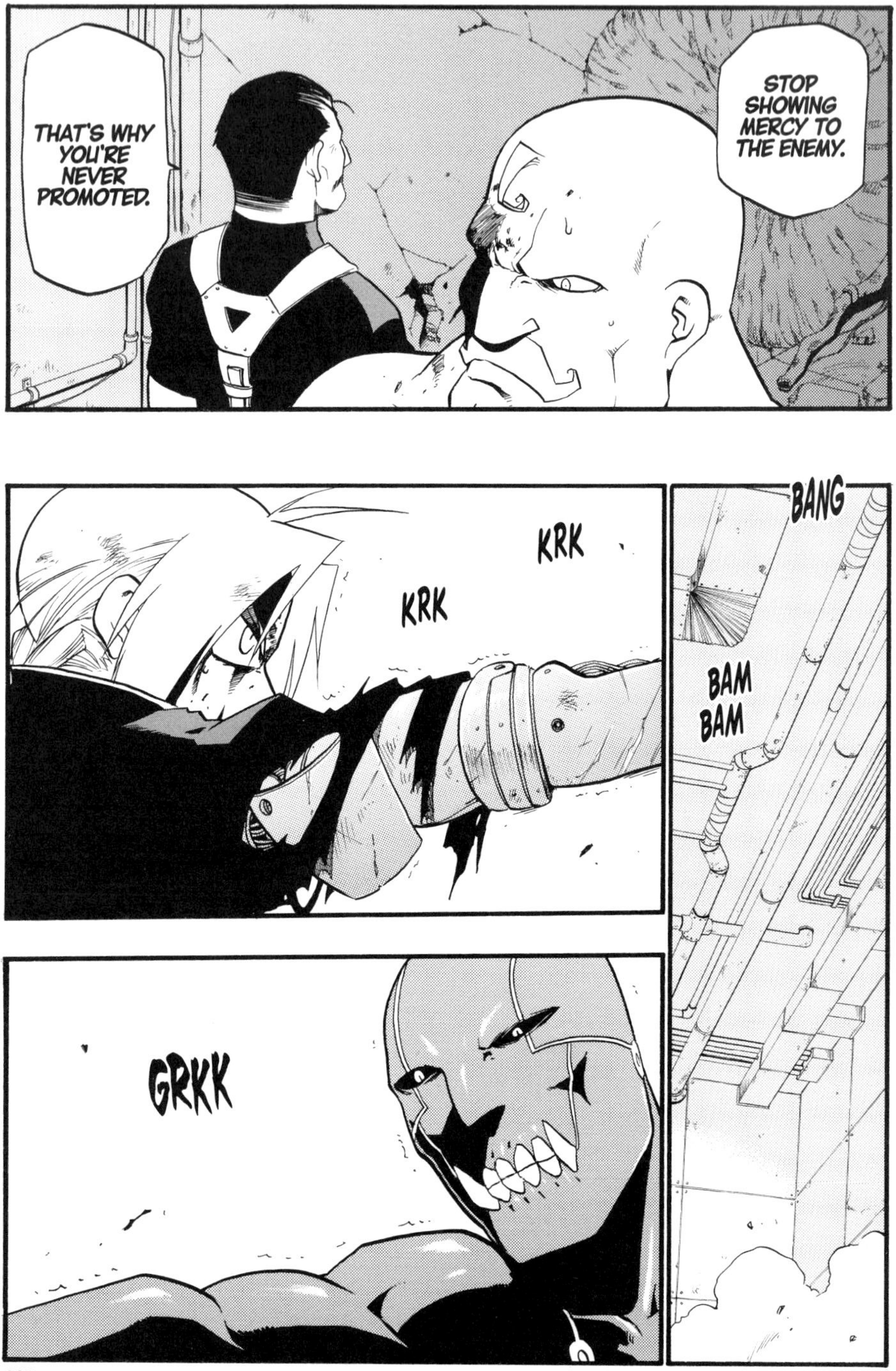
STOP SHOWING MERCY TO THE ENEMY.
THAT'S WHY YOU'RE NEVER PROMOTED.
BANG
BAM BAM
KRK
KRK
GRKK

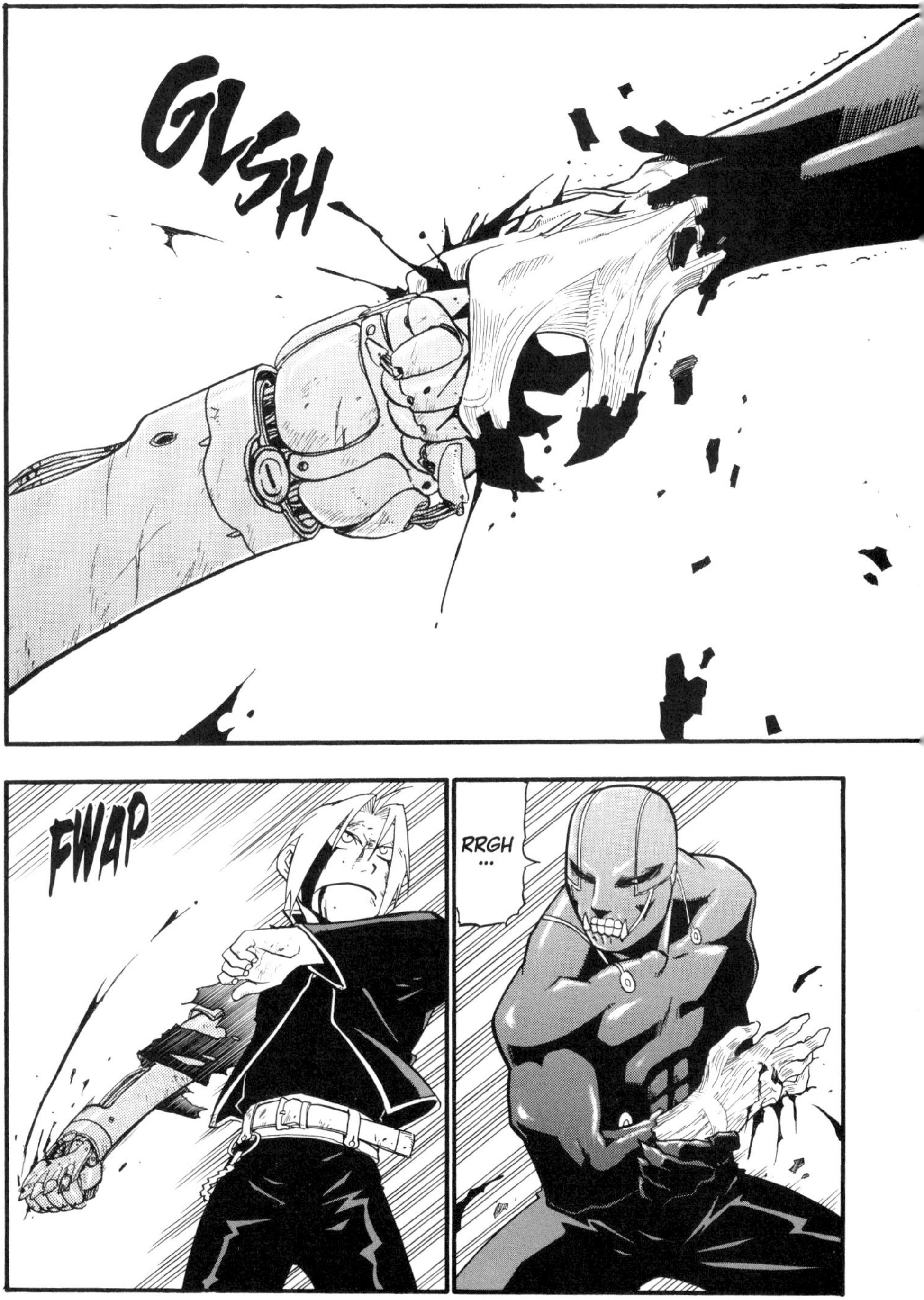
GUSH
RRGH ...
FWAP

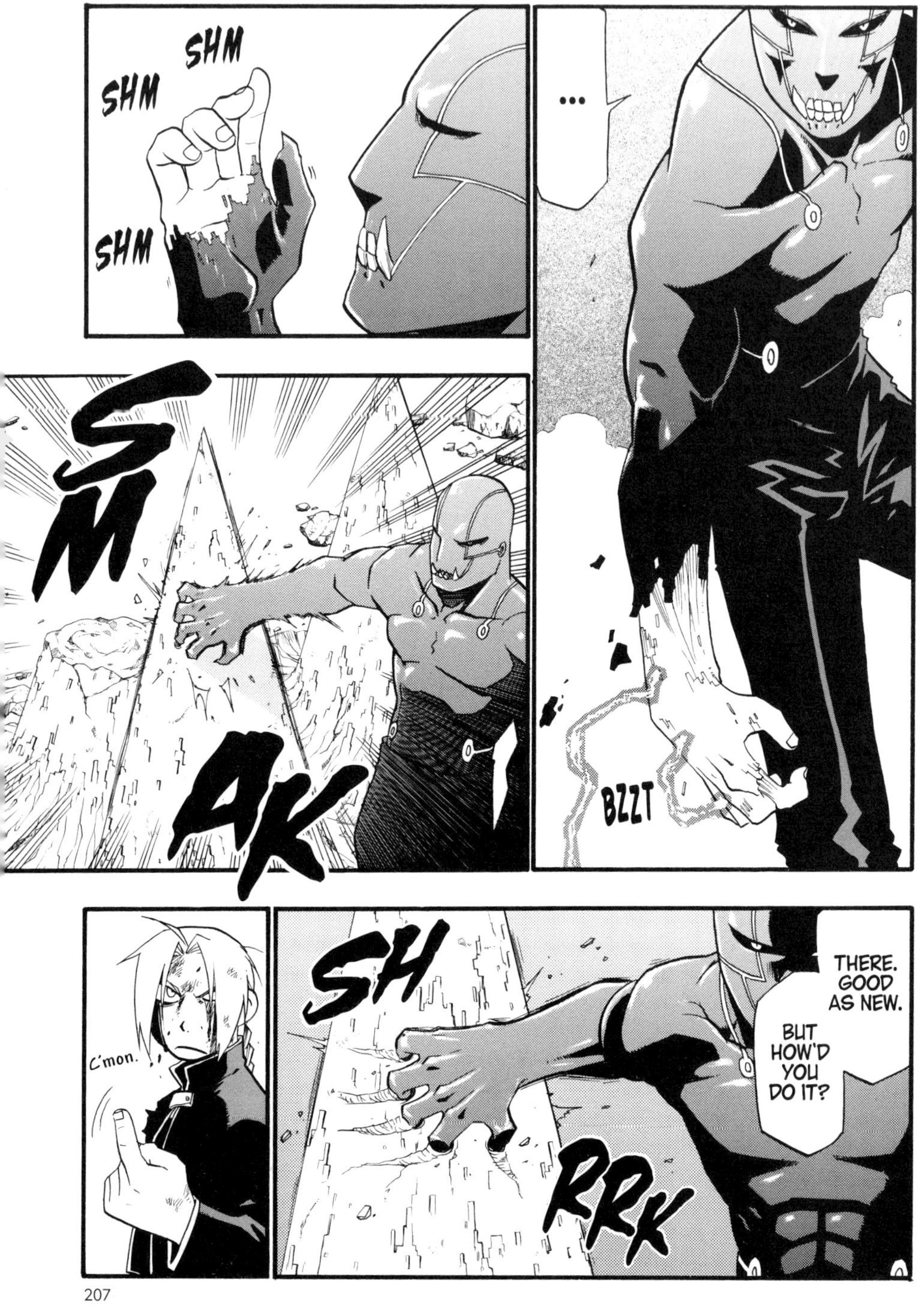
...
BZZT
SHM
SHM
SHM
SMAK
SH
THERE. GOOD AS NEW.
BUT HOW'D YOU DO IT?
RRK
C'mon.

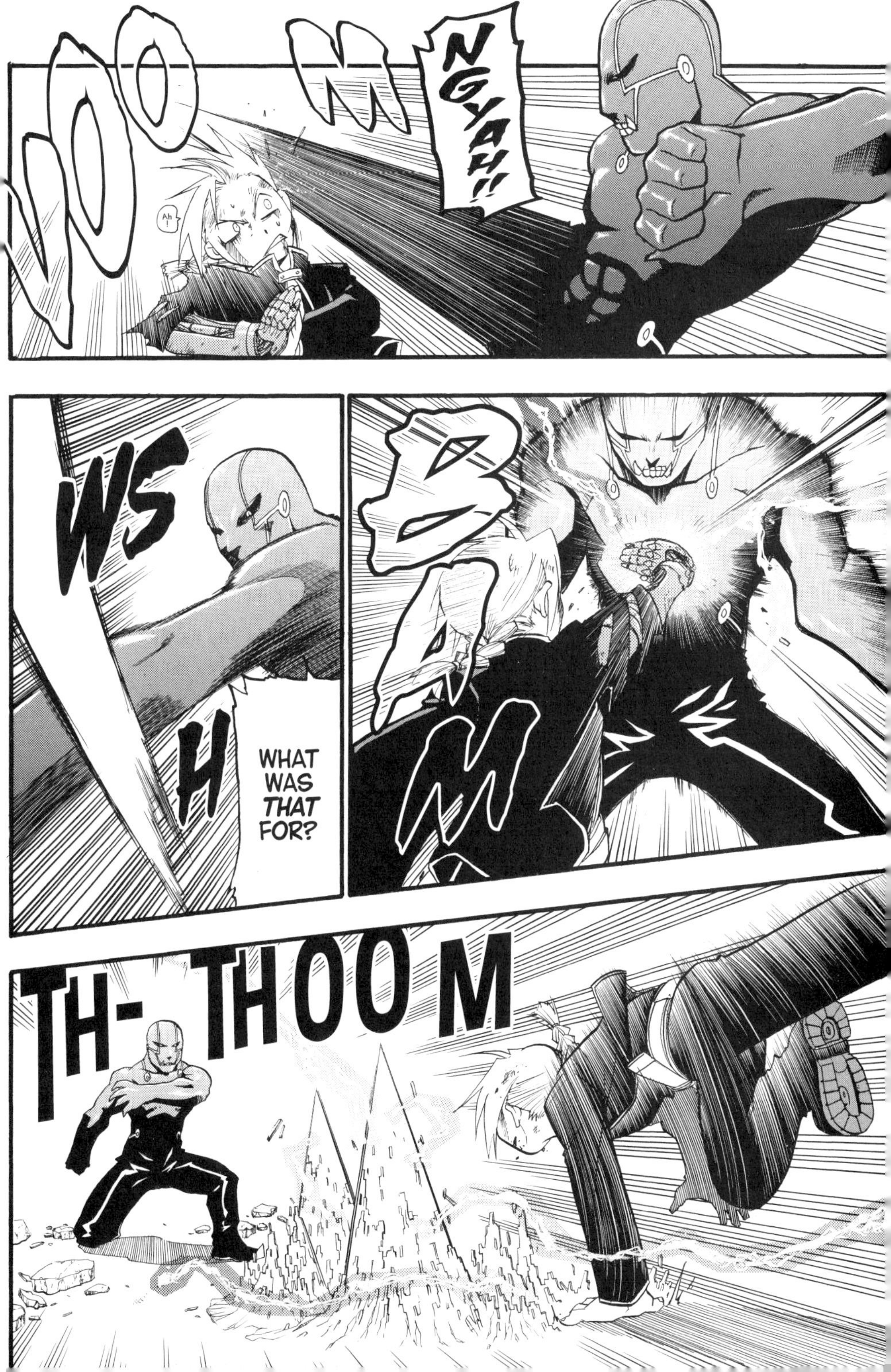
NGYAH!!
Ah!
BAM
WSH
WHAT WAS THAT FOR?
TH- THOOM

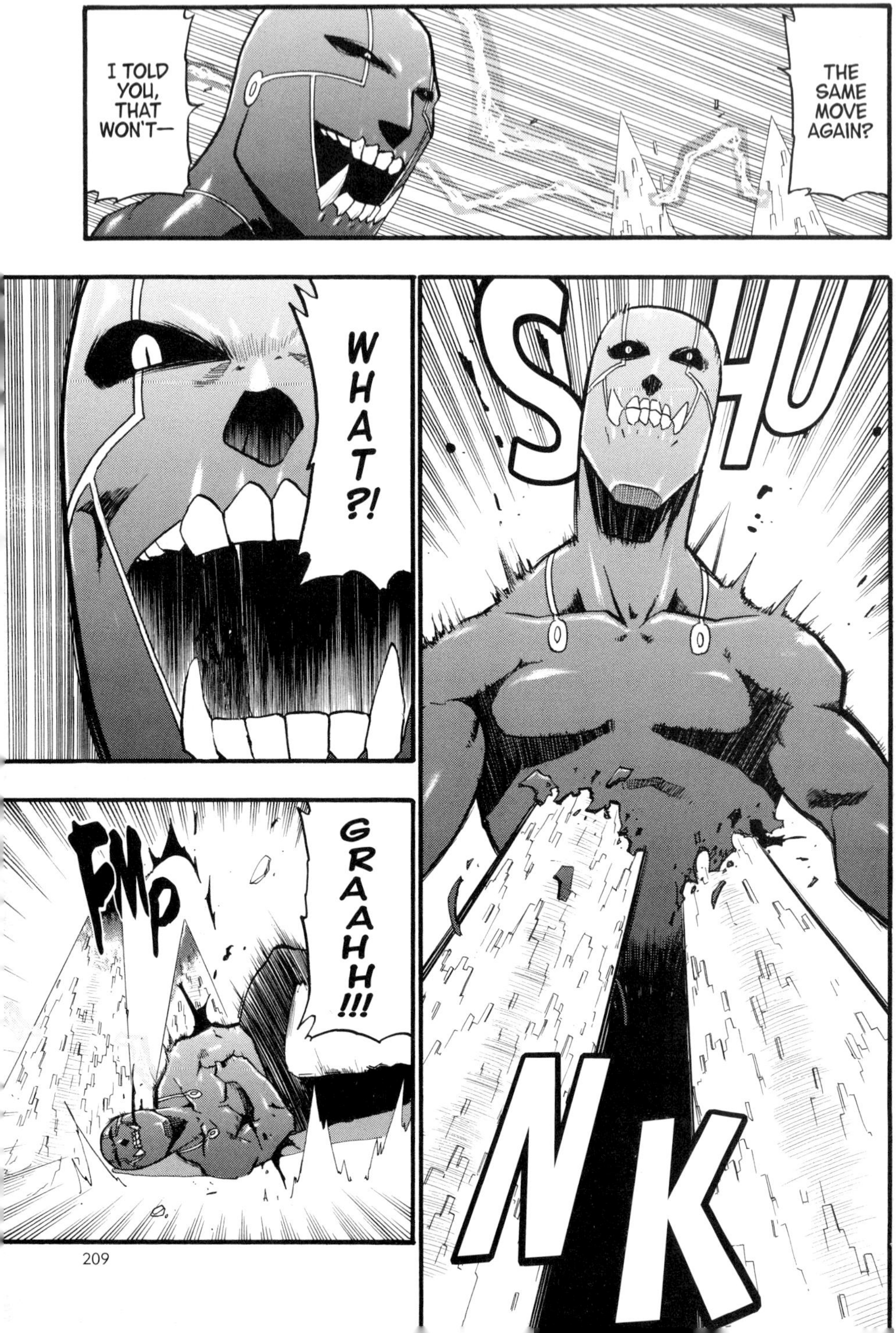
THE SAME MOVE AGAIN?
I TOLD YOU, THAT WON'T—
SHU
NK
WHAT?!
GRAAHH!!!
FMP

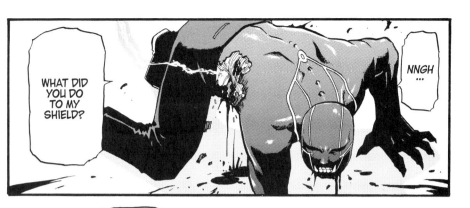

NNGH ...
WHAT DID YOU DO TO MY SHIELD?
IT WAS EASY ENOUGH ONCE I THOUGHT ABOUT IT. YOU CAN'T MAKE SOMETHING OUT OF NOTHING.
THEREFORE YOUR "SHIELD" IS BEING CREATED FROM **SOMETHING.**
YOU TOLD ME YOURSELF THAT YOU'RE CREATED FROM THE SAME BIOLOGICAL MATERIAL AS HUMANS.
AND I THOUGHT, "WHAT'S AN ELEMENT IN THE BODY THAT COULD BECOME A SHIELD THAT'S STRONGER THAN STEEL?"
THE SUBSTANCE THAT MAKES UP ONE-THIRD OF OUR BODIES...
CARBON!

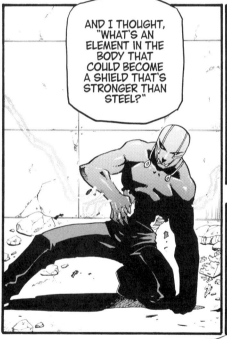

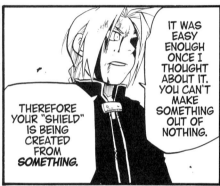

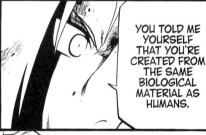

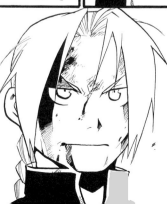

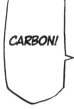

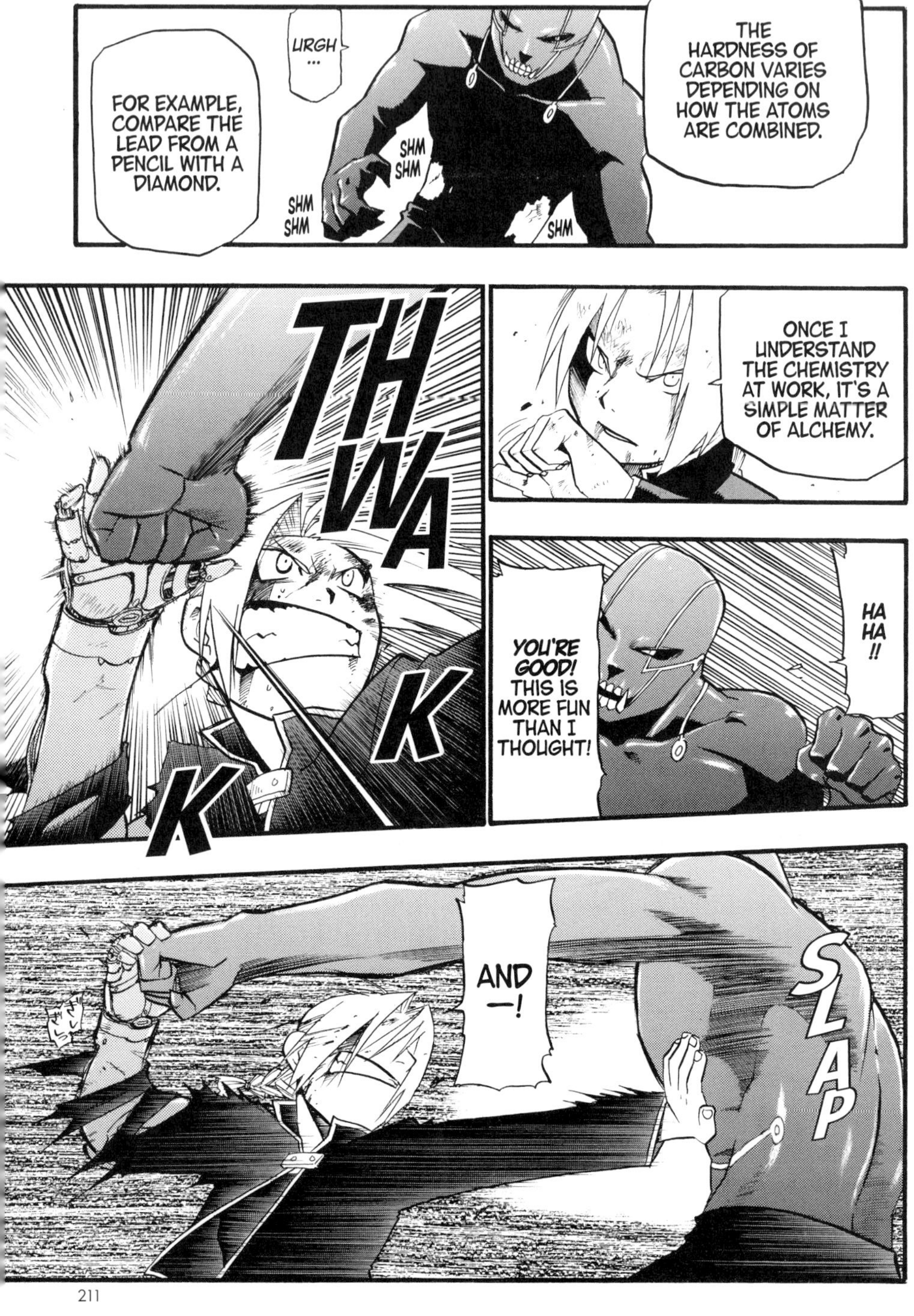
THE HARDNESS OF CARBON VARIES DEPENDING ON HOW THE ATOMS ARE COMBINED.
URGH...
SHM SHM
SHM
SHM SHM
FOR EXAMPLE, COMPARE THE LEAD FROM A PENCIL WITH A DIAMOND.
ONCE I UNDERSTAND THE CHEMISTRY AT WORK, IT'S A SIMPLE MATTER OF ALCHEMY.
HA HA !!
YOU'RE GOOD! THIS IS MORE FUN THAN I THOUGHT!
THWAKK
SLAP
AND—!

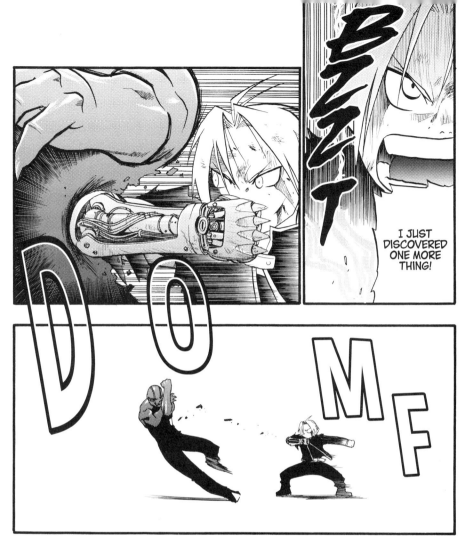

BZZT

I JUST DISCOVERED ONE MORE THING!

DOMF

YOU CAN'T HARDEN YOUR BODY AND REGENERATE AT THE SAME TIME!

GUGH

RRIP RRIP

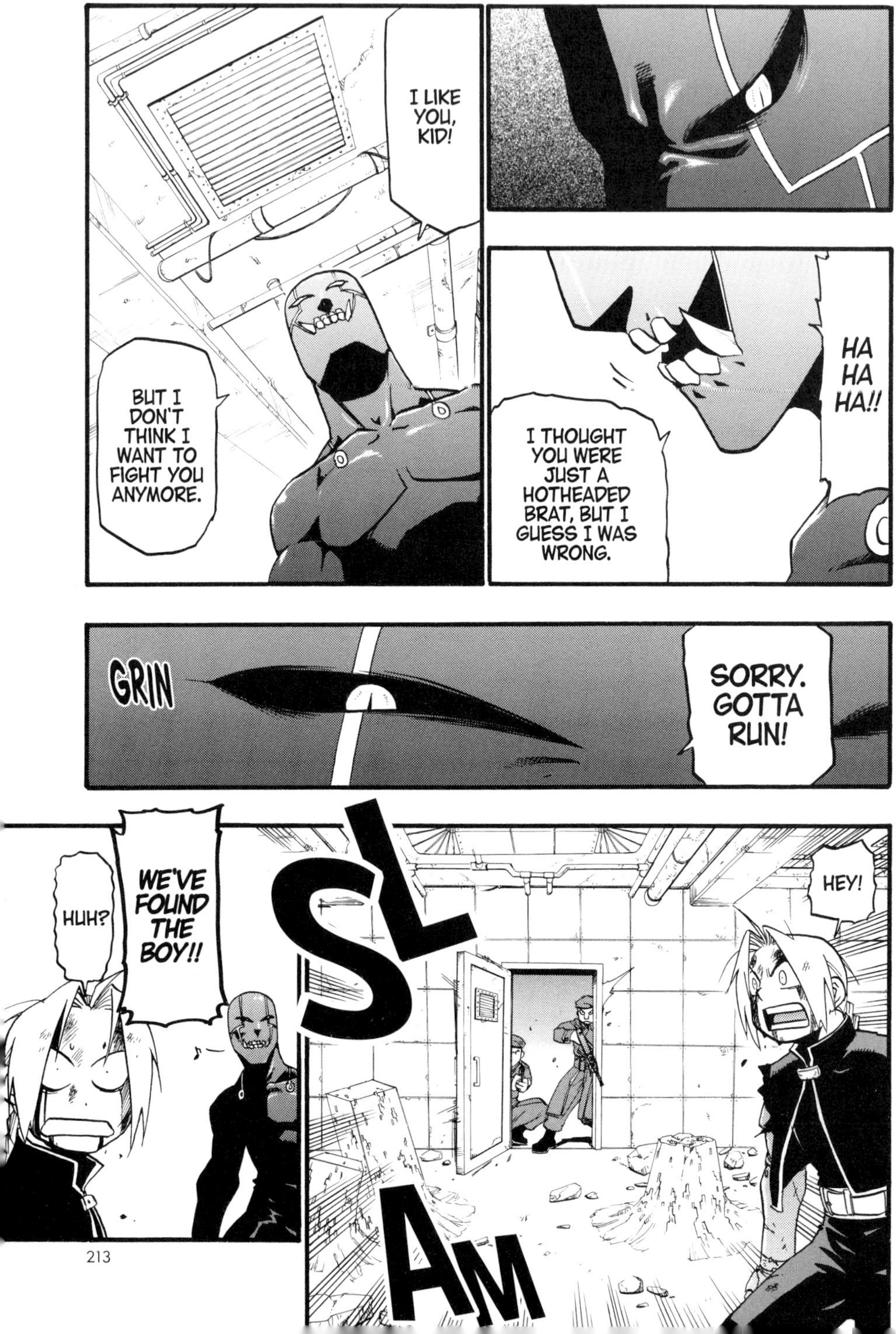
HA HA HA!!
I THOUGHT YOU WERE JUST A HOTHEADED BRAT, BUT I GUESS I WAS WRONG.
I LIKE YOU, KID!
BUT I DON'T THINK I WANT TO FIGHT YOU ANYMORE.
SORRY. GOTTA RUN!
GRIN
HEY!
SLAM
WE'VE FOUND THE BOY!!
HUH?

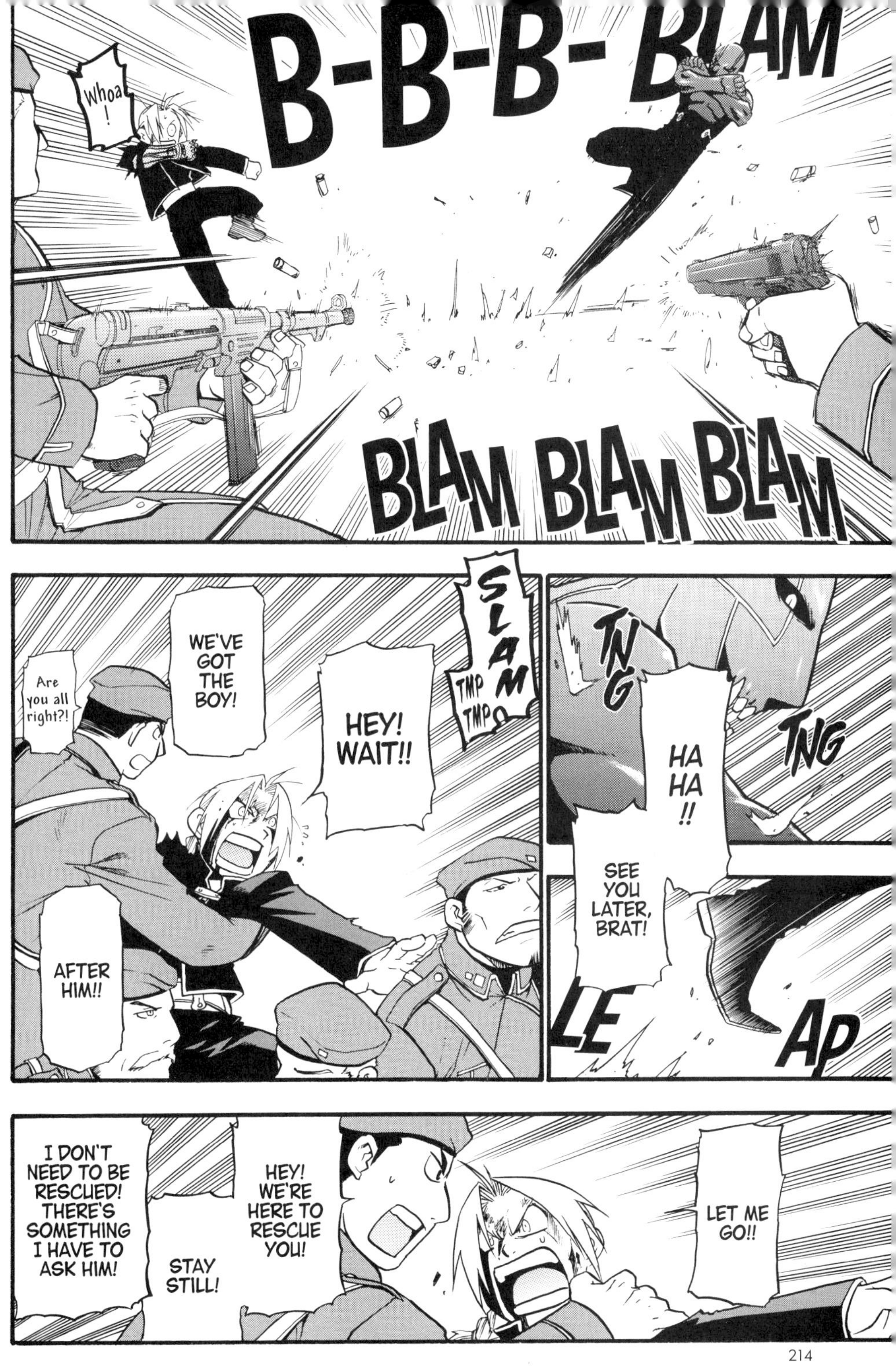
B-B-B-B-BLAM
Whoa!
BLAM BLAM BLAM
TNG
TNG
HA HA!!
SEE YOU LATER, BRAT!
LEAP
SLAM
TMP TMP
HEY! WAIT!!
WE'VE GOT THE BOY!
Are you all right?!
AFTER HIM!!
LET ME GO!!
HEY! WE'RE HERE TO RESCUE YOU!
STAY STILL!
I DON'T NEED TO BE RESCUED! THERE'S SOMETHING I HAVE TO ASK HIM!

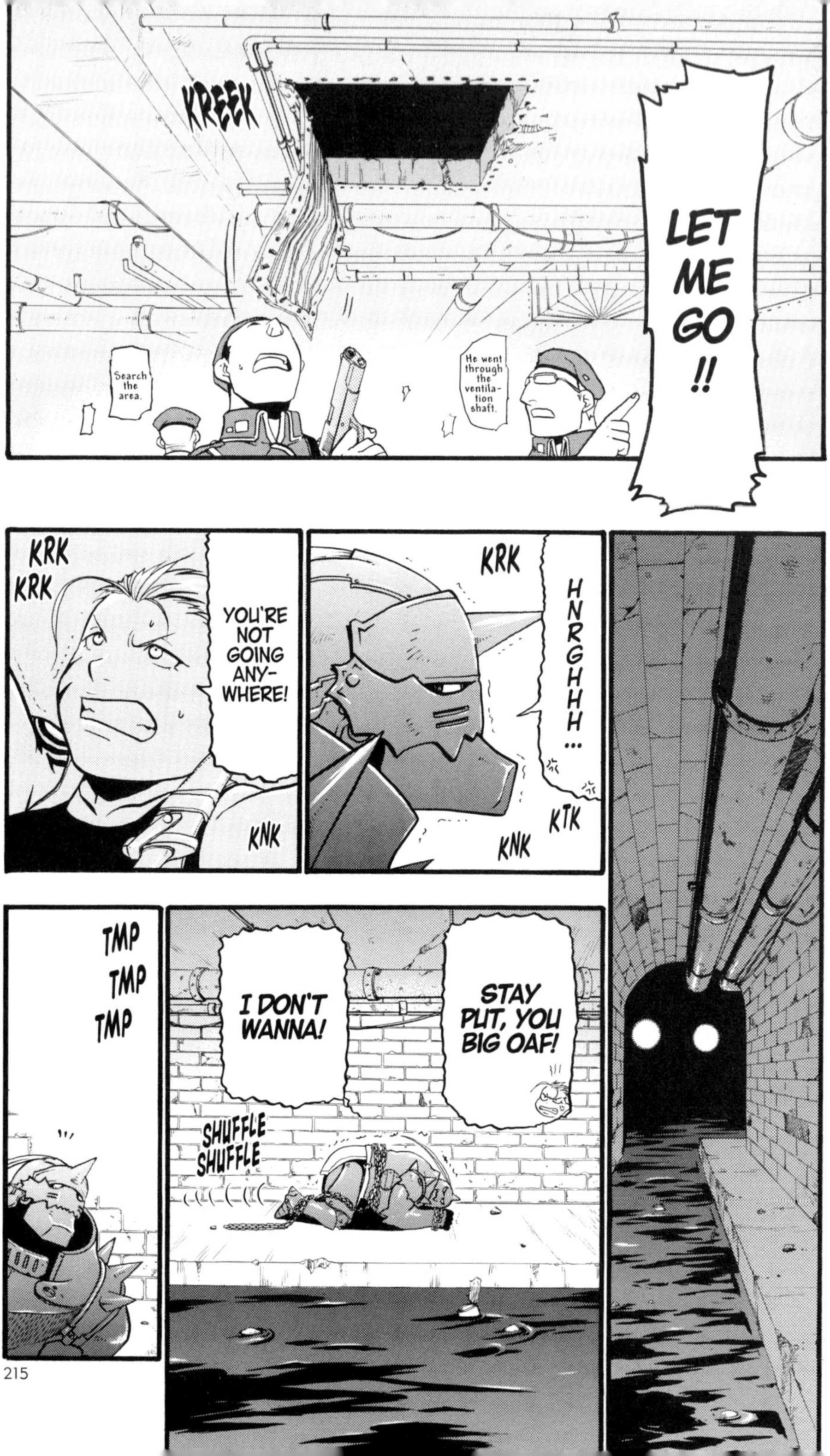
LET ME GO!!
KREEK
He went through the ventila-tion shaft.
Search the area.
KRK
HNRGHHH...
KTK
KNK
KRK KRK
YOU'RE NOT GOING ANY-WHERE!
KNK
STAY PUT, YOU BIG OAF!
I DON'T WANNA!
SHUFFLE SHUFFLE
TMP TMP TMP

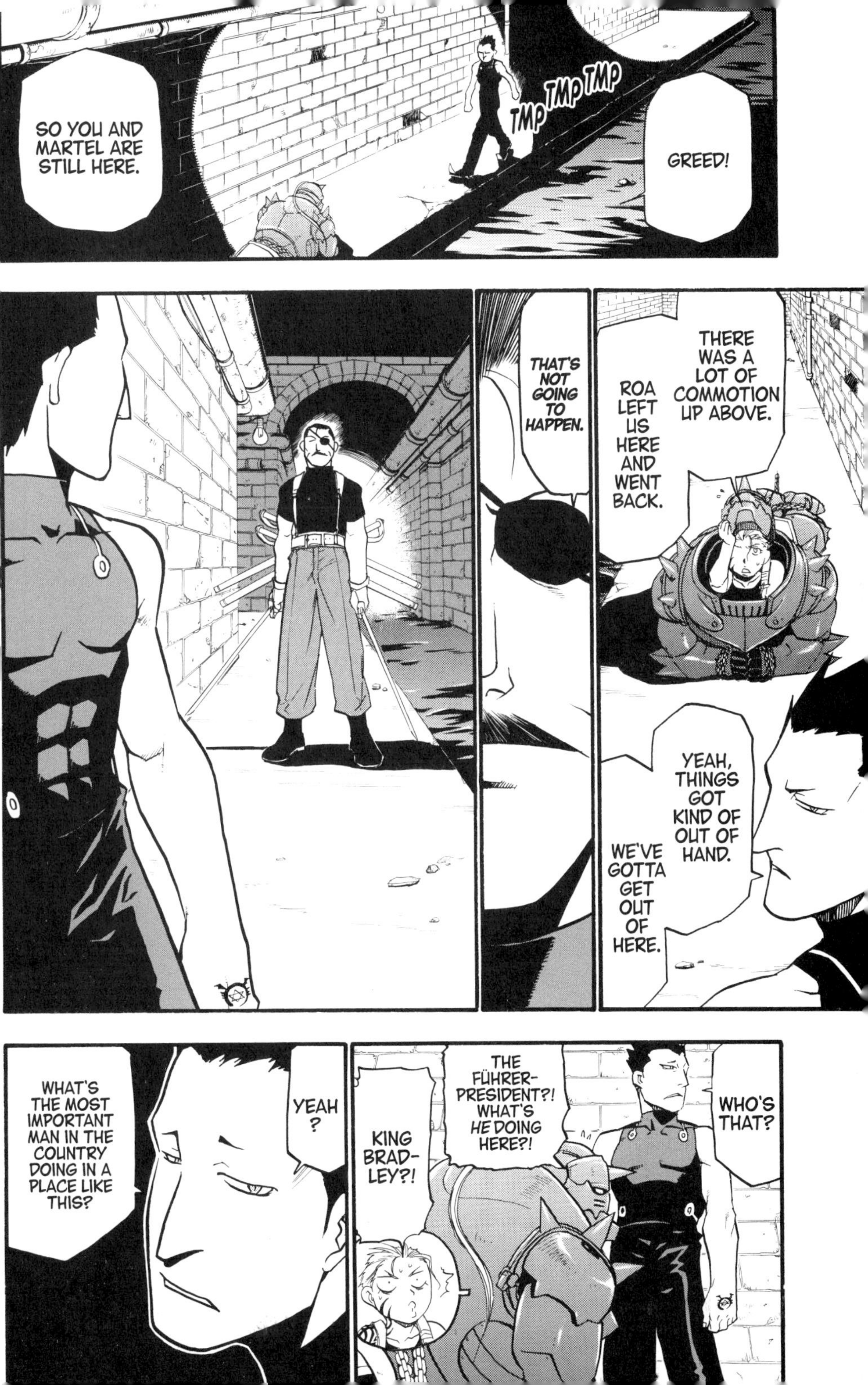
GREED!
TMP TMP TMP
SO YOU AND MARTEL ARE STILL HERE.
THERE WAS A LOT OF COMMOTION UP ABOVE.
ROA LEFT US HERE AND WENT BACK.
YEAH, THINGS GOT KIND OF OUT OF HAND.
WE'VE GOTTA GET OUT OF HERE.
THAT'S NOT GOING TO HAPPEN.
WHO'S THAT?
THE FÜHRER-PRESIDENT?! WHAT'S HE DOING HERE?!
KING BRADLEY?!
YEAH?
WHAT'S THE MOST IMPORTANT MAN IN THE COUNTRY DOING IN A PLACE LIKE THIS?

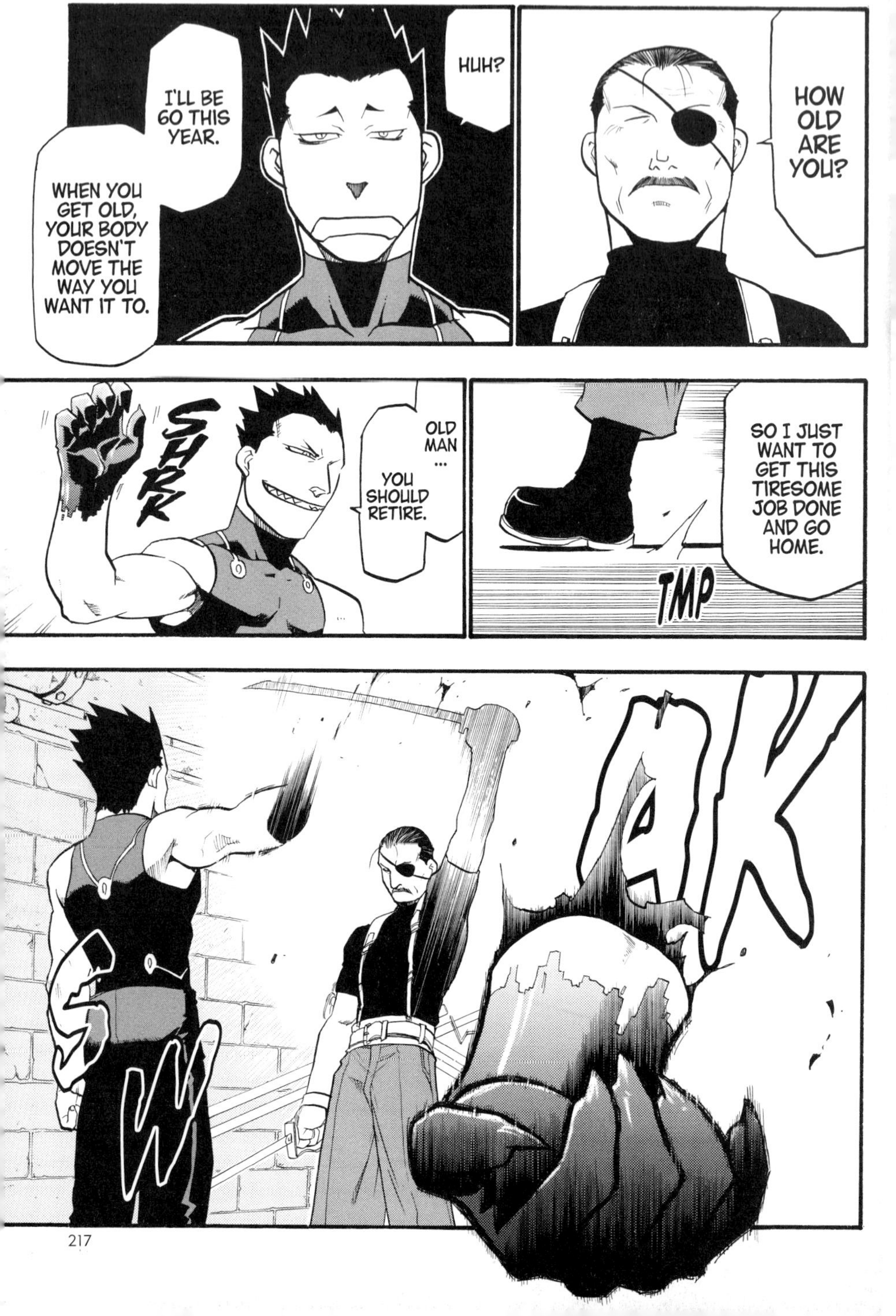
HOW OLD ARE YOU?
HUH?
I'LL BE 60 THIS YEAR.
WHEN YOU GET OLD, YOUR BODY DOESN'T MOVE THE WAY YOU WANT IT TO.
SO I JUST WANT TO GET THIS TIRESOME JOB DONE AND GO HOME.
TMP
SHRK
OLD MAN ...
YOU SHOULD RETIRE.
...
AK

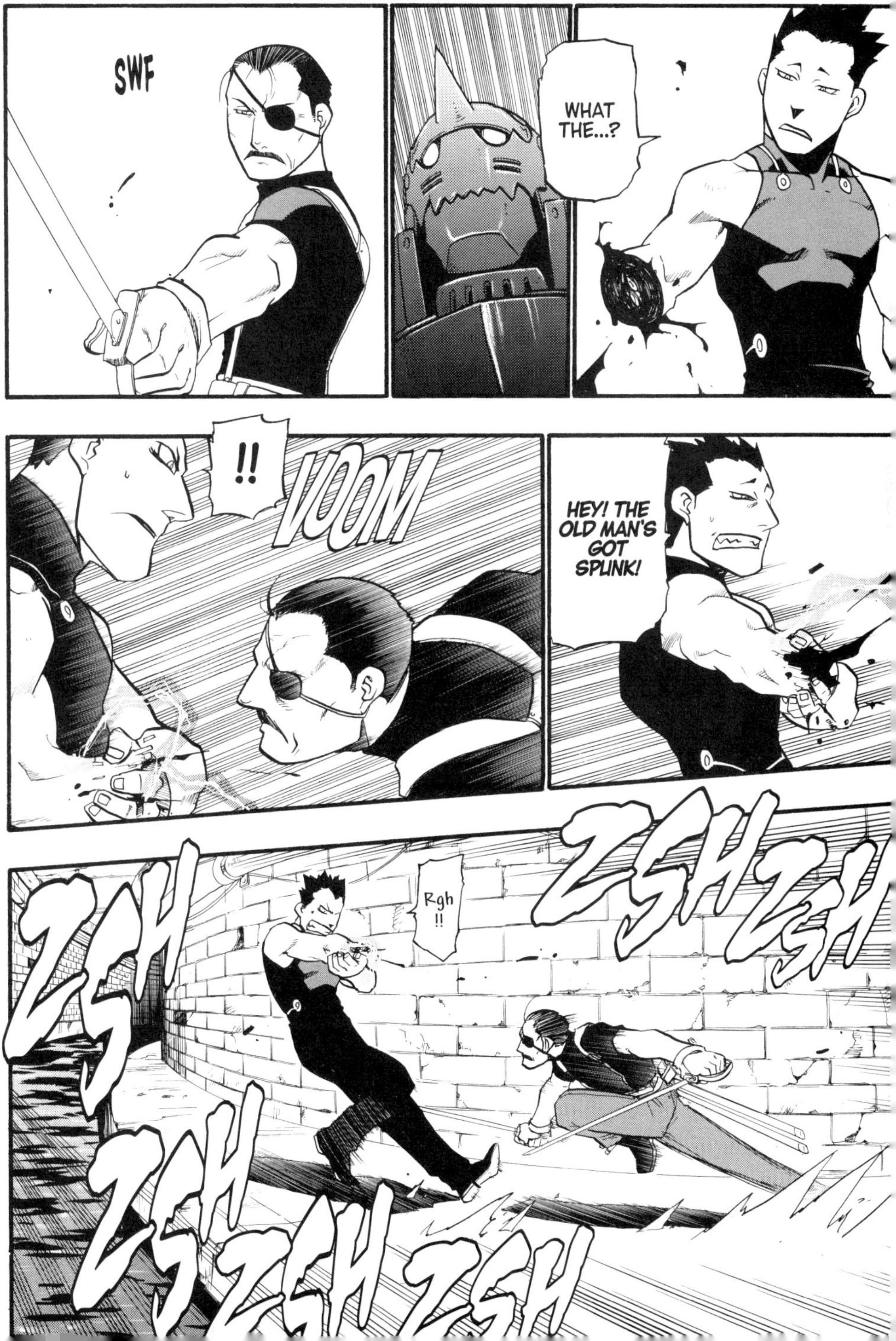
WHAT THE...?
SWF
HEY! THE OLD MAN'S GOT SPLUNK!
!!
VOOM
ZSH ZSH ZSH
Rgh !!
ZSH
ZSH ZSH ZSH ZSH

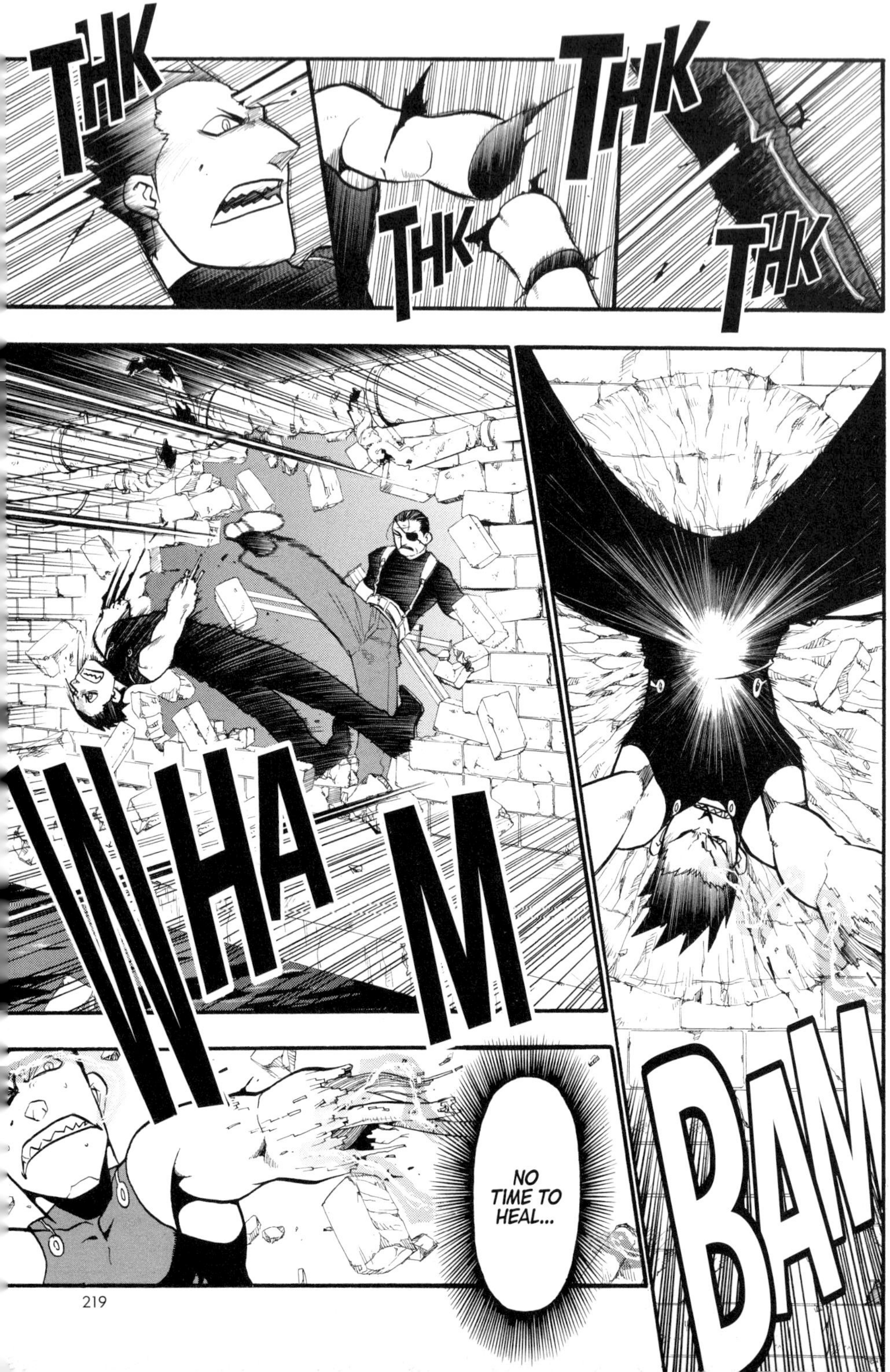
THK
THK
THK
THK
BAM
WHAM
NO TIME TO HEAL...

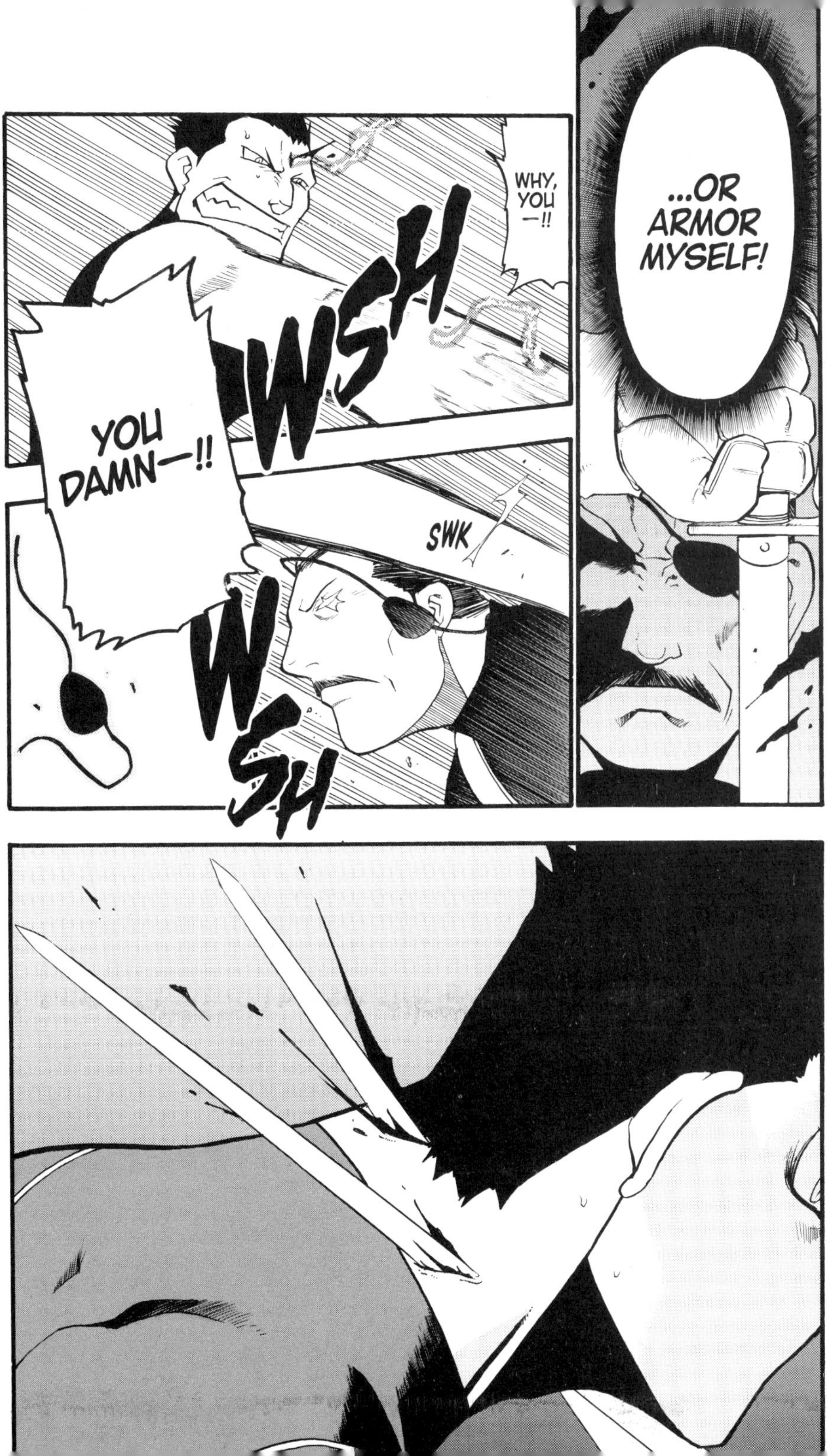
...OR ARMOR MYSELF!
WHY, YOU—!!
WSH
YOU DAMN—!!
SWK
WSH

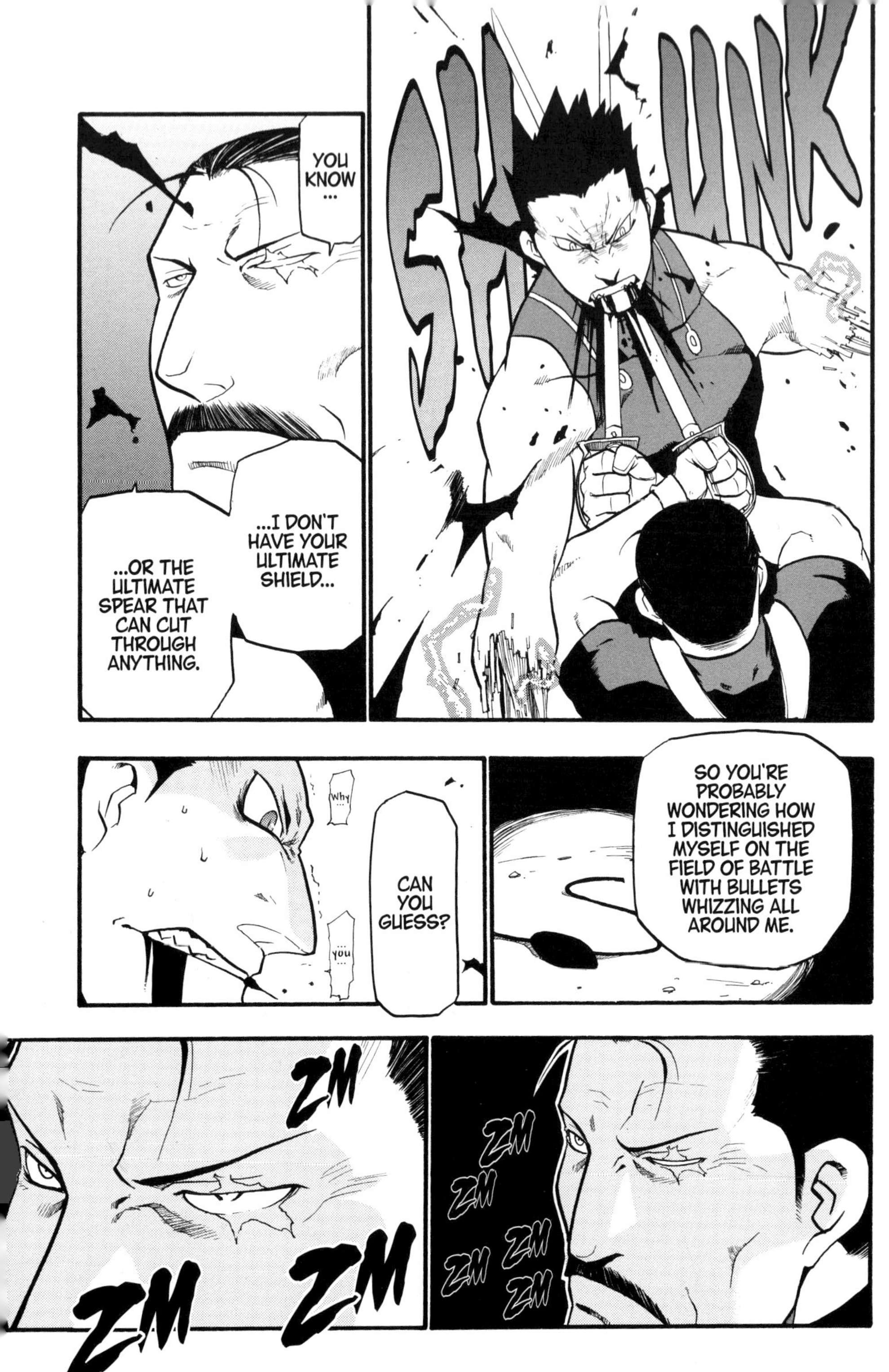
YOU KNOW ...
...I DON'T HAVE YOUR ULTIMATE SHIELD...
...OR THE ULTIMATE SPEAR THAT CAN CUT THROUGH ANYTHING.
SO YOU'RE PROBABLY WONDERING HOW I DISTINGUISHED MYSELF ON THE FIELD OF BATTLE WITH BULLETS WHIZZING ALL AROUND ME.
CAN YOU GUESS?
Why ...
... you
ZM
ZM
ZM
ZM
ZM
ZM
ZM
ZM
ZM

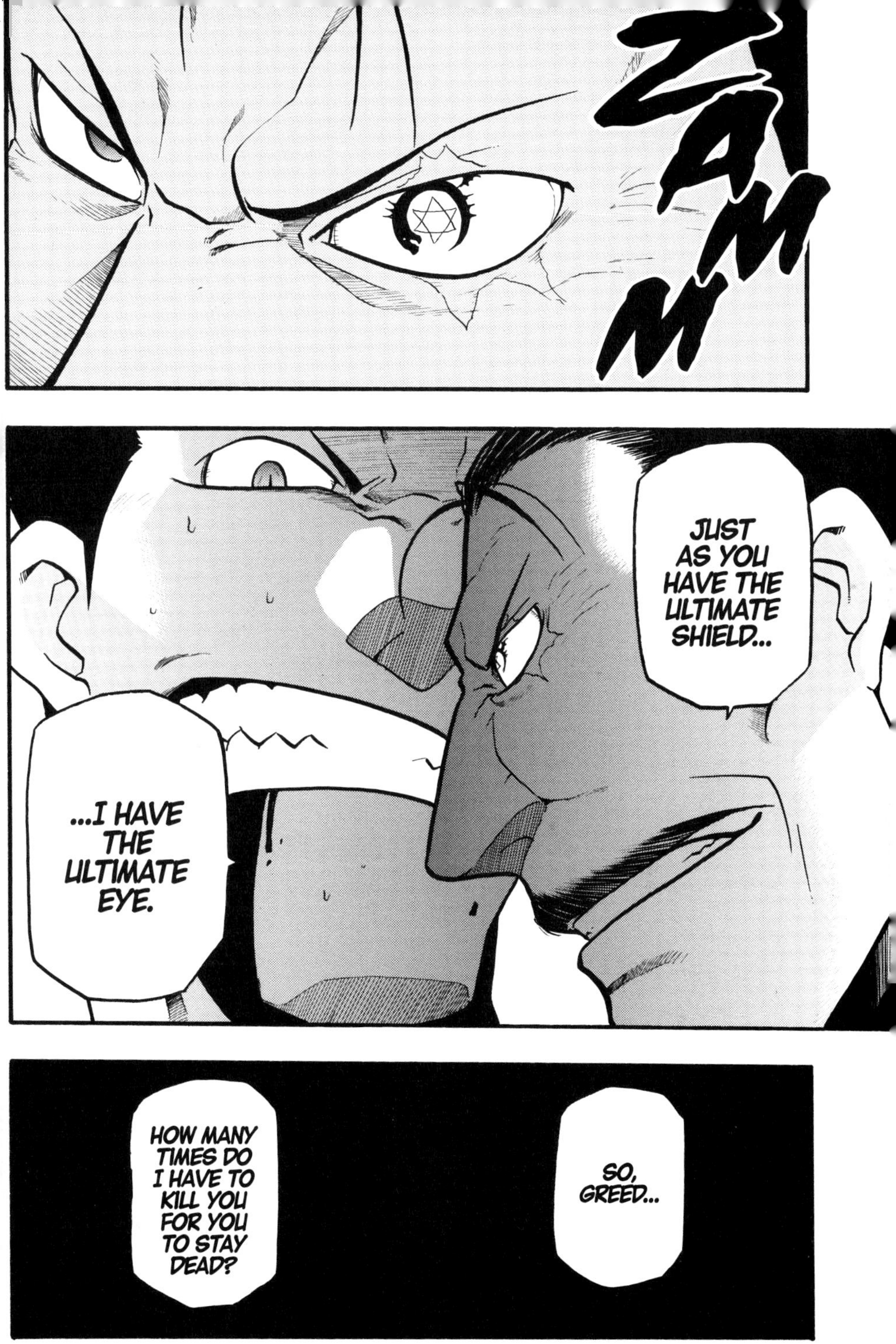
ZAMM
JUST AS YOU HAVE THE ULTIMATE SHIELD...
...I HAVE THE ULTIMATE EYE.
SO, GREED...
HOW MANY TIMES DO I HAVE TO KILL YOU FOR YOU TO STAY DEAD?

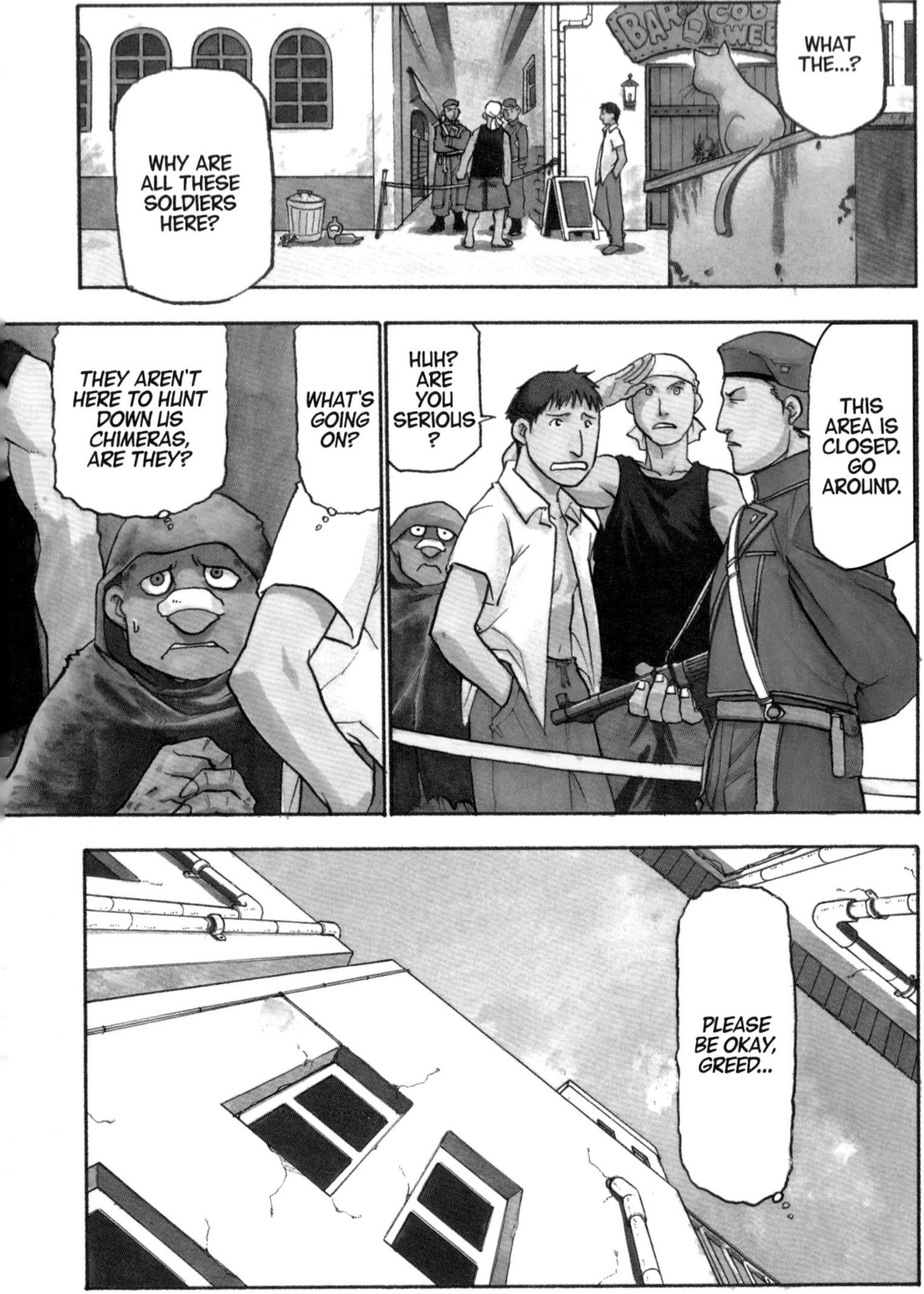
WHAT THE...?
WHY ARE ALL THESE SOLDIERS HERE?
THIS AREA IS CLOSED. GO AROUND.
HUH? ARE YOU SERIOUS?
WHAT'S GOING ON?
THEY AREN'T HERE TO HUNT DOWN US CHIMERAS, ARE THEY?
PLEASE BE OKAY, GREED...

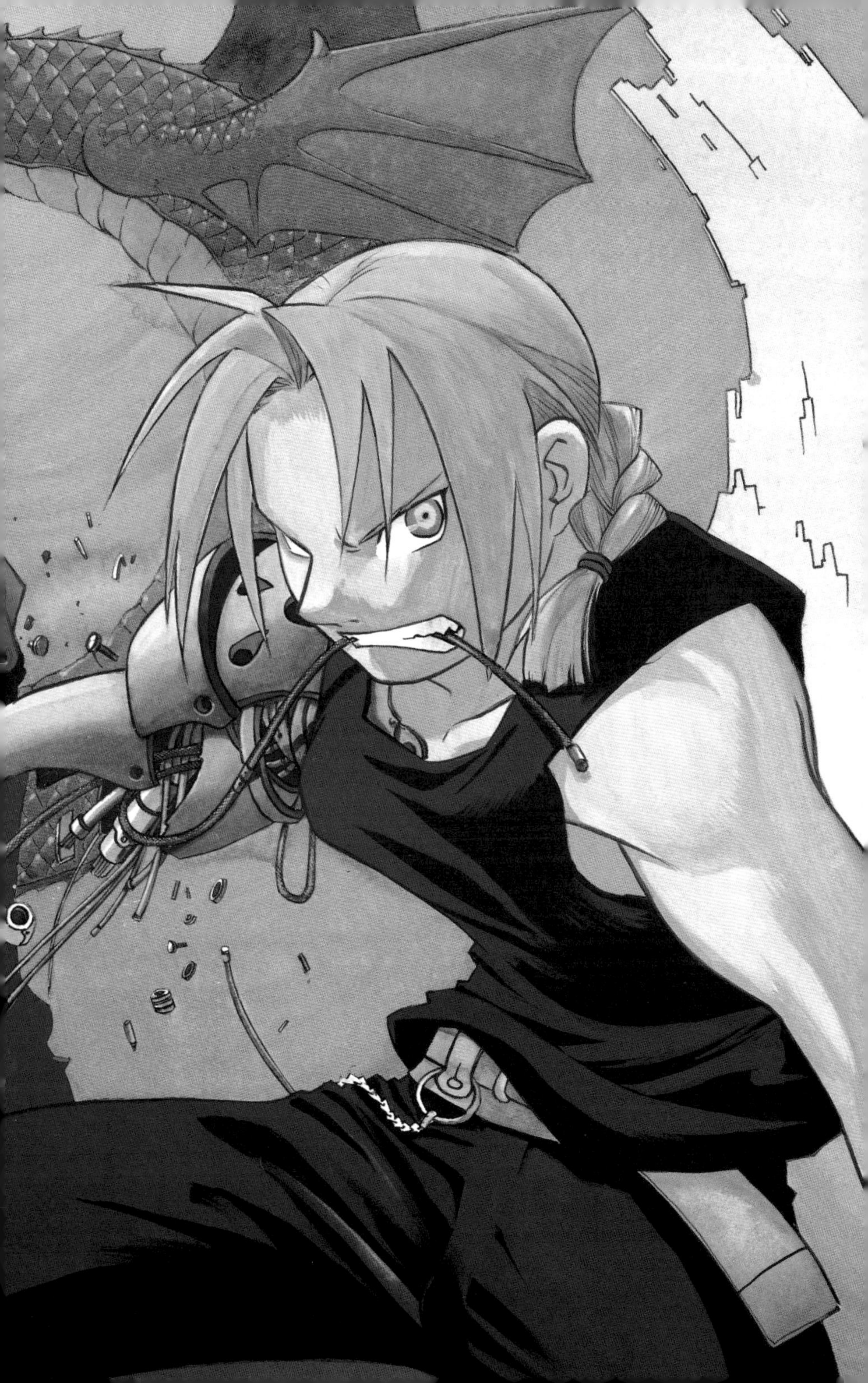

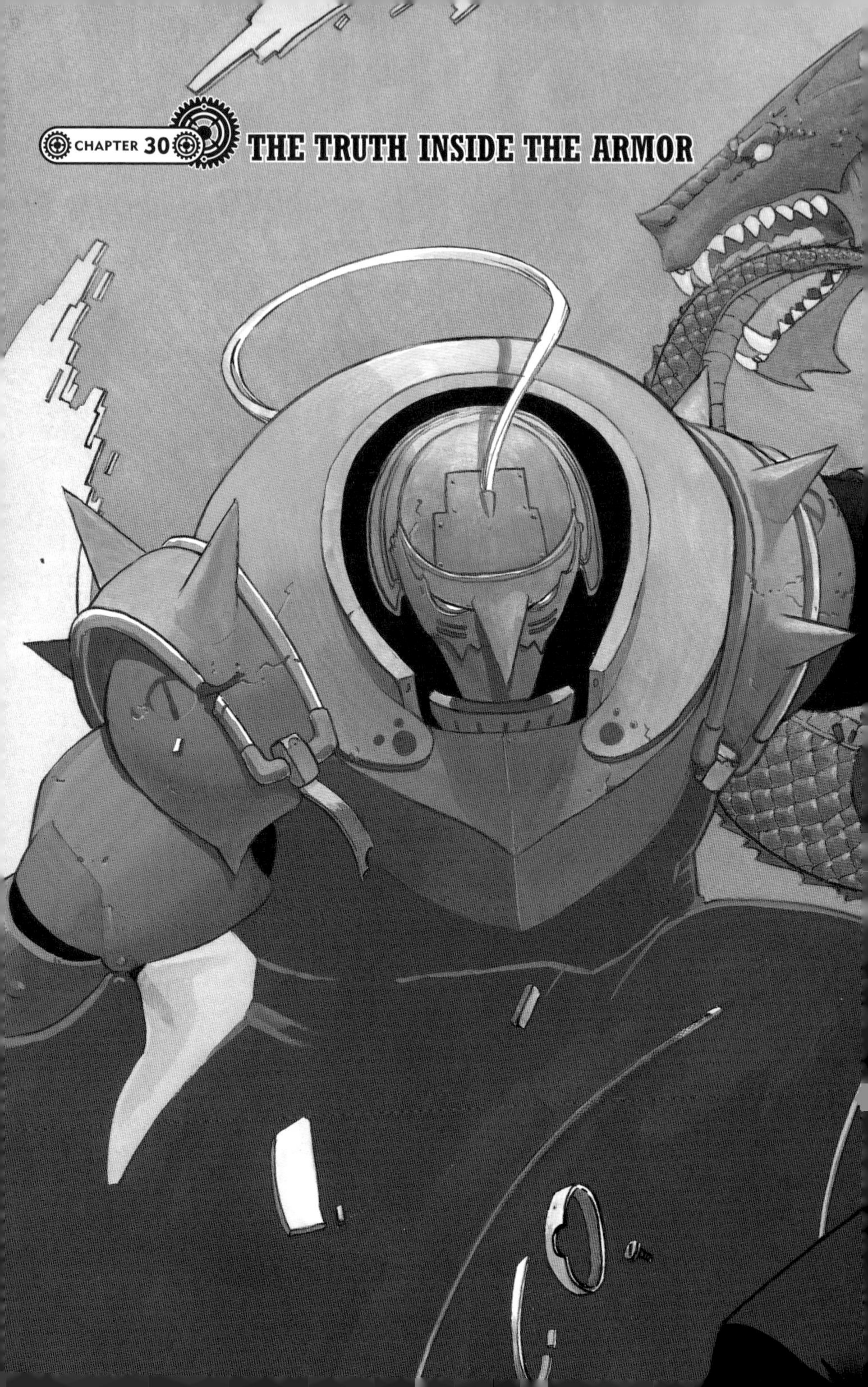
CHAPTER 30
THE TRUTH INSIDE THE ARMOR

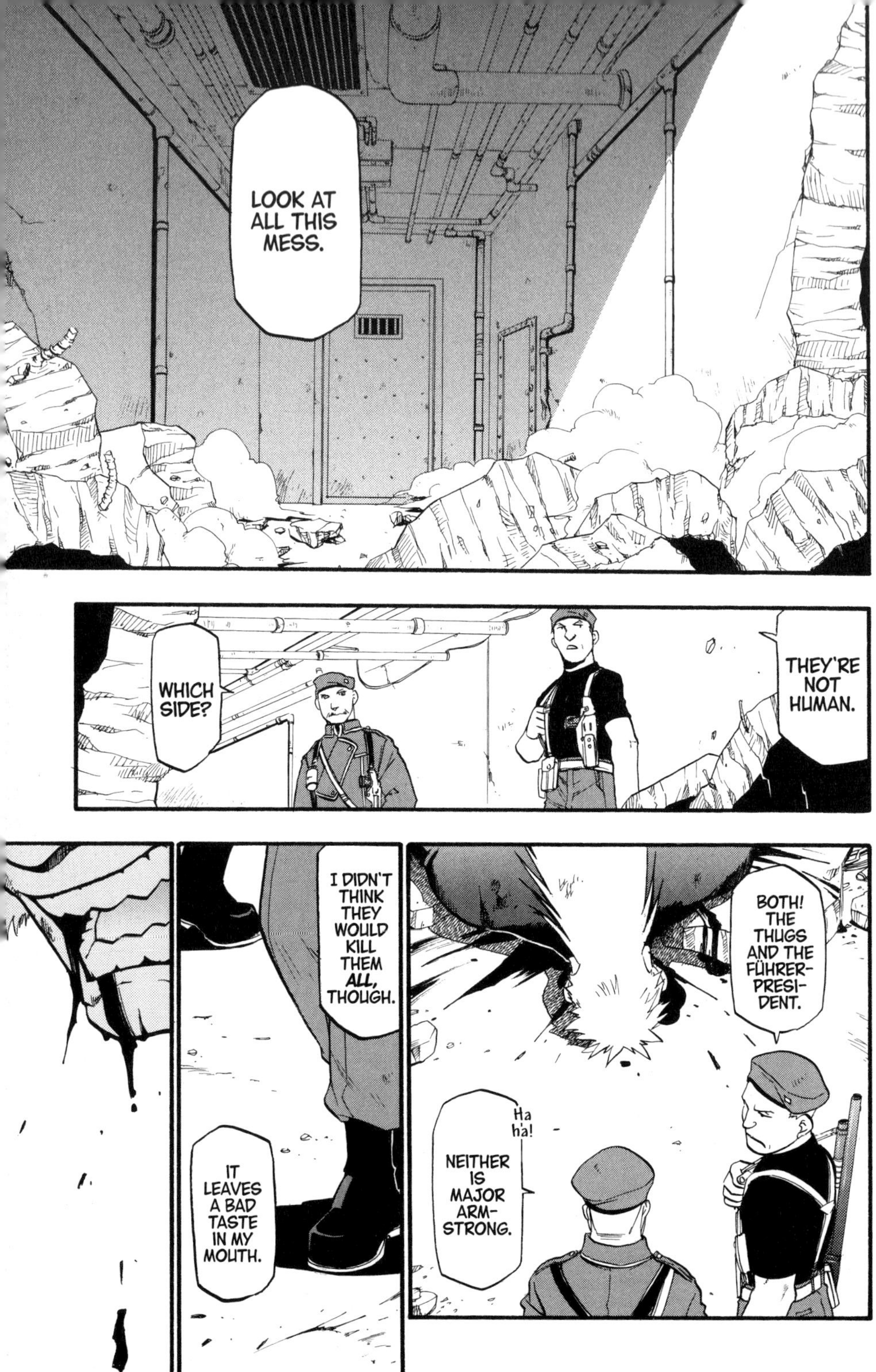
LOOK AT ALL THIS MESS.
THEY'RE NOT HUMAN.
WHICH SIDE?
BOTH! THE THUGS AND THE FÜHRER-PRESIDENT.
Ha ha!
NEITHER IS MAJOR ARM-STRONG.
I DIDN'T THINK THEY WOULD KILL THEM **ALL,** THOUGH.
IT LEAVES A BAD TASTE IN MY MOUTH.

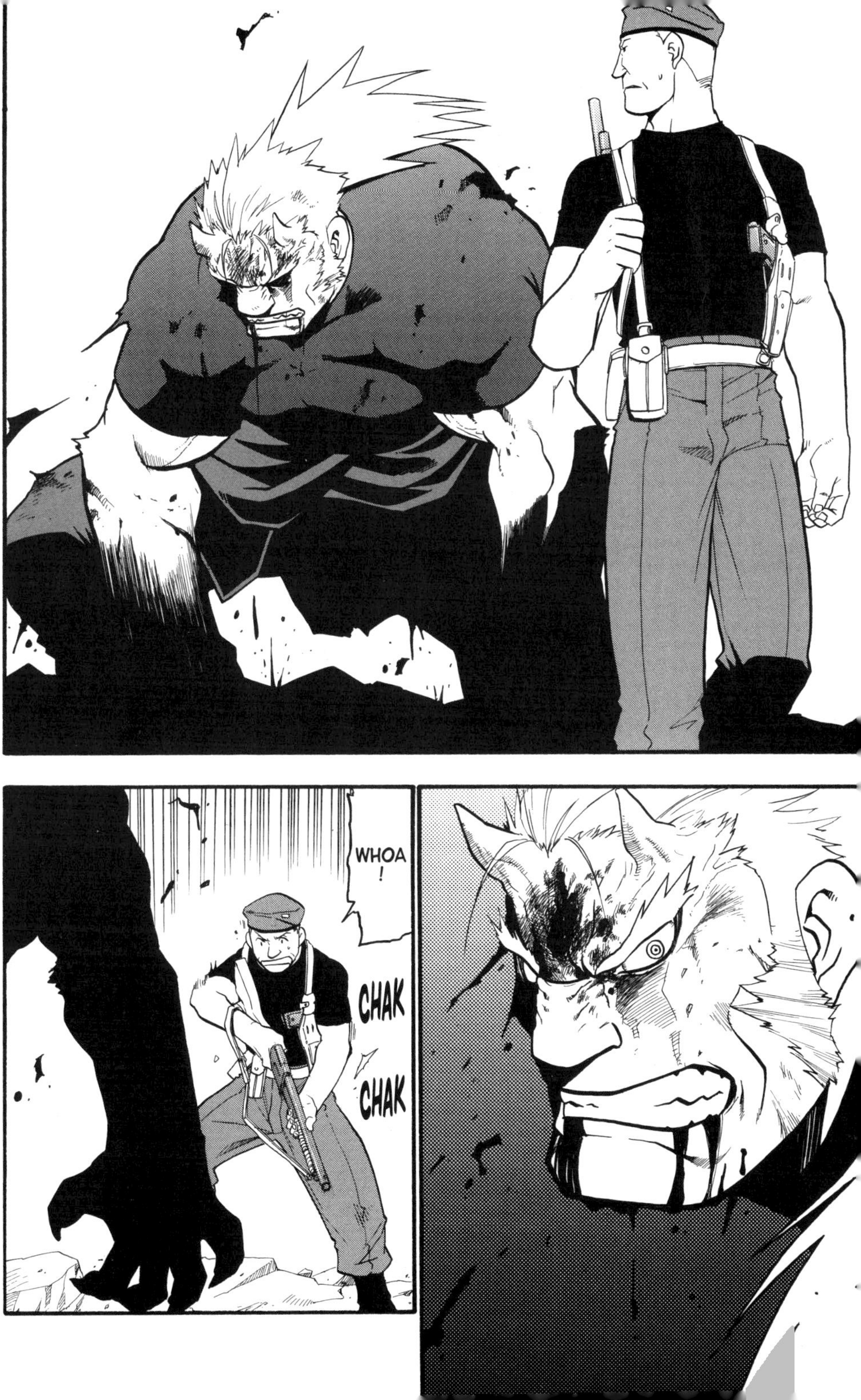
WHOA!
CHAK
CHAK

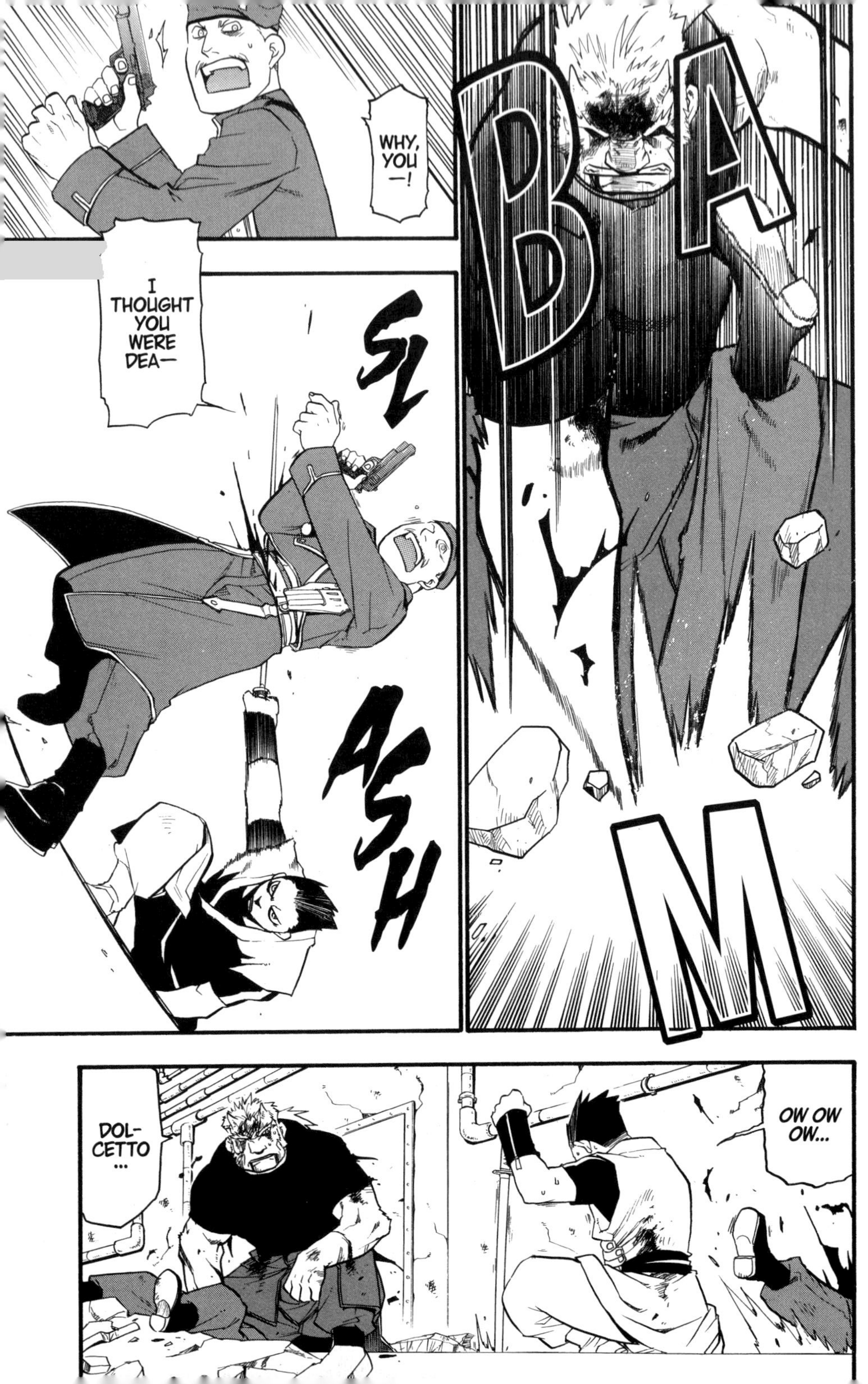
BAM
WHY, YOU—!
I THOUGHT YOU WERE DEA—
SLASH
OW OW OW...
DOL-CETTO ...

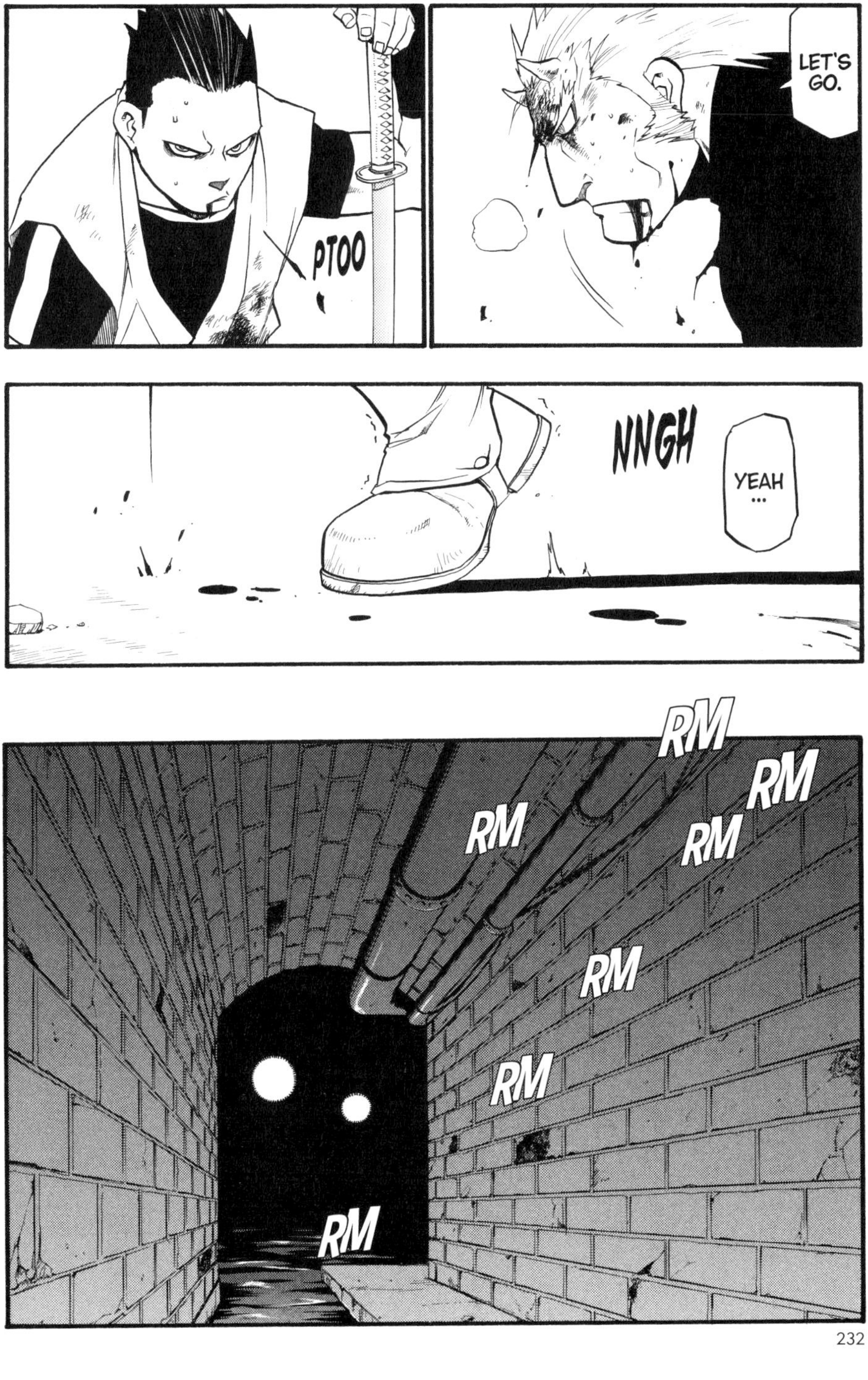
LET'S GO.
PTOO
YEAH ...
NNGH
RM
RM
RM
RM
RM
RM
RM

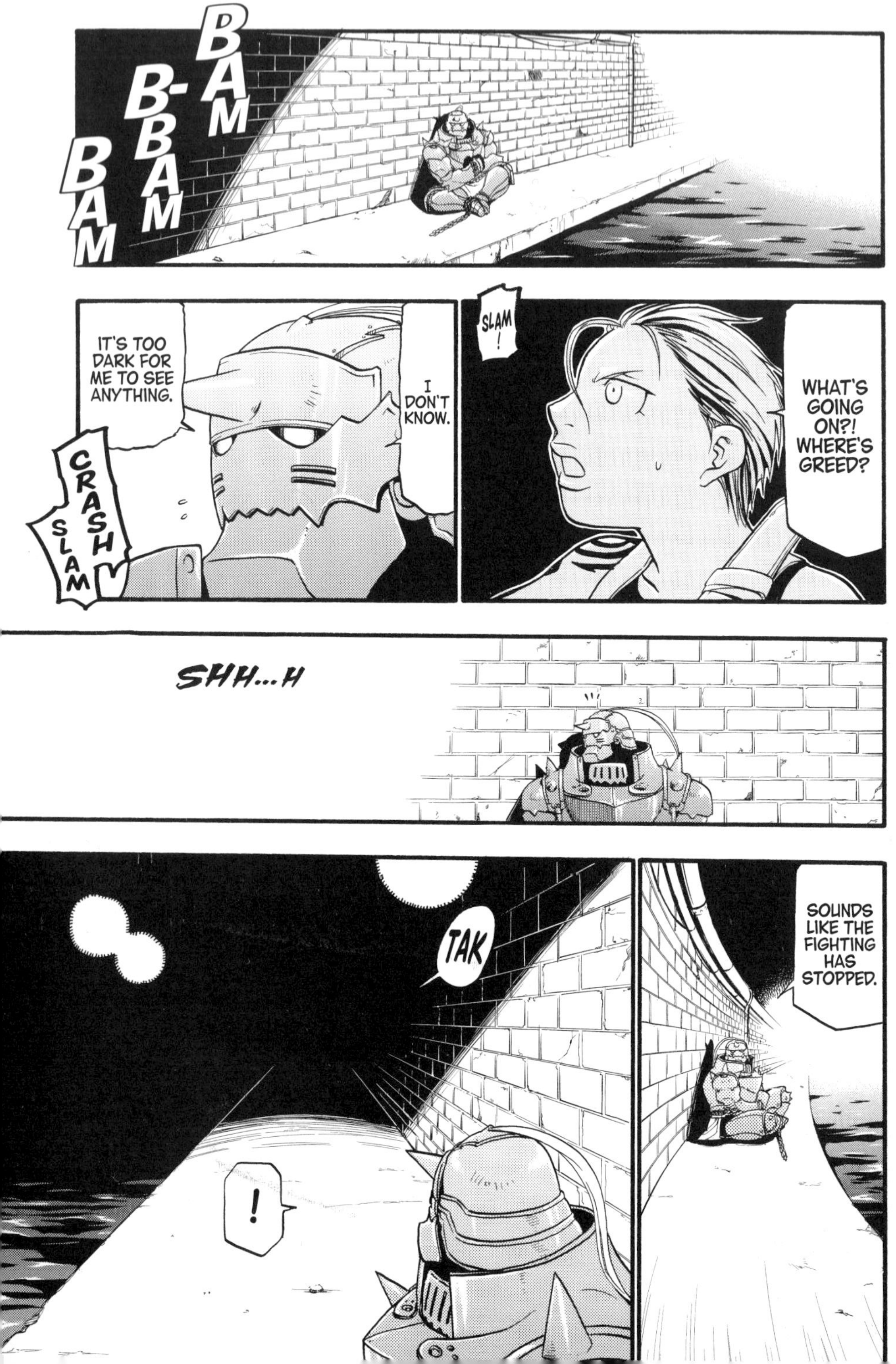
BAM
B-BAM
BAM
SLAM!
WHAT'S GOING ON?! WHERE'S GREED?
I DON'T KNOW.
IT'S TOO DARK FOR ME TO SEE ANYTHING.
CRASH
SLAM
SHH...H
SOUNDS LIKE THE FIGHTING HAS STOPPED.
TAK
!

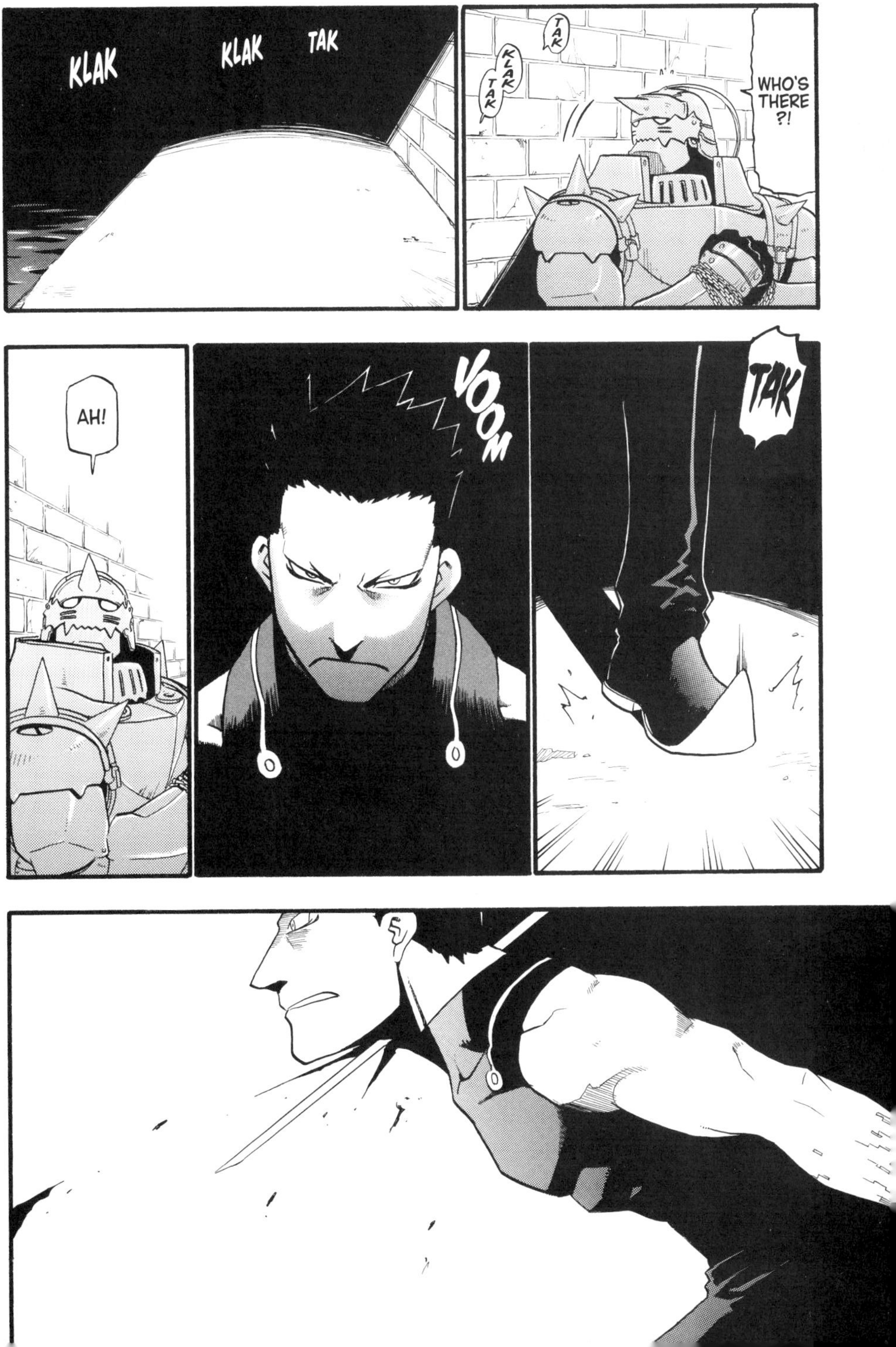
TAK
KLAK
TAK
WHO'S THERE?!
TAK
KLAK
KLAK
TAK
VOOM
AH!

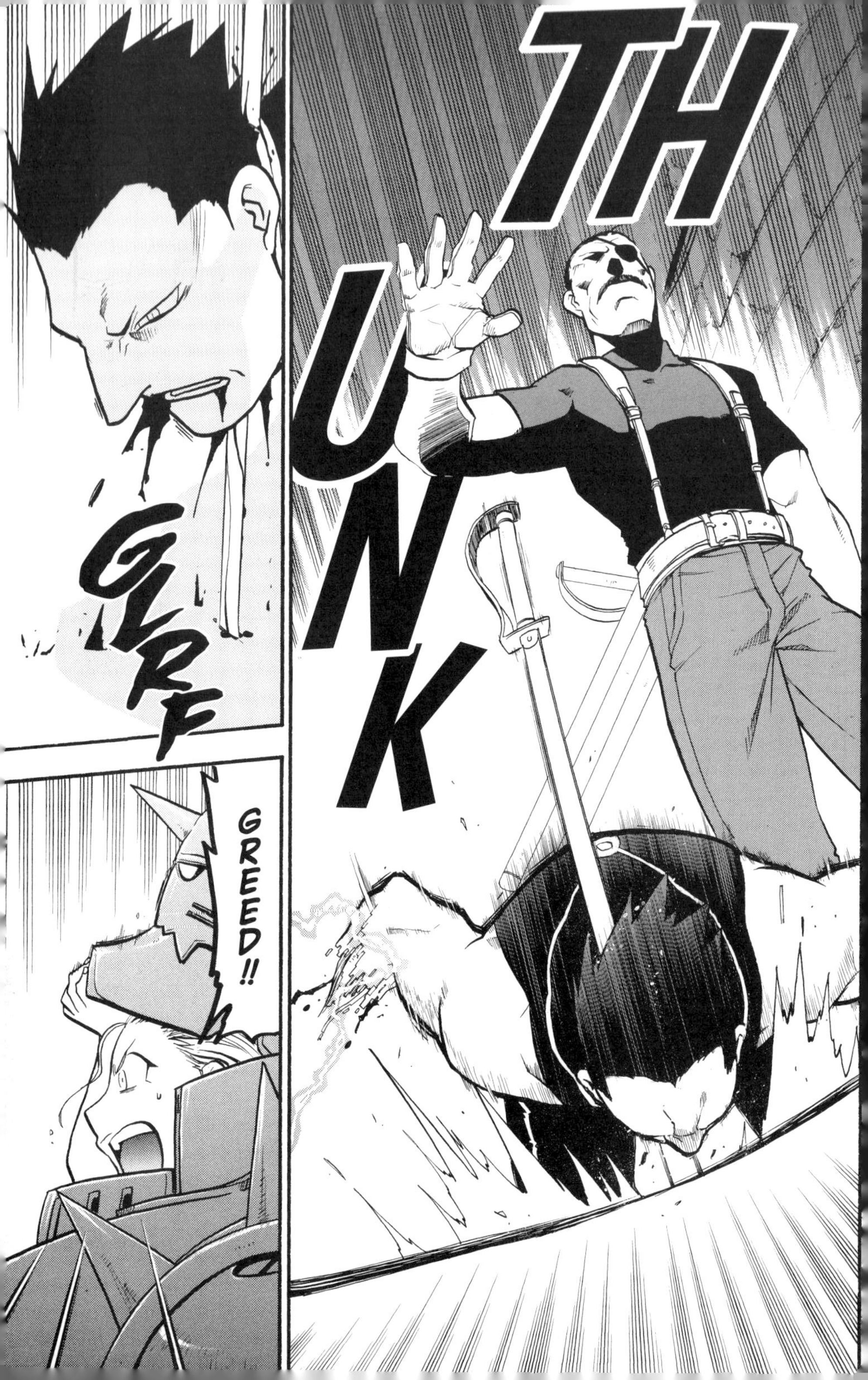
THUNK
GLRF
GREED!!

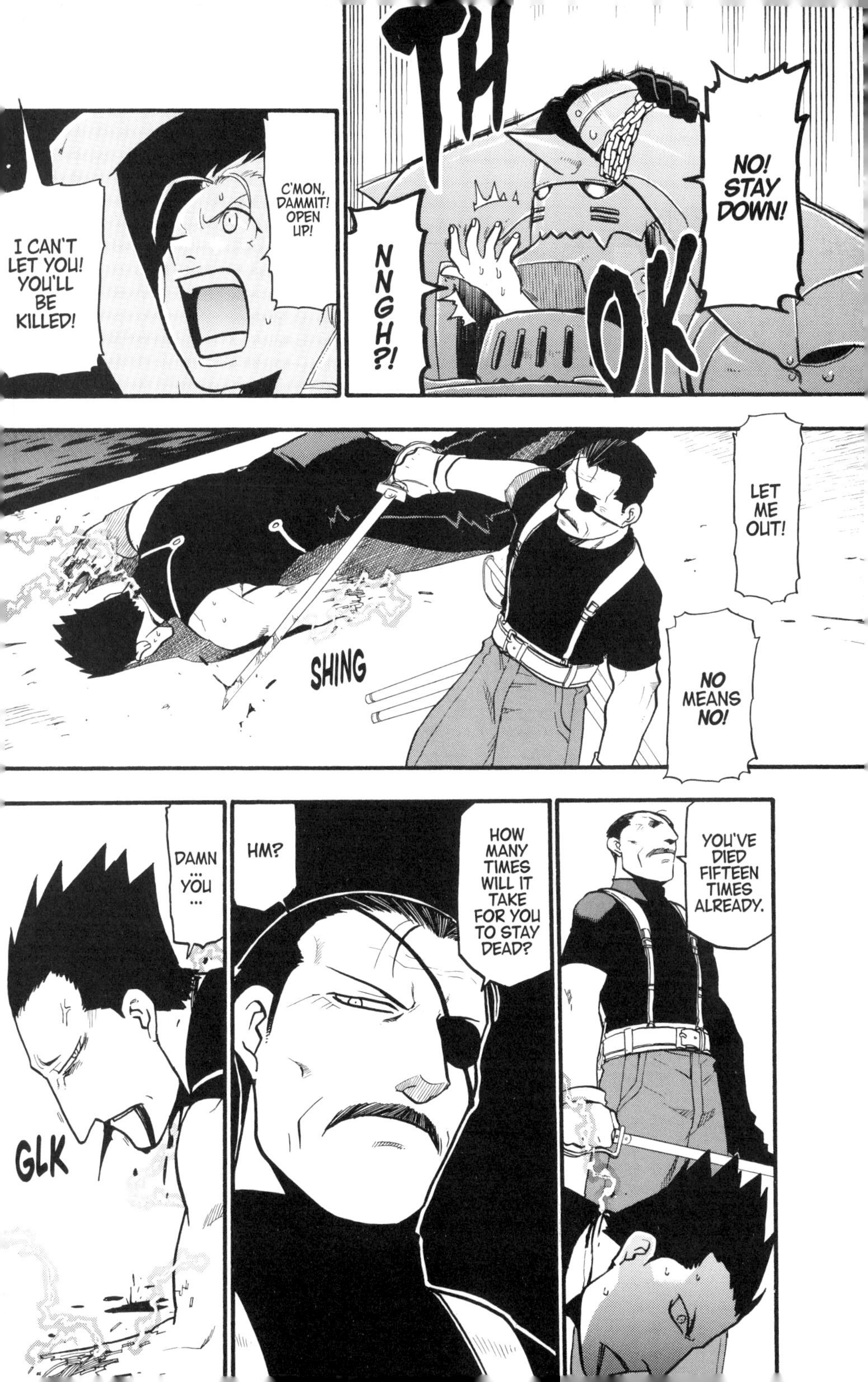
TH
NO! STAY DOWN!
OK
NNGH?!
C'MON, DAMMIT! OPEN UP!
I CAN'T LET YOU! YOU'LL BE KILLED!
LET ME OUT!
NO MEANS NO!
SHING
YOU'VE DIED FIFTEEN TIMES ALREADY.
HOW MANY TIMES WILL IT TAKE FOR YOU TO STAY DEAD?
HM?
DAMN ... YOU ...
GLK

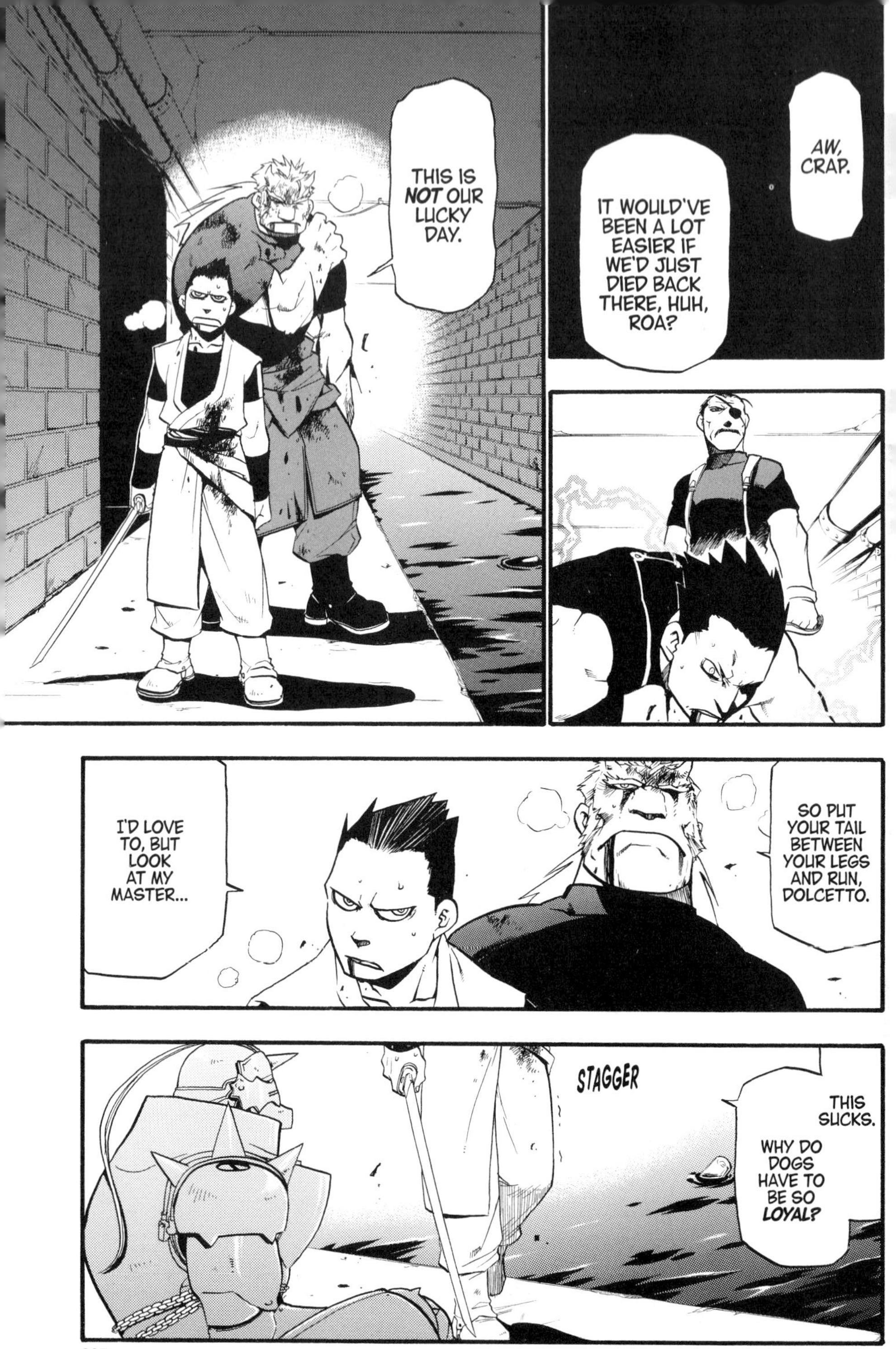
AW, CRAP.
IT WOULD'VE BEEN A LOT EASIER IF WE'D JUST DIED BACK THERE, HUH, ROA?
THIS IS NOT OUR LUCKY DAY.
SO PUT YOUR TAIL BETWEEN YOUR LEGS AND RUN, DOLCETTO.
I'D LOVE TO, BUT LOOK AT MY MASTER...
THIS SUCKS.
WHY DO DOGS HAVE TO BE SO LOYAL?
STAGGER

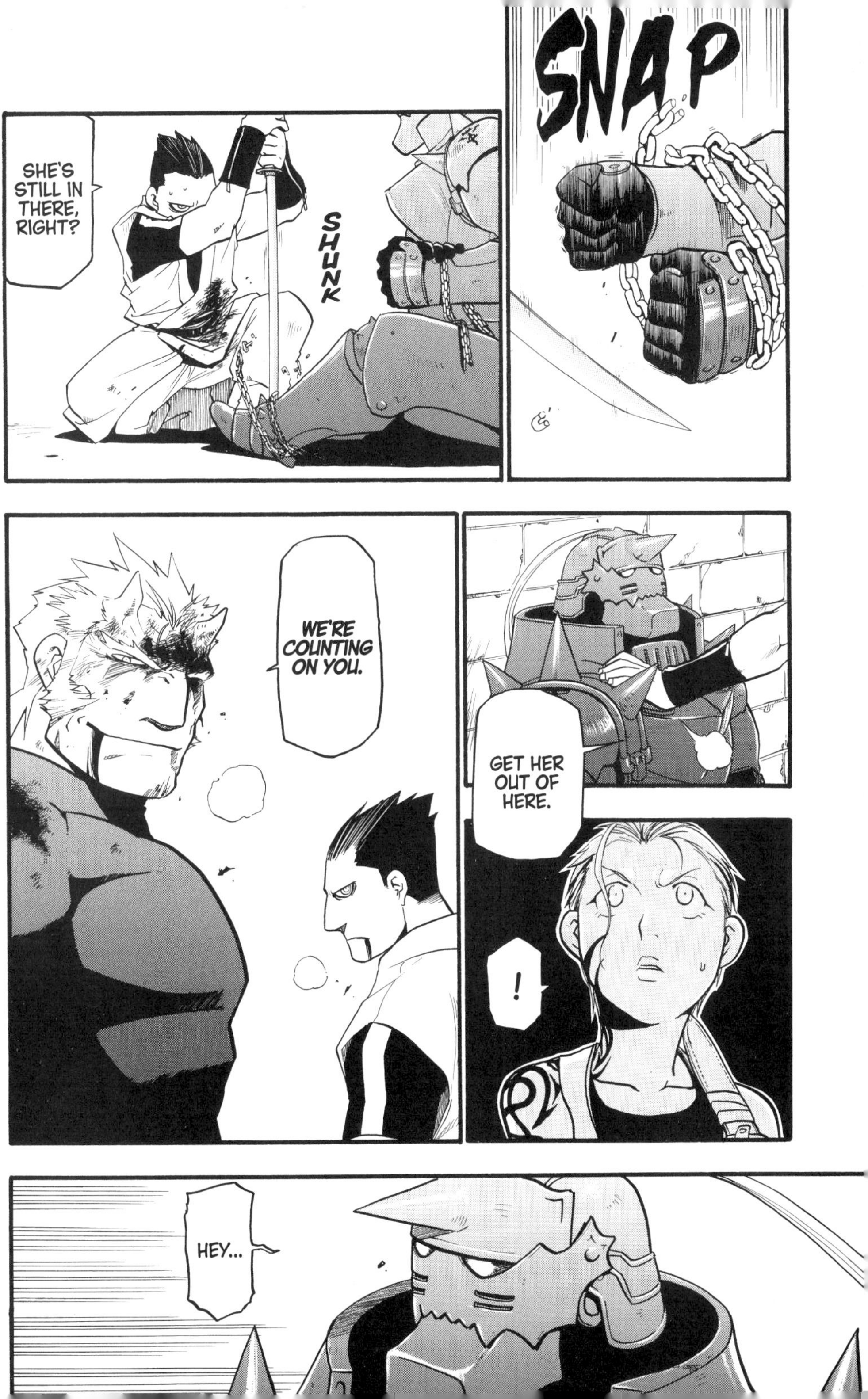
SNAP
SHE'S STILL IN THERE, RIGHT?
SHUNK
GET HER OUT OF HERE.
!
WE'RE COUNTING ON YOU.
HEY...

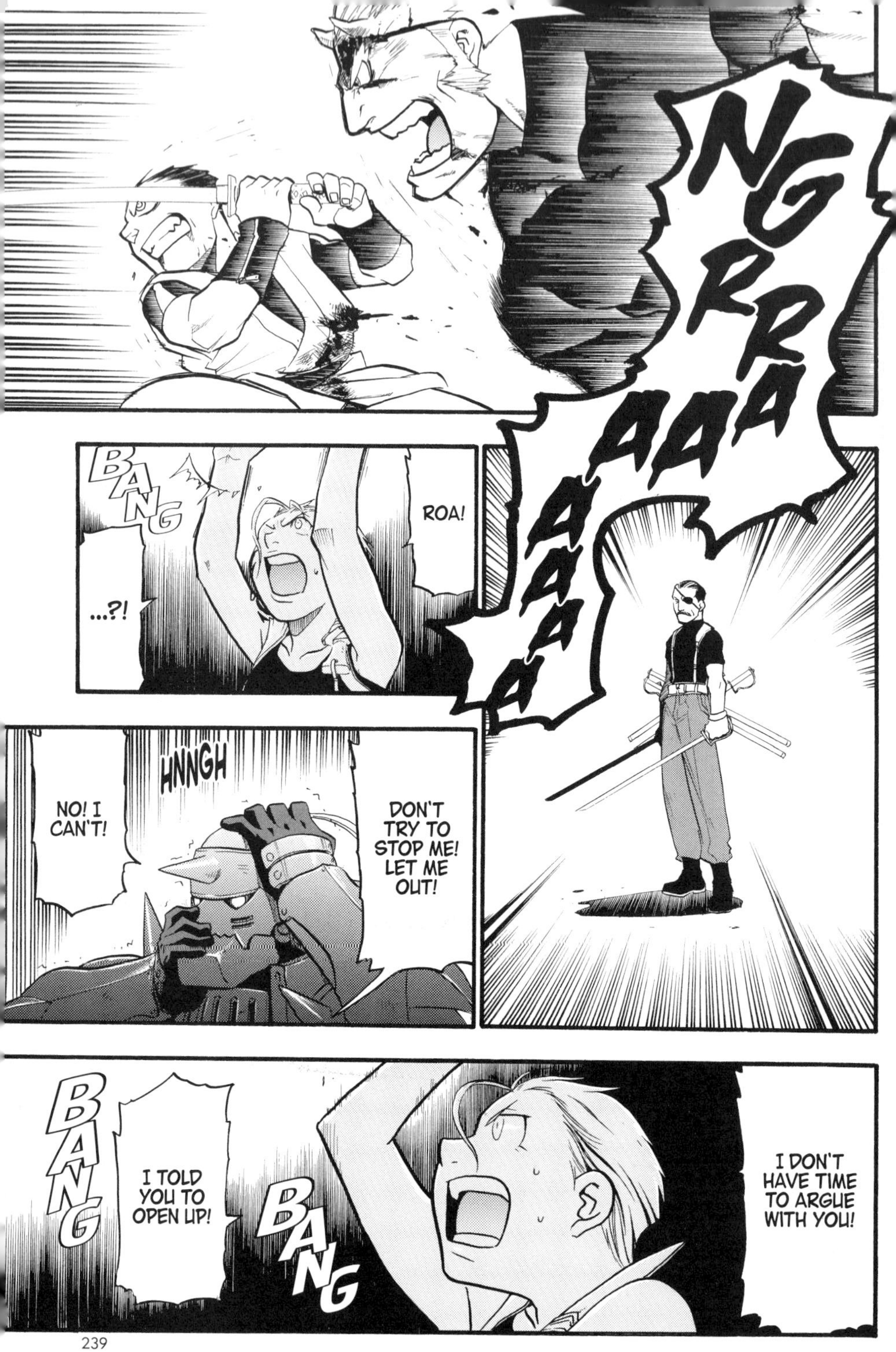
NGRRAAAAAAAAA
ROA!
BANG
...?!
DON'T TRY TO STOP ME! LET ME OUT!
HNNGH
NO! I CAN'T!
I DON'T HAVE TIME TO ARGUE WITH YOU!
BANG
I TOLD YOU TO OPEN UP!
BANG

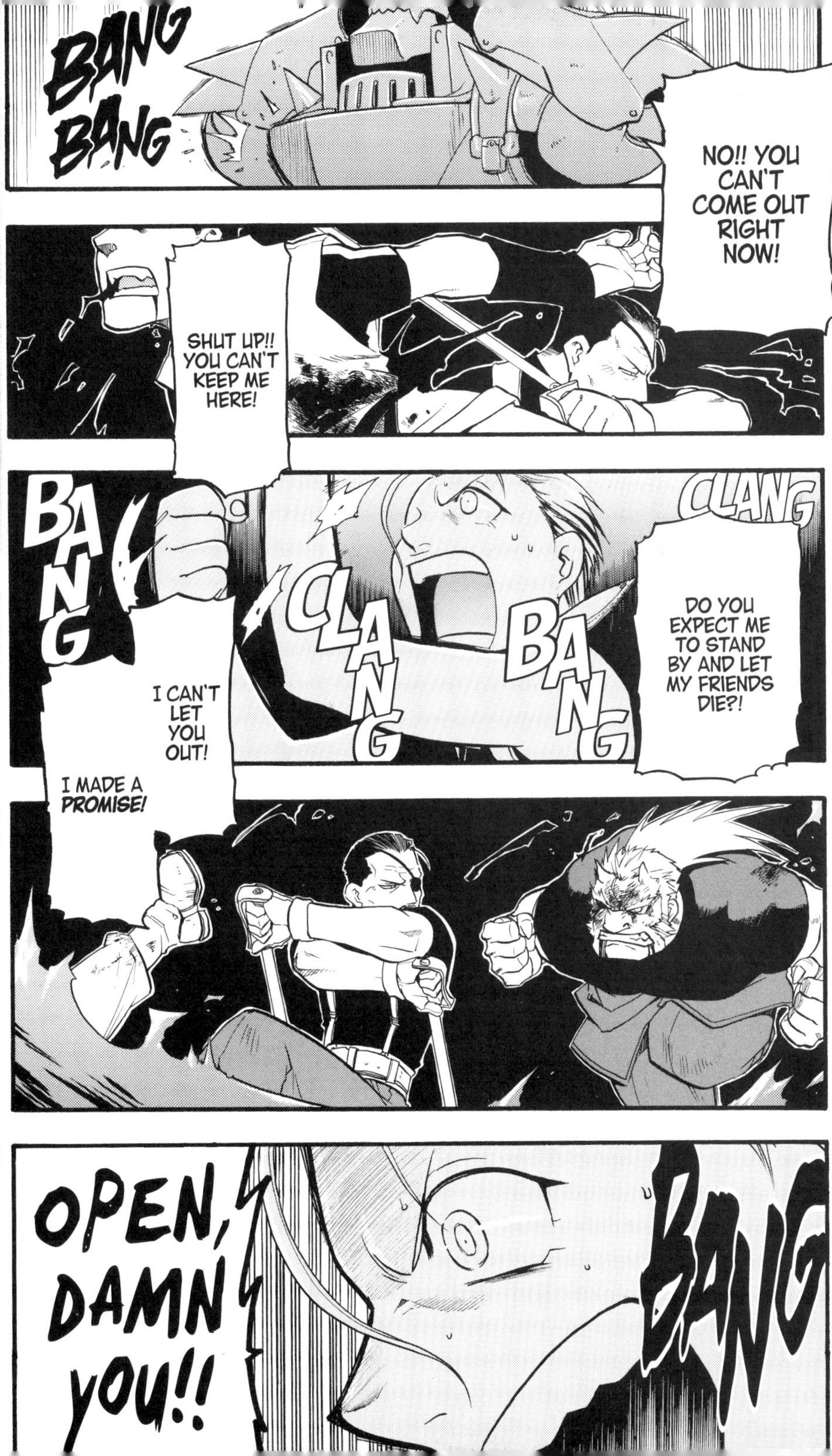
BANG BANG
NO!! YOU CAN'T COME OUT RIGHT NOW!
SHUT UP!! YOU CAN'T KEEP ME HERE!
CLANG
DO YOU EXPECT ME TO STAND BY AND LET MY FRIENDS DIE?!
BANG
CLANG
BANG
I CAN'T LET YOU OUT!
I MADE A PROMISE!
BANG
OPEN, DAMN YOU!!

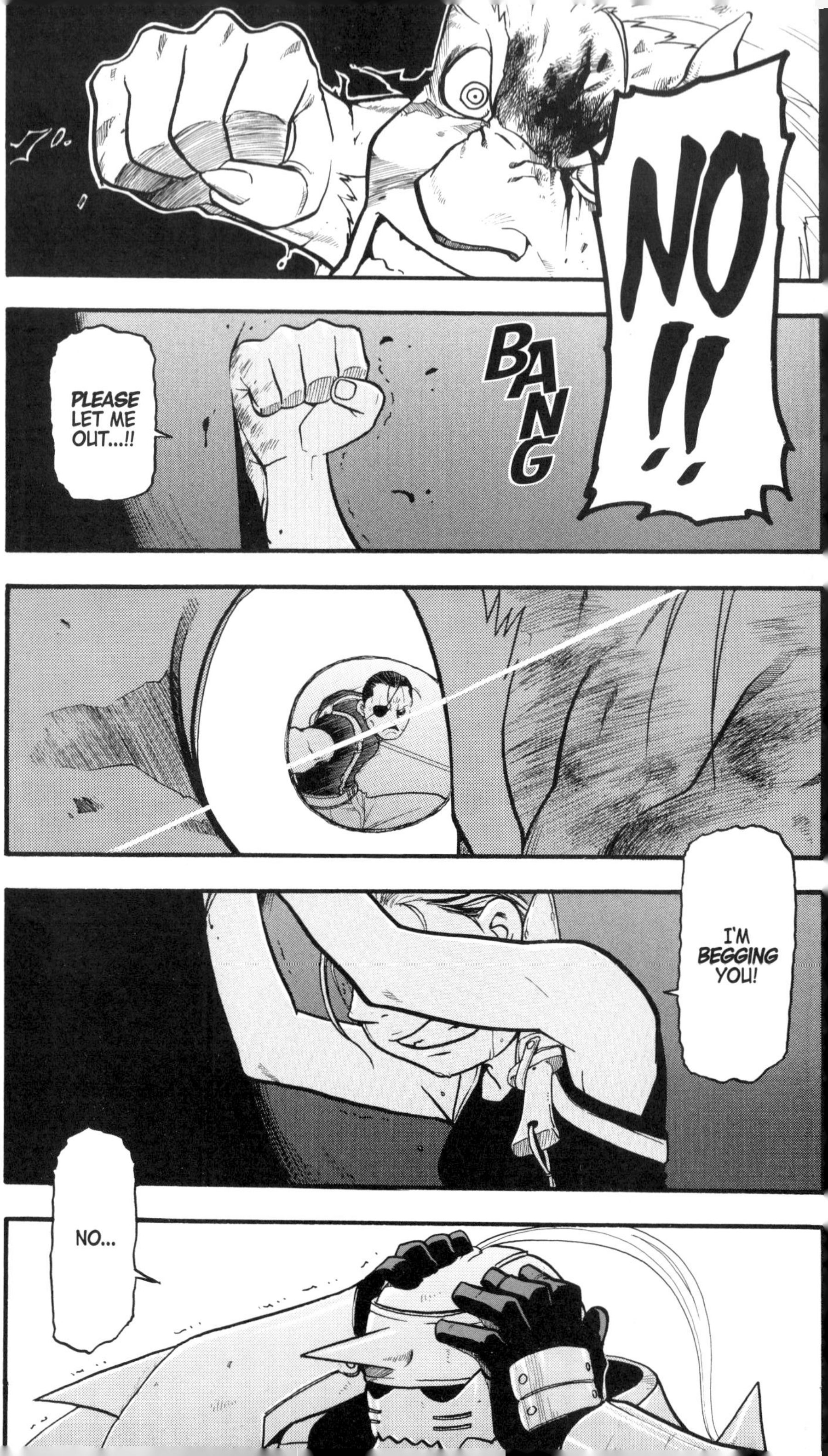
NO!!
BANG
PLEASE LET ME OUT...!!
I'M BEGGING YOU!
NO...

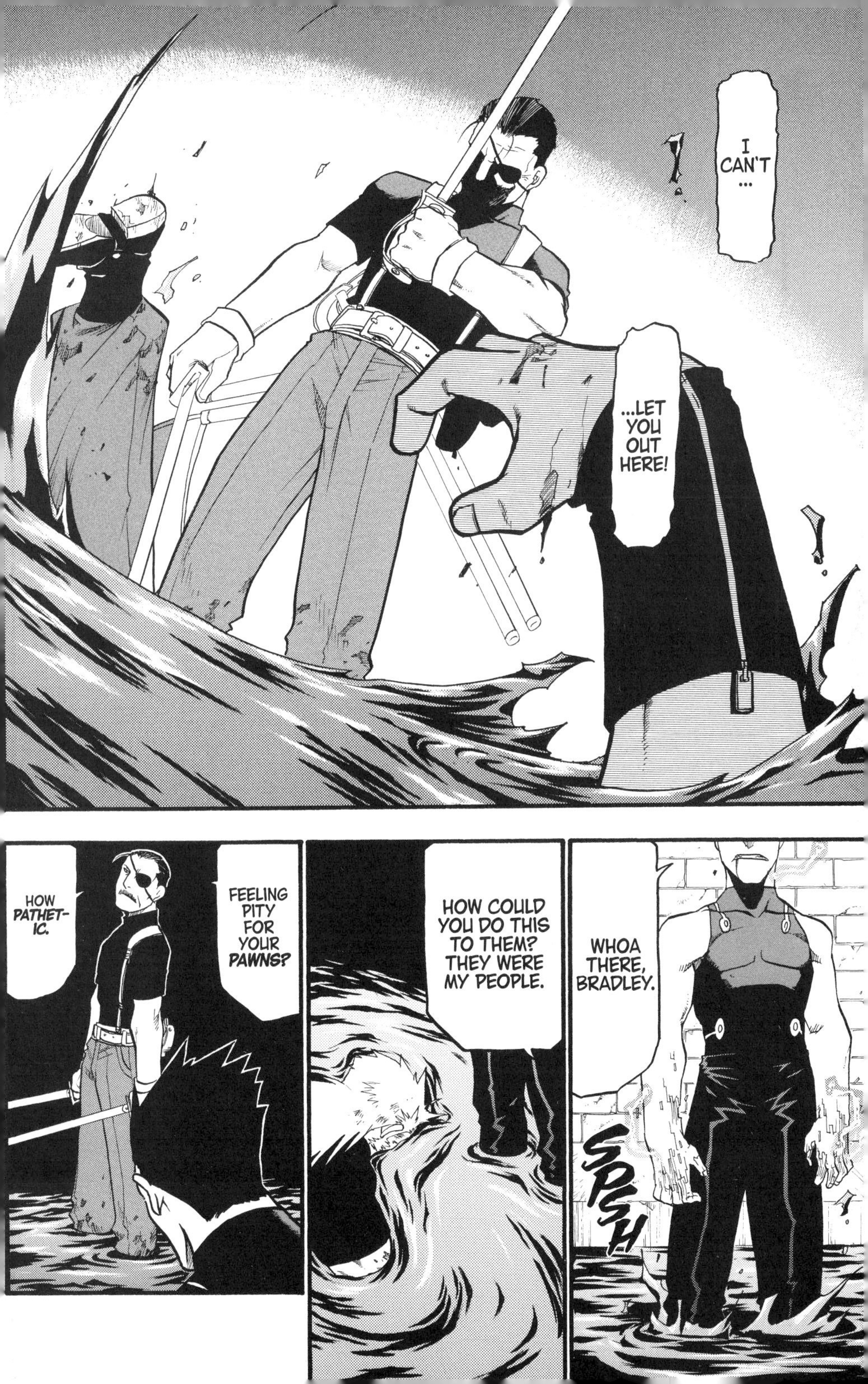
I CAN'T ...
...LET YOU OUT HERE!
WHOA THERE, BRADLEY.
SPSH
HOW COULD YOU DO THIS TO THEM? THEY WERE MY PEOPLE.
FEELING PITY FOR YOUR PAWNS?
HOW PATHETIC.

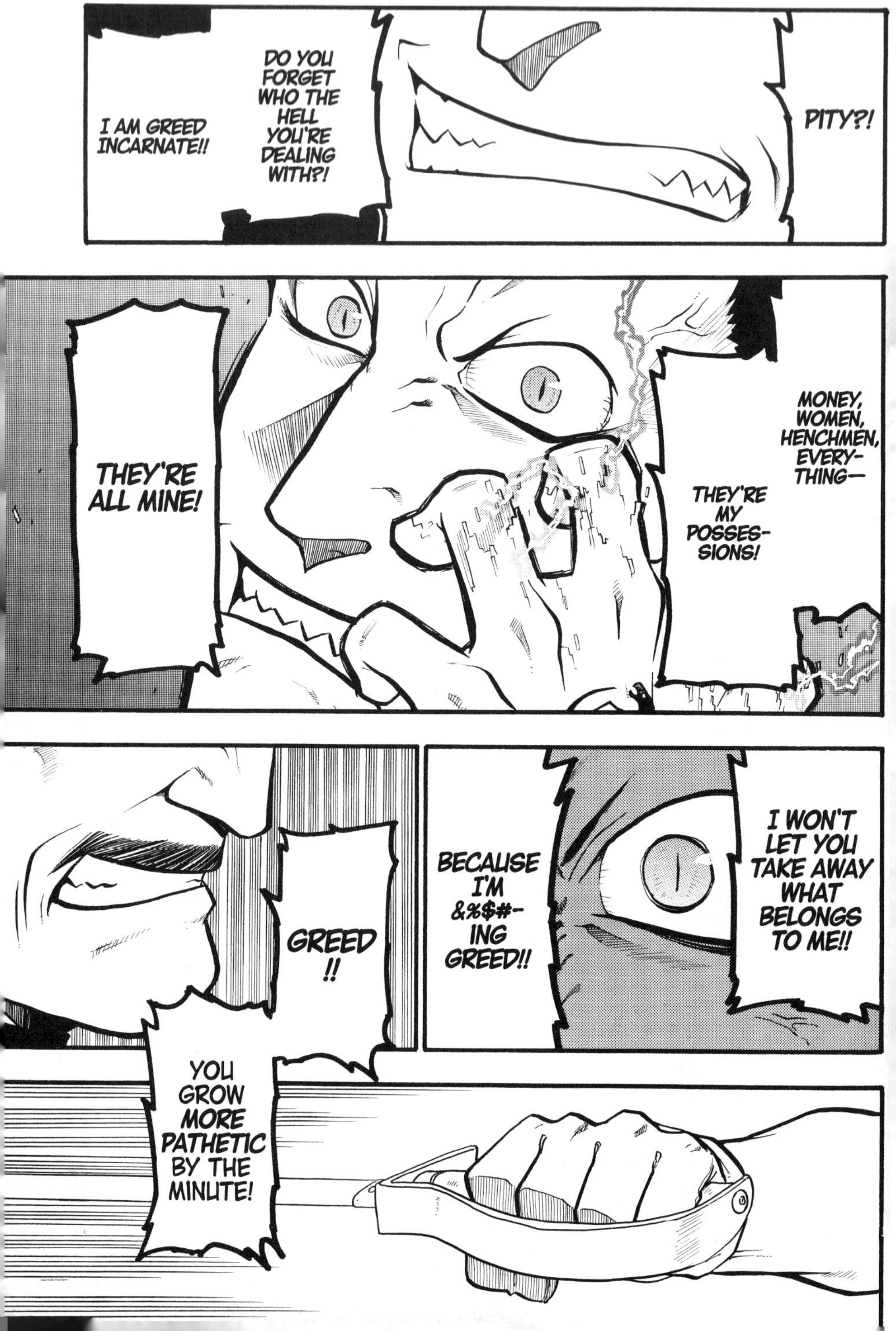

PITY?!
DO YOU FORGET WHO THE HELL YOU'RE DEALING WITH?!
I AM GREED INCARNATE!!
MONEY, WOMEN, HENCHMEN, EVERYTHING—
THEY'RE MY POSSESSIONS!
THEY'RE ALL MINE!
I WON'T LET YOU TAKE AWAY WHAT BELONGS TO ME!!
BECAUSE I'M &%$#-ING GREED!!
GREED!!
YOU GROW MORE PATHETIC BY THE MINUTE!

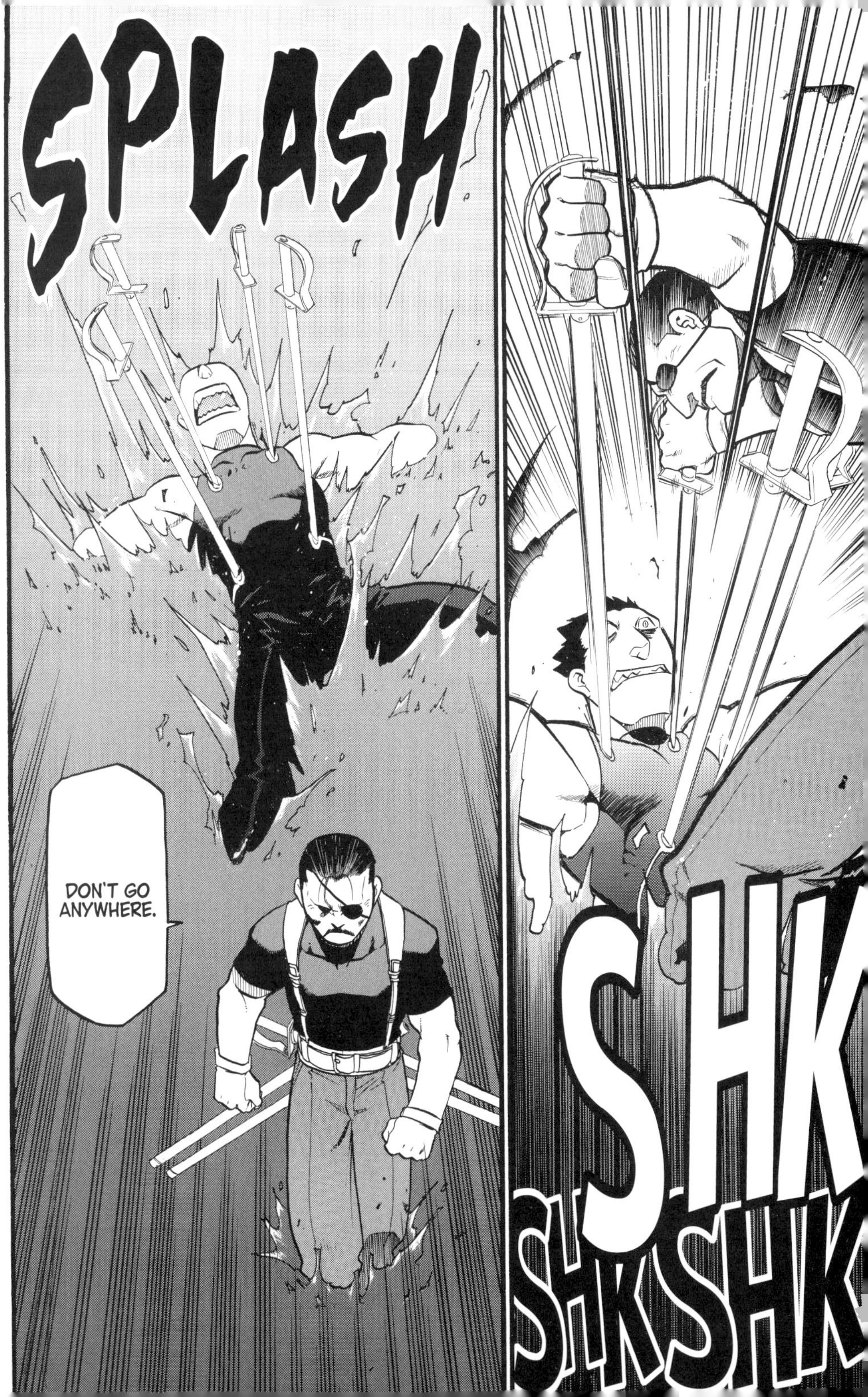
SHK
SHKSHK
SPLASH
DON'T GO ANYWHERE.

CLANK

I NEED TO ESCAPE...

I...

YOU'RE EDWARD'S YOUNGER BROTHER, AREN'T YOU?

ARE YOU HURT?

DO YOU NEED HELP?

SLSH

HOLD IT.

I'M FINE.

N-NO, SIR!

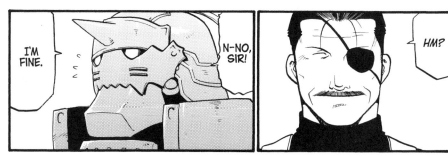

HM?

RGH...!

I CAN FIND MY WAY OUT ON MY OWN...

...SO IF YOU'LL EXCUSE ME...

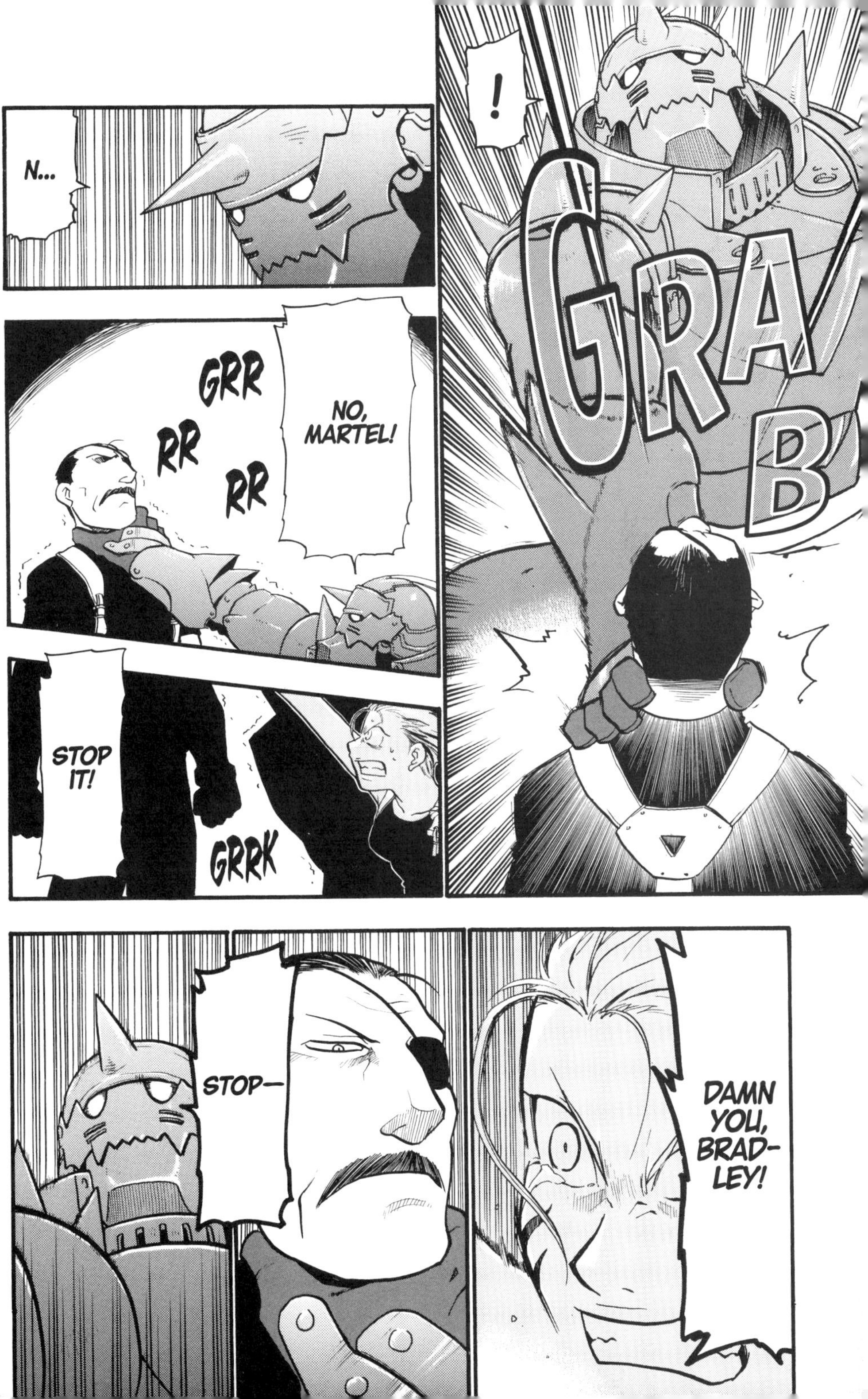
!
GRAB
N...
NO, MARTEL!
GRR
RR
RR
STOP IT!
GRRK
DAMN YOU, BRAD-LEY!
STOP—

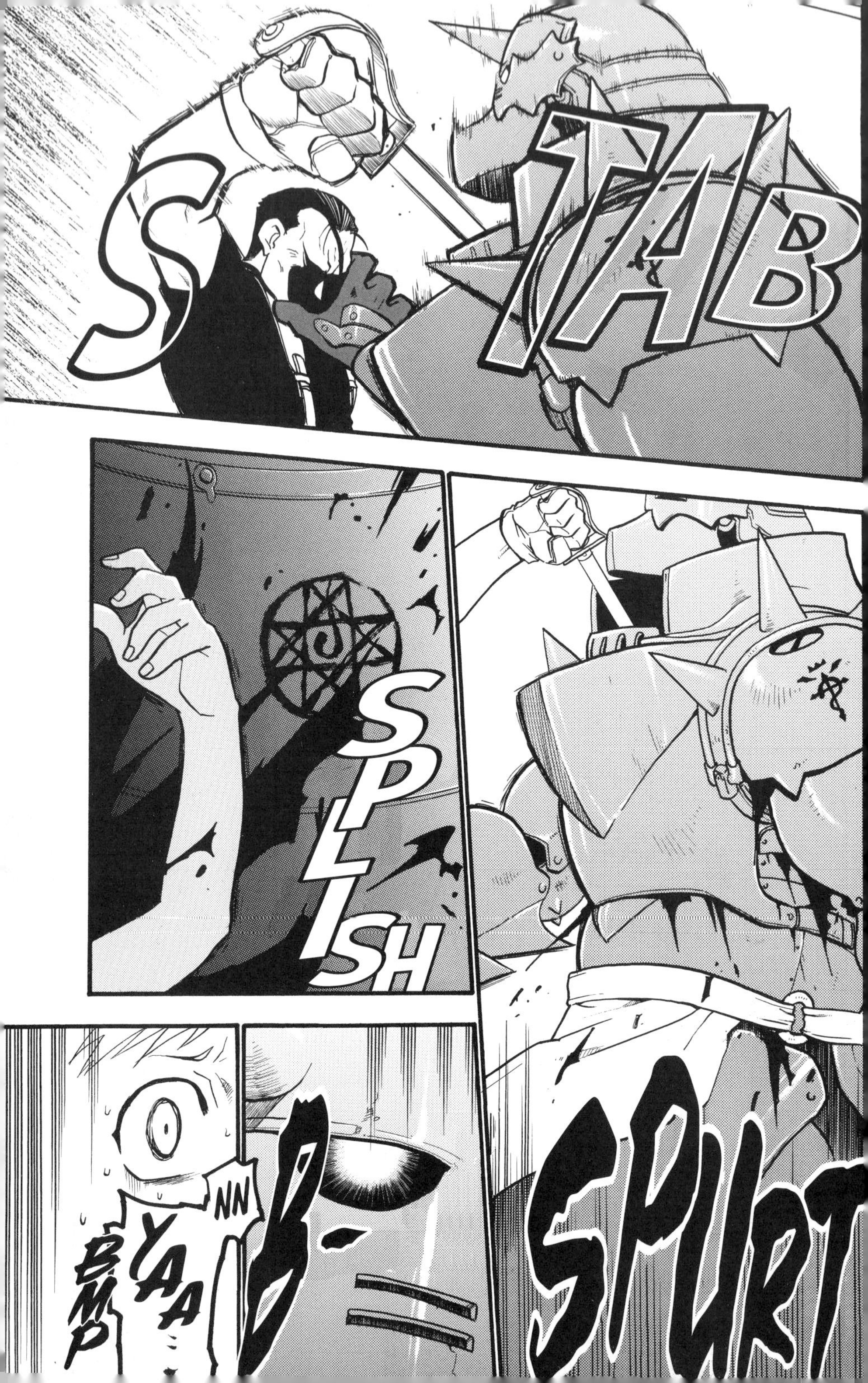
STAB
SPURT
SPLISH
B-
NN
YAAA
BMP

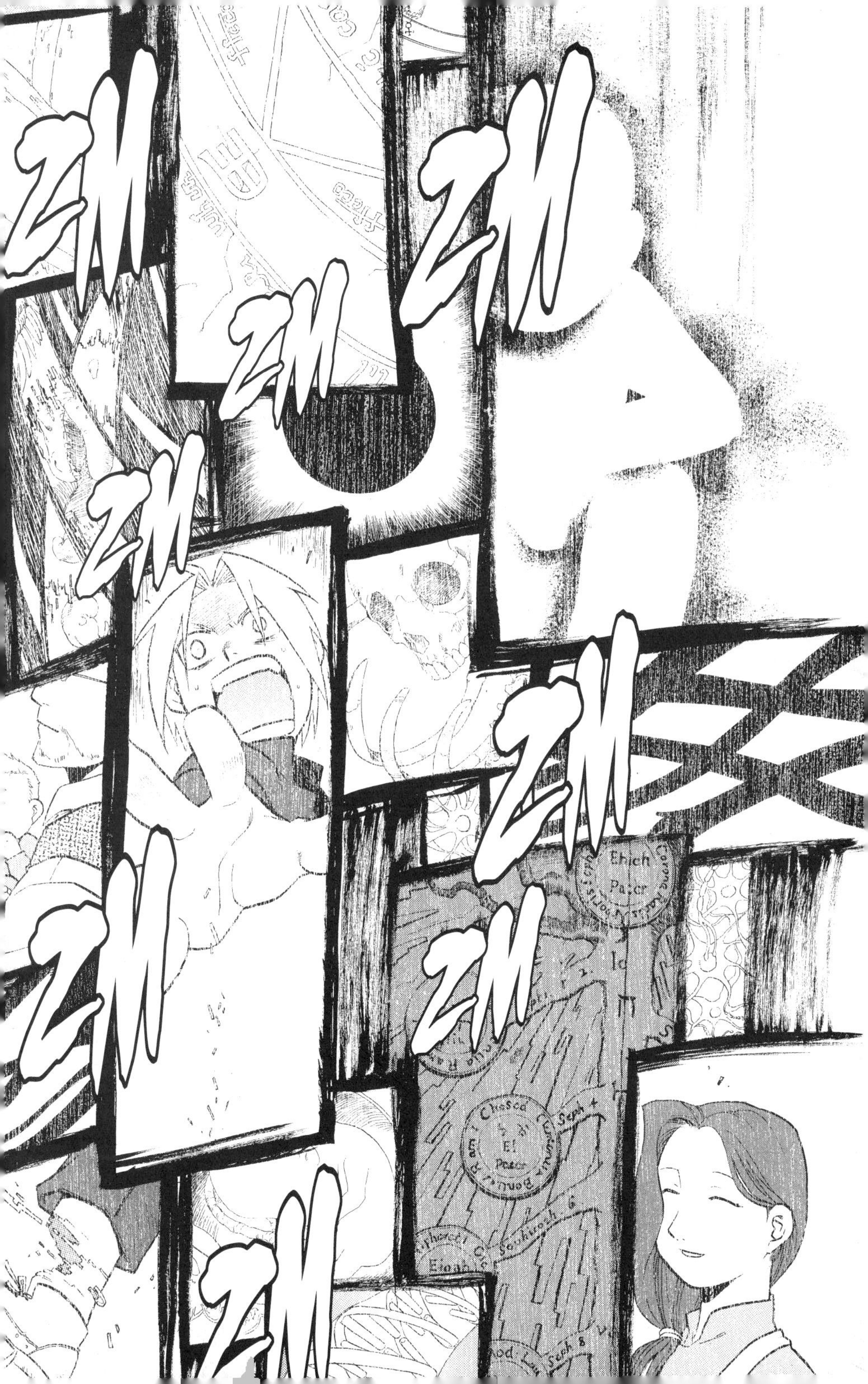
ZM
ZM
ZM
ZM
ZM
ZM
ZM
ZM

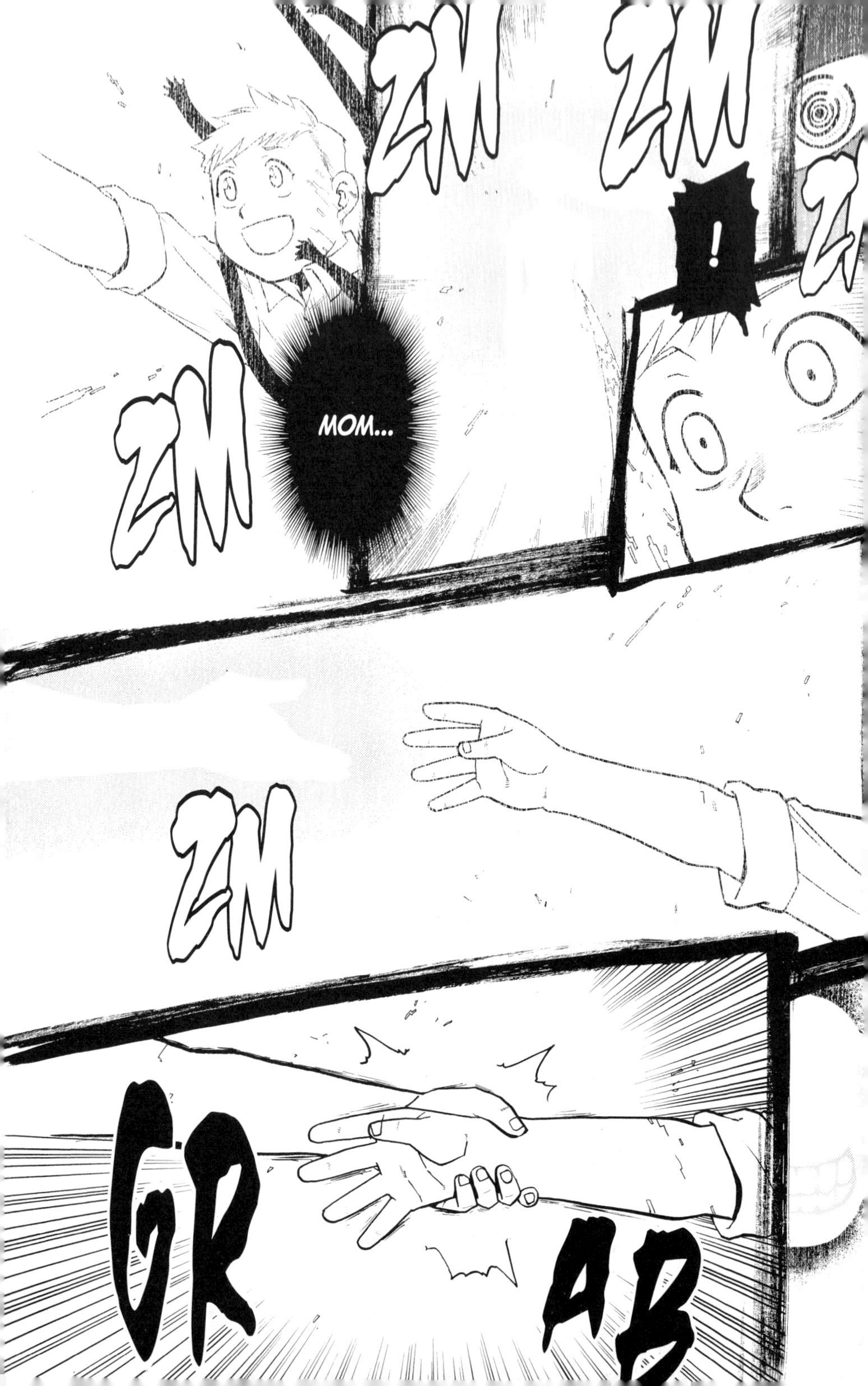
ZM
!
ZM
MOM...
ZM
ZM
GRAB

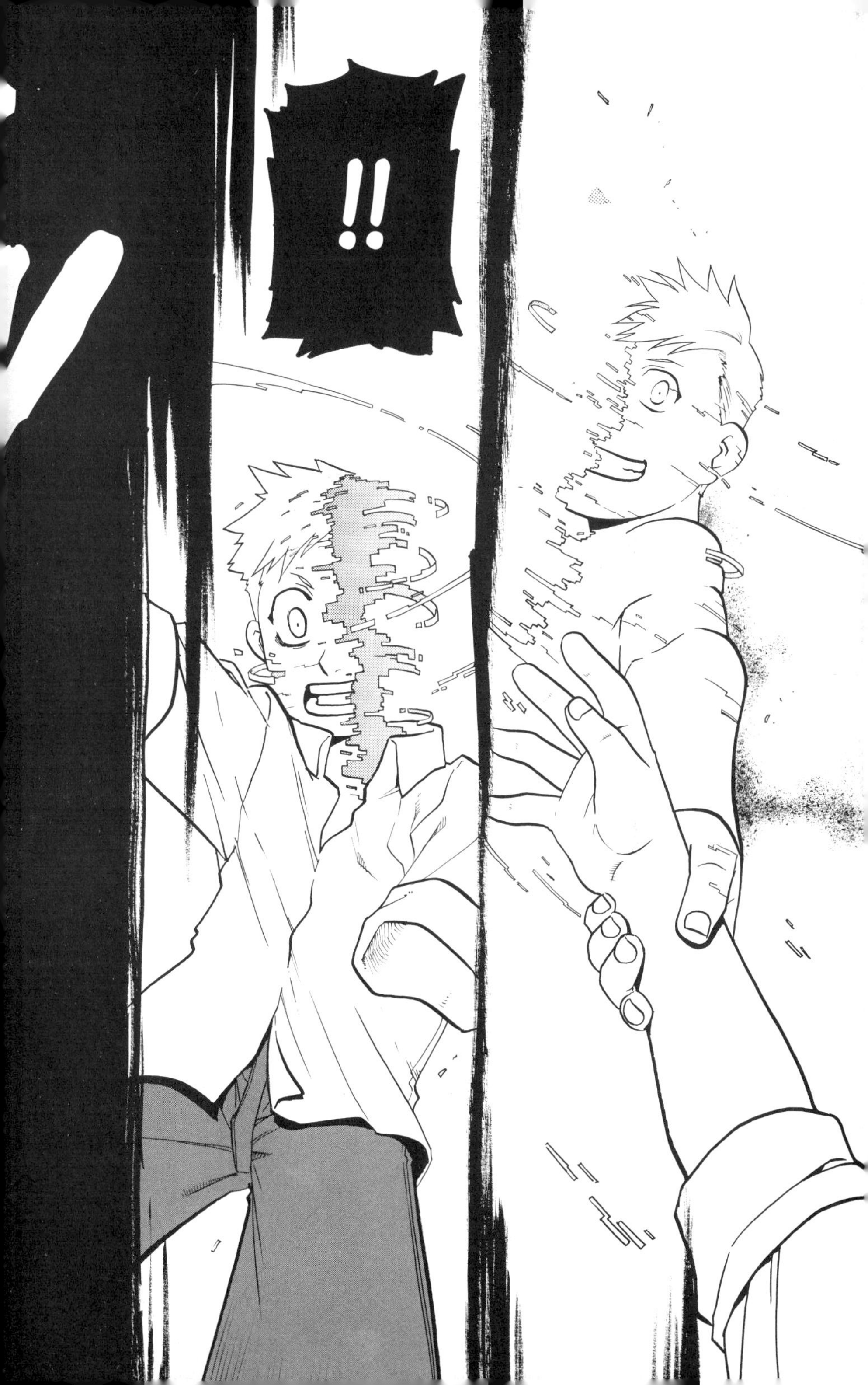
!!

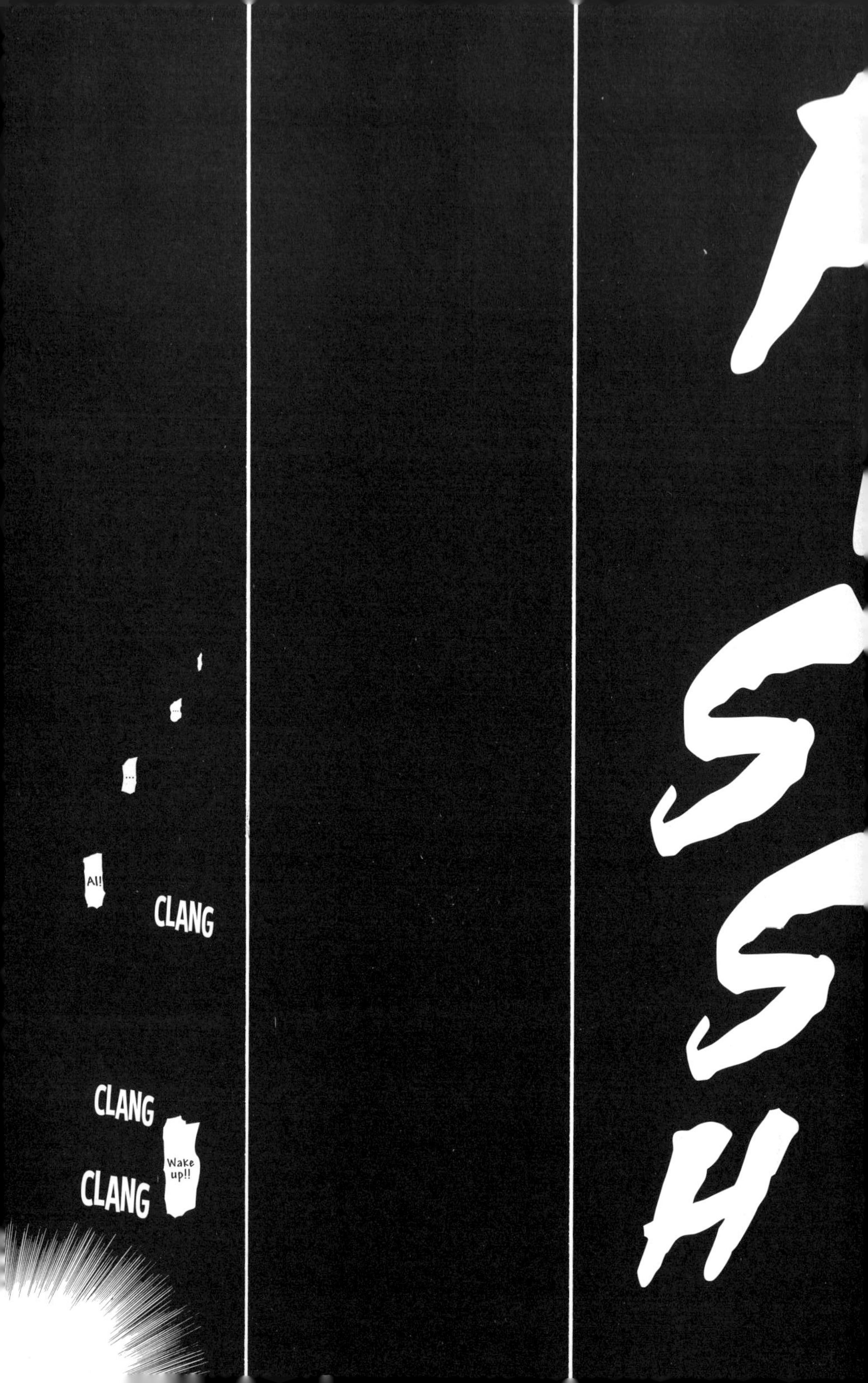
SSH
…
…
AI!
CLANG
CLANG
Wake up!!
CLANG

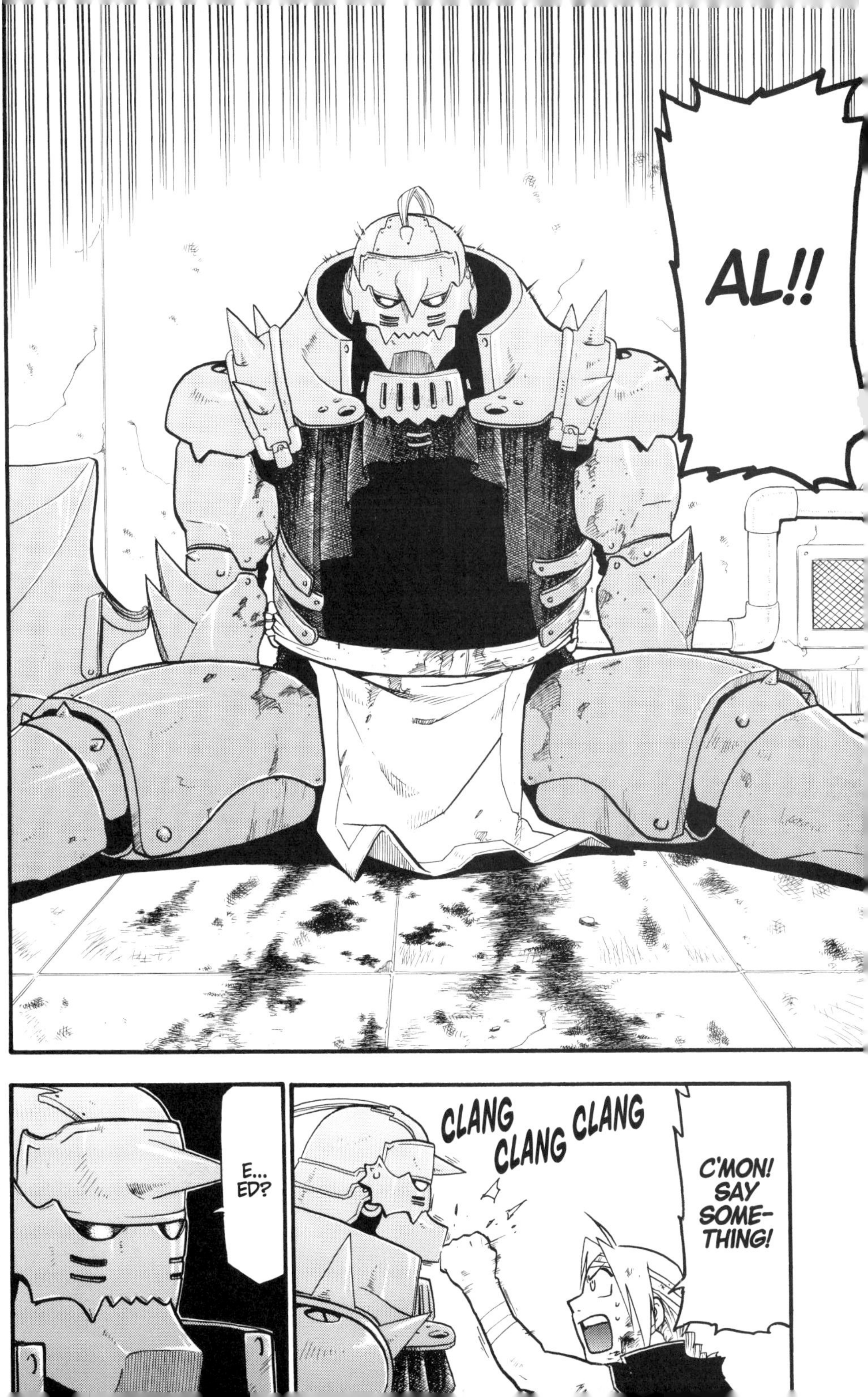
AL!!
CLANG CLANG CLANG
C'MON! SAY SOME-THING!
E... ED?

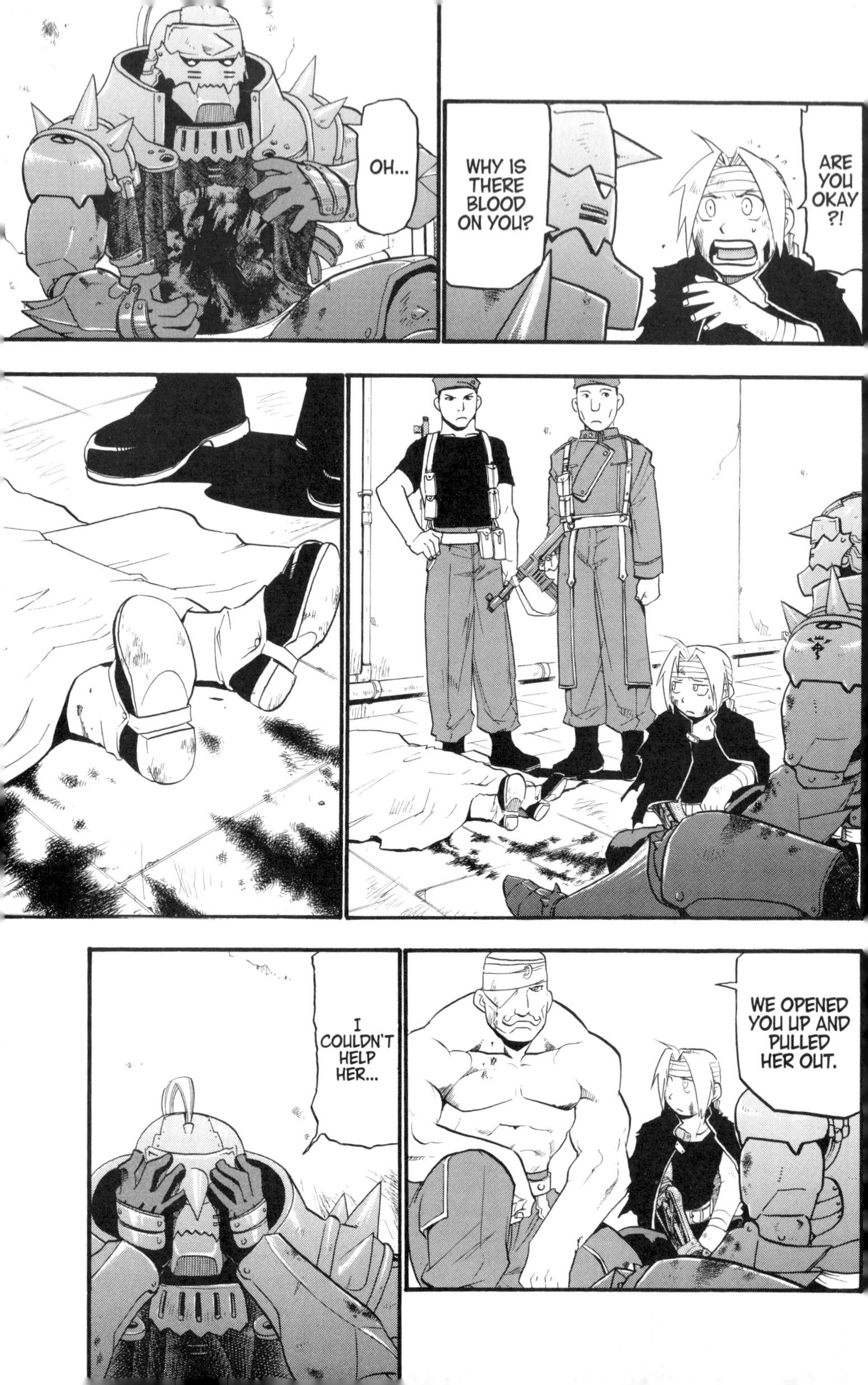
ARE YOU OKAY?!
WHY IS THERE BLOOD ON YOU?
OH...
WE OPENED YOU UP AND PULLED HER OUT.
I COULDN'T HELP HER...

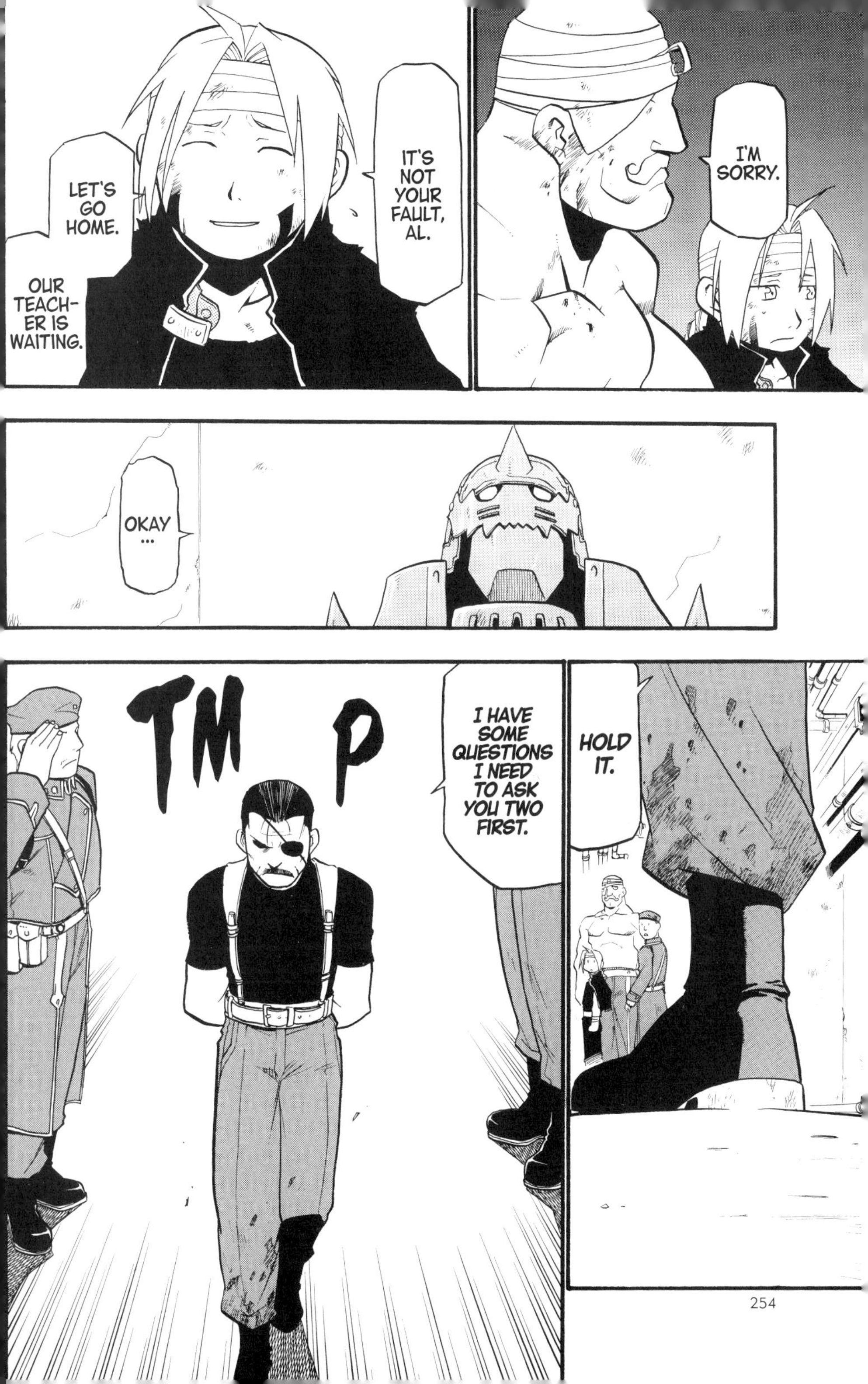
I'M SORRY.
IT'S NOT YOUR FAULT, AL.
LET'S GO HOME.
OUR TEACHER IS WAITING.
OKAY...
HOLD IT.
I HAVE SOME QUESTIONS I NEED TO ASK YOU TWO FIRST.
TMP

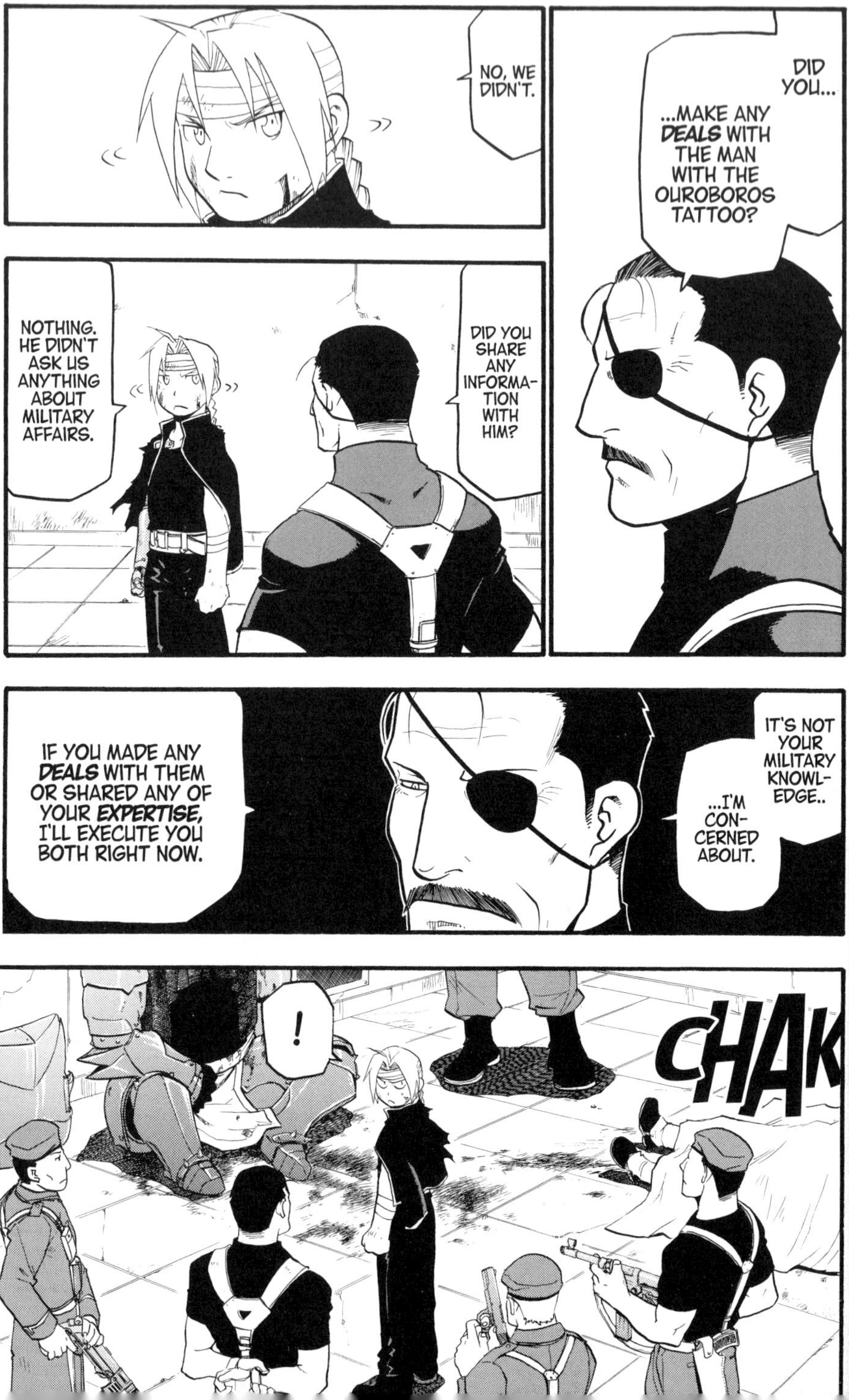
DID YOU...
...MAKE ANY **DEALS** WITH THE MAN WITH THE OUROBOROS TATTOO?
NO, WE DIDN'T.
DID YOU SHARE ANY INFORMATION WITH HIM?
NOTHING. HE DIDN'T ASK US ANYTHING ABOUT MILITARY AFFAIRS.
IT'S NOT YOUR MILITARY KNOWLEDGE..
...I'M CONCERNED ABOUT.
IF YOU MADE ANY **DEALS** WITH THEM OR SHARED ANY OF YOUR **EXPERTISE**, I'LL EXECUTE YOU BOTH RIGHT NOW.
CHAK
!

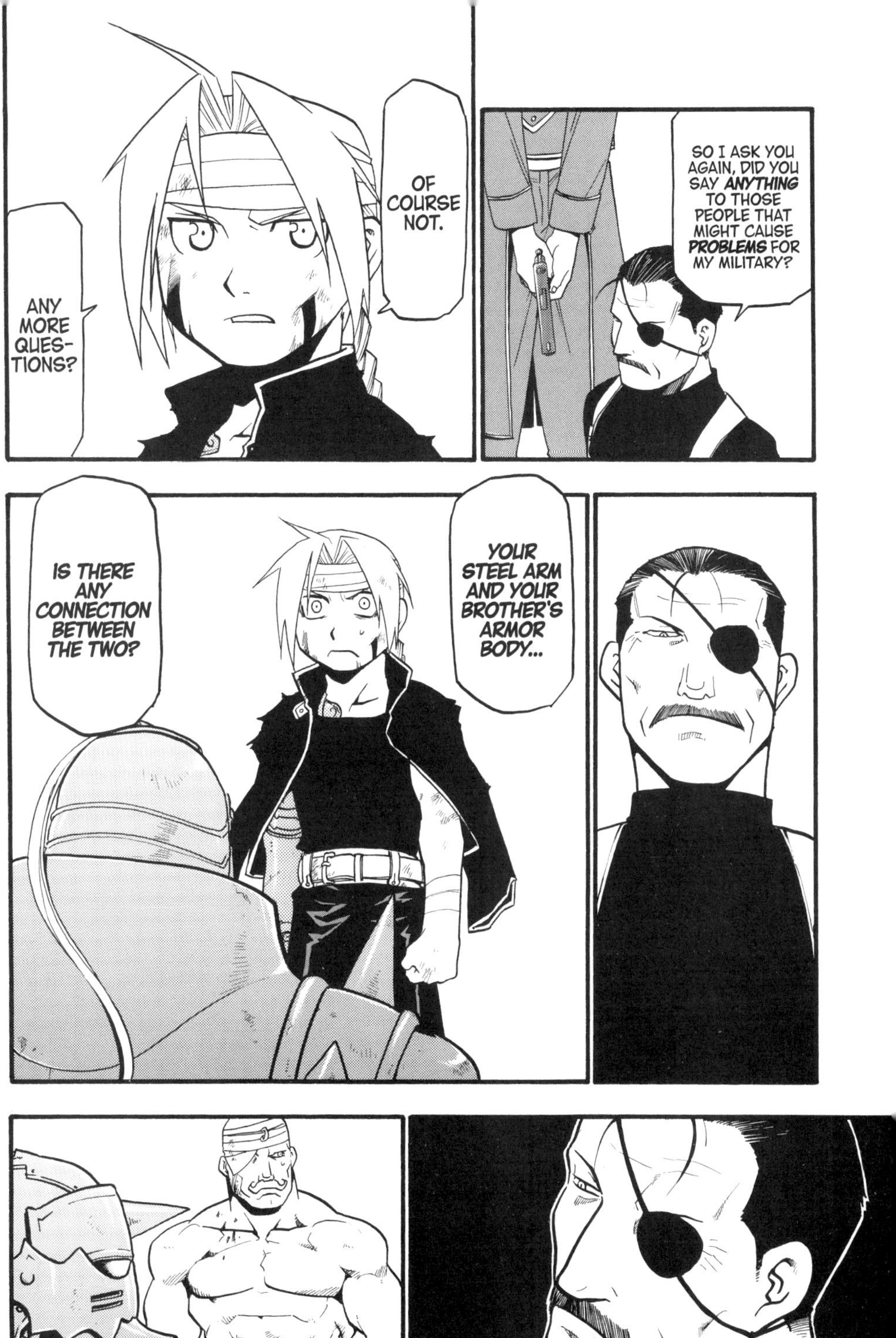
SO I ASK YOU AGAIN, DID YOU SAY ANYTHING TO THOSE PEOPLE THAT MIGHT CAUSE PROBLEMS FOR MY MILITARY?
OF COURSE NOT.
ANY MORE QUES-TIONS?
YOUR STEEL ARM AND YOUR BROTHER'S ARMOR BODY...
IS THERE ANY CONNECTION BETWEEN THE TWO?

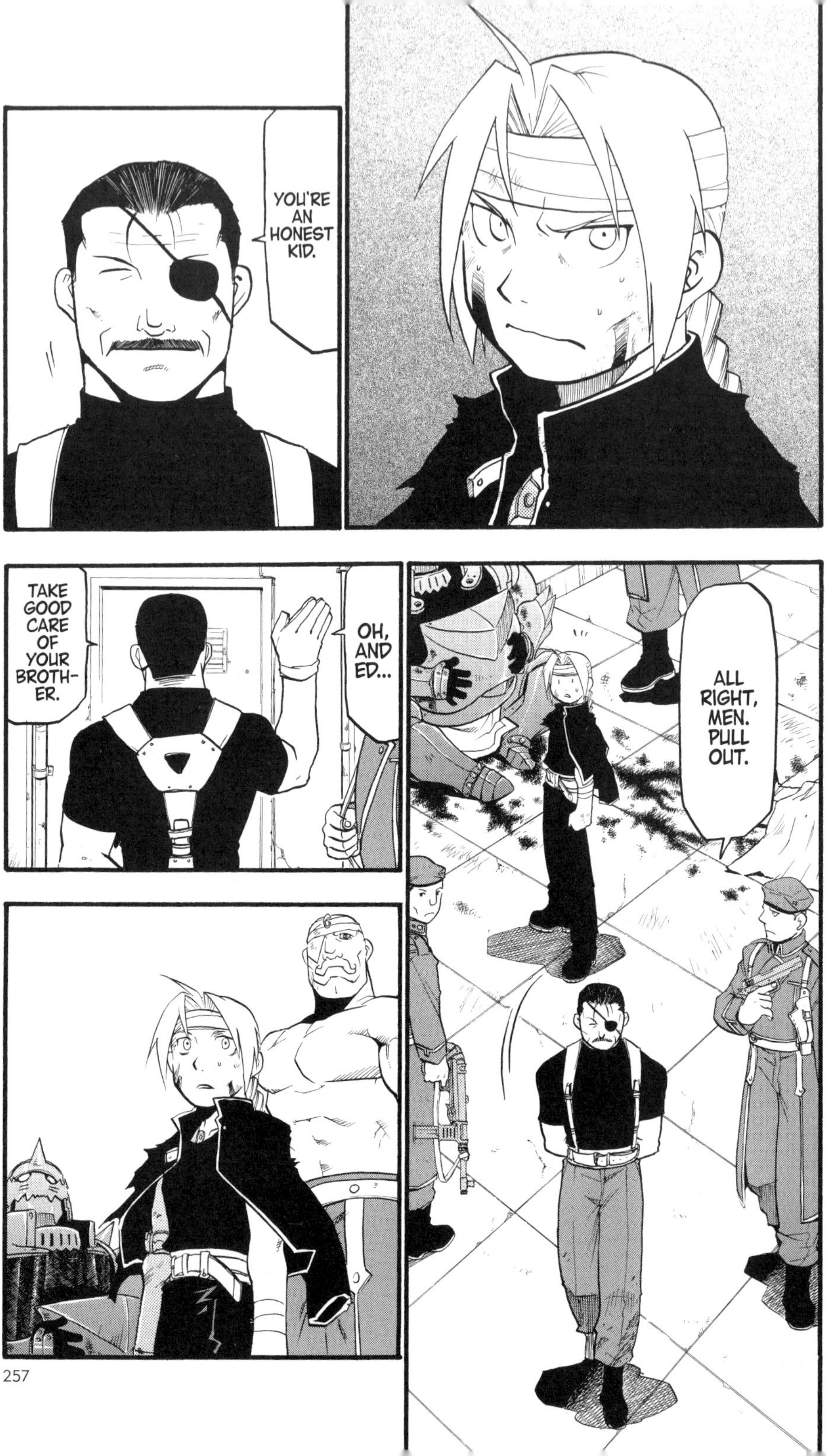
YOU'RE AN HONEST KID.
ALL RIGHT, MEN. PULL OUT.
OH, AND ED...
TAKE GOOD CARE OF YOUR BROTHER.

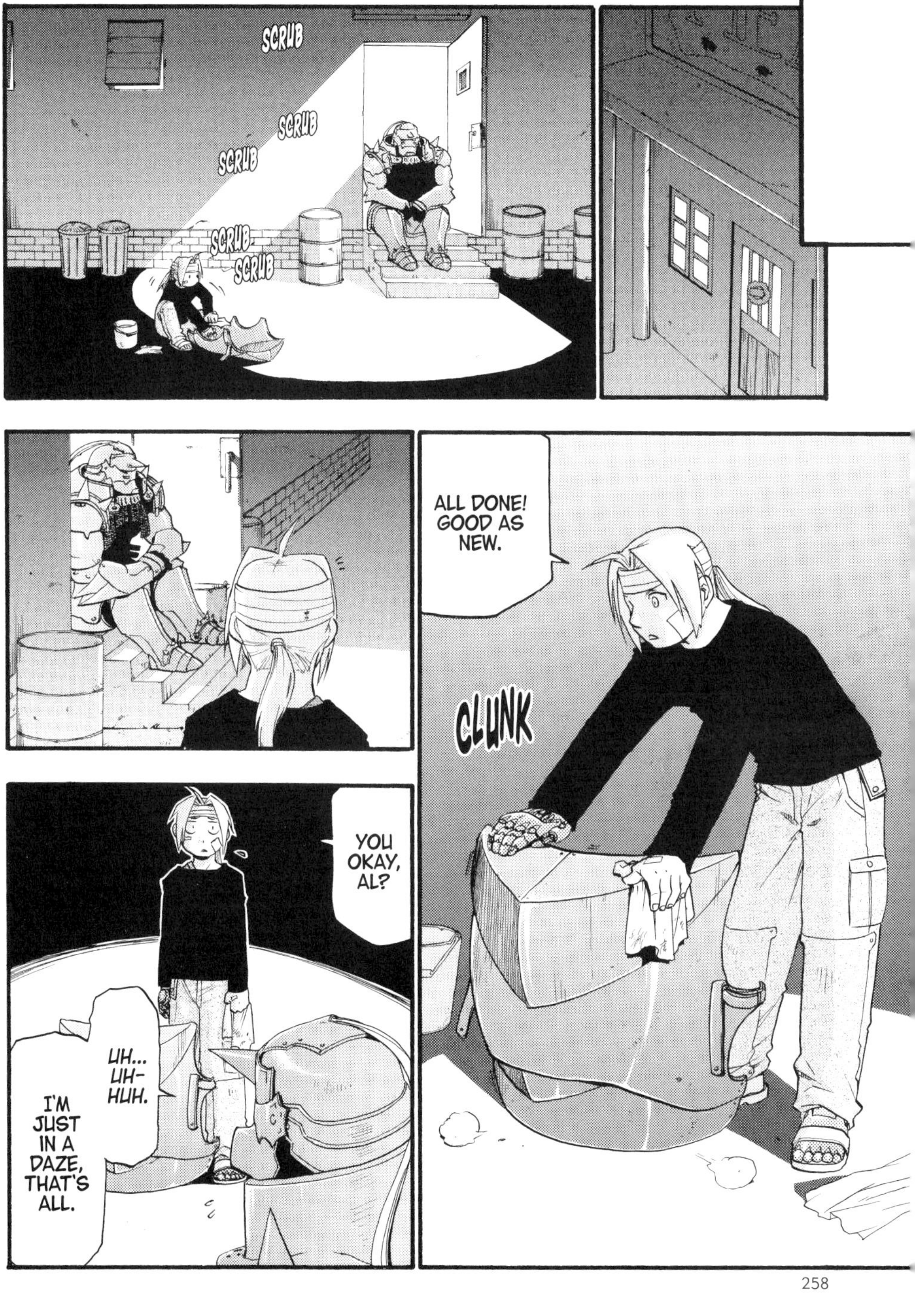
SCRUB
SCRUB
SCRUB
SCRUB
SCRUB
ALL DONE! GOOD AS NEW.
CLUNK
YOU OKAY, AL?
UH... UH-HUH.
I'M JUST IN A DAZE, THAT'S ALL.

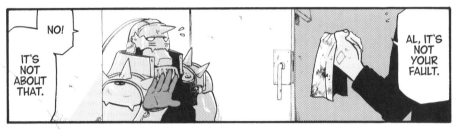

AL, IT'S NOT YOUR FAULT.
NO!
IT'S NOT ABOUT THAT.
I GOT IT BACK. THE *MEMORY* OF WHEN MY BODY WAS TAKEN AWAY.
W-WHAT WAS IT LIKE?!
UH, IT WAS PRETTY WEIRD!
Kinda like this.
BUT I DIDN'T FIND OUT ANYTHING ABOUT TRANSMUTING HUMAN BODIES.
I SEE...

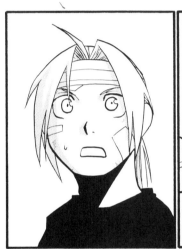

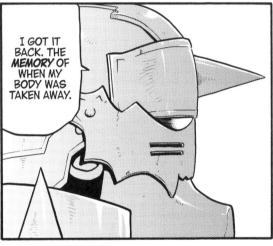

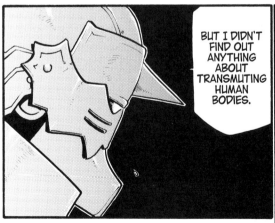

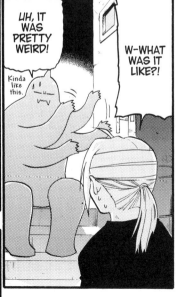

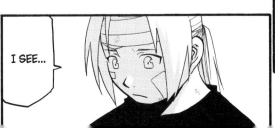

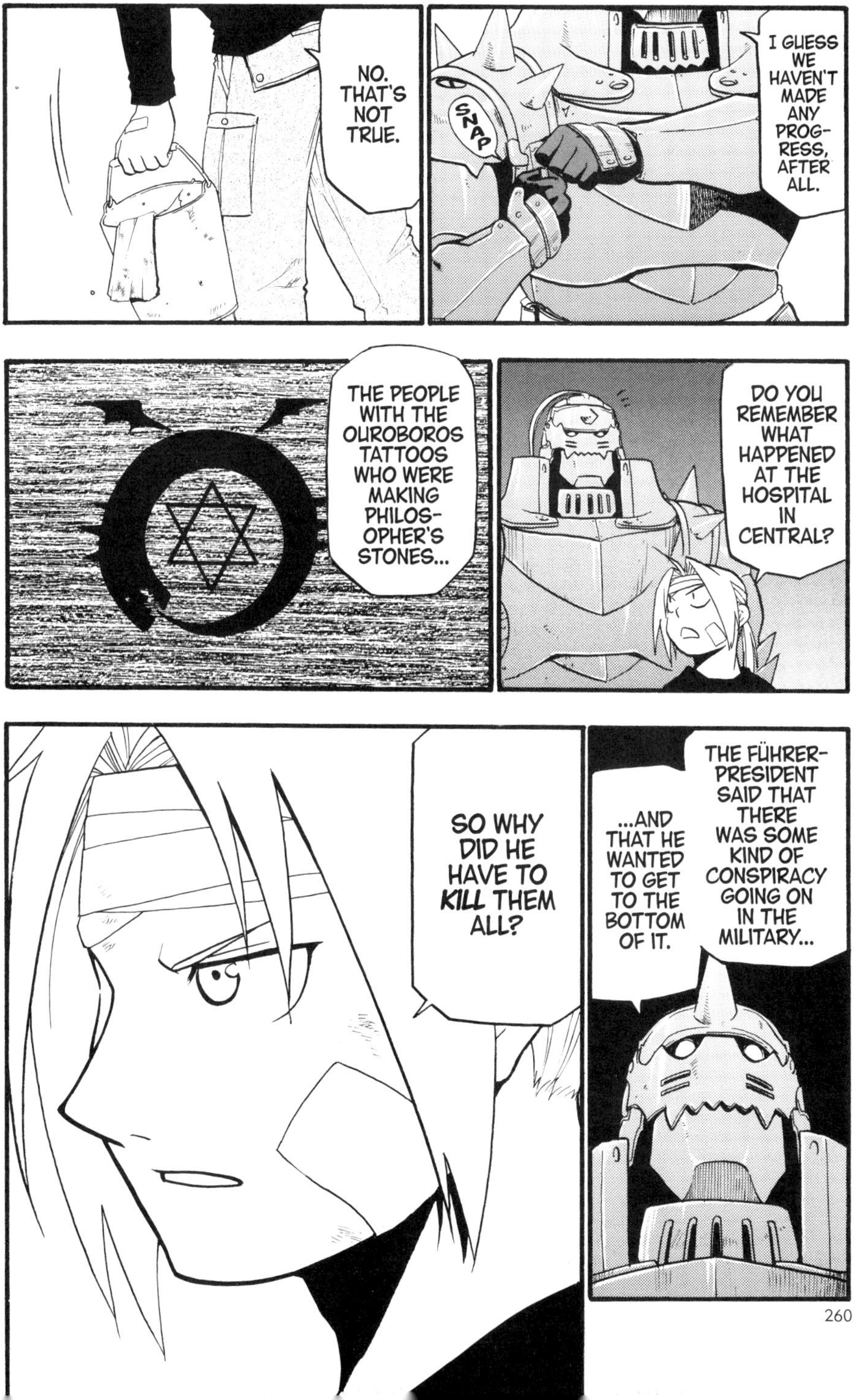
I GUESS WE HAVEN'T MADE ANY PROG-RESS, AFTER ALL.
SNAP
NO. THAT'S NOT TRUE.
DO YOU REMEMBER WHAT HAPPENED AT THE HOSPITAL IN CENTRAL?
THE PEOPLE WITH THE OUROBOROS TATTOOS WHO WERE MAKING PHILOS-OPHER'S STONES...
THE FÜHRER-PRESIDENT SAID THAT THERE WAS SOME KIND OF CONSPIRACY GOING ON IN THE MILITARY...
...AND THAT HE WANTED TO GET TO THE BOTTOM OF IT.
SO WHY DID HE HAVE TO KILL THEM ALL?

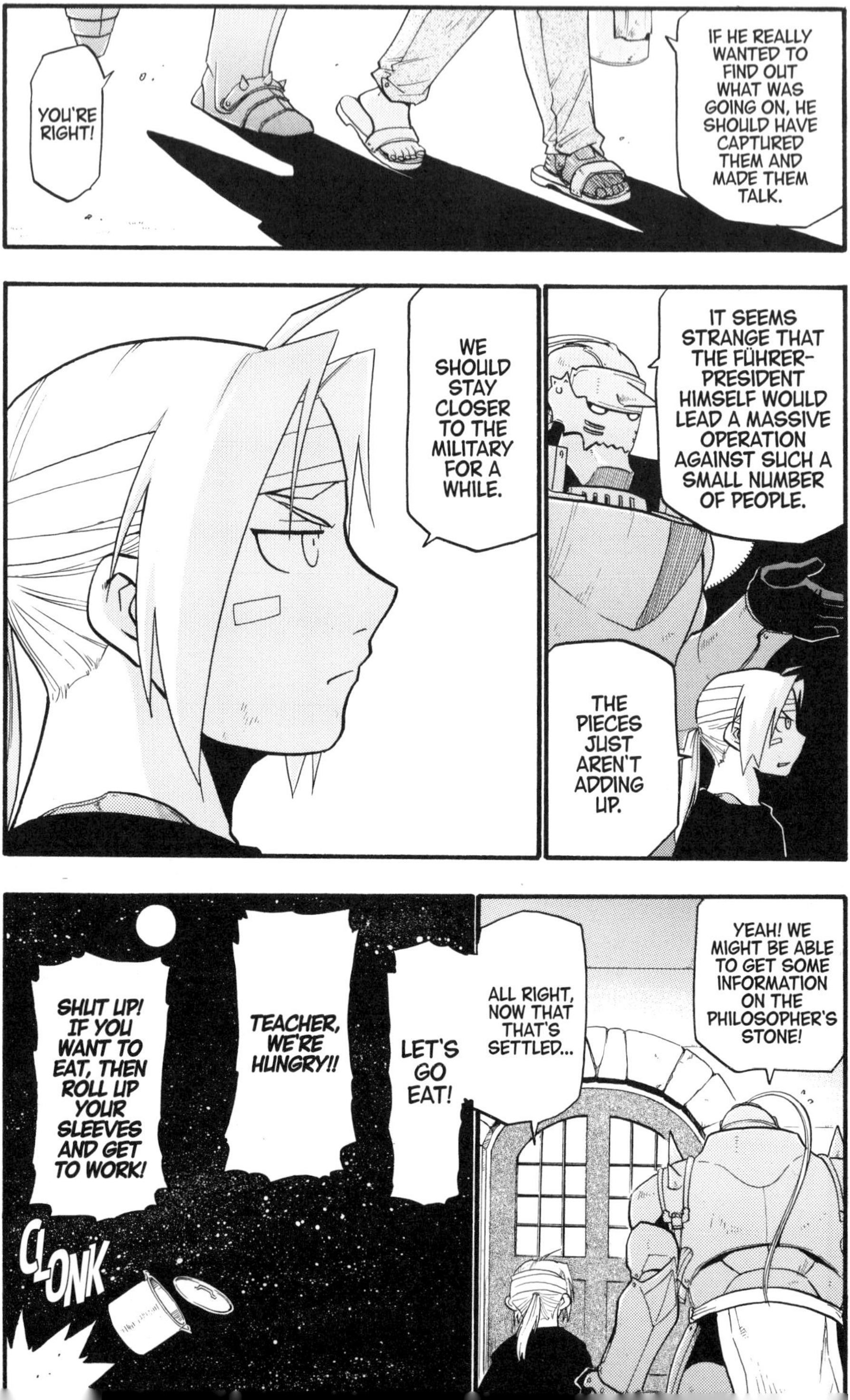
IF HE REALLY WANTED TO FIND OUT WHAT WAS GOING ON, HE SHOULD HAVE CAPTURED THEM AND MADE THEM TALK.
YOU'RE RIGHT!
IT SEEMS STRANGE THAT THE FÜHRER-PRESIDENT HIMSELF WOULD LEAD A MASSIVE OPERATION AGAINST SUCH A SMALL NUMBER OF PEOPLE.
THE PIECES JUST AREN'T ADDING UP.
WE SHOULD STAY CLOSER TO THE MILITARY FOR A WHILE.
YEAH! WE MIGHT BE ABLE TO GET SOME INFORMATION ON THE PHILOSOPHER'S STONE!
ALL RIGHT, NOW THAT THAT'S SETTLED...
LET'S GO EAT!
TEACHER, WE'RE HUNGRY!!
SHUT UP! IF YOU WANT TO EAT, THEN ROLL UP YOUR SLEEVES AND GET TO WORK!
CLONK

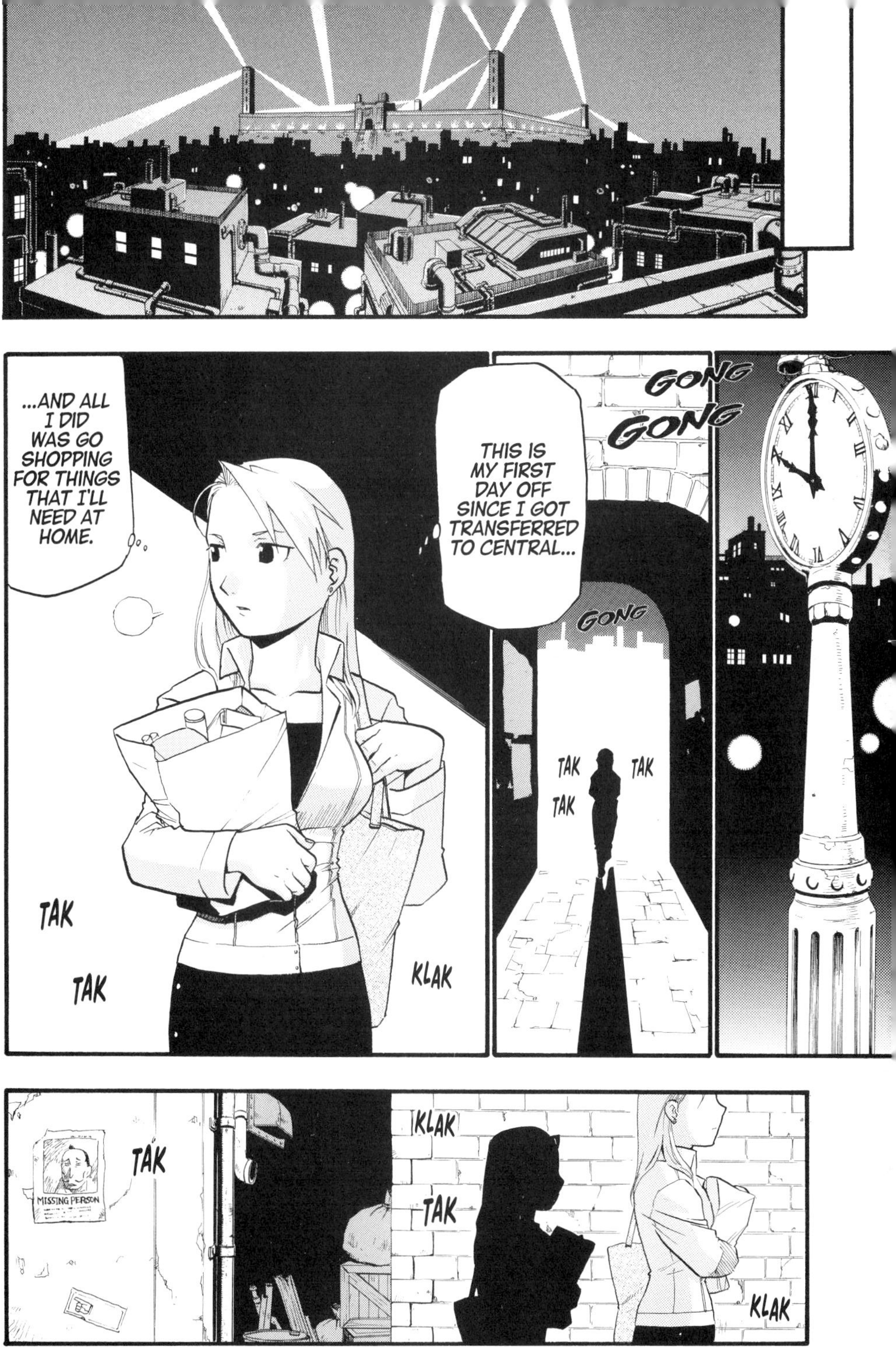
GONG
GONG
THIS IS MY FIRST DAY OFF SINCE I GOT TRANSFERRED TO CENTRAL...
GONG
TAK
TAK
TAK
...AND ALL I DID WAS GO SHOPPING FOR THINGS THAT I'LL NEED AT HOME.
TAK
TAK
KLAK
KLAK
TAK
KLAK
MISSING PERSON
TAK

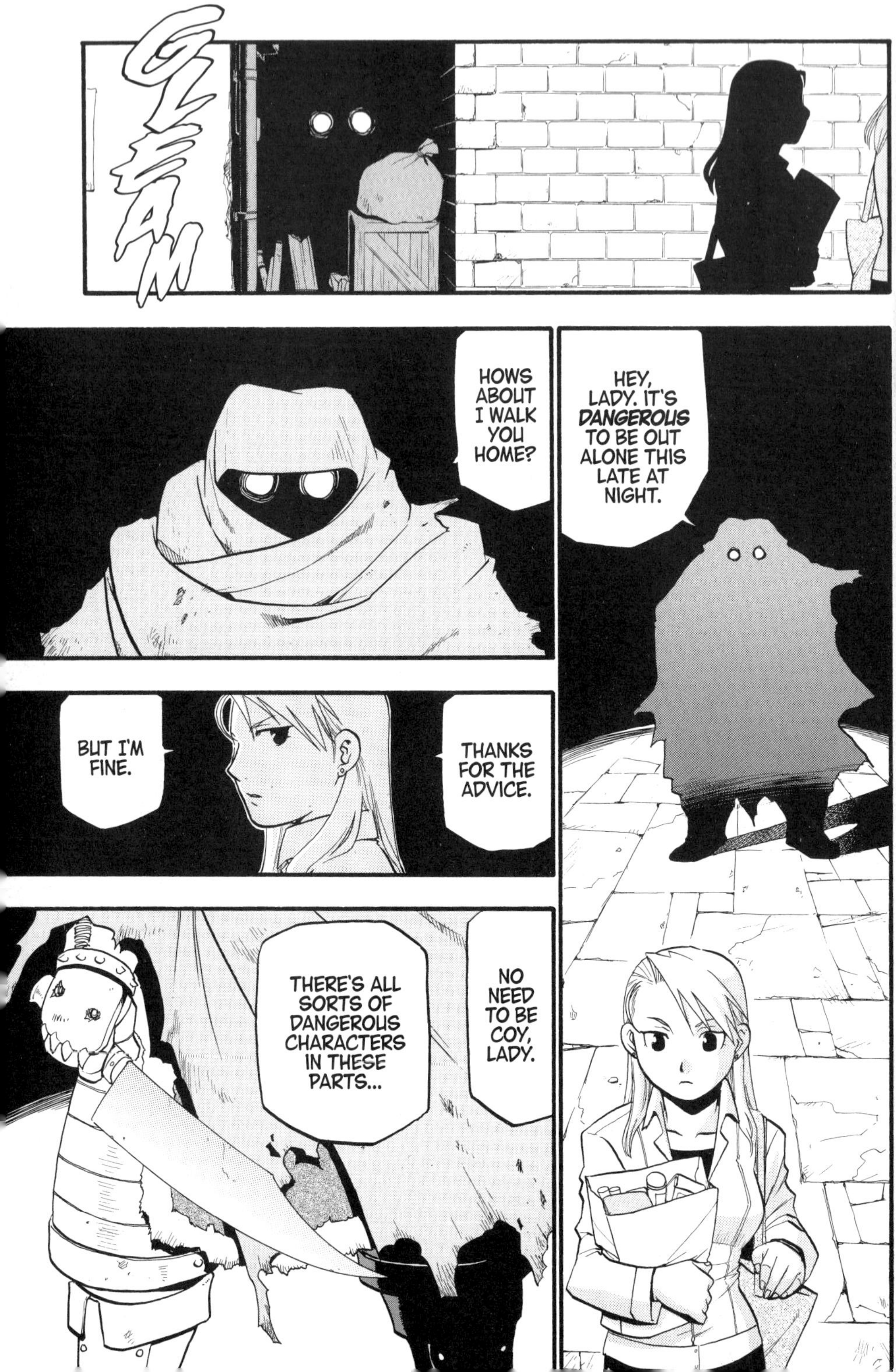
GLEAM
HEY, LADY. IT'S DANGEROUS TO BE OUT ALONE THIS LATE AT NIGHT.
HOWS ABOUT I WALK YOU HOME?
THANKS FOR THE ADVICE.
BUT I'M FINE.
NO NEED TO BE COY, LADY.
THERE'S ALL SORTS OF DANGEROUS CHARACTERS IN THESE PARTS...

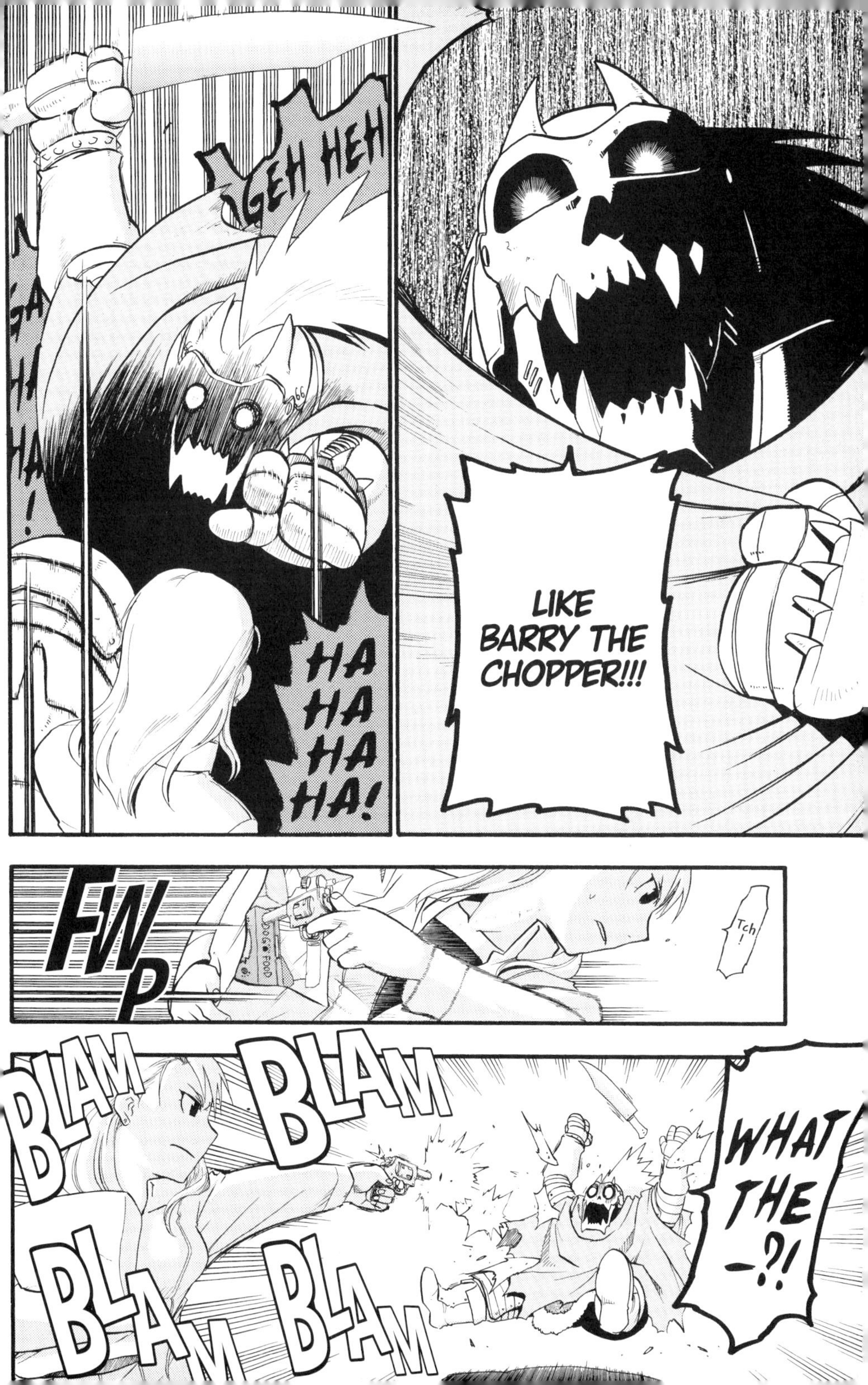
LIKE BARRY THE CHOPPER!!!
GEH HEH
GA HA HA HA!
HA HA HA HA!
Tch!
FWP
WHAT THE—?!
BLAM
BLAM
BLAM
BLAM

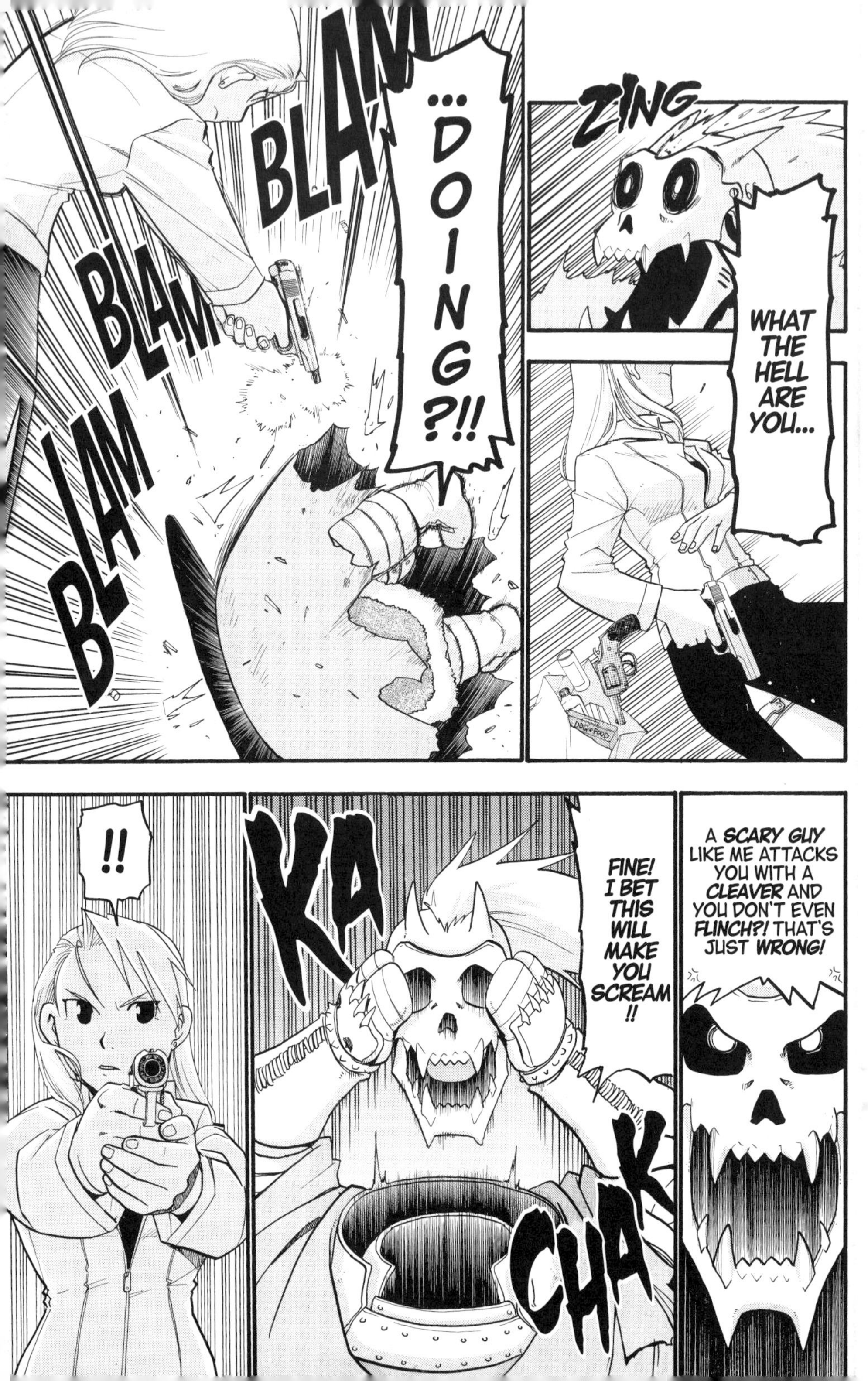
ZING
WHAT THE HELL ARE YOU...
DOG FOOD
...DOING?!!
BLAM
BLAM
BLAM
BLAM
A SCARY GUY LIKE ME ATTACKS YOU WITH A CLEAVER AND YOU DON'T EVEN FLINCH?! THAT'S JUST WRONG!
FINE! I BET THIS WILL MAKE YOU SCREAM!!
KA
CHAK
!!

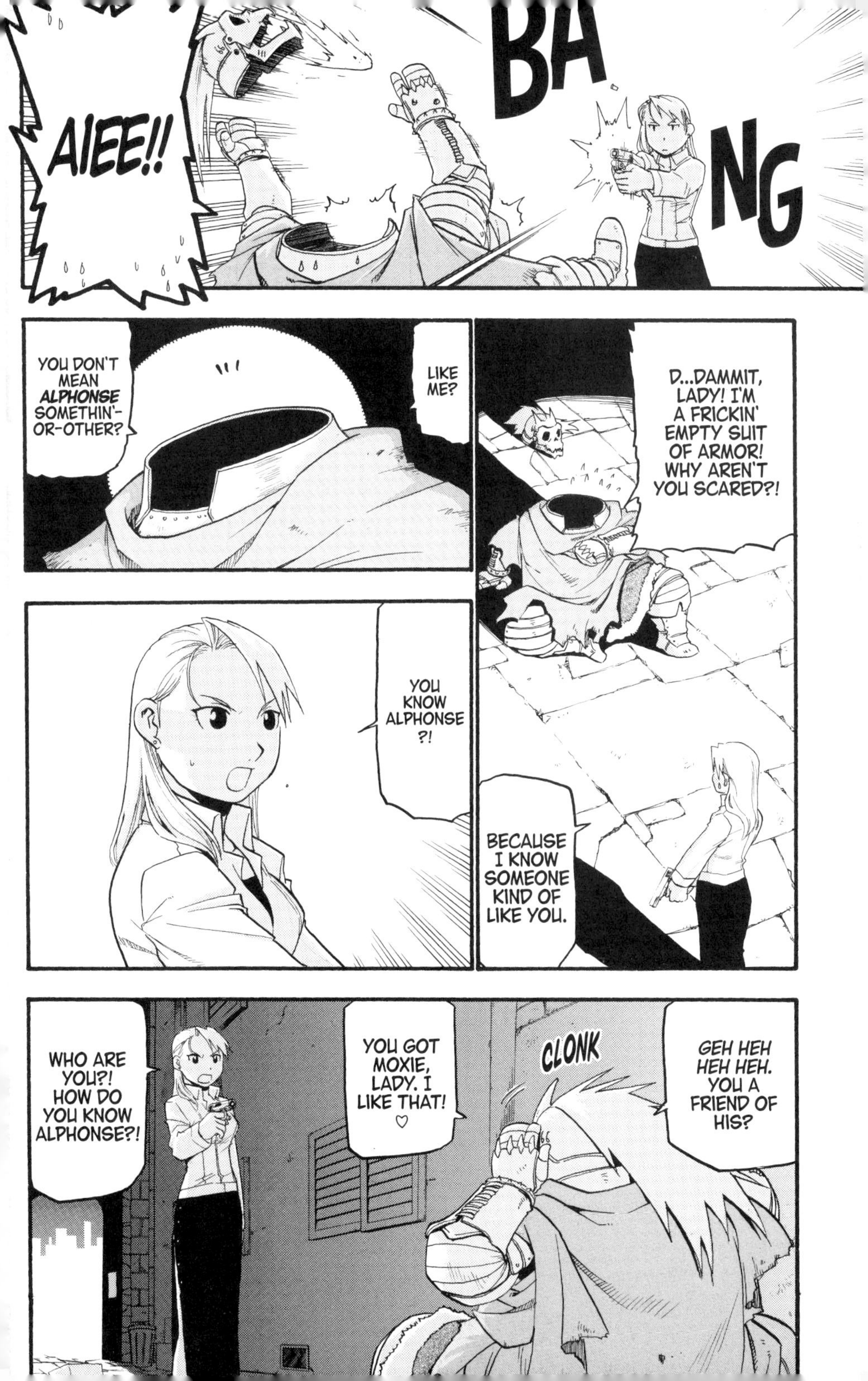
BA
NG
AIEE!!
D...DAMMIT, LADY! I'M A FRICKIN' EMPTY SUIT OF ARMOR! WHY AREN'T YOU SCARED?!
BECAUSE I KNOW SOMEONE KIND OF LIKE YOU.
LIKE ME?
YOU DON'T MEAN ALPHONSE SOMETHIN'-OR-OTHER?
YOU KNOW ALPHONSE ?!
GEH HEH HEH HEH. YOU A FRIEND OF HIS?
CLONK
YOU GOT MOXIE, LADY. I LIKE THAT! ♡
WHO ARE YOU?! HOW DO YOU KNOW ALPHONSE?!

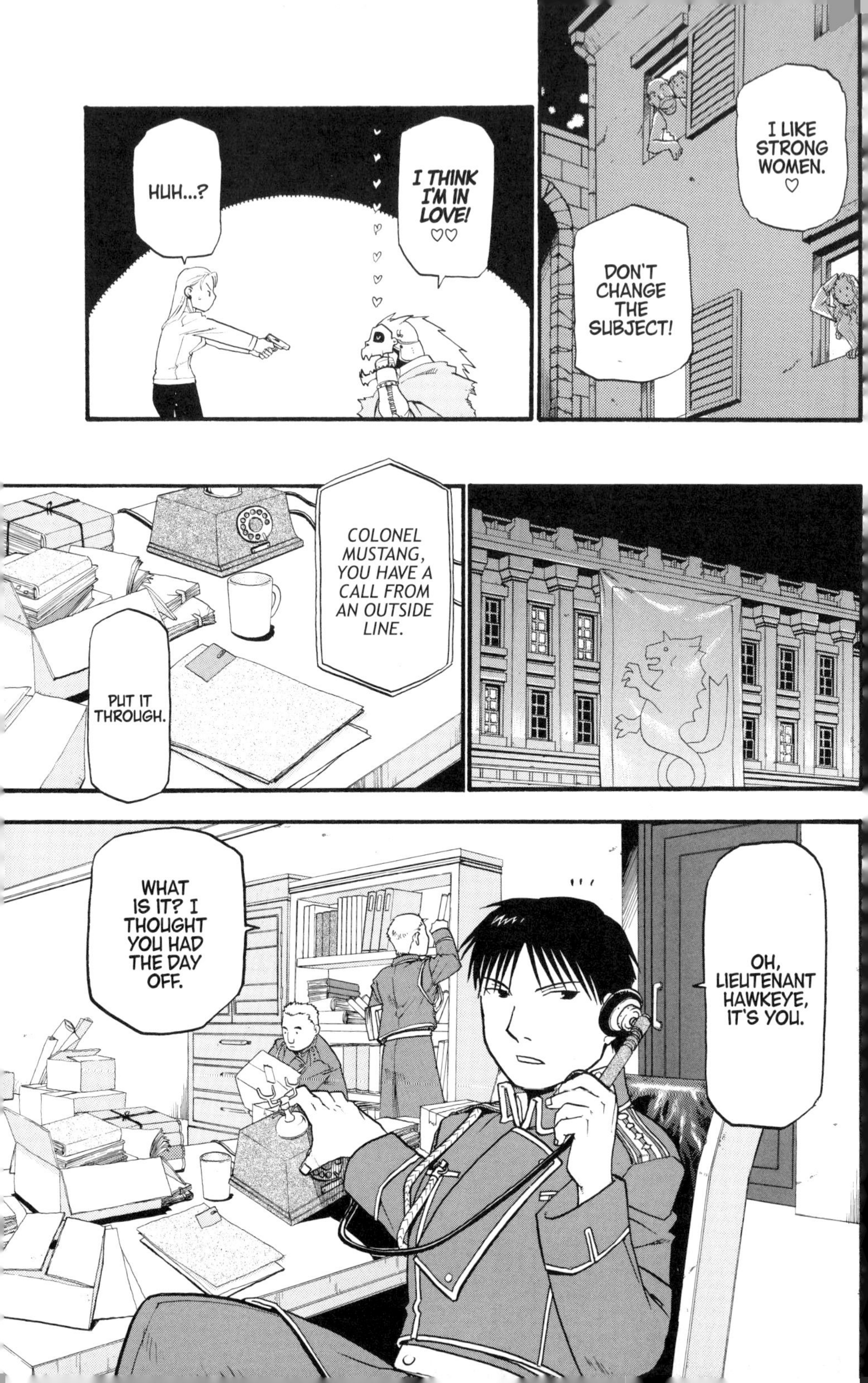
I LIKE STRONG WOMEN. ♡
DON'T CHANGE THE SUBJECT!
I THINK I'M IN LOVE! ♡♡
HUH...?
COLONEL MUSTANG, YOU HAVE A CALL FROM AN OUTSIDE LINE.
PUT IT THROUGH.
OH, LIEUTENANT HAWKEYE, IT'S YOU.
WHAT IS IT? I THOUGHT YOU HAD THE DAY OFF.

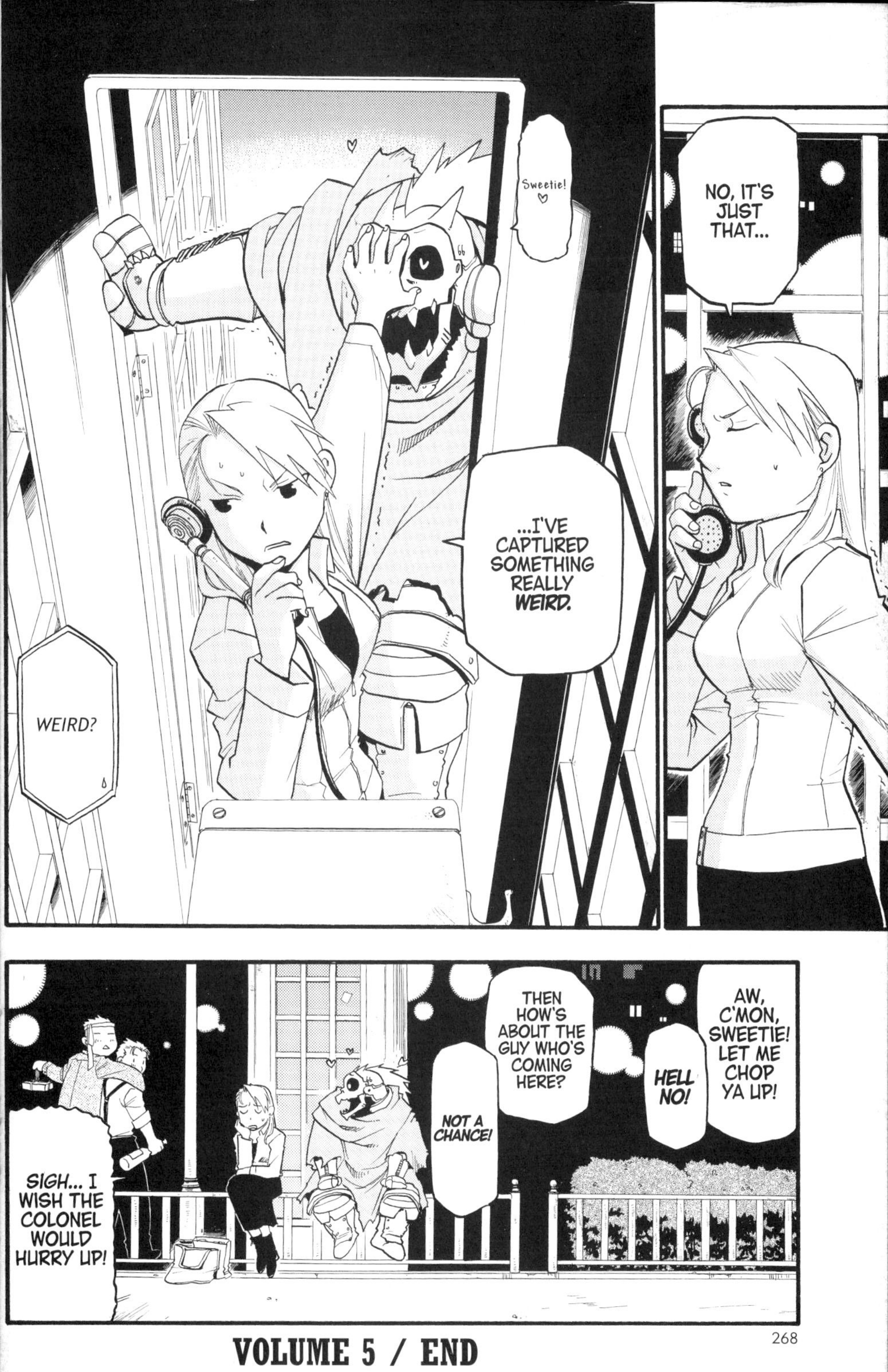
NO, IT'S JUST THAT...
Sweetie!
...I'VE CAPTURED SOMETHING REALLY **WEIRD.**
WEIRD?
AW, C'MON, SWEETIE! LET ME CHOP YA UP!
HELL NO!
THEN HOW'S ABOUT THE GUY WHO'S COMING HERE?
NOT A CHANCE!
SIGH... I WISH THE COLONEL WOULD HURRY UP!

VOLUME 5 / END

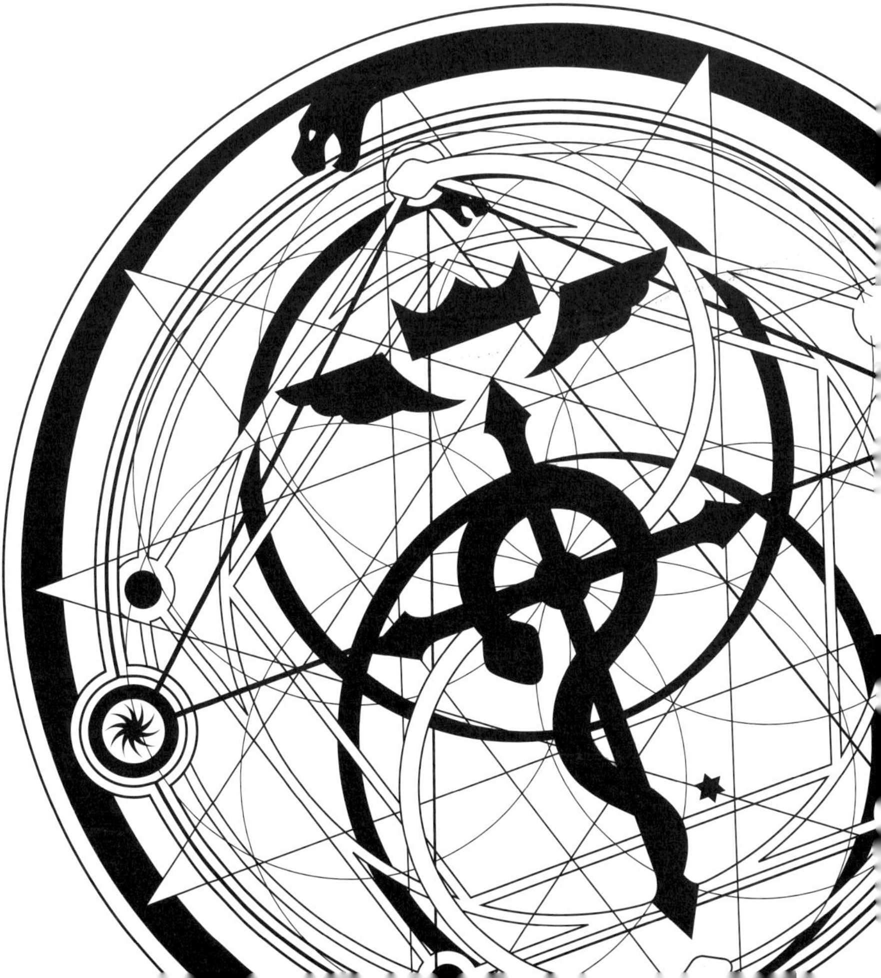

FULLMETAL EDITION

FULLMETAL ALCHEMIST

CONCEPT SKETCHES

05

The Elric brothers' teacher!

エルリック兄弟の
師匠

Here!
こん！

→

Dreads
ドレッド

連載開始頃、そのうち
こんなキャラ出ますよ〜と
担当さんにFAXしたやつ。

師匠は 外観固まるの 早かったなぁ

From around when we began serialization of Fullmetal Alchemist in the manga magazine. I sent a fax to my editor saying, "I'm going to add a character like this!" Her design came together really quickly.

The instructor of our
protagonist brothers

主人公兄弟の師匠

「精神を鍛えるには
まず肉体から」様
どこぞで 主婦を やっております。
30〜40歳代

She's from the school of "To train your spirit, first you must train your body." She's off being a housewife somewhere. 30–40 years old.

連載とかまったく考えてなかった頃の
スケッチブックらくがき。
ぼけーっと色々な女の人をらくがき
してた。たぶん原型。

This is from my sketchbook, which I'd draw in when I absolutely couldn't think about the serialization. I'd just sit around, zoning out and doodling various female characters. I think this was Izumi's prototype.

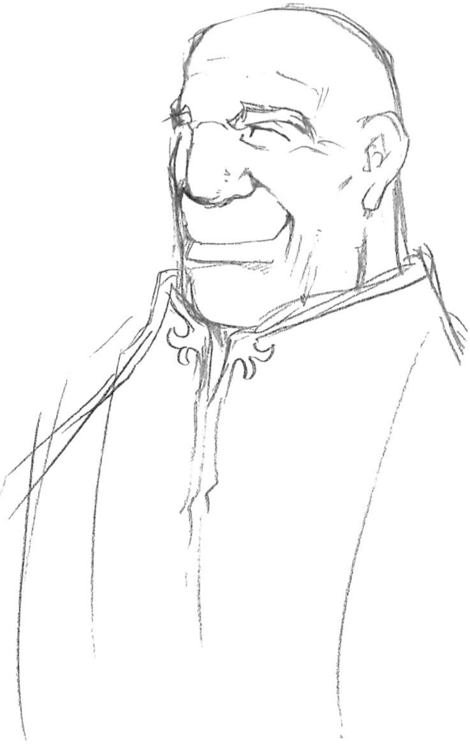

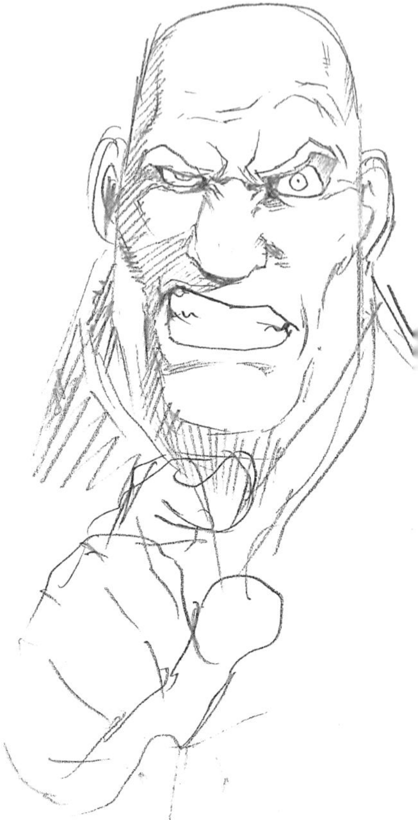

イズミ師匠の設定って
スパッと決まってしまったので
初期ラフが ほとんど無いよ。

しょうがないので
コーネロ様 初期ラフを
出すよ。

Because I decided on Izumi's design so quickly,
I barely have any roughs of her in the early stages.
So in lieu of that, here's an early rough of Cornello.

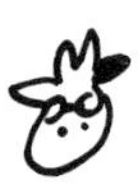

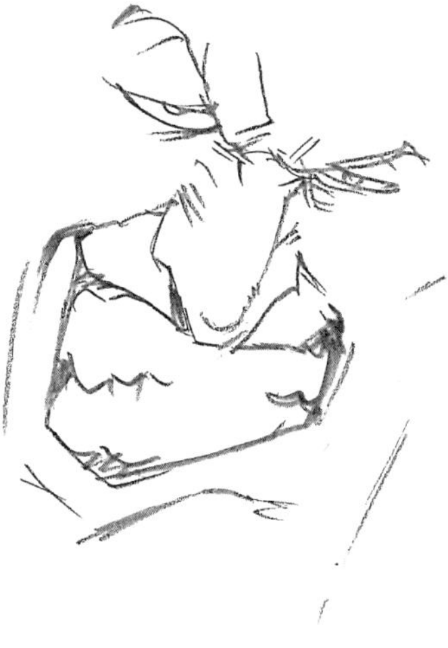

← 悪い顔が
ステキだよ。

His evil face is marvelous.

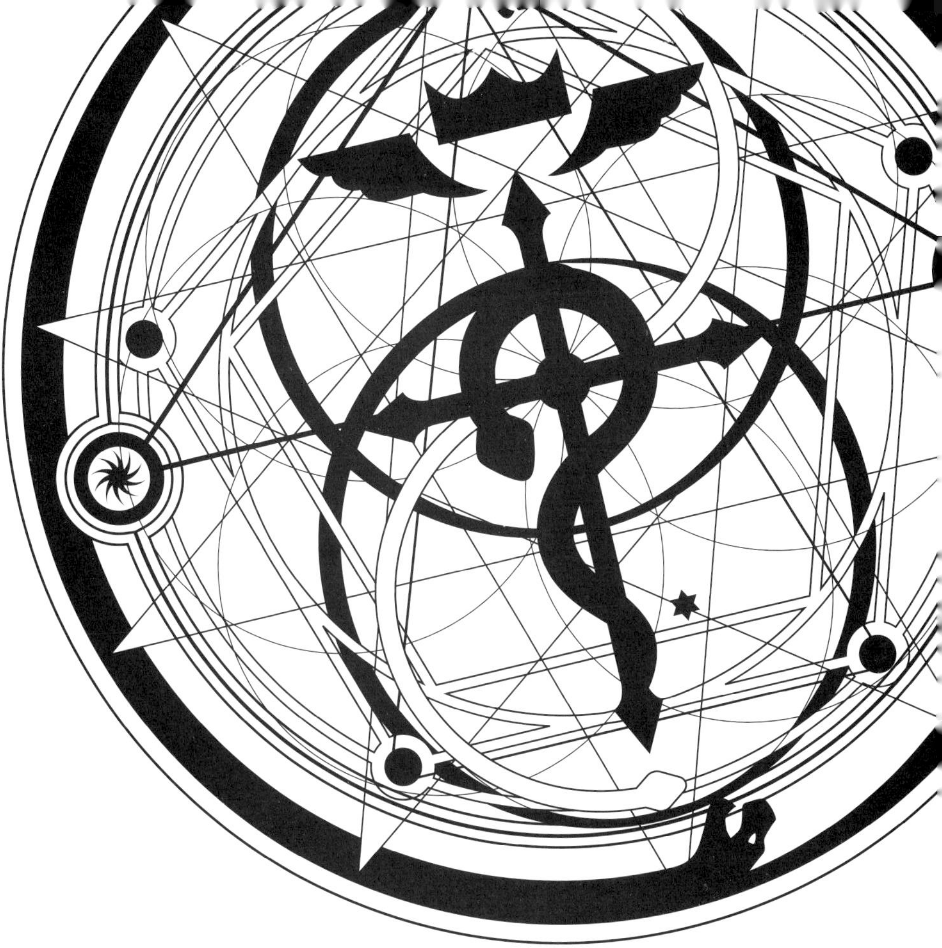

ABOUT THE AUTHOR

Born in Hokkaido, Japan, Hiromu Arakawa first attracted attention in 1999 with her award-winning manga *Stray Dog*. Her series *Fullmetal Alchemist* was serialized from 2001 to 2010 with a story that spanned 27 volumes and became an international critical and commercial success, receiving both the Shogakukan Manga Award and Seiun Award and selling over 70 million copies worldwide. *Fullmetal Alchemist* has been adapted into anime twice, first as *Fullmetal Alchemist* in 2003 and again as *Fullmetal Alchemist: Brotherhood* in 2009. The series has also inspired numerous films, video games and novels.

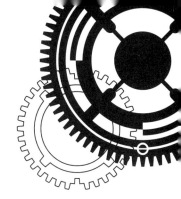

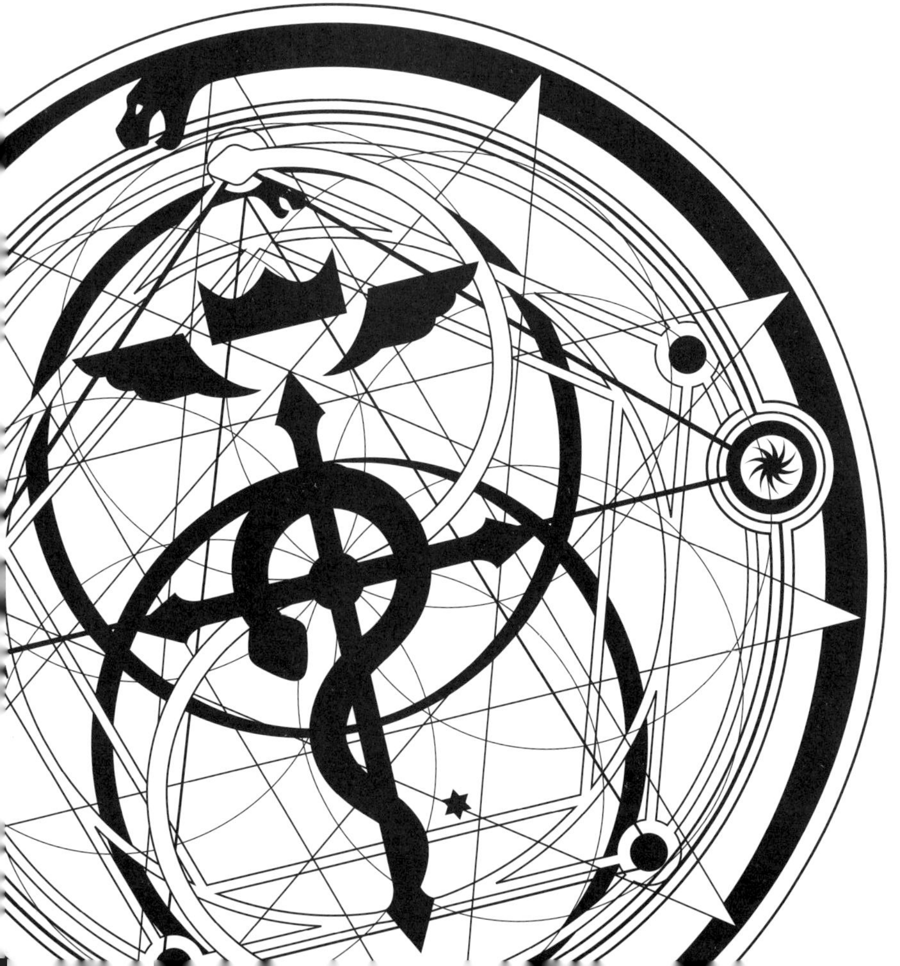

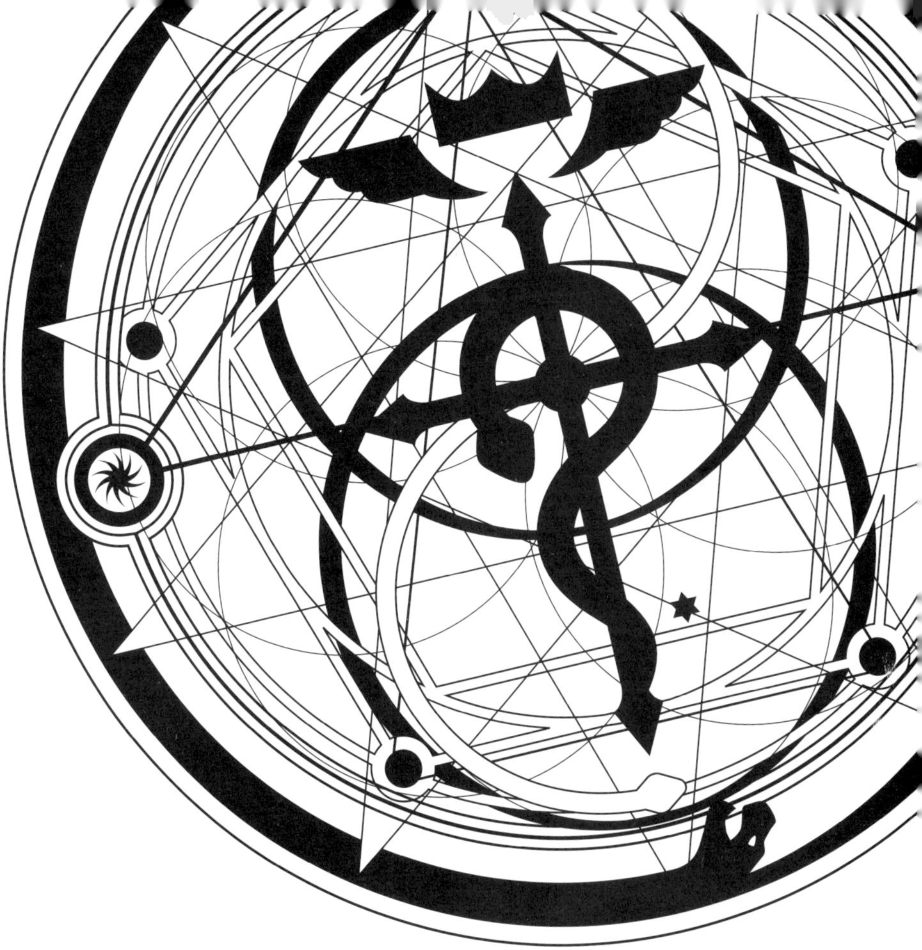

FULLMETAL EDITION

FULLMETAL ALCHEMIST

VOLUME 05

Story and Art by HIROMU ARAKAWA

Translation: AKIRA WATANABE
English Adaptation: JAKE FORBES
VIZ Media Edition Editor: JASON THOMPSON, URIAN BROWN
Touch-Up Art & Lettering: STEVE DUTRO
Design: ADAM GRANO
Editor: HOPE DONOVAN

FULLMETAL ALCHEMIST KANZENBAN vol. 5
© 2011 Hiromu Arakawa/SQUARE ENIX CO., LTD.
First published in Japan in 2011 by SQUARE ENIX CO., LTD.
English translation rights arranged with SQUARE ENIX CO.,
LTD. and VIZ Media, LLC. English translation © 2019 SQUARE
ENIX CO., LTD.

The stories, characters and incidents mentioned in this
publication are entirely fictional.

No portion of this book may be reproduced or transmitted
in any form or by any means without written permission
from the copyright holders.

Printed in Canada

Published by VIZ Media, LLC
P.O. Box 77010
San Francisco, CA 94107

10 9 8 7 6 5 4 3 2 1
First printing, May 2019

PARENTAL ADVISORY
FULLMETAL ALCHEMIST is rated T for Teen and is recommended
for ages 13 and up. This volume contains mildly strong language,
tobacco/alcohol use and fantasy violence.

VIZ MEDIA
viz.com

W9-DBT-720

This is the last page.

Fullmetal Alchemist reads right to left.